The New *York Magazine*

MW00909694

1998 Savvy Shoppers' Survey

Everything from Pearls to Plumbers,
Rated for Quality, Style, Service and Value.

Published by:
Custom Databanks, Inc.
New York, NY 10022-4168

For our husbands, who leave the shopping to us

The New York Edge
Copyright © 1997 by
Susan B. Dollinger and Jane R. Lockshin

Published by Custom Databanks, Inc.
60 Sutton Place South, Suite 14BN New York, NY 10022-4168

ISBN 1-889782-51-3

First printing

Cover Design: Solutions, Inc.

10 9 8 7 6 5 4 3 2 1
Second Edition

The New York Edge

Contents

Furniture & furnishings 167

Home & home office **248**

Home renovation **256**

Personal & repair services

Introduction

Welcome to the Second Edition of *The New York Edge*. The 1998 survey offers more—over 2,300 stores and services, 700 changes compared to last year's survey, all new ratings, and even more focused evaluations and comments.

This year, our favorite addition is a new category–Sample Sales. The stores listed in this chapter provide a way for you to shop wholesale—every true shopper's goal! And over the coming year, we will be expanding our web site to provide even more information for shoppers. Do visit us on the internet at www.nyedge.com.

Each savvy New Yorker has secret sources for the best quality, value and service. By surveying scores of New York's smartest shoppers and then checking on their recommendations, *The New York Edge* brings you the best shopping information available for the second year in a row.

The New York Edge covers the shopping experience from "Best Bargains" to "Price Is No Object." It brings you news of stores and services for everyone from infants to the elderly and for men, women and children.

The New York Edge contains up-to-date intelligence on more than 2,300 stores and services. In describing each, we first define its *Edge*—why it made our list. We then describe what the establishment has to offer. And our survey ranks two-thirds for quality, style, service and value. Most of the stores and services we list are terrific. Some, unfortunately, are coasting along on reputations they no longer deserve. We feel it's important that you know that, too, which is why you'll find some pans among our picks.

As two busy New York career women, we work hard to combine demanding jobs and quality family life. We know that living well takes time and money, scarce resources for most of us. *The New York Edge* highlights our best tips garnered from years of shopping, but it's much more than our opinions alone. The strength of this book is the collective shopping intelligence of some of New York's most sophisticated shoppers. Scores of extremely knowledgeable New Yorkers let us know which stores and services they use and what they think about them. Our survey participants provide great tips on best buys which we pass on to you. Where to haggle and how to do it. Which high-end Madison Avenue furniture stores offer discounts. Who knocks off Armani. Who discounts Hickey-Freeman. We quote our panel's views and ratings in this book.

Talk to us

The participation of New York shoppers makes *The New York Edge* special among shopping guides. We welcome your comments, recommendations and requests and invite you to participate in next year's survey. Send a stamped (2 ounces) self-addressed business size envelope to *The New York Edge*, % Custom Databanks, Inc., 60 Sutton Place South, Suite 14BN, New York, NY 10022-4168, marked "Attention: Survey Department."

In appreciation for your response, you will receive a free copy of next year's book.

The ratings

A broad spectrum of New York shoppers, primarily professional associates and friends of the authors, were surveyed for their opinions and ratings. Each store and service was rated in terms of quality, style, service and value. Ratings are scaled as follows:

The ratings: excellent 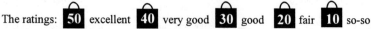 very good good fair **10** so-so

These ratings are subjective. In the case of value in particular, the ratings are relative and related to expected service and quality. A deluxe store and a discounter may both receive high ratings for value, given the shoppers' expectations for each type of store. With regard to deluxe, your initial response may be: How can such a high-priced store provide good value? These ratings reflect the quality and service provided by deluxe stores, so price becomes secondary when judging value.

Those judging the stores and services in this book are primarily women, ranging in age from 20 to 70 years old. The typical panel member is a 40-year-old vice president of a New York corporation who lives in Manhattan. She shops frequently for clothes, furniture and services.

The information

The New York Edge is arranged by category (and by subcategory) in alphabetical order from "Clothing & accessories to "Travel & vacation." The table of contents lists these categories and subcategories In addition, there's a complete index at the back of the book.

Hours are included for each store. For multistore chains, typical hours are listed—you may want to call an individual store to check its specific hours. Most stores accept credit and charge cards and deliver or send by UPS or FedEx. Stores that do not accept credit cards or do not send are noted. Subcategories and neighborhoods are listed for each store. A list of neighborhoods and a map of Manhattan follows.

Sue Dollinger   *Jane Lockshin*

October 30, 1997

About the authors

Sue Dollinger and Jane Lockshin are New York career women with a major sideline in shopping. Sue is a vice-president of a major international bank and a former president of the Financial Women's Association of New York. Jane is president of Custom Databanks, Inc., and a member of the New York YWCA's Academy of Women Achievers. Both are married parents with hard-won survival skills in getting the best out of New York in the least amount of time and for the least amount of money

Neighborhoods

**MANHATTAN
NEIGHBORHOODS**

1. LOWER MANHATTEN

2. SOHO / TRIBECA

3. LOWER EAST SIDE
   CHINATOWN

4. GREENWICH VILLAGE

5. FLATIRON
   EAST VILLAGE

6. CHELSEA

7. GRAMERCY PARK
   MURRAY HILL

8. MIDTOWN WEST

9. MIDTOWN EAST

10. UPPER EAST SIDE

11. UPPER WEST SIDE

12. UPPER UPPER EAST SIDE

13. UPPER UPPER WEST SIDE

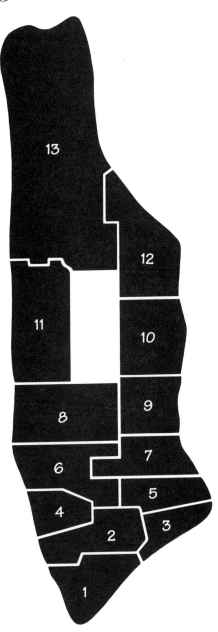

Clothing & accessories

Add

461 West Broadway
between Houston and Prince Streets / 539-1439
Daily 11am–8pm.

Accessories
SoHo/TriBeCa

| 35 | 40 | 35 | 30 |
| quality | style | service | value |

The Edge: Great accessories that become necessities. Find scarves, wallets, jewelry—including silver jewelry, some with stones—and much, much more.

Gallery of Wearable Art

34 East 67th Street
between Madison and Park Avenues / 425-5379
Tues–Sat 10am–6pm.

Accessories
Upper East Side

| 45 | 45 | 45 | 40 |
| quality | style | service | value |

The Edge: Entrance-making clothing. Unusual, one-of-a-kind, eye-catching clothing (evening and day dresses and jackets). Sizes 6 to 18 but can custom make to other sizes. *"Unusual, unique items."*

Julie Artisan's Gallery

687 Madison Avenue
near 62nd Street / 688-2345
Mon–Sat 11am–6pm (closed Sat July–Aug).

Accessories
Upper East Side

| 50 | 48 | 46 | 33 |
| quality | style | service | value |

The Edge: If "traffic-stopping" is you. One-of-a-kind clothing and jewelry designed by American artists. Cutting-edge jewelry including vintage Bakelite bracelets from $90 to $650. *"Can't afford anything, but love to look." "Wonderful."*

New York Exchange for Women's Work

149 East 60th Street
between Lexington and 3rd Avenues / 753-2330
Mon–Sat 10am–6pm.

Accessories
Midtown East

| 43 | 33 | 39 | 36 |
| quality | style | service | value |

The Edge: Style from yesteryear. Unique handcrafted gift items. Find knit toys, lingerie, children's clothing, painted furniture, and gift items. Best known for dresses, sweaters, and knits for babies. With the Elder Craftsmen now closed, many of its craftspeople are selling here. If you love nostalgia, you'll love the New York Exchange. *"Great place for unique gifts." "Too expensive."*

New York Firefighter's Friend

Accessories
SoHo/TriBeCa

263 Lafayette Street
near Prince Street / 226-3142
Mon–Sat 10am–6pm .

quality style service value

The Edge: Everything short of the Dalmatian. If you're into fires and fire department memorabilia, this is the place. Find caps, T-shirts, sweatpants, and shorts with the FDNY insignia, plus men's steel-toed rubber boots and children's boots. There's the *Big Red Book of Fire Trucks,* vintage fire hose nozzles for collectors, Dalmatians, and fire fighters pictured on everything. *"Fun yellow rain slickers."*

Only Hearts

Accessories
Upper West Side

386 Columbus Avenue
near 79th Street / 724-5608
Mon–Sat 11am–8pm, Sun noon–7pm.

30 30 35 30
quality style service value

The Edge: The name says it all. Lingerie and giftware with a heart motif.

A. T. Harris Formal Wear

Bridal, wedding & formal
Midtown East

11 East 44th Street
near 5th Avenue / 682-6325
Mon–Wed and Fri 9am–5:45pm, Thurs 9am–6:45pm, Sat 10am–3:45pm; and by appointment.

The Edge: For generations. Quality formal rentals, including cutaways and tails. Rents and sells a full range of conservatively styled formal wear (cutaways, tails, and tuxedos), including accessories: shirts, Chesterfield topcoats, shoes (for sale only), studs, cufflinks, and kid or suede gloves. Tuxedos are worsted wool. Rentals (from $125 plus tax) include everything but shoes.

Anne Bowen

Bridal, wedding & formal
Midtown West

80 West 40th Street, Penthouse West
at 6th Avenue / 921-8600
Weekdays by appointment 9am–5pm.

The Edge: Alternative wedding gowns. Evening wear in silk charmeuse, chantilly lace, and silk crepe. Custom orders only. No credit cards. No delivery.

Baldwin Formals

Bridal, wedding & formal
Midtown West

52 West 56th Street
between 5th and 6th Avenues / 245-8190
Mon and Thurs 8:30am–7pm, Tues–Wed and Fri 8:30am–6pm, Sat 10am–4pm.
Opens one hour later July–Aug.

The Edge: Rents formal wear. Rents and sells formal wear, including gowns, suits, overcoats, and top hats. Shoes for sale only. Rentals } $95 to $165.

Betsy

Bridal, wedding & formal
Upper East Side

540 Park Avenue, Suite 212
near 60th Street at the Regency Hotel / 753-7590

Weekdays 10am–6pm.

quality style service value

The Edge: Gorgeous designer evening gowns. European-styled evening gowns and coats. Simple, but high style. From $1,500 to $10,000. Deluxe. *"Sensational but pricey—and then there's the staff's attitude."*

Blue
125 St. Marks Place
between 1st Avenue and Avenue H / 228-7744
Mon–Sat noon–8pm, Sun noon–6pm .

Bridal, wedding & formal
Flatiron/East Village

quality style service value

The Edge: For weddings, a good alternative to Wang. A great young line of ultra-feminine clothing. For day to evening—fun fabrics and trims that are upbeat and cutting edge. Best known are her wedding and bridesmaid lines (not what you'd expect), in sophisticated New York styling. Wedding gowns from $600 to $1,200; bridesmaid, from $185 to $550. Wonderful fabrics—chiffon, silk shantung, peau de soie, and taffeta—in rich colors and styling. Nice suits (pants and skirts), well fitted in soft wools. *"You can't go wrong here." "Bridesmaid dresses that you really can wear after the wedding." "They have great style at great prices! But watch the work—they finally got it right after the wrong color, wrong size and unfinished hem!"*

Diane Wagner
90th Street
near Lexington Avenue / 663-1079
By appointment.

Bridal, wedding & formal
Upper East Side

quality style service value

The Edge: Sensational one-of-a-kind headpieces. Designs unique bridal headpieces, floral bouquets, and accessories. Her work is shown in *Modern Bride* and sold at Kleinfeld and Bergdorf. Beautiful work. Prices average $250 to $350. No credit cards. No delivery. Deluxe. *"Check this out."*

Eleny Couture
7A West 56th Street
between 5th and 6th Avenues / 245-0001
By appointment daily 10am–6pm.

Bridal, wedding & formal
Midtown West

quality style service value

The Edge: Sexy! Original designs for evening and bridal gowns. Sexy statement dresses. *"It can be a bit much."*

Jack and Company Formal Wear
128 East 86th Street
near Park Avenue / 722-4609
Weekdays 10am–7pm.

Bridal, wedding & formal
Upper East Side

The Edge: Formal wear—less expensive rentals and sales. In business since 1925, it sells and rents formal wear. Rentals from $99 to $136, and if you buy you can apply the rental fee to the purchase price. Tuxes sell for $169 to $500. Stocks a full range of sizes in middle-of-the-line tuxes in fabrics that are often blends.

Jane Wilson-Marquis

Bridal, wedding & formal
SoHo/TriBeCa

155 Prince Street
between West Broadway and Thompson Street / 477-4408
By appointment

The Edge: For *Age of Innocence* styling. Romantic wedding gowns priced from $1,000 to $6,000. Very dramatic, often looking like a period piece.

Just Once Ltd.

Bridal, wedding & formal
Midtown West

292 5th Avenue, 3rd Floor
between 30th and 31st Streets / 465-0960
Weekdays 11am–6:30pm, Sat 11am–3pm by appointment.

The Edge: Rents quality bridal and formal gowns and headpieces. Great designer clothing to buy at $500 to $3,500 or to rent at $400 to $800. Rent headpieces from $75. Sizes from petite 2 to misses 14.

Kleinfeld and Son

Bridal, wedding & formal
Brooklyn

8202 5th Avenue and 8209 3rd Avenue
near 82nd Street, Brooklyn / 718-238-1500
By appointment, Tues and Thurs 11am–9pm, Wed,
Fri and Sat 11-6.

44	44	43	39
quality	style	service	value

The Edge: Selection, selection, selection. Virtually no one gets married without a pilgrimage to Kleinfeld. It has it all—from veils to pumps—for the bride, her mom, and her attendants. It's always a scene, packed with brides from every state. Dressing rooms are full with staff grabbing dresses and sometimes brides checking out other brides and their choices. However, it's one of the most complete sources for bridal wear and accessories in New York, perhaps the U.S. If you've seen a dress somewhere, it's likely that this place has it! Good prices, lower than most elsewhere. Thousands of dresses are in stock, with every major supplier represented. Prices from moderate to high end. Mom has a separate store. Appointments are required. Their vans leave from the Parker Meridien at 10am and noon Monday to Friday and 9am and 1pm on Saturday (cost: $10 per person, reservations required). *"It's got a bridal dress for anywhere." "An experience if nothing else." "Got my dress there. Every bride's worst nightmare, but 25% off."*

La Sposa Veils

Bridal, wedding & formal
Midtown West

252 West 40th Street
near 8th Avenue / 354-4729
Weekdays 9am–6pm, Sat 9am–5pm.

The Edge: Fantasy wedding party dresses for those young attendants. Offers its own custom veils ($125 to $1,000), fabrics, and junior bridal/Communion dresses ($300 to $500) from its Just Once line. Featured in *Brides* magazine. Discounter.

Michelle of Australia Bridal

Bridal, wedding & formal
Midtown West

24 West 57th Street
between 5th and 6th Avenues / 245-3390
By appointment

The Edge: Price! Bridal gowns starting at $295. A wide variety of styles from straight to full-skirted dresses in silk satin, chiffon, and tulle. Also flower girl and bridesmaid dresses. More moderately priced lines. Sizes 2 to 20.

Nancy Wedding Center, Inc.
118 Bowery Street
near Grand Street / 966-6686
Daily 9am–7pm.

Bridal, wedding & formal
SoHo/TriBeCa

quality style service value

The Edge: Elaborate traditional Chinese wedding gowns. The source of the wedding gowns in the movie *The Wedding Banquet*. Features elaborate traditional Chinese red wedding dresses and very ornate Western wedding dresses for the bride and bridal party. Fun just to visit. Open Christmas Day.

One of a Kind Bride
89 5th Avenue, Suite 902
between 16th and 17th Streets / 645-7123
Weekdays by appointment 10am–6pm.

Bridal, wedding & formal
Flatiron/East Village

The Edge: Put your own wedding look together. Couture bridal dresses, favoring tailored sophisticated styles. Collection to view and try on. Quality dresses. Priced from $3,500 to $7,000.

Paul's Veil and Net
42 West 38th Street
between 5th and 6th Avenues / 391-3822
Weekdays 8:30am–4pm, Sat 8:30am–2pm.

Bridal, wedding & formal
Midtown West

quality style service value

The Edge: Great source of bridal veils and crowns, accessories, and supplies. Priced from $50 to $500. Accessories include garters, money bags, pillows, and the like. Flower accessories sold separately. No credit cards. No delivery. *"Anything you want, they'll make—reasonably."*

RK Bridal
2276 Broadway
near 82nd Street / 362-9512
Mon–Wed and Fri 10am–6:15pm, Thurs 10:30am–7pm, Sat 10am–4pm.

Bridal, wedding & formal
Upper West Side

The Edge: Seventh Avenue prices. Wedding gowns from $200 (is it possible?) to $2,000. The shop will ship anywhere. Call to see what it's featuring and if it can get what you want.

Reem Bridals
588 Broadway
between Houston and Prince Streets / 431-9232
By appointment.

Bridal, wedding & formal
SoHo/TriBeCa

quality style service value

The Edge: Great for headpieces. Intricate embroidery on soft fabrics. Wired headpieces to match. Dresses priced from $1,800 to $4,500. No credit cards. *"A little inconvenient to get to, but go!"* *"Couldn't be nicer—great advice on what's best for you!"*

Sander Witlin

27 East 61st Street
near Madison Avenue / 421-0869
Weekdays 10am–6pm.

Bridal, wedding & formal
Upper East Side

quality style service value

The Edge: The source for the ladies who lunch and glitter at night. Custom-made gala gowns. Makes gowns and day suits, but best known for its evening wear. Priced from $2,000 to $4,500. Deluxe. *"A little over the top."*

Vera Wang Bridal House Ltd.

991 Madison Avenue
near 77th Street / 628-3400
Mon–Sat 9am–6pm by appointment
(but no appointment needed at the Thurs open house 6–7pm).

Bridal, wedding & formal
Upper East Side

quality style service value

The Edge: Gorgeous modern gowns. The look is simple and elegant with the fabric and cut making the look. Gowns are priced from $3,000 to $7,000. Appointments necessary, except on Thusday evening when the salon hosts an open house for viewing—not trying on—gowns. *"Understated, sophisticated, small collection." "If you can get an appointment in a timely manner, they will make you feel like a princess." "Very snooty."*

Yumi Katsura Bridal House

907 Madison Avenue
between 72nd and 73rd Streets / 772-3760
Weekdays 11am–5pm, Sat 10am–4pm.

Bridal, wedding & formal
Upper East Side

quality style service value

The Edge: Elegant—but not Vera Wang. Over 2,000 wedding styles, with prices starting at $2,200 and averaging $3,000 to $4,000. Simple sophisticated styling. *"Expensive."*

A. Feibush

27 Allen Street
near Canal Street / 226-3964
Weekdays 9am–5pm, Sun 9am–4pm (closed Sun June–Aug).

Buttons, beads & trims
Lower East Side/Chinatown

quality style service value

The Edge: Zipper heaven. Zippers: all styles, colors, metals, teeth, and shapes, plus matching threads. No delivery. No credit cards. Discounter.

Gordon Button Company

222 West 38th Street
between 7th and 8th Avenues / 921-1684
Weekdays 9:30am–5:30pm.

Buttons, beads & trims
Midtown West

quality style service value

The Edge: High-fashion quality buttons at Seventh Avenue prices. Large button wholesaler since 1925. Offers styles featured in the current season's moderate to bridge lines. You won't find Tender Buttons' wonderful upper end or antique collection of buttons, but you'll find everything else at great prices. No credit cards. No delivery. Discounter.

Hersh 6th Avenue Buttons, Inc.

1000 6th Avenue
near 37th Street / 391-6615
Mon 9:30am–5:45pm, Tues–Fri 9am–5:45pm, Sat 11am–4pm.

Buttons, beads & trims
Midtown West

quality style service value

The Edge: Can't find the right button? They'll make it here. Dressmaking and millinery supplies. A full range of notions, including buckles, buttons, cording, ribbons, zippers, and the like. Zippers can be cut to size. The range of buttons includes antique to more modern styles, and for special needs they can create a custom button dyed to a specific color. Prices for buttons from $7 to $45 (a gross).

M&J Trimming

1008 Avenue of the Americas
near 37th Street / 391-6200
Weekdays 9am–6pm, Sat 10am–5pm.

Buttons, beads & trims
Midtown West

quality style service value

The Edge: You need it—they have it. Great source for dressmaking accessories. Find buttons, flowers, feathers, tassels, threads, trims, and more. Hundreds of items on display. Mail order requires a $50 minimum. Discounter. *"Has it all." "Expensive but good." "The trims are fabulous."*

So-Good

28 West 38th Street
between 5th and 6th Avenues / 398-0236
Weekdays 9am–5pm.

Buttons, beads & trims
Midtown West

quality style service value

The Edge: Ribbons galore! A store filled with beautiful patterned ribbons and flowers (roses and peonies in all sizes). The sign says "$10 minimum order," but ignore that—we've bought less. Ribbons are what make this place. Ribbons for present packages, great styles for your hair, and clothing trim. The ribbon prices range from 25¢ to $5 a yard, with wholesale prices on very large orders. Very reasonable prices. No credit cards. Discounter. *"Best selection ever!"*

Tender Buttons

143 East 62nd Street
between Lexington and 3rd Avenues / 758-7004
Weekdays 11am–6pm, Sat 11am–5:30pm.

Buttons, beads & trims
Upper East Side

quality style service value

The Edge: Everyone's favorite button source. A small store chock full of great, top-quality (new and antique) button treasures and cufflinks. A terrific way to update an old outfit, repair a cleaner's mistakes, and provide oomph for clothing. From moderate prices into the hundreds and thousands of dollars for antique cufflinks. No credit cards. No delivery. *"Great selection of buttons, but not cheap." "The most incredible source."*

Aquascutum of London

714 Madison Avenue
near 64th Street / 975-0250
Mon–Wed and Fri–Sat 10am–6pm,
Thurs 10am–7pm, Sun noon–5pm.

Clothing
Upper East Side

quality style service value

The Edge: A bit dated, but it's the English look. Famous for its raincoats. Not as pricey as Burberry. Sales, at the end of January and after July 4th, reduce prices dramatically. *"Predictable, classic English." "Classic (but can be dull) decent raincoats."*

Burberry Limited

9 East 57th Street
between Madison and 5th Avenues / 371-5010
Mon–Wed and Fri–Sat 9:30am–6pm,
Thurs 9:30am–7pm, Sun noon–5pm.

Clothing
Midtown East

quality style service value

The Edge: Classic British clothing that tries to be a bit more contemporary. Traditional English clothing (blouses, slacks, suits, sweaters, and topcoats), including—of course—its signature trench coat with the famous plaid lining. Deluxe. *"Same old, same old, but good at what it does." "Nice shirts that last." "Heirloom quality to their coats." "The same old stuff." "Better buys at Woodbury."*

Burlington Coat Factory

Mon–Sat 9am–9pm, Sun 10am–6pm.

Clothing
Multiple locations

quality style service value

The Edge: Good discounts on moderately priced brand-name coats. Five floors of casual to dress clothing for men, women, and children (children for outerwear only). All sizes, including plus sizes. Brands are the more inexpensive lines—Jones New York, Kasper, Liz Claiborne—discounted 25% to 30%. *"If you need an inexpensive item." "The coat source." "The space is worth a look." "Shoddy showrooms, but bargains."*

Locations: Chelsea: 116 West 23rd Street, at 6th Avenue (229-1300) / **Lower Manhattan:** 45 Park Place, between Church Street and West Broadway (571-2630)

Calvin Klein

654 Madison Avenue
at 60th Street / 292-9000
Mon–Wed and Fri–Sat 10am–6pm, Thurs 10am–8pm.

Clothing
Upper East Side

quality style service value

The Edge: That clean American look. Classic clothing, plus home accessories and luggage. All Calvin's clothing has a sleek masculine tailoring, but cut from fabulous fabrics to look sexy. In luggage, the sleek look favored is traditional salesman's cases. The home collection includes china, flatware, glassware, and linens, plus sterling gift items. Very, very expensive. *"Overpriced but good fabric, fine fit and workmanship." "Classic designs."*

Charivari

Mon–Wed and Fri 10am–7pm, Thurs 10am–8pm,

Clothing
Multiple locations

Sat 10am–6:30pm, Sun 12:30– 6pm.

quality style service value

The Edge: Always original. Prides itself on always being the first, or among the first, to discover new designers. Cutting-edge clothing sold now in two locations, including avant-garde Japanese designs. Merchandise for both men and women. Deluxe. *"Cutting edge."*

Locations: Midtown West: 18 West 57th Street, between 5th and 6th Avenues (333-4040) / **Upper East Side:** 1001 Madison Avenue, near 78th Street (650-0078) / **Upper West Side:** 257 72nd Street, near Columbus Avenue (787-7272)

Christian Dior

703 5th Avenue
at 55th Street / 223-4646
Mon–Wed and Fri–Sat 10am–6pm,
Thurs 10am–7pm, Sun 11am–5pm.

Clothing
Midtown East

quality style service value

The Edge: Luxury. Three floors carrying the full Dior range, including his less expensive lines, plus fragrances and cosmetics. Ready-to-wear for women only. Accessories for men and women are featured. This year the ladies who lunch are flocking to Dior to buy his $1,200 handbag, with a dangling metal Dior label. Quilted or plain leather, shoulder or hand held—the 1997–98 status symbol. Deluxe. *"Every item has great detail and tailoring."*

Comme des Garçons

116 Wooster Street
between Prince and Spring Streets / 219-0660
Mon–Sat 11am–7pm, Sun noon–6:30pm.

Clothing
SoHo/TriBeCa

quality style service value

The Edge: High-fashion Japanese designs. Designer Rei Kawakubo favors cutting-edge designs for men and women. Expect playful high-quality expensive clothing priced from $15 for socks to $6,000 for evening gowns. Bold colors and patterns. Deluxe.

Daffy's Fifth Avenue

Mon–Sat 10am–9pm, Sun noon–7pm.

Clothing
Multiple locations

quality style service value

The Edge: Best for the young on a tight budget and for inexpensive children's clothing. Crammed full of fashion-forward, inexpensive sportswear, shoes, and accessories for the entire family. Wonderful children's things. Lots of basic inexpensive items for the college set. Some higher-end European and American names, but mostly lower-end items. You have to hunt here to find treasures. Discounts from 40% or more. For children's clothing, Daffy's prices seem to top out at $30. No delivery. 30% off. *"Have to be willing to dig through the racks of clothes. Can find good buys if you're patient." "Hit or miss, but good values." "You really have to search. Good for lingerie." "Good for kids' clothing." "Clothes are picked over." "Used to be good.""Getting worse all the time." "Clothes are too crammed."*

Locations: Flatiron/East Village: 111 5th Avenue, near 18th Street (529-4477) / **Midtown East:** 335 Madison Avenue, near 44th Street (557-4422) / **Midtown West:** 1311 Broadway, Herald Square near 34th Street (376-4477)

Davide Cenci

Clothing
Upper East Side

801 Madison Avenue
between 67th and 68th Streets / 628-5910
Mon–Wed and Fri–Sat 10:30am–6:30pm, Thurs 10:30am–7:30pm .

quality style service value

The Edge: Expensive, classic Italian styling. Offers classic Italian menswear from casual to formal. Luxurious Italian fabrics and styling. Sells A. Testoni footwear. Both made-to-measure and hand-finished suits. Off-the-rack suits from $750 and made-to-measure from $1,900. Now a women's clothing collection which favors a very tailored Italian preppy look. Women's suits from $1,200. *"Divine—but pricey."*

Dollar Bill's

Clothing
Midtown East

32 East 42nd Street
between Madison and 5th Avenues / 867-0212
Weekdays 8am–7pm, Sat 10am–6pm, Sun 11am–5pm.

quality style service value

The Edge: High-end Italian, discounted. New and improved with its move to a new location. Two full floors of men's and now fine women's clothing—largely close-outs from mostly top Italian designers, but some American finds. For men: a full range of clothing—sportswear to suits. For women: limited casual wear, more office suits. Italian suits for women which appear to be made for them in the $500 range; some items by Jenny, Versace, Calvin Klein, and similar quality designers. Men always seem to find some Armani items, often Missoni sweaters, Versace, and Zegna. Great accessories, including handbags, briefcases, ties, and sunglasses. 33% off. *"Sometimes produces a gem at a bargain." "Women's store is very improved, but still best for men." "Good accessories."*

Enz's

Clothing
Flatiron/East Village

48 West 8th Street
near 6th Avenue / 475-0997
Daily 11am–8pm.

The Edge: Fashion-forward, even for the downtown crowd. Clothing and boots from London. The current look—rubber clothing, bustiers, and body piercing! No delivery.

Etro

Clothing
Upper East Side

720 Madison Avenue
between 63rd and 64th Streets / 317-9096
Weekdays 10am–7pm, Sat 10am–6pm.

quality style service value

The Edge: High-end fabrics custom tailored. Now finally in New York. A somewhat more contemporary Ferragamo. Beautiful fabrics in great alive colors and patterns. Six floors. You pick the fabric and items from the ready-to-wear collection they'll make it for you to size.

Filene's Basement

Clothing
Multiple locations

Mon–Sat 9:30am–9pm, Sun 11am–7pm.

quality style service value

The Edge: Well-known discounter. Lower-end discount clothing for the entire family. No delivery. 30% to 35% off. *"Not like the original in Boston." "Good buys, but lots of work to find them." "Disappointing."*

Locations: Chelsea: 620 Avenue of the Americas, between 18th and 19th Streets (620-3100) /
Upper West Side: 2224 Broadway, near 79th Street (873-8000)

Giorgio Armani
760 Madison Avenue
near 65th Street / 988-9191
Mon–Wed and Fri-Sat 10am–6pm, Thurs 10am–7pm .

Clothing
Upper East Side

quality   style   service   value

The Edge: It's Armani. Elegant, easy, unconstructed clothing in wonderful rich fabrics with a
conservative but up-to-date look. Find suits to evening wear. These are clothes you can wear
anywhere, from the office to the Academy Awards! Deluxe. *"A classic, if you can afford it."*
"Great, but overpriced."

Issey Miyake
992 Madison Avenue
near 77th Street / 439-7822
Weekdays 10am–6pm, Sat 11am–6pm.

Clothing
Upper East Side

quality   style   service   value

The Edge: Miyake's signature detailing. Features jackets, shirts, slacks, and coats. Very
expensive. Women's pants from $185 to $300. Jackets from $800 to $1,800, with some to $3,000.
Deluxe.

Kenzo
805 Madison Avenue
near 68th Street / 717-0101
Mon–Wed and Fri–Sat 10am–6pm, Thurs 10am–7pm.

Clothing
Upper East Side

quality   style   service   value

The Edge: Wild patterns made bolder by their exuberant colors. Japanese designer influenced
by his years in Paris (since the 1960s). Kenzo is noted for his bold-looking fabrics—wild flowers
and animals cut to tailored styles.

Krizia
769 Madison Avenue
at 66th Street / 879-1211
Mon–Wed and Fri–Sat 10am–6pm, Thurs 10am–8pm .

Clothing
Upper East Side

quality   style   service   value

The Edge: Sensuous evening gowns. Sensuous evening gowns, along with ultra-simple lines and
easy tweed suits. Features the signature feline sweaters and offers Mariuccia Mandelli's complete
line of clothing. For men: suits and jackets, sportswear, and accessories, including ties, belts,
umbrellas, and fragrances. Also glassware and dishes. Deluxe.

Laura Ashley
398 Columbus Avenue
near 79th Street / 496-5110
Mon–Wed and Sat 11am–7pm,
Thurs–Fri 11am–8pm, Sun noon–6pm.

Clothing
Upper West Side

quality   style   service   value

The Edge: That sweet English country look—best for youngsters. Lots of florals. Best for children's clothing for boys and girls age six months to 12 years. The home furnishings are English country and well priced. *"Excellent quality and service." "Only for the prissies among us."*

Le Firme

37 West 57th Street, Suite 401
between 5th and 6th Avenues / 888-3433
Weekdays 9am–6pm, Sat 10am–4pm .

**Clothing
Midtown West**

quality style service value

The Edge: The Italian names you covet, made almost affordable. Wonderful high-end Italian designer clothing. Expect to find Max Mara, Versace, and similar labels. Great selection—slacks, silk shirts, sweaters, suits, coats, and at times some evening wear. Now lingerie and swimwear from Gruppo La Perla. For men: smaller but similarly high-quality lines of Italian sportswear (jackets, shirts, and sweaters). To complement the fashion look, great accessories (belts and handbags), and for men, ties. 5,000 square feet filled with high fashion. Alterations available on purchased items at a flat fee—$8 on separates and $12 on coats and suits. Discounter. *"Lots to choose from." "A real find." "Have to keep checking to see if anything's there." "Best for women."*

Moschino

803 Madison Avenue
between 67th and 68th Streets / 639-9600
Mon–Sat 10am–6pm.

**Clothing
Upper East Side**

quality style service value

The Edge: The Cheap and Chic line—the rage in Rome. 20,000 square feet spread over five floors. Features the full Moschino lines, including the high-end signature collection and the fun young Cheap and Chic. Also a men's line, children's line, and fragrances. *"High style—clothes for one season. Expensive."*

Polo/Ralph Lauren

867 Madison Avenue
near 72nd Street / 606-2100
Mon–Wed and Fri–Sat 10am–6pm, Thurs 10am–8pm.

**Clothing
Upper East Side**

quality style service value

The Edge: The Connecticut preppy look in Manhattan! Traditional preppy look in a full line of clothing and shoes for boys (from age 4), men, and women. Also antique jewelry and housewares. Best feature is the shop itself, which is in the beautifully restored Rhinelander mansion. Very expensive. *"Classics that never go out of style."*

SYMS

42 Trinity Place
near Rector Street / 797-1199
Mon–Wed 9am–6:30pm, Thurs–Fri 9am–8pm,
Sat 10am–6:30pm, Sun noon– 5:30pm.

**Clothing
Multiple locations**

quality style service value

The Edge: Designer discount clothing for men and women. Price is reduced depending on how long the item remains unsold. Most of the merchandise is from more moderate lines—for women: Jones New York and Evan Picone. A full range of merchandise and accessories, but best for moderately priced suits for men, separates and casual wear, and coats. Some higher-end pieces in the downtown store are on the fourth floor. 33% off. *"Occasional buys in clothing and suits." "Some great values in sportswear." "Mostly tired and seldom this year's."*

Locations: / Lower Manhattan: 42 Trinity Place, near Rector Street (797-1199) / **Midtown East:** 400 Park Avenue, at 54th Street (317-8200)

Saint Laurie Ltd.
897 Broadway
between 19th and 20th Streets / 473-0100
Weekdays 10am–6:30pm, Sat 9:30am–6pm, Sun noon–5pm.

Clothing
Flatiron/East Village

quality style service value

The Edge: Traditional men's and women's suits. Suits, sport jackets, and slacks made in-house. For women: a petite and tall department with sizes from 2 to 18. Made-to-measure available with delivery in four weeks. Swatch club for mail order. *"Tried and true." "Past its prime."*

Steven-Alan
60 Wooster Street
between Broome and Spring Streets / 334-6354
Daily noon–8pm.

Clothing
SoHo/TriBeCa

quality style service value

The Edge: Hip young sexy clothing. Alan has the knack for finding young talent and buying their best. Expect a wide range of items from day to evening clothing, plus accessories and some shoes. Catch the fabulous sequined skirt by Rebecca Danenberg—about $226 in crème. Practical water-resistant watches by Casio in clear-plastic pastel-color tinted shades—very attractive ($125). Silver sandals—a '50s Miami Beach look for $28. Great vinyl hip huggers. Leather-free bags from Paris designer Herve Chapelier and fun bags from Kate Spade. *"Worth a trip."*

Steven-Alan Outlet
330 East 11th Street
between 1st and 2nd Avenues / 982-2881
Daily 1–8pm.

Clothing
Flatiron/East Village

quality style service value

The Edge: The source for trendy wear discounted. The discoverer of top young talent—Wendy Mulin, Pixie Yates, Sara Kozlowski, Living Doll, Bernadette Corporation, Rebecca Danenberg, and more. Prices are truly excellent, about half of retail. No delivery. Discounter.

Yohji Yamamoto
103 Grand Street
near Mercer Street / 966-9066
Mon–Sat 11am–7pm, Sun noon–6pm.

Clothing
SoHo/TriBeCa

The Edge: Yamamoto's own tailored and minimalist line. His signature collection, often in deep, dark colors. Rich sensual fabrics. Striking cuts. Very expensive. Coats start at $1,800. Deluxe.

Zara
750 Lexington Avenue
near 59th Street / 935-2853
Weekdays 10am–8pm, Sat 10am–7pm, Sun noon–6pm .

Clothing
Midtown East

quality style service value

The Edge: For the young hip crowd. Trendy medium-priced clothing from Spain. Blazers from $100. *"I can't wear their cut—too bad, because the shapes are cute."*

A/X Armani Exchange
568 Broadway
near Prince Street / 431-6000
Weekdays 10am–8pm, Sat 10am–8pm, Sun noon–7pm.

Clothing-casual
SoHo/TriBeCa

quality style service value

The Edge: It's Armani. Lower-priced casual Armani items, including jeans and sport shirts. An upscale The Gap. Jeans ($48 to $68), sport shirts, and sweaters. *"Great style, particularly if you like Black and White." "Better value at J. Crew or Banana Republic."*

Abercrombie & Fitch
199 Water Street
near South Street Seaport / 809-9000
Mon–Sat 10am–9pm, Sun 11am–8pm.

Clothing-casual
Lower Manhattan

quality style service value

The Edge: Rugged outdoor clothing. Same name, new management since the 1980s. Focus is on quality sports clothing, including rugged outdoor clothing. Sells only its own label. *"Good classic things." "Lovely things."*

Back From Guatemala
306 East 6th Street
between 1st and 2nd Avenues / 260-7010
Daily noon–10:30pm.

Clothing-casual
Flatiron/East Village

quality style service value

The Edge: Love it—it's so original. Very wearable—handcrafted collectibles from around the world. A unique collection of clothing, jewelry, and artifacts from over 30 countries. Expect to find musical instruments, masks, hats, scarves, sweaters, jewelry (ethnic and semiprecious), deities, puppets, frames, incense and holders, serapes, wall hangings, and more. Reasonable prices. *"Great—a young original look." "Plenty of affordable treasures."*

Banana Republic
Mon–Sat 10am–8pm, Sun noon–6pm.

Clothing-casual
Multiple locations

quality style service value

The Edge: Classic casual clothing that's meant to be worn. Colors tend to be muted (khaki, gray, brown, and olive). You'll find slacks, bush jackets, Oxford cloth shirts, fleece-lined suits, and accessories (canvas and leather belts, canvas duffels, and shoulder bags). *"An old standard that remains interesting." "Nice styling. Where Ralph Lauren began in the '70s." "Quality down, prices up. Careful." "Quality and style have dropped since The Gap took them over."*

Locations: Flatiron/East Village: 89 5th Avenue, near 16th Street (366-4630) / **Midtown East:** 130 East 59th Street, near Lexington Avenue (751-5570) / **SoHo/TriBeCa:** 205 Bleecker Street, near 6th Avenue (473-9570) / 522 Broadway, between Prince and Spring Streets (925-0308) / **Upper East Side:** 1131 3rd Avenue, near 67th Street (288-4279) / 1136 Madison Avenue, near 85th Street (570-2465) / **Upper West Side:** 215 Columbus Avenue, near 71st Street (873-9048)

Benetton
Mon–Sat 10am–9pm, Sun noon–8pm.

Clothing-casual
Multiple locations

quality style service value

The Edge: Like The Gap, sometimes snappier. Some years it's good; others, less so. You'll find sneakers, pants, and accessories. A range of sweaters from basic colors to bright colors, some with flash patterns which are fun if you're young. Now luggage—a great molded-resin suitcase on wheels in hot colors for $235. Moderate prices. *"Best for sweaters."*

Locations: Flatiron/East Village: 749 Broadway, near 8th Street (533-0230) / **Midtown East:** 597 5th Avenue, near 48th Street (223-4444) / **Midtown West:** 666 5th Avenue, near 53rd Street (399-9860) / **Upper East Side:** 805 Lexington Avenue, near 62nd Street (752-5283)

Canal Jeans

504 Broadway
off Spring Street / 226-3663
Sun–Thurs 11am–7pm, Fri–Sat 10am–8pm.

Clothing-casual
SoHo/TriBeCa

quality style service value

The Edge: Latest SoHo looks. You'll always find vintage jeans and motorcycle jackets. Bins of clothes, from used clothing to very trendy new looks sourced from close-outs. Also painter's pants, T-shirts, and cotton sweaters in good colors. *"Where the teenie boppers go to buy old clothes."*

Cockpit

595 Broadway
near Prince Street / 925-5455
Mon–Sat 11am–7pm, Sun 12:30–6pm.

Clothing-casual
SoHo/TriBeCa

quality style service value

The Edge: Clothing related to aviation. Great jackets related to flying—bomber, flight, leather, and unisex jackets, plus other aviation-related items. *"Fun—clever."*

Emporio Armani

110 5th Avenue
at 16th Street / 727-3240
Mon–Sat 11am–7pm, Sun 1–6pm.

Clothing-casual
Chelsea

quality style service value

The Edge: It's Armani. Sportswear less (but still) expensive than Giorgio Armani's main line. Casual sweaters, jeans, slacks, soft tailored dresses, and Emporio shoes. Relax at the Armani Cafe at the 601 Madison Avenue store, which serves espresso and light fare. *"Elegant European style for a certain figure." "Fashion for the anorexic set."*

Gap

Weekdays 9:30am–8pm, Sat 10am–7pm, Sun noon–5pm.

Clothing-casual
Multiple locations

quality style service value

The Edge: Basic inexpensive casual clothing. Basically T-shirts, flannels, sweatshirts, sweaters, and jeans. The basics are priced right and the jeans are great!! The rest doesn't seem to last, but, then, it isn't priced to last. Everyone shops here, from preteens to adults, and it's certainly "a must" for the college crowd. *"Reliable." "Great swimsuits—the Financial Center store has the best sales."*

Locations: Chelsea: 91-97 7th Avenue, between 16th and 17th Streets (989-1110) / 122 5th Avenue, near 17th Street (989-0550) / **Flatiron/East Village:** 133 2nd Avenue, near St. Marks (353-2090) / **Gramercy Park/Murray Hill:** 113 East 23rd Street, near Lexington Avenue (533-6670) / 445 5th Avenue, near 39th Street (532-8633) / 549 3rd Avenue, near 36th Street (213-6007) / 113 East 23rd Street, near Park Avenue (533-6670) / **Greenwich Village:** 345 Avenue of the Americas, near West 4th Street (727-2210) / **Lower Manhattan:** 89 South Street, 2nd Floor, South Street Seaport, Pier 17 (374-1051) / 157 World Trade Center Building 5, near Chambers Street (432-7086) / **Midtown East:** 757 3rd Avenue, near 47th Street (223-5140) / 657-659 3rd Avenue, near 42nd Street (697-3590) / 900 3rd Avenue, near 54th Street (754-2290) / 527 Madison Avenue, near 54th Street (688-1260) / 734 Lexington Avenue, near 59th Street (751-1543) / **Midtown West:** 250 West 57th Street, near Broadway (315-2250) / 1466 Broadway, near 42nd Street (768-2987) / 1212 Avenue of the Americas, near 48th Street (730-1087) / 60 West 34th Street, near Broadway (643-8960) / **Upper East Side:** 1131 3rd Avenue, near 66th Street (472-5559) / 1066 Lexington Avenue, near 75th Street (879-9144) / 1164 Madison Avenue, near 86th Street (517-5763) / 1511 3rd Avenue, near 85th Street (794-5781) / **Upper West Side:** 2101 Broadway, near 73rd Street (787-6698) / 335 Columbus Avenue, near 76th Street (873-9272) / 1988 Broadway, near 67th Street (721-5304) / 2373 Broadway, near 86th Street (873-1244) / 535 Columbus Avenue, near 86th Street (874-8377)

Henry Lehr

Clothing-casual
Upper East Side

772 Madison Avenue
near 66th Street / 535-1021
Mon–Wed and Fri–Sat 10am–6pm,
Thurs 10am–7pm, Sun noon–5pm.

quality style service value

The Edge: Upscale European country-western sportswear look. Find great prewashed jeans from Blue System, Replay, and Rivet with a great fit for $100 in sizes 2 to 14. Sportswear from $59 to $500, with slacks from $200. *"Only wear their jeans—they fit." "Pricey."*

House of Nubian

Clothing-casual
Chelsea

35 West 8th Street
near 5th Avenue / 475-7553
Mon–Thurs noon–9pm, Fri–Sat noon–11pm, Sun 1–8pm.

The Edge: African clothing items. A variety of African bags, clothing, hats, incense, jewelry, and oils. In addition, hand-carved African figures, most under $75. Prices ranging from 50¢ to $1,000.

J. Crew

Clothing-casual
Lower Manhattan

203 Front Street
South Street Seaport / 385-3500
Jan–Apr, Mon–Sat 10am–7pm, Sun 11am–6pm;
May–Dec, Mon–Sat 10am– 9pm, Sun 11am–8pm.

quality style service value

The Edge: Wonderful classic sportswear that appeals to all ages. Styling and colors are excellent. Good fabrics, including cottons, silks, wools, and cashmeres. Find shoes, jeans, shorts, shirts, skirts, and pants, plus accessories. Women's sizes mostly 2 to 12, some 14s. Men's suit sizes from 38 to 46. Great sales. For the college crowd to seniors, you can't go wrong. *"Great store for casual wear." "Fabulous cotton turtles, shorts—basics." "Fabulous return policy." "Mediocre quality but good looks, good service."*

Old Navy Clothing Company

610 Avenue of the Americas
near 18th Street / 645-0663
Mon–Sat 9:30am–9pm, Sun 11am–7pm.

Clothing-casual
Chelsea

quality style service value

The Edge: Less expensive Gap-style casual clothing. This Gap subsidiary offers less expensive Gap-type clothing. Basically T-shirts, flannels, sweatshirts, sweaters, and jeans. Not made to last, but it certainly will get you through the season. *"Great buys if you select carefully." "A lotta bang for the buck." ""Great sales, great kids ware, great outlet in Reading." "Sizing is variable. Store is always crowded." "Very inexpensive version of Gap clothes—but quality is poor."*

Peter Elliot

1070 Madison Avenue
near 81st Street / 570-2300
Weekdays 10:30am–7pm, Sat 10:30am–6pm, Sun 1–5pm.

Clothing-casual
Upper East Side

quality style service value

The Edge: Beloved by all—classic men's and women's sportswear. The basics, attractive and well fitting, conservative styling. Largest selection is menswear. *"Great choices and guidance."*

TG-170

170 Ludlow Street
between Houston and Stanton Streets / 995-8660
Tues–Sun noon–8pm.

Clothing-casual
Lower East Side/Chinatown

The Edge: Solves teenage crises. Owner Terri Gillis knows how to buy great hip clothing—hipster pants and tops, tight and short clothing. Designers/lines include Rebecca Danenberg, Bernadette Corporation, Jeffrey Costello, Maura McCarthy, Living Doll, and Pixie Yates. Sexy fun lingerie by Girlie NYC. Prices are low, under $100. Discounter.

Urban Outfitters

Mon–Sat 10am–10pm, Sun noon–8pm.

Clothing-casual
Multiple locations

quality style service value

The Edge: Weekend work clothing. The Gap look at higher prices. No delivery. *"All the latest urban trends, with 'awesome' accessories, including hair pieces and the cutest gifts." "Very young (college) and trendy clothes." "Great inexpensive gifts." "Lower quality but fairly priced." "Snotty employees; terrible return policy.Overpriced junk."*

Locations: Chelsea: 374 Avenue of the Americas, between Washington Street and Waverly Place (677-9350) / **Midtown East:** 127 East 59th Street, between Park and Lexington Avenues (688-1200) / **SoHo/TriBeCa:** 628 Broadway, between Houston and Bleecker Streets (475-0009)

Weiss & Mahoney

142 5th Avenue
near 19th Street / 675-1915
Weekdays 9am–7pm, Sat 10am–6:30pm, Sun 11am–5pm.

Clothing-casual
Chelsea

quality style service value

The Edge: A New York City army-navy surplus store. Some used items, but mostly new. Priced from $5.

Wings

Mon–Sat 9am–9pm, Sun 10am–8pm.

Clothing-casual
Multiple locations

quality style service value

The Edge: Basic weekend clothing, jeans, and sweats, at good prices. Features brand-name jeans like Jordache, Levis, and Wrangler, plus sweats and sneakers from Reebok, Nike, and New Balance. Oshkosh jeans for kids for $30 to $50. All sizes. No delivery.

Locations: Gramercy Park/Murray Hill: 155 East 23rd Street, between Lexington and 3rd Avenues (460-8963) / **Midtown West:** 270 West 38th Street, near 8th Avenue (768-4220) / **Upper East Side:** 666 Broadway, between Bleecker and Bond Streets (254-9002) / 1523 3rd Avenue, near 86th Street (628-6214) / **Upper West Side:** 2824 Broadway, near 110th Street (666-8330)

Pan Am Sportswear and Menswear

50 Orchard Street
between Grand and Hester Streets / 925-7032
Sun–Wed 9am–6pm, Thurs 9am–8pm, Fri 9am–4pm.

Clothing-casual-men
Lower East Side/Chinatown

quality style service value

The Edge: Good discounts on basic suits. Designer suits, including Hugo Boss, Perry Ellis, and Ralph Lauren, with raincoats from Christian Dior. 50% off. *"Good value."*

Tobaldi Huomo

83 Rivington Street
near Orchard Street / 260-4330
Sun–Thurs 9:30am–6pm, Fri 9:30am to one hour before sunset.

Clothing-casual-men
Lower East Side/Chinatown

quality style service value

The Edge: Very cutting-edge high-style Italian menswear. Features very flashy designer suits and sportswear. Discounter. *"Can negotiate."*

Agnes B.

1063 Madison Avenue
near 81st Street / 570-9333
Mon–Sat 11am–7pm, Sun noon–6pm.

Clothing-casual-women
Upper East Side

quality style service value

The Edge: Conservative, but zippy, French-styled sports clothes. Well-made, well-cut French clothing for men, women, and children at this location. For women: find wonderful leggings, slacks, T-shirts, sweaters, and accessories. The look is "Audrey Hepburn" in smaller sizes. For men: find suits (priced about $615) to size 48. Great faux fur coats this season. *"Trendy." "I wear a size 4 and can't fit into their clothing."*

Ann Crabtree

1310 Madison Avenue
near 93rd Street / 996-6499

Clothing-casual-women
Upper East Side

Weekdays 10:30am–6:30pm, Sat 10am–6pm.

quality style service value

The Edge: Sportswear for the ladies who lunch. Mostly elegant European and Calvin Klein sportswear. The look is New York chic. Full retail. Misses' sizes 4 to 12. *"Classic European style— good sales."*

Calypso

Clothing-casual-women

280 Mott Street
SoHo/TriBeCa
between Prince and Houston Streets / 965-0990
Mon–Sat 11am–7pm, Sun noon–7pm.

The Edge: Lots of resort clothing. Christiane Celle, the owner, favors small European houses. Befitting her East Hampton past, there's lots of casual wear, but also sophisticated sportswear to coats. *"Seems like their clothing is shrinking."*

Eileen Fisher Boutique

Clothing-casual-women

Mon–Sat noon–8pm, Sun noon–7pm.
Multiple locations

quality style service value

The Edge: Easy living Features unstructured cuts in loose, casual clothing in pastel colors made from natural fabrics. Moderately priced, easy care, pull-on clothing. Lots of handwashed silks. *"Very comfortable, easy-to-live-in clothes."* *"Good styles, but poor tailoring."*

Locations: Flatiron/East Village: 314 East 9th Street, near 1st Avenue (529-5715) / 103 5th Avenue, between 17th and 18th Streets (924-4777) / **Midtown East:** 521 Madison Avenue, near 53rd Street (759-9888) / **Upper East Side:** 1039 Madison Avenue, near 79th Street (879-7799) / **Upper West Side:** 341 Columbus Avenue, near 76th Street (362-3000)

Express

Clothing-casual-women

Weekdays 10am–8pm, Sat 10am–7pm, Sun noon–6pm.
Multiple locations

quality style service value

The Edge: Inexpensive teenager heaven featuring good-looking clothing. Beloved by the high school set. Mostly casual, comfortable, and colorful clothing. You'll find sweaters, slacks, gauzy skirts, and dresses. Watch for promotions, when prices get even lower.

Locations: Midtown West: 7 West 34th Street, between 5th and 6th Avenues (629-6838) / 901 Avenue of the Americas, near 33rd Street (971-3280) / **Upper East Side:** 667 Madison Avenue, near 61st Street (754-2721) / **Upper West Side:** 321 Columbus Avenue, near 75th Street (580-5833)

Fox's

Clothing-casual-women

Mon–Wed and Fri–Sat 10am–6pm, .
Multiple locations
Thurs 10am–8pm, Sun noon–5pm

quality style service value

The Edge: The buyers have a great eye. You never know what you'll find. Best for sportswear—slacks, skirts, shirts, and sweaters. Sometimes dresses, and very occasionally evening dresses. Low, low prices—cashmere sweaters for $80 to $90, silk shirts for less than $40, and similar prices on other items. Good-looking, up-to-date items. They'll find great things that go together and look well on you and they have no problem ordering other sizes. No credit cards. No delivery. Discounter. *"My favorite shop—no one has lower prices." "Too bad the secret's out! Great selection, awesome prices—50% off." "The Stamford, Conn., team thinks you're shopping Madison Avenue—they couldn't be more helpful."*

Locations: Connecticut: 1115 High Ridge Road, in Border's/ Bed, Bath & Beyond Mall, Stamford (203-322-3561) / **Long Island:** 80 Main Street, Mineola (516-294-8321) / 12 Elm Street, Huntington (516-424-5221) / **New Jersey:** 230 East Ridgewood Avenue, Ridgewood (201-444-1842) / 184 Route 10 West, Whippany (201-884-3634) / **Westchester:** 15 Waverly Place, Eastchester (914-793-1573)

Harriet Love

126 Prince Street
between Wooster and Greene Streets / 966-2280
Daily 11:30am–7pm.

Clothing-casual-women
SoHo/TriBeCa

quality style service value

The Edge: Young fun clothing. Moderately priced jewelry and casual young clothing with a vintage look. Nice suits and dresses with a '40s look. The sweaters are soft and feminine. However, no longer that wonderful vintage source it was when it was on West Houston Street. *"Pricey."*

Labels for Less

Weekdays 10am–7pm, Sat 10am–6pm, Sun noon–5pm.

Clothing-casual-women
Multiple locations

quality style service value

The Edge: Conservative, less expensive suits and sportswear. Fabrics of choice appear to be polyesters rather than silks, wools, or cottons. Find pants and skirts at $40+, suits averaging $99, and handbags at $39. No delivery. 20% off. *"Good for casual stuff." "Have to shop these stores." "Pass!"*

Locations: Flatiron/East Village: 204 Park Avenue South, near 17th Street (529-7440) / 286 1st Avenue, near 16th Street (674-6223) / **Gramercy Park/Murray Hill:** 130 East 34th Street, near Lexington Avenue (689-3455) / **Lower Manhattan:** 95 Wall Street, near Water Street (514-9388) / **Midtown East:** 639 3rd Avenue, near 42nd Street (682-3330) / 345 Madison Avenue, near 45th Street (697-6659) / 800 3rd Avenue, near 50th Street (752-2443) / 551 Madison Avenue, near 55th Street (888-8390) / **Midtown West:** 1345 Avenue of the Americas, near 57th Street (956-2450) / 1124 Avenue of the Americas, near 44th Street (302-7808) / 130 West 48th Street, near 6th Avenue (997-1032) / **Upper East Side:** 1430 2nd Avenue, near 75th Street (249-4080) / 1302 1st Avenue, near 68th Street (249-4800) / 175 East 96th Street, near 3rd Avenue (987-3637) / **Upper West Side:** 181 Amsterdam Avenue, near 68th Street (787-0850)

Limited

Weekdays 10am–8pm, Sat 10am–7pm, Sun noon–6pm.

Clothing-casual-women
Multiple locations

quality style service value

The Edge: The high school set loves these clothes. Young, fun clothing, great sportswear, and a contemporary look at moderate prices. *"Trendy stylish clothing made to last one season—but who needs more than one season for a trend?"*

Locations: Upper East Side: 691 Madison Avenue, near 62nd Street (838-8787) / **Lower Manhattan:** 4 World Trade Center, near Liberty Street (212-488-9790)

Limited Editions for Her

439 West 55th Street, 12th Floor-use freight
between 9th and 10th Avenues / 582-7114
Tues–Fri 8:30am–4pm.

Clothing-casual-women
Midtown West

quality style service value

The Edge: Incredibly low prices for casual wear. Use the freight entrance. Prices from the 1950s—truly low, low prices. Tends to favor casual clothing. The brand name sold is Carlyle, with most of its clothing made in Hong Kong. A well-dressed crowd shops here—for value and style. No deliveries. Discounter. *"Great. Let's keep it a secret."*

Omo Norma Kamali

11 West 56th Street
west of 5th Avenue / 957-9797
Mon–Sat 10am–6pm.

Clothing-casual-women
Midtown West

quality style service value

The Edge: Kamali designs. The full line, covering jewelry, bathing suits, swimwear, shoes, lingerie, suits, and wedding gowns. *"The best bathing suits."*

Patricia Field

10 East 8th Street
near 5th Avenue / 254-1699
Mon–Sat noon–8pm, Sun 1–7pm.

Clothing-casual-women
Flatiron/East Village

quality style service value

The Edge: Trend-setting clothing. Fun items for the club crowd. This year's hot item—a yellow patent-leather skirt at $125. Now featuring designers Kitty Boots, Living Doll, and Deborah Maruit. Never the same items. Be prepared—Field loves Day-Glo colors and looks. *"Wild styling." "First in clubware."*

Putumayo

147 Spring Street
near West Broadway / 966-4458
Mon–Sat 11am–7pm, Sun noon–6pm.

Clothing-casual-women
SoHo/TriBeCa

quality style service value

The Edge: Moderately priced upbeat South American casual clothing. Beloved by the high school set. Clothes and accessories from South America and India. Patterned sun dresses and wrap skirts and comfortable loose-styled clothing. Year-round bulky cotton sweaters. Woven sashes, South American jewelry, straw hats, bags, and more.

Scoop

532 Broadway
between Prince and Spring Streets / 925-2886
Mon–Thurs 11am–8pm, Fri–Sat 11am–8:30pm, Sun 11am–7pm.

Clothing-casual-women
SoHo/TriBeCa

The Edge: Something for everyone. From cutting-edge Todd Oldham jeans to Calvin's sexy T's to less expensive lines, including Doll House, Free People, DKNY, Kors, Fiorucci, and more.

Aida's & Jimi's Merchandising Co.

41 West 28th Street, 2nd Floor
between 6th Avenue and Broadway / 689-2415
Weekdays 9am–6pm.

Clothing-children
Midtown West

The Edge: Well priced! Known for featuring better American-made girls' dresses. Carries infants' sizes 12 to 24 months, toddlers 2T to 4T, and girls 4 to 14. Brand names favored. Discounter.

Ben's for Kids

1380 3rd Avenue
near 79th Street / 794-2330
Mon–Wed and Fri 10am–5pm, Thurs 10am–8pm, Sat 11am–5pm.

Clothing-children
Upper East Side

quality style service value

The Edge: Reliable neighborhood children's store. Meets all baby's needs, from toys to clothes to furniture and accessories (no disposables). Practical, more moderate focus. Prices from $10 to $60. Sizes from newborn to 4 years old. *"One of the better children's supply stores in Manhattan."* *"Good selection of moderately priced children's furnishings."*

Bonpoint

1269 Madison Avenue
near 91st Street / 722-7720
Mon–Sat 10am–6pm.

Clothing-children
Upper East Side

quality style service value

The Edge: Exclusive French-designed children's clothing. French children's clothing (newborn to size 16). Good fabrics and quality workmanship. Favors prissy styles of yesteryear. Everything from the basics to party dresses. Inspired children's antique-style furniture. A grandma's favorite resource. Prices are outta sight—T-shirts from $60 and skirts at $118 gives you the sense. Deluxe. *"Gorgeous things but pricey—even grandmothers shouldn't buy here."*

Children's General Store

2473 Broadway
near 92nd Street / 580-2723
Mon–Sat 10am–6pm, Sun noon–5pm.

Clothing-children
Upper West Side

The Edge: Calling all kids. Kids love the place. From playthings that are fun to play with (and hold up) to chic clothing and health-care necessities—this is the place.

Children's Place

173 East 86th Street
between Lexington and 3rd Avenues / 831-5100
Mon–Sat 10am–9pm, Sun 11am–7pm.

Clothing-children
Upper East Side

quality style service value

The Edge: Functional. Now clothing for real children. Affordable (but not discounted) functional basic clothing to wear to school and play.

Chocolate Soup

946 Madison Avenue
near 75th Street / 861-2210
Mon–Sat 10am–6pm.

Clothing-children
Upper East Side

quality style service value

The Edge: Fun, colorful, creative children's clothing. Doesn't ever seem to change. You'll find cotton T-shirts and leggings (wide range of colors), Oshkosh overalls hand-painted with whimsical, colorful storybook themes, knit sweaters, Hawaiian shirts, fun jewelry, small toys, and the old reliable Danish school bag that's unbelievably durable. Newborn to preteen sizes. A small, quality selection. *"Best T-shirts in town."*

Coco & Z

222 Columbus Avenue
near 70th Street / 721-0415
Mon–Sat 11am–7pm, Sun noon–5pm.

Clothing-children
Upper West Side

quality style service value

The Edge: Absolutely adorable and affordable children's clothing. Wonderful children's clothing in sizes infant to 8 from small California manufacturers (Malina, Tess et Cie, Baby Armadillo, and Cow and Lizzard) and some European designers. Casual, perky clothing, often with animal and flower designs and almost always with unusual and pretty patterns. There's a lot of black clothing, even for infants. Will make up gift baskets and maintains a baby registry. *"Very helpful service."*

Dinosaur Hill

306 East 9th Street
near 2nd Avenue / 473-5850
Daily 11am–7pm.

Clothing-children
Flatiron/East Village

quality style service value

The Edge: An international collection of children's toys and clothing. Hand-painted, hand-embroidered, and hand-knit clothing and toys from around the world for children from six months to six years old. Not expensive. An East Village look for kids, but very limited selection. Wonderful Brontosaurus when your kids go through that stage. *"Nice, but small sizes, mostly 8 and under."*

East Side Kids

1298 Madison Avenue
near 92nd Street / 360-5000
Weekdays 9:30am–6pm, Sat 9am–6pm.

Clothing-children
Upper East Side

quality style service value

The Edge: A fun place to take your children to buy shoes. Full stock of infants' to teenagers' basic to party shoes and boots. In summer, stocks sandals and camp shoes. Large range of designer shoes in sizes from 2 to adult 10. Priced from $24 (Keds) to $195. *"Love the popcorn machine and the grandstand for sitting!"*

Exclusive Oilily Store

870 Madison Avenue
near 70th Street / 628-0100
Mon–Wed and Fri–Sat 10am–6pm,
Thurs 10am–7pm, Sun noon–5pm.

Clothing-children
Upper East Side

quality style service value

The Edge: Adorable kids' clothing. Fashions for children and mom from the Dutch company Oilily. Styles are comfortable, pants are rolled, tops are oversized, dresses are long, and coats are lined to span the seasons. The kids' clothing is very cute but expensive, with sweatshirts for infants at $53 and denims for toddlers at $95. Its women's clothing is an acquired taste. Deluxe. *"Enchanting."*

Gap Kids and Baby Gap

Weekdays 9am–9pm, Sat 10am–9pm, Sun 11am–8pm.

Clothing-children
Multiple locations

33	42	32	40
quality	style	service	value

The Edge: Basic, good-looking kids and infants clothing. Find jeans, plaid flannel shirts, sweaters, T-shirts, shoes, caps, jackets, and Gap-style infants' clothing. Children's sizes from newborn to 13 years. Prices are moderate, with jeans from $19.50 to $30.

Locations: Chelsea: 354 Avenue of the Americas, near West 4th Street (777-2420) / **Lower Manhattan:** 89 South Street, 1st level, South Street Seaport, Pier 17 (786-1707) / **Midtown East:** 657 3rd Avenue, near 42nd Street (697-9007) / 545 Madison Avenue, near 55th Street (980-2570) / **Midtown West:** 60 West 34th Street, upper level, near Broadway (643-8995) / 250 West 57th Street, near Broadway (956-3140) / 1212 Avenue of the Americas, near 48th Street (764-0285) / 1466 Broadway, near 42nd Street (302-1266) / **Upper East Side:** 1037 Lexington Avenue, near 75th Street (988-4460) / 1535 3rd Avenue, at 87th Street (423-0444) / **Upper West Side:** 2373 Broadway, near 86th Street (873-2044)

Greenstone & Cie

442 Columbus Avenue
near 81st Street / 580-4322
Mon–Sat 10am–7pm, Sun noon–6pm.

Clothing-children
Upper West Side

45	40	40	40
quality	style	service	value

The Edge: High-end European styling. Features unique, imported European children's clothing and sturdy American lines. Sizes from three months to 12 years. A full range of styles, from play to school to party. *"A 'must have'—that great dog-face winter hat."*

Jacadi

1281 Madison Avenue
near 91st Street / 369-1616
Mon–Wed and Fri–Sat 10am–6pm,
Thurs 10am–7pm, Sun noon–5pm.

Clothing-children
Upper East Side

47	47	30	33
quality	style	service	value

The Edge: Fabulous French fashions for children. Full range of French clothing from infant to age 12. Deluxe. *"Only—maybe—on sale."*

Kidding Around

60 West 15th Street
near 6th Avenue / 645-6337
Weekdays 10am–7pm, Sat 11am–7pm, Sun 11am–6pm.

Clothing-children
Chelsea

The Edge: Well-chosen clothes and toys. Wonderful selection of children's clothing and toys. Great party wrappings.

Kids "R" Us

1298-1311 Broadway
near 34th Street / 643-0714
Mon and Fri 9am–9pm, Tues–Wed and Sat 9am–8pm,
Thurs 9am–9:30pm, Sun 11am–7pm.

Clothing-children
Midtown West

quality style service value

The Edge: Inexpensive basics. Features Carters, Jet Set, Oshkosh, etc. from infants' to girls' and boys' sizes. The atmosphere is chaotic. No delivery. Discounter. *"Out of stock a lot."*

Kids Are Magic

2293 Broadway
near 82nd Street / 875-9240
Mon–Wed 10am–8pm, Thurs–Sat 10am–9pm, Sun 10am–7pm.

Clothing-children
Upper West Side

quality style service value

The Edge: The Bolton's of children's clothing. Favors hipper looks. Features a full range of price points, including Baby Dior, French Toast, Sahara Club, Rachel's Kids, Flapdoodles, Calvin Klein, and more. Sahara Club is the big seller. Cheap jeans from $13, dresses and sweaters from $16, coats from $60. No shoes. Sizes from newborn to girls' size 14 and boys' size 20. The store is best for infantwear and girls' dresses. However, through the maze of boyswear you will, with patience, find treasures. The owners are former buyers from Century 21. Good at minimum for the basics. Expect savings of 40% and more. No delivery. Discounter. *"Like most discounters, hit or miss."*

La Layette et Plus

170 East 61st Street
between Lexington and 3rd Avenues / 688-7072
Mon–Sat 11am–6pm.

Clothing-children
Upper East Side

quality style service value

The Edge: Attention, Grandma: top-of-the-line clothing for newborns. Simply fabulous elegant children's clothing. Top of the line, from practical to dress for all occasions. Gorgeous, gorgeous items. Linens and furnishings equally grand. Deluxe.

Lisa Polanski, Inc.

121 7th Avenue
between President and Carroll Streets, Park Slope / 718-622-8071
Weekdays 11am–8pm, Sat 11am–7pm, Sun 11am–6pm.

Clothing-children
Brooklyn

The Edge: Everything you need and want for your child—discounted. Expect all the better names, including Doc Martens shoes.

Little Folks

123 East 23rd Street
near Park Avenue / 982-9669
Mon–Thurs 9:30am–7pm, Fri 9am–5pm, Sun noon–5pm.

Clothing-children
Gramercy Park/Murray Hill

quality style service value

The Edge: Uptown service at downtown prices in an almost midtown location. The basics to party items for infants to girls' and boys' size 14. Features Aprica, Levis, Maclaren, Oshkosh, Perego, and more. Moderately priced snowsuits at $45 to $88, down jackets at $75 to $120, and girls' dress coats at $80 to $100. Periodic sales (past-season items) reduce prices to 40% off. Also furniture, strollers, cribs, and car seats.

M. Kreinen Sales

301 Grand Street
near Allen Street / 925-0239
Sun–Thurs 9am–5pm, Fri 9am–3pm.

Clothing-children
Lower East Side/Chinatown

quality style service value

The Edge: Reliable for the basics. Mostly basic items, but some better things. Children's clothing by Carters, Oshkosh, Quiltex, Trimfit, Flapdoodles, Little Me, and others. Find pants, jackets (including down), sweaters, and more. Priced from $10 to $50. No credit cards. 20% off.

Magic Windows

1186 Madison Avenue
between 86th and 87th Streets / 289-0028
Mon–Sat 10am–6pm, Sun noon–5pm (closed Sun July–Aug).

Clothing-children
Upper East Side

quality style service value

The Edge: One-stop shopping for children's clothing from all the best designers. Classic traditional clothing from Florence Eiseman, Vive La Fête, and Sylvia Whyte. Sizes from infant to junior size 9. Find clothing for all occasions, from infants' receiving blankets, monogrammed and plain sweaters (at $52 to $86), dresses (including wonderful party dresses into the $100s), blazers ($80 to $120), and coats ($60 to $250). Shoes for infants to toddlers. Two stores with the annex dedicated to teens. For teens: the hot labels are Zoi Ltd., Monkey Wear, and Nicole Miller. Party dresses range from $120 to over $500. Fills that tough preteen niche when you're seeking something special and willing to pay dearly. *"Good for kids' special occasions."*

Space Kiddets

46 East 21st Street
between Park and Broadway / 420-9878
Mon–Tues and Fri 10:30am–6pm, Wed–Thurs 10:30am–7pm,
Sat 10:30am– 5:30pm.

Clothing-children
Gramercy Park/Murray Hill

quality style service value

The Edge: Fun, funky children's clothing. Small selection, but adorable clothing for newborns to size 14. Styles range from classic to funky. The hot funky look includes hot-pink bell bottoms, lion-faced socks, Andy Warhol shirts, and the like. A great resource for hard-to-satisfy preteens. Labels include Les Tout, In Vitro T-shirts, Smith jeans. Moderate prices—$20+ for T-shirts and $49 for jeans. *"My favorite."*

Spring Flowers

1050 3rd Avenue
at 62nd Street / 758-2669
Mon–Sat 10am–6pm.

Clothing-children
Upper East Side

quality style service value

The Edge: Party dresses for the discriminating. First-rate party dresses, separates, and private school uniforms, as well as hats, scarves, shoes, and all accessories from infant to preteen. Favors French and English clothing by such designers as Cacharel, Floriane, Magil, and Petit Bateau. Prices are very high, so you pay for the "ease" of pleasing those difficult ones. *"Lots for the difficult-to-please preteen. "*

Wicker Garden's Baby/Children

1327 Madison Avenue
between 93rd and 94th Streets / 410-7001
Mon–Sat 10am–6pm.

Clothing-children
Upper East Side

quality style service value

The Edge: High styled clothing and hand-painted wicker furniture. Wonderful collection of children's clothing, shoes, linens, and furniture. Clothing from layettes to practical school clothing, play clothes, and party dresses. Infant furniture (on the second floor) includes iron and wood cribs, some with canopies. Also bureaus and armoires hand-painted with pastoral scenes. Also antique quilts and linens to adorn the cribs. Deluxe. *"Not the place to think about price."*

Aldo Ferrari, Inc.
321 5th Avenue
near 32nd Street / 685-5131
Mon–Sat 10am–6pm.

Clothing-men
Gramercy Park/Murray Hill

The Edge: Inexpensive. Its own label European-style clothing (suits, shirts, raincoats, jackets, cashmere sweaters, and accessories). Low prices, from $20 for men's shirts. No delivery.

Alfred Dunhill of London
450 Park Avenue
between 56th and 57th Streets / 888-4000
Weekdays 9am–6:30pm, Sat 9am–6pm.

Clothing-men
Midtown East

quality style service value

The Edge: Elegant and sober. Offers three levels of suits, shirts, ties, and shoes: off the peg, special order, and custom tailored. Fine fabrics and good tailoring. Custom tailoring means the garment is sewn entirely by hand. Accessories include attaché cases, luggage, and Dunhill lighters. A well-known, top source for very expensive menswear. Deluxe. *"Old Guard."* *"Good buys on neckties in the Kowloon [Hong Kong] store."*

Bijan
699 5th Avenue
near 55th Street / 788-7500
By appointment.

Clothing-men
Midtown East

quality style service value

The Edge: Exclusivity. European styling for dress and casual clothing. For those who want to shop by appointment only (or chance the doorman not letting you in). Entry is easier from the St. Regis Hotel lobby. Prices are extreme. Service and quality make the place. Deluxe.

Brooks Brothers
Weekdays 8:30am–6:30pm, Sat 10am–5pm.

Clothing-men
Multiple locations

quality style service value

The Edge: Memories of childhood shopping trips. They have it all for boys to men from underwear to tuxedos! Conservative, well-tailored clothing unchanging year after year. Find three-button blazers and suits. A small women's department with ultra-preppy men's clothing cut for women. *"Defines conservatism."*

Locations: Lower Manhattan: One Liberty Plaza, near Broadway (267-2400) / **Midtown East:** 346 Madison Avenue, near 45th Street (682-8800)

Eisenberg and Eisenberg

Clothing-men
Flatiron/East Village

85 5th Avenue, 6th Floor
near 16th Street / 627-1290
Mon–Wed and Fri 9am–6pm, Thurs 9am–7pm, Sat 9am–5pm, Sun 10am–4pm.

The Edge: Inexpensive men's formal wear. Since 1898 has offered a full range of men's clothing—from casual to tuxedos—at discount. Tuxedos priced from $190 to $550 for sale and $75 to $115 for rental. Mostly its own label. Alterations included.

Ermenegildo Zegna

Clothing-men
Midtown East

743 5th Avenue
near 57th Street / 421-4488
Weekdays 10am–7pm, Sat 10am–6pm.

43	43	40	33
quality	style	service	value

The Edge: Best-styled, best-quality Italian men's clothing. You can't get more top-of-the-line than this. Prices are high—$1,100 to $2,350 for rack suits. (See the entry for Gilcrest, which says that its suits are made in the same factory as Zegna's.) Deluxe. *"Nice ties and jackets." "Very high prices."*

Euromoda Ltd.

Clothing-men
Lower East Side/Chinatown

56 Orchard Street
South of Grand Street / 219-3972
Sun–Fri 10am–6pm.

45	50	45	45
quality	style	service	value

The Edge: A top choice. Beautiful top-of-the-line suits featuring fine Italian fabrics at $695, tailoring included. Fine, well-tailored suits 40% off. *"My husband's favorite."*

Gianni Versace

Clothing-men
Upper East Side

816 Madison Avenue
near 68th Street / 744-5572
Mon–Sat 10am–6pm.

42	45	38	33
quality	style	service	value

The Edge: Au courant high-fashion men's clothing. Features casual to business wear. Very expensive: rack suits for $1,700 to $3,000, custom shirts at $230 to $700. The fabrics are luxurious. Suits in sizes 36 to 50. Hot sellers are leather jackets (to size 58), priced from $3,200 to $6,000. Cutting-edge and very expensive. Deluxe. *"Crazy/mad colors."*

Gilcrest Clothes Company

Clothing-men
Flatiron/East Village

900 Broadway, 3rd Floor
near 20th Street / 254-8933
Weekdays 7:30am–5:30pm, Sat 8:30am–5pm,
Sun 9:30am–4:30pm.

45	48	45	46
quality	style	service	value

The Edge: Good discounts on classic men's business suits. Features a full line of business clothing. Suits from $249 to $600, with most from $400 to $500. Features Boss (at $499) and Zegna (at $599). The hottest look is European, primarily Italian-styled suits. Also offers shirts, ties, and coats. No charge for alternations. It claims to sell designer suits at the lowest prices in town. Wide range of sizes (to 54 long). *"Great men's suits, good service." "40% off."*

Gorsart

9 Murray Street
between Broadway and Church Street / 962-0024
Mon–Wed and Fri 9am–6pm, Thurs 9am–7pm, Sat 9am–5:30pm.

Clothing-men
Lower Manhattan

quality style service value

The Edge: Conservative men's suits. The hottest store item is described as "gray stripe or navy"—
and that says it all! Suits from $295 to $750. Sizes to 50 long. Also shirts and shoes. Discounter.

Harrison James

5 West 54th Street
between 5th and 6th Avenues / 541-6870
Weekdays 10am–7pm, Sat 10am–6pm.

Clothing-men
Midtown West

The Edge: Upscale. Service-oriented men's haberdasher. Features a full line of men's clothing,
furnishings, and accessories. Luxurious.

Harry Rothman's

200 Park Avenue South
near 17th Street / 777-7400
Mon–Wed and Fri 10am–7pm, Thurs 10am–8pm,
Sat 9:30am–6pm, Sun noon– 5pm.

Clothing-men
Flatiron/East Village

quality style service value

The Edge: More moderately priced men's clothing. Carries Canali, Hickey Freeman, Joseph
Abboud, and Perry Ellis. Find suits, coats, shirts, ties, shoes, socks, and sweaters. 20% off. *"The
standards."*

J. Press

7 East 44th Street
between 5th and Madison Avenues / 687-7642
Mon–Sat 9am–6pm.

Clothing-men
Midtown East

quality style service value

The Edge: The Connecticut look. Full range of clothing, from shorts to tuxedos. Fabrics and
styling are traditional. Sizes to 52. Suits from $500 to $800. Jackets from $300. In summer, sports
clothing, slacks, and shorts come in bright colors with patterned/madras fabrics. *"Tried and true."*

Jekyll and Hyde Ltd.

93 Greene Street
between Prince and Spring Streets / 966-8503
Mon–Wed 11:30am–7pm, Thurs 11:30am–7:30pm,
Fri–Sat noon–7:30pm, Sun noon–6:30pm.

Clothing-men
SoHo/TriBeCa

The Edge: Forward, contemporary-looking clothing. English and Italian men's clothing, from
sportswear to dress (no shoes). Its current best-sellers are five-button suits from $725. Suits to size
46. *"Expensive merchandise."*

Jodamo International Ltd.

321 Grand Street
corner Orchard Street / 219-055
Mon–Wed 9am–7pm, Thurs 9am–8pm, Fri 9am to one hour before sunset, Sun 9am– 6pm.

Clothing-men
Lower East Side/Chinatown

The Edge: Bang for the buck. High-end European designers sold exclusively. From casual to dress, this is the place for men, with reasonable service and high-style designs at good prices. Discounter. *"Negotiations are required. For the lowest prices, wait until the end of the day when the sales help/owners seem to want to really move merchandise."*

L.S. Men's Clothing
19 West 44th Street
between 5th and 6th Avenues / 575-0933
Mon–Thurs 9am–7pm, Fri 9am–4:30pm, Sun 10am–5pm.

Clothing-men
Midtown West

40 20 40 50
quality style service value

The Edge: Where the law firm associates buy their uniforms. Discounts brand-name suits, some Hickey Freeman and Perry Ellis, among others. Suits mostly priced from $260 to $350 (retail at $495+). Also custom-tailored suits from Italian and English fabrics priced from $475. Custom suits take four weeks for delivery. 50% off.

Moe Ginsburg
162 5th Avenue
near 21st Street / 242-3482
Mon–Wed and Fri 9:30am–7pm, Thurs 9:30am–8pm,
Sat–Sun 9:30am–6pm.

Clothing-men
Gramercy Park/Murray Hill

40 38 40 44
quality style service value

The Edge: Five showroom floors running the gamut from shoes to formal wear. Offers some named designers along, for the most part, with its own brand. Primarily moderately priced lines. Full range of sizes, including a Big and Tall Department. 35% off. *"Fair selection and reasonably priced."*

Napoleon
725 5th Avenue
Trump Tower at 57th Street / 759-1110
Mon–Sat 10am–6pm.

Clothing-men
Midtown East

48 48 48 35
quality style service value

The Edge: One of the top men's boutiques. Features expensive Italian sportswear. Lots of Ermenegildo Zegna, among others. Good service. Deluxe. *"Terrific style and fabrics to die for. Great service, great quality."*

New Republic Clothiers
93 Spring Street
near Broadway / 219-3005
Mon–Sat noon–7pm, Sun noon–6pm.

Clothing-men
SoHo/TriBeCa

The Edge: An elegant retro look. Designs new clothing with the classic elegance of 1940s styling. Features a full range of clothing—sportswear and business. Also a small selection of good traditional English-made shoes.

Paul Smith
108 5th Avenue
near 16th Street / 627-9770
Mon–Sat 11am–7pm, Sun noon–6pm.

Clothing-men
Chelsea

48 45 41 34
quality style service value

The Edge: Where Prince Charles would shop. Traditional clothing with a twist (unusual fabrics, patterns, or colors). Look for its royal-looking Nova Suede slippers with Polartec linings in strong colors—purple with maroon, black spiced with yellow and purple, olive with blue. Prices are high, matching the quality. *"Nice but expensive." "Great look."*

Paul Stuart

Clothing-men
Midtown East

10 East 45th Street
at Madison Avenue / 682-0320
Mon–Wed and Fri 8am–6:30pm, Thurs 8am–7pm,
Sat 9am–6pm, Sun noon–5pm.

quality   style   service   value

The Edge: High quality in every way. Meets all the needs of the Wall Street man, from casual to work to formal. Good fabrics, good looks, good quality. *"My boss is addicted—and I must add that it has gorgeous suits." "If you're a woman, the salesmen tend to ignore you."*

Riflessi

Clothing-men
Gramercy Park/Murray Hill

260 Madison Avenue
near 39th Street / 679-4875
Mon–Sat 10am–7pm, Sun noon–5pm.

The Edge: Excellent prices, less than half of retail. Suits, sports jackets, shirts, and ties from all the great designers, including suits by Zegna, Loro Piana Tasmania, and Canali, and sports jackets by Valentino Uomo and Zegna, among others.

Sulka & Company

Clothing-men
Midtown East

430 Park Avenue
near 55th Street / 980-5200
Weekdays 9am–6pm, Sat 10am–5pm.

quality   style   service   value

The Edge: One of the top haberdasheries. Since 1895, fine-quality English-style clothing, including sports jackets, slacks, shirts cut from Sulka's own patterns, silk pajamas, robes, and smoking jackets. Known for its sports jacket with 18-karat-gold buttons. Made-to-measure and custom orders. Expensive. Deluxe. *"Luxury defined."*

Sussex Clothes

Clothing-men
Flatiron/East Village

893 Broadway
near 19th Street / 777-4486
Mon–Wed and Fri 9:30am–6pm, Thurs 9:30am–7pm, Sat 10am–5:30pm, Sun 11am–5pm.

The Edge: Deals for the guys. A discount men's clothing store providing service and good selection. Features Hart Schaffner & Marx suits, Ralph by Ralph Lauren, Cerutti 1881, and other fine lines. Suits retail between $525 and $880 (Cerutti line). Discounter.

Trend Clothiers

Clothing-men
Midtown East

40 East 41st Street
between Madison and Park Avenues / 889-4686
Weekdays 11am–7pm.

The Edge: Moderately priced traditional American and European men's suits. Specializes in French and Italian designer suits and its own line of American-cut suits. Also overcoats, shirts, ties, and shoes. Tailoring on premises. No delivery.

Aaron's

627 5th Avenue
near 17th Street, Brooklyn / 718-768-5400
Mon–Wed and Fri–Sat 9:30am–6pm, Thurs 9:30am–9pm.

Clothing-women
Brooklyn

33	27	23	35
quality	style	service	value

The Edge: End of season deals and steals. In business for more than 60 years, Aarons's offers over 100 current lines ranging from Adrienne Vittadini to Zelda, plus many West German and Italian lines as well. Sportswear, dresses, suits, and coats at discounts of 25% to 33%, with further markdowns until it's all gone at the end of the season. Misses' and petite sizes 4 to 16. *"Good value when you hit it right."*

Anik

1355 3rd Avenue
between 77th & 78th Streets / 861-9840
Mon–Sat 11am–8pm, Sun noon–7pm.

Clothing-women
Upper East Side

30	30	20	20
quality	style	service	value

The Edge: Nice things for the working woman. An Emanuelle (Ungaro) look—but much less expensive. Clean lines, good colors—nice for young professionals and that first job. *"Trendy yet chic."* *"Not relaxed—definitely salespeople on commission."*

Ann Taylor

Weekdays 10am–8pm, Sat 10am–7pm, Sun noon–6pm.

Clothing-women
Multiple locations

35	37	36	31
quality	style	service	value

The Edge: Young professionals' clothes. Same price range as Talbots, but better-looking sportswear and young career clothing, shoes, and accessories. Great sales. Misses' sizes 4 to 12, with some 14s. *"Good selection of career wear."* *"Free tailoring at the uptown store, if you have the store charge card."* *"Shoes fell apart."* *"Great sales."* *"Bad jacket seam."* *"Need a special figure to wear their clothes."*

Locations: Lower Manhattan: 4 Fulton Street, South Street Seaport (480-4100) / 225 Liberty Street, World Financial Center (945-1991) / **Midtown East:** 575 5th Avenue, near 47th Street (922-3621) / 645 Madison Avenue, near 60th Street (832-2010) / 805 3rd Avenue, near 50th Street (308-5333) / **Midtown West:** 100 West 33rd Street, at 6th Avenue (564-3992) / **Upper East Side:** 1320 3rd Avenue, near 75th Street (861-3392) / 1055 Madison Avenue, near 80th Street (988-8930) / **Upper West Side:** 2015-17 Broadway, near 69th Street (873-7344) / 2380 Broadway, near 87th Street (721-3130)

Anna Sui

113 Greene Street
between Prince and Spring Streets / 941-8406
Mon–Sat noon–7pm, Sun noon–6pm.

Clothing-women
SoHo/TriBeCa

38	43	35	28
quality	style	service	value

The Edge: Femmes fatales shop here. Glamorous contemporary clothing including hats. Known for her fabrics and her hip and sexy designs. A wide range of items, from casual leather jackets to sexy date wear. Fabrics are great. Best this year: low-slung sexy short leather skirt (about $385). Great slinky slip dresses. *"Wonderful patterns and designs."*

Bagutta Boutique

402 West Broadway
between Spring and Broome Streets / 925-5216
Weekdays 11am–7pm, Sat 11am–7:30pm, Sun noon–6:30pm.

Clothing-women
SoHo/TriBeCa

quality style service value

The Edge: High-fashion upscale European look. Wonderful top European-designed clothing. The latest looks from the hottest collections. Features a full range of clothing to accommodate a woman's full-day needs—skirts, slacks, dresses, jackets, and suits. Shirts run $200 to $1,200. Designers include Alexander McQueen, Prada, Helmut Lang, and more. Smaller sizes. Deluxe.

Betsey Johnson

Mon–Sat 11am–7pm, Sun noon–7pm.

Clothing-women
Multiple locations

quality style service value

The Edge: Fashion-forward clothing for the high school and/or club crowd. Avant garde without being totally way out. From day to evening—hip and sexy items. Moderately priced from $20 to $200. *"Has really fun party dresses." "Great funky girlie-wear."*

Locations: SoHo/TriBeCa: 130 Thompson Street, near Houston Street (420-0169) / **Upper East Side:** 251 East 60th Street, near 2nd Avenue (319-7699) / 1060 Madison Avenue, between 80th and 81st Streets (734-1257) / **Upper West Side:** 248 Columbus Avenue, near 71st Street (362-3364)

Betsy Bunky Nini

980 Lexington Avenue
between 71st and 72nd Streets / 744-6716
Mon–Wed and Fri–Sat 10:30am–6pm, Thurs 10:30am–7pm,
Sun noon–5pm (closed Sun July–Aug).

Clothing-women
Upper East Side

The Edge: Sexy. European clothing from such designers as Barbara Bui, Complice, Vestimenta, Industria, G. Gigli, State of Montana, and others. A very "today" look. If you need it today they'll messenger it to your home. *"Trendy."*

Bolton's

Mon–Sat 10am–7pm, Sun noon–5pm.

Clothing-women
Multiple locations

The Edge: For inexpensive wardrobe "fillers." Sportswear a specialty, but also stocks dresses and coats. An okay source for the basics. Carries moderately priced lines—skirts priced from $20 and up (to $79). Misses' sizes to size 16. No delivery. 25% off. *"Great for utility stuff."*

Locations: Gramercy Park/Murray Hill: 53 West 23rd Street, near 6th Avenue (924-6860) / 4 East 34th Street, near 5th Avenue (684-3750) / **Lower Manhattan:** 90 Broad Street, near Stone Street (785-0513) / **Midtown East:** 225 East 57th Street, near 3rd Avenue (755-2527) / **Midtown**

West: 27 West 57th Street, near 6th Avenue (935-4431) / 110 West 51st Street, near 6th Avenue (245-5227) / 27 West 57th Street, between 5th and 6th Avenues (935-4431) / **Upper East Side:** 1180 Madison Avenue, near 86th Street (722-4419)

Chanel Boutique

15 East 57th Street
between 5th and Madison Avenues / 355-5050
Mon–Wed and Fri 10am–6:30pm, Thurs 10am–7pm,
Sat 10am–6pm, Sun noon– 5pm.

Clothing-women
Midtown East

quality style service value

The Edge: It's Chanel. Everything Chanel from ready-to-wear, accessories, and jewelry to fragrances and cosmetics. Suits priced in the thousands of dollars. Deluxe. *"Chanel's prices have gone up dramatically in the past few years." "Great accessories."*

Country Road

Mon–Sat 11am–8pm, Sun noon–6pm.

Clothing-women
Multiple locations

quality style service value

The Edge: The movie *Out of Africa* look. A contemporary conservative look designed by this Australian sportswear company. Very good fabrics, tending to be in muted colors, well crafted into coat trousers, sweaters, and silk shirts. Some sleek suits for career wear and a less formal evening wear. Materials are good quality. *"Classics." "Great suits." "Not as good as it used to be." "Prices are okay—watch for the sales."*

Locations: Lower Manhattan: 199 Water Street, near John Street (248-0810) / **Midtown East:** 335 Madison Avenue, near 43rd Street (949-7380) / **SoHo/TriBeCa:** 411 West Broadway, near Spring Street (343-9544) / **Upper East Side:** 1130 3rd Avenue, near 66th Street (744-8633)

Dana Buchman

65 East 57th Street
near Park Avenue / 319-3257
Weekdays 10am–7pm, Sat 10am–6pm, Sun noon–5pm.

Clothing-women
Midtown East

quality style service value

The Edge: Elegant tailored yet feminine clothing for the executive woman. Classic elegant suits and shirts in fine fabrics. Feminine yet appropriately conservative. Mix 'n' match sizes to fit well and easily. Popular among our respondents. *"I love this store." "Free alternations a plus." "Good for everyday life." "Fit can be a problem."*

Dressing Room

49 Prince Street
between Mulberry and Lafayette Streets / 431-6658
Mon–Sat noon–7pm, Sun 1–6pm.

Clothing-women
SoHo/TriBeCa

The Edge: The source for fashion to stand out in. Small shop where you'll find the newest looks this year from Pixie Yates, Sacre Coeur, Girlie NYC, Rookie, and Margie Tsai. Moderate prices— dresses from $100.

Emanuel Ungaro

792 Madison Avenue

Clothing-women
Upper East Side

near 67th Street / 249-4090
Mon–Wed and Fri–Sat 9:30am–6:30pm, Thurs 9:30am–7:30pm.

quality style service value

The Edge: It's Ungaro's entire couture collection. The couture line is sexy, made from rich fabrics and put together in unusual combinations. Offers day to evening wear. Day dresses priced at about $1,800. Also offers Parallel and Solo Donna bridge lines designed by Emanuel. Deluxe. *"Luxury."*

Episode Sportswear

805 3rd Avenue
near 49th Street / 754-2442
Weekdays 10am–7pm, Sat 10am–6pm, Sun noon–5pm.

Clothing-women
Midtown East

quality style service value

The Edge: Chic-styled work clothing. Well-styled sportswear and suits made from natural fibers. Colors and styles tend to be muted. Check out their VIP program: Buy $1,000+ in any two-month period and enjoy a 10% discount forever (regardless of purchase amount) and an extra 5% on your birthday! The VIP program applies to any Episode store. *"Stylish work uniforms."*

Escada Boutique

7 East 57th Street
between 5th and Madison Avenues / 755-2200
Mon–Wed and Fri–Sat 10am–6pm, Thurs 10am–7pm.

Clothing-women
Midtown East

quality style service value

The Edge: The full Escada line. The full line—from ready-to-wear to couture—is sold here. Extremely expensive chic, if not flashy, sports line. Priced from $400 for slacks and $1,400 for jackets. Catalogs are available to clients spending $10,000 plus. Giselle on the Lower East Side stocks Escada, as does First Choice in Wayne, N.J., and Woodbury Commons Deluxe. *"If you can afford it—go! Make sure to ask for Elaine Cohen."*

Fashion Plaza

77 Orchard Street
near Broome Street / 966-3510
Sun–Thurs 9:30am–6pm, Fri 9:30am–3pm.

Clothing-women
Lower East Side/Chinatown

quality style service value

The Edge: The source for ladies' work uniforms. Mostly more conservative and upper moderately priced suits—Albert Nippon and Grossman, some Louis Feraud. Good prices. Open Christmas Day.

Fishkin Knitwear

314 Grand Street
near Allen Street / 226-6538
Mon–Thurs 10am–5pm, Fri 10am–4pm, Sun 9am–4:30pm.

Clothing-women
Lower East Side

quality style service value

The Edge: Mid-price-range clothing carried at discount. Full range of women's discount clothing (sportswear, sweaters, shoes, silk shirts, dresses). Coats sold in the fall. Sometimes carries Dana Buchman, DKNY, Liz Claiborne, and Eileen Fisher. Sizes 2 to 18, petites to 3X. 30% off. *"Great for sweaters and bathing suits." "Some fine cashmeres."*

Forman's

Sun–Wed 9am–6pm, Thurs 9am–8pm,
Fri 9am–2pm (to 4pm Fri in summer).

Clothing-women
Multiple locations

36	34	36	39
quality	style	service	value

The Edge: Moderately priced designer sportswear at discount. Designers include Evan Picone, Jones of New York, Gianni, and Kasper at 20% to 30% off retail prices. Petites to size 24 sold in four locations, now including an uptown, East 42nd Street location. *"My Mom loves the Sunday radio-advertised specials."*

Locations: Lower East Side/Chinatown: 82 Orchard Street, near Delancey Street (228-2500) / **Lower Manhattan:** 59 John Street, near William Street (791-4100) / **Midtown East:** 145 East 42nd Street, between Lexington and Park Avenues (681-9800)

Giselle Sportswear, Inc.

143 Orchard Street
near Delancey Street / 673-1900
Sun–Thurs 9am–6pm, Fri 9am–4pm.

Clothing-women
Lower East Side/Chinatown

50	48	38	43
quality	style	service	value

The Edge: Best of the Lower East Side. Three floors filled with discounted (20% offered) middle- to top-priced designer sportswear, including Escada (top floor—you need to ask for it), Emanuel, Mondi, Ungaro, Valentino, and Laurel. If you buy several things which add up, bargain hard with the man behind the counter downstairs and you can often lower the price even more (we've seen a woman achieve 40%), particularly if it's getting past mid-season. Sundays are too crowded for effective bargaining. They'll send your purchases via UPS anywhere in the U.S. without charge. Don't miss the cut-off dates for returns as the staff is impossible to deal with in that event, no matter what the reason. (When we say "impossible," that means no cash refund and no credit exchanges after the return cut-off.) *"Fourth floor terrific." "Expensive but discounted 30%. More so as the season goes on." "Negotiate or overpay."*

Givenchy Boutique

954 Madison Avenue
near 75th Street / 772-1040
Mon–Sat 10am–6pm.

Clothing-women
Upper East Side

47	40	48	47
quality	style	service	value

The Edge: It's Givenchy. Elegant ready-to-wear in sizes 4 to 16. Evening gowns are Givenchy's specialty. Special orders are possible. Very expensive: dresses run $1,800 to $3,000. Deluxe.

Hirshleifer's

2080 Northern Blvd.
in the Americana Mall, Manhasset / 516-627-3566
Mon–Sat 10am–6pm, Sun noon–6pm.

Clothing-women
Long Island

50	40	40	40
quality	style	service	value

The Edge: Now you don't have to go to Bergdorf. High-end, primarily European designer duds, including Chanel, Armani, and the like. Great selection and taste. Deluxe. *"Old-fashioned service."*

If Boutique

94 Grand Street
between Greene and Grand Streets / 334-4964

Clothing-women
SoHo/TriBeCa

Mon–Sat 11am–7pm, Sun 11am–6:30pm.

quality style service value

The Edge: For those sized under 10—high style. Features Vivien Westwood and Colonna, along with Moschino and Cheap & Chic and Couture. Also shoes and accessories. It's expensive: jackets priced from $500 to $1,500, bags from $200 to $600, and skirts/pants from $200 to $800. Carries sizes 4 to 8, with some 10s. One-of-a-kind very elegant look. A favorite source for *Vogue* magazine stylists.

Intermix

125 5th Avenue
between 19th and 20th Streets / 533-9720
Mon–Sat 11am–8pm, Sun noon–6pm.

Clothing-women
Flatiron/East Village

The Edge: Hip shop with clothing appropriate for work to dates. The shop features some of the best clothing from some of the new hot young designers, including Vivienne Tam, Byron Lars, Kate Spade, and the like. Moderate prices. *"The buyers have great taste."*

Jaeger

818 Madison Avenue
near 69th Street / 794-0780
Mon–Sat 10am–6pm.

Clothing-women
Upper East Side

| 41 | 38 | 38 | 33 |

quality style service value

The Edge: Classic clothing made for the Queen, not Princess Di. Classic suits and sportswear from an English institution known for its mainstream timeless clothing. It's the Talbots look, updated somewhat and featuring much better fabrics. *"Beautiful items. Expensive." "Doesn't fit U.S. bodies."*

Joseph

804 Madison Avenue
near 68th Street / 570-0077
Mon–Wed and Fri–Sat 10am–6:30pm, Thurs 10am–7pm.

Clothing-women
Upper East Side

| 40 | 35 | 30 | 30 |

quality style service value

The Edge: Cutting-edge young look. In-house designer features flare pants this year, but who knows what next year will bring. Prices for pants from $275, dresses from $200 to $400, and skirts from $110 to $150 in misses' sizes 2 to 12.

Kanae + Onyx

75 East 7th Street
between 1st and 2nd Avenues / 254-7703
Weekdays noon–8pm, Sat 1–8pm, Sun 1–7pm.

Clothing-women
Flatiron/East Village

The Edge: The place for sexy little dresses. A cutting-edge look for the club crowd. Dresses priced $80 to $140 and slinky vinyl leggings run $65 to $75. *"Wonderful dresses to go out in." "For those young and dating in New York—this is a find."*

Kenar

96 Orchard Street
near Houston Street / 254-8899
Daily 10am–5pm.

Clothing-women
Lower East Side/Chinatown

quality style service value

The Edge: The Kenar line at 20% off. Further discounts possible if you negotiate and it isn't Sunday when the store is crowded.

Klein's of Monticello

105 Orchard Street
near Delancey Street / 966-1453
Mon–Sat 10am–5pm.

Clothing-women
Lower East Side/Chinatown

quality style service value

The Edge: The Barneys look discounted on the Lower East Side. High-fashion European clothing, including many Barneys labels, discounted. Features pants and skirt suits, silk shirts, and accessories, including those fabulous designer silver (thousand-dollar) buckled belts, hats, scarves, and jewelry. Small but excellent selection of clothing sourced from smaller European design houses. Labels include Les Copains, Malo cashmere, Vestimenta, and similar quality items. Clothing tends to be in muted colors with lots of black and brown. Virtually all items are for women. For men: cashmere sports jackets only. 25% off. *"High-style original clothing." "Fine clothes—high end." "The owners think the shop is Barneys."*

Lea's Designer Fashion

119 Orchard Street
near Delancey Street / 677-2043
Weekdays 9:30am–5pm, Sun 9am–5pm.

Clothing-women
Lower East Side/Chinatown

quality style service value

The Edge: Discounts high-end top designers. Features an especially large collection of Louis Feraud, Kenzo, Albert Nippon, and other top designers. Suits for $250 to $1,000, skirts from $50, and pants from $60. If you buy a lot and if it's not a Sunday, talk price—greater discounts are possible. 30% off. *"The Lower East Side source for Feraud."*

Lee Anderson

23 East 67th Street
near Madison Avenue / 772-2463
Mon–Sat 11am–6pm.

Clothing-women
Upper East Side

quality style service value

The Edge: Pret-à-porter and custom clothing in classic styles with a European twist. Mostly skirts, shirts, pants, and peacoats. Prices are high, with $275 skirts, $325 pants, and $195+ shirts—and all from the in-house designer. Wonderful peacoat jackets in great colors. Deluxe.

Linda Dresner

484 Park Avenue
near 58th Street / 308-3177
Mon–Sat 10am–6pm (closed Sat in summer).

Clothing-women
Midtown East

quality style service value

The Edge: Very hip, selective, expensive clothing. Features Europeans like Jil Sander, Prada, Jean Muir, and more in misses' sizes 6 to 12, with shoes in sizes 7 to 9. Prices are high: pants $600+, shoes $300+, and suits $1,500+. Find jewelry, bags, and accessories that complement the line.

Loehmann's

Weekdays 10am–9pm, Sat 10am–9pm, Sun 11am–6pm.

Clothing-women
Multiple locations

quality style service value

The Edge: The Back Room. The Back Room is where you can sometimes find the best labels, like Anne Klein, Calvin Klein, DKNY, and Emanuel at the end of the season. Expect to find bathing suits (in season), coats, shirts, shoes, and slacks. Always a good source for glittery beaded evening dresses (for those who still wear them). Bus service on weekends to the Riverdale store (from in front of the Metropolitan Museum and Lincoln Center), which remains the best store—call 212-265-0512 for reservations and times. Discounter. *"Riverdale store is the best of the lot." "If you have the patience, it's worth the trip." "Not the store it used to be." "Has gone downhill over the years." "Many clothes look old and dated."*

Locations: Bronx: 5740 Broadway, near 236th Street, Riverdale (718-543-6420) / 2500 Halsey Street, Bronx (718-409-2000) / 901 Zerega Avenue, Bronx (718-829-6619) / **Brooklyn:** 19 Duryea Place, Brooklyn (718-469-9800) / **Chelsea:** 101 7th Avenue, between 16th and 17th Streets (352-0856) / **Long Island:** 1296 Broadway, Hewlett (516-374-5195) / 301 West Jericho Pike, Huntington Station (516-423-2020) / **Queens:** 6006 99th Street, Flushing (718-271-4000) / **Westchester:** 29 Tarrytown Road, White Plains (914-948-8090)

Margot Green
772-0892
By appointment.

Clothing-women
Mail/phone

quality style service value

The Edge: Wonderful knits and silks. Has her own boutique where she specializes in custom-knit adaptations of top European designers. Also silks and wool fashions. Quality custom work. Spends January through March in Palm Beach. Discounter.

Max Mara
813 Madison Avenue
near 68th Street / 879-6100
Mon–Wed and Fri–Sat 10am–6pm, Thurs 10am–7pm.

Clothing-women
Upper East Side

quality style service value

The Edge: Italian women's clothing—conservative to very stylish, depending on the line. Various lines and price points for coats ($700 to $4,000), suits ($600 to $1,100), skirts, pants, shoes, and evening wear. Dresses are cut well in fine fabrics. Misses' and petite sizes from 2 to 14. Publishes *MM* magazine twice a year, featuring its fashions and living trends. Remember Le Firme for Max Mara discounted. *"Sale items are good value, but the selection's not great during sales."*

Miriam Rigler
14 West 55th Street
near 5th Avenue / 581-5519
Mon–Sat 10am–6pm.

Clothing-women
Midtown West

quality style service value

The Edge: Miriam can put together what's right for you. Features moderately discounted women's sportswear, day dresses, knits, custom suits, and evening wear from less-well-known higher-end expensive European designers as well as her own designs. Caters to tourists and working women. Best for their conservative office and "mother of the bride" clothing. *"For work suits that are just a little bit different." "Don't let the sometimes dowdy windows deter you—go in!"*

Morgan De Toi
500 7th Avenue
between 37th and 38th Streets / 869-4760

Clothing-women
Midtown West

Weekdays 10am–6pm.

The Edge: Much-needed affordable French chic. The place where Europe's hottest looks are copied, making them almost affordable. The store copies Prada, among other designers. Expect branch outlets in New York that will carry Morgan shoes, handbags, and stationery along with the fashion line. Featured in *Vogue, Allure,* and *Marie Claire,* among other top fashion magazines.

Nicole Miller

780 Madison Avenue
near 66th Street / 288-9779
Weekdays 10am–7pm, Sat 10am–6pm.

Clothing-women
Upper East Side

39	40	39	35
quality	style	service	value

The Edge: Excellent little black dresses for evening. Favored by young career women. Complete line of sportswear, day dresses, and evening wear. Moderate prices, excellent styling. *"She has the quintessential evening wear." "Good styling at less than haute prices."*

Remin's

62 Purchase Street
at Purdy, Rye / 800-245-6671
Mon–Sat 9:30am–5:45pm, Sun noon–5pm.

Clothing-women
Westchester

35	35	35	38
quality	style	service	value

The Edge: High-end designs favored by the chairman of the board's wife. European designer clothing always discounted (20%). A full range of clothing, from casual weekend wear to conservatively tailored clothing good for the office. Some evening wear. Even through it's a discounter, it's very expensive and there won't be a lot of labels you know. 45 minutes from Manhattan; then a 2-minute walk from the Rye train station. Discounter. *"I've been going there for years and I do very well. It's sometimes too 'old-ladyish,' yet I'm always complimented on the clothes I bought there."*

Rodier

Mon–Wed and Fri–Sat 10am–6:30pm,
Thurs 10am–8pm, Sun noon–6pm.

Clothing-women
Multiple locations

42	33	35	35
quality	style	service	value

The Edge: The French version of Talbots. Lots of coordinated knits, slacks, shirts, and accessories. Conservative styling. Sales are seasonal and excellent.

Locations: Midtown West: 610 5th Avenue, near 50th Street (Rockefeller Center) (489-9427) / **Upper East Side:** 1310 3rd Avenue, near 75th Street (439-0104)

S&W

165 West 26th Street
near 7th Avenue / 924-6656
Mon–Wed 10am–6:30pm, Thurs 10am–8pm,
Fri 10am–3pm, Sun 10am–6pm.

Clothing-women
Midtown West

37	34	30	37
quality	style	service	value

The Edge: Negotiate or overpay for mid-range designer clothing. Designer clothing, including sportswear, dresses, evening wear, coats, suits, and accessories— moderately discounted. Expect to find Perry Ellis, Calvin Klein, Kenar, Kasper, and similar brands. You can usually get more off the price if you push, possibly to 40%. *"Must go often." "Staff is pushy."*

Saint Laurent Rive Gauche

855 Madison Avenue
near 70th Street / 988-3821
Mon–Sat 10am–6pm.

Clothing-women
Upper East Side

quality style service value

The Edge: The Paris legend! Timeless, well-cut clothing from pants to gowns. Well-cut styles, excellent tailoring, and wonderful fabrics at extremely high prices. Deluxe. *"Very, very expensive but timeless."*

Searle

Mon–Wed and Fri–Sat 10am–6pm, Thurs 10am–7pm,
Sun noon–5pm (closed Sun July–Aug).

Clothing-women
Multiple locations

quality style service value

The Edge: Conservative, well-made clothing in beautiful fabrics. Find everything for the Upper East Side matron—dresses, suits, sweaters, and coats—all beautifully tailored in lovely fabrics. Expensive. *"Good style and tailoring." "I love their coats." "Pricey, but beautifully styled and great fabrics." "Great chenille sweaters, jackets, and coats."*

Locations: Upper East Side: 1035 Madison Avenue, at 79th Street (717-4022) / 860 Madison Avenue, at 70th Street (772-2225) / 609 Madison Avenue, between 57th and 58th Streets (753-9021) / 1051 3rd Avenue, at 61st Street (838-5990)

Shulie's

175 Orchard Street
near Houston Street / 473-2480
Sun–Fri 9:30am–5:30pm.

Clothing-women
Lower East Side/Chinatown

quality style service value

The Edge: Tahari's line at 20% off. Tahari for women, from sportswear to dresses. The complete line is there or can be gotten. Also classic but spunky moderately priced shoes in an adjacent shop, accessible from the store. Prices are priced at 20% off, but negotiate for additional savings. *"Hard-to-find sizes."*

St. John Boutique

665 5th Avenue
near 53rd Street / 755-5252
Mon–Wed and Fri–Sat 10am–6pm, Thurs 10am–7pm.

Clothing-women
Midtown East

quality style service value

The Edge: Knits that travel well and look good. The Nancy Regan White House look beloved by the executive crowd, especially those who travel on business. Elegant lady-like knit suits, always available in navy, white, and black plus the current year's colors, with silk shirts and accessories to complement the outfit. The more contemporary line is Griffith and Grey, featuring woven knit patterns. Misses' sizes 2 to 14, with some 16s. Free alterations. Expensive, with suits in the $700 to $1,200 range. Deluxe. *"The rite of passage for executive women. Terrific—it's all I wear." "Good for travel business suits."*

Sue's Discount Better Dresses

638 Lexington Avenue
near 54th Street / 752-5574

Clothing-women
Midtown East

Weekdays 9:30am–6:30pm, Sun 11am–5pm.

The Edge: Gets close-outs of Grossman and Nippon suits. The source for basic business work clothing. A small shop selling very conservative suits, mostly Grossman and Nippon, that they buy right. Standard blouses and some dresses. 25% off. *"Good prices." "Pushiest salespeople in town."*

Tahari

225 Liberty Street
near Vesey Street / 535-1515
Weekdays 10am–7pm, Sat 11am–5pm, Sun noon–5pm.

Clothing-women
Lower Manhattan

The Edge: Tailored suits designed to take the busy executive from the office to evening. Graceful silk, rayon, and gabardine dresses, nicely cut slacks, and ultra-feminine silk blouses. Outlet at Woodbury Commons, on 7th Avenue, and at the New Jersey factory. *"Fantastic suits and dresses. Great evening dresses."*

Tahari Outlet Store

Weekdays 10am–7pm, Sat 11am–5pm, Sun noon–5pm.

Clothing-women
Multiple locations

38	38	35	38
quality	style	service	value

The Edge: Bargain Tahari. You never know what it will have—but the prices appeared better than at the store sales or at the mega-discount locations (Woodbury Commons and the like). The nicest help, and apparently most of everything they manufacture gets to the outlet shop eventually. The staff are truly special ladies—helpful and cheerful—it's worth going for that alone. No delivery. Discounter. *"Great for work suits as well as formals." "Good value but slim pickin's." "Woodbury Commons, the New Jersey outlet store, appears better." "Especially good at the end of the season."*

Locations: Midtown West: 525 7th Avenue, 19th Floor, at 38th Street (921-5164) / **New Jersey:** 501 Broad Avenue, Ridgefield (201-943-5000)

Talbots

Weekdays 10am–8pm, Sat 10am–7pm, Sun noon–6pm.

Clothing-women
Multiple locations

41	33	41	37
quality	style	service	value

The Edge: Ultra-conservative casual to business clothing. Known for the Connecticut look, featuring tailored slacks, skirts, suits, evening wear, and shoes. Full range of styles—if it's not in the store, call the toll-free number (800-882-5268) for quick delivery. Sizes from petite to misses' 20. See the twice-yearly sale when prices get really low. *"Great sales. Will call other stores to complete outfits and find sizes." "My favorite really, but a bit frumpy."*

Locations: Midtown East: 525 Madison Avenue, near 54th Street (838-8811) / **Upper East Side:** 1251-1255 3rd Avenue, near 72nd Street (988-8585) / **Upper West Side:** 2289-2291 Broadway, at 82nd Street (875-8753)

Todd Oldman

123 Wooster Street
between Prince and Spring Streets / 219-3531

Clothing-women
SoHo/TriBeCa

Mon–Sat 11am–7pm, Sun noon–6pm.

quality style service value

The Edge: Extravagant new looks. A top cutting-edge designer favoring wonderful fabrics with terrific colors. In his latest season he used 1,700 colors in what appeared to be a simple (but gorgeous) print.

Valentino
747 Madison Avenue
near 65th Street / 772-6969
Mon–Sat 10am–6pm.

Clothing-women
Upper East Side

quality style service value

The Edge: Classic sexy Italian clothing. A favorite of all our all-time favorite stylish ladies—Audrey Hepburn, Jacqueline Onassis, and Sophia Loren. Broad range of prices, depending on the line, from Couture to Miss V and Studio V. Deluxe. *"Exceptional in every way."*

Vivaldi Boutique
1288 3rd Avenue
at 74th Street / 734-2805
Mon–Wed and Fri–Sat 11am–7pm,
Thurs 11am–8pm, Sun noon–5pm.

Clothing-women
Upper East Side

quality style service value

The Edge: A great neighborhood spot for the right Upper East Side look. Favors European designers, including Claude Montana, Georges Rech, Angelo Tarlazzi, and Emmanuelle Kahn. Clothes from day to evening, plus accessories that complement the look. Very expensive. *"Wonderful taste—of course, you pay for it!"*

Wang
219 Mott Street
between Prince and Spring Streets / 941-6134
Daily noon–7pm.

Clothing-women
SoHo/TriBeCa

The Edge: There's more than one Wang to watch. Designs by sister Sally all sold at Sally's and sister Jennifer's joint shop. Clothing tends to be moderately priced, feminine yet appropriate for the office. Mostly skirts (from $100), dresses ($200), and jackets ($175 to $300) to complement. Great looks with an Oriental feel.

Wathne
4 West 57th Street
between 5th and Madison Avenues / 262-7100
Mon–Wed and Fri–Sat 10am–6pm, Thurs 10am–8pm.

Clothing-women
Midtown West

quality style service value

The Edge: What you'd expect to wear on the weekend at the great châteaux. High-quality classic French-styled country wear.

Abracadabra
10 Christoper Street
near 6th Avenue / 627-5745

Costumes
Greenwich Village

Mon–Sat 11am–7pm, Sun noon–5pm.

quality style service value

The Edge: Great costume rentals. One of the largest selections of costumes in the city. Also makeup, masks, props, wigs, and supplies for magicians. *"They have every costume imaginable."*

Allan Uniform Rental Service

121 East 24th Street
between Lexington and Park Avenues / 529-4655
Weekdays 9am–5pm.

Costumes
Gramercy Park/Murray Hill

The Edge: Costume rentals. Period, animal, and masquerade costumes for rent in adult sizes.

Gordon Novelty Company

933 Broadway
between 21st and 22nd Streets / 254-8616
Weekdays 9am–4:30pm.

Costumes
Gramercy Park/Murray Hill

The Edge: Wonderful costumes. A 65-year-old company that features a vast selection of costumes and accessories for magicians.

Alan Flusser at Saks

611 5th Avenue
near 49th Street, in Saks / 888-7100
Weekdays 10am–7pm, Sat 10am–6:30pm, Sun noon–6pm.

Custom
Midtown East

30	35	35	30
quality	style	service	value

The Edge: Upscale investment banker look. Designed Michael Douglas's suits in the movie *Wall Street*. The custom line is now sold at Saks on the sixth floor. Suits from $1,600. Deluxe.

Alexander Kabbaz

903 Madison Avenue
between 72nd and 73rd Streets / 861-7700
Weekdays 7am–7pm, Sat 10am–6pm.

Custom
Upper East Side

The Edge: Exceptionally fine custom-made shirts and suits. More modern styling. Wide range of fabrics and good tailoring. Very expensive, with shirts from $350 (a six-shirt minimum) and suits from $2,850. Shirts from Swiss fabric exclusively. Deluxe.

Arthur Gluck Shirtmakers

47 West 57th Street
between 5th and 6th Avenues / 755-8165
Mon–Thurs 9am–5pm, Fri 9am–2pm.

Custom
Midtown West

The Edge: Could be the best shirts in town. Wide choice of fine fabrics. Gluck special features include mother-of-pearl buttons and hand-sewn monograms. Shirts are $200 each, with a minimum order of six. Orders take two months. Worn-out cuffs and collars are replaced as needed. Gluck will launder its shirts at $8 per. Customers are reputed to include Henry Kissinger and Lew Wasserman. For women: men's-style shirts cut to fit. Deluxe.

Ascot Chang

7 West 57th Street
between 5th and 6th Avenues / 759-3333
Mon–Sat 9:30am–6pm.

Custom
Midtown West

quality style service value

The Edge: Fine custom work. Hong Kong shirtmaker offers ready-made and custom shirts and Italian made-to-measure suits. 2,000 fabrics and 12 different collar styles to choose from. Also silk pajamas, dressing gowns, and accessories. Very expensive. Deluxe. *"Expensive, but good." "Will wear forever—perfect measurement and tailoring."*

Brioni

55 East 52nd Street
between Park and Madison Avenues / 355-1940
Mon–Sat 9am–6pm.

Custom
Midtown East

quality style service value

The Edge: Impeccable tailoring. Traditionally styled Italian-shaped custom suits. Extensive selection of all the best fabrics (cashmeres, silks, and wools) to choose from. Priced from $2,700. Deluxe. *"Expensive, but the highest quality."*

Cheo Tailors

30 East 60th Street
between Madison and Park Avenues / 980-9838
Weekdays by appointment 10am–6pm, Sat 11am–3pm.

Custom
Midtown East

The Edge: Quality London-trained tailor. Exquisite custom suits made exclusively from European wools. Suits take two to three months to make. No delivery. Deluxe.

Chris-Arto Custom Shirt Company

39 West 32nd Street, 6th Floor
between 5th Avenue and Broadway / 563-4455
Weekdays 7:30am–4:30pm.

Custom
Midtown West

The Edge: Luxurious custom shirts. Shirts are well fitted and made from a choice of hundreds of quality fabrics. Multiple fittings. A minimum of five shirts is required for the first order. Prices are $165 to $175 per shirt. Also custom-made pajamas. Telephone orders for established customers only. No credit cards. No delivery. Deluxe.

Gilberto Designs

142 West 36th Street, 8th Floor
between 7th Avenue and Broadway / 695-4925
Weekdays 9am–4pm, Sat 9:30am–3pm (closed Sat July–Aug).

Custom
Midtown West

The Edge: Knockoffs for men. Custom suits, jackets, tuxedos, and overcoats. Can knock off any jacket. It manufactures its own line in fine Italian and English fabrics, with suits priced from $800 to $2,500, shirts from $75 (minimum order of four), and ties from $60. All work is done on site. Allow three weeks for a suit.

H. Herzfeld

507 Madison Avenue

Custom
Midtown East

near 52nd Street / 753-6756
Weekdays 9am–6pm, Sat 9am–5:30pm.

quality style service value

The Edge: Fine custom shirts. Conservative English-styled clothes. Known for its shirts, sweaters, and ties, but suits and slacks also. *"Old guard, good haberdasher."*

House of Maurizio

18 East 53rd Street
between Madison and 5th Avenues / 759-3230
Weekdays by appointment 8:30am–5pm.

Custom
Midtown East

quality style service value

The Edge: One of the top-of-the-line custom tailors. For 34 years, exquisite custom suits starting at $3,000, as well as blazers and coats. Thousands of fabrics from England and Italy. Custom shirts from $195 and custom ties from $75. Suits take four to five weeks. No credit cards. Deluxe.

Ilana Designs

150 East 69th Street
between Lexington and 3rd Avenues / 570-9420
By appointment—leave a message on the machine anytime.

Custom
Upper East Side

quality style service value

The Edge: Copies of the great designs. Located in the Imperial House (ask the doorman). Does alterations and makes custom suits and dresses to order. Can copy top European and American designers (Armani, Lacroix, Tiel). Will work on any fabrics. Not counting the fabric, women's jackets priced from $650, skirts from $250, and suits from $900. No credit cards.

John Anthony

153 East 51st Street
between Lexington and 3rd Avenues / 888-4070
By appointment.

Custom
Upper East Side

quality style service value

The Edge: Superb tailoring. Known for his elegant ball gowns (around $10,000) and day suits (about $6,000). "Stratospheric" is insufficient to describe these extraordinary prices, but superb tailoring and fabrics. Deluxe. *"Appointments required (call Scott)."*

Leonard Logsdail

9 East 53rd Street
between 5th and Madison Avenues / 752-5030
Weekdays 9am–5pm.

Custom
Midtown East

The Edge: Conservative elegance. Great tailoring. Quality English wool custom suits at $2,500+. Before you get your suit, it will have crossed the Atlantic four times. Longsdail fits your suit here, sends it to London for hand-stitching, ships it back for your fitting, back again to London for finishing, and then back home to the States for your closet. Allow eight weeks for an order. No credit cards. Deluxe.

Mandana

1175 Lexington Avenue
near 80th Street / 988-0800
Weekdays 9am–6pm, Sat 10am–4pm.

Custom
Upper East Side

quality style service value

The Edge: Good copies of top designer clothing. Offers alterations and copies of top designer clothing, such as Valentino evening dresses and Armani suits. Workmanship looks good. Allow two weeks to complete a suit. Very expensive— suits from $1,200. No delivery. Deluxe.

Mark Christoper of Wall Street
26 Broadway, Lobby Store
509-2355
Weekdays 8am–6pm, Sat–Sun by appointment.

Custom
Lower Manhattan

The Edge: A downtown source for custom-tailored menswear. Suits from $700 and shirts from $145 are all handmade on the premises in wool, silk, and cotton. Suits take five weeks. There's a four-shirt minimum order. Annual sale in December. Some tailoring for women—but not really for the ladies. Will copy anything well.

Mr. Ned
85 5th Avenue
near 16th Street / 924-5042
Weekdays 8am–6pm, Sat 8am–4pm.

Custom
Flatiron/East Village

quality style service value

The Edge: Semi-custom suits priced well. Features suits from $525 to $750 in a wide range of fabrics, including wools and cashmere, from all the top European houses. *"30% off."* *"My husband has been getting suits there for years! It's the only way to buy."*

New Bouquet Fashions, Inc.
26A Elizabeth Street
near Canal Street / 374-9086
Daily 11am–7pm.

Custom
SoHo/TriBeCa

quality style service value

The Edge: The secret source for high style. Where a cross section of the city meets. Excellent tailoring—you bring your own fabrics. At the shop expect to find anyone from Park Avenue matrons to Chinatown families to Ultra-Orthodox ladies commuting across the bridge from Brooklyn. Can do complex work and copy anything. Limited English spoken. Ladies' suits from $255 ($325 with skirt and slacks), excluding fabrics. No credit cards. No delivery. *"Absolutely first-rate down to the button holes."* *"I trusted them with the gown to my granddaughter's wedding."*

One-of-a-Kind
767 Lexington Avenue
near 60th Street / 371-4842
Weekdays 10am–5pm.

Custom
Upper East Side

The Edge: Elegant designer clothing copied well. Since 1971, originals and copies of designer lines, Armani and Chanel especially. Suits from $1,000, depending on fabric. Designer Surang Yamnaim was featured in *New York* magazine in 1991 as one of the best. House calls for $75 per hour. No credit cards. No delivery. Deluxe.

Susan Grant
223-0346
By appointment.

Custom
Midtown East

quality style service value

The Edge: High-end designer knockoffs. Mix and match. Susan Grant makes selected copies of quality jackets, skirts, and slacks cut in Armani, Chanel, or Ungaro style, in a range of sizes which can be custom-ordered in a large variety of fabrics and trims. Jackets run upward of $600, with slacks and skirts about $200. Nice detailing. Some knits on hand. Orders take two to three weeks. Grant likes to know who's coming to her small private shop—so when you call, either give her an existing client as a reference or your employer's name so she can get comfortable as to who you are. No credit cards. *"Great styles. Great buttons." "Easy shopping, nice looks, but expensive."*

Uma Reddy Ltd.

Custom
Midtown West

30 West 57th Street, Room 6E
between 5th and 6th Avenues / 757-7240
Weekdays by appointment 9:30am–5:30pm.

40	45	48	32
quality	style	service	value

The Edge: Another top tailor. Mostly English wool and Italian silk suits, with extra fabric kept on hand for alterations. Suits take four to six weeks. Priced from $3,200. Also custom ties ($95 to $125) and shirts ($165+). Prices depend on materials. No credit cards. Deluxe.

Vincent Nicolosi

Custom
Midtown East

510 Madison Avenue
at 53rd Street / 486-6214
Mon–Sat 10am–4pm.

The Edge: Where author Tom Wolfe's whites come from. High-end classic elegant suits appropriate for the board room. Some women's things, for women who like the classic quality man's tailored look. Deluxe.

William Fioravanti

Custom
Midtown West

45 West 57th Street
between 5th and 6th Avenues / 355-1540
Weekdays by appointment 9am–5pm.

The Edge: Quality custom, all hand-worked, suits and coats. Uses only fabrics imported from England and Italy. He's so booked up that new customers need a referral for an appointment. Suits take 10 to 12 weeks. Very expensive. No credit cards. No delivery. Deluxe. *"Fabulous work." "Snooty."*

Winston-Tailors

Custom
Midtown East

11 East 44th Street
between Madison and 5th Avenues / 687-0850
Weekdays 9am–5:30pm, Sat 10am–3pm (closed Sat June–Aug).

The Edge: The Chip II line. Conservative made-to-measure two-and three-button American-style suits, sports jackets, and coats. Custom tailoring for women. Fabrics most often are imported English wools. Private label manufacturer at the same address and telephone number as Chip II. Suits are priced from $750 to $1,200 (average $875).

Barneys New York
Mon-Fri 10-8 Sat 10-7 Sun noon-6.

Department stores
Multiple locations

44 | 45 | 38 | 29
quality style service value

The Edge: Still hard to ignore for cutting-edge fashion. Go to Bergdorf and Barneys for large selections and some of the best cutting-edge looks in the city. A wide choice of top designer and designed-for-Barneys clothing, from casual to formal wear. Styles from traditional to the cutting-edge is what it's known for. Chelsea Passage has items for the home. Jewelry from costume to real. Designers include Donna Karan, Chanel, Vera Wang, Jil Sander, Prada, and Thierry Mugler; and for men, Boss, Gieves & Hawkes, and Comme des Gartttttons. Always on the lookout for new talent. Men particularly love the Barneys warehouse sale—but it's the same merchandise. Deluxe. *"For the rich and skinny." "Cutting-edge fashion in drab colors." "The twice-yearly sale is your best bet (particularly for men)." "Really pretentious, but some terrific items."*

Locations: Lower Manhattan: Two World Financial Center, at 225 Liberty Street (945-1600) / **Upper East Side:** 660 Madison Avenue, at 61st Street (826-8900)

Bergdorf Goodman
754 5th Avenue
between 57th and 58th Streets / 753-7300
Mon–Wed and Fri–Sat 10am–6pm, Thurs 10am–8pm.

Department stores
Midtown West

44 | 43 | 39 | 31
quality style service value

The Edge: Real clothes for real ladies. Features a full range of women's designer fashion, from conservative to more high fashion. Top prices, but check the sales—they're fantastic. All the great names have boutiques in the store, including Chanel, Jil Sander, Prada, Blass, Claude Montana, Valentino, Armani, and more. Wonderful accessories, including costume and quality day jewelry. The home accessories are wonderful and include an outlet of Kentshire for a traditional English look. It's less cutting-edge than Barneys. Great news—Susan Ciminelli's spa has arrived! Deluxe. *"Nicest clothes in the city." "Top-notch clothing for top-notch wallets." "Bergdorf's treasure is Miriam Pfifferling, on the sixth floor—she'll search out the best buys in the store for you." "Great sales." "Always fabulous service." "The women's store is better than the men's store."*

Bergdorf Goodman Men's Store
745 5th Avenue
between 57th and 58th Streets / 753-7300
Mon–Wed and Fri–Sat 10am–6pm, Thurs 10am–8pm.

Department stores
Midtown West

45 | 43 | 41 | 36
quality style service value

The Edge: Wide range of quality designer fashions for men. Already a 45,000-square-foot store and getting bigger. Features a full range of men's designer fashion, from conservative to more high fashion. Top prices, but check the sales. Find a combination of traditional and high-fashion menswear with all the great names—Oxxford, Hickey-Freeman, Armani, Versace, and the like. To Boot is its shoe concession. Deluxe. *"Excellent selection, attentive staff. Expensive." "Men's store better than women's."*

Bloomingdale's
3rd Avenue or Lexington Avenue
between 59th and 60th Streets / 705-2000

Department stores
Midtown East

Weekdays 10am–8:30pm, Sat 10am–7pm, Sun 11am–7pm.

The Edge: Good all-around department store. What Bloomies has is range—from clothing to furniture and virtually anything in between. Especially good for young designers. Seems to be coming back! Prices range from moderate to very high. *"You can find anything." "A decent selection of everything." "If you have a Gold Visa, it's a great value." "Too much of a tourist trip to deal with." "Only the third floor and only on big sales days is Bloomies worth the effort of shopping in a discotèque."*

Century 21

Department stores
Lower Manhattan

22 Cortlandt Street
between Broadway and Church Street / 227-9092
Mon–Wed 7:45am–7pm, Thurs 7:45am–8:30pm,
Fri 7:45am–8pm, Sat 10am–7pm.

The Edge: One of the best values in the city. Full-range discount department store for the entire family. Features clothing with a contemporary look as well as small appliances, shoes, and cosmetics. Range from the basics to top European designs, with focus on moderately priced items. You'll never fail to find great things in the children's department. The men's department is strong, always with good basics and a range of sportswear that will please. We love the lingerie section, which often has Hanro, La Perla, Hue, Donna Klein, and Wolford, as well as more moderate lines— Hanes, Berkshire, etc. Women's clothing is hit or miss. The shoe department has moderately priced shoes. No try-ons except in the two locked dressing rooms in the women's European designer department (designers include such names as Dolce & Gabbana, Donna Karan, and the like at times). The high-end designer clothing is often just individual pieces, often missing buttons. The store is strong on cosmetics, and if you buy enough, you'll get store coupons—which creates a discount value on cosmetics. Many irregulars, so pay attention to your purchase. No delivery. 40% off. *"Great buys, but you have to be willing to dig and keep looking." "Fabulous for kids. 40% off." "Don't even think of going during lunchtime." "Worth it." "Great values—best for men." "Shopping secret of the chic and glamorous." "Sometimes great—sometimes zippo."*

Henri Bendel

Department stores
Midtown West

712 5th Avenue
near 56th Street / 247-1100
Mon–Wed and Fri–Sat 10am–7pm,
Thurs 10am–8pm, Sun noon–6pm.

The Edge: Not the old Bendel's but still interesting. Not the Bendel's we loved that had cutting-edge, understated chic. This small store is a full women's department store, featuring cosmetics, hair accessories, leggings, and casual to evening clothing by new designers and top-flight known talent. The Young Creators shop is where you'll find some cutting-edge new talent, while Bendel's Fancy has established designers. The tableware shop still has lovely modern things you'll remember. *"Some unique items—lovely service." "For the sales: great, great makeup collection." "You have to watch quality."*

Kmart

Department stores
Multiple locations

Weekdays 7-9 Sat 9-9 Sun 11-8.

The Edge: Suburbia in the City—for your casual clothing and housware needs. Find moderate to low priced clothing, housewares, and small appliances. *"I buy my rain flats here—great prices."*

Locations: Chelsea: 8th Street, at Lafayette Street (673-1540) / **Midtown West:** 34th Street, between 7th and 8th Avenues (760-1188)

Lord & Taylor

424 5th Avenue
between 38th and 39th Streets / 391-3344
Mon–Tues 10am–7pm, Wed–Fri 10am–8:30pm,
Sat 9am–7pm, Sun 11am–6pm.

**Department stores
Midtown West**

quality style service value

The Edge: Good selection of dresses. Features some of the top designers, including Anne Klein, Calvin Klein, Oscar de La Renta, and Ralph Lauren, but the focus is on more moderate price points. Has menswear and a well-stocked children's department. Has a particularly well-stocked swimsuit department (in season). A great resource for preteen boys, with such great labels as CK, Izod, Polo, Hilfiger, Reebok, Mike, Dockers, and Speedo. *"Still a standby for basics." "When they have a sale, they have a sale!" "Staid." "High styling."*

Macy's

Broadway at Herald Square
at 34th Street / 695-4400
Mon and Thurs–Fri 10am–8:30pm,
Tues–Wed and Sat 10am–7pm, Sun 11am– 6pm.

**Department stores
Midtown West**

quality style service value

The Edge: You can find anything. Mid-price focus. A huge store that, while badly organized, has everything for everyone—plus a full range of housewares, with kitchenware, appliances, and tableware particularly strong. One of the best sources for a wide range of teenagers' clothing. Beloved for the Thanksgiving Day parade and Fourth of July fireworks. *"Good for household items." "Good for men's and boys' underwear." "Good sales." "Just too big and crowded, to be avoided." "[In the Brooklyn store,] terrible service, no dressing rooms, few cash registers open."*

Saks Fifth Avenue

611 5th Avenue
between 49th and 50th Streets / 753-4000
Mon–Wed and Fri–Sat 10am–7pm,
Thurs 10am–8pm, Sun noon–6pm.

**Department stores
Midtown East**

quality style service value

The Edge: Terrific New York chic—the place to shop now. Somewhat more affordable than Barneys and Bergdorf, it features a very good New York style. Has it all for children, women, and men—from cosmetics and jewels and day wear to formal wear. For preteen girls (ages 10 to 15), check out the party dresses; they're not baby looking, they're just right, but very, very expensive ($500+). Good designs and wide style range tending to a more tailored look. Wonderful sales really early in the season. Check the Saks First program, which offers discounts when you reach prearranged (high) spending levels. *"One of NYC's best specialty stores!" "Best all-around department store." "Best store in town."*

T.J. Maxx

620 6th Avenue
between 18th and 19th Streets / 229-0875
Mon–Sat 9:30am–9pm, Sun 10am–6pm.

**Department stores
Chelsea**

<table>
<tr><td>32</td><td>31</td><td>27</td><td>36</td></tr>
<tr><td>quality</td><td>style</td><td>service</td><td>value</td></tr>
</table>

The Edge: Great value, if you can find something. 60,000 square feet of off-price designer clothing, shoes, gifts, jewelry, and housewares—at good but not rock-bottom prices. More moderately priced items and designers—Liz Claiborne, Levi's, Jones New York at times. Respondents think prices appear discounted 30% to 50%. No delivery. Discounter. *"I always find something worthwhile every time I go." "Here and there something." "Hit or miss. Best discounts for children's wear and housewares." "Good value on bare basics and staples." "An occasional find—but not worth the effort of the search."*

Takashimaya

693 5th Avenue
near 54th Street / 350-0100
Mon–Wed and Fri–Sat 10am–6pm, Thurs 10am–8pm.

Department stores
Midtown East

<table>
<tr><td>45</td><td>47</td><td>40</td><td>31</td></tr>
<tr><td>quality</td><td>style</td><td>service</td><td>value</td></tr>
</table>

The Edge: Oriental sensibility. This is the American flagship store of this 162-year-old Japanese company. The first two floors feature an art gallery and flowers. On the third and fourth floors find Japanese items, including stationery, clothing, furniture, and accessories. It has wonderful things with simple lines, top fabrics, and quality. The top floor looks like a duty-free shop, selling high-end European goods to Japanese tourists. There's a Japanese cafe and tea salon downstairs. Deluxe. *"A museum you can shop in." "Very expensive, but beautiful, unusual things." "Great gifts. Lunch in the cafe is very special."*

Chelsee Eyes, Inc.

20 West 20th Street, Suite 804
between 5th and 6th Avenues / 242-4823
Weekdays 10am–5pm, evenings and Sat by appointment.

Eyeglasses
Chelsea

The Edge: Value. Discount eyewear boutique featuring designer (all the top names) eyewear and prescription lenses. Great Italian sunglasses. Takes checks with ID. No credit cards.

Gruen Optika

Weekdays 9:30am–7pm, Sat 10am–5:30pm,
Sun noon–5pm (closed Sun July–Aug).

Eyeglasses
Multiple locations

<table>
<tr><td>45</td><td>40</td><td>40</td><td>35</td></tr>
<tr><td>quality</td><td>style</td><td>service</td><td>value</td></tr>
</table>

The Edge: Chic but conservative styling. High-fashion designer glasses. Selection includes Armani, Donna Karan, and Gaultier. Priced from $100 to $1,000+.

Locations: Midtown East: 599 Lexington Avenue, near 52nd Street (688-3580) / **Upper East Side:** 740 Madison Avenue, near 64th Street (988-5832) / 1076 3rd Avenue, near 63rd Street (751-6177) / 1255 Lexington Avenue, near 82nd Street (628-2493) / **Upper West Side:** 2382 Broadway, near 87th Street (724-0850)

Morgenthal-Frederics Opticians

685 Madison Avenue
between 61st and 62nd Streets / 838-3090
Weekdays 9am–7pm, Sat 10am–5:30pm, Sun noon–6pm.

Eyeglasses
Upper East Side

<table>
<tr><td>45</td><td>50</td><td>30</td><td>25</td></tr>
<tr><td>quality</td><td>style</td><td>service</td><td>value</td></tr>
</table>

The Edge: Whether you need 'em or not, you'll want to wear 'em. Great glasses from all the great designers—Oliver Peoples, L.A. Eyeworks, Christian Roth, and Matsuda—plus their own designs. Jackie O reputedly loved this place for glasses (and at minimum she was famous for her sunglasses). *"New York chic." "Best in town."*

A&N Fabrics

268 West 39th Street
between 7th and 8th Avenues / 719-1773
Weekdays 9am–5:45pm, Sat 9am–5pm.

Fabric
Midtown West

The Edge: All types of fabrics and industrial fabrics. Features more moderate lines, but has a wide selection of fabric types and colors. Offers decorating services and will make drapes, tablecloths, bedclothes, etc. Willing to find hard-to-get items for you. See Harry—he'll meet or beat any price!

B&J Fabrics

263 West 40th Street
between 7th and 8th Avenues / 354-8150
Weekdays 8am–5:45pm, Sat 9am–4:45pm.

Fabric
Midtown West

quality style service value

The Edge: Three floors of fine, mostly European ladies' fashion fabrics. Three floors of European silks, brocades, and natural fibers—mostly dressy fabrics. Bargain fabrics are on the third floor. Priced from $200 to $300 per yard. Discounter. *"Outstanding chiffons, brocades, silks. Excellent selection of cottons, linen, and wool."*

Beckenstein's Men's Fabrics

121 Orchard Street
near Delancey Street / 475-6666
Sun–Fri 9am–5:30pm.

Fabric
Lower East Side/Chinatown

quality style service value

The Edge: You can't find a more complete source for men's suit fabric. Find higher fashion, better lines, quality fabrics at a small discount. Discounter. *"Great selection." "You have the whole gamut of fabric here."*

Felsen Fabrics

264 West 40th Street
between 7th and 8th Avenues / 398-9010
Weekdays 8:30am–5:45pm, Sat 9am–4:45pm.

Fabric
Midtown West

quality style service value

The Edge: Bridal fabrics. Primarily fabrics for bridal wear. Will send swatches and accepts telephone and fax orders. Discounter. *"Good woolens and other fabrics."*

Kordol Fabrics

194 Orchard Street
near Houston Street / 254-8319
Sun–Fri 8am–5pm.

Fabric
Lower East Side/Chinatown

The Edge: Wide selection of suit fabrics for men and women. Good prices on linens, silks, and cottons. Discounter.

Mendel Goldberg Fabrics

72 Hester Street
between Allen and Orchard Streets / 925-9110
Sun–Thurs 9:30am–6pm, Fri 9:30am–4:30pm.

Fabric
Lower East Side/Chinatown

quality style service value

The Edge: One-stop shopping for a great look. Wonderful European fabrics from cottons and wools to top-of-the-line laces and silks. Alice Goldberg goes to Europe at least three times a year and comes back with designer fabrics you'll see on the runways of the top designers. Buttons to complement. Service is attentive, which is a surprise given that it's the Lower East Side. Will recommend tailors and work with you for what's right for you to wear. Reasonable prices. Discounter. *"Best fabric selection, best service, and lowest prices (for the quality) in town." "Want the Chanel, Prada, and the like look—they have the fabrics and buttons used." "See Sammy or Alice."*

Paron Fabrics

Mon–Sat 9am–5pm.

Fabric
Multiple locations

quality style service value

The Edge: Designer fabrics. The main store on 57th Street sells a good variety of linens, wools, imported silk, and other clothing fabrics. The clearance center on the second floor of 57th Street sells fabrics at 50% off. Paron West on West 40th Street specializes in designer and big-name fabrics. *"Very expensive but beautiful." "Sales are outstanding: good basics, good fancy goods, but can be more expensive than others."*

Locations: Midtown West: 206 West 40th Street, near 7th Avenue (768-3266) / 56 West 57th Street, near 6th Avenue (247-6451)

Poli Fabrics

227 West 40th Street
between 7th and 8th Avenues / 768-4555
Weekdays 8:30am–5:45pm, Sat 9am–4:45pm.

Fabric
Midtown West

quality style service value

The Edge: European and American designer fabrics. Claim to sell high-fashion fabrics at close-to-wholesale prices. Discounter. *"Great selection and 50% discount."*

Rosen & Chadick

246 West 40th Street
between 7th and 8th Avenues / 869-0136
Weekdays 8:30am–5:45pm, Sat 9am–5pm.

Fabric
Midtown West

quality style service value

The Edge: Largest selection on Fabric Street. Has everything from European silks, beaded lace, designer evening and bridal fabrics to a wide range of quality designer fabrics, woolens, cashmeres, cottons, and more. Moderate to very expensive. Will discount prices further for large bulk orders. *"Wonderful fabrics, tends to be expensive." "You need it, they have it in any season." "Very nice people who are helpful."*

Trebor Textiles, Inc.
215 West 40th Street
between 7th and 8th Avenues / 221-1610
Weekdays 8:30am–6pm, Sat 9:30am–4:30pm,
Sun 11am–4pm.

Fabric
Midtown West

quality   style   service   value

The Edge: More fabric basics. A large selection of wools, silks, and velvets. Discounter.

Weller Fabrics, Inc.
24 West 57th Street
between 5th and 6th Avenues / 247-3790
Weekdays 9am–6:30pm, Sat 9am–6pm.

Fabric
Midtown West

quality   style   service   value

The Edge: Lovely upscale European fabrics. An excellent source for ladies' designer fabrics. Wonderful silks, brocades, laces, and woolens. Full price and fine quality. *"Top of the line in looks and quality."*

Alixandre
150 West 30th Street, 13th Floor
near 7th Avenue / 736-5550
Weekdays 9am–5pm, Sat 9am–2pm.

Furriers
Midtown West

quality   style   service   value

The Edge: Fabulous classic furs designed by Oscar de la Renta, Valentino, and Yeohlee. Top-quality furs, from the softest shearlings to sable. The styling is divine, featuring designs by Valentino, Oscar de la Renta, and Yeohlee. These furs are often featured in *W*. Appointments are required—ask for Brad or Larry Schulman, sons of the senior Schulmans, Edwin and Stanley. The line is sold at Bergdorf and Neiman Marcus, among other places. While discounted from the prices at retail outlets, Alixandre's prices are at the high end of what you'll find on 7th Avenue. Wild mink coats start at $7,500, shearling jackets at $1,500, and fur-trimmed cashmere cloth coats at $2,300. Deluxe. Discounter. *"See Stanley or Edwin—they know what's best." "Fabulous-looking cashmere coats." "My first stop celebrating my promotion."*

Ben Kahn Salon
150 West 30th Street, 2n Floor
near 7th Avenue / 279-0633
Weekdays by appointment 9am–5pm, Sat 9am–2pm.

Furriers
Midtown West

quality   style   service   value

The Edge: Gorgeous furs. Quality furs from shearling to sable. Priced from $2,000 to $40,000. Deluxe. Discounter. *"Tops."*

Ben Thylan Furs
345 7th Avenue, 24th Floor
between 29th and 30th Streets / 753-7700
Weekdays 9am–5pm, Sat by appointment.

Furriers
Midtown West

quality   style   service   value

The Edge: Best for fur-lined raincoats. Couture furrier with designs by the Thylans and their associates. Classic and uncluttered styles. Fur coats and fur-lined raincoats. Relatively new for them are wool, cashmere, and camel's hair coats with or without fur trimming. Discounter. *"Beautiful."*

Birger Christensen

150 West 30th Street
near 7th Avenue / 947-7910
By appointment.

Furriers
Midtown West

quality style service value

The Edge: Another 7th Avenue fur source. Danish and Swedish furrier. B. Christensen is the exclusive designer. Features a full range of furs, from shearling coats to sable. This is the line now sold at Saks and Macy's. Stores and remodels furs as well. No credit cards. Deluxe. Discounter. *"Excellent furrier."*

Christie Bros.

333 7th Avenue, 11th Floor
near 28th Street / 736-6944
Weekdays 9am–5pm, and by appointment.

Furriers
Midtown West

quality style service value

The Edge: Traditional styling, quality furs. Features mostly classic but also contemporary styled furs from minks to sables. Deluxe. Discounter.

Frederick Gelb

345 7th Avenue, 19th Floor
between 29th and 30th Streets / 239-8787
Weekdays 9am–5pm, Sat 9am–2pm.

Furriers
Midtown West

The Edge: Favors European styling. Features female mink coats, wild mink, sheared mink, beaver, and shearlings, plus sporty fur-lined reversible coats and jackets in leather and microfiber. All sizes.

Goldin Feldman

345 7th Avenue
between 29th and 30th Streets / 594-4415
Weekdays 9am–5pm, Sat 9am–1pm.

Furriers
Midtown West

quality style service value

The Edge: Fine furs. Since 1909. Classic designs. Features a full range of furs—wild mink, Canadian fisher, Russian sable, and much more. Buy off-the-rack or order a custom-made fur. Deluxe. Discounter. *"A notch or two above other 7th Avenue furriers."*

J. Mendel

723 Madison Avenue
between 63rd and 64th Streets / 832-5830
Mon–Sat 10am–6pm.

Furriers
Upper East Side

The Edge: Tops in both price and styling. Tradition with an edge. Wonderful fur coats and wraps made from the finest furs and fabrics. This year's craze: mink backpacks. Beautiful styling—simple but elegant. Styles and lines by Gilles Mendel and Alfredo Cabrera. Great sales—don't be afraid to ask about price and possible bargains. Deluxe. *"The best in town." "Can negotiate—discuss when things are on sale."*

Michael Forrest

345 7th Avenue
between 29th and 30th Streets / 564-4726
Weekdays 9am–5pm.

Furriers
Midtown West

quality style service value

The Edge: 7th Avenue furrier. Another choice for wholesale furs. Anne Klein had been the designer, but now features its own in-house designers. Deluxe. Discounter.

Mohl Furs

345 7th Avenue
between 29th and 30th Streets / 736-7676
Weekdays by appointment 9am–5pm.

Furriers
Midtown West

quality style service value

The Edge: YSL furs. Yves St. Laurent's styling shows. Full line of furs: mink, sable, and others. Deluxe. Discounter.

Amy Downs

103 Stanton Street
near Ludlow Street / 598-4189
Wed–Sun 1–6pm.

Hats
SoHo/TriBeCa

The Edge: Cutting-edge style. Somewhat eccentric hats. Traditional styles accented with trims designed to be show stoppers. Reasonable prices combined with high style make this place a find. Prices from $40. Downs used to sell to Barneys and Charivari, now exclusively here.

Georgia Hughes Designs

45 East 89th Street
entrance on Madison Avenue / 996-5183
By appointment.

Hats
Upper East Side

quality style service value

The Edge: Truly unique fashion-forward hats. Features one-of-a-kind handmade and silk-lined hats. Hats from $200 to $265, fur-lined or trimmed hats from $200 to $700. Also sold at Barneys. Annual sale in January. No credit cards. *"Beautiful and timeless."*

Hat Shop

120 Thompson Street
between Prince & Spring / 219-1445
Tues–Sat noon–7pm (also Mon in Dec), Sun 1–6pm.

Hats
SoHo/TriBeCa

The Edge: Something for everyone. Hats from about 40 different designers, including Tracy Watts, Brenda Lynn, Francois V., and Chyna Chapeau. The shop features stock hats to custom creations.

Lola Ehrlich Millinery

2 East 17th Street
near 5th Avenue / 366-5708
Weekdays 11am–7pm, Sat 11am–6pm.

Hats
Flatiron/East Village

quality style service value

The Edge: Dazzling hats. One-of-a-kind creations in a variety of colors, shapes, and textures. A classic look with a au currant twist. Prices $200 to $350 mostly for a custom hat, with bridal pieces beginning at $500. When you view the designer collection shows, the headpieces are often Lola's pieces. When Gwyneth Paltrow made the cover of *Vogue* this is the place she went for a chapeau. Expensive. Deluxe.

Manny's Millinery Supply Company

26 West 38th Street
near 5th Avenue / 840-2235
Weekdays 9:30am–5:30pm, Sat 10am–4:30pm.

Hats
Midtown West

quality style service value

The Edge: The source in the "hat district" for millinery supplies. Carries millinery supplies, including decorations like silk flowers, ribbons, beads, and feathers, as well as finished hats. Hats are very reasonable—add oomph by adding the various decorations they sell. The silk flowers are also a wonderful add-on to suits. Be creative! Great bargains here if you take the basics and design your own. Discounter. *"Great if you're creative." "The finished hats are so-so."*

Tracey Tooker

1211 Lexington Avenue
at 82nd Street / 472-9603
Mon–Sat 11am–7pm.

Hats
Upper East Side

quality style service value

The Edge: If you're going to Ascot, this is the place to shop. Wonder where Bianca (Jagger) goes for those creations? Wonder no more. Find contemporary, creative creations. Ready-made and custom hats in cloth fabrics, fake furs, and real fur. Expensive (from $175).

Vander Linde Designs

111 East 56th Street, 2nd Floor
in the Lombardy Hotel / 758-1686
Weekdays 10am–5pm, Sat by appointment.

Hats
Midtown East

quality style service value

The Edge: Ensembles for Brooke and her crowd. In business for 45 years. Custom-made hats and suits for all seasons sold at a suite in the Lombardy Hotel. Hats stand alone or as part of a suit ensemble. Exquisite fabrics and trimmings from Paris. Cocktail hats from $250 and day hats from $150. Deluxe.

Whittall & Son

485 7th Avenue, Room 1411
near 36th Street / 594-2626
Weekdays 10am–5:45pm.

Hats
Midtown West

quality style service value

The Edge: Where tradition speaks loudly. Traditionally styled women's hats and sportswear below wholesale. Best for hats. No delivery.

Worth & Worth

331 Madison Avenue
near 43rd Street / 867-6058
Weekdays 9am–6pm, Sat 10am–5pm.

Hats
Midtown East

quality style service value

The Edge: Well-stocked men's hat store. Oldest hat shop in New York. Features a wide selection of fur, felt, and straw fedoras, cowboy hats, and caps, as well as ties, leather gloves, and belts. You'll find its own line of hats, plus the Stetson and Christys of London brands. Also umbrellas and ties. The fedora is its most popular look.

A La Vieille Russie

781 5th Avenue
near 59th Street / 752-1727
Weekdays 10am–6pm, also Sat Oct–May 11am–4pm.

Jewelry & watches
Midtown East

50	46	46	31
quality	style	service	value

The Edge: Breathtaking jewels and museum-quality furniture. The business originated in 1850 in Kiev. Features fabulous Russian objets d'art, including those by Peter Carl Fabergé, 18th- and 19th-century European jewelry, silver snuff boxes, etc. On the second floor, museum-quality 18th-century French and Russian furniture, paintings, porcelains, and candelabra. Some great items include enamel, emerald, and gold icons, snuff boxes, animal-shaped earrings, gorgeous Georgian brooches, and Victorian engagement rings. Deluxe. *"Malcolm Forbes's source for imperial Easter eggs." "The best jewels in the city!"*

Aaron Faber Gallery

666 5th Avenue
near 53rd Street / 586-8411
Mon–Wed and Fri 10am–6pm, Thurs 10am–7pm, Sat 11am–6pm.

Jewelry & watches
Midtown West

44	40	34	24
quality	style	service	value

The Edge: Interesting and different jewelry, particularly its vintage watches. Jewelry for all occasions in all styles. Find estate and art deco jewelry along with collectible watches and sterling-silver contemporary items. *"Interesting and different." "Good choice of antique engagement and wedding rings."*

Asprey Limited

725 5th Avenue
Trump Tower at 56th Street / 688-1811
Mon–Sat 10am–5:30pm.

Jewelry & watches
Midtown East

46	42	46	36
quality	style	service	value

The Edge: On the Queen's list of "palace" sources. New York outpost of a British institution. Features home accessories, antique and modern silver pieces and clocks, antique jewels, and fabulous South Sea pearl necklaces. Day to evening pearls from $500 to $500,000. Jewelry ranges from contemporary to antique—Edwardian, Georgian, Victorian, art deco pieces. A good source for expensive gift items, including fine leather goods, china, and crystal. For those with lots of cash, Asprey sells a $32,000 alligator jewelry case. On the lower levels, luggage and briefcases. Deluxe. *"Beautiful things, but hard to buy."*

Boris Le Beau Jewelers

721 Madison Avenue
near 63rd Street / 752-4186
Weekdays 10am–5:30pm, Sat noon–5pm.

Jewelry & watches
Upper East Side

40	27	37	27
quality	style	service	value

The Edge: Modern styling. Expensive 18-karat-gold and platinum jewelry, most of which features semiprecious and precious stones. Lots with large South Sea pearls. Most pieces are designed by the owner, Madeleine Van Eerde Le Beau. Also colored enamel and gold jewelry. Prices $200 and up, mostly in the thousands of dollars.

Buccellati
46 East 57th Street
near 5th Avenue / 308-5533
Mon–Sat 10am–6pm.

Jewelry & watches
Midtown East

45	40	45	40
quality	style	service	value

The Edge: Simply gorgeous Milan styling. Buccellati's golden weave designs are treasures. Some jewelry includes precious stones— emeralds, rubies, sapphires. For the home, antique and new Florentine silver, including hand-hammered sterling-silver candlesticks, trays, tureens, and tea and coffee services. Lace-like ornamentation. Also watches. elaborate sterling flatware in 23 patterns, and silver-plate centerpieces and flatware. Deluxe. *"Tremendous."*

Bulgari
730 5th Avenue
near 57th Street / 315-9000
Mon–Sat 10am–5:30pm.

Jewelry & watches
Midtown West

46	47	41	38
quality	style	service	value

The Edge: Statement baubles. Contemporary Italian designs. Large-scale jewels in unusual color and stone combinations. Favors gold and steel jewelry with stones. For men: cufflinks of semiprecious stones in the shape of animals. Also table-top items. Great presents. Everything made in Rome. Deluxe. *"Perhaps a bit vulgar, but real nice." "Sales staff has attitude."*

Camilla Dietz Bergeron
794-9100
Weekdays by appointment 9am–5pm.

Jewelry & watches
Upper East Side

48	48	45	48
quality	style	service	value

The Edge: Perfect taste, exquisite selection, and good prices. There's life after Wall Street. Camilla, a principal with Furman, Selz, Dietz, etc., left Wall Street, turning her avocation into a profession. Camilla and her partner Gus Davis offer antique and estate jewelry from rings to tiaras (at times). Day and evening jewelry, gold, pearls, and stones (diamond and colored). Wide price range: many earrings for less than $1,000, with other jewelry over $1,000 and evening jewelry higher. Featured in *Vogue* for her antique cufflinks, and is often in *W* and *Town & Country*. Call for an invitation to see the collection. Returns for store credit only. No credit cards. Deluxe. *"The only place I go!" "Husbands get TLC and you can always exchange."*

Cartier
Mon–Sat 10am–5:30pm.

Jewelry & watches
Multiple locations

44	44	34	32
quality	style	service	value

The Edge: Best for its period pieces. Les Must de Cartier has made the place more democratic. While there are still unique gems, much of the store is more affordable. On the first floor you'll find diamonds and other precious stones and gold combinations in unique settings, plus the famous Tank watch. On the second floor, find gift items, briefcases, sterling-silver tableware, scarves, handbags and leather goods, and, of course, classic stationery and invitations. *"Beautiful things. Expensive."*

Locations: **Midtown East:** 653 5th Avenue, near 52nd Street (753-0111) / 725 5th Avenue, Trump Tower at 56th Street (308-0840)

Cellini

Mon–Sat 10am–5:45pm.

Jewelry & watches
Multiple locations

The Edge: **Nice modern styles.** Features glitzy jewelry and watches. Lots of stones—precious and semiprecious. A fine watch collection. The Waldorf stores cater to visitors.

Locations: **Midtown East:** 509 Madison Avenue, at 53rd Street (888-0505) / 301 Park Avenue, in the Waldorf Astoria (751-9824)

Chopard

725 Madison Avenue
between 63rd and 64th Streets / 247-3300
Weekdays 10am–6pm.

Jewelry & watches
Upper East Side

The Edge: **Best for moveable stones.** Known for jewelry pieces with gems that float in their settings. Outpost of a Vienna store, featuring watches and jewelry.

Christopher Walling

608 5th Avenue
near 50th Street / 581-7700
Weekdays by appointment 10am–5pm.

Jewelry & watches
Midtown West

The Edge: **One-of-a-kind jewels.** Very expensive jewelry. Large settings featuring gold and precious stones (diamonds, diamond-cut pink sapphires and rubies) priced from $900 to many thousands of dollars, but mostly in the low to mid five figures. For example, a beautiful pair of statement earrings in South Sea pearls and precious stones is $42,000 (Walling loves working with large South Sea pearls). Deluxe. *"Breathtaking." "See Allan."*

David Webb

445 Park Avenue
near 57th Street / 421-3030
Weekdays 10am–5:30pm, Sat 10am–5pm.

Jewelry & watches
Midtown East

The Edge: **Statement jewels to be shown off.** Favors large-scale jewelry and semiprecious stones, often in unusual combinations. Webb likes to mix precious and semiprecious stones with nonprecious materials. Lots of pieces with coral, seashells, and rock crystal. Also evening purses made of wrought gold. Opulent and expensive. Deluxe.

Demner

740 Madison Avenue
near 64th Street / 794-3786
Mon–Sat 10:45am–5:30pm (closed Sat July–Aug).

Jewelry & watches
Upper East Side

The Edge: Elegant jewels. Favors contemporary evening jewelry, some of which is made for Demner in Italy. An elegant collection of diamond necklaces and other jewelry with large precious and semiprecious stones. Also some day jewelry. To some, what's best is the period pieces—Victorian- and Edwardian-style jewels, plus important 20th-century designs. Deluxe. *"Great stuff! Expensive." "Can negotiate price."*

Edith Weber & Company

Jewelry & watches
Upper East Side

994 Madison Avenue
between 77th and 78th Streets / 570-9668
Mon–Sat 11am–4:30pm.

quality style service value

The Edge: Collects historic jewels—items owned by people of note. Diverse offerings of antique and estate jewelry. Offers antique jewelry from the 17th to 19th centuries. Favors semiprecious and precious stones.

Ellagem

Jewelry & watches
Midtown West

580 5th Avenue, Room 3110
near 47th Street / 398-0101
By appointment through Ella weekdays 10am–5pm.

quality style service value

The Edge: One-of-a-kind breathtaking jewels. Expensive evening jewelry designed by Ella Gafter and her daughter Talila. Pieces all include precious stones, most often diamonds; emeralds from Colombia and Africa; rubies from Burma and Vietnam; sapphires from Ceylon, Thailand, and Burma; South Sea pearls from Australia and Akoya pearls from Japan. One-of-a-kind pieces manufactured by Italian craftsman. Priced from $10 to $50,000! See Ellagem's collection at Saks, Neiman Marcus, and Demner. No credit cards. Deluxe. *"Incredibly beautiful."*

Fortunoff

Jewelry & watches
Midtown East

681 5th Avenue
between 53rd and 54th Streets / 758-6660
Mon and Thurs 10am–7pm, Tues–Wed and Fri–Sat 10am–6pm.

quality style service value

The Edge: 47th Street style uptown, but not 47th Street's low, low prices. Find 14- and 18-karat-gold and sterling-silver jewelry in mostly standard designs. The selection is large, including some antiques. Fortunoff has good prices on its contemporary flatware patterns in sterling, stainless, and gold and silver plate. Jewelry appears to be full retail. *"Great affordable giftware." "Excellent bridal registry." "Fortunoff is a store that truly stands behind what it sells—even years later." "The Long Island store is much bigger and better!" "Commercial."*

Fragments

Jewelry & watches
SoHo/TriBeCa

107 Greene Street
between Spring & Prince Streets / 334-9588
Weekdays 11:30am–7pm, Sat noon–7pm, Sun noon–6pm.

quality style service value

The Edge: Delicate and romantic jewels. Used to be featured at Bendel's—now its own place. Collected by the stars—antique-style romantic pieces. Lovely Austrian crystals encased in leaded glass, silver ID bracelets, and more. Lovely pieces from low hundreds (for costume) into the thousands of dollars (for gold with stones). *"Cutting edge yet beautiful."*

Fred Leighton
773 Madison Avenue
near 66th Street / 288-1872
Mon–Sat 10am–6pm (closed Sat July–Aug).

Jewelry & watches
Upper East Side

quality style service value
48 48 45 27

The Edge: Period elegance is favored. Originally a small Greenwich Village clothing store selling only black and white clothing. Re-created into a jewelry store specializing in really fabulous antique jewels. Offers diamonds (including colored diamonds), the highest-quality pearls, and wonderful chokers and tiaras for those who need them. Top-quality designs by all the greats—Cartier, Van Cleef, Mauboussin, Boucheron, court jewels, and the like. Very expensive. Deluxe. *"Great."* *"Spectacular things. "*

George Paul Jewelers
51 East 58th Street
between Park and Madison Avenues / 838-7660
Weekdays 11am–5:30pm, Sat 11am–4pm.

Jewelry & watches
Midtown East

The Edge: Good source for watch bands. Buys and sells estate jewelry. Though the jewelry is pleasant, it's best as a source for watch bands.

H. Stern
645 5th Avenue
near 51st Street / 688-0300
Mon–Sat 10am–5:30pm.

Jewelry & watches
Midtown East

quality style service value
44 42 45 35

The Edge: Flashy gems set in 18-karat gold in a broad price range. Brazilian company featuring three-tone gold jewelry and sterling-silver pieces for day wear. Specialty is diamonds, rubies, emeralds, and sapphires crafted in contemporary settings. The second-floor gallery is filled with home gift items. Deluxe. *"Unusual, beautiful things."*

Harry Winston
718 5th Avenue
near 56th Street / 245-2000
Weekdays 10am–5:30pm,
Sat 10:30am–5pm (closed Sat in summer).

Jewelry & watches
Midtown West

quality style service value
48 43 45 38

The Edge: Investment-quality jewels. Features large superb-quality stones in classic settings. You'll find gold and diamond jewelry from $5,000 up to diamond solitaires in the millions. Noted for selling some of the most famous world-renowned stones. Deluxe. *"Think opulence and glamour."* *"Crème de la crème."*

Historical Design, Inc.
306 East 61st Street
between 1st and 2nd Avenues / 593-4528
Mon–Sat 10am–6pm.

Jewelry & watches
Upper East Side

The Edge: Wiener Werkstatte period pieces. Beautiful designer jewelry, including pieces by Joseph Hoffman.

Ilias Lalaounis

733 Madison Avenue
near 64th Street / 439-9400
Mon–Sat 10am–5:30pm (closed Sat July–Aug).

Jewelry & watches
Upper East Side

quality style service value

The Edge: Jewelry designs in ancient Greek styles. Large-scale heavy gold jewelry, hand-finished in Athens and mostly in 18- to 22-karat gold. Deluxe.

J. Mavec & Company Ltd.

946 Madison Avenue
between 74th and 75th Streets / 517-7665
Weekdays 11am–5:30pm, Sat by appointment.

Jewelry & watches
Upper East Side

quality style service value

The Edge: Lovely Georgian antique jewelry. Features antique jewelry (Georgian) through the 20th century and glass objects. A special collection is noted for its animals, florals, and religious objects. Prices from $500 to $100,000.

Josie Atplace

1050 2nd Avenue, Gallery 50F
near 56th Street / 838-6841
Mon–Sat 11am–6pm.

Jewelry & watches
Midtown East

quality style service value

The Edge: Nice jewelry from the turn of the century to the 1950s. Mostly diamonds and precious stones set in gold. Features smaller pieces.

Judith Ripka Jewellery

673 Madison Avenue
at 61st Street / 355-8300
Mon–Sat 10am–6pm.

Jewelry & watches
Upper East Side

quality style service value

The Edge: Lovely pavé creations. Jewels crafted in 18-karat celedon gold, gold, and platinum, in styles that, while traditional looking, are somehow modern. For men: cufflinks, belt buckles, and watches. The stacked gold rings with semiprecious stones are a find.

La Valencia

899 Madison Avenue
near 72nd Street / 472-9600
Mon–Sat 10am–6pm.

Jewelry & watches
Upper East Side

The Edge: Fine Italian 18-karat jewelry. Some plain gold, others with semiprecious stones and/or diamonds. Expensive, with prices from the hundreds to the thousands of dollars. Simple gold-knot earrings were $500, about as basic as you get here.

Lawrence W. Ford

608 5th Avenue
near 49th Street / 581-4600
Mon–Thurs 10am–3:30pm.

Jewelry & watches
Midtown West

quality style service value

The Edge: Beautiful antique pieces. Primarily wholesale. Expect to see expensive antique pieces and some wonderful treasures. No credit cards. Discounter.

Lloyd Jensen
716 Madison Avenue
near 63rd Street / 980-3966
Mon–Sat 10am–6pm.

Jewelry & watches
Upper East Side

The Edge: Vintage watches. Varying period pieces and designers from unknowns to the top— Cartier, Rolex, Patek Philippe, and others. Deluxe.

Manfredi
737 Madison Avenue
near 64th Street / 734-8710
Weekdays 10am–5:30pm, Sat 11am–5pm (closed Sat July–Aug).

Jewelry & watches
Upper East Side

30 | 27 | 33 | 20
quality style service value

The Edge: Contemporary precious and semiprecious stones set into 18-karat gold. Jewels plus crystal, silver, and wood table-top items.

Marina B
809 Madison Avenue
near 68th Street / 288-9708
Mon–Sat 10am–5:30pm (closed Sat July–Aug).

Jewelry & watches
Upper East Side

42 | 30 | 33 | 27
quality style service value

The Edge: Extravagant gems. One-of-a-kind pieces set in 18-karat gold with precious stones and modern settings.

Maurice Badler
578 5th Avenue
near 47th Street / 575-9632
Mon–Sat 10am–5pm.

Jewelry & watches
Midtown West

40 | 38 | 38 | 45
quality style service value

The Edge: Fortunoff styling at exceptionally good prices. Sells retail, wholesale, and mail order in the heart of the jewelry district. Basic day jewelry, some copies of designer jewels, with evening glitter an option. Prices are 47th Street prices, about 50% of retail. To obtain a $3 catalog, write Badler Catalog, 578 5th Avenue, Department F, New York, NY 10036. *"Affordable." "Good copies."*

Mikimoto
730 5th Avenue
between 56th and 57th Streets / 664-1800
Mon–Sat 10am–5:30pm.

Jewelry & watches
Midtown West

45 | 20 | 30 | 20
quality style service value

The Edge: Only pearls are sold at this branch of the famous Tokyo store. Sells pearl-accented gifts—mirrors, frames, boxes, and of course, jewelry. Features a full range of good-quality pearls— saltwater, irregular freshwater, South Sea pearls—in all sizes, styles, and colors. *"Not what it was, but trying to make a comeback in styling."*

Paul Seiden Jeweler

52 West 47th Street
between 5th and 6th Avenues / 869-5147
Weekdays 10am–5pm.

Jewelry & watches
Midtown West

quality style service value

The Edge: Among the best on 47th Street copying Bulgari. Excellent styling. Copies Tiffany, Van Cleef, and Bulgari at 47th Street prices. Features a wide range from day to evening jewels. Lots of statement jewels—earrings with precious stones (large sizes) in the $5,000 to $10,000 range. Discounter. *"Worth a look, particularly for their statement, but not crazily priced, evening jewels."*

Reinstein/Ross

Mon–Sat 11:30am–7pm, Sun noon–6pm.

Jewelry & watches
Multiple locations

quality style service value

The Edge: Contemporary-styled 22-karat-gold jewelry. Find 22-karat-gold jewelry set with unusual semiprecious and precious stones and some freshwater pearls. Beautiful styling. It's somehow reminiscent of Greek jewelry, but modern. Known for its custom wedding bands in gold with warm colors—22-karat "apricot" gold, 20-karat "chartreuse" gold, and 20-karat "peach" gold. Lovely rings with tiny golden braids. For the truly personal gift, wide bands with an engraved message on the inside or outside. *"Lovely, but much copied and overpriced."* *"Will let you bring your own stones (including fakes) for their pieces."*

Locations: SoHo/TriBeCa: 122 Prince Street, near Greene Street (226-4513) / **Upper East Side:** 29 East 73rd Street, near Madison Avenue (772-1901)

Robert Lee Morris

400 West Broadway
near Spring Street / 431-9405
Weekdays 11am–6pm, Sat 11am–7pm, Sun noon–6pm.

Jewelry & watches
SoHo/TriBeCa

quality style service value

The Edge: Very creative styling. Mostly jewelry, with some belts, bags, scarves, and other artistic inspirations. Silver jewelry or metals dipped in gold. Some home accessories, including candlesticks, pewter, and aluminum alloy bowls. Prices from $500 to $1,000. Sold at Bergdorf also. *"Very nice things, but a bit expensive."* *"Doesn't wear well."*

Saity Jewelry

450 Park Avenue
between 56th and 57th Streets / 223-8125
Mon–Sat 10am–6pm.

Jewelry & watches
Midtown West

quality style service value

The Edge: Native American jewelry. Features a large quality collection of Native American jewelry—Hopi, Zuni, and Navajo— priced from $200, including rings, bracelets, and necklaces. Over 10,000 Native American pieces. Also offers modern jewelry from Nepal, Tibet, Africa, and Europe.

Sally Hawkins Gallery

448 West Broadway
near Prince Street / 477-5699
Daily 11am–7pm.

Jewelry & watches
SoHo/TriBeCa

The Edge: Modern, moderately priced jewelry. Sterling-silver and gold, some with semiprecious stones and crystals, at very moderate prices ($30 to $1,000). Favored by Oscar de La Renta, Carolyn Roehm, and others to complement their collections. Fun pieces—colorful plastic designs, new sculptured pieces in silver and gold, and surprises each season.

Seaman Schepps

485 Park Avenue
near 58th Street / 753-9520
Weekdays 10:30am–6:30pm, Sat 11am–5pm.

Jewelry & watches
Midtown East

quality style service value

The Edge: Jewelry with bright-colored enameling and stones in this well-known look. Favors jewels with shells and lots of styles in animal shapes. Prices tend to be high—$1,000 and up.

Stephen P. Kahan Ltd.

25 East 61st Street
near Madison Avenue / 750-3456
Weekdays 10:30am–5:30pm,
Sat 11am–5pm (closed Sat July–Aug).

Jewelry & watches
Upper East Side

quality style service value

The Edge: Elegant jewelry to be shown. Features contemporary and antique jewelry from the grand designers, including early David Webb. Favors large precious stones set in statement pieces. Mostly (95%) wholesale, but he'll let you up.

Swatch

Weekdays 9am–6pm, Sat 10am–6pm, Sun 10am–5pm.

Jewelry & watches
Multiple locations

quality style service value

The Edge: The full Swatch watch line. The well-known Swatch line, priced from $40 to $100.

Locations: Lower Manhattan: 89 South Street, Pier 17, South Street Seaport (571-6400) /
Midtown West: 500 5th Avenue, near 42nd Street (730-7530)

Tiffany & Company

727 5th Avenue
near 57th Street / 755-8000
Mon–Wed and Fri–Sat 10am–6pm, Thurs 10am–7pm.

Jewelry & watches
Midtown East

quality style service value

The Edge: Their signature blue box and white ribbon bows. Best for its own label and surprisingly inexpensive wedding presents. Jewelry surrounds you on the first floor. Designers include Elsa Peretti, Paloma Picasso, and Schlumberger. The watch selection is among the largest in the city. Go to the second floor for clocks, silver (flatware, jewelry, table-top items), knickknacks, leather accessories, scarves, and stationery. The accessories, handbags, and briefcases are classic and up-to-date chic. Our favorite is the third floor—wedding present heaven and surprisingly inexpensive. Its own and top-name china and glass table items range from reasonably priced to high end. Corporate accounts get a small discount. Deluxe. *"Best for special presents." "The Tiffany label is still valuable." "High prices. Reliable." "Often very crowded, but always great for gifts."*

Tourneau

Weekdays 10am–8pm, Sat 10am–6pm, Sun 11am–6pm.

Jewelry & watches
Multiple locations

quality style service value

The Edge: Large selection of watches from all major companies. Will let you trade in your old watch for a credit toward a new one. Its prices are list, not discounted, but it offers a good selection. Also does repairs.

Locations: Midtown East: 488 Madison Avenue, between 51st and 52nd Streets (758-6346) / 500 Madison Avenue, near 52nd Street (750-6098) / 200 West 34th Street, at 7th Avenue (563-6880) / **Upper East Side:** 12 East 57th Street, at Madison Avenue (758-7300)

Van Cleef & Arpels

744 5th Avenue
near 57th Street / 644-9500
Weekdays 10am–5:30pm, Sat 10am–5pm.

Jewelry & watches
Midtown West

quality style service value

The Edge: Serious gems. Two Van Cleefs—one is in Bergdorf off on the side of the main floor, and the serious statement gems are next door in the main salon. Magnificent colored gemstones in invisible settings. Things at Bergdorf tend to be more daytime and less expensive. Deluxe. *"You know it's the real thing." "Beautiful things for beautiful prices." "I find it intimidating."*

Wong's Jade Corp.

27 West 47th Street, Store #9 & 10
between 5th and 6th Avenues / 354-9554
Weekdays 9:30am–5:30pm.

Jewelry & watches
Midtown West

quality style service value

The Edge: Beads, beads, beads. A large selection of a beads of all kinds—jade, onyx, rose quartz, and more, including gold beads as a fill, sold individually with clasps to make your own jewelry or Wong's will make it for you. Imports and manufactures jade Oriental art and pearls, semiprecious beads, and pearl stringing. Low prices, high quality.

Yaeger Watch Corp.

578 5th Avenue
International Jewelers Exchange/47th Street / 819-0088
Weekdays 10am–5pm, Sat 10am–4pm.

Jewelry & watches
Upper West Side

The Edge: All brand-name watches discounted. Yaeger says it will meet or beat any price. In repairs we list Manhattan Band (great for repairs), which also sells every brand-name watch at great prices. Compare prices. No credit cards. Discounter.

Gale Grant Ltd.

485 Madison Avenue
near 52nd Street / 752-3142
Mon–Sat 10am–6pm.

Jewelry & watches-costume
Midtown East

quality style service value

The Edge: The source for great costume jewelry. Good imitations of all the top designers, for all occasions from office to evening. Huge selection, with colors to accent all your outfits. *"Something for every occasion." "I'll feel at home here when I'm 85."*

Ilene Chazanof

254-5564
Mon–Sat by appointment.

Jewelry & watches-costume
Flatiron/East Village

quality style service value

The Edge: The best tag sale in the city. The shop is crammed full of vintage handbags (many lizards), a full range of jewelry (costume to real) and household accessories (crystal, platters, and silver picture frames). Fine jewelry— including cufflinks, pins, bracelets, and earrings—are in glass display cases. Lots of sterling silver from top lines like Georg Jensen and much, much more. You must call ahead since Ilene insists on knowing who's coming to her fourth-floor loft store. Reasonable prices. *"Always fun—lots of treasures." "Plan on spending hours here."*

Jaded

1048 Madison Avenue
near 80th Street / 288-6631
Mon–Sat 10:30am–6:30pm, Sun noon–5pm.

Jewelry & watches-costume
Upper East Side

quality style service value

The Edge: Costume jewelry that looks as real as it gets. Mostly day jewels, with some costume jewelry for evening wear. Prices from $100 to $3,000. *"Worth a look, but seems expensive for costume."*

Linda Morgan Antiques

152 East 70th Street
near Lexington Avenue / 628-4330
Weekdays 10:30am–6pm, Sat 11am–5pm (closed Sat in summer).

Jewelry & watches-costume
Upper East Side

The Edge: Victorian accessories. French costume jewelry from the 1920s and 1930s. English Victorian jewelry. Some crocodile and lizard handbags. No delivery.

Ro Star, Inc.

27 West 47th Street, Suite 11, Plaza Arcade
between 5th and 6th Avenues / 221-3144
Weekdays 9:30am–4:30pm.

Jewelry & watches-costume
Midtown West

quality style service value

The Edge: Top-quality CZs (cubic zirconia)—can't tell they're not real. The TV show *20/20* took a Ro Star stone and a $50,000 Harry Winston diamond to 47th Street where apparently half the dealers picked the Ro Star CZ. Already set pieces include pierced earrings set in 14-karat gold, rings, and pendants. Also unset CZs in a range of shapes and sizes. A 1-karat pair of pierced earrings was priced at $36. The store can be hard to find. Go midway down the Plaza Arcade on the right side, going from 47th to 48th Street. No credit cards. No delivery. Discounter. *"It's my favorite place (with Jewelry Display of New York) to take traveling businessmen for a little surprise (presented in a Cartier look-alike box) for their wives."*

Jewelry Display of New York

32 West 47th Street
near 6th Avenue / 768-3623
Weekdays 9am–5pm.

Jewelry & watches-supply
Midtown West

quality style service value

The Edge: Best source in the jewelry district for upscale jewelry gift boxes at great prices. Go straight downstairs for wonderful gift boxes. Features cotton-filled (white, gold, silver) Japanese-style patterned-paper–wrapped ring-size boxes, Cartier-style red boxes, Florentine leathers with gold trim lines, velvets (in pink, gray, and black) and jewelry traveling rolls, paper wrap, bows, and bags. If you make jewelry, see their jewelry tools. Charge for delivery via UPS. Discounter.

Platt Box Company, Inc.

66 West 47th Street
near 6th Avenue / 869-9140
Weekdays 9:30am–5pm.

Jewelry & watches-supply
Midtown West

quality style service value

The Edge: Jewelry boxes and displays. Go to the back far right off the main floor. They'll imprint a label on boxes for a sizable order. Boxes range from under $1 to several dollars for those Cartier/Harry Winston–style red boxes with velvet interiors. No credit cards. Discounter.

Altman Luggage

135 Orchard Street
near Delancey Street / 254-7275
Sun–Fri 9am–6pm.

Leathers
Lower East Side/Chinatown

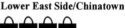

quality style service value

The Edge: Wide selection and good prices. Discounts all major luggage brands (Boyt, Samsonite, Travelpro), pens, and briefcases. Prices in a spot-check appeared to be discounted 20%. *"Wide selection, good prices." "Negotiable on price."*

Barbara Shaum

60 East 4th Street
near Broadway / 254-4250
Wed–Fri 1–8pm, Sat 1–6pm.

Leathers
Flatiron/East Village

quality style service value

The Edge: Custom-designed sandals with an upscale look. Shaum designs a full range of leather items which have been featured in *Gentlemen's Quarterly* and *Mirabella*. Custom sandals are her specialty. Priced from $100 to $400.

Bettinger's Luggage Shop

80 Rivington Street
between Orchard and Allen Streets / 674-9411
Sun–Fri 9:30am–6pm.

Leathers
Lower East Side/Chinatown

quality style service value

The Edge: Among the best luggage prices in the city. An 81-year-old shop. Carries top-line luggage and briefcases, including Andiamo, Boyt, Lucas, Travelpro, and more. In our spot-check, it was cheaper than anyone else on luggage. Bargaining is standard. Does repairs. 35% to 40% off.

"Small shop crammed with goodies." "Knowledgeable staff." "Know what you want before you go." "Negotiate."

Bottega Veneta
635 Madison Avenue
near 59th Street / 371-5511
Weekdays 10am–6pm, Sat 11am–6pm.

Leathers
Midtown East

quality style service value

The Edge: An Italian landmark. Expensive soft Italian leather items in great colors, including handbags, accessories (gloves and wallets), shoes, briefcases, and luggage. Widely copied, especially the woven leathers. Deluxe. *"Super merchandise." "Great soft sale shoes for city walking." "Very expensive." "Staff seem arrogant."*

Coach Store
Mon–Wed and Fri 8:30am–7pm, Thurs 8:30am–8pm,
Sat 10am–6pm, Sun noon– 5pm.

Leathers
Multiple locations

quality style service value

The Edge: Durable, simple classic accessories. Features durable soft leathers. Find belts, briefcases, diaries, handbags, luggage, wallets, and small accessories. Its discount stores sell Coach at 20% to 30% off—the closest are in Amagansett on Long Island or Woodbury Commons in Central Valley, N.Y. *"Timeless classics, great quality." "Predictable styles with good color sense." "Durable, but stuffy styles." "Best leather bags in town." "Best outlet, Amagansett Long Island."*

Locations: Lower Manhattan: 193 Front Street, near John Street (947-1727) / 5 World Trade Center, Concourse Level, near Vesey Street (488-0080) / **Midtown East:** 342 Madison Avenue, near 44th Street (599-4777) / 595 Madison Avenue, near 57th Street (754-0041) / 725 5th Avenue, 3rd Floor, Trump Tower at 57th Street (355-2427) / **Upper East Side:** 710 Madison Avenue, near 63rd Street (319-1772)

Crouch & Fitzgerald
400 Madison Avenue
near 46th Street / 755-5888
Mon–Sat 9am–6pm.

Leathers
Midtown East

quality style service value

The Edge: Just $69 per bag at the August sale. Since 1939. Classic styled handbags in leathers and exotic skins. Carries all the best-known manufacturers plus its own private-label designs in fine-quality leathers. Also wallets, belts, and other small leather goods. The luggage department is upstairs. *"The annual sales event offers real value." "Only for sales."*

Deco Jewels
131 Thompson Street
between Houston and Prince Streets / 253-1222
Daily noon–8pm.

Leathers
SoHo/TriBeCa

The Edge: Fun and young. Well, not quite leathers—fabulous plastic handbags from the '40s and '50s, a unique collection.

Eclectiques

483 Broome Street
corner of Wooster Street / 966-0650
Wed–Sun 12:30–5:30pm.

Leathers
SoHo/TriBeCa

The Edge: Designer vintage trunks, bags, and steamers. Store focuses on designer 18th-century to 1920s lines. Moderate prices.

Fendi

720 5th Avenue
near 56th Street / 767-0100
Mon–Sat 10am–6pm.

Leathers
Midtown West

quality style service value

The Edge: Classic Italian styling. Find leather shoes, bags, briefcases, wallets, and suitcases. Deluxe. *"Gorgeous bags." "Expensive, wait for the sales." "Pricey." "More of the same, same, same."*

Ferragamo

725 5th Avenue
near 56th Street / 759-7990
Mon–Wed and Fri–Sat 10am–6pm, Thurs 10am–7pm.

Leathers
Midtown East

quality style service value

The Edge: Quiet, elegant styling. Known most for its traditional shoes (casual to formal) with styles for women and men. But don't forget the clothes and accessories. Gorgeous sportswear made in soft sensuous wools and silks. Great tailoring and detail. Deluxe. *"Shoes and clothing in styles that last for years." "Has its cult." "Best-quality shoes anywhere." "Overpriced, but good style." "Get to the Ferragamo pre-sale (twice a year) and the salesman will send you shoes at sale price the day of the sale. Not everything is at pre-sale, though."*

Fine and Klein

119 Orchard Street
near Delancey Street / 674-6720
Sun–Fri 9am–5pm.

Leathers
Lower East Side/Chinatown

quality style service value

The Edge: Large selection of discounted name-brand and knockoff pocketbooks. Good-quality pocketbooks in a wide price range from $100 up. Accepts phone orders, if you know what you want. 30% off. *"Wide variety of handbags, many knockoffs." "Wide range of quality." "Less interesting stock as more style-conscious stores are on the scene." "Helpful staff." "Sales help not very helpful [but perhaps that's because they were shopping on a Sunday]."*

Furla

Mon–Wed and Fri–Sat 10am–6pm, Thurs 10am–6:30pm.

Leathers
Multiple locations

quality style service value

The Edge: Good colors and up-to-date styling. Good-looking Italian handbags in the moderate to upper price range. Deluxe. *"Gorgeous and classic!" "Great wallets and bags." "New line scratches, but old totes great." "Pretty but not durable."*

Locations: Upper East Side: 727 Madison Avenue, between 63rd and 64th Streets (755-8986) /
Upper West Side: 159 Columbus Avenue, near 67th Street (874-6119)

Ghurka
41 East 57th Street
between Madison and Park Avenues / 826-8300
Mon–Wed and Fri–Sat 10am–6pm, Thurs 10am–7pm.

Leathers
Midtown East

quality style service value

The Edge: Expensive, but wears forever. Handbags in a range of sizes and styles—canvas and leather, artist portfolios, and picnic baskets. Quality leather products that last. *"Fine quality and style." "Great travel bags."*

Gucci
685 5th Avenue
near 54th Street / 826-2600
Mon–Wed and Fri–Sat 9:30am–6pm,
Thurs 9:30am–7pm, Sun noon–6pm.

Leathers
Midtown East

quality style service value

The Edge: Coming back—new design team! Find boots, briefcases, key cases, luggage, purses, shoes, and wallets in wonderful colors and beautiful leather textures. Also silk scarves and clothing, including shirts, suits, sweaters, and trousers. Deluxe. *"Terrific service, great value." "Go to the outlet in New Jersey." "They've changed enough that I no longer go there." "Check out the new look."*

Handbag Warehouse
105 Sheer Plaza
on Newtown Road, at Old Country Road, Plainview / 516-694-3770
Weekdays 9am–5pm.

Leathers
Long Island

The Edge: Prices are great. Designer bags as found in the best department stores at half price. Prices here range from $45 to $70, with evening clothes priced at $165 to $395. No credit cards. No delivery. Discounter.

Hermès
11 East 57th Street
between 5th and Madison Avenues / 751-3181
Mon–Wed and Fri–Sat 10am–6pm, Thurs 10am–8pm.

Leathers
Midtown East

quality style service value

The Edge: Top-quality leathers that last a lifetime. Expensive, luxurious leathers in wonderful shades. From small leather items to the Kelly bag, as well as shoes, luggage, and saddles, plus clothing (including silk scarves, gloves, trousers, riding clothes) and home needs (china, linens, bath towels, and bar tools). Now furniture from the Pippa collection. Check out the sales, which last only a few days (summer is one), when buys are fabulous, but are as crowded as the subway at rush hour. Deluxe. *"Beautiful scarves at exorbitant prices." "Scarves to collect as a hobby." "Suarez has a great, great Kelly copy!"*

Il Bisonte
72 Thompson Street
near Spring Street / 966-8773

Leathers
SoHo/TriBeCa

Sun–Mon noon–6pm, Tues–Sat noon–6:30pm.

40	40	40	35
quality	style	service	value

The Edge: Italian leather goods stamped with bison logo. Bags are soft and simply styled and come in natural colors. Prices moderate to high. *"Good all-around bags."*

Jobson's Luggage

Leathers
Midtown East

666 Lexington Avenue
between 55th and 56th Streets / 355-6846
Mon–Sat 9am–6pm, Sun 11am–5pm.

43	43	47	40
quality	style	service	value

The Edge: If you're hard-hitting at bargaining, among the best prices in the city. Large selection of discounted luggage, attaché cases, and small leather goods. Brands include Andiamo, Halliburton, American Tourister, Lark, Travelpro, and Boyt. Free monogramming, free repair and delivery. Carries Mont Blanc and Shaeffer pens. Pluses are a convenient midtown location and large selection of high-quality luggage. Negatives are that you really have to push to get the best price. Management told our researchers that pricing is almost wholesale—but to get that price level you must be pushy, since posted prices are close to retail. *"10% above cost!" "Free initials/monograms."*

Judith Leiber on Madison

Leathers
Upper East Side

987 Madison Avenue
between 76th and 77th Streets / 327-4003
Mon–Sat 10am–6pm.

48	45	40	30
quality	style	service	value

The Edge: Luxurious. Now in her own store. Known for her fabulous evening handbags, including her signature miniatures—animal purses encrusted with Austrian crystals. Her collection includes leather handbags for day, small leather items, belts, jewelry boxes, and now jewelry. Very, very expensive. Purses into the many thousands. Day bags at about $2,000. Deluxe. *"Original styles. High priced."*

Kate Spade

Leathers
SoHo/TriBeCa

59 Thompson Street
between Broome and Spring Streets / 965-0301
Mon–Sat 11am–7pm, Sun noon–6pm.

38	40	30	28
quality	style	service	value

The Edge: Sets today's styles. A small but select collection of basic stylish handbags, limited but good-looking clothing, and classic cotton women's PJs—the white and red trim adds zest. Handbags $80 to $400. At Barneys and now in Soho. Great patent leathers. For fall, Harris tweed pocketbooks. *"Overpriced, but beautiful and functional." "Nice pajamas."*

Lancel

Leathers
Upper East Side

690 Madison Avenue
near 62nd Street / 753-6918
Mon–Sat 10am–6pm.

38	40	35	35
quality	style	service	value

The Edge: Classic French handbags in bold colors. A full range of leather items in bold colors and exotic skins.

Leather Facts

Leathers

262 West 38th Street — **Midtown West**
between 7th and 8th Avenues / 382-2788
Weekdays 9:30am–6pm, Sat by appointment.
The Edge: Custom-made dresses, skirts, pants, jackets, and coats. Dresses from $150 to $700, pants from $80 to $300. Leather coats are the biggest seller, at $150. Leathers in a wide variety of colors. Clothing can be custom-made. No credit cards.

Leather Outlet
327 Avenue of the Americas
near 3rd Street / 229-1500
Mon–Thurs 11am–9pm, Fri–Sat 11am–11pm, Sun 1–8pm.

Leathers
Greenwich Village

quality style service value

The Edge: Hip leather jackets for the college set. Sells only jackets, which are priced from $100 to $250. A hot seller is a hip-length jacket for men. Discounter.

Lederer de Paris, Inc.
613 Madison Avenue
near 58th Street / 355-5515
Weekdays 9:30am–6pm, Sat 10am–6pm.

Leathers
Midtown East

quality style service value

The Edge: Copies the top fashion houses like Chanel and Hermès. Known for a full range of quality leather items, plus canvas hunting bags, garment bags, shooting and riding jackets, and Wellington boots. Much less expensive than the originals.

Lexington Luggage
793 Lexington Avenue
near 61st Street / 223-0698
Mon–Sat 9am–6pm, Sun 11am–5pm.

Leathers
Upper East Side

quality style service value

The Edge: If you're hard-hitting at bargaining, among the best prices in the city. Large selection (250 brands) of discounted luggage, attaché cases, and small leather goods. Pluses are a convenient midtown location and large selection of high-quality luggage. Negatives are that you really have to push to get the best price. *"Lots of pressure to buy."*

Louis Vuitton
49 East 57th Street
between Park and Madison Avenues / 371-6111
Weekdays 10am–6pm, Sat 10am–5:30pm, Sun noon–5pm.

Leathers
Midtown East

quality style service value

The Edge: Their famous logo. Known for its signature handbags made of laminated vinyl on Egyptian cotton canvas and adorned with that famous logo. Find train cases, steamer trunks, golf bags, kitty carriers, wig boxes, and attaché cases. The line is expanding now to more traditional styles in strong colors. Deluxe. *"Great, but the prices are a joke!"*

Luggage Plus
92 Orchard Street
near Delancey Street / 673-0274
Sun–Thurs 10am–5:30pm, Fri 10am–2pm.

Leathers
Lower East Side/Chinatown

quality style service value

The Edge: Moderately priced luggage, discounted. Find luggage, backpacks, and briefcases. Discounter.

Prada

Leathers
Midtown East

45 East 57th Street
between Madison and Park Avenues / 308-2332
Mon–Wed and Fri–Sat 10am–6pm, Thurs 10am–7pm.

41	44	39	28
quality	style	service	value

The Edge: Fashion-forward, yet conservative, bags and shoes. Highest-quality leathers, including exotic skins and embossed leather. Full range of leather items, from shoes to beautiful handbags, briefcases, and accessories. Casual clothing in exceptional fabrics. Simply gorgeous. Deluxe. *"Great bags, but the cost is high." "Love those bags!" "Fab styles."*

Suarez

Leathers
Midtown East

450 Park Avenue
between 56th and 57th Streets / 753-3758
Weekdays 10am–6pm, Sat 10am–5pm.

46	44	45	45
quality	style	service	value

The Edge: The best for less. Discounts name-brand bags 30% to 50% and sells copies of the top labels, including Bottega Veneta, Chanel, Hermès, Prada, Gucci, and Mark Cross. Same look and high quality (mostly made in the same factories), but without the labels. Prices mostly in the $250 to $450 range. Twice-a-year bag sale. Now shoes too. Some accessories. Beloved by all. *"Fabulous designer totes." "Gorgeous and classic quality." "Good knockoffs." "The Suarez family serves its customers best." "Nice people—you always find something." "The bag sale is great!"*

T. Anthony Ltd.

Leathers
Midtown East

445 Park Avenue
near 56th Street / 750-9797
Weekdays 9:30am–6pm, Sat 10am–6pm (to 5pm Sat July–Aug).

47	43	43	37
quality	style	service	value

The Edge: The Hermès look, but not quite the prices. Well known for its luggage in all sizes from small overnight bags to massive pieces, leather-trimmed soft-canvas luggage, and classic hard-frame pieces. Accessories include handbags, wallets, billfolds, key cases, briefcases, portfolios, looseleafs of all sizes, and agendas, as well as English umbrellas by Swain Adeney Brigg. Leathers in vivid colors and exotic skins. Clientele reputedly includes King Fahd of Saudi Arabia and Elton John. Very expensive. Deluxe. *"High-end luggage of excellent quality."*

Madison Avenue Maternity & Baby

Maternity
Upper East Side

1043 Madison Avenue
between 79th and 80th Streets / 988-8686
Weekdays 10am–7pm, Sat 10am–6pm, Sun noon–5pm.

30	30	30	30
quality	style	service	value

The Edge: Very stylish. The source for high-styled, high-quality French and Italian clothing for mom and baby. A fine collection of sophisticated clothing, which makes you feel chic. Custom gift packages can be shipped worldwide.

Motherhood Maternity

Maternity
Chelsea

641 Avenue of the Americas
near 20th Street / 741-3488

Daily 10am–7pm.

quality style service value

The Edge: Maternity career clothing. Career suits in silks and wools, as well as casual wear, lingerie, and underwear. In-house designers, plus Rand, Japanese Weekend, and St. Simone. Prices are moderate to high.

Secaucus Outlets

American Way
off Meadowlands Parkway, Secaucus / 201-348-4780
Mon–Wed 10am–6pm, Thurs 10am–9pm,
Fri–Sat 10am–7pm, Sun noon–6.

**Outlet Centers
New Jersey**

quality style service value

The Edge: 100 outlets—some finds within the chaos. Among the 100 stores are Calvin Klein, Mondi, Joan & David, and others. The stores are attached to factories and warehouses which makes getting around difficult, and without a car, not possible. Discounter. *"Occasional buys, but too much junk." "Not such a great selection of clothes." "Stick to department store sales."*

Tanger Factory Outlet Center

Long Island Expressway
Exit 73, Riverhead / 516-369-2724
Sun–Thurs 10am–7pm, Fri–Sat 10am–8pm.

**Outlet Centers
Long Island**

quality style service value

The Edge: 67 stores—medium-priced labels favored. More casual clothing—moderately priced lines including Gap, Levis, Timberland, and more. No delivery. Discounter. *"20% off." "Nice, still enjoyable and pleasant."*

Woodbury Commons

New York State Thruway - Interstate 187
Exit 16 Route 32, Central Valley / 914-928-4000
Daily 10am–8pm.

**Outlet Centers
Orange County**

quality style service value

The Edge: 150 stores Lots of the big names—Barneys New York, Polo Ralph Lauren, Calvin Klein, Donna Karan, TSE Cashmere, Timberland, First Choice (Escada line), and others. Much of the merchandise is past-season sales items, and some items are made for the outlets and product seconds—still some great things. Transportation from Manhattan is provided daily by Short Line and Gray Line buses. No delivery. Discounter. *"One-stop Christmas shopping." "Fashionable stores. Very reasonable prices. Plan to spend the day." "Worth the trip." "Quality has declined as crowds have increased." "Much merchandise merely made for the outlet store." "Better prices at store sales.""Crowded parking lot. On weekends lines form to enter the 'hot' shops."*

About Time

13 Prince Street
at Elizabeth Street / 941-0966
Mon by appointment, Tues–Sun 11am–8pm.

**Previously owned
SoHo/TriBeCa**

quality style service value

The Edge: Great 1940s suits. Cutting-edge vintage. Finds from new less-known designers and the classics. The shop carefully selects timeless/fun pieces from top names like Geoffrey Beene, Courrèges, Halston, and Yohji Yamamoto to comers. From day to evening, the shop's selection is good. A great source for 1940s designer suits. *"Run, don't walk—this is one of the best new places in town." "No good dressing rooms; good vintage."*

Alice Underground

481 Broadway
between Grand and Broome Streets / 431-9067
Sun–Fri 11am–7pm, Sat 11am–8pm.

Previously owned
SoHo/TriBeCa

quality style service value

The Edge: Vintage heaven!! Casual to formal period clothing from the 1930s to the 1970s. Strong on the '50s and '60s. Vintage jeans and antique linens too. Find $1 scarves and $200 leather jackets. Great beaded sweaters. Look at the merchandise carefully—there are lots of really worn items. No delivery. *"Beautiful vintage clothes and accessories." "Basics for college."*

Andy's Chee-Pee's

691 Broadway
between West 3rd and West 4th Streets / 420-5980
Mon–Sat 11am–9pm, Sun noon–8pm.

Previously owned
SoHo/TriBeCa

quality style service value

The Edge: Fun used stuff, mostly for the younger set. Vintage clothing for women and men. Day dresses to wedding gowns and formal wear. Period pieces from the 1920s, but most from the 1950s to the 1970s. Used Levis are a specialty ($30 a pair). A large selection of suede and leather jackets (from $35 to $150). Collector's items are priced at $600. A large selection of bell-bottom pants. Most of the merchandise is well worn. No delivery. *"Great for vintage jeans."*

Antique Boutique

712 Broadway
near Washington Place / 460-8830
Mon–Thurs 11am–9pm, Fri–Sat 11am–10pm, Sun noon–8pm.

Previously owned
Flatiron/East Village

quality style service value

The Edge: Vintage clothing in good condition. Another favorite source for the younger set. You'll never know what you'll find: sequined sweaters, bathing suits, jeans, wedding dresses, and more. Shop here to dress for the club scene. No delivery. *"Great for vintage Levis." "Overpriced vintage knockoffs that are too trendy."*

Cancer Care Thrift Shop

1480 3rd Avenue
between 83rd and 84th Streets / 879-9868
Mon–Tues and Fri 11am–6pm, Wed–Thurs 11am–7pm,
Sat 10am–4:30pm, Sun 12:30–5pm (closed Sun July–Aug).

Previously owned
Upper East Side

quality style service value

The Edge: Designer evening dresses—sometimes. Mostly clothing, with some furniture. When in the neighborhood, check out the costume jewelry, vintage lingerie, and designer evening dresses. Wonderful finds on occasion, like Chanel costume jewelry and designer items. A good place to donate clothing. For larger donations, items can be scheduled for pickup. No delivery. *"Today's window: a fabulous gray sequined Armani evening pants suit!"*

Cheap Jack's Vintage Clothing

841 Broadway
near 13th Street / 777-9564
Mon–Sat 11am–8pm, Sun noon–7pm.

Previously owned
Flatiron/East Village

quality style service value

The Edge: Huge selection of vintage treasures. You'll never know what to expect, from evening dresses to leather and wool coats, military clothing, tweed jackets, suits, shirts, tuxedos, and slacks of all kinds, with the largest selection for men. Beaded sweaters and wool skirts for women. Levis jeans priced from $5 to $2,000 (collector's items), with most $35 to $65. More expensive than many other vintage stores. Now two floors! No delivery. *"A good eye can find interesting trendy clothes—fun."*

Designer Resale

324 East 81st Street
between 1st and 2nd Avenues / 734-3639
Mon–Wed and Fri 11am–7pm, Thurs 11am–8pm,
Sat 10am–6pm, Sun noon–5pm.

Previously owned
Upper East Side

quality style service value

The Edge: Great value. Used clothing in perfect condition. Favors top designers—an elegant Upper East Side look, befitting the address. Three rooms to date, filled with the right stuff. *"A well-edited collection."*

Dorothy's Closet

335 Bleecker Street
near Christopher Street / 206-6414
Daily 11am–7pm.

Previously owned
Greenwich Village

quality style service value

The Edge: Carefully selected vintage clothing. A small shop with limited, but excellent, vintage clothing from the 1950s to 1970s for men and women. Expect the always-useful little black cocktail dress, luxurious lingerie, fitted women's jackets, vests, and great accessories. Good selection of vintage Levis from $10. Everything in good condition. No credit cards. No delivery. *"Cute, attentive, good value."*

Encore

1132 Madison Avenue
near 84th Street / 879-2850
Mon–Wed and Fri 10:30am–6:30pm, Thurs 10:30am–7:30pm,
Sat 10:30am–6pm, Sun noon–6pm (closed Sun July–Aug).

Previously owned
Upper East Side

quality style service value

The Edge: The Barneys of the thrift shop world. Sells barely used top American and European designer clothing in perfect condition. Clothes for day and for those splashy evening events. Some men's clothing. If you're lucky you'll find great things, particularly in small sizes. No credit cards. No delivery. Discounter. *"Lots of good things in small sizes."*

Gentleman's Resale

303 East 81st Street
between 1st and 2nd Avenues / 734-2739
Weekdays 11am–7pm, Sat 10am–6pm, Sun noon–5pm.

Previously owned
Upper East Side

The Edge: Finally—value for the boys. Deals exclusively with men's fashion. From tuxedos to office and casual ware, this place stocks it. Favors the better labels—Burberry, Perry Ellis, Boss, Armani, and Ralph Lauren, among others. A 24-hour return policy—an unusual feature.

Good-Byes
230 East 78th Street
between 2nd and 3rd Avenues / 794-2301
Weekdays 11:30am–6pm, Sat 10:30am–5pm.

Previously owned
Upper East Side

40	40	30	50
quality	style	service	value

The Edge: A practical affordable option. High-quality secondhand clothing, accessories, and toys for children from infants through age 14. Everything is cleaned and in great condition and looks like new. Accepts consigned clothes (the shop keeps 50% of the sale price). Prices from $10 to $100. No credit cards. No delivery.

INA
Daily noon–7pm.

Previously owned
Multiple locations

45	45	40	47
quality	style	service	value

The Edge: Avant-garde cutting-edge designers. Carries top European and Japanese designers like Alaida, Comme des Garçons, Gaultier, and Matsuda. Some vintage Chanel. A truly special source for day to evening wear. A small selection of handbags, shoes, and accessories. Merchandise comes from fashion insiders—magazine shoots, samples, walkers, etc., so is in very good condition. The Thompson Street location is more upscale, the Prince Street location younger. No delivery. *"Well edited. Nice people. Decent dressing room." "Prices seem high for used, but not for the quality, given the designers sold."*

Locations: SoHo/TriBeCa: 101 Thompson Street, between Houston and Spring Streets (941-4757) / 21 Prince Street, between Mott and Elizabeth Streets (334-9048)

Irvington Institute Thrift Shop
1534 2nd Avenue
near 80th Street / 879-4555
Mon–Tues and Fri–Sat 10am–6pm,
Wed–Thurs 10am–8pm, Sun noon–5pm.

Previously owned
Upper East Side

38	33	30	38
quality	style	service	value

The Edge: A great place for your own donations. Mostly very basic clothing, not in perfect condition, and some furniture. Find costume jewelry, vintage clothing, and accessories. A good source for furniture for that first post-college apartment. Irvington House is perhaps the best place to donate used items. It will give you a set appointment for pickup and provide good valuations to be used for tax deductions. As part of the trust and estate service, it will pick up the entire contents of the house or apartment—furniture, clothing, knickknacks, and the like—leaving the place spotless. *"Good value if you're lucky." "Go often—occasional finds." "I found my favorite YSL jacket there."*

Jana Starr Antiques
236 East 80th Street
between 2nd and 3rd Avenues / 861-8256
Mon–Sat noon–6pm or by appointment .

Previously owned
Upper East Side

40	45	40	38
quality	style	service	value

The Edge: Starr and her former partner, Jean Hoffman, are among the best sources for exquisite Victorian wedding gowns. Picture-perfect Victorian white and Irish lace bridal dresses from the 1890s to the 1960s. Favors gowns from 1890 to 1930. Wedding dresses are priced from $300, with most averaging $1,000 to $1,200, but some much more. Some 1930s evening gowns, with shoes, veils, and jewelry to match. Also christening gowns. Jana Starr has been featured in *Vogue* and *Martha Stewart*. Provides props to photographers and stylists. *"Lovely turn-of-the-century looks."*

Jean Hoffman

207 East 66th Street
between 2nd and 3rd Avenues / 535-6930
Mon–Sat noon–6pm or by appointment .

Previously owned
Upper East Side

40	45	40	38

quality   style   service   value

The Edge: Hoffman and her former partner, Jana Starr, are among the best sources for exquisite Victorian wedding gowns and dresses. Quality vintage items from 1890 to 1950 in perfect condition. Features absolutely beautiful vintage Victorian wedding gowns, plus a limited selection of other period clothing and accessories (linens, lace, jewelry, antique gifts, and silver items). *"Very nice things."*

Kavanagh's Designer Resale Shop

146 East 49th Street
between 3rd and Lexington Avenues / 702-0152
Weekdays 11am–6pm (to 7pm in summer), Sat 11am–4pm.

Previously owned
Midtown East

48	45	45	50

quality   style   service   value

The Edge: Elegant things. Expect to find top-designer clothing and accessories for all occasions. Favors Beene, Blass, Chanel, Galanos, Herrera, La Croix, Lang, Mugler, Oscar, Ungaro, Valentino, Versace, St. Laurent, and more. Owner Mary Kavanagh (former director of personal shopping at Bergdorf) describes her clothing collection as antique and "pre-owned" and her shop as a bit of Madison Avenue. Items tend to be in their original shape—buttons, labels, and cufflinks. *"Expensive for resale, but great selection—Chanel in great condition." "Sales fantastic, decent dressing rooms."*

Legacy

109 Thompson Street
between Christopher and Spring Streets / 966-4827
Daily noon–7pm.

Previously owned
SoHo/TriBeCa

The Edge: Another vintage source, plus some new designs inspired by old styles. Find floral day dresses with great details, cocktail dresses some with beading and sequins, and lovely Victorian white dresses. Wonderful fabrics—silks, satin, brocades included. Lots of gowns reasonably priced, many under $1,000.

Love Saves the Day

119 2nd Avenue
near 7th Street / 228-3802
Daily noon–9pm.

Previously owned
Flatiron/East Village

The Edge: 1950s and 1960s kitsch items. While the clothing collection is small, it's first-rate. From day wear to bridal wear, you'll never know what to expect. A great source for Halloween costumes (they really get into the holiday!). Even better, though, for TV sitcom collectibles from the

1950s and 1960s. Tremendous selection of period collectibles. Collectible toys from *Star Wars* to Barbie.

Memorial Sloan-Kettering Thrift Shop

1440 3rd Avenue
near 81st Street / 535-1250
Mon–Wed and Fri 10am–5:30pm,
Thurs 10am–8pm, Sat 10am–5pm.

**Previously owned
Upper East Side**

quality style service value

The Edge: The designer selection. Offers mostly clothing and accessories, with some furniture and housewares. And this is an excellent place to donate used clothing and household items for favorable tax deductions. Will pick up if the donation is furniture or a large amount of clothing. No delivery.

Michael's Resale

1041 Madison Avenue
between 79th and 80th Streets / 737-7273
Mon–Wed and Fri–Sat 9:30am–6pm, Thurs 9:30am–8pm.
Bridal parties by appointment.

**Previously owned
Upper East Side**

quality style service value

The Edge: Slightly used designer clothing. Find designer day to evening clothes. You never know what you'll find. Favors top designers and stocks wedding gowns. Priced from $40 to $900. No delivery. *"Got to hit it right." "Best are small sizes."*

New and Almost New

65 Mercer Street
near Broome Street / 226-6677
Sept–May, Wed–Sun noon–6:30pm; June–Aug, Tues–Sat noon–6:30pm.

**Previously owned
Chelsea**

The Edge: You never know. Some of the best—Armani, Chanel, Klein—European and American designer clothing labels. Great prices.

Nicolina of New York

247 West 46th Street
between 8th and Broadway / 302-6426
Sun–Tues 10am–8pm, Wed–Sat 10am–10pm.

**Previously owned
Midtown West**

The Edge: Best known for new clothes in old styles by local artists. Features accessories and unique ready-to-wear with styling from the early 1920s to the 1940s. A few men's items (cufflinks, ties, shirts, vests, and some clothing). Loose and flowing women's clothing favored.

Out of the Closet Thrift Shop

136 West 18th Street
between 6th and 7th Avenues / 633-6965
Mon–Sat noon–7pm, Sun noon–5pm.

**Previously owned
Chelsea**

quality style service value

The Edge: Lots of high-style clothing. Favors cutting-edge designer looks—Dolce & Gabbana, Miyake, and more. Carries a full range of clothing and accessories, including shoes—Fisher was a buyer at Barneys and her purchases reflect that look. Owner Terin Fisher sells her own jewelry—wrought seed-pearl jewelry. Tailoring available on site. No credit cards. No delivery. Discounter. *"Everything is black." "Mostly bric-a-brac."*

Reminiscence
74 5th Avenue
between 13th and 14th Streets / 243-2292
Mon–Sat 11am–8pm, Sun noon–7pm.

Previously owned
Chelsea

quality style service value

The Edge: Retro 1950s and 1970s clothing, some jewelry and accessories. Favored by our younger respondents. Funky items, often badly worn. Ever-changing. *"1980s prices—worth looking."*

Screaming Mimi's
382 Lafayette Street
near Great Jones Street / 677-6464
Weekdays 11am–8pm, Sat noon–8pm, Sun noon–6pm.

Previously owned
Flatiron/East Village

quality style service value

The Edge: Fashion-forward is an understatement. Vintage clothing and new "hot" designers—Dollhouse, Living Doll, Girlie NYC, and Blackheat. Vintage styles from the 1950s to the 1970s in clothing, accessories, and gloves. Whatever it has is fashion-forward! The mezzanine level features period housewares. *"Clothing styles are out of this galaxy." "Fun to look, better to find and wear."*

Spence-Chapin Thrift Shop
1430 3rd Avenue
between 81st and 82nd Streets / 737-8448
Mon–Wed and Fri 10am–7pm, Thurs 10am–8pm,
Sat 10am–5pm, Sun noon–5pm.

Previously owned
Upper East Side

quality style service value

The Edge: Vintage lingerie and accessories, which at times are great. Two floors, including a separate designer area upstairs. Vintage lingerie and linens are favorites. Accessories (handbags, jewelry, and hats) are sometimes great. Proceeds benefit the Spence-Chapin Adoption Resource Center. Good donations. Will pick up furniture. No delivery. *"Give there. Go there."*

Spooly D's
51 Bleecker Street
between Bowery and Lafayette Street / 598-4415
Tues–Sat 9am–7pm, Sun noon–6pm.

Previously owned
SoHo/TriBeCa

The Edge: Sexy vintage gowns. Vintage gowns from the 1920s and 1930s—romantic and clingy. Gowns are priced from $200. Casual clothing includes the hot Halston-cut jeans, skirts, pants, and jackets. Skirts and pants from $150, jackets from $300.

Transfer International
594 Broadway
between Prince and Houston Streets / 355-4230
Tues–Sun 1–7pm and by appointment.

Previously owned
SoHo/TriBeCa

The Edge: Best European labels. Prada, Gucci, Chanel, Hermès, and the like.

Trash and Vaudeville
4 St. Mark's Place
between 2nd and 3rd Avenues / 982-3590

Previously owned
Flatiron/East Village

Mon–Thurs noon–8pm, Fri 11:30am–8pm,
Sat 11:30am–9pm, Sun 1–7:30pm.

35	38	28	36
quality	style	service	value

The Edge: Beyond funky. Clothing, accessories, and footwear for the very young. Styles from leather bras and G-strings to statement East Village–style prom wear! If you need body jewels, faux tattoos, and other East Village essentials, this is the place. This year's look featured red-hot patent-leather boots with locks—bondage for the feet. Some new clothing from Europe. Delivers mail-order items only. *"Not for everyone—although Elle is catching up with red patent-leather boots this season."*

Addison on Madison

698 Madison Avenue
near 62nd Street / 308-2660
Mon–Sat 10:30am–6:30pm.

Shirts & blouses
Upper East Side

43	42	42	35
quality	style	service	value

The Edge: Breadth of selection and great sales. Sells only business shirts and shirt accessories (silk ties, cufflinks, and pocket squares). High-quality fabrics used exclusively. European styling combined with an American fit. Prices are good, given the quality. *"I'm addicted to their sales!"*

Custom Shop

Weekdays 8:30am–5:30pm.

Shirts & blouses
Multiple locations

28	36	30	30
quality	style	service	value

The Edge: Inexpensive dress shirts. Wide selection of fabrics—cotton and cotton blends. Allow six weeks for delivery. Minimum order is four shirts.

Locations: Lower Manhattan: 115 Broadway, near Pine Street (267-8535) / **Midtown East:** 338 Madison Avenue, near 44th Street (867-3650) / 18 East 50th Street, 10th Floor, between 5th and Madison Avenues (223-3600) / 555 Lexington Avenue, near 50th Street (759-7480) / **Midtown West:** 618 5th Avenue, near 49th Street (245-2499)

Penn Garden Shirts

63 Orchard Street
near Grand Street / 431-8464
Sun–Wed and Fri 9am–6pm, Thurs 9am–8pm.

Shirts & blouses
Lower East Side/Chinatown

The Edge: Designer shirts and menswear, discounted. Features designer sweaters by Boss, Jhane Barnes, and Coogi, and shirts by Gianfranco Ferre, among others. Men's shirts, socks, and sweaters discounted. Known for its sweaters.

Shirt Store

51 East 44th Street
between Vanderbilt and Madison Avenues / 557-8040
Weekdays 8am–6:30pm, Sat 10am–5pm.

Shirts & blouses
Midtown East

45	43	45	40
quality	style	service	value

The Edge: Ready-to-wear and custom-made pure-cotton shirts. Shirts sold direct from the manufacturer for $37 to $85 for ready-to-wear and $85 to $250 for custom-made. Swatches and pictures are available for mail order. Monogramming and alterations also available. Semiannual sales (January and June). There's a 10% corporate discount program for companies of 100 employees or more. Full line of accessories. *"Good value and sales." "Great selections, sweet value."*

Victory, the Shirt Experts

125 Maiden Lane
between Pearl and Water Streets / 480-1366
Mon–Sat 8:30am–6pm.

Shirts & blouses
Lower Manhattan

quality style service value

The Edge: Quality moderately priced shirts. Manufactures and sells cotton two-ply broadcloth to Sea Island broadcloth in ready-to-wear and made-to-measure shirts. Will taper, shorten sleeves, and monogram shirts. Prices from $45 to $95 for Sea Island cotton. Sells ties, cufflinks, and belts. Discounter.

A. Testoni

665 5th Avenue
between 52nd and 53rd Streets / 223-0909
Weekdays 10am–7pm, Sat 10am–6pm, Sun noon–5pm.

Shoes, socks & stockings
Midtown East

quality style service value

The Edge: Tops. Shoes from this company originating in Bologna, Italy, are tops in both design and quality. Also handbags, belts, scarves, ties, and luggage. *"Classic design."*

Anbar Shoes

60 Reade Street
1 block north of Chambers Street / 964-4017
Weekdays 9am–6:30pm, Sat 11am–6pm.

Shoes, socks & stockings
Lower Manhattan

quality style service value

The Edge: Discounts moderately priced shoes. 20,000 pairs of shoes sold on two floors. Priced from $21 to $70. No delivery. *"Excellent value and offerings for hard-to-find sizes—very small or very large."*

Andrea Carrano Boutique

850 Madison Avenue
near 70th Street / 570-1443
Mon–Sat 10am–7pm, Sun noon–6pm.

Shoes, socks & stockings
Upper East Side

quality style service value

The Edge: Great classic flats in wonderful colors. Classic to trendy Italian shoes made from glove-soft leathers and fine suedes. Features the baby-styled, sophisticated flats like Jackie O used to wear.

Bally of Switzerland

Weekdays 10am–6:30pm, Sat 10am–6pm, Sun noon–5pm.

Shoes, socks & stockings
Multiple locations

quality style service value

The Edge: Classic quality shoes for women and men. Classic, traditional, well-made shoes in glove-soft leathers. Fans call the styles understated and timeless, others say dull. The 45th Street store carries shoes for men only. The 59th Street store carries women's shoes also. For savings, check the Bally Outlet Store in New Rochelle (914-576-3230). *"Still makes leather-lined handbags. Even Chanel can't say that." "Very expensive, good value." "Great bags and shoes." "The best shoes in town." "Delicate. Men's shoes not durable." "Handbags and shoes that don't last."*

Locations: Midtown East: 347 Madison Avenue, near 45th Street (986-0872) / **Upper East Side:** 628 Madison Avenue, near 59th Street (751-9082)

Belgian Shoes

60 East 56th Street
between Madison and Park Avenues / 755-7372
Weekdays 9:30am–4:15pm.

Shoes, socks & stockings
Midtown East

quality   style   service   value

The Edge: Perfect for the country-club set, casual loafers. Handmade, soft leathers, solid and two-tone casual loafers made in Belgium in 50 color combinations. Priced from $200. *"Specific styling for specific tastes." "Very comfortable." "Seams hurt my toes. They wear out quickly."*

Botticelli

666 5th Avenue
near 53rd Street / 582-2984
Weekdays 10am–7:30pm, Sat 10am–7pm, Sun 11am–7pm.

Shoes, socks & stockings
Midtown West

quality   style   service   value

The Edge: Italian leather staples from the classic to the trendy. Men's store filled with classic Italian footwear, socks, ties, and leather jackets. Footwear includes office, formal, and casual styles. Shoes are hand-stitched and priced from $125. *"Very high quality."*

Broadway Sneakers

Daily 9am–8pm.

Shoes, socks & stockings
Multiple locations

quality   style   service   value

The Edge: Unbelievable choice of sneaker labels. Carries 67 sneaker labels, but the largest selection is in Nike and Reebok. Also hiking shoes and in-line skates. Running gear from socks to windbreakers at a modest discount. No delivery. *"The no-return policy can be a problem."*

Locations: Midtown West: 25 West 45th Street, between 5th and 6th Avenues (944-9844) / **SoHo/TriBeCa:** 430 Broadway, between Canal and Howard Streets (334-9488) / 323 Canal Street, near Broadway (966-1125)

Bruno Magli

677 5th Avenue
near 53rd Street / 752-7900
Mon–Wed and Fri 10am–6:30pm, Thurs 10am–7pm,
Sat 10am–6pm, Sun noon– 5pm.

Shoes, socks & stockings
Midtown East

quality   style   service   value

The Edge: An Italian institution. Casual to dressy shoes made of soft Italian leathers in basic colors with good feminine styling. Priced from $150 to $1,000.

CSC Imports

148 Orchard Street
between Stanton and Rivington Streets / 477-5858
Daily 8:30am–6:30pm.

Shoes, socks & stockings
Lower East Side/Chinatown

The Edge: Discounts on work boots. Small shop that carries mostly men's shoes and some women's, including New Balance, Nike, Timberland, and more. Prices are 10% to 15% off retail and most sales are on work boots. As at most discounters, don't come here for the service. *"Service is nonexistent."*

Cole-Haan

Mon–Sat 10am–7pm, Sun noon–6pm.

Shoes, socks & stockings
Multiple locations

quality style service value

The Edge: Conservative, nicely styled shoes and boots. Classic shoes for men, women, and children in casual to dress styles. Also belts, handbags, luggage, and umbrellas. *"Long-lasting quality with style that lasts." "Boring styles—a shame given the quality of the leather."*

Locations: Midtown West: 620 5th Avenue, near 50th Street (765-9747) / **Upper East Side:** 667 Madison Avenue, near 60th Street (421-8440)

Diego Della Valle

41 East 57th Street
between Madison and Park Avenues / 644-5945
Mon–Sat 10am–6pm.

Shoes, socks & stockings
Midtown East

quality style service value

The Edge: Updated classic shoes, an expensive Nine West look. Find Diego's own line plus name-brand shoes like Calvin Klein and J. P. Tod in casual to dressy styles. Children's shoes (priced from $70 to $110) to adult sizes. *"Today's style."*

Eric Shoes

Mon–Wed and Fri 11am–7pm, Thurs 11am–8pm,
Sat 10am–6pm, Sun 1–6pm.

Shoes, socks & stockings
Multiple locations

quality style service value

The Edge: Great style. Sells current designs from all the top designers, including Robert Clergerie, Miss Maud, and Fratelli Rosseti, plus its own label. Expensive. *"Great shoes, but overpriced." "No narrows."*

Locations: Upper East Side: 1333 3rd Avenue, near 76th Street (288-8250) / 1222 Madison Avenue, near 88th Street (289-5762)

Fogal

Mon–Wed and Fri–Sat 10am–6:30pm, Thurs 10am–8pm.

Shoes, socks & stockings
Multiple locations

quality style service value

The Edge: Great hosiery. Hosiery for men and women in hundreds of hues, designs, and patterns. Prices are high (from $16.50), but the hose is long-lasting. Wide range of fabrics, from cottons and wools to wonderful cashmere-silk blends. *"A last resort for great hosiery." "Only at sales."*

Locations: Upper East Side: 680 Madison Avenue, between 61st and 62nd Streets (759-9782) / 510 Madison Avenue, near 53rd Street (355-3254)

French Sole

985 Lexington Avenue
near 72nd Street / 737-2859
Weekdays 10am–7pm, Sat 11am–6pm.

Shoes, socks & stockings
Upper East Side

quality style service value

The Edge: Chanel-inspired ballet slippers. Slippers by Hirica come in 122 solid and/or two-color patterns. Made from French glove leather with adjustable drawstring bows and street soles. Shoes priced at $45 to $50 for flats and $60 to $75 for quilted styles. Also Italian sneakers and winter boots priced from $45 to $250 for boots. *"Adorable."*

Friedman Hosiery

326 Grand Street
near Orchard Street / 674-3292
Sun–Thurs 9am–6pm, Fri 9am–3pm.

Shoes, socks & stockings
Lower East Side/Chinatown

quality style service value

The Edge: Hose and underwear for the whole family, discounted. Find BVD, Berkshire, CK, Christian Dior, Dufold, Hanes, and Jockey, as well as some high-end European hose (Wolford). All sizes from infant to adult. Prices are discounted 20%. Can negotiate for another 10% off on larger orders. *"Good value." "A small selection of upscale hose."*

Gabby's Shoe Outlet

11 South Street
at Stewart Avenue, Garden City / 516-222-4545
Weekdays 10am–9pm, Sat 10am–6pm, Sun 11am–6pm.

Shoes, socks & stockings
Long Island

The Edge: For value. Over 25,000 designer shoes for men and women at outlet prices. For women: designers include Via Spiga, Anne Klein, Joan & David, Stuart Weitzman, and others. For men: Buffalino, Aerosoles, Bruno Magli, Stanley Blacker, Johnston & Murphy, and more. No delivery. Discounter.

Gelman Custom

404 East 73rd Street
near 1st Avenue / 249-3659
Weekdays by appointment 7am–7pm, Sat 7am–5pm.

Shoes, socks & stockings
Upper East Side

The Edge: Custom shoes and boots. Adjusts shoes and boots for comfort and to alleviate foot problems. Priced at $450+ for size 10 pumps. Takes three weeks to complete. Deluxe.

Great Feet

1241 Lexington Avenue
near 84th Street / 249-0551
Mon–Wed and Sat 9:30am–5:30pm,
Thurs–Fri 9:30am–7:30pm, Sun noon–4:30pm.

Shoes, socks & stockings
Upper East Side

quality style service value

The Edge: Enormous stock of stylish children's shoes. From casual to dress pumps in a full range of styles and sizes. Go at off-times to avoid the crowds. Good at fitting your child. Check out the "frequent buyer" program—buy 12 pairs and get the 13th free. *"Wonderful imported children's wear." "Only place for kids—long waits." "Good neighborhood store." "Price commensurate with service."*

Harry's Shoes

2299 Broadway
near 83rd Street / 874-2035
Mon and Thurs–Sat 10am–6:45pm,
Tues–Wed 10:30am–6:45pm, Sun noon– 5:30pm.

Shoes, socks & stockings
Upper West Side

quality style service value

The Edge: Family shoe store with everything. One-stop shopping for family shoe basics that include casual and dressy shoes, sneakers, and boots. Labels include Easy Spirit, Sebago, Dexter, and Rockport. Not stylish. *"Comfort shoes for adults. Only other place for kids." "Great for comfy, not stylish shoes."*

Helene Arpels, Inc.

470 Park Avenue
between 57th and 58th Streets / 755-1623
Mon–Sat 10am–6:30pm (closed Sat July–Aug).

Shoes, socks & stockings
Midtown East

quality style service value

The Edge: Elegant styling for the ladies who lunch. Handmade shoes in soft leathers—from elegant low heels to sexy satin and leather pumps, some with skinny high heels. Favored by the "crowd"—Nancy Reagan, Brooke Astor, and friends. Some handmade sweaters and dresses are produced exclusively for the store. No returns. Very expensive—shoes priced from the hundreds to thousands of dollars per pair. Deluxe.

J. M. Weston

812 Madison Avenue
at 68th Street / 535-2100
Mon–Sat 10am–6pm (to 5pm Sat June–Aug).

Shoes, socks & stockings
Upper East Side

quality style service value

The Edge: For over 100 years, classic handmade luxury footwear. Priced from $600. Parisian shoe company with branches in New York. Wide range of sizes and widths. Some classic women's shoes. Keep a record of each customer's size for phone orders. Deluxe. *"Best shoes. Last forever. Expensive."*

Joan & David

Mon–Sat 11am–7pm, Sun 1–7pm (closed Sun in summer).

Shoes, socks & stockings
Multiple locations

quality style service value

The Edge: Known for its shoes, but check out the clothing. Its own label shoes, boots, belts, bags, and some clothing. Conservative moderately priced shoes. Features a limited range of men's shoes. The clothing is great—fine fabrics, good detailing, and muted colors. Lovely slacks, skirts, sweaters, and silk shirts. *"Great shoes." "Great leather with less-than-inspired styling."*

Locations: **Chelsea:** 104 5th Avenue, near 15th Street (627-1780) / **Upper East Side:** 816 Madison Avenue, near 68th Street (772-3970)

John Fluevog Shoes

104 Prince Street
near Greene Street / 431-4484
Mon–Sat 11am–7pm, Sun noon–6pm.

Shoes, socks & stockings
SoHo/TriBeCa

quality style service value

The Edge: Outrageous women's and men's shoes. Shoe styles are extreme, but seem to appeal to high schoolers. *"Great heel shapes."*

Kenneth Cole

353 Columbus Avenue
between 76th and 77th Streets / 873-2061
Mon–Sat 11am–7:30pm, Sun noon–7pm.

Shoes, socks & stockings
Upper West Side

quality style service value

The Edge: Trendy and classic styles. Classic shoes.

Leach-Kale

1261 Broadway, Suite 815-816
near 31st Street / 683-0571
Weekdays by appointment 7:30–4:30pm.

Shoes, socks & stockings
Midtown West

The Edge: Custom shoes. A place to go for custom shoes. Prices start at $700, with the second pair for $500. They pay attention to foot problems. No credit cards. Deluxe.

Leggiadro

700 Madison Avenue
near 62nd Street / 753-5050
Mon–Sat 10:30am–6pm.

Shoes, socks & stockings
Upper East Side

quality style service value

The Edge: Hundreds of stocking options. Broad selection of imported pantyhose, stockings, knee-highs, and leggings.

Lismore Hosiery

334 Grand Street
between Ludlow and Orchard Streets / 674-3440
Sun–Fri 10:30am–5:30pm.

Shoes, socks & stockings
Lower East Side/Chinatown

quality style service value

The Edge: Inexpensive hose. Sells its own line, plus Berkshire, Calvin Klein, Dior, and Hanes socks, tights, and pantyhose. Priced from $1 to $24. Open Christmas Day. Discounter.

Little Eric Shoes

Weekdays 10am–7pm, Sat 10am–6pm, Sun noon–6pm.

Shoes, socks & stockings
Multiple locations

quality style service value

The Edge: The first to feature Italian designer shoes for children. A full range of shoes, including sneakers, school shoes, dress shoes, and boots. Some women's shoes. *"Extremely beautiful and expensive kids' shoes."*

Locations: Upper East Side: 1331 3rd Avenue, near 76th Street (288-8987) / 1118 Madison Avenue, near 83rd Street (717-1513)

Louis Chock
74 Orchard Street
near Grand Street / 473-1929
Sun–Thurs 9am–5pm, Fri 9am–1pm.

Shoes, socks & stockings
Lower East Side/Chinatown

quality style service value

The Edge: Good Lower East Side source for discounted hosiery for the entire family. All the better brand-name (but not the very top-of-the-line) hosiery (Berkshire, Calvin Klein, Hanes), underwear, and sleepwear discounted. 25% off. *"Strange combo of panty house and electronics."*

M. Stever Hosiery Company
31 West 32nd Street
near 5th Avenue / 563-0052
Daily 7:45am–5:20pm.

Shoes, socks & stockings
Midtown West

The Edge: Lingerie discounted. The basics—hose, lingerie, and active wear at discount prices. For men: socks only. Sells both retail and wholesale. Discounter.

Manolo Blahnik
15 West 55th Street
between 5th and 6th Avenues / 582-3007
Weekdays 10:30am–6pm, Sat 11am–5:30pm.

Shoes, socks & stockings
Midtown West

quality style service value

The Edge: Cutting-edge Italian-made shoes. Offers wonderful daytime styles and fabulous evening shoes, including bridal shoes. Expensive. Deluxe. *"Sexy, flattering, and expensive."* *"Ridiculously priced."*

Maraolo
Weekdays 11am–8pm, Sat 10am–7pm, Sun 1–6pm.

Shoes, socks & stockings
Multiple locations

quality style service value

The Edge: Well known for good conservative Italian women's shoes from casual to business styles. Highly rated by those over 40! Also features Armani, DKNY, and Donna Karan shoes, bags, and belts. Some men's shoes also. *"Good value at the higher end."* *"Value only during the sales."*

Locations: Midtown East: 551 Madison Avenue, near 55th Street (308-8793) / **Upper East Side:** 1321 3rd Avenue, near 76th Street (535-6225) / 835 Madison Avenue, near 69th Street (628-5080) / 782 Lexington Avenue, near 61st Street (832-8182)

Medici Shoes
161 5th Avenue
near 22nd Street / 260-4253

Shoes, socks & stockings
Gramercy Park/Murray Hill

Weekdays 10am–8pm, Sun 11:30am–7:30pm.

quality style service value

The Edge: European clothing, shoes, and accessories. Moderate prices. Classic, stylish shoes. Discounter. *"The selection is nice but the salespeople can be pushy."*

Nana

138 Prince Street
near West Broadway / 274-0749
Mon–Sat 11am–7pm, Sun noon–6pm.

Shoes, socks & stockings
SoHo/TriBeCa

The Edge: Moderately priced trendy young clothes and lots and lots of shoes. Downtown: trendy clothing, backpacks, candles, hair dye, and its own shoe line. Uptown: mostly shoes, its own and Doc Martens.

Nine West

Weekdays 10am–7:30pm, Sat 10am–6pm, Sun noon–5pm.

Shoes, socks & stockings
Multiple locations

quality style service value

The Edge: At last—moderately priced, high-style, classic shoes. A full range of good-looking-flats, heels, and boots—staples to higher fashion. Priced from $50 to $150. *"Great for shoes. Good sales."*

Locations: Lower Manhattan: 313 World Trade Center, concourse level (488-7665) / **Midtown East:** 757 3rd Avenue, near 47th Street (371-4597) / 750 Lexington Avenue, near 59th Street (486-8094) / **Upper East Side:** 1195 3rd Avenue, near 69th Street (472-8750) / 711 Madison Avenue, near 63rd Street (752-8030) / **Upper West Side:** 2305 Broadway, near 83rd Street (799-7610)

99X

84 East 10th Street
between 3rd and 4th Avenues / 460-8599
Mon–Sat noon–8pm, Sun noon–7pm.

Shoes, socks & stockings
Flatiron/East Village

The Edge: For the punk and high school set: sturdy, funky shoes and clothing. The latest in looks at this large, t wo level store, noted for its large selection of Dr. Martens; also Getta Grips and John Fluevog shoes. Sneakers by Puma, Fred Perry, etc. Lots of clothing for the club scene made by young designers including Fresh Jive. *"The shop is a scene in itself—hot music."*

Peter Fox Shoes

Mon–Sat 11am–7pm.

Shoes, socks & stockings
Multiple locations

quality style service value

The Edge: Fun, stylish shoes. Whimsical women's shoes, boots, and slippers. Known for its *Age of Innocence* evening and bridal shoe look. Bridal shoes at the SoHo location only. Wonderful embroidered bridal shoes from $340 and boots from $460. *"High style, excellent quality and fit."* *"Good for large sizes."*

Locations: SoHo/TriBeCa: 105 Thompson Street, near Spring Street (431-6359) / **Upper East Side:** 806 Madison Avenue, near 67th Street (744-8340)

Plus 9

11 East 57th Street, 3rd Floor
between Madison and 5th Avenues / 593-3030
Mon–Sat 10:30am–6pm.

Shoes, socks & stockings
Midtown East

quality style service value

The Edge: Quality women's classic pumps and flats in sizes 9 and over. Features styles and designers you'd find at the Bergdorf shoe saloon, including Bruno Magli, Cole-Haan, Pancaldi, Stuart Weitzman, Via Spiga, and others. Sizes 9½AA to 12AA and 10½B to 13B. Priced from $110 to $250. Great looks. *"Good for me." "Chic for big sizes."*

Richie's Discount Children's Shoes

183 Avenue B
between 11th and 12th Streets / 228-5442
Daily 10am–5pm.

Shoes, socks & stockings
Flatiron/East Village

The Edge: Alphabet City's recommended place for children's shoes. For 80 years a family business! We're not wild about Alphabet City, but this place delivers the latest shoes at 15% to 25% off list. Labels include Babybotte, Jonathan Bennett, Jumping Jacks, Keds, Shoe B'Doo, Stride Rite, and European brands. Infant to teenage sizes and styles. No delivery. Discounter.

Robert Clergerie

41 East 60th Street
between Park and Madison Avenues / 207-8600
Weekdays 10am–6pm, Sat 11am–6pm.

Shoes, socks & stockings
Midtown East

quality style service value

The Edge: Shoes that define "with it" chic. Cutting-edge French shoes for those who "dress." Deluxe. *"Beauties." "Prefer buying at Barneys and IF—same style, better service."*

Sacco Shoes

Weekdays 11am–8pm, Sat 11am–7pm, Sun noon–7pm.

Shoes, socks & stockings
Multiple locations

The Edge: Discounted Italian classics. Mostly Italian classic pumps and flats at moderate prices. Discounter.

Locations: Chelsea: 94 7th Avenue, near 16th Street (675-5180) / **Upper West Side:** 324 Columbus Avenue, near 75th Street (799-5229) / 2355 Broadway, near 86th Street (874-8362)

Shoe City

133 Nassau Street
near City Hall / 732-3889
Weekdays 8am–6pm, Sat 10am–4pm.

Shoes, socks & stockings
Lower Manhattan

The Edge: Best for Timberland discounts. Basic moderately priced sneakers and shoes, including Timberland.

Shoofly

465 Amsterdam Avenue
between 82nd and 83rd Streets / 580-4390
Mon–Sat 11am–7pm, Sun noon–6pm.

Shoes, socks & stockings
Upper West Side

quality style service value

The Edge: Classic to funky shoe and hat shop for infants and young women. Features European shoes, bow ties, gloves, hair accessories, hats, shoes, and suspenders at reasonable prices. Priced from $50. *"Glitter shoes to die for." "Cute clothes for kids. 10% off."*

Sigerson Morrison
242 Mott Street
between Houston and Prince Streets / 219-3893
Mon–Sat 11am–7pm, Sun noon–6pm.

Shoes, socks & stockings
SoHo/TriBeCa

The Edge: A fashion happening. A small shop that features top designer looks created by the two young owners—Karl Sigerson and Miranda Morrison, both graduates of FIT. This is a "secret source" of the fashion elite, but not so secret as it's often featured in *Elle*. *"Love the red patent look." "Great colors, new looks."*

Sole of Italy
125 Orchard Street
near Delancey Street / 674-2662
Sun–Fri 9:30am–6pm.

Shoes, socks & stockings
Lower East Side/Chinatown

The Edge: Moderately priced Italian lines, discounted. Shoes in sizes 4½ to 11 from lots of unknown designers. Styling tends to be trendier. Priced from $50.

Stephane Kelian
Mon–Fri 10-6 Sat 11-6.

Shoes, socks & stockings
Upper East Side

quality style service value

The Edge: High-style designer shoes for women (and some for men). Features Gaultier, Montana, and Kelian's own line. Prices average $350 a pair. Deluxe.

Locations: SoHo/TriBeCa: 120 Wooster Street, near Prince Street (925-3077)

Steve Madden
540 Broadway
between Spring and Price Streets / 343-1800
Mon–Thurs 10:45am–8pm, Fri–Sat 10:45am–8:30pm,
Sun 11:30am–7:30pm.

Shoes, socks & stockings
SoHo/TriBeCa

quality style service value

The Edge: Funky club-looking shoes. Hot looks in shoes and boots. Great platforms. Prices $99 to $128. *"Great and very stylish shoes." "Strangest shoes on earth, very clunky."*

Tall Size Shoes
3 West 35th Street
near 5th Avenue / 736-2060
Mon–Wed and Sat 9:30am–6pm, Thurs–Fri 9:30am–7pm.

Shoes, socks & stockings
Midtown West

quality style service value

The Edge: Meets your needs. Features moderately priced women's shoes to size 14 in widths other than medium—widths from narrow to wide. Stocks designers like Amalfi, Evan Picone, and Via Spiga. Priced from $40 to $225. Plus Nine is more upscale, favoring the higher end of the price range. *"More basic styles." "Good for me."*

To Boot

256 Columbus Avenue
near 76th Street / 724-8249
Mon–Sat noon–8pm, Sun 1–6pm.

Shoes, socks & stockings
Upper West Side

quality style service value

The Edge: Stylish men's shoes. Carries a wide selection of casual to dressy top-designer shoes. Also at Bergdorf. No delivery. *"Top quality, great prices, terrific service—a fun place to shop." "Quality, but you pay for it."*

Tootsi Plohound

Weekdays 11am–7:30pm, Sat 11am–8pm, Sun noon–7pm.

Shoes, socks & stockings
Multiple locations

quality style service value

The Edge: Young offbeat shoes. Cutting-edge shoes that tend to be clunky. Favorites are men's classics—but for women. *"Shoe styles to die for."*

Locations: Gramercy Park/Murray Hill: 137 5th Avenue, between 20th and 21st Streets (460-8650) / 413 West Broadway, between Spring and Prince Streets (925-8931) / **Upper East Side:** 1116 3rd Avenue, between 65th and 66th Streets (249-0671)

Vamps

Mon–Sat 10am–7pm, Sun noon–6pm.

Shoes, socks & stockings
Multiple locations

quality style service value

The Edge: Very affordable style. Features casual to bridal shoes from Anne Klein, DKNY, Via Spiga, and Aerosole—slightly discounted. A great source for styles from hush puppies and boots to evening and bridal shoes. Dyes evening shoes within 24 hours. Prices range from $39 to $150. Now a second store and more sizes, including above-average widths. No delivery. *"Good selection of the latest styles." "Affordable and very nice, best for casual and evening shoes, including bridal."*

Locations: Upper East Side: 1421 2nd Avenue, near 74th Street (744-0227) / 1412 3rd Avenue, near 80th Street (737-7122)

Walter Steiger

Mon–Sat 10am–6pm.

Shoes, socks & stockings
Multiple locations

quality style service value

The Edge: Trendy gorgeous French shoes and, believe it or not, stunning golf shoes. Sexy, high-heeled designer evening shoes, casual shoes, and absolutely stunning two-tone golf shoes. Makes you want to go to the course! Very expensive, priced from $245 to $295. Some shoes custom-made—they're much more expensive and take six to eight weeks for delivery. Deluxe. *"This year, great checked shoes with stacked heels."*

Locations: Midtown East: 417 Park Avenue, near 55th Street (826-7171) / **Upper East Side:** 739 Madison Avenue, between 64th and 65th Streets (570-1212)

Wolford Boutique

619 Madison Avenue
at 58th Street / 688-4850
Mon–Sat 10am–6pm.

Shoes, socks & stockings
Midtown East

quality style service value

The Edge: Enormously expensive—but long-lasting, extremely durable legwear. Very silky sensuous legwear which features a mixture of nylon, Lycra, and cotton in varying weights, which offers control and longer-lasting hose—given the high prices, these stockings have to earn their keep. Hose from $28 to $70, with bodysuits from $160. Several hose shops on the Lower East Side discount Wolford at least 20%, and Century 21 sometimes has heavily discounted discontinued lines and the prior season's hose. *"Synergy lines wear forever."*

Yaska Shoes

Weekdays 10am–7pm, Sat 11am–6pm.

Shoes, socks & stockings
Multiple locations

quality style service value

The Edge: Great sales on cutting-edge young shoes and classic work shoes with oomph. Wonderful European-style shoes, from classic pumps and flats to more trendy styles. Designers include Gritti, Visconto, and Pensato. Expensive at $95 to $450, with most $150 to $200, but the twice-yearly sales are great, particularly after the second markdown. For those seeking conservative, look past the very hip styles, since there's much to find. Sizes 6 to 12, with an extensive stock of larger sizes. *"From conservative pumps good for the office to trendy clunkers."*

Locations: Midtown East: 875 3rd Avenue, near 52nd Street (371-3633) / **Upper East Side:** 1088 Madison Avenue, near 82nd Street (734-0818)

Ashanti

872 Lexington Avenue
between 65th and 66th Streets / 535-0740
Mon–Wed and Fri–Sat 10am–6pm, Thurs 10am–8pm,
Sun 11am–5pm.

Special sizes
Upper East Side

quality style service value

The Edge: Good clothing for the larger woman. Clothing and accessories for the larger woman. Much of the clothing is Ashanti's own design. Off-the-rack clothing to size 28, custom clothing in larger sizes. Down the block from Forgotten Woman (another larger-size store).

Chelsea Atelier

128 West 23rd Street
between 6th and 7th Avenues / 255-8803
Mon–Sat noon–7pm, Sun noon–5pm.

Special sizes
Chelsea

The Edge: More Greenwich Village than uptown. Designs and makes clothing in one-size-fits-all plus misses' sizes 6 to 20. Stock is mostly 12s to 16s. Made in natural fabrics, including cotton, crêpe de chine, raw silk, rayon, and wool. Carries the Flax line by Angel Heart. Priced from $59 to $300. *"So-so style."*

Forgotten Woman

Mon–Wed and Fri–Sat 10am–6pm, Thurs 10am–7:30pm,

Special sizes
Multiple locations

Sun noon–5pm (closed Sun June–Aug).

quality style service value

The Edge: Favored source for larger clothing sizes. Two locations. Carries a full range of quality clothing for women sizes 14 to 24—casual clothing to formal wear with everything in between. Name designers like Ellen Tracy, as well as some exclusive house designers. Moderate to expensive, with coats from $100 to $2,500. The Lexington Avenue shop is down the street from Ashanti. *"Best of the 'big' boutiques, but Saks, Macy's, and Bloomies have great departments too."*

Locations: Midtown West: 60 West 49th Street, between 5th and 6th Avenues (247-8888) / **Upper East Side:** 888 Lexington Avenue, near 66th Street (535-8848)

Rochester Big & Tall

1301 Avenue of the Americas
near 52nd Street / 247-7500
Mon–Wed and Fri 9:30am–6:30pm,
Thurs 9:30am–8pm, Sat 9:30am–6pm.

Special sizes
Midtown West

quality style service value

The Edge: Enormous selection of hard-to-find large sizes. Stock includes suits, shoes, shirts, and more from Canali, Docker, Gant, Hickey Freeman, Levi, Oxxford, Zegna, and others. Sizes from 48 regular to 60 extra-long. *"Good selection, meets all needs."*

Berk of Burlington Arcade London

781 Madison Avenue
near 66th Street / 570-0285
Weekdays 10am–6pm, Sat 10am–5pm.

Sweaters
Upper East Side

quality style service value

The Edge: Top classic cashmeres. Up to six-ply cashmere items in a wide range of colors. Priced from $199 to $900. Capes and wonderful velvet slippers in deep autumn colors (slippers $185 to $200). Deluxe. *"Fine things." "Arrogant 'Don't Touch' attitude."*

Best of Scotland

581 5th Avenue
between 47 and 48th Streets / 644-0415
Mon–Sat 10am–5pm.

Sweaters
Midtown East

quality style service value

The Edge: Beautiful sweaters, somewhat less expensive than the best-known spots. Sweaters, cashmere capes, and stoles are priced from $160 to $325. Hundreds of colors. 30% off.

Cashmere-Cashmere

840 Madison Avenue
between 69th and 70th Streets / 988-5252
Weekdays 10am–6pm, Sat noon–6pm, Sun noon–5pm.

Sweaters
Upper East Side

quality style service value

The Edge: Quality and colors. Classic to high-fashion (to 10-ply) cashmere clothing and accessories in a range of excellent colors. Find blankets, dresses, robes, socks, sweatsuits, and sweaters. Prices start at $195. Great size range. Guests at the Four Seasons Hotel get a 10% discount. Deluxe. *"Good value." "Okay—good but not great."*

Granny-Made

381 Amsterdam Avenue
near 79th Street / 496-1222
Weekdays 11am–7:30pm, Sat 10am–6pm, Sun noon–5pm.

Sweaters
Upper West Side

45	40	40	35
quality	style	service	value

The Edge: Grandma-designed but machine-executed sweaters. Sweaters for children's through adult sizes. A full range of knit items, from ski caps to suits and dresses. Sweaters only for men. *"Lovely to look at."*

TSE Cashmere

827 Madison Avenue
Mon–Wed and Fri–Sat 10am–6pm, Thurs 10am–7pm.
at 69th Street / 472-7790

Sweaters
Upper East Side

44	46	40	40
quality	style	service	value

The Edge: Luxurious cashmeres. Classic cashmere turtlenecks, cardigans and polos, sportswear, coats, and natural-tone robes and blankets. Lots of cashmere blends—cashmere with silk, cashmere with cotton, etc. TSE has an outlet at Woodbury Commons, where you'll find these wonderful things discounted. Favors muted colors and more current styling. Deluxe. *"Best cashmere in New York. Very expensive." "The Woodbury Commons shop help will call when items you want go on sale."*

A. W. Kaufman

73 Orchard Street
between Broome and Grand Streets / 226-1629
Mon–Thurs 10:30am–5pm, Fri 10:30am–2pm, Sun 10am–5pm.

Underwear & lingerie
Lower East Side/Chinatown

42	40	32	43
quality	style	service	value

The Edge: Could be the best-stocked top-quality designer lingerie shop in the city. Crammed with quality lingerie, lounge wear, underwear, gowns, and robes at about 20% off. Features European (French, Swiss, and Belgian) lingerie. Virtually impossible to see what it has since the store is stocked so tightly and is often crowded. Labels include Calida, Christian Dior, David Brown, Hanro, Lejaby, Pluto, Wolford, and more. Phone orders are routine—if they have it, you get it; if they don't, you never hear from them. Service is abominable. The shop is always crowded, help is limited and slow, and you're not permitted to look without help. Absolutely no returns. *"High-end lingerie at a discount—25% off." "Cramped Lower East Side store, but good value on lingerie." "No service and no returns, no matter what."*

AM/PM

109 Thompson Street
between Prince and Spring Streets / 219-0343
Daily noon–7pm.

Underwear & lingerie
SoHo/TriBeCa

The Edge: Outrageous lingerie, including bustiers if you're so inclined. Lingerie from the demure (Hanro) to the outrageous. Scores of designers featured—a little of everything. No delivery.

Bra Smyth

905 Madison Avenue
near 72nd Street / 772-9400
Mon–Sat 10am–7pm.

Underwear & lingerie
Upper East Side

The Edge: Bras that fit. The staff will advise on fit and style appropriate to the need. Alterations are free at the Madison Avenue shop. Bras are arranged by style and color, with panties to match or complement. Favors La Perla, Chantal, and similar high-end European lingerie labels.

Brief Essentials

1407 Broadway
between 38th and 39th Streets / 921-8344
Weekdays 8:30am–5:30pm.

Underwear & lingerie
Midtown West

quality style service value

The Edge: The basics in moderately priced lingerie and exercise wear. Discounter.

Chas. Weiss Fashions

331 Grand Street
near Orchard Street / 966-1143
Sun–Thurs 11am–5pm.

Underwear & lingerie
Lower East Side/Chinatown

quality style service value

The Edge: Basic underwear, discounted. Mostly a bra and panty store. Basic functional, inexpensive items including jogging suits, nightgowns, and Danskins. Telephone orders make it convenient.

Enelra

48½ East 7th Street
between 1st and 2nd Streets / 473-2454
Sun–Wed noon–8:30pm, Thurs–Sat noon–9:30pm.

Underwear & lingerie
Flatiron/East Village

The Edge: Sexy lingerie. Runs the gamut from practical to sexy (her specialty) lingerie (teddies, slips, and nightgowns) to funky, including jeweled bustiers and to vinyl bondage wear (if you find that funky). Lingerie from $5 to $250.

Howron Sportswear

295 Grand Street
near Allen Street / 226-4307
Sun–Fri 9am–5:30pm.

Underwear & lingerie
Lower East Side/Chinatown

The Edge: The basics discounted. While it features men's sportswear (Countess Mara, Pierre Cardin, and Sansabelt), it's a better source for men's and women's underwear (Bali, Olga, Vanity Fair, and Warner) and hosiery (Berkshire, CK, Givenchy, Hanes, and Round the Clock). Wide range of sizes.

Joovay

436 West Broadway
near Prince Street / 431-6386
Daily noon–7pm.

Underwear & lingerie
SoHo/TriBeCa

quality style service value

The Edge: Feminine delicate lingerie. Features delicate colors, fine fabrics, and feminine trims. Stocks top lines like Christian Dior, Hanro, La Perla, and Pluto. Bras priced from $22 to $147, and panties from $9 to $95. *"Lovely things." "Only on sale, please."*

La Perla

Underwear & lingerie
Upper East Side

777 Madison Avenue
between 66th and 67th Streets / 570-0050
Mon–Sat 10am–6pm.

quality style service value

The Edge: Wonderful Italian imports. Expect to find a huge selection of La Perla's lovely, sexy, soft lingerie, plus bathing suits. To create a look, try on the Sculpture bra—it's a new you.

La Petite Coquette, Inc.

Underwear & lingerie
Flatiron/East Village

52 University Place
between 9th and 10th Avenues / 473-2478
Mon–Sat 11am–7pm, Sun noon–6pm.

50 45 45 35
quality style service value

The Edge: Racy sexy late-evening wear. A very small shop featuring sexy European lingerie. Great for pick-me-up indulgences. *"New store, great size, less intimidating."*

Le Corset

Underwear & lingerie
SoHo/TriBeCa

80 Thompson Street
between Spring and Broome Streets / 334-4936
Mon noon–7pm, Tues–Sat 11am–7pm, Sun noon–6pm.

The Edge: A special collection. This small cozy shop features very feminine underwear and lingerie—new and vintage. The new lingerie is sourced from small European designers, including Chantal Thomass, Fifi Chachnil, Pricess Tam-Tam, and Deborah Marquit—small suppliers. Expect lacy garter belts, corsets, silk stockings, silk and lace slip dresses, and nightwear. Also a special collection of vintage lingerie, all in perfect condition. For the athletic: high-tech, high-performance gear—"plastic-and-polyester" bras.

Ora Feder Lingerie

Underwear & lingerie
Upper East Side

20 East 69th Street, Suite 2A
between 5th and Madison Avenues / 517-7125
Tues–Sat 10am–6pm (closed Sat in summer).

quality style service value

The Edge: Worth wearing outside. Beautiful lingerie trimmed with Victorian lace or embroideries on silk and cotton lingerie. Also bras and underwear, garters, and lace handkerchiefs. Some vintage pieces occasionally. Items fitted as needed. Feder was a wholesaler to Bergdorf prior to opening this shop.

Peress

Underwear & lingerie
Upper East Side

739 Madison Avenue
near 64th Street / 861-6336
Mon–Sat 10am–6pm.

45 40 35 45
quality style service value

The Edge: Lovely intimate apparel. High-end lingerie in moderate to very expensive lines. Bras $13 to $150. Check the sales in January and August.

Roberta

Underwear & lingerie
Upper East Side

1252 Madison Avenue
near 90th Street / 860-8366

Mon–Sat 10am–6pm.

quality style service value

The Edge: Well-stocked neighborhood lingerie shop. Everything you'd want in a lingerie store, from basic to sexy styles. Extras include swimsuits and nursing bras. Offers top lines and attention to fit. Bras priced at $18 to $125. *"Easy shopping for it all."*

Rosenberg Grand Lingerie

Underwear & lingerie
Lower East Side/Chinatown

330 Grand Street
between Orchard and Ludlow Streets / 473-0969
Sun–Fri 10am–5pm.

quality style service value

The Edge: 25% off on brand-name underwear. Features Lollipop, Maidenform, Vanity Fair, and many other brands, but no Calvin Klein. No credit cards. No delivery.

Samantha Jones Lingerie

Underwear & lingerie
Upper East Side

996 Lexington Avenue
at 72nd Street / 308-6680
Weekdays 10:30am–7pm, Sat 10:30am–5pm, Sun 1–6pm.

quality style service value

The Edge: Sexy lingerie. Lingerie and accessories, including silk scarves and fragrances. Features La Perla, Lise Charmel, Samantha Jones, and other lines. *"Beautiful silks and slippers."*

Schachner Fashions

Underwear & lingerie
Lower East Side/Chinatown

95 Delancey Street
between Orchard and Ludlow Streets / 677-0700
Mon–Sat 9am–5:30pm, Sun 9am–6pm.

quality style service value

The Edge: Value for the lingerie basics. Features robes, sleepwear, underwear, and lounge wear discounted. Brands carried include Vanity Fair, Exquisite Form, Barbizon, Maidenform, Carnival, Warner's, Bali, and others. Open Christmas Day until 3pm.

Sue Ekahn / New York

Underwear & lingerie
Mail/phone

929-4432
By appointment.

The Edge: Custom lingerie and home wear. One of her specialties is custom bridal trousseaus and gifts for bridal attendants. A source of favorite gifts for the bride, including lovely garters made from antique ribbons and trim. Prices from $95. Ekahn used to be Diana Vreeland's personal shopper, and you can imagine how demanding *she* was. She'll make it or find it for you. No credit cards.

Victoria's Secret

Underwear & lingerie
Multiple locations

Weekdays 10am–8pm, Sat 10am–7pm, Sun noon–6pm.

quality style service value

The Edge: Nice-looking inexpensive lingerie. Owned by The Limited and in malls all over the U.S. The shop is devoted to attractive lingerie in a wide price range. Both sexy and functional items.

Locations: **Midtown East:** 34 East 57th Street, between Park and Madison Avenues (758-5592) /
Upper East Side: 693 Madison Avenue, at 62nd Street (838-9266)

Dornan
Uniforms
Midtown West

653 11th Avenue
between 47th and 48th Streets / 247-0937
Mon–Wed and Fri 8:30am–4pm, Thurs 8:30am–6pm.

The Edge: One-stop shopping for uniforms. Uniforms for chauffeurs, butlers, maids, and cooks
and (if you're on your coop/condo board) uniforms for doormen, handymen, superintendents, and
the like. Will customize and distribute uniforms worldwide.

Ideal Department Store
Uniforms
Brooklyn

1814-1816 Flatbush Avenue
between Avenues J and K, Brooklyn / 718-252-5090
Mon–Wed and Fri–Sat 10am–5:45pm, Thurs 10am–6:45pm.

The Edge: A lifesaver if you need one. Boy Scout and Girl Scout uniforms in children's sizes,
with some for adults.

Billy Martin's Western Wear
Western wear
Upper East Side

812 Madison Avenue
near 68th Street / 861-3100
Weekdays 10am–7pm, Sat 10am–6pm, Sun noon–5pm.

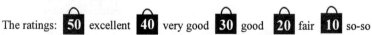

44	43	36	26
quality	style	service	value

The Edge: The source for top western gear. The city's best-known spot for top-quality and high-
priced western gear. Features boots, shirts, riding pants, western hats, parkas, jackets, and
accessories. Wonderful sterling-silver jewelry. Boots mostly priced from $350 to $695 (for lizard);
the most expensive boots cost $5,000! *"If you need a pair of boots, go!" "Great silver belt buckles
and sets. Good boots." "Overpriced."*

Whiskey Dust
Western wear
Greenwich Village

526 Hudson Street
between West 10th and Charles Streets / 691-5576
Mon–Sat 12:30–7pm, Sun 1–6pm.

The Edge: Vintage western gear for sale or rent. Features everything you'd need or want for a
country-western party—both vintage and new. Quality items in good condition. Prices are
reasonable—particularly if you're comparing them to Billy Martin's Western Wear. Rentals at 30%
off the retail price for a three-day period. An affordable alternative to buying for those western
theme parties. Rentals cater to the film industry. No delivery.

The ratings: **50** excellent **40** very good **30** good **20** fair **10** so-so

Cosmetics, bath & beauty

Aedes de Venustas

15 Christopher Street
between 6th and 7th Avenues / 206-8674
Mon–Sat noon–8pm, Sun 1–7pm.

Cosmetics, etc.
Greenwich Village

The Edge: The source for impossible-to-find items. A simply beautiful salon. The source for hard-to-find fragrances and beauty products from around the world. Some things are so perishable that they must be refrigerated. Products include Etro perfumes from Milan, D. R. Harris perfumes from Milan, "M" from St. Barts, and more. Fresh flowers are part of the packaging. Regulars include designer Todd Oldham, model Kristy Hume, Michael Kors, and others. Prices $6 for soap to $120 for its signature perfume, Palais Jamais.

Alcone Warehouse

5-49 49th Avenue, between Vernon and the East River
Long Island City / 718-361-8373
Weekdays 9am–4:30pm.

Cosmetics, etc.
Queens

The Edge: Professional theater makeup for all—via mail order. The Alcone warehouse provides makeup, makeup cases, brushes, and supplies through its mail-order service. Originally targeted to professional theater personnel, now for all.

Aveda Lifestyle Store

Weekdays 10am–7pm, Sat noon–7pm, Sun noon–6pm.

Cosmetics, etc.
Multiple locations

quality style service value

The Edge: The source for aroma-therapy hair products. Find biodegradable products made from flowers and plants for your hair and body, scented candles, fabric and household cleaners. Known best for hair-care products. Also haircuts, facials, body massages, and makeup. Prices are $65 for a haircut, shampoo, and blow dry; $75 to $100 for hair coloring; $45 (for a half hour) to $95 (for 1½ hours) for a massage; facials from $55 to $90; and body treatments from $110. The staff is friendly and helpful. Before your first session you're required to complete a questionnaire which prescribes the treatment you'll be provided. Home appointments are possible (but are not common and need arranging) by calling the West Broadway store. No delivery.

Locations: Chelsea: 140 5th Avenue, near 19th Street (645-4797) / **Midtown East:** 509 Madison Avenue, between 52nd and 53rd Streets (832-2416) / **SoHo/TriBeCa:** 456 West Broadway, between Prince and Houston Streets (473-0280) / 233 Spring Street, between 6th Avenue and Varick Street (807-1492)

Body Shop

Weekdays 9am–7pm, Sat 11am–7pm, Sun 11am–5pm.

Cosmetics, etc.
Multiple locations

quality style service value

The Edge: Environmentally safe lotions and soaps. Known for its custom-made baskets filled with your choice of fragrant soaps and lotions. Offers free makeovers with no purchase required—except for the sales pitch. 10% discount available with the Transmedia card.

Locations: Flatiron/East Village: 747 Broadway, between 8th Street and Waverly Place (979-2944) / **Gramercy Park/Murray Hill:** 135 5th Avenue, near 20th Street (254-0145) / **Lower Manhattan:** World Trade Center Concourse #340, Building 5 (488-7595) / 16 Fulton Street, South Street Seaport (480-9876) / **Midtown East:** 485 Madison Avenue, near 52nd Street (832-0812) / 479 5th Avenue, near 41st Street (661-1992) / **Midtown West:** 901 Avenue of the Americas, near 33rd Street (268-7424) / 1270 Avenue of the Americas, near 52nd Street (397-3007) / **Upper East Side:** 773 Lexington Avenue, near 61st Street (755-7851) / **Upper West Side:** 2159 Broadway, at 76th Street (721-2947)

Boyd's Chemist

655 Madison Avenue
near 60th Street / 838-6558
Weekdays 8:30am–7:30pm, Sat 9:30am–7pm, Sun noon–6pm.

Cosmetics, etc.
Upper East Side

quality style service value

The Edge: You name the beauty need and Boyd's have it. Known for its makeup instruction (including instructional diagrams) with its own and/or name-brand products. The store has nine full-time makeup consultants. Makeovers can be done off-site (caters to wedding makeups, party and press events). A great array of cosmetics—great colors and variety. Also brushes, soaps, jewelry, hair accessories, and more. Prescription service. High-end prices. *"Great advice." "Staff can be pushy." "Good if they understand your style."*

Caswell-Massey Company Ltd.

Weekdays 9am–7pm, Sat 10am–6pm.

Cosmetics, etc.
Multiple locations

quality style service value

The Edge: A bit of yesteryear. Old-fashioned shop, selling soaps, colognes, lotions, and powders. Favorite scents—rose, lavender, and freesia. Large selection of herbal, glycerin, coconut oil, oatmeal, and buttermilk treatments and gift packages.

Locations: Lower Manhattan: 225 Liberty Street, World Financial Center (945-2630) / **Midtown East:** 518 Lexington Avenue, near 48th Street (755-2254) / 725 5th Avenue, Trump Tower at 57th Street (421-6645) / **SoHo/TriBeCa:** 155 Spring Street, between Wooster and West Broadway (219-3661)

Cosmetic Show

919 3rd Avenue
at 56th Street / 750-8418
Weekdays 8am–7pm, Sat 10am–5pm, Sun 11am–5pm.

Cosmetics, etc.
Midtown East

quality style service value

The Edge: Not everything, but what they have is cheap. Worth the time to browse for cosmetics and perfumes from all the major houses, deeply discounted. Lines include Laslo, Lauder, Yves St. Laurent, Elizabeth Arden, and the like. Lots of gift packages (like those inducements you get at cosmetic counters). Not necessarily the latest colors or scents (much is overstocks or older styles), but virtually everything you use, if you're at all flexible. Also boxed candies and cookies. Yes, it's in the office building (side entrance) slightly off 3rd Avenue.

Cosmetic Too!

14 East 41st Street
between 5th and Madison Avenues / 698-2481
Weekdays 8am–7pm, Sat 10am–5pm, Sun 11am–5pm.

Cosmetics, etc.
Midtown East

quality style service value

The Edge: Cosmetic Show's sister shop. Cosmetics, perfumes, and candies from all the best houses. Not the latest labels, but something for everyone—and everything you can possibly use. Discounter.

Cosmetic World and Gift Center

393 5th Avenue, 2nd Floor
between 36th and 37th Streets / 213-4047
Weekdays 10am–6pm (also Sat 10am–6pm in December).

Cosmetics, etc.
Gramercy Park/Murray Hill

quality style service value

The Edge: Cosmetics showroom open to the public. Like the duty-free shops at airports. An eclectic mix of cosmetics, men's and women's fragrances, handbags, jewelry, and ties at discounts that range from 15% to 50% (50% on discontinued items). It stocks major brands and has a multilingual staff. Telephone and mail orders are possible.

Cosmetics Plus

Weekdays 8:30-7:30 Sat 10-6.

Cosmetics, etc.
Multiple locations

quality style service value

The Edge: It has virtually everything from everyone—at 10% to 20% off list. Find Borghese, Lancôme, Elizabeth Arden, and many others. Virtually all brands of cosmetics, hair treatments, and perfumes, as well as accessories, hair bands, hosiery, costume jewelry, nonprescription drugs, and fragrances for both women and men.

Locations: Lower Manhattan: 170 Broadway, near Maiden Lane (843-6656) / **Midtown East:** 500 Lexington Avenue, between 47th and 48th Streets (832-5460) / 605 3rd Avenue, near 40th Street (986-1407) / 875 3rd Avenue, at 53rd Street (319-2120) / 515 Madison Avenue, near 53rd Street (644-1911) / **Midtown West:** 275 7th Avenue, near 26th Street (727-0705) / 1320 Avenue of the Americas, at 55th Street (247-0444) / 171 West 57th Street, between 6th and 7th Avenues (399-9783) / 666 5th Avenue, near 53rd Street (757-2895) / 1601 Broadway, near 48th Street (757-3122) / 516 5th Avenue, near 43rd Street (221-6560) / **Upper East Side:** 1201 3rd Avenue, near 70th Street (628-5600) / 1388 3rd Avenue, near 79th Street (772-3633) / **Upper West Side:** 1920 Broadway, near 65th Street (875-8604) / 2151 Broadway, between 75th and 76th Streets (595-7727)

Crabtree and Evelyn

Mon–Sat 10am–6pm, Sun noon–5pm.

Cosmetics, etc.
Multiple locations

quality style service value

The Edge: You know it—it's the choice of luxury hotels to pamper you. Known for its custom gift baskets filled with your special picks. Baskets include sachets, baby products, shampoos and conditioners, soaps, gels, hangers, brushes, potpourri, and candles. All natural ingredients and no animal testing. It offers many fragrances (based on flowers and citrons), as well as cookies and jams. Relatively moderate prices.

Locations: Lower Manhattan: 141 World Trade Center, at Fulton Street, concourse level (432-7134) / **Midtown East:** 520 Madison Avenue, between 53rd and 54th Streets (758-6419) / **Midtown West:** 620 5th Avenue, near 49th Street (581-5022) / **Upper East Side:** 1310 Madison Avenue, near 93rd Street (289-3923)

Equinox Urban Spa and Clarins Institute

Cosmetics, etc.
Upper East Side

205 East 85th Street
between 2nd and 3rd Avenues / 439-8500
Mon–Thurs 5:30–10:30pm, Fri 5:30–1pm, Sat–Sun 8am–9pm.

30	30	30	30
quality	style	service	value

The Edge: Health and glamour, in one place. Full-service fitness facility made special by spa features—massages, facials, and treatments to make you glow all over. *"Facials with Gabrielle."*

Erbe

Cosmetics, etc.
SoHo/TriBeCa

196 Prince Street
between Sullivan and MacDougal Streets / 966-1445
Tues–Sat 11am–7pm.

The Edge: The place for "TLC." Where Kate Moss, Naomi Campbell, and their friends shop—for both the herbal treatments and much-needed "TLC" (tender, loving care). Erbe is tranquil, with soft lights, classical music, and some of the best products around. A full range of treatments from facials to body wraps to make you look and feel good. Toll-free mail-order number: 800-432-3723. *"Some basements are worth checking out."*

Floris

Cosmetics, etc.
Upper East Side

703 Madison Avenue
between 62nd and 63rd Streets / 935-9100
Mon–Wed and Fri–Sat 10am–6pm, Thurs 10am–7pm.

45	50	45	40
quality	style	service	value

The Edge: Old-fashioned English charm. A bit of Victorian England in this shop offering wonderful floral fragrances in soaps, room sprays, sachets, and dusting powders.

Il-Mikiage

Cosmetics, etc.
Midtown East

107 East 60th Street
between Lexington and Park Avenues / 371-0551
Mon and Thurs 9am–8pm, Tues–Wed 9am–7pm,
Fri 9am–3pm (to 5pm in winter), Sun 10am–6pm.

40	40	30	30
quality	style	service	value

The Edge: Shop alongside a celebrity clientele. Celebrity clientele—actresses and models—shop here to meet their makeup needs. Good products and good looks.

J. F. Lazartigue

Cosmetics, etc.
Upper East Side

764 Madison Avenue
between 65th and 66th Streets / 288-2250

Mon–Tues and Thurs–Sat 10am–6pm, Wed 10am–8pm.

quality style service value

The Edge: Personalized hair treatments and consultations. Provides personalized hair treatments (including consultation with hair analysis), massage, and products tailored to your specific needs. Hair treatments start at $75; products range in price from $20. Sold at top salons, Bergdorf, and the like.

Jay's Perfume Bar
14 East 17th Street
near 5th Avenue / 243-7743
Weekdays 9am–6pm, Sat 9am–4:30pm, Sun 10am–4pm.

Cosmetics, etc.
Flatiron/East Village

quality style service value

The Edge: Offered some of the lowest prices we found. In spot checks, Jay's appears slightly cheaper than other sources, but like many discounters, it doesn't have a complete selection of brands and fragrances. Find perfume copies as well.

Jean Laporte L'Artisan Parfumeur
870 Madison Avenue
near 71st Street / 517-8665
Mon–Sat 10am–6pm.

Cosmetics, etc.
Upper East Side

quality style service value

The Edge: Only natural fragrances for the home or body.

Kiehl's
109 3rd Avenue
between 13th and 14th Streets / 677-3171
Weekdays 10am–6:30pm, Sat 10am–6pm.

Cosmetics, etc.
Flatiron/East Village

quality style service value

The Edge: Everyone comes here—including top salons—to meet their clients' special body needs. Since 1851. Kiehl makes special treatments and preparations by hand which are distributed internationally. Only natural ingredients are used in the company's products, which include cleansers, scrubs, toners, moisturizers, eye-area preparations, men's creams, masks, body moisturizers, bath and shower products, sports items, suntan lotion, ladies' leg-grooming formulations, shampoos, conditioners, and treatments. People advise here but don't push. Good service via the 800 telephone number. Plenty of free samples are included in orders for you to get to know the product line.

M.A.C. Cosmetics
Mon–Sat noon–7pm, Sun 1–6pm.

Cosmetics, etc.
Multiple locations

42 48 38 38

quality style service value

The Edge: The not-so-secret source where models get done. M.A.C. = Makeup Art Cosmetics. Good makeup beloved for its ability to last the day. Its own line of cosmetics—light, easy to apply, and less expensive than other top lines. Good colors and selections. Cosmeticians provide good advice for what's right for you. A favorite is the M.A.C. travel bag—faux leather filled with travel-size favorites, including moisturizers, body treatments, exfoliating cleanser, and sea-kelp soap. Clients include model Linda Evangelista, Michelle Pfeiffer, and the like. Is this their secret? *"Makeup applications are terrific."*

Locations: Greenwich Village: 14 Christopher Street, near 6th Avenue (243-4150) / **SoHo/TriBeCa:** 113 Spring Street, near Spring Street (334-4641)

Perfumania

Weekdays 7:30am–8pm, Sat 7:30am–7:30pm, Sun 10am–6pm.

Cosmetics, etc.
Multiple locations

quality style service value

The Edge: Good discounts. Stocks hundreds of brands, but your favorites won't always be in stock. Sells perfume at 20% off retail for newer fragrances, to 40% to 75% off for older lines. It carries American and European brands and offers discounts on gift sets. Call first to check prices and stock, since like most discounters, it doesn't have everything. Will take credit cards and ship via UPS anywhere.

Locations: Flatiron/East Village: 755 Broadway, at 8th Street (979-7674) / **Midtown West:** One Penn Plaza, level across from LIRR (268-0049) / 20 West 34th Street, near 5th Avenue (736-0414) / 1585 Broadway, between 47th and 48th Streets (541-8047) / **Upper East Side:** 782 Lexington Avenue, near 60th Street (750-2810) / 342 Madison Avenue, near 44th Street (338-0146) / **Upper West Side:** 2321 Broadway, near 84th Street (595-8778)

Revlon Employee Store

767 5th Avenue
near 58th Street
Monday-Friday 10-4

Cosmetics, etc.
Midtown East

quality style service value

The Edge: Employee prices. In the basement (past the Vidal Sassoon salon) is the Revlon company store. Follow the signs—the shop is off the main corridor behind closed but unlocked doors. It's a wonderful source for a wide range of Revlon products, especially the more moderate lines at close to 50% off. While officially a company store only, they're flexible and ask no questions.

Ricky's

Mon–Thurs 8am–1pm, Fri 8am–midnight,
Sat 9am–midnight, Sun 10am–10pm.

Cosmetics, etc.
Multiple locations

quality style service value

The Edge: Bargain cosmetics. Find Nexxus, Paul Michell, and Sebastian hair products; Cover Girl, Lancôme, and Revlon makeup; as well as CK1 and Coal Water perfume. Lots of soaps, scrubs, oils, brushes, etc. Best for its wide range of hair and hair-care products. Low prices. Offers a pharmacy as well. Wouldn't quote prices over the phone. No delivery.

Locations: Chelsea: 466 Avenue of the Americas, at 11th Street (924-3401) / **Flatiron/East Village:** 718 Broadway, at Washington Place (979-5232) / 44 East 8th Street, between Broadway and Greene Street (254-5247) / 180 3rd Avenue, near 17th Street (228-4485) / **Gramercy Park/Murray Hill:** 501 2nd Avenue, near 28th Street (679-5435) / 585 2nd Avenue, near 32nd Street (685-5518) / **SoHo/TriBeCa:** 590 Broadway, near Houston Street (226-5552) / **Upper East Side:** 1675 3rd Avenue, near 94th Street (348-7400) / **Upper West Side:** 600 Columbus Avenue, near 89th Street (769-1050) / 2200 Broadway, near 78th Street (579-6959)

United Beauty Products

49 West 46th Street
between 5th and 6th Avenues / 635-3950
Weekdays 9:30am–5:45pm.

Cosmetics, etc.
Midtown West

The Edge: Sensational prices on hair care. You go to top salons and want to use what they use and wonder where they get it—wonder no more. U.B.P. supplies just about every top salon on the city with hairdryers, curlers, manicure/pedicure products, treatments, and color products. Great lines and great prices. Come here and save on all the products you'll need. Call toll free 800-635-3950 for products.

Zitomer

969 Madison Avenue
between 75th and 76th Streets / 737-2037
Weekdays 9am–8pm, Sat 9am–7pm, Sun 10am–6pm.

Cosmetics, etc.
Upper East Side

quality style service value

The Edge: An upscale general store featuring pharmaceuticals, cosmetics, and children's clothing. Dazzling neighborhood shop with a full-line drugstore and cosmetics center on the first floor, and on the second, adorable British and French designer children's clothing, lingerie, and toys. Enchanting gift items. *"A little of everything—great!" "Good value for a neighborhood store." "Service lousy. They wouldn't take my return of earrings that broke one day after I bought them—for over $100."*

Angela Cosmai

16 West 55th Street
between 5th and 6th Avenues. / 541-5820
By appointment.

Haircuts & hairstylists
Midtown West

The Edge: Cuts and color in an attractive brownstone. Shop in an attractive private brownstone. Clients include Anne Bass and Teri Garr. Women's haircuts for $100 to $125. Color with Cosmai: $225 half head, $400 full head. Deluxe.

Astor Place Hair Stylists

2 Astor Place
near Broadway / 475-9854
Mon–Sat 8am–8pm, Sun 9am–6pm.

Haircuts & hairstylists
Flatiron/East Village

quality style service value

The Edge: Good haircuts for $12. Is it ever *not* crowded? Haircuts and men's shaves provided by close to 100 professionals. Haircuts from $10, color from $25, straightening at $35 and up, and highlights for $50 and up. Provides manicures, pedicures, and, yes, waxing. Everyone goes, from staid bankers to orange-haired in-line skaters. No appointments taken. Cash only. *"Dominick is tops!" "We've learned to tip high and, yes, jump the line."*

Brunellier Salon

692 Madison Avenue
near 62nd Street / 758-7779
Mon–Wed and Fri–Sat 9am–5pm, Thurs 9am–6:30pm.

Haircuts & hairstylists
Upper East Side

quality style service value

The Edge: Specializes in hair-conditioning treatments. All agree: Service is first-rate. No credit cards.

Bumble and Bumble

146 East 56th Street
between 3rd and Lexington Avenues / 521-6500
Tues–Fri 9:30am–7:30pm, Sat 9am–5:30pm.

Haircuts & hairstylists
Midtown East

42	43	40	36
quality	style	service	value

The Edge: If you're 35 or under and want the look, this is the place. Widely known. A good resource for hair styling and makeup lessons and applications—but you need to know who the good stylists are. A bit of a scene—not a bad pickup place.

Donsuki

19 East 62nd Street
between 5th and Madison Avenues / 826-3397
Tues–Wed and Fri 9am–5:30pm,
Thurs 10am–6:30pm, Sat 9am–3pm.

Haircuts & hairstylists
Upper East Side

50	50	46	44
quality	style	service	value

The Edge: They know you work—so they'll do manicure, pedicure, and color all at once. From the moment you enter the door, you feel pampered by their gracious attitude. Great cuts and great color. Prices from $75 for one-process color and $100 for a cut. *"Dare I share this? Franco for color and Joseph for the cut—simply the best."*

Garren

712 5th Avenue
at Henri Bendel / 841-9400
Mon–Wed and Fri–Sat 10am–7pm, Thurs 10am–8pm.

Haircuts & hairstylists
Midtown West

The Edge: Another one of the top salons. Fashionable salon at Henri Bendel, featuring Garren as the top stylist. Cozy—just six chairs. Clients have included Linda Evangelista and Lucie de la Falaise. Other services include hair treatments, manicures, and pedicures. Priced $100 to $300 (for Garren) for a haircut only. Highlights from $325.

Jacques Dessange

505 Park Avenue
near 59th Street / 308-1400
Tues–Sat 9am–7pm.

Haircuts & hairstylists
Midtown East

30	40	30	25
quality	style	service	value

The Edge: A chic chain store. A chain of 600 salons around the world, but only one is in New York. Top stylists are Jerome and Bruno.

Julius Caruso Salon

22 62nd Street
near Madison Avenue / 759-7574
Mon–Sat 9am–5pm.

Haircuts & hairstylists
Upper East Side

40	45	45	40
quality	style	service	value

The Edge: See Nathan, a genius with color. It's been around forever as one of the city's top salons. Reputedly Nancy Regan used to be a regular in her pre–White House days. Recommended by one of our most stylish respondents.

Kenneth's Salon

301 Park Avenue
near 50th Street in the Waldorf Astoria / 752-1800
Mon–Tues and Thurs–Sat 9am–6pm, Wed 9am–8pm.

Haircuts & hairstylists
Midtown East

quality style service value

The Edge: The dean of the stylists. This is not where the models go now, but lots of fashion editors come here. The clientele is both an older, more established socialite crowd and working women who value the hours and the large number of good stylists. You can always get an appointment with someone good at any time. There's a separate men's styling area. Was First Lady Jacqueline Kennedy's White House stylist (she later used Joseph at the Thomas Morrisey Salon). Noted for chic service. In one hour you can get lunch, a hair styling, a manicure, and a pedicure—all while talking on the phone. Reliable, but expensive. *"I'm a regular—I love the place." "Aldo is tops!"*

La Coupe

22 East 66th Street
between 5th and Madison Avenues / 717-2060
Mon–Tues and Fri–Sat 8:30am–5pm, Wed–Thurs 8:30am–8pm.

Haircuts & hairstylists
Upper East Side

quality style service value

The Edge: A no-frills salon catering to busy professional women. Moderately priced haircuts ($30 to $85). Also manicures, pedicures, and waxing. Hair-care products are available for sale. Will mail products. Jutta and Bruno are the top stylists here.

Louis Guy D

41 East 57th Street
near Madison Avenue / 753-6078
Mon–Sat 9am–6pm.

Haircuts & hairstylists
Midtown East

The Edge: Hair salon specializing in longer hair. Only hair care—cuts and coloring. Best for longer hair. Sells its own hair-care products. Highlights for $100 to $200, depending on length. Haircut for $70 to $75. No credit cards.

Louis Licari Color Group

797 Madison Avenue, 2nd Floor
near 67th Street / 517-8084
Mon–Tues and Thurs–Fri 7:30am–6pm,
Wed and Sat 8:30am–4pm.

Haircuts & hairstylists
Upper East Side

quality style service value

The Edge: Full-service salon with early hours for working women. Full-service salon specializing in hair color. Supposed to be where Ivana Trump and Anna Wintour get their hair colored, although rumor has it that Wintour has left the salon over neglect (long waits to be taken care of). While the salon is noted for providing styles and color for many movies, including *The Age of Innocence,* for us mere mortals the treatment is less than special. The salon is crowded, noisy, and expensive. Top colorist is Louis, who charges $300 for highlights. Student nights are Wednesday nights, with color and cuts each under $20. *"Louis makes the place."*

Minardi Minardi Salon

29 East 61st Street
between Park and Madison Avenues / 308-1711

Haircuts & hairstylists
Upper East Side

Tues 8am–6pm, Wed 9am–9pm, Thurs 11am–9pm,
Fri 9am–7pm, Sat 9am–6pm.

quality style service value

The Edge: Tops for color treatments. Best known for color treatments, which are advanced. Unlike most highlight techniques, Beth Minardi cross-sections the hair with highlights applied in different directions for a more sun-bleached effect. Celebrity regulars include Tom Hanks, Sarah Jessica Parker, and Matt Dillon. Haircuts $60 to $150 (for Minardi). While color by Minardi is great, treatments are uneven, depending on the stylist. Coloring $65 and up. Highlights $175 and up. Training classes are Tuesday nights.

Oribe

691 5th Avenue, at Elizabeth Arden
near 54th Street / 319-3910
Mon–Sat 9am–5pm.

Haircuts & hairstylists
Midtown East

quality style service value

The Edge: Elizabeth Arden's full-service salon. Tends to attract an older crowd, unless you're in for the day on one of its package specials, which tend to be presents for prom girls or your mother-in-law. A good source for gifts, from a manicure to a full day of beauty treatments. Offers coloring, facials, hair styling, hair treatments, makeup, and massages. Oribe is the top hair stylist. He works with European designers including Dolce & Gabbana, Karl Lagerfeld, and Versace.

Peter Coppola

746 Madison Avenue
near 65th Street / 988-9404
Mon–Sat 9am–6pm.

Haircuts & hairstylists
Upper East Side

The Edge: Top salon for hair styling and color, but best of all, it opens at 7:30am for the working woman. Here are 16 stylists, headed by Burton Machen plus Sharon Dorram, a colorist who works on Demi Moore and Barbra Streisand. Clients include Naomi Campbell and Cindy Crawford. Geared to the working women, the salon opens early and is equipped with fax machines and portable telephones. Deluxe.

Salvatore Macri

520 Madison Avenue
between 53rd and 54th Streets / 355-0031
Weekdays 9:30am–5:30pm.

Haircuts & hairstylists
Midtown East

quality style service value

The Edge: An unusually good men's stylist. It's rare to find an up-to-date barber, who keeps to his appointments and provides (if asked) well-suited recommendations. The crowd is conservative (investment bankers, law firm partners), although he can do more casual styling. No credit cards. *"Sal's the best."*

Thomas Morrissey Salon

787 Madison Avenue
between 66th and 67th Streets / 772-1111
Mon–Wed and Fri–Sat 9am–6pm, Thurs 9am–8pm.

Haircuts & hairstylists
Upper East Side

quality style service value

The Edge: Top talent, as low-key and nice as you can get. How many salons get front-page second-section write-ups in the *New York Times* when the team bolted from Kenneth's? See Morrissey for color and Joseph for cutting and styling. Clients include Caroline Kennedy

Schlossberg, introduced to the salon by her mother, who used to be a regular. No credit cards. *"Joseph is a treasure!"*

Anushka Institute
241 East 60th Street
between 2nd and 3rd Avenues / 355-6404
Mon and Sat 9am–6pm, Tues and Thurs 10am–8pm, Wed and Fri 10am–7pm.

Personal care
Midtown East

The Edge: Pampering par excellence. A city spa (two floors in a town house) providing a full range of pampering from manicures and pedicures to massages. A good source for cellulite and body-contouring treatments. Massages (60 minutes) $65; facials, $60 to $90; pedicures, $36 to $65. The focus is fighting cellulite. Individual treatment rooms to ensure privacy.

Christiana & Carmen
128 Central Park South
between 6th and 7th Avenues / 757-5811
Weekdays 9am–7pm, Sat 9am–6pm.

Personal care
Midtown West

40 40 40 30
quality style service value

The Edge: High-end facials and body treatments. Celebrity clients include Candice Bergen, Demi Moore, and Michelle Pheiffer.

Diana Young
38 East 57th Street, 8th Floor
between Madison and Park Avenues / 753-1200
Mon–Thurs 10am–8pm, Fri 10am–6pm, Sat 9am–5pm.

Personal care
Midtown East

The Edge: Facials and more. Facials, exfoliation, hand and foot treatments, makeup applications, and other services.

Dorit Baxter Day Spa
47 West 57th Street, 3rd Floor
between 5th and 6th Avenues / 371-4542
Mon–Sat 9am–9pm.

Personal care
Midtown West

30 40 40 30
quality style service value

The Edge: A get-it-done place. A full-service salon—less luxurious than others, but nevertheless good. A 30-minute facial that leaves you ready to party, with no red skin or blotchy remains. Effects of the treatments last a week. For body treatment, Baxter uses materials from the Dead Sea for her two-hour sea-mineral-mud treatment and sea-salt body scrub (with a half-hour massage). Treatments run $60 for massage, $60 to $85 for facials, and $30 for pedicures. Less expensive alternative to the truly luxurious spas.

Eastside Massage Therapy Center
351 East 78th Street
between 1st and 2nd Avenues / 249-2927
Weekdays 11am–9:30pm, Sat 9am–7pm, Sun noon–6pm.

Personal care
Upper East Side

50 50 50 50
quality style service value

The Edge: Massages to alleviate New York's stress. Most of the center's clients are here for special treatments—alleviation of back and neck problems, athletes and dancers with overtaxed muscles, and the like. Salon directors Robin and Stuart Bragdon or their other masseurs are available for at-home calls. *"Lifesavers."*

Helen Lee Day Spa
205 East 60th Street
between 2nd and 3rd Avenues / 888-1233
Mon and Fri 9:30am–6pm, Tues–Thurs 9am–8:30pm, Sat 9am–5pm.

Personal care
Midtown East

The Edge: Chinese beauty secrets. Founded by Ford model Helen Lee, the spa features Chinese beauty secrets incorporated into its facial, waxing, pedicure, manicure, hair coloring, and other treatments.

Isabella Electrolysis
241 East 60th Street
between 2nd and 3rd Avenues / 355-6404
By appointment

Personal care
Midtown East

The Edge: Electrolysis plus videos! Electrolysis perhaps made less painful by the videos in the treatment room available for watching. No credit cards. No delivery.

Laura Geller Makeup Studios
1044 Lexington Avenue
at 74th Street / 570-5477
By appointment.

Personal care
Mail/phone

48	48	45	45
quality	style	service	value

The Edge: Where Broadway stars go for their makeup. Laura is now on the Home Shopping Network for advice and products. Does the makeup for many Broadway stars, including Ann Reinkin of *Chicago*. Just have your makup done or choose the works: haircut, facial, color, electrolysis, makeup lessons. Does weddings too. Bridal makeup costs $200; hair is an added $200. *"Couldn't be a nicer person, offering practical advice and instruction, matching her recommendations to your style." "A real find."*

Lia Schorr
686 Lexington Avenue
between 56th and 57th Streets / 486-9670
Weekdays 9am–8pm.

Personal care
Midtown East

35	40	40	28
quality	style	service	value

The Edge: Bargain student nights. High-quality treatments for men and women. Waxes, body scrubs, wraps, and more. Makeup applications as well as haircuts—but noted for its treatments. Well-trained staff—though sometimes aggressive in pushing products. Student nights are a bargain—provide training to the staff and special treatments to you.

Ling Skin Care
12 East 16th Street
near 5th Avenue / 989-8833
Weekdays 10am–7pm, Sat 9:30am–5pm.

Personal care
Flatiron/East Village

The Edge: Asian-style body care. Celebrity clients, including Marisa Tomei, Winona Ryder, and Carly Simpson, go for the 90-minute Ginseng Herbal Healing Facial ($80, or $100 with Ling).

Lori Klein
996-9390
By appointment.

Personal care
Mail/phone

quality style service value

The Edge: Marvelous looks. Lori, a former model, does makeovers and gives makeup lessons. She couldn't give you a better look. Does Barbara Walters before her shows. Great for weddings. Nice to everyone and flexible—if you need her at the last minute, she's there. Lori's in constant touch through her beeper. *"When I've had an early-morning TV appearance, Lori's here at 4:30am." "A real find."*

Mario Badescu
320 East 52nd Street
near 1st Avenue / 758-1065
Mon–Tues and Fri 10am–4pm, Wed–Thurs 11am–7pm,
Sat 9am–3:30pm.

Personal care
Midtown East

quality style service value

The Edge: Facials by hand only. 30 years' experience. Creates all the products in the salon's lab. Products are excellent, based on fresh fruits and other natural ingredients. Facials from $55. European-trained staff taught to go gentle and easy on your skin. Services include facials, massages, electrolysis, waxing, bleaching, manicures, and pedicures. *"Top drawer! "The best in town!"*

Myriam Vasicka
897 Park Avenue
between 78th and 79th Streets / 734-1017
Flexible hours 8am–6pm by appointment.

Personal care
Upper East Side

quality style service value

The Edge: Recommended electrolysis, but can be a bit pushy on appointments. Recommended by one of our more stylish respondents as her personal resource. No credit cards.

Noelle Day Spa
1100 High Ridge Road
Stamford / 203-322-3445
Mon 8:15-5:30 Wed Fri 9-6 Tue Thurs 9-8 Sat 8:30-5 Sun 10-5.

Personal care
Connecticut

The Edge: Finally the 'burbs have it all. Full service care with treatments from $6 to $405. Massages, facials and Pilates classes. *"The salon can be crowded and hectic at times, but the treatment rooms are always relaxing."*

Susan Ciminelli Day Spa
at Bergdorf Goodman's, 745 5th Avenue
between 57th and 58th Streets / 688-5500
By appointment.

Personal care
Midtown East

quality style service value

The Edge: A range of facial and body treatments. Facials, shiatsu massage, nutritional therapy, and Tibetan Reiki are specialties. The skin-care line is based on nutrient-rich seaweed.

Love Discount

2030 Broadway
near 69th Street / 877-4141
Sun–Thurs 7am–12:30am, Fri 7am–2am, Sat 8am–2am.

Pharmacies
Upper West Side

quality style service value

The Edge: Open really really late for your prescription needs. Full prescription service. Also sundries. No delivery. Discounter.

Prescriptions Limited

1151 Madison Avenue
near 86th Street. / 628-3210
Weekdays 9:30am–6pm, Sat 10am–2pm.

Pharmacies
Upper East Side

45 *45* *45* *45*

quality style service value

The Edge: Good prices for vitamins and dietary supplements.

Union Square Drugs

859 Broadway
between 17th and 18th Streets / 242-2725
Weekdays 7:30am–7pm, Sat 9am–4pm.

Pharmacies
Flatiron/East Village

The Edge: Good prices on prescription drugs and a notary on premises.

The ratings: excellent very good good fair so-so

Food & beverages

Aron Streit, Inc.
148-154 Rivington Street
between Suffolk and Clinton Streets / 475-7000
Sun–Thurs 8:30am–4:30pm.

Appetizers
Lower East Side/Chinatown

30	30	30	40
quality	style	service	value

The Edge: Passover nostalgia. Fresh-baked matzoth. Varieties include regular, whole-wheat, onion, and low-sodium. Also matzoth meal and farfel, and bags of matzoth broken in production. No credit cards. No delivery. *"Fresh, variety, mom and pop."*

Barney Greengrass
541 Amsterdam Avenue
between 86th and 87th Streets / 724-4707
Tues–Sun 8am–6pm.

Appetizers
Upper West Side

45	34	37	35
quality	style	service	value

The Edge: Best breakfast in town. Despite the crowds and lines (go before 10am or expect to wait) and atmosphere (none), you can't beat a Barney Greengrass breakfast of lox 'n' eggs, sturgeon, and other smoked fish. Bagels— of course—accompany all. There's table service and a large take-out counter. Clients allegedly include Calvin Klein and David Geffen. Mail order. *"A New York institution." "Great for breakfast, if you go early before the crowds." "Best nova in town."*

Caviarteria
502 Park Avenue
near 59th Street / 759-7410
Mon–Sat 9am–8pm, Sun 11am–4pm.

Appetizers
Midtown East

28	25	25	28
quality	style	service	value

The Edge: For those still living in the '80s, caviar. It's moved to a new location, redesigned the space (very upscale), and added a champagne bar for blinis and caviar. What's unchanged is that it sells good-quality caviar and foie gras at good prices. The least expensive caviars sold are American sturgeon and red caviar. For home use, find "broken egg" caviar, which brings the price down to almost affordable. Much of its business is mail order (call 800-4-CAVIAR). Deluxe. *"Great expensive business Christmas presents." "Overpriced."*

D'Artagnan, Inc.
399-419 St. Paul Avenue
Jersey City / 201-792-0748
Weekdays 9am–6pm.

Appetizers
New Jersey

50	40	40	40
quality	style	service	value

The Edge: For special occasions and special presents. Gift and special Christmas baskets filled with luxury foods, including prunes soaked in Armagnac, top-notch foie gras, pheasant terrine en herbette with fennel, duck galantine with apricots and foie gras, wild hare terrine with cherries, venison terrine, and cassoulet. For the health-conscious, baskets filled with free-range poultry, rabbit, wild boar from Texas, American buffalo, venison from New Zealand, free-range lamb from Australia, organic imported veal, and exotic meats like alligator tail and turtle. If that's not enough, there are whole suckling pigs and more! Delivers via overnight air anywhere and by messenger to New York. For telephone orders call toll free 800-327-8246 (800-DARTAGN). Very expensive.

Fine & Schapiro

138 West 72nd Street
between Broadway and Columbus Avenue / 877-2874
Daily 10am–10pm.

Appetizers
Upper West Side

quality	style	service	value
32	26	29	29

The Edge: A neighborhood institution offering kosher deli items. Basic dinners for at-home consumption include roast chicken, chicken in a pot, stuffed cabbage, and other standards. And, of course, the complete line of cold cuts. *"A good sandwich."*

Guss Pickles

35 Essex Street
near Hester Street / 254-4477
Sun–Thurs 9:30am–6pm, Fri 9:30am–3pm.

Appetizers
Lower East Side/Chinatown

quality	style	service	value
40	35	35	40

The Edge: A Lower East Side landmark. Inspired the movie *Crossing Delancey Street.* Features pickles, pickled tomatoes, sauerkraut, sweetkraut, and superb grated horseradish. Mail order available. Discounter. *"A New York tradition. Try the half-sours!" "The best."*

Homarus, Inc.

76 Kisco Avenue
Route 133 and Saw Mill River Parkway, Mt. Kisco / 914-666-8992
Oct 1–Apr 1, Sat 10am–3pm (retail shop and mail order).

Appetizers
Westchester

quality	style	service	value
40	30	30	40

The Edge: Wholesale smoked fish. Sells wholesale to all the fine hotels, restaurants, and shops (Zabar's and Stew Leonard's included). Offers freshly smoked (on premises) fish, including eel, Scottish salmon, and trout. Also baked salmon, jumbo shrimp, and sturgeon. Our favorite is a dill-wrapped gravlax. All-natural high-quality products. Mail order from October through early April only. Takes credit cards with mail orders. Great prices. Discounter.

Hors d'Oeuvres Unlimited

4209 Dell Avenue
at 43rd Street, North Bergen / 201-865-4545
Weekdays 7am–3pm, also Sat Dec–Jan 9am–2pm.

Appetizers
New Jersey

quality	style	service	value
15	20	30	50

The Edge: Inexpensive adequate hors d'oeuvres. Sells to restaurants, caterers, and hotels such as the Holiday Inn chain. Large selection, including asparagus rollups, clams casino, chicken sate, mushroom caps with nine fillings, shrimp toast, spinach phyllo, water chestnut wrapped in bacon, and lots more. Delivers daily to New York for a $25 delivery charge—call toll free 800-648-3787 for phone orders. *"So-so, but the price is right if you're feeding a crowd of college boys."*

Murray's Sturgeon Shop

2429 Broadway
between 89th and 90th Streets / 724-2650
Sun–Fri 8am–7pm, Sat 8am–8pm.

Appetizers
Upper West Side

quality style service value

The Edge: Absolutely outstanding smoked salmon. The prices may be the highest in the city for smoked fish, but some say no one has better tasting smoked salmon. In addition to smoked salmon, find caviar, egg salad, mushroom salad, sturgeon, whipped tuna salad, and of course, assorted terrific cream cheeses and bagels (from Columbia Hot Bagels). Prepares and sends platters. Clients are reputed to include Norman Lear, Barbra Streisand, and Robert Duvall. *"Delicious." "Good neighborhood value. Courteous and reliable."*

Petrossian

182 West 58th Street
at 7th Avenue southeast corner / 245-2217
Weekdays 10am–10pm, Sat 10am–8pm, Sun 10am–6pm.

Appetizers
Midtown West

quality style service value

The Edge: First-rate luxuries, priced accordingly. First-rate luxury items—including caviar, French chocolates, foie gras, Scottish salmon, and selected packaged goods—are sold in the "boutique" of this fashionable restaurant. Very creative gift baskets are a specialty and can include champagne and vodka (purchased through links to selected liquor stores). Prices are sky high. Delivers in New York; Fed Exes out of state. Deluxe. *"Great caviar bar." "Attentive staff." "Rip-off!"*

Russ & Daughters

179 East Houston Street
between Allen and Orchard Streets / 475-4880
Mon–Wed 9am–6pm, Thurs–Sat 9am–7pm.

Appetizers
Lower East Side/Chinatown

quality style service value

The Edge: A Lower East Side institution. Very good smoked fish and herring from around the world, plus the accouterments (cream cheese and bagels). The cream cheese and farmer cheese are very good. Also caviar, pickles, dried fruits, nuts, and candies. Prices are higher than at other Lower East Side outlets, but much lower than the uptown favorites. The quality is consistently good and the selection is broader than elsewhere downtown. *"Deli heaven!" "Close second to Balducci's." "On Friday afternoons and holidays—lines with a forever wait for service." "A New York City landmark." "Immaculate, fine quality."*

Sable's

1489 2nd Avenue
between 77th and 78th Streets / 249-6177
Weekdays 8am–8pm, Sat 8am–7:30pm, Sun 8am–5pm.

Appetizers
Upper East Side

quality style service value

The Edge: Used to be the team at Zabar's appetizer department. Ran Zabar's appetizer department for 11 years. Appetizers is what Sable's sells—chopped liver, cream cheese, salmon, smoked fish, etc. Platters and catering available. Delivers in the neighborhood. *"Wonderful service. Good deli fish selection." "Good—but you live in a city filled with great."*

Yonah Schimmel's Knishes Bakery

137 East Houston Street

Appetizers
Lower East Side/Chinatown

between 1st and 2nd Avenues / 477-2858
Daily 8am–6pm.

quality style service value

The Edge: Knishes like grandma's. A New York institution. Sells only knishes of all kinds, including potato, kasha, fruit and cheese, and more. Will make cocktail-size knishes and franks in the blanket. No credit cards. *"An institution." "Ordinary, but the kids love 'em." "Not what it once was."*

Baked Ideas
450 Broadway
near Grand Street / 925-9097
By appointment Mon–Sat 10am–6pm.

Bakery
SoHo/TriBeCa

The Edge: Delicious and pretty, a winning combination. Custom-designed cookies and cakes. Great holiday-oriented, icing-covered cookies (no one does them better). Baked items carried in the best food shops. Cookies can be used as party favors or place cards with guest names at $6 to $10 each. Works exclusively with butter-cream frostings, and can do anything in frosting. Has a great design sense—very creative. Cakes start at $100.

Bakery Soutine
104 West 70th Street
near Columbus Avenue / 496-1450
Weekdays 8am–7pm, Sat 9am–5pm (closed Sat July–Aug),
Sun 9am–3pm.

Bakery
Upper West Side

quality style service value

The Edge: Wonderful and creative. Specialties include chocolate cake (seven inch at $24) and miniatures ($1 each), including tiny fudge cakes, chocolate-raspberry-mousse cakes, honey-bourbon cakes, and crème brûlée. No credit cards.

Bijoux Doux
304 Mulberry Street
near Houston Street / 226-0948
By appointment.

Bakery
SoHo/TriBeCa

The Edge: Classically inspired wedding and special-occasion cakes. Ornate graceful cakes—for example, a wonderful model of a baroque Prague church for a wedding (it was the couple's favorite building). Everything is custom-made and requires consultation to ensure that you get what you want. The French-style cakes are wonderful and creative—and taste great! No credit cards.

Black Hound
149 1st Avenue
between 9th and 10th Streets / 979-9505
Weekdays noon–8pm, Sat noon–7pm (closed Sat in July),
Sun noon–6pm. Closed Aug.

Bakery
Flatiron/East Village

quality style service value

The Edge: Gifts worthy of any occasion. Thinks of itself as the Neiman Marcus of bakers. The flourless chocolate cake—made with cocoa, chocolate, very little sugar, and lots of eggs—is rich. Cookies are exceptional, very buttery, and the chocolate truffles are among the best in the city. Deliveries within Manhattan for large orders. For mail orders call toll free 800-344-4417. *"Wonderful gifts, beautifully wrapped!"*

Bonte Patisserie

1316 3rd Avenue
between 75th and 76th Streets / 535-2360
Mon–Sat 9am–6:30pm.

Bakery
Upper East Side

quality style service value

The Edge: Best French bakery in the city. The owner/baker came to New York to bake for Lutèce until he opened his shop in 1974. Everything is outstanding. Find fruit tarts (blueberry, plum, raspberry, and tart tatin), mousse cakes, a triangle cake (sponge cake, with meringue, almonds, and liquor), brioches, macaroons, petit fours (miniatures and large), and Grand Marnier and mocha cakes. The tarts appear to be held together just by the fruit alone, which is always of superb quality. Wonderful wedding cakes, with a vial of fresh flowers in the center. Decorations on other cakes are made from spun sugar. Did Julie Nixon's White House wedding cake. For the holidays, Bouche Noël. No credit cards. No delivery. *"Very French!" "The best pies." "Great, but during the holidays, service was a bit off."*

Cafe Lalo

201 West 83rd Street
near Broadway / 496-6031
Weekdays 9am–2pm, Sat–Sun 9am–4pm.

Bakery
Upper West Side

quality style service value

The Edge: Classic Viennese bakery. Takeout plus table service for coffee and desserts. Large selection and variety of cakes, cheesecakes, and pies. Accepts credit cards on deliveries only.

Caffè Roma

385 Broome Street
between Mulberry and Mott Streets / 226-8413
Daily 8am–midnight.

Bakery
SoHo/TriBeCa

35	35	30	30
quality	style	service	value

The Edge: The wonderful Italian rum cake. Caffè Roma is a lower-keyed less expensive Ferrara's. The decor is casual, old-fashioned soda shop–style table and chairs. It's an okay place to stop for nostalgia with your cappuccino and espresso with typical southern Italian pastry, biscotti, cannolis, and Italian cheesecake. The wonderful Italian rum cake can be decorated for special occasions. An inexpensive alternative to uptown party cakes. No credit cards. No delivery. *"Not as good as Ferrara's—but cheap."*

Ceci-Cela

55 Spring Street
near Mulberry Street / 274-9179
Daily 7am–7pm.

Bakery
SoHo/TriBeCa

The Edge: Finally a good French-style pastry shop near Mulberry Street. Features French pastries, plain and stuffed croissants, tarts, and rich cakes. No credit cards. No delivery.

Cheryl Kleinman Cakes

448 Atlantic Avenue
between Bond and Nevins Streets, Brooklyn / 718-237-2271
By appointment Mon–Sat 9am–5pm.

Bakery
Brooklyn

The Edge: Known for whimsical, highly personal custom cakes. Kleinman's personalized cakes take every shape from Fabergé eggs to porcelain jewelry boxes to the New York Yankees winning the pennant. Very creative, and perhaps more important, good-tasting cakes. Style preferences include lots of cakes done with a more traditional Old English garden look. Prices run about $6.50 per person. No credit cards.

Chez Laurence

245 Madison Avenue
at 38th Street / 683-0284
Weekdays 7am–10pm, Sat 8am–10pm.

Bakery
Gramercy Park/Murray Hill

quality style service value

The Edge: Standard French pastry fare. Features brioches, pains au chocolat, croissants, and standard French pastries.

Colette's Cakes

327 West 11th Street
between Greenwich and Washington Streets / 366-6530
By appointment.

Bakery
Greenwich Village

The Edge: High-styled delicious custom-made cakes. The specialty is whimsical, classic, and lavish cakes to order, beginning at $8 per person. Did "Madonna Goes Platinum" for a *New York* magazine contest. Very creative, good, tasty, rich moist cakes. It was good enough to be the cake of choice of the two Miller (Marie Chantal and Alexander) women at their weddings. No credit cards.

Cupcake Cafe

522 9th Avenue
near 39th Street / 465-1530
Weekdays 7am–7:30pm, Sat 8am–6pm, Sun 9am–5pm.

Bakery
Midtown West

quality style service value

The Edge: Butter-cream heaven. The artist-owner creates highly styled floral cakes that are good, rich, and butter-creamy. Offers all the standard flavors, plus Bohemian (maple-walnut), with icings to match or mix. Also wonderful coffee cake, crumb pies, doughnuts, and excellent pies. Expensive, priced from $30 to $35 for an eight-inch cake without decoration. No credit cards. *"Great cakes for all occasions." "Only if you like butter cream!" "The cupcakes are beautiful, but are too butter-creamy for my taste."*

Daniel's Bakery, Inc.

1570 1st Avenue
between 81st and 82nd Streets / 879-0139
Daily 7am–9pm.

Bakery
Upper East Side

quality style service value

The Edge: Greenberg-inspired bakery from a former Greenberg chef. If things look familiar, Daniel was a chef at William Greenberg Jr. Desserts and many of the cakes are inspired by that bakery. No delivery. *"Good quality for good prices—fresher than Greenberg's."*

De Robertis Pastry

176 1st Avenue
between 10th and 11th Streets / 674-7137
Tues–Thurs 9am–11pm, Fri–Sat 9am–midnight.

Bakery
Flatiron/East Village

quality style service value

The Edge: Best in the neighborhood. Features good to very good Sicilian pastries. When available, the fig tarts are exceptional. The chocolate-covered traditional cannolis are great! *"Casual and villagey—old-time goodness."*

Ecce Panis

1120 3rd Avenue
between 65th and 66th Streets / 535-2099
Weekdays 8am–8pm, Sat–Sun 8am–6pm.

Bakery
Upper East Side

41 | 39 | 36 | 34
quality style service value

The Edge: Could be the city's top bread source. Standard breads plus exotics, including chocolate (Friday through Sunday only), raisin-pecan-sourdough rye, focaccia-type loaves with onion and sun-dried tomatoes, walnut bread, and ciabatta and rosemary breads. Try the new olive bread. Its breads are served at the Sign of the Dove and Contrapunto, among other restaurants. It offers excellent biscotti (pistachio-almond, chocolate– macadamia nut, bourbon-pecan, and chocolate-hazelnut) and cookies (wonderful chocolate chip). Traditional Italian pan forté (fruit-and-nut Christmas cake) from Sienna in season. No delivery. *"Generous with tastings, plus a good selection."* *"Really amazing bread and attitude—so nice!"* *"The chocolate bread is best."* *"Great bread, despite the price."*

Eileen's Special Cheesecake

17 Cleveland Place
across from Lafayette and Spring Streets / 966-5585
Daily 9am–6pm.

Bakery
SoHo/TriBeCa

30 | 30 | 30 | 30
quality style service value

The Edge: More than a dozen types of cheesecake. The cheesecake is light but rich with a graham cracker crust. Flavors include fruit and chocolate. Also pies, including a Granny Smith apple pie which is quite good.

Erotic Baker

2440 Broadway
between 90th and 91st Streets / 362-7557
Tues–Fri 10am–6pm.

Bakery
Mail/phone

35 | 40 | 30 | 30
quality style service value

The Edge: Cake toppings only—you ask for it, they'll do it! Sculptured out of marzipan in designs as the name suggests. It's $35 for an eight-inch cake with marzipan topping. Give them three days' notice and they can do anything. Candy too.

Ferrara's

195 Grand Street
near Mulberry Street / 226-6150
Daily 8am–midnight.

Bakery
SoHo/TriBeCa

35 | 37 | 31 | 30
quality style service value

The Edge: One of the best pastry shops in Little Italy. A Little Italy landmark for 104 years, featuring Italian pastries, light lunches, cappuccino, and espresso. The style is glitzy (catering hall feel) with a few decent pastries. *"Delicious espresso and pastries."* *"Many homemade items."* *"Not to be missed."*

Gail Watson Custom Cakes

335 West 38th Street

Bakery
Midtown West

between 8th and 9th Avenues / 967-9167
By appointment Mon–Wed 9am–6:30pm.

The Edge: Serious chocolate cakes here. Watson does custom cakes (non-chocolate too). Favors artful tiered wedding cakes. Minimum with delivery is $100 for a cake that serves 25. Prices (depending on the detailing) run $4.25 per person up to $10 for molded flowers.

Gertel's

53 Hester Street
between Essex and Ludlow Streets / 982-3250
Sun–Thurs 6:30am–5:30pm, Fri 6:30am–3pm.

Bakery
Lower East Side/Chinatown

34	28	28	30
quality	style	service	value

The Edge: Old-fashioned kosher delights. Babkas, cakes, chocolate rolls, and strudels—with potato kugel on Thursdays. Breads include challah, cornbread, pumpernickel, and sour rye. Holiday cakes. There are a few tables for coffee and cake. *"Excellent breads. Traditional Jewish fare."*

Glendale Bake Shop

1290 Lexington Avenue
near 87th Street / 410-5959
Weekdays 6am–8pm, Sat 7am–7pm, Sun 7am–5pm.

Bakery
Upper East Side

30	28	30	28
quality	style	service	value

The Edge: Standard fare—save the calories. Baked goods from cheesecake to chocolate layer cakes, rye bread to pretzel rolls. A deli and gift department offers baskets, piñatas, and cookie jars. *"Commercial—supermarket quality." "The prices aren't that great, given the quality."*

Grossinger's Uptown

570 Columbus Avenue
near 88th Street / 874-6996
Mon–Thurs 7:30am–7pm, Fri 7:30am–sundown, Sun 7:30am–5pm.

Bakery
Upper West Side

40	30	40	40
quality	style	service	value

The Edge: A good kosher bakery. Best known for its cheese and ice cream (especially praline ice cream) cakes. Also challah, six-grain bread, and strudels. The prices are good. *"Great ice cream cake." "Good value." "It wouldn't be my birthday without their praline cake!"*

Houghtaling Mousse Pie Ltd.

389 Broome Street
near Mulberry Street / 226-3724
Weekdays 9am–6:30pm.

Bakery
SoHo/TriBeCa

The Edge: Rich dense desserts. The specialty is chocolate-truffle cake, intensely rich. The lemon mousse with shortbread pie is great. Ten varieties of mousse pies and six kinds of mousse cakes are featured. Sold at some of the finest city restaurants and food emporiums including Dean & Deluca and Fairway. Custom decoration and mail order are available. Deliveries with two days' notice, but only on Tuesday and Thursday. Prices at the shop are wholesale.

Krispy Kreme

265 West 23th Street
between 7th and 8th Avenues / 620-0111
Mon–Thurs 6am–midnight, Fri–Sat 6am–2am, Sun 6am–10pm.

Bakery
Chelsea

48	28	40	35
quality	style	service	value

The Edge: Best doughnuts in the city. Imported from New Orleans—15 varieties of wonderful doughnuts. Our favorite is its famous glazed doughnut. A celebrity hang-out. No credit cards. No delivery. *"Best doughnuts—especially when hot." "Decadent! Long lines." "Heavenly!"*

Little Pie Company

Bakery
Midtown West

424 West 43rd Street
between 9th and 10th Avenues / 736-4780
Weekdays 8am–8pm, Sat 10am–6pm, Sun noon–6pm.

quality style service value

The Edge: The best American-style pies! Wonderful fresh-fruit pies and other specialties that change with the season. Also cakes and muffins. A Martha Stewart source. No delivery. *"Prime quality. Long lines at holiday time—so reserve early." "It wouldn't be a holiday without a trudge to 43rd Street." "Superb!"*

Margaret Braun Cakes

Bakery
Mail/phone

33 Bank Street
at West 4th Street / 929-1582
By appointment.

The Edge: Braun, a former artist, expresses herself in her cakes. Dense flavors. Fabulous sweet-tasting cakes feature lifelike sugar portraits, which could include reproductions of photos, magazine covers, and the like. In a *New York* magazine contest she did a lifelike stage bill of Kathleen Battle returning to the Met. Also wedding cakes and custom-designed cakes for all occasions, priced from $250. Cakes run about $10 per person. No credit cards. *"10 for style and flavor." "Pricey but worth it."*

Marnie Carmichael / Noonie's Traditional Southern

45 Carmine Street, Suite 5A
near Bedford Street / 691-0673
By appointment.

Bakery
Greenwich Village

The Edge: Delicious, beautifully presented sweet-looking and -tasting gifts. Customized, creatively styled southern round pound cakes displayed in fancy hat boxes with a nosegay of fresh flowers packed in the middle. These customized cakes can be all her imagination and your pocketbook will allow! Cakes run $60 to $250 and up. These cakes are apparently a favorite gift item of Condé Nast, Gitano jeans, and Mike Ovitz, formerly of Creative Artists Agency (Ovitz traditionally sent her cakes to his Creative Artists Agency clients celebrating their Oscar wins!).

Marquet Patisserie

Bakery
Flatiron/East Village

15 East 12th Street
near 5th Avenue / 229-9313
Mon–Sat 7:30am–8pm.

The Edge: French perfection. Known for her elegant marquise cake rimmed with ladyfingers, filled with chocolate mousse, and topped with decorative chocolate. Also petit fours iced in pastel colors. Now offers a small menu of prepared foods, including our French favorite—sausage and lentils. Coffee and pastries served in the store. Inexpensive.

Patisserie Claude

Bakery
Greenwich Village

187 West 4th Street

between 6th and 7th Avenues / 255-5911
Daily 8am–8pm.

quality style service value

The Edge: Moderate prices make this a favorite. Features a full range of good, but conventional, home-style French bakery items, including nice fruit tarts (especially tarte tartin), croissants, and brioches. Nice napoleons also. No delivery. No credit cards.

Patisserie Lanciani

Bakery
Greenwich Village

414 West 14th Street
between 9th and 10th Avenues / 989-1213
Mon–Sat 8am–8pm, Sun 9am–8pm.

40 30 33 40

quality style service value

The Edge: A pleasant cafe plus a good French bakery. Good country French bread and pastries. Expect to wait in line for the few tables on Friday and Saturday nights. Owner Lanciani was the pastry chef at the Plaza Hotel and later at the Palace. His specialties are wonderful tarts, including French nut tarts, tarte tatin, and lemon tarts, as well as a signature white-chocolate-mousse cake. Of course, croissants, brioches, and the rest. Good special-occasion cakes. Special orders require at least three days' notice. Will accommodate customer preferences on special orders. *"A quiet spot to relax and treat yourself." "Love the lemon tarts."*

Patisserie Les Friandises

Bakery
Upper East Side

972 Lexington Avenue
between 70th and 71st Streets / 988-1616
Mon–Sat 9am–7pm, Sun 10am–5pm (closed Sun July–Aug).

The Edge: Good French tarts. Its specialty tarte tatin is sold in 6-, 8-, and 10-inch sizes for $10.50, $21, and $38, respectively. Also sticky buns and lemon tarts.

Ron Ben-Israel Cakes

Bakery
Midtown West

130 West 25th Street
between 6th and 7th Avenues / 627-2418
By appointment.

43 43 45 38

quality style service value

The Edge: Where Martha indulges! Sugar flowers are his specialty. The cakes are light, moist, and on the sweet side, with a minimum price of $250. His cakes have celebrity status, having been featured on Oprah's show and in *Martha Stewart Living* and *Modern Bride*. Required advance notice is 24 hours for simple cakes up to six months for highly complex, designed large cakes. No credit cards.

Rosie's Creations

Bakery
Mail/phone

362-6069
By appointment.

The Edge: Edible cake toppers that can be kept for years as mementos. Ricki Arno's husband nicknamed her Rosie—hence Rosie's Creations is her name for this unique business which uses her talents as an artist, confectioner, and baker. She'll make your wedding topper to resemble you and your groom, complete with faces, clothing, furniture, and hobbies. She's not cheap—toppers start at $2,000, plus the cost of the cake. Allow two to three months' notice. Requires 50% deposit.

Royale Pastry Shop

237 West 72nd Street
between Broadway and West End Avenue / 874-5642
Mon–Thurs 6am–8pm, Fri 6am–4pm, Sun 7am–7pm.

Bakery
Upper West Side

quality style service value

The Edge: At least it's kosher. Except for the rugelach and babka (which are particularly good here), you can miss this place. Features French and Danish pastries and breads, including Jewish rye, corn rye, challah, and whole-wheat. The rich frosted cakes are overly sweet and heavy. *"Great Passover matzoth and that's it." "Kosher, crowded, okay."*

Sant Ambroeus Ltd.

1000 Madison Avenue
between 77th and 78th Streets / 570-2211
Mon–Sat 9:30am–10:30pm, Sun 10:30am–6pm.

Bakery
Upper East Side

quality style service value

The Edge: Desserts are good, but it's beauty over taste. This is a bakery in front of a branch of a Milanese restaurant that serves mostly light pasta meals. You'll find eclairs, cream puffs, cupcakes dotted with candied fruit, and rich cakes made with chestnut purée, chocolate and orange liqueur, and whipped cream. The cakes are gorgeous and somehow more formal. Very expensive, plus there's a delivery charge. *"Beautiful cakes, but they don't taste as good as they look."*

Sylvia Weinstock Cakes

273 Church Street
between Franklin and White Streets / 925-6698
Weekdays by appointment 8am–6:30pm.

Bakery
SoHo/TriBeCa

quality style service value

The Edge: Sets the style in beautiful floral-bouquet specialty cakes. One of the first of the creative custom cake designers. Best known for her elegant English garden floral-bouquet cakes, but fun and imaginative designs are possible, including a Keds sneaker accurate down to the side label. Her celebrity clientele includes Eddie Murphy, Whitney Houston, and Natosha Richardson. Very expensive. No credit cards. Deluxe. *"Set's the standard for all the rest!" "Disappointed. Donald Trump's wedding cake s—d." "Love the look." "Uneven flavors—make sure you like what you get!"*

Umanoff & Parsons

467 Greenwich Street
near Watts Street / 219-2240
Weekdays 8:30am–5:30pm.

Bakery
SoHo/TriBeCa

The Edge: A wholesale bakery that sells retail. Features apple brown Betty, turtle cheesecake (with pecans, chocolate, and caramel), orange bundt cake, and three kinds of quiche (broccoli and cheddar, spinach and mushroom, and Lorraine). No credit cards. Delivers.

Veniero's Pasticceria

342 East 11th Street
near 1st Avenue / 674-7264
Daily 8am–midnight.

Bakery
Flatiron/East Village

quality style service value

The Edge: Excellent Sicilian pastry—best prices. Excellent biscotti, candies, crisp ricotta cheesecakes, and rum cakes. Best of all are its small (petit-four size) Italian pastries, which are great for dessert parties. Delivery service is a real bonus, but requires three to four days' notice. Prices are very reasonable. *"Number 1 pastry and coffee." "Mostly I get the minis, also available at Balducci's." "Great pastries, great place for dessert. Unfortunately, always very crowded." "Excellent Bavarian crème-filled cakes!" "New York's best Italian confectioner."*

William Greenberg Jr. Desserts
Weekdays 8am–6:30pm, Sat 8:30am–5pm.

Bakery
Multiple locations

quality style service value

The Edge: Old-fashioned American-style desserts. Best known for its dense, rich, bitter-chocolate-frosted chocolate cake, strawberry shortcake, brownies, and honey buns. Once a year, in late summer, the brownies go on sale for 10% off. The decorated cakes are works of art and priced to match. He did the enormous cake for President Clinton's New York City 50th-birthday-bash fund-raiser. Very expensive. No delivery. *"The best cookies in the world—let alone New York City—an institution!" "I love his pies at Thanksgiving." "Best birthday cake in town."*

Locations: Gramercy Park/Murray Hill: 518 3rd Avenue, between 34th and 35th Streets (686-3344) / **Upper West Side:** 2187 Broadway, between 77th and 78th Streets (580-7300)

B&E
511 West 23rd Street
near 10th Avenue / 243-6812
Mon–Thurs 9am–6:30pm, Fri–Sat 9am–7pm.

Beverages
Chelsea

The Edge: Substantial discounts. Sells all the standard brands of soda and beer at good prices.

Milkman
P.O. Box 794
Midtown Post Office / 279-6455
Weekdays 7am–3pm.

Beverages
Mail/phone

The Edge: Excellent-quality milk delivered at a reasonable price. Milk, juice, and bottled water delivered to your door—daily, weekly, or on request.

A. Zito and Son's Bakery
259 Bleecker Street
between 6th and 7th Avenues / 929-6139
Mon–Sat 6am–7pm, Sun 6am–3pm.

Bread
Greenwich Village

quality style service value

The Edge: Some say the best Sicilian bread in the city. Italian whole-wheat, semolina, and white breads, plus bread made with prosciutto and provolone, all handmade and baked in brick ovens. No credit cards. No delivery. *"Great crusty whole-wheat breads." "Every bread is excellent—just the smell is heavenly."*

Bagelry
1324 Lexington Avenue
between 88th and 89th Streets / 996-0567
Weekdays 7am–7:15pm, Sat 7am–6:45pm, Sun 7am–5:45pm.

Bread
Upper East Side

quality style service value

The Edge: Good bagels in a city known for bagels. Uses salt instead of sugar. Also find bialys and high-quality smoked fish from Maine's Duck Trap River Farms, including smoked trout, salmon, and peppered salmon. Free delivery in the neighborhood or mail order by phone (call toll free 800-43-BAGEL). No credit cards. *"Fresh bagels, good coffee."*

Bagels on the Square
7 Carmine Street
near 7th Avenue / 691-3041
Daily 24 hours.

Bread
Greenwich Village

quality style service value

The Edge: A good source for bagels and the fixings. Makes 18 varieties of old-fashioned, hand-formed bagels as well as 20 different kinds of cream cheeses to match. Mail order available. No credit cards.

Columbia Hot Bagels
2836 Broadway
corner 110th Street / 222-3200
Daily 24 hours.

Bread
Upper West Side

quality style service value

The Edge: Some say the best of the New York bagels. A wide selection of bagels. These are the bagels sold at Murray's and Zabar's, among other places. No credit cards. Delivers. *"My favorite bagel source." "Zabar's sells Columbias—they're good but not as good as H&H."*

D&G Bakery
45 Spring Street
between Mott and Mulberry Streets / 226-6688
Daily 8am–2pm.

Bread
SoHo/TriBeCa

quality style service value

The Edge: A. Zito's rival for the best bread in the city. Handmade, crusty, flavorful Sicilian bread, baked in a 100-year-old coal-fired brick oven. Breads includes white, whole-wheat, prosciutto, and provolone. D&G supplies bread to Balducci's, Jefferson Market, Fairway, and East Village Cheese, among others. Good prices. No credit cards. No delivery.

Ess-A-Bagel
Mon–Sat 6:30am–10pm, Sun 6:30am–5pm.

Bread
Multiple locations

quality style service value

The Edge: Another great bagel source. The standard bagel assortment. With the bagels—fish, cream cheese, and vegetarian spreads. Will Fed Ex bagels anywhere. *"Delicious!" "Sometimes too doughy." "Great, but crowded."*

Locations: Gramercy Park/Murray Hill: 359 1st Avenue, near 21st Street (260-2252) / **Midtown East:** 831 3rd Avenue, near 51st Street (980-1010)

H&H Bagels
Daily 24 hours.

Bread
Multiple locations

quality style service value

The Edge: Among the top contenders for the best bagels in New York City. Baked fresh daily with new batches every few hours. Prices are among the highest in the city. Deliveries on orders of 10 dozen or more. Mail order available (call toll free 800-NYBAGEL). Ships worldwide. Those who love it, love it, but others find the bagels too heavy. *"What New York is all about." "The best." "Great bagels—just too big."*

Locations: Midtown West: 639 West 46th Street, near 12th Avenue (595-8000) / **Upper East Side:** 1551 2nd Avenue, near 80th Street (734-7441) / **Upper West Side:** 2239 Broadway, near 80th Street (595-8000)

Kossar's Bialystoker Kuchen Bakery
367 Grand Street
between Essex and Norfolk Streets / 473-4810
Daily 24 hours.

Bread
Lower East Side/Chinatown

quality style service value

The Edge: Best bialys and onion boards in the city. Also bagels and onion rolls. Four items, that's it! The onions are fresh and ground by hand in the basement. Zabar's carries the bialys. No credit cards. No delivery. *"Best in class." "Best bialys in the city, but the service is slow." "Cheaper at Fairway."*

Orwasher's Bakery
308 East 78th Street
between 1st and 2nd Avenues / 288-6569
Mon–Sat 7am–7pm.

Bread
Upper East Side

quality style service value

The Edge: 36 types of bread and rolls sold to many top New York restaurants. Bread varieties made by hand. Breads include challah, cinnamon-raisin, Irish soda, onion boards, raisin-pumpernickel, and rye. Special-order breads by 3pm the day before you want them. The bread sells fast, so reserve or go early if you want to ensure a particular item. Also a small selection of standard imported cheeses. Very reasonable. No credit cards. No delivery. *"Excellent expensive breads." "A New York must." "Perfection defined—their rye, dark pumpernickel, and corn breads."*

Pick a Bagel
1475 2nd Avenue
near 77th Street / 717-4668
Daily 6am–midnight.

Bread
Upper East Side

quality style service value

The Edge: Bagels and their accouterments. A bagel cafe with delivery. *"Humongous bagels." "Bagels and muffins are good!" "Great nova and caviar."*

Vesuvio Bakery
160 Prince Street
near West Broadway / 925-8248
Mon–Sat 7am–7pm.

Bread
SoHo/TriBeCa

quality style service value

The Edge: Excellent, handmade Italian bread. No credit cards. No delivery.

Bazzini Importers
339 Greenwich Street
near Jay Street / 334-1280
Weekdays 8am–7pm, Sat 9:30am–6pm.

Candy, fruit & nuts
SoHo/TriBeCa

quality style service value

The Edge: The nuts are what's special. This is a wholesale operation open for retail sales. It supplies Dean & DeLuca and many of the best gourmet shops with nuts and dried fruits. Best are the butter-toffee peanuts, fresh-roasted cashews, and nut crunches. Also find candy and imported packaged cookies, coffee, condiments, gift baskets, and good baked goods. Deliveries for very large orders only. Good prices always, but even better prices if you buy more than five pounds. Discounter. *"I found the pistachios too salty."*

Economy Candy Corp.
108 Rivington Street
between Essex and Ludlow Streets / 254-1531
Weekdays 8:30am–6pm, Sat 10am–5pm.

Candy, fruit & nuts
Lower East Side/Chinatown

quality style service value

The Edge: Prices are about half those uptown. Find hundreds of kinds of chocolates (including baking varieties), dried fruits, nuts, and penny candies. The wide-ranging candy selection includes Baby Ruths, Baci, fresh halvah cut to order, chocolates of every conceivable kind, and boxed gift candies, as well as sugar-free varieties. Pick N' Mix gift baskets from $25. Prices are excellent, wholesale (for very large orders) or retail at near-wholesale prices. Mail-order catalog available.

5th Avenue Chocolatiere
510 Madison Avenue
near 53rd Street / 935-5454
Mon–Sat 9am–6pm, Sun 10am–5pm.

Candy, fruit & nuts
Midtown East

quality style service value

The Edge: The style of the old Kron Chocolatiere. Chocolates come packaged in attractive wooden crates. Specialties include fresh and dried fruits dipped in semisweet chocolate, fresh truffles, and bittersweet or milk chocolate molded into telephones, champagne bottles, records, tennis racquets, golf balls, and women's legs. Will make a chocolate version of anything you want with two weeks' notice. Charges for deliveries in Manhattan. Mail order elsewhere.

Godiva Chocolatier
Weekdays 9am–6pm.

Candy, fruit & nuts
Multiple locations

quality style service value

The Edge: Department store sweets—the Bergdorf of its kind. Sweets in gold boxes sold prepackaged or purchased loose. Mostly chocolates filled with cream fillings and some with nuts. *"Not specific to New York—they're in every mall."*

Locations: Lower Manhattan: 33 Maiden Lane, near Nassau Street (809-8990) / 225 Liberty Street, World Financial Center, Winter Garden (945-2174) / **Midtown East:** 560 Lexington Avenue, near 50th Street (980-9810) / 200 Park Avenue, at 45th Street (697-9128) / 701 5th Avenue, near 55th Street (593-2848) / **Midtown West:** 30 Rockefeller Plaza, near 50th Street (765-4336) / **Upper West Side:** 245 Columbus Avenue, between 71st and 72nd Streets (787-5804)

Kadouri & Son, Inc.
51 Hester Street
near Essex Street / 677-5441
Sun–Thurs 8am–6pm, Fri 8am–3pm.

Candy, fruit & nuts
Lower East Side/Chinatown

The Edge: Low, low prices. The shop looks run-down, but it sells nuts, dried fruit, coffees, beans, and herbs and spices at close-to-wholesale prices.

La Maison du Chocolat
25 East 73rd Street
between 5th and Madison Avenues / 744-7117
Weekdays 10am–6:30pm, Sat 10am–6pm.

Candy, fruit & nuts
Upper East Side

50 | 50 | 45 | 38
quality style service value

The Edge: Exceptional Parisian chocolates, the best in New York. This shop is an affiliate of a Parisian chocolate store on Rue du Faubourg Saint-Honoré. Very rich, fabulous chocolate in 27+ combinations. Specialties include fruit pâtés, rich and buttery chocolate truffles, arribas (bittersweet wafers filled with a thin layer of chocolate ganache), Valencia (fresh orange peel and orange liqueur), rochers (hazelnut and almond praline covered in dark or light chocolate), and chocolate-covered chestnuts in season. The chocolate truffles are bittersweet and extremely fresh, and should be eaten immediately—everything else within two weeks! Nan Kemper wouldn't end a dinner party without these chocolates. Very, very expensive and very very special! *"Enjoy—you only live once!"*

Li-Lac Chocolates
120 Christoper Street
between Bleecker and Hudson Streets / 242-7374
Labor Day–Memorial Day, Mon–Sat 10am–8pm, Sun noon–5pm;
Memorial Day– Labor Day, Tues–Sat noon–8pm, Sun noon–5pm.

Candy, fruit & nuts
Greenwich Village

48 | 45 | 48 | 43
quality style service value

The Edge: Loyalists call them the best chocolates in the world. A Greenwich Village tradition since 1923. Not fancy. Chocolates are made from blocks of chocolate from Peter's, a division of Nestlé. The chocolates are then melted, reformed, and filled—all by hand, daily, in small batches using fresh ingredients. No preservatives. Specialties include turtles, butter crunch, French cream rolls, and the Taste of New York collection—hand-molded solid-chocolate replicas of the Empire State Building and the Statue of Liberty. Messenger service delivers chocolates in Manhattan (you pay their charge), mail order elsewhere. *"Small but heavenly." "Turtles to die for."*

Mondel Chocolates
2913 Broadway
near 114th Street / 864-2111
Weekdays 11am–7pm, Sun noon–5pm (closed Sun July–Aug).

Candy, fruit & nuts
Upper West Side

40 | 40 | 40 | 40
quality style service value

The Edge: Chocolate happiness for Columbia students. Since 1943 Mondel has offered candy corn, chocolate-covered ginger and fruit, chocolate cups (filled with espresso, mint, or kirsch), hand-dipped apricots, hard candies, jellybeans, lollipops, and very good turtles. Find chocolates molded as alligators, cowboys, guitars, mice, pigs, Rolls-Royces, tennis racquets, and Volkswagens. Also holiday gift packages. Delivers.

Neuchâtel Chocolates
Weekdays 10am–6pm.

Candy, fruit & nuts
Multiple locations

quality   style   service   value

The Edge: Unique flavored truffles. Very fresh rich truffles. Intensely flavorful chocolates are packaged in constantly changing gift packages for all occasions, including bar/bas mitzvahs, weddings, and birthdays. Unique chocolate gifts.

Locations: Lower Manhattan: 60 Wall Street, near William Street (480-3766) / **Midtown West:** 2 West 59th Street, the Plaza Hotel (751-7742)

Perugina
520 Madison Avenue
between 53rd and 54th Streets / 688-2490
Weekdays 10am–6pm, Sat 11am–5pm.

Candy, fruit & nuts
Midtown East

quality   style   service   value

The Edge: Everyone knows these chocolates, or at least Baci. The shop features the familiar Baci, butter creams, pralines, gianduia, hard candies, chocolate ore liete, and lazzaroni cookies in attractive gift boxes and pretty porcelain bowls. Moderately expensive. *"Great gifts."* *"Overpriced." "Very good hard candies."*

Rich Art
7 East 55th Street
near 5th Avenue / 371-0364
Weekdays 10am–7pm, Sat 10am–6pm.

Candy, fruit & nuts
Midtown East

quality   style   service   value

The Edge: Perfection. Perfect chocolates from the Richart family of Lyons, France. Expect exceptional treats (filled chocolates in an assortment of flavors), pralines intensified with roasted nuts, ganaches (a floral bouquet of violet, rose, and jasmine with an infusion of mint), fruit coulis infused with apricots from the Rhône Valley, lemons or Aquitaine plums blended with Corinthian raisins, and more. Whimsical children's drawings of people, animals, sports, and more adorn the chocolates. For special occasions, order chocolates with appropriate inscriptions or for fabulous corporate gifts with your logo or personal messages inscribed. Prices are sky high—16 pieces (not close to a pound) for $25. Delivery charge is $10 per person. Delivers. Credit cards accepted. *Harpers Bazaar's* view: *"It's about savoring one gorgeous Richart chocolate, not inhaling the whole box."* *Elle's* opinion: *"It's almost too much pleasure."*

Sweet Life
63 Hester Street
near Ludlow Street / 598-0092
Sun–Fri 9am–6pm.

Candy, fruit & nuts
Lower East Side/Chinatown

quality   style   service   value

The Edge: An old-fashioned candy store. Features candy, chocolates, coffees, dried fruit, fruit slices, jams, nuts, 10 kinds of halvah, and teas. Gift baskets with stuffed animals and mugs, to enhance the present, are available. Good prices. Discounter. *"Sample the odd item—there's usually a good find."*

Toraya

Candy, fruit & nuts
Upper East Side

17 East 71st Street
near Madison Avenue / 861-1700
Mon–Sat 10am–6pm.

quality style service value

The Edge: Japanese tranquillity in the midst of New York's madness. A traditional Japanese confectionery. The tea and candy are downstairs in the shop, with a tea room in the back. The Tea Room does a traditional Japanese tea ceremony. Tea served from 11am to 6pm.

Wolsk's Confections

Candy, fruit & nuts
Lower East Side/Chinatown

81 Ludlow Street
near Delancey Street / 475-7946
Sun–Thurs 9am–5pm, Fri 9am–3pm.

quality style service value

The Edge: Number 1 for all your childhood favorites. Chocolates, 50 varieties of nuts fresh roasted at the store, and 30 kinds of dried fruit. Extensive gift basket options. Hundreds of penny candies. Discounter.

Alleva Dairy

Cheese
SoHo/TriBeCa

188 Grand Street
at Mulberry Street / 226-7990
Mon–Sat 8:30am–6pm, Sun 8:30am–3pm.

The Edge: The oldest Italian cheese store in the city. All the Italian cheese greats: ricotta and mozzarella (plain, smoked, and rolled around prosciutto), Mascarpone and Gorgonzola torta with basil. Plus fresh and dried pasta, with sauces to complement. Mail order available. Discounter.

Ben's Cheese Shop

Cheese
Lower East Side/Chinatown

181 East Houston Street
near Orchard Street / 254-8290
Mon–Thurs 8:30am–5:30pm,
Fri 7:30am–3:30pm, Sun 7:30am–6pm.

quality style service value

The Edge: The place for variety and quality in cream cheese and farmer cheese. This is the Lower East Side, so don't expect service and do expect Sunday crowds. Here the farmer cheese comes in multiple flavors, including nut and raisin, blueberry, strawberry, and pineapple. Cream cheese also in multiple flavors, including garlic, herb, scallion, and vegetable. The cheese is sold as well at Fairway, at close to Ben's prices. Unbelievably fresh. Inexpensive. No credit cards. No delivery. Discounter.

East Village Cheese Shop

Cheese
Flatiron/East Village

40 3rd Avenue
between 9th and 10th Streets / 477-2601
Weekdays 9am–6:30pm, Sat–Sun 9am–6pm.

quality style service value

The Edge: Limited selection of foods, but good quality at East Village prices. A fine but limited selection of basic imported cheese, good breads, and other items, including coffee, cold cuts, and olive oil. No credit cards. No delivery. Discounter. *"The prices are good but the help can be rude."*

Harry Wils & Company

Cheese
SoHo/TriBeCa

182 Duane Street
between Greenwich and Hudson Streets / 431-9731
Weekdays 9am–5pm.

The Edge: Fresh, fresh, fresh. Supplies butter, eggs, and yogurt to better restaurants and gourmet shops. Reasonable prices and top quality. No credit cards. No delivery.

Ideal Cheese Shop

Cheese
Upper East Side

1205 2nd Avenue
between 63rd and 64th Streets / 688-7579
Weekdays 9am–6:30pm, Sat 8:30am–6pm.

quality style service value

The Edge: For many, this is New York's only cheese shop. Hundreds of domestic and imported cheeses, in perfect condition, are available in this very small shop. Some rare cheeses are here only. A very select selection. Additional specialties include pâtés, smoked salmon, French saucisson, specialty meats, olives, cheese straws, and La Semeuse coffee (served at Lutèce). Price list available for mail order. Expensive. *"The best cheese in town!"*

Joe's Dairy

Cheese
SoHo/TriBeCa

156 Sullivan Street
near Houston Street / 677-8780
Tues–Sat 9am–6:30pm.

The Edge: Among the best mozzarella in the city. Exceptional mozzarella, made daily and all throughout the day. Smoked and plain mozzarella made daily, and on weekends smoked and pepper-cured prosciutto balls. Also find bocconcini (small marinated mozzarella balls with garlic and red pepper). No credit cards. No delivery.

LaMarca Cheese Shop

Cheese
Gramercy Park/Murray Hill

161 East 22nd Street
near 3rd Avenue / 673-7920
Weekdays 10am–6:45pm, Sat 10:30am–5:30pm (closed Sat in summer).

The Edge: Top quality, reasonable prices for Italian cheese, bread, and pasta. Offers fresh mozzarella made daily, plus a wide range of pastas and fresh soups. Terrific breads. Some from Marie's in Hoboken. Reasonable prices. Delivery during the week from 6 to 10pm. No credit cards.

Murray's Cheese Shop

Cheese
Greenwich Village

257 Bleecker Street
near Cornelia Street / 243-3289
Mon–Sat 8am–8pm, Sun 9am–6pm.

44 | 40 | 40 | 38
quality style service value

The Edge: Very high-quality cheeses at reasonable, often discounted, prices. Large selection of moderately priced excellent cheeses, with a limited variety of fresh pastas, sauces, breads, pitas, and sliced meats, and a whole line of gourmet groceries. No credit cards. *"Nice selection." "Be sure to check the weekly specials for the best prices." "Rude—cold."*

9th Avenue Cheese Market

525 9th Avenue
between 39th and 40th Streets / 564-7127
Daily 8am–7pm.

Cheese
Midtown West

quality style service value

The Edge: Hundreds of cheeses—best are Greek and Middle Eastern. Broad selection of traditional cheeses from all over, although Greek products are emphasized. Carries 15 kinds of feta cheese alone. Also find breads, caviars, coffees, dried fruits, jams, olives, Russian sausages, and more. Low prices.

Russo & Son Dairy Products

344 East 11th Street
between 1st and 2nd Avenues / 254-7452
Mon–Sat 9am–7pm, Sun 11am–3pm.

Cheese
Flatiron/East Village

The Edge: Quality classic Italian products. A small store that makes fresh mozzarella several times daily, smoked mozzarella, mozzarella with prosciutto, and salami. Also pastas, cheeses, sliced meats, and breads. Inexpensive. No delivery. Discounter.

Adriana's Caravan

409 Vanderbilt Street
Brooklyn / 800-316-0820
Daily 9am–8pm.

Coffees, teas & spices
Mail/phone

The Edge: Wide range of condiments and seasonings. It's virtually impossible to need something it doesn't have. While the selection is good and sometimes it's the only source, prices are high. You'll find spices and packaged and dried ingredients from all over the world. Mail, phone, and fax orders only.

Angelica's Traditional Herbs and Spices

147 1st Avenue
near 9th Street / 529-4335
Mon–Sat 10am–7:45pm, Sun 11am–6:45pm.

Coffees, teas & spices
Flatiron/East Village

quality style service value

The Edge: One of the best herb and spice shops in the city. Features thousands of Western and Chinese herbs. Also organic foodstuff, including organically grown grains (10 different types of rice) and 50 types of teas and dried fruits. No credit cards. No delivery.

Aphrodisia

264 Bleecker Street
near 10th Avenue / 989-6440
Mon–Sat 11am–7pm, Sun noon–5pm.

Coffees, teas & spices
Greenwich Village

quality style service value

The Edge: The oldest herb and spice store in the city. Features more than 1,000 different herbs and spices. Half the store is devoted to cooking and the other half to medicinal herbs. *"Can be rude, but then I'm not big on organic herbs and spices."*

Coffee Grinder

348 East 66th Street
between 1st and 2nd Avenues / 737-3490
Weekdays 9:30am–7pm, Sat 9:30am–6pm.

Coffees, teas & spices
Upper East Side

quality style service value

The Edge: Best known for its custom-blended coffees and teas. Also features coffee makers and coffee gift baskets, plus salad dressings and marmalades. *"Great selection."*

D'Amico Foods

309 Court Street
Brooklyn / 718-875-5403
Mon–Sat 8am–7pm.

Coffees, teas & spices
Brooklyn

The Edge: Great coffee specials. Roasts its own coffees—good quality at excellent prices. Lots of coffee choices, including the house blend, Costa Rican and Mocha Java; also Colombian Supremo, French and Viennese roast, Colombian Light, Kenya AA, and much more. A large mail-order business (shipping is $3.40). Frequent specials on mail-order coffees are offered, which make the prices even better. Discounter.

Empire Coffee and Tea

592 9th Avenue
between 42nd and 43rd Streets / 586-1717
Weekdays 8am–7pm, Sat 9:30am–6:30pm,
Sun 11am–5pm (closed Sun in summer).

Coffees, teas & spices
Midtown West

quality style service value

The Edge: Selection. 90 kinds of coffee and 75 varieties of loose teas from every imaginable region. Prices are reasonable if not downright low, but 9th Avenue in the 40s is not our favorite shopping area.

M. Rohrs

303 East 85th Street
between 1st and 2nd Avenues / 396-4456
Mon–Sat 7am–8pm, Sun 10am–6pm.

Coffees, teas & spices
Upper East Side

The Edge: Excellent coffees, before the current coffee craze. Since 1896. Features over 30 kinds of coffees and more than 19 kinds of loose tea, as well as candies, honeys, and accessories, including coffee pots, filters, tea pots, and strainers. Coffees and teas are sold in antique red-and-gold coffee tins. It's fighting the trend with "no coffee bar now envisioned." Prices are very good, and made even better by the high quality.

McNulty's Tea and Coffee Company

109 Christoper Street
between Bleecker and Hudson Streets / 242-5351
Mon–Sat 10am–9pm, Sun 1–7pm.

Coffees, teas & spices
Greenwich Village

quality style service value

The Edge: Broad selection of teas and coffees. More than 75 varieties of coffees and 25 varieties of teas, from the standard to the rare. Good prices. Call toll free 800-356-5200 for phone orders. *"Old world."*

Open Pantry

Coffees, teas & spices
Flatiron/East Village

184 2nd Avenue
near 11th Street / 677-2640
Daily 7:30am–11pm.

The Edge: Another good choice for coffees and teas. Full range of coffees and teas. Check out the weekly specials. Inexpensive.

Oren's Daily Roast

Coffees, teas & spices
Multiple locations

Mon–Thurs 7am–8pm, Fri 7am–7pm, Sat 10am–6pm.

36	36	32	23
quality	style	service	value

The Edge: Good prices and a wide selection of coffees. Coffee is roasted daily and brought to the shop's six locations. More than 50 kinds of coffees from all over the world, including flavored coffees. Expensive, with prices per pound starting at $9 and going to $39 for Jamaica Blue Mountain. *"Great selection. Pricey." "Fast service."*

Locations: **Flatiron/East Village:** 31 Waverly Place, near University Place (420-5958) / **Gramercy Park/Murray Hill:** 434 3rd Avenue, near 31st Street (779-1241) / **Midtown East:** 33 East 58th Street, between Madison and Park Avenues (838-3345) / **Upper East Side:** 1144 Lexington Avenue, between 79th and 80th Streets (472-6830) / 985 Lexington Avenue, near 71st Street (717-3907) / 1574 1st Avenue, between 81st and 82nd Streets (737-2690)

Porto Rico Importing Company

Coffees, teas & spices
Multiple locations

Weekdays 8am–8pm, Sat 9am–8pm, Sun noon–7pm.

42	46	50	42
quality	style	service	value

The Edge: Top quality, great value, and an enormous variety of coffees and teas. Huge selection of coffees and loose teas. Carries flavored coffees, spices, chocolates, and condiments. You'll find a full line of coffee and tea makers. Inexpensive. No credit cards (the Bleecker Street store does take credit cards). No delivery. Discounter. *"Great coffee—at half the price of Starbucks' beans." "Starbucks' quality at supermarket prices."*

Locations: **Flatiron/East Village:** 40½ St. Marks Place, between 1st and 2nd Avenues (533-1982) / **SoHo/TriBeCa:** 201 Bleecker Street, near 6th Avenue (477-5421)

Sensuous Bean

Coffees, teas & spices
Upper West Side

66 West 70th Street
near Columbus Avenue / 724-7725
Mon and Thurs–Fri 8:30am–9pm, Tues–Wed 8:30am–7pm,
Sat 8:30am–6pm, Sun 9:30am–6pm.

45	45	40	45
quality	style	service	value

The Edge: Really large selection of coffees and teas. All you'll find is coffee, tea, and coffee and tea makers. Features 72 kinds of coffee and 28 kinds of tea. The shop will blend coffees and teas to suit. This is a good source for La Semeuse. Prices are reasonable and quality good. *"Very knowledgeable help."*

Starbucks Coffee Company
Sun–Thurs 6:30am–midnight, Fri–Sat 6:30am–2am.

Coffees, teas & spices
Multiple locations

quality style service value

The Edge: If you don't mind paying $2 for a large cup of coffee, it's delicious. The Seattle coffee company with a conscience and a name synonymous with coffee. Find good freshly brewed coffee in three sizes and prices, and with European names. Espresso, cappuccino, latte, and standard brewed coffee offered, among others. Also muffins, bagels, and scones. Delivers mail order. *"Number 1. Excellent." "Great crumb cake." "Expensive." "Mochaccinos and frappuccinos. Yummy!" "I'm hooked on them!"*

Locations: Flatiron/East Village: 141 2nd Avenue, at 9th Street (780-0024) / 13 Astor Place, near Lafayette Street (982-3563) / **Gramercy Park/Murray Hill:** 585 2nd Avenue, at 32nd Street (684-1299) / 395 3rd Avenue, near 28th Street (686-2483) / **Lower Manhattan:** 38 Park Row, near Broadway (587-8400) / **Midtown East:** 400 East 54th Street, at 1st Avenue (688-8951) / **Midtown West:** 25 West 45th Street, between 5th and 6th Avenues (505-5175) / 1656 Broadway, near West 51st Street (397-7124) / **SoHo/TriBeCa:** 78 Spring Street, near Broadway (219-2961) / **Upper East Side:** 1117 Lexington Avenue, at 78th Street (517-8476) / 1128 3rd Avenue, at 66th Street (472-6535) / 1290 3rd Avenue, at 74th Street (772-6903) / 1445 1st Avenue, at 75th Street (472-7784) / 1559 2nd Avenue, at 81st Street (472-7972) / **Upper West Side:** 2379 Broadway, at 87th Street (875-8470) / 2252 Broadway, near 82nd Street (721-4157) / 152 Columbus Avenue, near 67th Street (721-0470) / 2681 Broadway, near 99th Street (280-1811)

Ten Ren Tea Company
75 Mott Street
near Canal Street / 349-2286
Daily 10am–8pm.

Coffees, teas & spices
SoHo/TriBeCa

quality style service value

The Edge: Asian remedies—teas for taste and medicinal herbs. A full range of Asian teas and some lovely simple tea sets. Teas are grown for Ten Ren on its own plantations on Taiwan. The shop holds a traditional tea service daily at an ornate mahogany table in the center of the store. You can try the tea you're considering buying. Also a large selection of herbal medicines.

Myers of Keswick
634 Hudson Street
near Jane Street / 691-4194
Weekdays 10am–7pm, Sat 10am–6pm, Sun noon–5pm.

English
Greenwich Village

quality style service value

The Edge: A bit of Britain in the city. Features British food products, including steak-and-kidney pie, Stilton, kippers, homemade sausage, baked hams, beans, teas, jams, and fruit sodas. No delivery. *"Fabulous quirky place. Loads of hard-to-find culinary delights for the sophisticated palate."*

Albert's

Fish & meat
Upper East Side

836 Lexington Avenue
between 63rd and 64th Streets / 751-3169
Weekdays 8am–7pm, Sat 8am–6pm, Sun noon–5pm.

44 **40** **40** **30**

quality style service value

The Edge: Custom-cut butcher shop known for game and suckling pigs. Also good-quality regular meats. Mostly a telephone and delivery business. Quality, as is price, is high.

Baldwin Fish Market

Fish & meat
Upper East Side

1584 1st Avenue
between 82nd and 83rd Streets / 288-9032
Mon–Sat 8am–7:30pm.

The Edge: Good, reliable neighborhood fish market. The selection is limited but it's always very fresh and includes fish, some shellfish, and well-kept fresh lobsters. Usually the standards—lobster, salmon, sole, swordfish, and tuna. Delivers within a 20-block radius. Accepts credit cards.

Catalano's in the Vinegar Factory

Fish & meat
Upper East Side

431 East 91st Street
between York and 1st Avenues / 628-9608
Daily 8am–8pm.

42 **40** **38** **35**

quality style service value

The Edge: Very fresh fish—good selection. A reliable neighborhood source for fish. It accepts personal checks. Expensive. No credit cards.

Central Fish Company

Fish & meat
Midtown West

527 9th Avenue
near 39th Street / 279-2317
Mon–Sat 8am–6:15pm.

The Edge: Affordable lobsters. Specializes in seafood—fresh Maine lobster, Brazilian lobster tails shipped flash frozen, Florida shrimp, frozen Gulf shrimp, plus the regulars like salmon and tuna. Come for the prices, not the service. No delivery. Discounter.

Citarella

Fish & meat
Upper West Side

2135 Broadway
near 75th Street / 874-0383
Mon–Sat 8am–9pm, Sun 9am–7pm.

46 **40** **41** **39**

quality style service value

The Edge: Universal agreement—the best fish store in the city. The fish is always fresh and well maintained. Now in addition to fish, it carries meats and prepared foods, including homemade sausage, pasta, sauces, custardy rice pudding, and rotisserie chicken. Best for fish, fowl, and meats. Prices are very high, but the quality is consistently good. Caters also. *"Excellent fish, but also very good meat and prepared foods. Terrific that they added bread." "A thing of beauty—best prices on the finest olive oil and balsamic vinegar." "I can't wait till they come east!"*

East Village Meat Market

Fish & meat
Flatiron/East Village

139 2nd Avenue

between St. Mark's Place and 9th Street / 228-5590
Mon–Sat 8am–6pm.

The Edge: A Polish/Ukrainian meat store featuring great kielbasa. Specialty items include double-smoked kielbasa (Polish sausage) and Polish and Lithuanian breads. No credit cards. No delivery.

Empire Purveyors
901 1st Avenue
between 50th and 51st Streets / 755-7757
Weekdays 7am–5pm, Sat 10am–5pm.

Fish & meat
Midtown East

The Edge: A wholesale meat operation. A wholesale meat operation selling meat at prices at about 30% off retail. Sells beef, veal, pork, chicken, and duck. No credit cards. Delivers in the neighborhood only.

F. Rozzo & Sons
159 9th Avenue
between 19th and 20th Streets / 242-6100
Weekdays 4am–3:30pm.

Fish & meat
Chelsea

quality style service value

The Edge: Wholesale seafood operation, sometimes open to the public. Occasional sales when this seafood-only place is officially open to the public. Buy here anytime for 100 pounds of seafood, plus or minus. Great lobster prices in those quantities. No delivery.

Faicco's
260 Bleecker Street
between 6th and 7th Avenues / 243-1974
Tues–Thurs 8am–6pm, Fri 8am–7pm, Sun 9am–2pm.

Fish & meat
Greenwich Village

quality style service value

The Edge: The place for first-rate Italian sausages. Known most for pork products, pork roasts, pork chops, and sausages. Its Italian sweet and hot sausages are among the best in the city. The provolone cheese and parsley sausage is a specialty. Offers, as well, a full range of meats and Italian prepared foods. No delivery.

Florence Meat Market
5 Jones Street
near West 4th Street / 242-6531
Mon 8:30am–1pm, Tues–Fri 9am–6:30pm, Sat 9am–6pm.

Fish & meat
Greenwich Village

quality style service value

The Edge: Quality meat market, less expensive than uptown. Full-line butcher shop priding itself on very old-fashioned service. No longer any prepared foods.

Giovanni Esposito & Sons Meat Shop
500 9th Avenue
at 38th Streets / 279-3298
Mon–Sat 8am–7:30pm.

Fish & meat
Midtown West

quality style service value

The Edge: Another good Italian butcher. Old-fashioned old-time store offering a full line of meat products, including wonderful Italian sausages. Good quality and good prices. Phone orders. Delivers throughout the city with a $50 minimum order. Payment by cash or personal check. Order the evening before or early in the morning as the truck leaves before 10am. *"Great homemade sausages and Italian meat."*

Hoi Sing Seafood

Fish & meat
Lower Manhattan

17-19 Catherine Street
between East Broadway and Henry Street / 964-9694
Daily 8:30am–7pm.

The Edge: Less expensive fish. No English spoken. Beautiful, much less expensive fish than uptown. You need to get used to shopping in Chinatown, however, as they don't feature uptown cleanliness. Prices are about half of uptown. No credit cards. No delivery.

Hung Phat Seafood & Meat

Fish & meat
SoHo/TriBeCa

225 Grand Street
east of the Bowery / 941-6363
Daily 9am–7pm.

The Edge: Quality fish at Chinatown prices. The *New York Times* describes this and its neighbor (Tan My My) as the best fish (Hung Phat) and produce (Tan My My) stores in the area. Excellent-quality fish, always kept well iced. Great selection and good prices, although not the lowest in the area. The range of fish is wide— five types of snapper, three different groupers, blue fish, mackerel, pickerel, razor clams, tuna, and much, much more. Prices are less than half of uptown. Why are items kept iced? This isn't uptown—iced often means on ice outdoors. No credit cards. No delivery.

Jefferson Market

Fish & meat
Chelsea

450 Avenue of the Americas
near 10th Street / 533-3377
Mon–Sat 8am–9pm, Sun 9am–8pm.

38	36	38	35
quality	style	service	value

The Edge: One of the best meat markets in the city. Top meats and fish. Also salads and prepared foods. The prepared shrimp is as good as it gets in New York, tasting like the cocktail shrimp featured at 21. Fifteen cuts of steak alone. Catering available. Prices are high, matching the quality. *"Good always." "Good, but better at Balducci's."*

Joe's Ninth Avenue Meat Market

Fish & meat
Midtown West

533 9th Avenue
near 40th Street / 947-8090
Mon–Sat 8am–6:30pm.

40	40	40	30
quality	style	service	value

The Edge: Reasonable prices. Specials on all basic meats. Good, not great, prices. No credit cards. No delivery.

Kurowycky Meat Products

Fish & meat
Flatiron/East Village

124 1st Avenue
between 7th and 8th Streets / 477-0344
Mon–Sat 8am–6pm (closed Mon July–Aug).

40	40	40	40
quality	style	service	value

The Edge: The best kielbasa! Come here for homemade kielbasa, plus a full line of the standard meats and wonderful Russian breads. Prices are very low. No credit cards. No delivery.

Leonard's Market

1241 3rd Avenue
near 71st Street / 744-2600
Weekdays 8am–7pm, Sat 8am–6pm.

Fish & meat
Upper East Side

30	23	23	23
quality	style	service	value

The Edge: Top-quality meats for over 80 years. Has now broadened the offerings to include a good selection of fresh fish and seafood. Some takeout, including Manhattan clam chowder. Very expensive, among the highest prices in town. *"Ridiculous prices!"*

Les Halles

411 Park Avenue South
between 28th and 29th Streets / 679-4111
Daily noon–midnight.

Fish & meat
Gramercy Park/Murray Hill

38	38	36	34
quality	style	service	value

The Edge: French-style meats. The butcher is French trained and cuts meat "French style." Specialties include pork stuffed with prunes, hangar steak, and boudin (blood sausage). Top-rate! Prepares picnic baskets (from $20) in summer. Requires a minimum order for delivery.

Lobel's Prime Meats

1096 Madison Avenue
between 82nd and 83rd Streets / 737-1372
Mon–Sat 9am–6pm (closed Sat July–Aug).

Fish & meat
Upper East Side

44	40	41	34
quality	style	service	value

The Edge: To some, this is the top butcher in New York. Caters to the "carriage crowd and working women," featuring a full line of gourmet meats, game, and exotic products (alligator and ostrich on special order with one-week notice). The steaks are buttery and chickens are from a breeder who reputedly feeds the chicken to Lobel's specifications. Offers house charges. 90% of its business is by telephone (out-of-town callers dial toll free 800-556-2357). *"Expensive, but fabulous for special dinner parties." "I love their steaks."*

Lobster Place

436 West 16th Street
between 9th and 10th Avenues / 255-5672
Retail hours, Mon–Sat 10am–8pm, Sun 10am–6pm;
wholesale hours, Mon–Sat 5am–2pm.

Fish & meat
Chelsea

30	30	20	10
quality	style	service	value

The Edge: Fresh, fresh seafood favored by New York's finest restaurants. The place for fresh Maine lobster and other seafood, including shrimp, crab, clams, oysters, and mussels. Reputed to supply Le Cirque, La Côte Basque, and the Four Seasons with seafood. Maintains a large wholesale operation, but now sells retail. Good prices discounted. No credit cards. No delivery.

Ocean Sea Food

19-21 Henry Street
near Catherine Street / 227-3067
Daily 9am–7pm.

Fish & meat
Lower East Side/Chinatown

The Edge: Another Chinatown favorite for fresh seafood. From lobsters to turtles to shrimp, this is the place. Limited English and typical Chinatown service—curt and efficient. Cash and carry only. Inexpensive. No credit cards.

Oppenheimer Meats, Inc.
2606 Broadway
between 98th and 99th Streets / 662-0246
Mon–Sat 8am–7pm.

Fish & meat
Upper West Side

quality style service value

The Edge: Excellent meats. Full range of meats and game. 42 years in business. About 50% of its business is by telephone and it delivers on the East Side for orders put in before 2pm. Specials are posted at the shop. House charge accounts. *"Great German cold cuts."*

Ottomanelli & Sons Prime Meat Market
285 Bleecker Street
off 7th Avenue / 675-4217
Weekdays 8am–6:30pm, Sat 7am–6pm.

Fish & meat
Greenwich Village

quality style service value

The Edge: Old-fashioned full-service Italian butcher shop. Not related to the uptown Ottomanelli Brothers. A full-line quality butcher featuring the standards, plus specialty items like chicken sausage, veal roast, and (in season) fresh game and venison.

Ottomanelli Brothers
1549 York Avenue
between 82nd and 83rd Streets / 772-7900
Weekdays 7am–6:30pm, Sat 7am–6pm.

Fish & meat
Upper East Side

quality style service value

The Edge: Old-fashioned full-service Italian butcher shop. Good quality for all the standards, plus game, fresh sausage, rolled roasts, osso buco, and other dinner items. Not-bad southern Italian specialties, including baked ziti, lasagne, chicken parmigiana, and pasta sauces, as well as basic fresh Italian breads.

Park East Kosher Butcher
1163 Madison Avenue
near 86th Street / 737-9800
Mon–Wed 6:30am–6:30pm, Thurs 6:30am–8pm,
Fri 6:30am–3pm.

Fish & meat
Upper East Side

quality style service value

The Edge: Excellent but pricey kosher butcher. All the regular meats, plus cooked chickens, barbecued turkey or duck, and some prepared foods (breast of veal, chopped liver, and more). Good service. Very expensive. This store is the Upper East Side source for kosher meat. *"Tops in quality and price!"* *"Unpleasant to all but their very good customers."*

Pisacane Midtown Corp.
940 1st Avenue
between 51st and 52nd Streets / 355-1850
Weekdays 7:30am–6pm, Sat 9am–5pm.

Fish & meat
Midtown East

quality style service value

The Edge: Excellent fish market. The shop stocks a wide variety of the freshest fish, including tanks of live Dungeness crabs, brook trout, lobsters, and live soft-shell crabs in season. Also find smoked salmon, cooked lobster, shrimp, and crabmeat. The prepared foods are very good, especially if kept simple. No credit cards. No delivery.

Premier Veal
555 West Street
near West 12th Street / 243-3170
Weekdays 4am–1pm.

Fish & meat
Greenwich Village

The Edge: Wholesale veal products. Top quality and excellent prices. Wholesale only, but will take retail orders depending on their mood. Very reasonable. No credit cards. Discounter.

Prime Access
P.O. Box 8187
White Plains / 800-314-2875
Daily 24 hours.

Fish & meat
Mail/phone

The Edge: Meats served at top New York restaurants. Unlike at most mail-order butchers, steaks are shipped fresh and need to be frozen or used within five days. The prime dry-aged steaks are flavorful and well marbled, with the outside fat trimmed so closely that they don't flare when grilled. Apparently these are the steaks used at Chanterelle, among other four-star restaurants. Have recently added veal and lamb to the line. Very, very expensive—well over $20 per pound for steak and lamb. Overnight and weekend shipping extra.

Rosedale Fish & Oyster Market
1129 Lexington Avenue
between 78th and 79th Streets / 861-4323
Weekdays 8am–6:30pm, Sat 8am–6pm.

Fish & meat
Upper East Side

quality style service value

The Edge: Top, top quality fresh fish. The Neuman family has owned Rosedale since 1906. The store is noted for superb service. Pricey but very good fish, including all the standards and whatever's fresh on Mr. Neuman's daily trip to the Fulton Fish Market. They can and will get any fish you want. Takeout includes lobster salad, fresh tuna salad, clam chowder, and poached salmon, with appropriate sauces. Clams, oysters, and salmon are routinely cooked or shucked to order. If you stick with simple fresh fish, the takeout is fine. Daily specials are posted in the window. Mr. Neuman will take customers on his daily trip to the Fulton Fish Market for an interesting 4am experience. House charges are available. *"They prepare your fish to perfection, but pricey."* *"Expensive."*

Salumeria Biellese
376-378 8th Avenue
near 29th Street / 736-7376
Weekdays 7am–6pm, Sat 9am–6pm.

Fish & meat
Midtown West

quality style service value

The Edge: Sets the standard in homemade sausage. Since 1925. You'll find 40 kinds of homemade sausages, including all the standards, plus sausage boudin blanc with truffles, sausage boudin noir, and sausage from rabbit, venison, and more. Reputed to be the sausage served at Le Cirque, among other top French and Italian restaurants. Also homemade prosciutto, salamis, and fresh hams. Now has a restaurant, Birichino (at 260 West 29th Street, serving moderately priced northern Italian food). The shop has added a catering and takeout service, including dinner dishes made with chicken and veal. Mail order is available if the order is large enough. No credit cards. *"Love it—I don't shop anywhere else now!"*

Schaller & Weber

1654 2nd Avenue
between 85th and 86th Streets / 879-3047
Mon–Sat 9am–6pm.

Fish & meat
Upper East Side

41	35	36	34
quality	style	service	value

The Edge: Yorkville neighborhood butcher. The shop features all the standard meats, plus 100 varieties of German deli meats and sausages. Unusual meats include smoked goose breast and suckling pig. No delivery. No credit cards. *"Used to be better."*

Schatzie's Prime Meats

1200 Madison Avenue
between 87th and 88th Streets / 410-1555
Mon–Sat 8am–6pm.

Fish & meat
Upper East Side

The Edge: Prime meats at very good prices. Quality prime meats, plus every kind of fresh game from mallard duck to venison (in season). Catering service available (no set-ups). The shop will prepare dishes and foods to order. For Thanksgiving it will, with several weeks' notice, prepare the entire dinner, including fresh-killed turkey, cranberry sauce, sweet potatoes, gravy, vegetables, pastas (lasagne, etc.), and pies for dessert. Advance notice is key during the holidays. Reasonable prices.

Sea Breeze Fishmarket

541 9th Avenue
near 40th Street / 563-7537
Mon 7:30am–6pm, Tues–Fri 7:30am–6:30pm, Sat 7am–6:30pm.

Fish & meat
Midtown West

The Edge: Reasonably priced quality fish. Expect to find the standards plus live lobsters, which are stored in saltwater tanks. Priced about half of what you'd pay uptown. No delivery. Discounter.

Vin Hin Company

129 Mott Street
close to Canal Street / 431-5297
Daily 8am–8pm.

Fish & meat
SoHo/TriBeCa

The Edge: Cheap, cheap fish. Little English is spoken here. The fish can be great or okay—what's always spectacular is the prices. No credit cards. No delivery. Discounter.

National Wholesale Liquidators

632 Broadway
between Houston and Bleecker Streets / 979-2400
Mon–Sat 9:30am–8pm, Sun 11am–7pm.

General stores
SoHo/TriBeCa

40	15	40	45
quality	style	service	value

The Edge: Close-outs of basic household and food supplies. Two packed floors holding everything from furniture to hairspray. Find furniture, furnishings, food, household supplies, and personal hygiene products. Ever-changing inventory (dependent on close-outs) in this store with a Woolworth/Kmart atmosphere. No delivery. Discounter.

Ralph's Discount City

93-95 Chambers Street
near Broadway / 267-5567
Weekdays 7:30am–7pm, Sat 8:45am–5pm, Sun 10am–5:30pm.

General stores
Lower Manhattan

The Edge: If you're lucky and have the time. Features cheap products from close-outs or overstocking, including health and beauty products, food, housewares, candy, and soda. Now in a new bigger store. No delivery. Discounter.

E.A.T. Gifts

1062 Madison Avenue
near 80th Street / 861-2544
Mon–Sat 10am–6pm, Sun noon–5pm.

Gifts
Upper East Side

43	45	38	29
quality	style	service	value

The Edge: Always-welcome comfort gifts. Stuffed animals, party favors, and basic jams and herbs available in attractive gift baskets. Very, very expensive. *"Overpriced for value." "Great gourmet gift items." "Typically New York, but not worth it."*

Fraser-Morris

102 President Street
at Hicks Street, Brooklyn / 718-802-9771
Mon–Sat 8:30am–7pm, Sun 10am–5pm (closed Sun July–Aug).

Gifts
Brooklyn

39	28	31	26
quality	style	service	value

The Edge: Standard mail-order gift packages their specialty. Features imported specialty items, package items, okay cheeses, chocolates, and biscuits. Fruit baskets feature the standard pile of fruit, cellophane wrapped and shipped. *"Good selection." "Snobbish, but stylish."*

Gift Baskets International

37 West 20th Street, 6th Floor
between 5th and 6th Avenues / 604-9022
Weekdays 9am–5pm.

Gifts
Chelsea

40	30	30	20
quality	style	service	value

The Edge: Easy gift solutions. Gift baskets in a wide variety of price ranges from $65, with most in the high $100s. Themes include Chocolate Decadence, Executive for Her, Golf Pro, New York, various baby baskets, and much, much more.

Manhattan Fruitier

105 East 29th Street
between Park and Lexington Avenues / 686-0404
Weekdays 9am–5pm.

Gifts
Gramercy Park/Murray Hill

43	45	45	35
quality	style	service	value

The Edge: Glorious, gorgeous healthy gifts. Expensive but beautiful fruit baskets that look like "edible Dutch still lives." Included in the baskets are the freshest fruits, plus biscotti graced with fresh flowers. Baskets could include chocolate, dried fruit, Australian crystallized ginger, or dried pear. Wonderful holiday items. Gift baskets from $50 to $200. Delivery in the New York area (within 50 miles) or by Federal Express elsewhere. Staff is accommodating and efficient. They even keep track of what you sent, when, and to whom, to avoid repeats. They couldn't be nicer to work with. For out-of-town orders, call toll free 800-841-5718. *"Good gifts." "Beautiful baskets, but they used to be larger for the basic $50 price." "The best baskets!" "The food is pretty, but not sweet."*

Bell Bates Company

97 Reade Street
between Broadway and Church Streets / 267-4300
Weekdays 9am–8pm, Sat 11am–5pm.

Health food
SoHo/TriBeCa

40	20	20	40
quality	style	service	value

The Edge: Gourmet health-food store. Features organic items, including foods, herbs, spices, and vitamins. A monthly flyer lists special bargains. No delivery.

Commodities

117 Hudson Street
near North Moore Street / 334-8330
Daily 10am–8pm.

Health food
SoHo/TriBeCa

40	30	40	40
quality	style	service	value

The Edge: Well-stocked health-food supermarket. Find dairy, frozen foods, grains, package foods, pasta, and produce. No delivery.

Health Nuts

835 2nd Avenue
near 45th Street / 490-2979
Weekdays 8:30am–8:30pm, Sat 10am–7pm.

Health food
Midtown East

40	33	33	40
quality	style	service	value

The Edge: Healthy items only. Find dietary supplements, organic items, personal-care products, and books and pamphlets on health issues. *"Excellent variety of natural food and ingredients."*

Healthy Pleasures

93 University Place
near 11th Street / 353-3663
Weekdays 8am–10pm, Sat–Sun 9am–9pm.

Health food
Flatiron/East Village

34	32	28	32
quality	style	service	value

The Edge: Health-food supermarket and salad bar. Items include organic milk and free-range roasted chickens. Limited delivery between 23rd and Houston Streets and between 3rd and 6th Avenues. *"Excellent variety and clean."*

Herban Kitchen

290 Hudson Street
between Dominick and Spring Streets / 627-2257
Daily 11am–11pm.

Health food
SoHo/TriBeCa

45	45	40	40
quality	style	service	value

The Edge: Health-food items, as you'd expect. Expect prepared foods, organic produce, and groceries—plus meals at the shop. Open for lunch and dinner, seven days a week. Eat at the establishment or take out food, including Caesar salad with grilled chicken, grilled vegetable sandwich, and vegetarian grain burgers. Organic ingredients only. Also cater. Deliver to the Village,

SoHo, and TriBeCa only. *"Beautifully prepared, scrumptious food. High quality—and they deliver!"*

Foods of India

121 Lexington Avenue
near 28th Street / 683-4419
Mon–Sat 10am–8pm, Sun 11am–6pm.

Indian
Gramercy Park/Murray Hill

quality style service value

The Edge: The full range of Indian cooking ingredients. A wholesaler that stocks a full range—from beans and flours to spices—for Indian cooking. Good prices. Discounter. *"Very good salads, especially the Caesar."*

Kalustyan Orient Export Trading

123 Lexington Avenue
between 28th and 29th Streets / 685-3451
Mon–Sat 10am–8pm, Sun and holidays 11am–7pm.

Indian
Gramercy Park/Murray Hill

The Edge: Features Indian and Middle Eastern spices and cooking ingredients. Offers cheeses, dried lemons, exotic vegetables, four kinds of homemade mango chutney, Middle Eastern sweets, delicious mango ice cream, fresh California dates (in season), grains, olives, roasted almonds, more than 20 kinds of rice, and sun-dried mulberries. Some Middle Eastern prepared foods. Same-day delivery available depending on destination. Inexpensive.

Bruno the King of Ravioli

Weekdays 8am–9pm, Sat–Sun 9am–8pm.

Italian
Multiple locations

quality style service value

The Edge: All sorts of homemade pasta. Homemade gnocchi, lasagne (sold frozen), pasta, ravioli, tortellini, and homemade sauces made in the factory behind the 45th Street store. Great varieties of raviolis. Nice biscotti, particularly those loaded with dried fruit. Delivers with a $50 minimum. Frozen or not, the lasagne is great. The owner just spent $30,000 redoing the 8th Avenue store, so he feels he should get "100" for style! Discounter. *"Excellent service." "Love the pasta and sauces!"*

Locations: Chelsea: 249 8th Avenue, near 23rd Street (627-0767) / **Midtown West:** 653 9th Avenue, between 45th and 46th Streets (246-8456) / **Upper West Side:** 2204 Broadway, between 78th and 79th Streets (580-8150)

DiPalo's Fine Food, Inc.

206 Grand Street
corner of Mott and Grand Streets / 226-1033
Mon–Sat 9am–6:30pm, Sun 9am–3pm.

Italian
SoHo/TriBeCa

quality style service value

The Edge: A neighborhood Italian spot for 70 years. Find good pastas, canned tomatoes, breads, olive oils, cheeses (fresh mozzarella, ricotta, Parmesan, and Gorgonzola), sausages, and of course, biscotti in this small storefront. The DiPalos go to Italy to search out cheeses and products to sell at the shop. Have the best prices in Little Italy. Will send UPS with two-day delivery for large orders. Service is wonderful, and best during the week when the store is less crowded. Discounter. *"Great shells."* *"Gracious owners. I had a large order and they volunteered a 10% discount!"*

Italian Food Center

Italian
SoHo/TriBeCa

186 Grand Street
near Mulberry Street / 925-2954
Daily 8am–7pm.

The Edge: Good prices on Italian products. Good assortment of Italian necessities, from olive oil to pasta to sauces and meats and breads. Discounter.

Manganaro's Food and Restaurant

Italian
Midtown West

488 9th Avenue
near 37th Street / 563-5331
Weekdays 8am–7pm, Sat 9am–7pm.

quality style service value

The Edge: Good basic Sicilian specialties and pastry. An Italian food store best known for its cheeses, Italian breads, canned tomatoes from San Marzano, dried and fresh pasta, olive oils, and fresh chestnuts at Christmas. Salads and sandwiches can be taken out or eaten at the shop with espresso. Does the six-foot sandwich, but the focus is on takeout and grocery items. Same-day delivery in Manhattan only. *"Good authentic Italian cheeses and specialty items."* *"Service can be difficult."*

Piemonte Ravioli Company

Italian
SoHo/TriBeCa

190 Grand Street
between Mott and Mulberry Streets / 226-0475
Tues–Sat 8:30am–6pm, Sun 8:30am–4pm.

quality style service value

The Edge: Perhaps the city's best pasta source: high-quality, enormous variety, and good prices. More than 25 varieties of pasta and assorted sauces made fresh daily. Favorites include cannelloni and the lobster, pumpkin, and porcini ravioli. Deliveries throughout Manhattan on large orders; for smaller orders, delivery by Fed Ex or UPS is possible, but they're concerned about spoilage in warm weather. Excellent prices, about half of uptown. Crowded on weekends. No credit cards. No delivery. Discounter. *"Best value—best taste."*

Raffetto's

Italian
SoHo/TriBeCa

144 West Houston Street
between Sullivan and MacDougal Streets / 777-1261
Tues–Fri 9am–6:30pm, Sat 8am–6pm.

quality style service value

The Edge: Good broad selection of pasta and sauces. Since 1906 has featured more than 50 kinds of fresh and dried pastas and sauces to complement the pastas. Cheese and spinach ravioli, pumpkin ravioli, and garlic-parsley fettuccine are among the specialties. Pasta sheets can be cut to your specification. Also breads, bread sticks, cheese, canned olive oil, imported Italian tomatoes, spices, and other basic Italian products. Inexpensive. No credit cards. No delivery. Discounter. *"One of the one best."*

Ravioli Store

Italian
SoHo/TriBeCa

75 Sullivan Street

between Spring and Broome Streets / 925-1737
Weekdays 10am–7pm, Sat–Sun 11am–5pm.

quality style service value

The Edge: Exotic pastas. The shop (owned by Geraldine Ferraro's son, John) features fresh pasta and ravioli, from the basic to the innovative, including tomato ravioli with five-cheese filling, tomato-basil pasta with walnut pesto, and lobster-mousse–filled ravioli. Dean & DeLuca carries Ravioli Store products. Prices have been lowered—now mostly $4.10 to $6.75.

Asia Market Corporation
71 1/2 Mulberry Street
between Canal and Bayard Streets / 962-2028
Daily 8am–7pm.

Oriental
SoHo/TriBeCa

The Edge: Thai, Indonesian, Philippine, and Malaysian canned goods. Also offers sauces, noodles, and fresh produce. The manager speaks English—which is a big plus for Chinatown. No credit cards.

Chinese American Trading Company
91 Mulberry Street
near Canal Street / 267-5224
Daily 9am–8pm.

Oriental
SoHo/TriBeCa

quality style service value

The Edge: Good prices and quality for Oriental food. Features a wide variety of imported Oriental foodstuffs. Inexpensive. No credit cards. No delivery. Discounter.

Fung Wong Bakery
30 Mott Street
near Chatham Square / 267-4037
Daily 8am–9pm.

Oriental
SoHo/TriBeCa

The Edge: Fortune cookie source. No English spoken here. Fortune cookies and almond cookies, plus traditional Chinese pastry. No credit cards. No delivery. Discounter.

Han Arum
25 West 32nd Street
between 5th and 6th Avenues / 695-3283
Daily 9am–9pm.

Oriental
Midtown West

The Edge: Largest Korean supermarket in Manhattan. Little, if any, English spoken. All the standard Korean items, plus a salad bar featuring 20 Korean dishes, as well as Korean baked goods and cookies. No delivery. Discounter.

Kam Man Food Products
200 Canal Street
between Mott and Mulberry Streets / 571-0330
Daily 9am–9pm.

Oriental
SoHo/TriBeCa

quality style service value

The Edge: One of the largest Asian supermarkets. Has everything from fresh fish, meats (including excellent barbecued pork and roasted duck), Chinese mushrooms, desserts, and teas to housewares and exotic Chinese remedies. The store features Chinese, Japanese, Vietnamese, Philippine, Thai, and Singapore products. Prices are great. Discounter. *"Good food, but the non-English-speaking help makes shopping difficult."*

Katagiri and Company

224 East 59th Street
between 2nd and 3rd Avenues / 755-3566
Mon–Sat 10am–7pm, Sun 11am–6pm.

Oriental
Midtown East

quality style service value

The Edge: The city's oldest Japanese food store. A very small gourmet supermarket stocked full with Japanese fresh foods, including sushi ingredients, vegetables (seaweeds too), rice, and exquisitely fresh fish. Also cooking utensils. Expensive. *"Recommended—if you can't get to Yaohan Plaza."*

Lung Fong Chinese Bakery

41 Mott Street
near Biddle Street / 233-7447
Daily 8am–8pm.

Oriental
SoHo/TriBeCa

quality style service value

The Edge: Chinese pastry. Chinese fortune and almond cookies, plus standard Chinese pastries. No credit cards. No delivery.

May May Gourmet Chinese Bakery

35 Pell Street
near Mott Street / 267-0733
Daily 8am–7pm.

Oriental
SoHo/TriBeCa

quality style service value

The Edge: Best dim sum source. Excellent selection of dim sum—an infinite variety, including Shanghai vegetable buns, pork buns, spareribs, shrimp buns, and lots more. Both fried and steamed options. Great prices. Simply steam or microwave and serve. Discounter. *"Great cocktail party options." "The only place to go!"*

Tan My My

249 Grand Street
near Chrystie Street / 966-7878
Daily 9am–8:30pm.

Oriental
Lower East Side/Chinatown

quality style service value

The Edge: Perhaps the best Chinatown source for fresh fish and vegetables. Prices are amazingly low, but, better still, the quality is as good as it gets anywhere in the city. The fish look as if they're still swimming and the fruits and vegetables look as though they've jumped from the ground to the store. Like most Chinatown places—no service and no English. No delivery. No credit cards.

Yaohan Plaza

595 River Road
Edgewater / 201-941-0055
Open daily.

Oriental
New Jersey

quality style service value

The Edge: Little Japan so close by. A giant Japanese supermarket in a shopping complex with only Japanese stores. Food bars are available for dining while you shop. Also stores selling cosmetics, clothing, and gift items. But the shops are best for the fresh vegetables imported from Japan, meat, fish, and other staples. A shuttle bus from the Port Authority will take you right there. *"Like being in Japan."*

Annie's

1204 Lexington Avenue
near 82nd Street / 861-4957
Mon–Sat 7:30am–7:30pm.

Produce
Upper East Side

quality style service value

The Edge: Quality conventional fruits, vegetables, and dairy products. Takes personal checks. Expensive. No credit cards.

Likitsakos

1174 Lexington Avenue
between 80th and 81st Streets / 535-4300
Weekdays 8am–9pm, Sat–Sun 8am–8pm.

Produce
Upper East Side

| 40 | 40 | 30 | 37 |

quality style service value

The Edge: Could be the freshest produce on the Upper East Side. Excellent selection of fresh, fresh produce. This store has taken the Upper East Side by storm. It's one of the top sources for just about any kind of produce, plus gourmet items from charcuterie and cheese to Greek and pasta-based prepared foods and staples (breads, coffees, oils, vinegar, and more).

Nature's Gifts

1297 Lexington Avenue
between 87th and 88th Streets / 289-6283
Weekdays 8am–9pm, Sat–Sun 8am–8pm.

Produce
Upper East Side

| 40 | 30 | 20 | 20 |

quality style service value

The Edge: Good prices on good produce. Items just outside the store are where the really good values are. Mostly sells fresh fruits and vegetables. Also butter, juice, milk, pastas, couscous, dressings, Eli's Breads, and Ciao Bella gelati. The takeout counter features fruit, Greek, health, and pasta salads. Local delivery with $20 minimum.

Paradise Market

1100 Madison Avenue
near 83rd Street / 570-1190
Weekdays 8am–7pm, Sat 8am–6pm.

Produce
Upper East Side

The Edge: Impeccable produce. Always favorably reviewed by the *New York Times* and *New York* magazine. Carries fresh and unusual produce, including wild mushrooms, fresh herbs, and all the standard produce, but selected for its quality. Extremely expensive. Payment by cash or check only. *"You eat their fruit, they eat your dollars—dumb!"*

Agata & Valentina

1505 1st Avenue
near 79th Street / 452-0690
Daily 8am–9pm.

quality style service value

The Edge: Excellent tastes. Another Balducci's-style gourmet shop, emphasizing Italian ingredients and Sicilian-style prepared foods. You'll find bakery items, breads, candies, caviar, gourmet dishes, cheeses, extra-virgin olive oil, fresh vegetables, gelati, meats, and smoked fish. Plus very fresh seafood, good pasta salads, and great desserts. Surprisingly, prices on some fruits and vegetables were in the supermarket range and on gourmet items prices were better than much of the competition. *"Fabulous takeout." "The seafood salad is as good as I've eaten anywhere." "Not as many 'specials' as Zabar's, but good quality and selection." "Has hard-to-find items."*

Balducci's

424 Avenue of the Americas
between 9th and 10th Streets / 673-2600
Daily 7am–8:30pm.

quality style service value

The Edge: Impeccable source for everything. You'll find breads, cheeses, fresh pastas and sauces, meats, produce, salads, smoked fish, and a full range of baked goods, candy, coffee/tea, condiments, dried fruits and nuts, oils, packaged items, prepared foods, and vinegars. In fish carries the standards plus specialties. Prepared foods are good, the simpler the better though. Known for its French cheeses. Well known for quality gift and picnic baskets. The shop is always crowded and the isles are narrow. Surprisingly, for such high-end quality, prices aren't bad. Delivers anywhere in the five boroughs. Mail order also. *"Number 1!" "A dream place to shop—and they deliver!" "Fresh veggies—a feast for the eyes too." "The meat department is tops. Seafood terrific! Fantastic takeout." "Expensive, but everything is worth it." "Every food product you'll ever want or need."*

Broadway Farm

2339 Broadway
near 85th Street / 787-8585
Daily 24 hours.

quality style service value

The Edge: Grocery store styled after Fairway. Like Fairway, it features quality inexpensive food items, coffee, cheeses, fruits and vegetables, smoked fish, specialty beers, and unusual imported items. Delivers from Central Park West to Riverside Drive between 70th and 93rd Streets. *"With Fairway nearby, why bother?"*

Butterfield Market

1114 Lexington Avenue
near 78th Street / 288-7800
Weekdays 7:30am–8pm, Sat 7:30am–5:30pm.

quality style service value

The Edge: Purveyor to the queen, and that says something. Apparently when Queen Elizabeth's boat is in town this store provided provisions. Service is excellent, with special attention to every customer. Carries a full range of high-quality food items from basic to gourmet. Caters to the phone-order trade. Very expensive. *"Wonderful quality in a small space. A long-time Upper East Side* *standard." "Check out 'the couple' adorable salt and paper shakers and the 'dancing couple' tea set.*

Dean & Deluca

560 Broadway
corner of Prince Street / 431-1691
Mon–Sat 8am–8pm, Sun 9am–7pm.

Superstores
SoHo/TriBeCa

43	42	35	29
quality	style	service	value

The Edge: Only the best of everything lands here. If it's a food or related item, chances are it's here. Find breads, candy, cheeses, coffees, dairy, desserts, the freshest of fish, fruits, prime meats, oils, pasta, prepared foods, vegetables, and vinegars. The foods displayed are picture perfect. D&D is, as expected, the best source for new, out-of-the-ordinary products. Some 150 cheeses are usually on hand, with great English and American cheeses. Prices are high, but what's always surprising is that not-as-good competitors often charge more. The place could be called "Tiffanys"—it has that quality. Joining the food are top-of-the-line, first-class kitchenware, including copper, earthenware, porcelain, stainless-steel pots, including pot crocks, steamers, and stock pots. Also baking equipment, cutlery, kitchen utensils and gadgets, table linen, and the best of the new cookbooks. Deluxe. *"The 'Barneys' of the food trade." "Not as good as it once was."* Style, terrific food, very high quality."

Fairway Market

Daily 7am–midnight.

Superstores
Multiple locations

41	33	32	40
quality	style	service	value

The Edge: The best prices and the best-quality produce and cheeses, if you can stand the crowds. Features a wide selection of produce, coffees, deli, breads, pastas and sauces, packaged cookies, olives, and cakes, but only so-so prepared foods. Among the best produce in town—certainly the best prices. Will put picnic baskets together in only 15 minutes—just call ahead. Catering service for platters of smoked fish, fresh fruit, cookies, sliced meats, pâté, and cheese and vegetables. The space is so narrow and crowded that you can hardly get around the store. The checkout lines are long, but move fast. Prices are even lower at their new 35,000-square-foot Harlem store located at 133rd Street and 12th Avenue. No delivery. 30% off. *"A madhouse, but fresh produce and good prices." "Much better selection than the standard City market." "Terrific produce." "Aisles too small—difficult to navigate." "Low prices."*

Locations: Upper Upper West Side: 2328 12th Avenue, near 132nd Street (234-3883) / **Upper West Side:** 2127 Broadway, near 74th Street (595-1888)

Gourmet Garage

453 Broome Street
near Mercer Street / 941-5850
Daily 7:30am–9pm.

Superstores
SoHo/TriBeCa

43	38	35	38
quality	style	service	value

The Edge: Gourmet food items at better prices. The original of this new trend for gourmet foods at good prices. Features greens, meat, dairy, prepared foods, coffees, and juices. Quality is high. Features good products from top distributors. No delivery. *"Great shopping."*

Grace's Marketplace

1237 3rd Avenue
near 71st Street / 737-0600
Mon–Sat 7am–8:30pm, Sun 8am–7pm.

Superstores
Upper East Side

quality style service value

The Edge: Selection and quality—but you pay for it. Inspired by Balducci's. A great selection of candy, condiments, baked goods, breads, cheeses, coffees, dairy, deli meats, dried fruits, nuts, pasta/sauces, smoked fish, fruits, and vegetables. Stocks over 200 cheeses. Good selection. Can be expensive: for example, a platter of sandwiches (mozzarella and sun-dried tomatoes essentially) for $160. *"Beautiful produce, imported veggies, and pasta." "Expensive, but worth it."*

International Groceries and Meat Market

529 9th Avenue
between 39th and 40th Streets / 279-5514
Mon–Sat 8am–6pm.

Superstores
Midtown West

The Edge: Excellent prices, good quality. Near the Port Authority, it specializes in food products from around the world. Expect to find it all, from flours and dried pastas to condiments and meat, fish, and cheeses. Greek products are a specialty. Local deliveries only. No credit cards.

Nader Food Market

1 East 28th Street
near 5th Avenue / 686-5793
Weekdays 9am–7pm, Sat 10am–6pm, Sun noon–5pm.

Superstores
Gramercy Park/Murray Hill

The Edge: Specializes in Middle Eastern food products. Find cooking ingredients, including bulgur wheat, lentils, spices, imported pistachio nuts, several kinds of halvah, dried fruits, and candies. Very good prices. No credit cards.

Ninth Avenue International Foods

543 9th Avenue
near 40th Street / 279-1000
Mon–Sat 8:30am–7pm.

Superstores
Midtown West

The Edge: Great Middle Eastern products. Features good prices on coffees (40 kinds), spices, chocolates, caviar spreads, European cheeses, grains (in bulk bags), and more. Great prices—for example, all coffees are sold at $6 a pound. It's a cash-and-carry place. Discounter.

Novello

333 East 38th Street
between 1st and 2nd Avenues / 697-5555
Daily 8am–8pm.

Superstores
Gramercy Park/Murray Hill

The Edge: 10,000 square feet devoted to gourmet foodstuffs from around the world. Expect to find appetizing pastas, cheeses, charcuterie, produce, bakery items, spices (including Novello's own line), and prepared foods. Catering service, gift baskets, and charge accounts available. An import from Tarrytown, in Westchester County.

Sahadi Importing Company, Inc.

187-189 Atlantic Avenue

Superstores
Brooklyn

near Court Street, Brooklyn / 718-624-4550
Weekdays 9am–7pm, Sat 8:30am–7pm.

quality style service value

The Edge: Wonderful prices on Middle Eastern delights. An old-fashioned turn-of-the-century–style store featuring Middle Eastern specialties. Really low prices and everyone is friendly and helpful. You'll find breads, candies, canned goods, cheeses, dried fruits, fresh coffee beans, frozen foods, jams, nuts, pastas, prepared foods, rice, and spices. Phone orders and delivery are possible through Sultan's Delight. Discounter.

Sultan's Delight

P.O. Box 090302
Brooklyn / 718-745-2121
Daily 8am–8pm.

Superstores
Mail/phone

quality style service value

The Edge: Ships for Sahadi Importing. Brooklyn prices on more than 250 Middle Eastern specialty items, including herbs, spices, nuts, dried beans, dried fruits, teas, rice, barley, flours, pastas, canned goods, and coffee. Sultan's Delight ships Sahadi Importing products worldwide. Will send you a catalog, if you provide a legal-size self-addressed and stamped return envelope. Call toll free 800-852-5046. Discounter.

Todaro Brothers

555 2nd Avenue
between 30th and 31st Streets / 532-0633
Mon–Sat 7am–9pm, Sun 7am–8pm.

Superstores
Gramercy Park/Murray Hill

quality style service value

The Edge: A much less expensive Balducci's. A large top-quality Italian market featuring appetizers, baked goods, bread, cheeses, coffee, dairy, Italian cold cuts, meat, imported pasta, poultry, prepared foods, sandwiches, sauces, smoked fish, and tea. Moderate prices on most items. A large wholesale operation. *"Good homemade mozzarella." "A small Balducci's."*

Zabar's Appetizers & Caterers

2245 Broadway
between 80th and 81st Streets / 787-2000
Weekdays 8am–7:30pm, Sat 8am–8pm, Sun 9am–6pm.

Superstores
Upper West Side

quality style service value

The Edge: Legendary for selection and price. The best of Zabar's includes its appetizer department, the annual New Year caviar price war, breads, candy, cheese, dried fruits, great coffee cakes, nuts, rugelach, sticky buns, pasta, and Zabar's coffees and teas. Not up to par are the prepared foods. Delivery and phone orders are available for large orders. Catering and picnic baskets are also available. Upstairs, find an unbelievable range of kitchen cookware at some of the best prices in the metro area. 25% off. *"Zabar's should be a New York City shrine!" "You can never get intelligent phone assistance." "A classic!" "A New York experience—terrific value and quality." "Fun place, lots of good munchies, but very crowded." "I can't take the lines and crowds." "Their takeout food can't be beat for quality and variety."*

Barocco Alimentari

297 Church Street
between Walker and White Streets / 431-0065
Weekdays 7:30am–6pm.

Takeout
SoHo/TriBeCa

The Edge: Takeout from Restaurant Barocca. This takeout shop adjacent to the Restaurant Barocca features Italian dishes. No delivery. *"Not what it was."*

Benny's Burritos To Go

Daily 11am–midnight.

Takeout
Multiple locations

The Edge: What New Yorkers expect of standard Mexican food. Offers 12-inch-long party-size burritos, guacamole, enchiladas, tacos, and chili. Inexpensive. No credit cards. No delivery. *"Not the best, but a good bet." "No style—mom and pop."*

Locations: Chelsea: 112 Greenwich Avenue, between Jane and West 13th Streets (633-9210) / **Flatiron/East Village:** 93 Avenue A, near 6Th Street (254-2054)

Between the Bread

Weekdays 7:30am–2:30pm.

Takeout
Multiple locations

The Edge: Either you love it or you think the prices are unconscionable. At breakfast, find a wide variety of fresh-fruit muffins, which seem to have a similar taste after a while, but the coffee is good and rich. At lunch, the standard salads, pasta, tuna, and steak. Very expensive. *"Great for business lunch delivery." "Greasy and overpriced."*

Locations: Midtown East: 141 East 56th Street, between Lexington and 3rd Avenues (888-0449) / **Midtown West:** 145 West 55th Street, between 6th and 7th Avenues (581-1189)

Canard and Company

1292 Madison Avenue
near 92nd Street / 722-1046
Weekdays 7am–9pm, Sat–Sun 7am–7:30pm.

Takeout
Upper East Side

The Edge: Catering and mail order. Gift baskets available. Santa Fe–style dishes, designer sandwiches, and excellent pies, coffee cakes, and chocolate-chip cookies made for the shop by Kathleen's. Catering is a specialty. For gifts, find custom gift baskets, fine candies, and jams and jellies. Also Beluga and Ossetra caviar and smoked salmon. *"A good place to get your takeout."*

City Bakery

22 East 17th Street
between 5th Avenue and Broadway / 366-1414
Mon–Sat 7:30am–6pm.

Takeout
Flatiron/East Village

The Edge: *The* **place for great takeout!** The fruit tarts are wonderful, as are the chocolate and brûlée tarts. At Christmas, a wonderful chestnut napoleon. Our favorite fruit tarts in season are blueberry, pear, and plum. Offers a limited seasonal luncheon menu and catering. Favors organic produce and meats. Now offering "dinner to go." The food menu features such items as grilled shrimp with avocado, grilled pineapple, brown rice, and black beans; balsamic-glazed baked chicken; pasta and vegetable dishes; and assorted salad combinations from the salad bar. The shop provides a taped recitation of the day's menu if you call the shop and press 1. Deliveries between the Battery and 96th Street, river to river. *"Great tarts and desserts." "Yes, real marshmallows." "A taste of Paris."*

David's Chicken

1323 3rd Avenue
corner of 76th Street / 628-2700
Weekdays 9am–9pm, Sat 10am–7:30pm, Sun 10am–8pm.

Takeout
Upper East Side

35	24	27	34
quality	style	service	value

The Edge: The Williams of the East Side. Rotisserie chicken, duck, turkey, capon, and rock Cornish hen, all moist and piping hot. Accompanying the chicken is egg barley, kasha varnishkes, mushrooms, string beans, and other cold salads. Also chicken soup with your choice of noodles or matzoth balls. *"Only grandma's chicken soup is better!" "The only good chicken in New York." "A bit greasy." "The soup can be salty."*

Dial-A-Dinner

350 5th Avenue / 643-1222
Daily 9am–10pm.

Takeout
Mail/phone

45	40	45	35
quality	style	service	value

The Edge: Food from your favorite restaurant in your home. Charges 20% over menu prices to deliver meals to your home. Restaurants include Arcadia, Harry Cipriani, Palm, Lobster Club, Mr. Chow, Table d'Hote, Bice, Mezzaluna, Les Halles, Nirvana, Jean Lafitte, Demarchelier, Due, Tse Yang, Provence, Tribeca Grill, San Domencio, Jezebel, Petrossian, Hatsuhana, and more. Delivery within 60 to 90 minutes.

E.A.T.

1064 Madison Avenue
between 80th and 81st Streets / 772-0022
Daily 7am–10pm.

Takeout
Upper East Side

41	40	36	22
quality	style	service	value

The Edge: Great food, but those prices and that attitude! Owned by Eli Zabar, Inc. Excellent sandwiches, salads, made-to-order appetizers, wonderful desserts, and catering. Prices are sky-high, and even with these prices they charge for delivery. *"The only $15 egg salad in New York!" "Prices are out of sight—not good value."*

El Pollo

Weekdays 11am–11pm, Sat–Sun noon–11pm.

Takeout
Multiple locations

30	10	30	40
quality	style	service	value

The Edge: Good cheap meals. Grilled roasted chicken served with a good sauce, crispy french fries or, even better, papa-rellenas (ground meat, fried potato, and raisins), and salads. No delivery. *"Delicious—good prices."*

Locations: SoHo/TriBeCa: 482 Broome Street, corner of Wooster Street (431-5666) / **Upper East Side:** 1746 1st Avenue, between 90th and 91st Streets (996-7810)

Fisher & Levy

875 3rd Avenue
near 53rd Street, concourse level / 832-3880
Weekdays 7:30am–5:30pm.

Takeout
Midtown East

The Edge: Specialty office catering. Will do everything from big functions to individual sandwich orders—breakfast to dinner. Also assortments of sandwiches (the shrimp is delicious) and salads.

Food Attitude

127 East 60th Street
between Lexington and Park Avenues / 980-1818
Weekdays 7am–7pm, Sat 8am–5pm, Sun 9am–4pm.

Takeout
Midtown East

The Edge: Good source for baked items and light lunches. Features brioches, croissants, desserts, quiche, salads, and soups. Makes a wonderful pear tatin in season. Good petit fours. Delivery only very locally, 3rd to 5th Avenues and 53rd to 67th Streets.

Friend of a Farmer

77 Irving Place
between 18th and 19th Streets / 477-2188
Sun–Fri 9:30am–10pm, Sat 9:30am–11pm.

Takeout
Flatiron/East Village

quality style service value

The Edge: Food you wished your mother made. Offers wholesome food (a meat-and-mashed-potato place). The desserts are especially good, particularly the fruit pies like cherry and apple. Also carries delicious cinnamon-raisin, white, and rye bread. A restaurant/takeout combo. *"Good home cookin'." "Great baked goods."*

Good & Plenty To Go

410 West 43rd Street
between 9th and 10th Avenues / 268-4385
Weekdays 7am–8pm, Sat–Sun 7am–6pm.

Takeout
Midtown West

quality style service value

The Edge: A Word of Mouth offshoot with good comfort food to take out. Owned by one of the original owners of Word of Mouth. Good, high-quality food includes rare sliced steak, divine cornbread, meatloaf, and, for nostalgia, macaroni and cheese. Desserts taste like you imagine grandma's did.

Hale & Hearty

849 Lexington Avenue
between 64th and 65th Streets / 517-7600
Mon–Thurs 8:30am–7pm, Fri 8:30am–6pm, Sat 10am–5:30pm.

Takeout
Upper East Side

quality style service value

The Edge: Healthy, well-prepared, but not exceptional, food. Menu favors soups, salads, and sandwiches for the office lunch crowd. No credit cards. Delivery available within a 10-block radius.

International Poultry Company
Weekdays 10am–9pm, Sat–Sun 10am–8pm.

Takeout
Multiple locations

40	30	30	30
quality	style	service	value

The Edge: A reasonable takeout alternative. Barbecued/grilled chicken served with salsa and soups, including chicken soup. Offers picnic baskets and catering.

Locations: Midtown East: 983 1st Avenue, near 54th Street (750-1100) / **Upper East Side:** 1133 Madison Avenue, between 84th and 85th Streets (879-3600)

Lorenzo & Maria's Kitchen
1418 3rd Avenue
between 80th and 81st Streets / 794-1080
Mon–Sat 10am–8pm.

Takeout
Upper East Side

37	33	33	30
quality	style	service	value

The Edge: Expensive, very good takeout, but you must know what's good. Top items include marinated shrimp with fresh dill, rare and tender leg of lamb, flaky salmon, crunchy French string beans, mashed or roast potatoes, and desserts, including crème caramel and rice pudding. Caters to telephone orders and delivers all over the city. The takeout menu changes daily, but many of the top choices mentioned above appear to be offered daily. The catering is flexible, with the kitchen accommodating a wide range of preferences. *"Best takeout in town, if you know what to order."*

Once Upon a Tart
135 Sullivan Street
near Houston Street / 387-8869
Mon–Sat 9am–8pm, Sun 9am–6pm.

Takeout
SoHo/TriBeCa

The Edge: Expensive catering service for mostly corporate clients. Catering items are primarily salads, soups, and sandwiches served in baskets and platters. The desserts are the best of all, including poached-pear tart and other fruit tarts (whatever's in season). Individual fruit tarts are $4 to $5. There are a few tables for eating in. No delivery.

Petite Abeille
107 West 18th Street
between 6th and 7th Avenues / 604-9350
Weekdays 7am–9pm, Sat–Sun 9am–7pm.

Takeout
Gramercy Park/Murray Hill

The Edge: Salads, quiches, and fabulous chocolate desserts. A Belgian cafe and catering shop. Delivers locally.

Poseidon Bakery
629 9th Avenue
between 44th and 45th Streets / 757-6173
Tues–Sat 9am–7pm, Sun 10am–4pm.

Takeout
Midtown West

40	30	30	40
quality	style	service	value

The Edge: Traditional Greek desserts and dinner items. Since 1925 has offered dinner pies, including meat and cheese, spinach and feta, spinach, potato, and cabbage and onion, plus party-size appetizers. Always available are 70 different types of streudels. Standard desserts accompany dinner. Find both fresh, handmade and machine-made phyllo dough. Will ship nationwide. Prices are reasonable. *"The only place to find fresh phyllo dough."*

Pranzo Fine Foods

1500 2nd Avenue
near 78th Street / 439-7777
Weekdays 7am–10pm, Sat–Sun 8am–9pm.

Takeout
Upper East Side

35 | 35 | 40 | 38
quality style service value

The Edge: Takeout favoring standard American and Italian favorites. For breakfast, more American than Italian, including assorted muffins and smoked-salmon platters. For evening, hors d'oeuvres include smoked-salmon triangles, assorted mini quiches, mini shrimp and crab cakes, and goat cheese bruschetta. Dinner specialties include salads, pastas, and grilled items representing various regional Italian specialties. Keep it simple and it's okay.

Remi To Go

145 West 53rd Street, in the aetrium
between 6th and 7th Avenues / 581-7115
Weekdays 6am–7pm.

Takeout
Midtown West

43 | 33 | 33 | 33
quality style service value

The Edge: Very good Italian takeout. Affiliated with the Restaurant Remi. Features business luncheon fare mostly: pasta salads, sandwiches, and some hot entrees. Full coffee bar and gourmet groceries. There are a few tables in the atrium to eat at. Caters to the business crowd for lunch and breakfast meetings. Local deliveries. *"Great food, great value—beats a deli!" "Too expensive for takeout."*

Taylor's

523 Hudson Street
between West 10th and Charles Streets / 645-8200
Weekdays 6am–9pm, Sat–Sun 7am–9pm.

Takeout
Greenwich Village

40 | 40 | 45 | 40
quality style service value

The Edge: The baked items are best. Breakfast specialties include muffins for start-the-day meetings. Dinner entrees include chicken pot pies, vegetable lasagne, and three-cheese pasta. Best are the baked goods, which include a chocolate-soufflé cake studded with walnuts, praline cookies, and iced cinnamon buns. No credit cards. No delivery.

TriBakery

186 Franklin Street
near Greenwich Street / 431-1114
Sun–Fri 7:30am–10:30pm, Sat 8am–10:30pm.

Takeout
SoHo/TriBeCa

30 | 30 | 30 | 30
quality style service value

The Edge: A new neighborhood casual spot offering takeout. A needed addition to the neighborhood, backed by Robert DeNiro, Bill Murray, and others. At the retail counter in this new neighborhood casual spot, takeout includes baked goods, ice cream, and basic home-cooking items. The kitchen closes at 10:30pm at the cafe, but you can still buy bread until they close the doors (midnight roughly). No delivery.

Trois Jean

154 East 79th Street
between Lexington and 3rd Avenues / 988-4858
Weekdays noon–6:30pm, Sat–Sun 10am–9pm.

Takeout
Upper East Side

quality style service value

The Edge: Very good traditional French fare. Takeout dishes include salads, cassoulet, and other traditional items. It's most famous for desserts, which include tarts, mousse, and crème brûlée, plus its chocolate pyramid, a birthday must. No delivery. *"Excellent food and service, attractive atmosphere." "The desserts are great."*

William Poll

1051 Lexington Avenue
between 74th and 75th Streets / 288-0501
Mon–Sat 9am–6:30pm.

Takeout
Upper East Side

quality style service value

The Edge: Some good things, but out-of-sight expensive. Best items are the frozen hors d'oeuvres (phyllo dough stuffed with spinach and cheese, meatballs, etc.). Known for its caviar, dips, and smoked salmon. Will make up sandwiches, which are small and expensive. At Christmas it offers handmade gingerbread houses, which incorporate music boxes and Christmas lights, for $150+.

Williams Bar-B-Que

2350 Broadway
between 85th and 86th Streets / 877-5384
Daily 9am–7:30pm.

Takeout
Upper West Side

quality style service value

The Edge: Traditional Friday-night Jewish dinners. Chicken and all the fixings, including chicken soup (with egg barley, mushrooms, and noodles), chopped liver, kasha varnishkes, potato pancakes, and more. Plus capon, duck, fried chicken, and turkey. No credit cards. *"Best in class— for Friday night dinners."*

Word of Mouth

1012 Lexington Avenue
between 72nd and 73rd Streets / 734-9483
Weekdays 10am–7pm, Sat 10am–6pm, Sun 11:30am–5:30pm.

Takeout
Upper East Side

quality style service value

The Edge: Good basic takeout. One of the first gourmet takeout stores. Specialties include meatloaf, sliced steak, lamb stew, salads, rice pudding, brownies, pecan bars, and peanut cup bars. Catering and picnic baskets available. Delivery for a fee. *"Wonderful lunch and brunch." "Very good takeout and catering."*

Acker Merrall and Condit

160 West 72nd Street
near Broadway / 787-1700
Mon–Sat 9am–10pm.

Wines & liquors
Upper West Side

quality style service value

The Edge: Strong selection of German and Alsatian wines. It's strongest in Californian, German, and Alsatian wines, but features a good selection of Australian, French, and Italian wines. Carries wine-related gift items, including corkscrews, baskets, books, and glassware. *"Unique items, great gifts."* *"Knowledgeable help, willing to spend time while you learn."*

Astor Wines & Spirits

12 Astor Place
corner of Lafayette Street / 674-7500
Mon–Sat 9am–9pm.

Wines & liquors
Flatiron/East Village

quality style service value

The Edge: Huge inventory of wines from around the world. The shop has a huge inventory and following. It's particularly strong on South American wines and champagnes and offers a large selection of moderately priced wines. *"Huge selection at great prices."* *"Excellent selection of kosher and hard-to-find wines."*

Burgundy Wine Company Limited

323 West 11th Street
between Greenwich and Washington Streets / 691-9092
Mon–Sat 10am–7pm.

Wines & liquors
Greenwich Village

quality style service value

The Edge: Great selection of—what else?—burgundies. Find a very good, large selection of top Burgundy and Rhône wines, often from smaller vineyards. An ever-changing inventory. Expensive.

Cork & Bottle

1158 1st Avenue
near 63rd Street / 838-5300
Mon–Thurs 9am–10pm, Fri–Sat 9am–11pm.

Wines & liquors
Upper East Side

quality style service value

The Edge: Good selection of wines. Cork & Bottle merged with Jim McMullen Wine & Liquor, which was owned by restaurateur Jim McMullen who is beloved by the Upper East Side senior set. Prices are okay for a local Upper East Side shop. *"Our favorite drop-by place!"* *"Good selection."*

Crossroads Wine & Liquor

55 West 14th Street
between 5th and 6th Avenues / 924-3060
Mon–Sat 9am–9pm.

Wines & liquors
Chelsea

quality style service value

The Edge: Good selection at good prices. A cluttered store featuring a large selection of wines with good coverage of Australian, Californian, French, Italian, and Oregonian wines, plus port. Also a large selection of champagnes in a wide range from inexpensive to very high end—carefully selected and priced well. A shabby-looking shop with anything but shabby service. 10% off. *"One of the best in town."* *"A must place to stop for your wine."*

First Avenue Wines & Spirits

383 1st Avenue
between 22nd and 23rd Streets / 673-3600
Mon–Sat 9am–8:30pm.

Wines & liquors
Gramercy Park/Murray Hill

quality style service value

The Edge: German wines. A broad selection of wines.

Garnet Wine & Liquor

929 Lexington Avenue
between 68th and 69th Streets / 772-3211
Mon–Sat 9am–9pm.

Wines & liquors
Upper East Side

quality style service value

The Edge: Excellent prices and huge selection. Features quality wines, liqueurs, ports, and standard liquors. A noteworthy selection of wines from California, Australia, France, and Italy. The place is often crowded. Weekly specials are advertised in flyers and in the Wednesday *New York Times*. The help is uneven. But if you know what you want, call—they'll most likely have it, and will deliver it within hours. Discounter. *"Best priced liquor." "The wine may be a value, but the attitude is horrendous."*

Gotham Wines & Liquors

2519 Broadway
at 94th Street / 876-4120
Mon–Sat 9am–9pm.

Wines & liquors
Upper West Side

quality style service value

The Edge: Excellent prices and service. The owners have a good knowledge of wines and offer a limited but quality selection. Watch for advertised specials in the *New York Times*. Mail order is available for out of the area. Discounter. *"Good prices, good selections."*

K&D Wines & Liquors

1366 Madison Avenue
between 95th and 96th Streets / 289-1818
Weekdays 9am–9:30pm, Sat 9am–9pm.

Wines & liquors
Upper East Side

quality style service value

The Edge: Good coverage of less expensive (under $10) wines. Good broad selection. Features less expensive wines (under $10) from Chile, Greece, and Australia. Wouldn't quote prices on the phone but advertises in the Wednesday *New York Times*. Mail order.

Morrell & Company

535 Madison Avenue
between 54th and 55th Streets / 688-9370
Mon–Sat 9am–6:45pm.

Wines & liquors
Midtown East

quality style service value

The Edge: Best for special gifts from a huge inventory of vintage wines. Offers often unique labels and vintages. The liquor store feels like a library. Excellent selection and service, but you pay for it. Offers wine-appreciation seminars periodically. *"Pricey, but quality choices."*

Park Avenue Liquors

292 Madison Avenue
between 40th and 41st Streets / 685-2442
Weekdays 8am–7pm, Sat 8am–5pm.

Wines & liquors
Midtown East

quality style service value

The Edge: Good selections. Features a wide range of hard-to-find wines from less-well-known Italian and California vineyards and a good selection of champagnes. Expensive.

Quality House

Wines & liquors
Gramercy Park/Murray Hill

2 Park Avenue
between 32nd and 33rd Streets / 532-2944
Weekdays 9am–6:30pm, Sat 9am–6pm (closed Sat July–Aug).

quality style service value

The Edge: Good selection, particularly of French wines and champagnes. Helpful staff. Prices are average to high, reflecting the level of service. No credit cards. No delivery. *"Great for gifts."*

Sherry-Lehmann Wine & Spirits Merchants

Wines & liquors
Upper East Side

679 Madison Avenue
near 61st Street / 838-7500
Mon–Sat 9am–7pm.

quality style service value

The Edge: A New York institution, offering a broad selection of wines. Great wines sold at okay prices, which on special become actually good prices. The selection of Californian, French, and Italian wines and champagnes, ports, and other after-dinner drinks is outstanding. The catalog is excellent, very extensive, and features some of the best prices. The store stocks plenty of inexpensive wines under $10. Free delivery in New York State for orders over $95. *"Number 1. Excellent." "Wonderful selection; patient, knowledgeable salespeople." "You name it and they have it. Very expensive. Very good delivery." "A New York City institution."*

67 Wine & Spirits Merchants

Wines & liquors
Upper West Side

179 Columbus Avenue
between 67th and 68th Streets / 724-6767
Mon–Thurs 9am–9pm, Fri–Sat 9am–10pm.

quality style service value

The Edge: First-rate selection of French and California wines. A large selection of Californian, French, Australian, and Italian wines and champagnes. Good, but not rock-bottom, prices. *"Good competitive neighborhood store." "Large special selection."*

Warehouse Wines & Spirits

Wines & liquors
Flatiron/East Village

735 Broadway
between Waverly Place and 8th Streets / 982-7770
Mon–Thurs 9am–9pm, Fri–Sat 9am–10pm.

quality style service value

The Edge: A large selection of premium liquor and wines. Okay prices. No delivery

The ratings: excellent very good good fair 10 so-so

Furniture & furnishings

Accscentiques

1418 2nd Avenue
near 74th Street / 288-3289
Wed–Fri 11am–7pm, Sat 11am–6pm,
Sun noon–5pm, Tues by appointment.

Accessories
Upper East Side

quality style service value

The Edge: An eclectic mix best for decorative accents. Features sachets and dried flowers,
decorative and other items, some small (pillows, picture frames) and some more significant (bed and
window) treatments. Also sofas and beds. *"For those who have it all!"*

Adrien Linford

1320 Madison Avenue
near 93rd Street / 289-4427
Daily 11am–7pm.

Accessories
Upper East Side

quality style service value

The Edge: Unique garden furniture and accessories. A good source for beautiful garden
furniture and accessories (gift items and tableware) crafted by artisans. *"Come here for the unusual
and for the beautiful—not for a bargain."*

Alphabet's

115 Avenue A
near St. Marks Place / 475-7250
Daily noon–8pm.

Accessories
Flatiron/East Village

quality style service value

The Edge: Unique adult games. Befitting Alphabet City, features adult toys, T-shirts, and eclectic
personal decorative gifts.

Bob Pryor Antiques

1023 Lexington Avenue
near 73rd Street / 688-1516
Mon–Sat 10:30am–5:30pm (closed Sat July–Aug).

Accessories
Upper East Side

quality style service value

The Edge: One-of-a-kind gift items. For over 22 years, unique gift items. Find unusual carved
wooden walking sticks, corkscrews, fire tools, picture frames, snuffboxes, and more. *"I try to
negotiate for 10% off."*

Candle Shop

118 Christopher Street

Accessories
Greenwich Village

between Bleecker and Hudson Streets / 989-0148
Mon–Thurs noon–8pm, Fri–Sat noon–9pm, Sun 1–7pm.

The Edge: Candles in all sizes, shapes, and hues. Hundreds of candles in a broad range of styles (paperweights, seasonals, conventional dinner) and candle holders made in an assortment of materials and styles. Also incense and oil lamps.

Clear Plastics

Accessories
SoHo/TriBeCa

45 Lispenard Street
between Church Street and Broadway / 925-6782
Weekdays 9:30am–6pm, Sat 10am–5pm.

The Edge: Plastic designs to order. Cuts plastic for shelves or dividers in any length and width. Sells plastic storage boxes. No credit cards.

Coca-Cola Fifth Avenue

Accessories
Midtown East

711 5th Avenue
near 55th Street / 418-9260
Mon–Sat 10am–8pm, Sun noon–6pm.

30	28	38	23
quality	style	service	value

The Edge: The Coke logo on everything. Over 600 items featuring Coca-Cola's logo and memorabilia, ranging from postcards to a vintage Coke vending machine. *"Great for gifts for all ages."*

Common Ground, Inc.

Accessories
Greenwich Village

19 Greenwich Avenue
between Christopher and 10th Streets / 989-4178
Weekdays noon–7pm, Sat 10am–6:30pm, Sun noon–6pm.

The Edge: Authentic Native American crafts. Features Native American, Mexican, and South American crafts and jewelry. Expect to find quality Navaho and other Native American rugs dating from the 1880s to the 1930s, with some contemporary Indian rugs. Priced from $1,500 to $20,000.

Craft Caravan

Accessories
SoHo/TriBeCa

63 Greene Street
between Broome and Spring Streets / 431-6669
Tues–Fri 10am–6pm, Sat–Sun 11am–6pm.

37	37	35	35
quality	style	service	value

The Edge: Traditional African crafts. In business 30 years, featuring traditional African handicrafts mainly from East and West Africa, priced from $1 to $5,000.

Dimson Homma

Accessories
Upper East Side

20 East 67th Street
near 5th Avenue / 439-7950
Mon–Sat 11am–6pm.

The Edge: Unusual wide-ranging collectibles. Expect to find exquisite jewelry and gift items from '40s Bulgari jewels to Chinese antiques. Wonderful taste.

Distant Origin

153 Mercer Street
between Prince and Houston Streets / 941-0024
Mon–Wed and Fri–Sat 11:30am–6:30pm,
Thurs 11:30am–7pm, Sun noon–6pm.

**Accessories
SoHo/TriBeCa**

quality style service value

The Edge: Eclectic furniture and accessories. From antique to modern, Mexico to Italy. Complementing the furniture, find accessories from all over the world, including silk lamps from Italy.

Felissimo

10 West 56th Street
between 5th and 6th Avenues / 247-5656
Mon–Wed and Fri–Sat 10am–6pm, Thurs 10am–8pm.

**Accessories
Midtown West**

quality style service value

The Edge: Unusual Oriental-feeling gifts. A less expensive Takashimaya. An entire town house selling accessories, bed and bath products, gifts, some clothing for men and women, table-top items, and unusual furniture. Top-floor tea room. Japanese owned and influenced. A catalog for the Christmas/New Year holidays only, call toll free 800-708-7690. *"Great place for unusual gifts with an Oriental feel."*

Flights of Fancy

1502 1st Avenue
near 78th Street / 772-1302
Mon–Tues and Thurs–Fri noon–7pm, Wed noon–8pm,
Sat 10am–6pm, Sun noon–6pm.

**Accessories
Upper East Side**

quality style service value

The Edge: Gifts from a bygone era. Special gift items, including reproduction jewelry, candles, Victorian and art deco jewelry and decorative items, pottery, and more. Wonderful Christmas ornaments. Prices range from under $10 to several thousand dollars. Watch for the annual summer sale, which reduces everything 20%.

41

41 Wooster Street
near Broome Street / 343-0935
Weekdays 10am–6pm, Sat noon–6pm.

**Accessories
SoHo/TriBeCa**

The Edge: Favorite shop for top decorators. Decorative arts, pottery, and costume jewelry. No credit cards.

Framed on Madison

740 Madison Avenue
between 64th and 65th Streets / 734-4680
Mon–Wed and Fri–Sat 10am–6pm, Thurs 10am–7pm,
Sun noon–5pm. (closed Sun July–Aug).

**Accessories
Upper East Side**

quality style service value

The Edge: Beautiful picture frames. Specializes in high-end picture frames in all shapes, sizes, and materials. A large, quality selection with mostly silver, silver-plate, and wood and antique frames. Priced from $7 to $2,000.

Gargoyles Ltd. of Philadelphia

200 Lexington Avenue, Suite 423
between 32nd and 33rd Streets / 255-0135
Weekdays 9:30am–5:30pm.

Accessories
Gramercy Park/Murray Hill

quality style service value

The Edge: An eclectic collection of potentially decorative items. New York showroom of an established Philadelphia company featuring vintage suitcases, equestrian equipment (helmets and trophies), general sporting goods, nautical items, trunks, and much, much more. *"New York's only garage sale!"*

Gifted Ones

150 West 10th Street
between Greenwich Street and Waverly Place / 627-4050
Mon–Sat noon–7:30pm.

Accessories
Greenwich Village

The Edge: Customized gift baskets. Imaginative baskets for all occasions filled with gourmet food, bath treats, spirits, and you-name-the-treasure. Customized to meet your gift needs.

Graham Arader

29 East 72nd Street
near Madison Avenue / 628-3668
Daily 10am–6pm.

Accessories
Upper East Side

quality style service value

The Edge: Rare prints of birds and botanicals.

H. M. Luther

61 East 11th Street
between Broadway and University Place / 505-1485
Weekdays 9am–5pm.

Accessories
Flatiron/East Village

quality style service value

The Edge: Favorite of top decorators. Unique accessories. No credit cards. *"Truly beautiful furniture, great style."* *"Pricey."*

Hammock World

66 East 7th Street
between 1st and 2nd Avenues / 673-1910
Mon–Sat 2–10pm.

Accessories
Flatiron/East Village

The Edge: Special Mexican things. Mexican pottery, clothing, and toys priced from $5 to $250.

Historic Design

306 East 61st Street
between 1st and 2nd Avenues / 593-4528
Mon–Sat 10am–6pm.

Accessories
Upper East Side

The Edge: Beautiful objects carefully selected. Decorative arts from 1880 to 1950, including Arts and Crafts, Vienna Secession, Wiener Werkstatte, Bauhaus, and art deco period pieces.

Hoshoni

309 East 9th Street
between 1st and 2nd Avenues / 674-3120
Tues–Sat noon–8pm, Sun noon–6pm.

Accessories
Flatiron/East Village

The Edge: Santa Fe in New York. Features exclusively New Mexican artisans creating furniture, accessories, and jewelry. Favors handmade custom-designed products, some exclusive to the store.

Hubert Des Forges

1193 Lexington Avenue
near 81st Street / 744-1857
Mon–Thurs 10am–6pm, Fri 10am–5pm.

Accessories
Upper East Side

quality style service value

The Edge: An eclectic shop crammed full of odd antique accessories. Items from the 18th-century through the 1940s. *"Expensive."*

John Rosselli International

Weekdays 10am–5pm.

Accessories
Multiple locations

| 40 | 50 | 40 | 30 |
quality style service value

The Edge: Decorative accessories from the 17th century to the present. Unique accessories, some antique, some reproduction. Prices to $20,000. Accessories featured at John Rosselli Antiques on 72nd Street. Supposed to be "to the trade only," but this is the '90s so visit anyway. No credit cards. No delivery. *"Beautiful reproductions."*

Locations: Upper East Side: 523 East 73rd Street, near York Avenue (772-2137) / 255 East 72nd Street, near 2nd Avenue (737-2252)

La Boutique Fantasque

620 5th Avenue
Rockefeller Promenade at 50th Street / 332-1830
Daily 10am–10pm.

Accessories
Midtown West

The Edge: One of the few Russian folk art stores in the city. Features hand-painted matroska (nesting dolls), lacquered boxes, and Fabergé-style eggs. The matroska dolls come in every size and feature presidents and Russian leaders.

Linda Horn Antiques

1015 Madison Avenue
between 78th and 79th Streets / 772-1122
Mon–Sat 10am–6pm (closed Sat July–Aug).

Accessories
Upper East Side

| 43 | 50 | 37 | 33 |
quality style service value

The Edge: Very ornate English and European 19th-century antiques. Features an eclectic collection of small furniture, accessories (including crystal pitchers and decanters, many with sterling-silver stoppers), picture frames, and walking sticks. The focus is whimsical ornate styles, many in bamboo, lacquer, marble, or papier-mâché. Deluxe. *"I love her style."*

Man-Tiques Ltd.

Accessories
Midtown East

1050 2nd Avenue
between 55th and 56th Streets / 759-1805
Mon–Sat 11am–5:30pm.

quality style service value

The Edge: Unique antique gift items for hard-to-please men. Selection includes canes, German beer steins, porcelain shaving mugs, scientific instruments, walking sticks, and more. The canes seemed particularly nice. *"Wonderful things from bygone days."*

Marco Polo

Accessories
Upper East Side

1135 Madison Avenue
between 84th and 85th Streets / 734-3775
Weekdays 10:30am–5:30pm, Sat noon–4:30pm.

quality style service value

The Edge: English gift items. Find items expected in a proper Victorian home, including cut crystal, letter openers, magnifying glasses, pens and inkwells, sterling-silver picture frames, sterling-silver capped boudoir jars, and more. Both antique and modern pieces. *"Good English-style knickknacks."*

Matt McGhee

Accessories
Greenwich Village

22 Christoper Street
near Waverly Place / 741-3138
Jan–Thanksgiving, Tues–Sat noon–7pm; Thanksgiving–Dec, Mon–Sat noon– 8pm, Sun 1–5pm.

The Edge: Wonderful traditional Christmas ornaments. At Christmas stocks old-fashioned tree ornaments and stocking stuffers, including carved wooden figures of angels, nativity scenes, and more. Also hand-painted Limoges porcelain boxes and unique pewter figures.

Mediterranean Shop

Accessories
Upper East Side

780 Madison Avenue
near 66th Street / 879-3120
Mon–Sat 10am–5:30pm.

quality style service value

The Edge: Reproductions of antique French and Italian faïence. Specialty papers and ceramics. Designs range from a 12th-century Palio collection to the Moustiers and Rouen patterns of the late 18th century. *"Florence in New York."*

Moss

Accessories
SoHo/TriBeCa

146 Greene Street
near Houston Street / 226-2190
Tues–Sat 11am–7pm, Sun noon–6pm.

The Edge: Eclectic household items. Wonderful fabrics favor sheers and metallics. Unusual gift items, including an inflatable plastic frame and table light that turns on by simply tilting it to the right or left.

Mxyplyzyk

Accessories
Greenwich Village

125 Greenwich Avenue
near 13th Street / 989-4300
Mon–Sat 11am–7pm, Sun noon–5pm.

quality style service value

The Edge: Stylish home furnishings, adorable children's toys, and other knickknacks. Home accessories, including magazine racks, lamps, picture frames, vases, hardware, and the like. Favorite toys for kids: colorful tricycles and scooters—who says these have to be boring? Bikes made with color pieces painted out of steel frames and PVC-plastic seats. Plenty for pet lovers— bathrobes with Dalmatian trim plus many animal-logo items.

Pierre Deux

870 Madison Avenue
near 71st Street / 570-9343
Mon–Sat 10am–6pm.

Accessories
Upper East Side

The Edge: French country wares—fabrics and home furnishings. Features fabrics from all the regions of France, including Souleiado hand-screened fabrics in traditional Provençal patterns. Also a wide range of home furnishings, such as napkins, pewter, place mats, and tablecloths in addition to flatware and faïence by Moustiers. 18th- and 19th- century handcrafted French country furniture and antiques, mostly from Provence. Deluxe.

Pillowry

132 East 61st Street
between Park and Lexington Avenues / 308-1630
Weekdays 11:30am–5:30pm, Sat by appointment.

Accessories
Upper East Side

The Edge: Pillows of all sorts. Old and one-of-a-kind pillows made from tapestries, rugs, and textiles dating from the 16th century to modern times. Most things are 19th- to early 20th-century. Priced from $50 to $3,200.

Piston's

1050 2nd Avenue
near 57th Street / 753-8322
Weekdays 10am–4pm, Sat 10am–2pm and by appointment.

Accessories
Midtown East

quality style service value

The Edge: Rare 17th- to 19th-century decorative brass, copper, and pewter accessories. Accessories include candlesticks, copper kettles, pewter plates, curtain tiebacks, cornices, and more. No credit cards.

Planet Hemp

423 Broome Street
between Crosby Street and Broadway / 965-0500
Sun–Wed noon–6pm, Thurs–Sat noon–8pm.

Accessories
SoHo/TriBeCa

The Edge: It's all hemp. SoHo mini–department store with home furnishings. Home furnishings include blankets, wallpaper, curtain panels, rugs, etc. Most of the clothing is made of 100% hemp.

Plexi-Craft

514 West 24th Street
between 10th and 11th Avenues / 924-3244
Weekdays 9am–5pm.

Accessories
Chelsea

The Edge: Customized Plexiglass shelving, tables, and stands. Custom- and ready-made plastic furnishings. Discounter. Catalogue $2.

Pondicherri

454 Columbus Avenue
near 82nd Street / 875-1609
Sun–Wed 11am–7pm, Thurs–Sat 11am–8pm.

Accessories
Upper West Side

quality style service value

The Edge: Pottery from Indonesia and Africa. Pottery, plus fabrics made into decorative
household items, including bed linens and tableware. Very large selection. Pillows from $10.50 to
$80.

Portantina

895 Madison Avenue
near 72nd Street / 472-0636
Mon–Sat 10:30am–6pm.

Accessories
Upper East Side

quality style service value

The Edge: Small Italian objets d'art from the 17th and 18th centuries. Wonderful Venetian
treasures. *"Costly but choice selection."*

Primavera Gallery

808 Madison Avenue
near 68th Street / 288-1569
Mon–Sat 11am–6pm (closed Sat July–Aug).

Accessories
Upper East Side

quality style service value

The Edge: Glorious 20th-century art and jewelry. Features furniture, jewelry, and decorative
items. Wonderful art deco furniture from top designers. Also decorative items such as glass by
Lalique and Jean Luce. Art deco and art nouveau jewelry, including designs by Boucheron, Cartier,
David Webb, Lalique, Van Cleef & Arpels, and Tiffany. High-end. *"Such beautiful taste!"*

Rita Ford Music Boxes

19 East 65th Street
between 5th and Madison Avenues / 535-6717
Mon–Sat 9am–5pm.

Accessories
Upper East Side

quality style service value

The Edge: Wonderful music boxes and carousels. Features contemporary music boxes and
carousels. Contemporary carousels are handmade by artists. Music boxes from inexpensive to
unbelievably costly. Unique Christmas tree music boxes are designed for the shop. Pricing into the
mega-thousands. Repairs music boxes as well. *"Fun, fun, fun."* *"Very expensive, but wonderful."*

Russian Arts

451 Avenue of the Americas
near 11th Street / 242-5946
Tues–Sat noon–6:30pm.

Accessories
Chelsea

The Edge: Soviet memorabilia. Expect military uniforms, Russian dolls, and decorative items.
Priced from $1 to $2,000.

Saint Remy

818 Lexington Avenue
near 62nd Street / 486-2018
Weekdays 10:30am–7pm, Sat 10:30am–6pm.

Accessories
Upper East Side

quality style service value

The Edge: Fabrics and porcelain from Provence. Expect to find tiny floral potpourri, printed cottons, sachets, scented drawer liners, wreaths, and wonderful hand-painted French country pottery.

Serendipity
225 East 60th Street
between 2nd and 3rd Avenues / 838-3531
Mon–Thurs 11:30am–12:30am, Fri 11:30am–1am,
Sat 11am–2am, Sun 11:30am– midnight.

Accessories
Midtown East

quality style service value

The Edge: Every child's (and the child is everyone) favorite restaurant. Known for frozen hot chocolate, foot-long hot dogs, and ice-cream sundaes. The front of the store is a gift boutique featuring an eclectic selection of hand-painted T-shirts, vests, coffee mugs, and more.

Slatkin & Company
131 East 70th Street
between Park and Lexington Avenues / 794-1661
Mon–Sat 10am–6pm (closed Sat July–Aug).

Accessories
Upper East Side

quality style service value

The Edge: Well-chosen traditional accessories. Small furniture items. Best known for its English country styled accessories, including candles, hand-painted porcelains, picture frames, and table linens. *"Gifts to take to Balmoral weekends!"*

Stardust
38 Gramercy Park
near 3rd Avenue / 677-2590
Weekdays 11am–7pm, Sat 11am–6pm, Sun noon–5pm.

Accessories
Gramercy Park/Murray Hill

The Edge: Antiques and reproductions cast from the original molds. Features English and American furniture, jewelry, and paintings from Victorian times to the 1930s. Some reproductions.

Susan P. Meisel Decorative Arts
133 Prince Street
between Wooster Street and West Broadway / 254-0137
Sept to mid-July, Tues–Sat 10am–6pm;
mid-July and Aug, by appointment.

Accessories
SoHo/TriBeCa

quality style service value

The Edge: Eclectic collection. The shop features American and English nautical and scientific items, pinup art, and pond boats from the 1930s to the 1960s.

Terracotta
259 West 4th Street
between Perry and Charles Streets / 243-1952
Tues–Sat noon–7pm, Sun noon–6pm.

Accessories
Greenwich Village

The Edge: An artisan gift store. Features home and personal accessories. For home: candles, gifts, picture frames, pretty pillows, and more. For you: wonderful hats, jewelry, and ties. Priced from $5 to $300.

Things Japanese
Accessories
Midtown East

127 East 60th Street
between Lexington and Park Avenues / 371-4661
Mon and Wed–Sat 11am–5pm, Tues 11am–6pm.

40	30	40	45
quality	style	service	value

The Edge: Japanese decorative items. Features dolls, ivory carvings, lacquerware, pottery, and wood block prints. Some vintage kimonos. *"Unusual and unique!"*

Tim McKoy Gallery
Accessories
Greenwich Village

318 Bleecker Street
near Christopher Street / 242-3456
Tues–Sun noon–7pm.

The Edge: Specializes in antique dolls. Dolls range in price from $200 to $5,000.

Timbuktu
Accessories
Flatiron/East Village

238 East 6th Street
between 2nd and 3rd Avenues / 388-0951
Thurs–Sun 1–6pm.

The Edge: Moroccan treasures. From tea glasses to iron works, wonderful, unique Moroccan items for the home. Favorite items include traditional lanterns and those ceramic tile tables. *"Reasonable prices and great taste."*

U.S.E.D.
Accessories
Greenwich Village

17 Perry Street
near 7th Avenue / 627-0730
Daily 1:30–8pm.

The Edge: Eclectic knickknacks. The owner buys what he likes—much of which is used (hence the name) decorative items, including boxes, glassware, and games. No delivery.

Urban Archaeology
Accessories
SoHo/TriBeCa

285 Lafayette Street
between Prince and Houston Streets / 431-6969
Weekdays 8am–6pm, Sat 10am–4pm (closed Sat July–Aug).

43	43	43	33
quality	style	service	value

The Edge: You never know what they've found—truly unique urban treasures. An eclectic mix of treasures gathered from buildings, homes, and offices with no rhyme or reason for their salvage. Find antique and reproduction garden furniture, bathroom fixtures, bookcases, columns, lighting, mantels, mirrors, old paneled doors, and more. Wide price range. *"Stylish and up-to-the-minute. The experts on architecture."*

William Wayne & Company
Accessories
Upper East Side

850 Lexington Avenue
at 64th Street / 288-9243
Daily 10:30am–6:30pm.

The Edge: Treasures from the turn of the century. Find small furniture and accessories, including desk lamps, bamboo magazine racks, sconces, and more. Old-world styling. The Christmas ornaments are lovely. *"Great timely gifts." "Cramped, but interesting inventory."*

XYZ Total Home
15 East 18th Street
between 5th Avenue and Broadway / 388-1942
Daily 11am-8pm.

Accessories
Flatiron/East Village

The Edge: Unique and affordable home accessories and gifts. Find custom made pillows and bedding and unique home design accessories and furniture. Recently opened in a landmark building, XYZ Total Home operates its own factory as well. New to the City and to us—let us know what you think.

Zona
97 Greene Street
between Spring and Prince Streets / 925-6750
Mon–Wed and Fri–Sat 11am–6:30pm,
Thurs 11:30am–7pm, Sun noon–6pm.

Accessories
SoHo/TriBeCa

The Edge: Beautiful unique accessories. Handmade, mostly sterling-silver, jewelry, plus home accessories, including small furniture, candles, pottery, soaps, and more. *"Terrific vacation home things." "Beautiful but high priced." "Expensive."*

Alice's Antiques
72 Greene Street
near Spring Street / 874-3400
Daily 11:30am–7pm.

American
SoHo/TriBeCa

The Edge: Best known for its antique American iron beds. Iron beds are available in a range of sizes from single to king. Decorator discount possible to (we believe) 20%. *"Average Victoriana."*

Barton-Sharpe Ltd.
66 Crosby Street
below Spring Street / 925-9562
Mon–Sat 10am–6pm, Sun noon–5pm (closed Sat July–Aug).

American
SoHo/TriBeCa

The Edge: Exact reproductions of English and Shaker-inspired American furniture. Find wonderful fabrics along with the furniture reproductions. *"The salesmen know their merchandise and follow up on orders."*

Hirschl & Adler Galleries, Inc.
21 East 70th Street
between 5th and Madison Avenues / 535-8810
Tues–Fri 9:30am–5:15pm,

American
Upper East Side

Sat 9:30am–4:45pm (closed Sat May 24–Labor Day).

quality style service value

The Edge: Museum-quality American folk furniture. Furniture and accessories, including corner cupboards, blanket chests, paintings, quilts, needlework, weather vanes, and sculptures. Deluxe. No credit cards. *"Quality—unusual items." "Good quality."*

Peter Roberts Antiques

134 Spring Street
near Greene Street / 226-4777
Mon–Sat 11am–7pm, Sun noon–6pm.

American
SoHo/TriBeCa

quality style service value

The Edge: Signed pieces of American Arts and Crafts and Mission furniture. Full range of furniture. Accessories include copper, lighting, and pottery, as well as reproduction Gustav Stickley rugs and runners. No credit cards.

United House Wrecking

535 Hope Street
I-95 Exit 9 or Merritt Parkway Exit 36, Stamford / 203-348-5371
Mon–Sat 9:30am–5:30pm, Sun noon–5pm.

American
Connecticut

quality style service value

The Edge: Connecticut's largest antiques emporium, with used decorative hardware at good prices. Started as a demolition business in 1954, the Lodato family salvaged doors, mantels, stained glass, and other architectural remnants of value. Find antiques, accessories, accent pieces, lawn and garden furniture, lighting fixtures, and more. Also reproductions and decorative brass hardware. *"The brass hardware, used and reproductions, are great buys. I found beautiful brass door knobs there at a fraction of New York prices."*

A Repeat Performance

156 1st Avenue
near 10th Street / 529-0832
Mon–Sat 10am–8pm, Sun 2–8pm.

Antiques
Flatiron/East Village

30 30 40 40

quality style service value

The Edge: Eclectic collection of period furniture and household accessories. Period odds and ends favoring the witty. Complementing the furniture, expect some clothing and costume jewelry, decorative items, and period shades. Cozy and cluttered.

Amy Perlin Antiques

1020 Lexington Avenue, 2nd Floor
between 72nd and 73rd Streets / 744-4923
Weekdays 10am–5pm.

Antiques
Upper East Side

50 50 50 40

quality style service value

The Edge: Eclectic shop with 18th-century accessories and furniture. Decorator discounts to 25% are possible. No credit cards. *"Unique."*

Ann Morris Antiques

239 East 60th Street
near 2nd Avenue / 755-3308
Weekdays 9am–6pm.

Antiques
Midtown East

quality style service value

The Edge: Mostly English country furniture. Allegedly to the trade only. Mostly English country furniture, with some furniture from Scotland and France. Favorite of top decorators. 25% decorator discount.

Annex Antiques Fair and Flea Market

Avenue of the Americas
at 26th Street / 243-5343
Year-round, Sat–Sun sunrise–sunset.

Antiques
Midtown West

quality style service value

The Edge: Ever-changing eclectic treasures. Come early and bring a flashlight. Collectibles range from costume and estate jewelry to furniture and home and personal accessories. Make sure to bargain hard. $1 admission. No credit cards. No delivery.

Arkitektura

96 Greene Street
near Spring Street / 334-5570
Tues–Fri 10:30am–5:30pm, Sat noon–5pm (closed Sat in Aug).

Antiques
SoHo/TriBeCa

quality style service value

The Edge: Licensed replicas (and originals) of 1930s to 1990s furniture. A loft-size showroom featuring a large array of contemporary (1930s to 1990s) furniture priced from $1,000 to $40,000. It manufactures its own lighting ($295 to $650).

Chelsea Antiques Building

110 West 25th Street
between 6th and 7th Avenues / 929-0909
Daily 10am–6pm.

Antiques
Midtown West

quality style service value

The Edge: 10 floors of decorative items. 100 dealers and a cafe.

Depression Modern

150 Sullivan Street
near Houston Street / 982-5699
Wed–Sun noon–7pm (closed Sun in Aug).

Antiques
SoHo/TriBeCa

quality style service value

The Edge: Furniture from the Depression period. Find quality furniture, lamps, rugs, and decorative accessories. The garden features vintage summer furniture. No credit cards.

George N. Antiques

67 East 11th Street
between Broadway and University Place / 505-5599
Weekdays 10:30am–5:30pm.

Antiques
Flatiron/East Village

The Edge: Fine period furniture and chandeliers. Mostly to the trade, but some retail. Primarily 19th and 20th century with some 18th-century pieces. Favors French and English, with some American, continental, and Italian furniture.

Hyde Park Antiques

836 Broadway
near 13th Street / 477-0033
Weekdays 9am–5:30pm, Sat 10am–2:30pm (closed Sat July–Aug).

Antiques
Flatiron/East Village

quality style service value

The Edge: A vast inventory of fine 18th-century English furniture. Two floors of furniture and accessories (paintings, mirrors, and English and Chinese porcelains). Items priced from $1,000 to $500,000. No credit cards. *"Extensive selection."*

James Hepner Antiques

130 East 82nd Street
between Park and Lexington Avenues / 737-4470
Weekdays 11am–5pm; other hours, call for appointment.

Antiques
Upper East Side

The Edge: Quality 17th- to 19th-century antiques. Often unique pieces. Great taste. No credit cards.

Lee Calicchio Ltd.

134 East 70th Street
near Lexington Avenue / 717-4417
Weekdays 11am–5pm (closed Fri in Aug), Sat by appointment.

Antiques
Upper East Side

quality style service value

The Edge: Quality 18th- and 19th-century French and continental furniture. Furniture, plus accessories, including crystal pieces, lamps, and objets d'art. 15% off to decorators.

Manhattan Art & Antiques Center

1050 2nd Avenue
at 56th Street / 355-4400
Mon–Sat 10:30am–6pm, Sun noon–6pm.

Antiques
Midtown East

quality style service value

The Edge: Fine antiques from more than 100 dealers. Offers period furniture, jewelry, silver, porcelains, Americana, Orientalia, Africana, and other objets d'art. *"Interesting place to browse."*

Secondhand Rose

138 Duane Street
between West Broadway and 4th Street / 393-9002
Weekdays 10am–6pm, Sat–Sun noon–5pm.

Antiques
Midtown East

quality style service value

The Edge: More used than antique furniture and knickknacks. Features furniture from the 1920s to the 1950s like that found at grandma's.

William Lipton Ltd.

27 East 61st Street
between Park and Madison Avenues / 751-8131
Weekdays 10am–6pm, Sat noon–5pm
(Sat in summer by appointment).

Antiques
Upper East Side

quality style service value

The Edge: Unique objets d'art. Specialty is Asian antiques.

ABC Trading Company

Appliances
Lower East Side/Chinatown

31 Canal Street
between Essex and Ludlow Streets / 228-5080
Sun–Fri 10am–6pm.

quality style service value

The Edge: Appliances geared for the export market. Features small and large appliances (refrigerators, air conditioners, televisions) converted for the export market. Wouldn't quote prices over the phone. 25% off.

Bernie's Discount Center

Appliances
Midtown West

821 Avenue of the Americas
between 28th and 29th Streets / 564-8582
Weekdays 9:30am–6pm, Sat 11am–4pm (closed Sat July–Aug).

quality style service value

The Edge: Discounts appliances and electronics. Since 1948. Sells a full range of small to large appliances. *"Great prices."*

Bloom and Krup

Appliances
Flatiron/East Village

504 East 14th Street
between Avenues A and B / 673-2760
Mon–Sat 9am–6pm, Sun 11am–4pm.

quality style service value

The Edge: Service over price. Since 1928. Principally appliances and plumbing fixtures. Good service and installation, with prices about 10% to 20% higher than the discounters. *"High priced, but worth it for the service."*

Dembitzer Brothers

Appliances
Lower East Side/Chinatown

5 Essex Street
near Canal Street / 254-1310
Mon–Thurs 10am–4:30pm, Fri 10am–2pm, Sun 10am–4:30pm.

quality style service value

The Edge: Appliances for export. Features discounted appliances, especially those geared for overseas shipment. Staff speaks six languages. Won't quote prices over the phone.

Electrical Appliances Rental Sales Company

Appliances
Midtown West

40 West 29th Street
between 6th Avenue and Broadway / 686-8884
Weekdays 8:30am–5:30pm.

The Edge: Wide range of appliances. Sells a wide range of appliances, from fans and heaters to refrigerators. Rents TVs and VCRs (VCRs from $30 per day).

Home Sales Enterprises

Appliances
Mail/phone

513-1513
Weekdays 9am–5pm, Sat 9am–1pm.

quality style service value

The Edge: Discount buying service for major appliances. Often really low prices and a wide range of products. Call up with make and model numbers and then schedule delivery, sometimes for the next day. Requires payment by certified check or cash, but price includes delivery. No credit cards. Discounter.

LVT Price Quote Hotline

Appliances
Mail/phone

P.O. Box 444
Commack / 800-582-8884
Mon–Sat 9am–6pm.

The Edge: Appliances by phone—efficient and has among the lowest prices. Instant prices by phone on a wide range of small and large appliances, air conditioners, electronic equipment, and more. Virtually all the top brands. Order by calling with the manufacturer and model number of the item you want. Delivers to New York, New Jersey, Connecticut, and Pennsylvania. Among the lowest prices we found in our spot-check on price, plus it had most of the items we were checking. Very polite and efficient. No credit cards. Discounter.

Peninsula Buying

Appliances
Mail/phone

838-1010
Weekdays 9am–5pm, Sat 9–11am.

35	30	30	50
quality	style	service	value

The Edge: Appliance buying services offering low prices. Claim to sell 5% above wholesale and were among the best prices discovered in our spot survey. However, ordering required patience since they can be slow to answer and provide prices. A more limited selection than others we checked.

Price Watchers

Appliances
Mail/phone

718-470-1620
Weekdays 9am–6pm, Sat 9am–5pm.

50	30	50	50
quality	style	service	value

The Edge: Great prices on electronics and appliances. Discount buying service for TVs, video equipment, and large appliances. Phone with the make and model number and compare prices. Payment via cash, money order, or certified check. When we spot-tested prices, they were among the lowest quoted to our research team.

Acquavella Galleries, Inc.

Art & artifacts
Upper East Side

18 East 79th Street
between 5th and Madison Avenues / 734-6300
Weekdays 10am–5pm.

50	50	40	30
quality	style	service	value

The Edge: Features 19th- and 20th-century art and antiques. Find master paintings, drawings, and sculptures showing works from impressionist, post-impressionist and postwar contemporary artists.

Altar Egos

Art & artifacts
SoHo/TriBeCa

110 West Houston Street
between Sullivan and Thompson Streets / 677-9588

Tues–Sun 1-8pm.

The Edge: Exclusively religious objects. Find books, music, candles, holy water, incense, and jewelry from every religion from East to West.

Andre Emmerich

41 East 57th Street
between 5th and Madison Avenues / 752-0124
Tues–Sat 10am–5:30pm.

Art & artifacts
Midtown East

50	50	50	50
quality	style	service	value

The Edge: Contemporary American and European artists. Includes works by David Hochney, Hans Hofmann, and others.

Art Insights Gallery

161 West 72nd Street
between Columbus and Amsterdam / 724-3715
Mon–Sat 10:30am–7pm, Sun noon–6pm, or by appointment.

Art & artifacts
Upper West Side

30	20	30	30
quality	style	service	value

The Edge: Specializes in 20th-century graphics, paintings, drawings, and sculpture. Features original works by Erte, Haring, McKnight, Gorman, Fazzino, Rizzi, Neiman, Kostabi, Li Zhong Liang, Agam, Rauschenberg, Tarkay, Maimon, Behrens, and Vasarely.

Associated American Artists

20 West 57th Street
between 5th and 6th Avenues / 399-5510
Tues–Sat 10am–6pm.

Art & artifacts
Midtown West

The Edge: Since 1934, features works on paper. Artists include Rufino Tamayo, Robert Motherwell, Sam Francis, Adolph Gottlieb, Fernando De Szyszlo, Francisco Toledo, Helen Frankenthaler, Richard Diebenkorn, Wayne Thiebaud, Paul Jenkins, Milton Avery, and Werner Drewes. Spotlights 20th-century art.

Brooke Alexander

59 Wooster Street
between Spring and Broome Streets / 925-4338
Wed–Sat noon–6pm.

Art & artifacts
SoHo/TriBeCa

40	40	40	40
quality	style	service	value

The Edge: Paintings, drawings, and sculptures. Find works by Ahearn, Bordo, Bosman, Burckhardt, Chase, Cole, De Keyser, Dickson, Dorner, Guzman, Jacquette, McCollum, Morton (estate), Mullican, Nadin, Nechvatal, Otterness, Mangold, Raetz, Salcedo, Thek (estate), Tobias, Torress, Tuttle, Winter, and Zaugg.

De Nagy

724 5th Avenue
at 57th Street / 262-5050
Tues–Sat 10am–5:30pm.

Art & artifacts
Midtown West

The Edge: Focus on photography.

Elizabeth Harris Gallery

529 Broadway, 6th Floor
between 9th and 10th Avenues / 463-9666
Tues–Sat 10am–6pm.

Art & artifacts
SoHo/TriBeCa

The Edge: Emerging modern artists. Find paintings, sculpture, and ceramics.

Feller's Judaica and Gift Gallery

1205 Lexington Avenue
between 81st and 82nd Streets / 472-2300
Mon–Thurs 11am–6pm, Fri 10:30am–2pm, Sun noon–5pm.

Art & artifacts
Upper East Side

quality style service value

The Edge: Small store featuring Judaica. Find candlesticks, books, pictures, traditional religious items, and the like. The back of the store caters to children with such items as a Hebrew spelling board and books. *"Excellent service, accommodating, knowledgeable."*

Frank J. Miele Gallery

1086 Madison Avenue
between 81st and 82nd Streets / 249-7250
Weekdays 10am–6pm, Sat 10am–5pm, Sun noon–5pm.

Art & artifacts
Upper East Side

The Edge: Focus on modern folk art.

Gagosian Gallery

Weekday 10am–6pm; summer, weekdays 10am–6pm.

Art & artifacts
Multiple locations

The Edge: The gallery of the moment! Noted for its collection of modern and contemporary paintings, sculpture, and drawings.

Locations: SoHo/TriBeCa: 136 Wooster Street, near Spring Street (228-2828) / **Upper East Side:** 980 Madison Avenue, between 76th and 77th Streets (744-2313)

Gallery of Graphic Arts

1601 York Avenue
near 85th Street / 988-4731
Mon–Sat 11am–6:30pm.

Art & artifacts
Upper East Side

quality style service value

The Edge: Graphic art from around the globe. Find graphic art priced from $50 to $4,000. Specializes in problem framing. *"Great framing."*

J. Levine Co.

5 West 30th Street
between Broadway and 5th Avenue / 695-6888
Mon–Wed 9am–6pm, Thurs 9am–7pm,
Fri 9am–2pm, Sun 10am–5pm.

Art & artifacts
Upper East Side

quality style service value

The Edge: If they don't stock it, question why you want it. All aspects of Jewish faith are represented since the store's founding in 1890 in Lithuania (since 1905 in the U.S.). The first floor is devoted to gifts and mezuzahs. The second floor has thousands of books, children's items, and

CDs. Afternoon prayers are at 1:40pm, and there's a monthly lunchtime class on mysticism and spirituality.

James Graham & Sons, Inc.

Art & artifacts
Upper East Side

1014 Madison Avenue
near 78th Street / 535-5767
Sept–June, Tues–Sat 10am–5:30pm, Mon by appointment; July–Aug, weekdays 10am–5:30pm.

The Edge: Fine 19th- and early 20th-century American and European art. Find 19th- and early 20th-century American and European painting and sculpture.

James Lowe Autographs

Art & artifacts
Midtown East

30 East 60th Street, Suite 304
between Madison and Park Avenues / 759-0775
Weekdays 9:30am–4:30pm, Sat by appointment.

quality style service value

The Edge: Signed memorabilia from the makers and shakers. Celebrated signatures on autographed photos, documents, and letters from the Revolution on. Covers all areas of history, literature, music, and more. Civil War and 19th-century photographs a specialty. No credit cards.

Kraushaar Galleries, Inc.

Art & artifacts
Midtown West

724 5th Avenue
near 56th Street / 307-5730
Sept–May, Tues–Fri 9:30am–5:30pm, Sat 10am–5pm;
June–July, weekdays 10am–5pm; Aug, by appointment.

The Edge: 20th-century artists. Specializes in Maine artists from 1900 to 1950. Expensive, with prices into the hundreds of thousands.

Leo Castelli Gallery

Art & artifacts
SoHo/TriBeCa

420 West Broadway
between Spring and Prince Streets / 431-5160
Tues–Sat 10am–6pm.

quality style service value

The Edge: Well-known gallery featuring the latest in contemporary paintings.

Lost City Arts

Art & artifacts
SoHo/TriBeCa

275 Lafayette Street
near Prince Street / 941-8025
Weekdays 10am–6pm, Sat–Sun noon–6pm.

The Edge: Whimsical Americana decorative items. Features furniture and decorations from the 1930s (mostly) to the 1950s, as well as architectural ornamentation. Memorabilia from beloved places and images. Favors pop American decorative items. Priced from $2 to $20,000.

Mary Boone Gallery

Art & artifacts
Midtown West

745 5th Avenue
between 57th and 58th Streets / 752-2929
Tues–Fri 10am–6pm, Sat 10am–5pm.

quality   style   service   value

The Edge: Featuring contemporary art.

Pace Wildenstein Gallery
32 East 57th Stret
between Madison and Park Avenues / 421-3292
Tues–Sat 9:30am–6pm.

Art & artifacts
Midtown East

quality   style   service   value

The Edge: First-rate modern artists.

Phyllis Lucas Gallery & Old Print Center
981 2nd Avenue
at 52nd Street / 755-1516
Mon–Thurs 9:30am–7pm, Fri–Sat 9:30am–6pm.
Closed Sat Jun-Aug.

Art & artifacts
Midtown East

quality   style   service   value

The Edge: Early American prints. Features Early American prints, including engravings, lithographs, and signed limited-edition lithographs. Some reproductions. No credit cards. *"Wonderful collection of antique prints."*

Poster America
138 West 18th Street
near 6th Avenue / 206-0499
Tues and Fri–Sat 11am–6pm, Sun noon–5pm (closed Sun June–Aug).

Art & artifacts
Chelsea

The Edge: Collectible posters from 1910 to 1965. Posters, graphic designs, and original advertising art. Priced from $400 to $2,000.

Robert Miller
41 East 57th Street
at Madison Avenue / 980-5454
Tues–Sat 10am–6pm.

Art & artifacts
Midtown East

The Edge: Focus on photographs.

Rosenberg & Stiebel, Inc.
32 East 57th Street, 6th Floors
between Madison and Park Avenues / 753-4368
Weekdays 10am–5pm, or by appointment.

Art & artifacts
Midtown East

quality   style   service   value

The Edge: Fabulous collection of old-master paintings and drawings. A top art gallery featuring exceptional-quality old-master works. Some porcelains, sculpture, and more contemporary works. No credit cards. Deluxe. *"Expensive, but quality."*

Untitled/Fine Art in Print
159 Prince Street
near West Broadway / 982-2088
Mon–Sat 10am–10pm, Sun 11am–7pm (Sun in summer to 9pm).

Art & artifacts
SoHo/TriBeCa

The Edge: Unique books and postcards. Favors beautiful reproduction postcards, which make wonderful note cards and invitations.

Wally Findlay Galleries

14 East 60th Street
between 5th and Madison Avenues / 421-5390
Weekdays 9:30am–5:30pm, Sat 9:30am–5pm.

Art & artifacts
Midtown East

quality   style   service   value

The Edge: Quality collection. Represents a score of leading European and American 20th-century post-impressionist artists.

West Side Judaica

2412 Broadway
between 88th and 89th Streets / 362-7846
Mon–Thurs 10:30am–7pm, Fri 10:30am–3pm,
Sun 10:30am–5pm.

Art & artifacts
Upper West Side

quality   style   service   value

The Edge: A strong collection. Something for everyone, from books and music to objects of faith. *"Good neighborhood store."*

Works Gallery

1250 Madison Avenue
near 90th Street / 996-0300
Winter, Mon–Thurs 10am–7pm, Fri–Sat 10am–6pm,
Sun noon–5pm; summer, Mon–Sat 10am–6pm.

Art & artifacts
Upper East Side

quality   style   service   value

The Edge: For those who like crafts. Quality craft items by gallery artists. Favors crystal and ceramics, but also fine jewelry and watches. Artists include Atelier Janiye.

Barry of Chelsea Antiques

154 9th Avenue
between 19th and 20th Streets / 242-2666
Tues–Sat noon–6pm, Sun noon–7pm.

Art deco/art nouveau
Chelsea

quality   style   service   value

The Edge: Great art deco lighting. Good selection of antique, especially art deco, lighting, including antique hanging lamps. Restores vintage lamps. Prefers dealing with decorators.

Delorenzo

958 Madison Avenue
near 75th Street / 249-7575
Weekdays 10am–6pm, Sat 10am–5:30pm.

Art deco/art nouveau
Upper East Side

quality   style   service   value

The Edge: Collector of art deco furniture and accessories turned dealer. Delorenzo features French art deco furniture from top designers. Also rugs and lighting fixtures, including torchères and table and floor lamps. Sells furniture as art. No credit cards. Deluxe. *"Top high-end deco pieces and prices."*

Joia Interiors, Inc.

149 East 60th Street
between Lexington and 3rd Avenues / 759-1224
Mon–Thurs 10am–6pm, Fri call for hours.

Art deco/art nouveau
Midtown East

quality style service value

The Edge: Good source for vintage art deco furniture and accessories. The real thing, plus well-executed reproductions. Carries a full range of furniture. Accessories include Lalique designs and paintings.

Macklowe Gallery Ltd.

667 Madison Avenue
near 60th Street / 644-6400
Weekdays 10:30am–6pm, Sat 10:30am–5:30pm
(closed Sat July–Aug).

Art deco/art nouveau
Upper East Side

quality style service value

The Edge: Large collection of art nouveau furniture and jewelry. Features furniture and accessories from late European, French, art nouveau, and art deco periods. Decorative items include wonderful Tiffany lamps. Jewelry includes designs from Cartier, David Webb, Fouquet, Van Cleef, and others. Incredible furnishings. Prices mostly $2,500 to $10,000.

Maison Gerard

36 East 10th Street
near Broadway / 674-7611
Weekdays 11am–6pm, Sat by appointment.

Art deco/art nouveau
Flatiron/East Village

quality style service value

The Edge: 90% of the shop is filled with top French art deco furniture. Furniture, accessories, objets d'arts and jewelry.

Minna Rosenblatt

844 Madison Avenue
near 69th Street / 288-0257
Mon–Sat 10am–5:30pm.

Art deco/art nouveau
Upper East Side

quality style service value

The Edge: Small-scale art nouveau and art deco objects. Find Tiffany lamps and vases and Steuben perfume bottles. Featured artists include Daum, Galle, and more. No credit cards.

Oldies, Goldies & Moldies

1609 2nd Avenue
near 83rd Street / 737-3935
Tues–Fri noon–7pm, Sat 11am–6pm,
Sun 11am–5pm (closed Sun July–Aug).

Art deco/art nouveau
Upper East Side

quality style service value

The Edge: More used than antique, but functional, furniture and accessories. Prices are reasonable. Furniture and accessories are largely pieces from the Victorian era to the early 1950s, with the owners' preference being art deco and art moderne. Most pieces are small. Also a large selection of lighting and accessories.

Retro Modern

58 East 11th Street, 2nd Floor
between Broadway and University Place / 674-0530

Art deco/art nouveau
Flatiron/East Village

Weekdays 11am–6pm, Sat 1–5pm.

The Edge: Fine period pieces. Focus on lighting—from the 1920s through the 1960s, including art deco, neoclassic, and moderne original designs. Designers include Oscar Bach, John Salterini, Kurt Versen, Walter Von Nessen, and Josef Hoffmann. Prices from the high hundreds into the thousands. No credit cards.

Christie's

502 Park Avenue
near 59th Street / 546-1000
Weekdays 9:30am–5:30pm, Sat 10am–5pm, Sun 1–5pm.

Auction houses
Midtown East

quality style service value

The Edge: The December jewelry and spring art sales. Features a wide range of collectibles, including furniture, historical letters and documents, jewelry, paintings, and silver. Spring and fall art courses are available (call 212-546-1092 for details). Auctions and showing times are posted in the Friday *New York Times*. *"You have to know what you're doing, but great value." "A New York institution. Expensive."*

Christie's East

219 East 67th Street
near 2nd Avenue / 606-0400
Weekdays 9:30am–5pm, Sat 10am–5pm, Sun 1–5pm.

Auction houses
Upper East Side

quality style service value

The Edge: Less serious collectibles. Less expensive collectibles, including drawings, furniture, rugs, paintings, and 20th-century decorative arts.

Sotheby's

1334 York Avenue
near 72nd Street / 606-7000
Weekdays 9am–5:30pm, Sat 10am–5pm.

Auction houses
Upper East Side

quality style service value

The Edge: The spring art sales. Noted auction house featuring a wide range of items from those lesser priced at the arcade to high-end paintings, jewelry, and silver. Auction details and showing times listed in the Friday *New York Times*. The one- to three-day short course for collectors costs $300 to $500. The courses address the wide array of collectibles Sotheby's auctions. *"Very good jewelry, rug, and furniture auctions." A New York institution."*

William Doyle Galleries

175 East 87th Street
between 3rd and Lexington Avenues / 427-2730
Daily 8am–5pm for pickup. Call for auction dates and times.

Auction houses
Upper East Side

quality style service value

The Edge: Auction house with unique estate sales sometimes. Right after the big two international houses, Sotheby's and Christie's, is William Doyle. The owner's New York social connections sometimes generate unique estate sale merchandise. The 30 auctions per year feature mostly jewelry, paintings, furniture, and silver, but also books, prints, photographs, toys, and dolls. Favors 17th- and 18th-century estate furniture. The gallery features a tag-sale area for items that didn't get sold at auction or are less expensive. Check out the 7pm Monday lectures on current sales. *"Excellent knowledgeable staff."*

Charles P. Rogers Brass Bed Company

899 1st Avenue
between 50th and 51st Streets / 594-8777
Weekdays 10am–7pm, Sat 10am–6pm, Sun noon–6pm.

Beds & bedding
Midtown East

quality style service value

The Edge: Over 50 brass and iron beds. Shows over 50 bed models in four-posters, contemporary and hand-painted styles, replicas of original designs, and old-time beds. All sizes available in stock or by special order. Worldwide delivery available. *"Excellent selection of daybeds." "Don't use for active teenagers—my two managed to bend a corner tube by leaning on it."*

Dial-A-Mattress

31-10 48th Avenue
near Van Dam Street, Long Island City / 718-472-1200
Daily 24 hours.

Beds & bedding
Mail/phone

quality style service value

The Edge: Beloved by all—the place to call for mattresses. Widely used by our respondents. Same day you phone your order it's delivered and assembled (provided it's in stock). 30-day return policy. Delivery within 4 hour window; for an extra $10, delivery within a 2 hour period. Good prices. 20% off. *"Used once—was perfect." "Excellent inventory." "It's just as they advertise— you call and they deliver. And the prices are good."*

Chairs and Stools, Etc.

222 Bowery
between Prince and Spring Streets / 925-9191
Weekdays 9am–5pm, Sat 10am–3pm.

Chairs & tables
SoHo/TriBeCa

The Edge: Chairs and stools, tables, tabletops, and bases. Wholesale and retail orders. Wide variety of mostly basic styles. Discounter.

Bellini

1305 2nd Avenue
near 68th Street / 517-9233
Mon–Wed and Fri 10am–6pm, Thurs 10am–8pm,
Sat 10am–5:30pm, Sun noon– 5pm.

Children
Upper East Side

quality style service value

The Edge: Unique, sophisticated baby furniture and accessories befitting the New York baby! Contemporary and European-made cribs, which are color coordinated with bedding and furniture for a pulled-together designer look. Furniture converts to junior beds and changing tables transform to dressers. Colors are sophisticated and there are matching decorative accessories as well as carriages, high chairs, and strollers.

Ages Past Antiques
China, crystal & silver
Upper East Side
450 East 78th Street
near 1st Avenue / 628-0725
Mon–Sat 11am–5pm, but it's a good idea to call ahead.

The Edge: British memorabilia. A small shop featuring 19th-century English pottery and porcelain, including platters, figurines, cups and saucers, and commemorative items. A source for royalty commemorative memorabilia.

Alice Kwartler
China, crystal & silver
Midtown East
123 East 57th Street
between Park and Lexington Avenues / 752-3590
Mon–Sat 11am–6pm.

50 | 50 | 50 | 35
quality style service value

The Edge: Where Edith Wharton would shop for gifts. Find turn-of-the-century (and later) silver, crystal, decorative items, and some antique cufflinks. Wonderful Tiffany pieces, including an enormous selection of tea sets, picture frames, candlesticks, vases, and trays. Also a large selection of cufflinks and stud sets. Great gifts. Engraving available. Very expensive—for example, silver frames from $400 to $800. Deluxe. *"Gorgeous stuff, but very expensive." "You can always find a gift here—for every occasion."*

Avventura
China, crystal & silver
Upper West Side
463 Amsterdam Avenue
near 83rd Street / 769-2510
Weekdays 10:30am–7pm, Sun 11am–6pm.

50 | 50 | 43 | 40
quality style service value

The Edge: Simply superb contemporary Italian items. Very unique pieces. Features Murano glass and Italian ceramic work, including dishes, flatware, serving pieces, and tables. Some jewelry. Bridal registry. *"An inventory that makes selection easy."*

Baccarat, Inc.
China, crystal & silver
Midtown East
625 Madison Avenue
near 59th Street / 826-4100
Mon–Wed and Fri–Sat 10am–6pm,
Thurs 10am–7pm; in holiday season, also Sun.

47 | 45 | 46 | 33
quality style service value

The Edge: You know it. Fabulous and expensive crystal. While its specializes in crystal, you'll also find Limoges china and silver by Christofle and Puiforcat. Full retail. During the Christmas season it's open Sunday. Deluxe. *"I use the outlet store in Vermont."*

Bardith Ltd.
China, crystal & silver
Multiple locations
Weekdays 11am–5:30pm; in holiday season, also Sat 11am–5pm.

50 | 50 | 50 | 45
quality style service value

The Edge: Quality antique English porcelain (18th century on), trays, and papier-mâché. Complete china sets and accessories from all the name houses. Wonderful trays and tray tables. Decorator discounts. No credit cards. Deluxe. *"Negotiate for 10% off."*

Locations: Upper East Side: 901 Madison Avenue, near 72nd Street (737-3775) / 31 East 72nd Street, between Madison and Park Avenues (737-8660)

Bernardaud Limoges
499 Park Avenue
near 59th Street / 371-4300
Weekdays 10am–7pm, Sat 10am–6pm.

China, crystal & silver
Midtown East

quality style service value

The Edge: The full line of Bernardaud at full price. Features Bernardaud Limoges and crystal (Saint Louis, Baum, Baccarat, Lalique). Deluxe. *"Terrific selection of beautiful things—but not cheap." "Very helpful staff." "I call Lanac for Bernardaud discounted."*

Block China Warehouse Store
57 Brighton Avenue
near Ocean Avenue, Long Branch / 908-222-1144
Mon–Sat 10am–5pm, Sun 11am–4pm.

China, crystal & silver
Mail/phone

quality style service value

The Edge: The outlet for Block china and Atlantis crystal. Also offers Salton/Maxim housewares. Phone orders welcomed. Discount depends on the popularity of the design. For discontinued or older brands, discount can range to 70%.

Brodean
338 Columbus Avenue
at 76th Street / 877-4000
Daily 10am–8pm.

China, crystal & silver
Upper West Side

quality style service value

The Edge: Country-style furniture and furnishings. China and furnishings favoring English antique furniture, but mostly country-style china, silver, and linens. 80 different designer flatware patterns (stainless steel to sterling), crystal glassware, and fine linens. Designers include Anna Weatherley Designs, MacKenzie Childs, Buccellati, and Old Newbury Crafters. Bridal registry.

Cardel
621 Madison Avenue
near 58th Street / 753-8690
Mon–Sat 10am–6pm.

China, crystal & silver
Midtown East

quality style service value

The Edge: Hundreds of crystal and silver platters. China from all the great houses, plus traditional housewarming and wedding presents. *"Pricey." "Beautiful crystal, china, and gifts." "Excellent service."*

Ceramica
59 Thompson Street
between Spring and Broom Streets / 941-1307
Mon–Sat 11:30am–7pm, Sun 11:30am–6pm.

China, crystal & silver
SoHo/TriBeCa

quality style service value

The Edge: Absolutely fabulous Italian tableware. Best known for its large selection of Majolica (Italian) tableware, featuring rich bold colors in traditional 15th-century and contemporary motifs. Styling includes strong colors and complex patterns. Complete dinner sets and platters and bowls always available. Items imported from Deruta, Italy. *"Such beautiful china." "Unusual patterns."*

Ceramica Gift Gallery

1009 Avenue of the Americas
between 37th and 38th Streets / 354-9216
Weekdays 9:30am–6pm, Sun noon–5pm.

**China, crystal & silver
Midtown West**

The Edge: Discount prices on top-brand china, crystal, and silver. Bridal registry giftware at discount prices. Carries all the expected, and even the hard-to-find, at discount. Brands like Georg Jensen and Royal Copenhagen at very good prices.

Christofle

680 Madison Avenue
near 62nd Street / 308-9390
Weekdays 10am–6pm, Sat 10am–5:30pm.

**China, crystal & silver
Upper East Side**

The Edge: The Christofle line at full retail. Features its own brand of flatware (stainless to sterling), plus crystal by Baccarat and St. Louis, china by Haviland and Ceralene, and its own elegant table linens. Also gold, gold and silver, sterling-silver, and silver-plate bowls, ice buckets, pitchers, sugar bowls and creamers, tea services, and trays. Bridal registry. Deluxe. *"Always a standard for excellence."*

Daum Boutique

694 Madison Avenue
near 62nd Street / 355-2060
Mon–Sat 10am–6pm.

**China, crystal & silver
Upper East Side**

The Edge: Only Daum crystal, including decorative and limited-edition items.

Eastern Silver Company

54 Canal Street, 2nd Floor
near Orchard Street / 226-5708
Sun–Thurs 9:30am–5pm, Fri 9:30am–1pm.

**China, crystal & silver
Lower East Side/Chinatown**

The Edge: Table-top items at discount prices. Specializes in table-top gift items, such as candlesticks, decanters, vases, and the like in crystal, pewter, and silver.

Eastside China

Brooklyn / 718-633-8672
Mon 10am–7pm, Tues–Wed and Sun 10am–6pm,
Thurs 10am–8pm, Fri 10am– 2pm.

**China, crystal & silver
Mail/phone**

The Edge: China, crystal, and silver discounter. Discounts all major brands of crystal and china, including Bernardaud, Limoges, Mikasa, Oneida, Royal Doulton, Wedgwood, Baccarat, and Lenox. Bridal registry and corporate gifts. Very good prices, particularly on china, often the lowest in the city. They give wonderful telephone service. Call and order. If it's not in stock, they'll get it for you. *"Good prices, fair service."*

Fishs Eddy

Mon–Sat 10am–9pm, Sun 11am–8pm.

**China, crystal & silver
Multiple locations**

quality style service value

The Edge: Functional chinaware. Functional china, glassware, and food-related accessories. Seconds or overruns from restaurants and hotels sold by the piece or in sets. Has its own patterns now, as well. 25% off. In 1997 it featured Palace Hotel dishes and glasses (rimmed in 18-karat gold leaf)—boxes and boxes of never-used dishes. *"As amusing as it is useful!" "Great eclectic dishes and glasses." "For all your fun dinnerware."*

Locations: Flatiron/East Village: 889 Broadway, near 19th Street (420-9020) / **Upper West Side:** 2176 Broadway, near 77th Street (873-8819)

Gem Antiques
1088 Madison Avenue
near 82nd Street / 535-7399
Mon–Sat 10:30am–5:30pm.

China, crystal & silver
Upper East Side

The Edge: Antique and modern European and American porcelains and paper weights. Find Coichy, Baccarat, Gouda, Grueby, Moorcroft, Newcomb, Ohr, Pilkington, Rookwood, and Saint Louis. Features unique pieces. Priced from $100 to $15,000. Deluxe.

Guild Antiques
1095 Madison Avenue
near 82nd Street / 472-0830
Mon–Sat 10am–5pm.

China, crystal & silver
Upper East Side

quality style service value

The Edge: Simply first-rate 18th- and 19th-century English furniture and Chinese export porcelains. Full sets of dishes and serving pieces. Also small-scale 18th- and early 19th-century English furniture. *"Good decorative pieces, but not on the level of Levy or Sacks."*

Hoffman Gampetro Antiques
1050 2nd Avenue, Gallery 37
between 55th and 56th Streets / 755-1120
Mon–Sat 10:30am–5:30pm.

China, crystal & silver
Midtown East

quality style service value

The Edge: Wonderful collection of Arts and Crafts movement silver. English ceramics and etched glass complement the silver.

Hoya Crystal Gallery
689 Madison Avenue
near 62nd Street / 223-6335
Mon–Sat 10am–6pm.

China, crystal & silver
Upper East Side

quality style service value

The Edge: Top crystal designed by Japanese artists. Simple to elaborate designs. You'll find wonderful decorative accessories, including art pieces, candlesticks, decanters, and vases. Top items. The Japanese Steuben. Deluxe. *"A place for terrific gifts." "Beautiful, unusual crystal. Not the standard stuff."*

Interieurs
114 Wooster Street
between Prince and Spring Streets / 343-0800

China, crystal & silver
SoHo/TriBeCa

Sun–Mon noon–6pm, Tues–Sat 11am–7pm.

The Edge: Exceptional taste. From France, glasswork by Marisa Osorio-Farinha made in the same traditional Venetian process. Hand-blown plates and glassware—with a contemporary colorful fun look. Wonderful pale china, including Jean-Paul Pichon handmade oversize Provençal bowls ($195).

Jamar
1714 Sheepshead Bay Road
Brooklyn / 718-615-2222
Tues–Sat 11am–5:45pm.

China, crystal & silver
Brooklyn

quality style service value

The Edge: Discount china, crystal, and silver. Claims to match or beat any advertised price on silver, crystal, china, and gift items. Tends to feature the more widely available, moderately priced items.

James II Galleries
11 East 57th Street, 4th Floor
between 5th and Madison Avenues / 355-7040
Weekdays 10am–5:30pm, Sat 10:30am–4:30pm
(closed Sat June–Aug).

China, crystal & silver
Midtown East

quality style service value

The Edge: Exquisite antique table items. Find Victorian china, furniture, glass, jewelry, pottery, and silver. The history of each piece is outlined. The china includes all the famous top English brands. Floral patterns are favored. Stocked items include full dinner sets, plus children's tea sets, dessert sets, silver serving pieces, pitchers, trays in all sizes, Victorian silver-plates, and mother-of-pearl–handled fish forks and knives. Deluxe. *"Very fine, expensive collection." "Helpful staff."*

James Robinson
480 Park Avenue
near 58th Street / 752-6166
Weekdays 10am–5pm, Sat 10:30am–4:30pm
(closed Sat July–Aug).

China, crystal & silver
Midtown East

quality style service value

The Edge: Wonderful 17th- to 19th-century fine English tableware and jewelry. Some old English porcelain. Best known for Georgian cut-glass stemware, bowls, and centerpieces and estate jewelry priced from $500 to $250,000. Also carries 17th- to 19th-century English hallmark silver and hand-forged sterling-silver flatware antique reproductions in 18 classic patterns. The silver tends to have simple classic lines. Flatware is sometimes discounted 25%. Find portable canvas silver chests, practical gift items. The jewelry collection includes a very large selection of antique engagement rings from the late 1880s to 1920s. Now Helen Woodhull's jewelry collection, with jewelry inspired by ancient motifs. Deluxe. *"Beautiful, upscale jewelry!" "Incredibly expensive, but if you can afford it, it's worth it."*

Jean's Silversmiths
16 West 45th Street
near 5th Avenue / 575-0723
Mon–Thurs 9am–4:30pm, Fri 9am–3:30pm; also Sat in Dec.

China, crystal & silver
Midtown West

quality style service value

The Edge: Discontinued silver and china patterns. Sells discontinued and current flatware and china patterns and some antique silver, gold, and diamond jewelry. Carries almost 1,000 silver patterns. Wonderful table accessories, including candlesticks and trays in every size. New silver flatware is discounted. Also polishes silver (for about $4 per piece) via a commercial polish process, which takes out all nicks and scratches, or butler's satin, which provides a duller finish. A reputable dealer in vintage silver. Will deliver jewelry the day you buy it, but not silver, which requires polishing. 10% off. *"Refinishes silver like new." "Replating service the best. Great antiques." Good service, good value, expensive." "A great place to find discontinued patterns (used)."*

L.S. Collection

469 West Broadway
south of Houston Street / 673-4575
Weekdays 11:30am–7pm, Sat 11:30am–8pm, Sun noon–6pm.

China, crystal & silver
SoHo/TriBeCa

quality style service value

The Edge: Unique modern gifts. L.S. (Lazy Susan) has brought its giftware collection (china, glasses, hand-blown crystal, sterling, etc.) from Japan to the U.S. Many items in the $500 price category. Elegant tableware. *"Good place for unusual gifts." "Expensive, unique things."*

La Terrine

1024 Lexington Avenue
near 73rd Street / 988-3366
Mon–Sat 10:30am–6pm.

China, crystal & silver
Upper East Side

quality style service value

The Edge: Hand-painted, mostly Portuguese and Italian, ceramics. Practical and attractive ceramics, including coffee mugs, covered butter dishes, large pasta bowls, pitchers, and platters. Also hand-painted imported tabletops from France, Italy, and Portugal. Complete dinner services can be special ordered. Cloth place mats and napkins from Provence and India and simply wonderful paper napkins. The mugs range from $15 to $20; platters and large pasta bowls run up to the $100 area. *"Such pretty tableware!" "It used to be unusual, now it seems as if these hand-painted ceramics are everywhere."*

Lalique

680 Madison Avenue
near 61st Street / 355-6550
Weekdays 10am–6pm, Sat 10am–5:30pm.

China, crystal & silver
Upper East Side

quality style service value

The Edge: Wonderful art deco glass. Art deco Lalique pieces from stemware to gift items, including crystal vases and clocks. Catalog costs $10. Deluxe. *"I love their warehouse sales in New Jersey for discontinued merchandise."*

Lanac Sales

73 Canal Street
between Allen and Canal Streets / 925-6422
Sun–Thurs 9am–6pm, Fri 10am–2pm.

China, crystal & silver
Lower East Side/Chinatown

quality style service value

The Edge: Prices are among the best in the city. Discount prices on chinaware, cut glass, silverware, flatware, and gifts. Stocks or is able to get virtually all major brands. Was able to quote on everything in our spot-check price comparison, from Georg Jensen silver to Royal Copenhagen and Bernardaud china. Individually the prices matched or beat their competitors on virtually every item in our sample. Bridal registry available. Most items in stock, with immediate shipment. *"Always the lowest prices!"*

Leo Kaplan Ltd.

967 Madison Avenue
near 75th Street / 249-6766
Mon–Sat 10am–5:30pm (closed Sat in summer).

China, crystal & silver
Upper East Side

quality style service value

The Edge: Beautiful items for the collector. 18th-century English porcelain and stemware, including all the top period designers. Wonderful paperweights and art nouveau glass from Baccarat, Daum, Galle, and Webb. Very expensive. Deluxe.

Locaters, Inc.

2217 Cottontail Lane
Little Rock / 800-367-9690
Weekdays 9am–5pm, Sat 10am–3pm, Central Time.

China, crystal & silver
Mail/phone

The Edge: Replaces irreplaceable stemware, china, and sterling. A phone-order business finding discontinued china and stemware from the major brands. Stocks a huge selection of patterns.

Malvina L. Solomon

1021 Lexington Avenue
between 73rd and 74th Streets / 535-5200
Weekdays 11am–5:30pm, Sat 11am–5pm.

China, crystal & silver
Upper East Side

quality style service value

The Edge: Vintage jewelry and American art pottery. Vintage jewelry, including wonderful Bakelite items. American art pottery from Fulper, Rookwood, Ohr, and others.

Michael C. Fina

3 West 47th Street
near 5th Avenue / 869-5050
Mon–Wed and Fri 9:30am–6pm, Thurs 9:30am–7pm,
Sat 10:30am–6pm.

China, crystal & silver
Midtown West

quality style service value

The Edge: Well-known discounter of giftware. Now 20,000 square feet of gift items—twice the space as in the old shop. Features over 5,000 patterns. Offers discounts on all major brands of china, cookware, crystal, giftware, jewelry, sterling, and more. 15% off. *"Wide range and selection. One call and all your needs are met." "Often long delays to get silver. Not much in stock." "Good for showers."*

Nat Schwartz

549 Broadway
between 25th and 26th Streets, Bayonne / 800-526-1440
Mon–Wed and Fri 9:30am–6pm, Thurs 9:30am–8pm,
Sat 10am–5pm.

China, crystal & silver
Mail/phone

The Edge: Small discounts on all major lines of silver, crystal, and china. Features all the top lines.

Nelson & Nelson

445 Park Avenue
between 56th and 57th Streets / 980-5825
Mon–Sat 10:30am–5:30pm.

China, crystal & silver
Midtown East

quality style service value

The Edge: Magnificent silver objects. Should one want to live well—befitting the grand style of yesteryear—this is the place. Fine sterling hollowware, crystal, enamels, and jewelry. Some important pieces from the 17th century, most from the 19th and early 20th centuries. Lovely period jewels. A very unique selection. It's a family-run business, owned by Steve, Marge and Pat Nelson. Ask—they tend to better the posted prices. Antiques purchased. Repair service available. *"Some flexibility on price." "Courteous, knowledgeable, authentic, and pricey."*

Niels Bamberger

1070 Madison Avenue
near 80th Street / 737-7118
Weekdays 9am–5:30pm.

China, crystal & silver
Upper East Side

quality style service value

The Edge: Vintage Scandinavian china. Find vintage and new pieces of Scandinavian china, sterling-silver tableware accessories, and porcelains. Stocks wonderful Royal Copenhagen china patterns. Deluxe. *"Courteous and knowledgeable."*

Orrefors

58 East 57th Street
near Park Avenue / 752-1095
Weekdays 10am–6pm, Sat 10am–5pm.

China, crystal & silver
Midtown East

quality style service value

The Edge: Scandinavian glassware. Large selection, full retail prices.

Pottery Barn

Weekdays 10am–8pm, Sat 10am–7pm, Sun noon–6pm.

China, crystal & silver
Multiple locations

quality style service value

The Edge: Lower-end basic housewares. For housewares (no delivery on these items) and furniture (sold through its catalog). The furniture—full-size chairs, sofas, tables, and queen-size beds—is delivered. Best known, however, for its basic china, candlesticks, coffee mugs, platters, and wine glasses. The sister chain, Williams-Sonoma, is more upscale and features cooking equipment and cookbooks for "true cooks," as well as good-looking china, glasses, and general tableware. *"Pleasant, current styling at good prices." "Their catalog makes shopping a breeze."*

Locations: Chelsea: 100 7th Avenue, near 16th Street (633-8405) / **Greenwich Village:** 51 Greenwich Avenue, near 6th Avenue (807-6321) / **Midtown East:** 117 East 59th Street, between Park and Lexington Avenues (753-5424) / **SoHo/TriBeCa:** 600 Broadway, near Houston Street (505-6377) / **Upper East Side:** 1451 2nd Avenue, near 76th Street (988-4228) / 250 West 57th Street, at 8th Avenue (315-1855) / **Upper West Side:** 2109 Broadway, near 73rd Street (595-5573)

Replacement Ltd.

1089 Knox Road
(P.O. Box 26029), Greensboro / 910-697-3000
Daily 8am–10pm.

China, crystal & silver
Mail/phone

The Edge: A top source for discontinued hard-to-find flatware, china, and crystal patterns. Handles discontinued flatware, china, crystal, and collectibles (56,000 patterns, three million pieces). Features hard-to-find patterns from all the top labels and manufacturers no longer in business. Claims to be the largest replacement company in the world. If you're in North Carolina, go see the showroom.

Royal Copenhagen Porcelain / Georg Jensen

683 Madison Avenue
near 61st Street / 759-6457
Mon–Sat 10am–6pm.

China, crystal & silver
Upper East Side

quality style service value

The Edge: The full-price retail outlet for Scandinavian tablewares. The shop features a large selection of Royal Copenhagen and seemingly all the Georg Jensen silver patterns. Also more moderate lines, including Orrefors and Kosta Boda crystal and Dansk wood pieces. The Georg Jensen collection includes the full range of flatware, plus sterling table-top items. Deluxe. *"Beautiful wares."*

S. J. Shrubsole

104 East 57th Street
between Lexington and Park Avenues / 753-8920
Weekdays 9:30am–5:30pm, Sat 10am–5pm.

China, crystal & silver
Midtown East

quality style service value

The Edge: Features very rare (the rarest) high-quality antique silver and period jewelry. A small collection of treasures, some dating from the late 1700s but most from the 19th century: silver bowls, flatware, picture frames, serving pieces, tea sets, etc. Also wonderful unique period jewelry. You can expect to find work from renowned silversmiths like Paul Revere. Very fine Victorian and Edwardian jewelry. Antique English and American silver cufflinks and studs. Prices mostly from $1,000 to $25,000. Deluxe.

S. Wyler, Inc.

941 Lexington Avenue
near 69th Street / 879-9848
Mon–Sat 9:30am–5:30pm.

China, crystal & silver
Upper East Side

quality style service value

The Edge: From the practical to the sublime antique English silver and porcelain. The shop is crammed full of one-of-a-kind 18th- and 19th-century English silver and porcelain. Some silver reproductions. Excellent quality and style. A large inventory of flatware, picture frames, serving pieces, and tea sets. Priced from $100 to the six figures. *"Presents for royalty!"*

Scully & Scully

504 Park Avenue
near 59th Street / 755-2590
Mon–Sat 9am–6pm.

China, crystal & silver
Midtown East

quality style service value

The Edge: Great for basic English country house–style gift items. The store features china, glassware, desk sets, those hard-to-find wooden salad bowls with pewter (not silver) bases, brass fire tools, enameled boxes, English print place mats, globes, and more. China patterns include Ceraline, Crown Derby, Herend, and Wedgwood. 18th-century reproduction English and American-made furniture, including classic Queen Anne and Chippendale chairs scaled to children's sizes. *"Great wedding registry for Muffy, Buffy, and the New Canaan set!" Very stuffy, old English." "Great source for English lacquerware place mats." "Expensive."*

Simon Pearce

Mon–Sat 11am–7pm, Sun noon–6pm.

China, crystal & silver
Multiple locations

quality style service value

The Edge: Primarily handmade modern but somehow traditionally styled glass tableware. Heavy glass pieces including vases to glasses. Some pottery. Not expensive. Simple but elegant styling. All handmade in its workshop in Quechee, Vermont. Sells seconds (with small, not particularly noticeable defects)—discounted 30%—without its label.

Locations: Midtown East: 500 Park Avenue, near 59th Street (421-8801) / **SoHo/TriBeCa:** 120 Wooster Street, near Spring Street (334-2393)

Solanee, Inc.

866 Lexington Avenue
near 65th Street / 439-6109
Weekdays 10am–6pm, Sat 11am–5pm.

China, crystal & silver
Upper East Side

The Edge: Traditional French pottery and glassware. Features or can get virtually all patterns of Segries and hand-painted pottery from Moustiers, France. Also stocks glassware from Brittany. Can order complete Segries dinner sets. The catalog costs $20.

Steuben Glass

715 5th Avenue
near 56th Street / 752-1441
Mon–Wed and Fri–Sat 10am–6pm, Thurs 10am–7pm.

China, crystal & silver
Midtown East

quality style service value

The Edge: Top-quality American-designed glass. Find all sorts of glass items, stemware, tableware accessories (vases, bowls, candlesticks), and palm-sized animals. Steuben glass is a standard White House gift to heads of state. Corporate discounts. Call toll free 800-424-4240 for phone orders. Deluxe.

Stupell Ltd.

29 East 22nd Street
near Broadway / 260-3100
Mon–Sat 10am–6pm.

China, crystal & silver
Gramercy Park/Murray Hill

The Edge: All major china and crystal patterns. Wonderful selection of traditional to modern table settings, including Venetian glassware, silver and stainless flatware, and linens. Gift items, including picture frames and porcelains.

Tudor Rose Antiques

28 East 10th Street
between University Place and Broadway / 677-5239
Weekdays 10:30am–6pm, Sat 10am–5pm.

China, crystal & silver
Flatiron/East Village

quality style service value

The Edge: Victorian knickknacks. Victorian crystal and sterling gift items, including candlesticks, crystal, flatware, frames, and bowls. Offers a bridal registry and corporate gifts program.

Villeroy & Boch

974 Madison Avenue
near 76th Street / 535-2500
Mon–Sat 10am–6pm.

China, crystal & silver
Upper East Side

quality style service value

The Edge: The entire line of china, plus silver flatware and crystal. Look here to see the entire line. But don't forget the Villeroy & Boch outlet shops, which offer good-quality seconds that are virtually indistinguishable from the first-quality merchandise. Prices at the 24 outlet stores are discounted 40%, with frequent special sales reducing prices to 55% off. Call with phone orders to the city's closest one, in Norwalk, Connecticut (203-831-2821).

Waterford/Wedgwood

713 Madison Avenue
near 63rd Street / 759-0500
Weekdays 10am–5pm, Sat 10am–6pm.

China, crystal & silver
Upper East Side

quality style service value

The Edge: Full selection of Waterford/Wedgwood. Very expensive traditional china, glassware, lamps, and linens. The store is on two levels, with the higher-priced items upstairs.

Williams-Sonoma Outlet

231 10th Avenue
between 23rd and 24th Streets / 206-8118
Weekdays 11am–6pm, Sat 10am–5pm.

China, crystal & silver
Chelsea

quality style service value

The Edge: Three floors of discontinued, returned, and close-out merchandise from Williams-Sonoma. A creaky, dingy warehouse space with a staircase that serves as the only access to the various floors. The main level features china, glass, and cookware. The second floor has decorative items for the house. Good prices (25% to 50% off retail) but very uneven stock, featured in an out-of-the-way location. No delivery. *"You never know, you may find something good."*

Williams-Sonoma, Inc.

Weekdays 10am–8pm, Sat 10am–7pm, Sun noon–6pm.

China, crystal & silver
Multiple locations

quality style service value

The Edge: High-styled, well-priced kitchen accessories and cooking items. Nicely styled basic pottery and china, bowls, platters, pitchers, teapots, and specialty food items. A wide range. Bridal registry with a nationwide listing. Everyone seems to register for wedding gifts here. Features cooking equipment and cookbooks from around the world for "true cooks" as well as general tableware. Delivers by UPS. Phone and fax orders 24 hours daily. Call 800-541-2223 to order. *"Good cookware at top prices." "Has the best selection of kitchenware in a setting that's appealing to shop in." "Often crowded and less-than-adequate service." "Sometimes you find just what you want." "I've gotten some excellent buys here."*

Locations: Chelsea: 110 7th Avenue, near 17th Street (541-2223) / **Midtown East:** 20 East 60th Street, between Madison and Park Avenues (980-5155) / **Upper East Side:** 1309 2nd Avenue, near 69th Street (288-8408) / 1175 Madison Avenue, near 86th Street (289-6832)

Wolfman Gold & Good Company
117 Mercer Street
between Prince and Spring Streets / 431-1888
Mon–Wed and Fri–Sat 11am–6pm,
Thurs 11am–7pm, Sun noon–5pm.

China, crystal & silver
SoHo/TriBeCa

quality style service value

The Edge: Simple, elegant, mostly white dishes. Features simple but elegant, and mostly white, dishes and serving pieces from France and England. Glassware ranges from the practical to the more formal. Find antique silver, crystal decanters, some silver-plate serving pieces, and English-style linens. Sometimes wonderful wicker butler trays. Understated country elegance is the style. *"Expensive, but appealing inventory." "Great white goods."*

Yellow Door
1308 Avenue M
near East 13th Street, Brooklyn / 718-998-7382
Weekdays 10am–5:45pm, Sun 11am–5pm.

China, crystal & silver
Brooklyn

quality style service value

The Edge: High-end giftware, discounted. China, giftware, jewelry, and tableware from all the top names, including Alessi, Baccarat, Lalique, and Villeroy & Boch. Discounts from 20% to 30% off retail. *"Good prices." "Slow phone service."*

Archetype Gallery
115 Mercer Street
between Prince and Streets / 334-0100
Wed–Fri 10am–6pm, Sat–Sun noon–6pm.

Contemporary
SoHo/TriBeCa

quality style service value

The Edge: Cutting-edge furniture and accessories. Features a large and diverse selection of contemporary furniture and accessories (door knobs, glassware, jewelry, lighting, and textiles) made by artists. Priced from $9 to $5,000, with occasional items to $20,000.

Carlyle Custom Convertibles Ltd.
Mon–Wed and Fri 10am–7pm, Thurs 10am–8pm,
Sat 10am–6pm, Sun noon–5pm.

Contemporary
Multiple locations

quality style service value

The Edge: Finally, beautiful convertible sofas. Top-quality convertible sofas, beautifully crafted and covered with fine fabrics, along with matching chairs and ottomans. Wonderful trims. Discontinued items and samples (not always on the floor) are often discounted, bringing them into a more reasonable price range. Ask about sale items. Photographs of these items and fabric samples are usually available. Deluxe. *"Investment furniture." "They stand behind their merchandise, but charged me $50 for a call during their warranty period—not nice. Also not as comfortable as their ads imply!"*

Locations: Chelsea: 122 West 18th Street, between 6th and 7th Avenues (675-3212) / **Upper East Side:** 1375 3rd Avenue, between 78th and 79th Streets (570-2236) / 1056 3rd Avenue, between 62nd and 63rd Streets (838-1525)

Classic Sofa

Contemporary
Gramercy Park/Murray Hill

5 West 22nd Street
between 5th and 6th Avenues / 620-0485
Mon, Wed, and Fri–Sat 10am–6pm;
Tues and Thurs 10am–8pm; Sun noon–5pm.

30	30	25	20
quality	style	service	value

The Edge: Quality traditional furniture deliverable within two weeks. Custom chairs and sofas, handmade to your specifications in its own workroom. Down-filled and delivered within two weeks. Very, very expensive, with prices starting at $2,495. Deluxe.

Door Store

Contemporary
Multiple locations

Mon–Wed and Fri–Sat 10am–6pm,
Thurs 10am–8pm, Sun noon–5pm.

27	32	38	28
quality	style	service	value

The Edge: Come here for furniture price, not longevity. Inexpensive functional country pine furniture, with immediate delivery.

Locations: Chelsea: 123 West 17th Street, between 6th and 7th Avenues (627-1515) / **Gramercy Park/Murray Hill:** 1 Park Avenue, near 33rd Street (679-9700) / **Midtown East:** 599 Lexington Avenue, near 53rd Street (832-7500) / **Upper East Side:** 1201 3rd Avenue, near 70th Street (772-1110)

Foremost Furniture Showrooms

Contemporary
Midtown West

8 West 30th Street
between 5th Avenue and Broadway / 889-6347
Mon–Wed and Fri 10am–6pm, Thurs 10am–7pm,
Sat 10am–5pm, Sun 11am–5pm.

31	29	35	39
quality	style	service	value

The Edge: Discounts brand-name furniture. Discounts on Henredon, Stanley, and Century. 48,000 square feet of display space on four floors, laid out by floor and room plans. *"New York's best resource."*

Jensen-Lewis

Contemporary
Chelsea

89 7th Avenue
near 15th Street / 929-4880
Mon–Wed and Fri–Sat 10am–7pm,
Thurs 10am–8pm, Sun noon–5pm.

40	44	36	35
quality	style	service	value

The Edge: Basic apartment furnishings and housewares. Furnishings and lighting for every room in a range of styles, from Shaker to contemporary. Offers bunk beds, durable porch and patio furniture, housewares, kitchen accessories, and small bureaus. *"Stylish tables, bookcases, and amenities."*

Knoll

Contemporary
SoHo/TriBeCa

105 Wooster Street

near Prince Street / 343-4000
Weekdays 10am–6pm, Sat–Sun noon–5pm
(closed Sat–Sun Memorial Day–Labor Day).

quality style service value

The Edge: Classic and contemporary furniture designs. Formerly available only through decorators, now retail also.

Lively Set
33 Bedford Street
near Carmine Street / 807-8417
Daily 11am–7pm.

Contemporary
Greenwich Village

The Edge: Chic metals. Known for furniture and furnishings from the '30s and '40s. Expect to find American pottery and affordable metal furniture. Medical cabinets start at $750.

Maurice Villency
200 Madison Avenue
near 35th Street / 725-4840
Mon and Thurs 10am–9pm,
Tues–Wed and Fri–Sat 10am–6pm, Sun noon–5pm.

Contemporary
Gramercy Park/Murray Hill

quality style service value

The Edge: Best known for contemporary leather sofas and chairs. Features a large showroom filled with a wide range of modern furniture, including leather sofas and chairs, lacquer furniture, and wall units. Prices $1,800 to $6,000. Catalog $10. *"I've had good experience with their leather furniture."*

Modern Age
102 Wooster Street
between Spring and Prince Streets / 966-0669
Tues–Fri 11am–6pm, Sat–Sun noon–6pm.

Contemporary
SoHo/TriBeCa

quality style service value

The Edge: Cutting-edge furniture and accessories. Features two floors of modern furniture and home accessories from top modern designers, including Gijs Papavoine, Philippe Starck, Jasper Morrison, Borek Sipek, Gerard Van den Berg, Niels Bendtsen, and Marie-Christine Dorner. Prices range from $350 to $10,000. Important contemporary furniture as seen in the Museum of Modern Art. *"Gorgeous modern furniture. Expensive."* *"Unusual modern look."*

North Carolina Furniture Showrooms
12 West 21st Street, 5th Floor
near 5th Avenue / 260-5050
Mon–Wed and Fri–Sat 10am–6pm,
Thurs 10am–8pm, Sun noon–5pm.

Contemporary
Gramercy Park/Murray Hill

quality style service value

The Edge: Furniture direct from the manufacturer. Offers furniture and bedding from hundreds of top furniture houses, including Hekman, Henredon, Hickory, Stanley, and more. Features styles ranging from 18th-century reproductions to contemporary furnishings. Discounts range from 40% to 45% off the suggested retail price. Credit cards for deposits only. You shop primarily by catalog.

Nuovo Melodrom
60 Greene Street
between Spring and Broome Streets / 219-0013

Contemporary
SoHo/TriBeCa

Weekdays 9am–6:30pm, Sat–Sun noon–6pm.

The Edge: Designer contemporary furniture exclusively. Represents almost a dozen contemporary furniture designers, including Anonimo, Barocco, Bistrot, Bucciarelli (sold exclusively here), Haus Killer/Hoffmann, Jean Michel Frank, Mies van der Rohe, Noguchi, Palio, Piuma, and more. The classics are generally in stock, with a standard chrome frame and black leather upholstery. Lead time for special orders is six to eight weeks. 50 different canvas colors available on upholstered items. Priced from $1,000 to $5,000.

Pace Collection

321 East 62nd Street
between 1st and 2nd Avenues / 838-0331
Weekdays 10am–6pm.

Contemporary
Upper East Side

quality style service value

The Edge: Fabulous moderns. Represents some of the finest contemporary designers. Very simple but sophisticated styling, using fine materials and good workmanship.

Portico Home

379 West Broadway
between Broome and Spring Streets / 941-7800
Mon–Sat 11am–7pm, Sun noon–6:30pm.

Contemporary
SoHo/TriBeCa

quality style service value

The Edge: Clean country styling in furniture and bed and bath accessories. Special-order Shaker adaptation furniture priced from $500 to $5,000. Accessories include candles, candlesticks, linens, natural bath products, and potpourri. *"Wonderful country look." "Extensive soaps and lotions." "Original."*

SEE Ltd.

920 Broadway
near 21st Street / 228-3600
Mon–Sat 10am–7pm, Sun noon–6pm.

Contemporary
Gramercy Park/Murray Hill

quality style service value

The Edge: SEE equals Spatial Environmental Elements—need we say more. Avant-garde furniture sold direct. 70 different designers featured. Priced from $1,000 to $10,000. *"Interesting furniture, but high priced."*

Scott Jordan Furniture

137 Varick Street
near Spring Street / 620-4682
Mon–Wed and Fri–Sat 11am–6pm,
Thurs 11am–8pm, Sun noon–5pm.

Contemporary
SoHo/TriBeCa

quality style service value

The Edge: Traditional, quality crafted furniture. Quality traditionally styled furniture made in solid hardwoods. *"Fabulous furniture—the antiques of tomorrow."*

Shabby Chic

93 Greene Street
near Prince Street / 274-9842
Mon–Sat 10am–7pm, Sun 11am–7pm.

Contemporary
SoHo/TriBeCa

quality style service value

The Edge: Expensive overstuffed furniture. Furniture with the old English country look. Faded, classical slipcovered furniture, throw pillows, linens, and period accessories. Pieces are made in cream and white, slipcovered in your choice of fabric. Very expensive (couches $4,000 to $7,000, slipcovered).

Winslow Furniture
464 Broome Street
near Mercer Street / 219-9244
Mon–Sat 11am–5pm, Sun 1–5pm.

Contemporary
SoHo/TriBeCa

The Edge: Reasonably priced custom-made furniture. Winslow manufactures his adaptation of Mission to modern furniture. Priced from $500 to $5,000.

Workbench
Mon–Sat 10am–7pm, Sun noon–6pm.

Contemporary
Multiple locations

quality style service value

The Edge: Price is the driver for these simply styled pieces. A large selection of Shaker-style basics, from trundle beds and desks to storage units and toy chests in a variety of finishes. The inexpensive lower-end furniture is scaled to apartment living. *"If you like teak. Great sales."* *"Excellent and typical teak and rosewood furniture."* *"Very good value and on time delivery too!"*

Locations: Gramercy Park/Murray Hill: 470 Park Avenue South, near 32nd Street (481-5454) / **SoHo/TriBeCa:** 176 Avenue of the Americas, between Prince and Spring Streets (675-7775) / **Upper East Side:** 336 East 86th Street, between 1st and 2nd Avenues (794-4418) / **Upper West Side:** 2091 Broadway, near 72nd Street (724-3670)

Wyeth
151 Franklin Street
near Varick Street / 925-5278
Mon–Sat 11am–6pm.

Contemporary
SoHo/TriBeCa

The Edge: The source for the finest metal furnishings. Steel furniture in sleek clean lines–practical and stylish. *"Expensive, but gorgeous, stuff."*

Bridge Kitchenware
214 East 52nd Street
between 2nd and 3rd Avenues / 688-4220
Weekdays 9am–5:30pm, Sat 10am–4:30pm.

Cookware & cutlery
Midtown East

quality style service value

The Edge: Exceptionally well-stocked cooking store for serious cooks. Since 1945, offering professional cooking equipment, china, and serving accessories— everything you could possibly need. Few stores carry as many specialty cookware items. Much of the wares hang overhead or are piled in open containers. A virtual warehouse of cooking supplies. Full retail prices. *"Not discount but very complete."* *"We love this place—essential."* *"Overpriced, but remains a culinary Mecca."*

Broadway Panhandler

477 Broome Street
near Wooster Street / 966-3434
Weekdays 10:30am–7pm, Sat 11am–7pm,
Sun noon–6pm (closed Sun July–Aug).

Cookware & cutlery
SoHo/TriBeCa

quality style service value

The Edge: Best for bakeware. Good neighborhood source (SoHo and East Village) for top-quality kitchenware pots and pans from basic to gourmet quality. Baking and pastry equipment are the store's chief attraction. 20% off. *"Lots of Le Cruset and Celphalon Pots." "Wonderful selection, limited service, pricey."*

Daroma Restaurant Equipment Corp.

196 & 231 Bowery
near Prince Street / 226-6774
Weekdays 9am–5pm, Sat 9am–3:30pm.

Cookware & cutlery
Lower East Side/Chinatown

quality style service value

The Edge: Unbelievable prices. Sells restaurant supplies and equipment, including professional refrigerators and stoves. Large selection. As with most discounters, come here for the prices, not the service.

E. Rossi

191 Grand Street
near Mulberry Street / 226-9254
Mon–Sat 10am–7pm, Sun 10am–5pm.

Cookware & cutlery
SoHo/TriBeCa

The Edge: A wholesale source for Italian cooking needs. Mostly wholesale, but you can buy hand-cranked pasta makers, ravioli plates, rolling pins and boards, cappuccino makers, coffee pots, heavy crockery bowls for serving and making pasta, and general gadgets needed for Italian kitchens. Discounter.

Empire Restaurant Supply

114 Bowery
at Grand Street / 226-4447
Weekdays 7:30am–5pm, Sat 9am–noon.

Cookware & cutlery
SoHo/TriBeCa

quality style service value

The Edge: Great prices. One of the best restaurant-supply stores. Features everything from the basics to commercial ranges.

Gringer & Sons, Inc.

29 1st Avenue
at 2nd Street / 475-0600
Weekdays 8:30am–5:30pm, Sat 8:30am–4:30pm.

Cookware & cutlery
Flatiron/East Village

quality style service value

The Edge: Selection and price. Restaurant-supply store featuring a good selection of kitchen appliances made from stainless-steel. Also a wide range of standard appliances from major manufacturers. *"Great place for appliances. Good selection, best prices." "You have to go there—I called for information (twice) and they never called back."*

Hung Chong Import

Cookware & cutlery
SoHo/TriBeCa

14 Bowery
between Pell and Doyers Streets / 349-1463
Daily 9am–7pm.

The Edge: Good source for Chinese cooking instruments at lower prices than uptown. Features kitchenware and some hardware. Family to restaurant-size equipment. Prices are 50% below uptown. Supplies many Chinese restaurants. Not much English spoken. No credit cards. Discounter.

J. B. Prince

Cookware & cutlery
Gramercy Park/Murray Hill

36 East 31st Street, 11th Floor
between Park and Madison Avenues / 683-3553
Mon and Wed–Fri 9am–5pm, Tues 9am–6pm.

The Edge: Convenience. More like a showroom for its large mail-order business in professional cookware equipment for amateur chefs. Specialty cookware and cookbooks. Helpful staff. No delivery.

Lamalle Kitchenware

Cookware & cutlery
Gramercy Park/Murray Hill

36 West 25th Street, 6th Floor
between 6th Avenue and Broadway / 242-0750
Weekdays 9am–6pm, Sat 10am–6pm (closed Sat June–Aug).

The Edge: The shop for serious kitchen professionals. In operation since 1927, now owned by Fisher & Levy's owner, Lamalle caters to chefs seeking quality oven- and bakeware, assorted specialty tools, cutlery, and more. You'll find an enormous selection of Apilco French porcelain.

Lechter's

Cookware & cutlery
Multiple locations

Mon–Sat 10am–8pm, Sun 11am–6pm.

35	32	32	38
quality	style	service	value

The Edge: Low-end basic housewares. Basic source for moderately priced (not discounted) kitchenware. *"Good selection of basic household utensils." "Ordinary items." "Good value—when you need it, they have it."*

Locations: Flatiron/East Village: 55 East 8th Street, near Mercer Street (505-0576) / 292 1st Avenue, near 17th Street (677-6481) / **Greenwich Village:** 401 Avenue of the Americas, near 8th Street (741-0016) / **Lower Manhattan:** 5 World Trade Center, near Liberty Street (inside mall) (432-0844) / **Midtown East:** 475 5th Avenue, near 41st Street (889-4754) / **Midtown West:** 901 Avenue of the Americas, near 33rd Street (268-7303) / 250 West 57th Street, near Broadway (956-7290) / 10 West 34th Street, between 5th and 6th Avenues (564-3226) / 60 East 42nd Street, near Madison Avenue (682-8476) / **SoHo/TriBeCa:** 536 Broadway, near Spring Street (274-0890) / **Upper East Side:** 1198 3rd Avenue, near 69th Street (744-1427) / 1504 3rd Avenue, near 85th Street (988-3730) / **Upper West Side:** 2141 Broadway, near 75th Street (580-1610) / 2503 Broadway, near 93rd Street (864-5464) / 2875 Broadway, between 111th and 112th Streets (864-5591)

Matas Restaurant Supply

Cookware & cutlery
SoHo/TriBeCa

210 Bowery
between Prince and Spring Streets / 966-2251

Weekdays 8am–5pm; also Sat in summer 10am–4pm.

The Edge: The basics in cookware, more for restaurants. 30,000 items, including dishes, glassware, and pots. Known for basic restaurant supplies. Discounter.

New Cathay Hardware Corporation

Cookware & cutlery
SoHo/TriBeCa

49 Mott Street
near Bayard Street / 962-6648
Daily 10am–7pm.

The Edge: One of the largest sources for Chinese cooking items. Meets all Chinese cooking needs. Much cheaper than uptown! Items priced from $5 to the low hundreds. Stocks one of the largest selections of Oriental cookware in the city. Discounter.

Platypus

Cookware & cutlery
Multiple locations

Weekdays 11am–6pm, Sat 11am–7pm, Sun noon–6pm.

42	42	41	34
quality	style	service	value

The Edge: Eclectic household items. Hard to describe the themes—home accessories, kitchenware, some furniture, plus chocolates and coffees. Kitchenware (china, cutlery, glassware, and equipment) from around the world. The tableware, mostly from Italy and France, has a chunky country feel. *"The freshest coffee!" "Great inventory."*

Locations: Lower Manhattan: Two World Financial Center, 225 Liberty Street (786-0577) /
SoHo/TriBeCa: 126 Spring Street, near Greene Street (219-3919)

Cobweb

Country
SoHo/TriBeCa

116 West Houston Street
between Thomas and Sullivan Streets / 505-1558
Weekdays noon–7pm, Sat noon–5pm (closed Sat July–Aug).

45	50	50	50
quality	style	service	value

The Edge: Antique Spanish and Central and South American furniture. Two-story shop filled with a mix of antique Spanish and Central and South American rustic and formal furniture, plus accessories. Accessories include antique tiles, chandeliers, earthenware water jugs, hand-painted ceramic plates, iron washstands, terra-cotta bowls, and wooden plant stands.

Le Fanion

Country
Greenwich Village

299 West 4th Street
near Bank Street / 463-8760
Weekdays 11am–7pm, Sat noon–6pm.

45	45	45	40
quality	style	service	value

The Edge: Antique furniture and decorative items from the south of France. Features 18th- and 19th-century country French furniture, plus decorative items (including contemporary handmade pottery) painted in Provence.

Martell Antiques

53 East 10th Street
near Broadway / 777-4360
Weekdays 10am–5:30pm, Sat 11am–5pm (closed Sat in Aug).

Country
Flatiron/East Village

The Edge: Dedicated to antique formal French country furniture. Mostly 18th- and early 19th-century formal French country furniture. Priced from $5,000 to $15,000. No credit cards.

Adorama Camera

42 West 18th Street
between 5th and 6th Avenues / 675-6789
Mon–Thurs 9am–6:30pm, Fri 9am–1:30pm, Sun 9:30am–5:30pm.

Electronics, etc.
Chelsea

The Edge: Wide range of camera equipment. Mail order for amateurs and professionals featuring basic cameras to dark-room equipment. Everything for photography at good prices. See its 14+-page ads in most photography publications. Very large inventory.

B&H Photo & Electronics

420 9th Avenue
between 33rd and 34th Streets / 807-7474
Mon–Tues 9am–6pm, Wed–Thurs 9am–7:15pm,
Fri 9am–2pm, Sun 10am– 4:45pm.

Electronics, etc.
Chelsea

The Edge: The photographer's source. Features professional photo, video, and imaging equipment. Very good prices on cameras, lenses, and supplies. More than 200 styles of top-brand cameras. Features both new and used equipment. A monthly flyer features specials. Also has a large catalog. Ships worldwide. Discounter. *"If you can get attention, the advice is good." "Best camera shop in the city." "You should know what you want."*

Brookstone Company

Daily 10am–9pm.

Electronics, etc.
Multiple locations

The Edge: Unique, fun gadgetry gifts. Here necessities include items from cordless head phones and foot massagers to garden hoses, hammocks, and more. *"Gadgets are terrific!" "Downscale version of the Sharper Image." "Like all gadget stores, fun to browse. And good values here."*

Locations: Lower Manhattan: 18 Fulton Street, South Street Seaport (344-8108) / **Midtown West:** 16 West 50th Street, between 5th and 6th Avenues (262-3237)

Canal Hi-Fi

319 Canal Street
near Broome Street / 925-6575
Daily 10am–6:30pm.

Electronics, etc.
SoHo/TriBeCa

The Edge: Discounts on quality audio components. Find professional sound equipment, speakers, and compact disc players from Pioneer and Sony, among others. No delivery. Discounter.

CompUSA

420 5th Avenue
between 37th and 38th Streets / 782-7700
Weekdays 8:30am–8pm, Sat 10am–7pm, Sun 11am–6pm.

Electronics, etc.
Gramercy Park/Murray Hill

quality   style   service   value

The Edge: A computer superstore. Good advice, great selection—all you'll need in the computer area. *"Good help who know their products."*

Computers

7 Great Jones Street
near Broadway / 254-9000
Weekdays 10am–6:30pm.

Electronics, etc.
SoHo/TriBeCa

quality   style   service   value

The Edge: Software and computers for sale or rent. In business since 1978. Sells hardware, software, and accessories for computers and desktop-publishing systems. Also magazines and books. You can rent and use the equipment at the store. Discounter.

Crocodile Computers

240 West 73rd Street
between Broadway and West End Avenue / 769-3400
Weekdays 10:30am–7pm, Sat 11am–5pm.

Electronics, etc.
Upper West Side

quality   style   service   value

The Edge: Sells refurbished and new computers. Brands include Macs and IBMs and compatibles, all with store warranty. No credit cards. Discounter. *"Good value—if you can get what you want."*

Foto Electric Supply Company

31 Essex Street
near Grand Street / 673-5222
Sun–Thurs 9am–6pm, Fri 9am–3pm.

Electronics, etc.
Lower East Side/Chinatown

quality   style   service   value

The Edge: Discounts small appliances, cameras, sunglasses, and watches. Like the items found in most duty-free shops. *"Customers must know the products."*

Harvey Electronics

2 West 45th Street
near 5th Avenue / 575-5000
Mon–Wed and Fri 9:30am–6pm, Thurs 10:30am–8pm,
Sat 10am–6pm, Sun noon– 5pm.

Electronics, etc.
Midtown West

quality   style   service   value

The Edge: The place for state-of-the-art home theaters. Offers top-of-the-line audio and video equipment, plus a design and installation division. Very expensive. *"Very good service. Knowledgeable staff. Low pressure." "Excellent service, but limited selection and high prices."*

Hi Fi Electronics

152 Delancey Street
at Clinton Street / 260-7222
Daily 10am–7:30pm.

Electronics, etc.
Lower East Side/Chinatown

The Edge: New and refurbished equipment by Fisher, Pioneer, Sony, etc. Refurbished equipment carries a three-month warranty.

J&R Computer World

15 Park Row
near Broadway / 238-9100
Mon–Sat 9am–6:30pm, Sun 10:30am–6:30pm.

Electronics, etc.
Lower Manhattan

quality style service value

The Edge: One stop shopping. A great source for computers, fax machines, office equipment, and the like. Stocks a huge inventory. Authorized dealer for Apple, AST, Canon, Hewlett-Packard, NEC, Toshiba, and more. Order by fax or phone—24 hours a day, seven days a week—call toll free 800-232-8180. 20% off. *"Great for discount items." "Very large selection, good prices." "Phone ordering is very easy and convenient—but sometimes you have to wait for service."*

Manhattan Electronics Corporation

16 West 45th Street
near 5th Avenue / 354-6462
Weekdays 9am–5pm, Sat 9:30am–4pm.

Electronics, etc.
Midtown West

The Edge: Exclusively computer equipment and parts. New equipment only. Discounter.

Micro U.S.A. Computer Depot

55 Avenue of the Americas
near Canal Street / 941-0270
Weekdays 10am–6pm, Sat 11am–5pm.

Electronics, etc.
SoHo/TriBeCa

The Edge: Computers and software at good prices. Sells custom-made IBM-compatible computers, accessories, software, and supplies at good prices. No delivery. Discounter.

Olden Camera

1265 Broadway
near 31st Street / 725-1234
Weekdays 9am–7pm, Sat 9am–6pm, Sun 10am–5pm.

Electronics, etc.
Midtown West

quality style service value

The Edge: Discounts on new and used camera equipment. Sells new and used cameras, cellular phones, computers, faxes, and video equipment at discounted prices.

Phone Boutique

828 Lexington Avenue
near 63rd Street / 319-9650
Mon–Sat 10am–6:30pm.

Electronics, etc.
Upper East Side

quality style service value

The Edge: Buys, sells, and repairs vintage telephones. Vintage telephones range from 1920s candlesticks in black metal and brass to more current 1950s styles. Phones can be updated with pushbuttons. Repairs start at $45. Also sells answering machines, fax machines, and telephone-related accessories. Rents cellular phones and beepers. *"Expensive."*

Sharper Image

Weekdays 10am–7pm, Sat 10am–6pm, Sun noon–5pm.

Electronics, etc.
Multiple locations

quality style service value

The Edge: Executive toys and comforts. Wonderful catalog featuring binoculars, desk accessories, fitness equipment, globes, high-end stereo equipment, massage chairs, power fish tanks, and telescopes. *"A living catalog."*

Locations: Lower Manhattan: 89 South Street, Pier 17, between South and Fulton Streets (693-0477) / **Midtown West:** 4 West 57th Street, between 5th and 6th Avenues (265-2550) / **Upper East Side:** 900 Madison Avenue, near 73rd Street (794-4974)

Software Etc.

Weekdays 10am–7pm, Sat 10am–6pm, Sun 11am–6pm.

Electronics, etc.
Multiple locations

quality style service value

The Edge: Kowledgeable staff. Computer accessories, books, and software sold at good prices.

Locations: Flatiron/East Village: 101 5th Avenue, between 17th and 18th Streets (727-3280) / 743 Broadway, near Astor Place (979-7678) / **Lower Manhattan:** 150 Broadway, near Maiden Lane (233-5913) / **Midtown East:** 595 5th Avenue, near 48th Street (752-7305) / 162 East 53rd Street, near 3rd Avenue (753-7780) / **Midtown West:** 1282 Broadway, near 33rd Street (967-9070) / 666 5th Avenue, near 52nd Street (315-4744) / 1120 Avenue of the Americas, near 44th Street (921-7855) / **Upper East Side:** 128 East 86th Street, near Lexington Avenue (423-1844) / **Upper West Side:** 2300 Broadway, near 83rd Street (362-3460)

Sound City

58 West 45th Street
between 5th and 6th Avenues / 575-0210
Weekdays 9am–7pm, Sat 9am–6pm.

Electronics, etc.
Midtown West

quality style service value

The Edge: Good variety and selection. Discounts all major brands of stereo, video, photo, and home electronics. *"Very good range of price and styles." "Good service, knowledgeable."*

Spectra Research Group

762 Madison Avenue
between 65th and 66th Streets / 744-2255
Mon–Sat 10am–6pm.

Electronics, etc.
Upper East Side

The Edge: State-of-the-art audio-visual and surveillance equipment. Surveillance equipment and general consumer electronic goods. Discounts possible depending on the amount you buy.

Stereo Exchange

627 Broadway
near Houston Street / 505-1111
Weekdays 11am–7:30pm, Sat 10:30am–7pm, Sun noon–7pm.

Electronics, etc.
SoHo/TriBeCa

quality style service value

The Edge: Repairs and sells used high-end stereos. Features top-end stereos and components for stereo, video, and audio systems. Refurbished items carry a 30-day warranty. Discounter. *"Knowledgeable staff, good value." "Good for selling your used equipment."*

Vicmarr Stereo and TV
88 Delancey Street
near Orchard Street / 505-0380
Sun–Thurs 9am–7pm, Fri 9am–2pm.

Electronics, etc.
Lower East Side/Chinatown

The Edge: Full-line electronics shop. Offers a large selection of basic electronic products, including answering machines, camcorders, car audio systems, microwave ovens, stereos, telephones, etc. Good prices. Discounter.

Waves
110 West 25th Street, 10th Floor
between 6th and 7th Avenues / 989-9284
Weekdays noon–6pm, Sat–Sun 10am–6pm.

Electronics, etc.
Midtown West

The Edge: Vintage electronics. Sells old radios, record players, and telephones. Also repairs radios.

Willoughby's Camera Store
136 West 32nd Street
between 6th and 7th Avenues / 564-1600
Weekdays 8:30am–9pm, Sat–Sun 10am–7pm.

Electronics, etc.
Midtown West

The Edge: Variety and selection. Good selection of computers, cameras, and electronics.

Wiz
Mon–Sat 10am–8pm, Sun 11am–7pm.

Electronics, etc.
Multiple locations

37	26	28	39
quality	style	service	value

The Edge: Chain of audio/video discount stores. Discounts TVs, CDs, computers, fax machines, automatic cameras, etc. Claim to meet any price. It's like most discounters, so don't go there for the service. 20% off. *"Good prices and selection but no service."*

Locations: Flatiron/East Village: 726 Broadway, near Astor Place (677-4111) / 17 Union Square West, near 15th Street (741-9500) / **Gramercy Park/Murray Hill:** 337 5th Avenue, near 33rd Street (447-0100) / **Midtown East:** 212 East 57th Street, between 2nd and 3rd Avenues (754-1600) / **Midtown West:** 871 Avenue of the Americas, at 31st Street (594-2300) / **Upper East Side:** 1536 3rd Avenue, at 86th Street (876-4400) / **Upper West Side:** 2577 Broadway, at 97th Street (663-8000)

Barry Friedman Ltd.
32 East 67th Street
between Madison and Park Avenues / 794-8950
Weekday 11am–6pm; June–Aug, weekdays 10am–5:30pm.

Empire & Biedermeier
Upper East Side

50	50	50	30
quality	style	service	value

The Edge: Features Vienna Secession furniture, paintings, and accessories. With Vienna Secessionist pieces, also Italian modern pieces from the 1920s and 1930s. Periodic special exhibitions with a catalog produced for the show. No credit cards.

Eileen Lane Antiques

150 Thompson Street
near Houston Street / 475-2988
Daily 11am–7pm (closed Sun June–Aug).

Empire & Biedermeier
SoHo/TriBeCa

quality style service value

The Edge: Large selection of Biedermeier and art deco furniture. Two-story furniture and accessory warehouse. Its specialty is Biedermeier and Empire furniture matched with accessories, including art deco pieces, vintage alabaster chandeliers, and more. Chandeliers priced $1,350 to $4,500.

Karl Kemp & Associates Ltd.

34 East 10th Street
between Broadway and University Place / 254-1877
Weekdays 10am–5pm, Sat noon–5pm (closed Sat in summer).

Empire & Biedermeier
Flatiron/East Village

The Edge: Small superb collection. Known for top-quality Empire, Biedermeier, and art deco furnishings. A small collection, but in excellent condition. Some accessories, which on our last visit included a stunning tea set, vases, and mirrors. No credit cards.

Niall Smith

Mon–Sat noon–6pm (closed Sat June–Aug).

Empire & Biedermeier
Multiple locations

quality style service value

The Edge: Neoclassic early 19th-century European furniture and accessories. Wonderful for Biedermeier. No credit cards. No delivery.

Locations: Greenwich Village: 344 Bleecker Street, between West 10th and Christopher Streets (255-0660) / **SoHo/TriBeCa:** 96 Grand Street, between Greene and Mercer Streets (941-7354)

Ritter Antik

35 East 10th Street
between Broadway and University Place / 673-2213
Weekdays 10am–5:30pm, Sat noon–5pm.

Empire & Biedermeier
Flatiron/East Village

quality style service value

The Edge: Best for its Biedermeier collection. Known for expensive Biedermeier furniture. Also features Russian, French, Austrian, and Scandinavian pieces from the 16th to the 18th century. No credit cards.

Victor Antiques Ltd.

223 East 60th Street
between 2nd and 3rd Avenues / 752-4100
Weekdays 10am–6pm, Sat noon–5pm.

Empire & Biedermeier
Midtown East

quality style service value

The Edge: Loft-size store—lots of Biedermeier. Features 18th-century to art deco (mostly items from the 19th century) European and Scandinavian furniture. Favors Biedermeier furniture, with prices from $4,000.

Agostino Antiques Ltd.
808 Broadway
near 11th Street / 533-3355
Weekdays 9am–5pm.

English
Flatiron/East Village

quality style service value

The Edge: Large selection of 18th- and 19th-century English furniture. Used to be to the trade only, but now takes retail clients. Features two floors of primarily 18th- and 19th-century English furniture and accessories, plus some French and continental pieces. Priced from $1,000 to many hundreds of thousands. Also an English reproduction collection, priced from $400 to $15,000. High quality. Decorator discount possible to 20%. No credit cards. *"So beautiful—so expensive."*

Eagles Antiques
1097 Madison Avenue
near 83rd Street / 772-3266
Weekdays 9:30am–5:30pm, Sat 10am–5:30pm.

English
Upper East Side

quality style service value

The Edge: Quality period English formal furniture. Specializes in formal 18th- and 19th-century English period furniture, including some unique Georgian pieces priced from $9,000 to $50,000; 17th- to 19th-century Aubusson pillows, priced from $1,000 to $5,000; and 16th- to 19th-century antique accessories, including porcelain lamps and candlesticks. No credit cards. Deluxe. *"Pricey, but worth it."*

Florian Papp
962 Madison Avenue
near 76th Street / 288-6770
Weekdays 9am–5:30pm, Sat 10am–5pm.

English
Upper East Side

quality style service value

The Edge: Museum-quality, formal 17th- to 19th-century English furniture. Third-generation family business. Three floors of furniture and accessories priced from $2,000 to $300,000. Deluxe. No credit cards. No delivery. *"Magnificent quality."*

Kentshire Galleries
37 East 12th Street
near University Place / 673-6644
Weekdays 9am–5pm, Sat 10:30am–3pm (closed Sat May–Oct).

English
Flatiron/East Village

quality style service value

The Edge: A large selection of very expensive English antique furniture and furnishings. Ever-changing stock on seven floors, but staples include fine English china, Majolica plates, crystal decanters, and desk accessories. An excellent selection of furniture from Queen Anne through William IV. Maintains a small gift annex at Bergdorf. Deluxe. No credit cards. *"Extensive selection." "Need lots and lots of money for these collector items."*

Malcolm Franklin, Inc.
762 Madison Avenue

English
Upper East Side

between 65th and 66th Streets / 288-9054
Weekdays 10am–5:30pm, Sat 10am–4pm (closed Sat June–Aug).

quality style service value

The Edge: Rare Queen Anne furniture. Features 17th- to early 19th-century English furniture, plus wonderful porcelain and brass accessories. Priced from $2,000 to $40,000. No credit cards. Deluxe.

Philip Colleck of London Ltd.

English
Flatiron/East Village

830 Broadway
near 12th Street / 505-2500
Weekdays 10am–5:30pm or by appointment.

quality style service value

The Edge: Museum-quality 18th-century formal English furniture. Features Adam, Chippendale, and Queen Anne furniture. Full range of furniture, plus decorative accessories, including museum-quality gilded mirrors. No credit cards. Deluxe.

Stair & Company

English
Upper East Side

942 Madison Avenue
near 74th Street / 517-4400
Weekdays 9:30am–5:30pm, Sat 11am–4pm (closed Sat July–Aug).

quality style service value

The Edge: Quality 18th- and early 19th-century English furniture. Since 1812 in New York and London (24 Bruton Street). Two floors of mostly furniture, but also accessories, including carpets, chandeliers, Chinese export porcelains, lacquerware, mirrors, paintings, and screens. Furniture prices range from $5,000 to $250,000. No credit cards. No delivery. Deluxe. *"Gracious English tone." "I fantasize about living in Buckingham Palace one day!"*

Trevor Potts Reproductions

English
Upper East Side

1065 Lexington Avenue
between 75th and 76th Streets / 570-5573
Weekdays by appointment 9:30am–5pm; also Sat after Labor Day.

quality style service value

The Edge: Filled with reproductions of English Regency painted and gilded furniture. High-style quality reproductions of antique English furniture. No credit cards.

Cap-Sud, Inc.

European
SoHo/TriBeCa

50 Bond Street
near Lafayette Street / 260-9114
Weekdays 11am–7pm, Sat–Sun noon–6pm.

quality style service value

The Edge: French or Mexican? Only your decorator will know! Handmade in Mexico but looks like Louis XIII and XIV furniture, available but custom order. Wool carpets inspired by 1930s patterns. Made-in-France sofas and bistro chairs. Also accessories and lighting.

Dalva Brothers

European
Midtown East

44 East 57th Street
between Madison and Park Avenues / 758-2297

Mon–Sat 10am–5:30pm (closed Sat July–Aug).

50	50	43	40
quality	style	service	value

The Edge: Five floors of fine 18th-century French furniture and accessories. Wonderful antique furnishings, including clocks and porcelains. Deluxe. No delivery. No credit cards.

Didier Aaron, Inc.

European
Upper East Side

32 East 67th Street
between Park and Madison Avenues / 988-5248
Weekdays 9:30am–6pm, Sat by appointment.

50	50	50	43
quality	style	service	value

The Edge: Impeccable 18th- and 19th-century French furniture. While mostly French 18th- and 19th-century furniture, also some non-French antiques (Anglo-Indian, English, Irish, Italian, Russian, and others). Features exceptional pieces. Some old-master and 19th-century paintings and drawings. No credit cards. Deluxe.

Frederick P. Victoria and Son, Inc.

European
Midtown East

154 East 55th Street
between 3rd and Lexington Avenues / 755-2549
Weekdays 9am–5pm.

50	50	50	40
quality	style	service	value

The Edge: Collector-quality 19th-century French furniture. Fine selection of 18th-century French clocks, crystal chandeliers, and works of art from around the globe. A favorite shop of top decorators. Prices from $5,000 to $350,000. No credit cards. Deluxe.

French & Company, Inc.

European
Upper East Side

17 East 65th Street
between 5th and Madison Avenues / 535-3330
By appointment.

40	40	40	40
quality	style	service	value

The Edge: Museum-quality 18th-century French and English furniture. A small, select collection of high-quality antique furniture, plus some old-master paintings. Caters to museums seeking important furniture. Deluxe. *"Beautiful, but expensive."*

Grange Furniture

European
Gramercy Park/Murray Hill

200 Lexington Avenue
near 32nd Street / 685-9057
Weekdays 9am–6pm.

35	40	50	50
quality	style	service	value

The Edge: Quality expensive reproductions of French period furniture. Features a full range of quality reproductions of period French furniture, including 18th-century French Provençal, 19th-century Louis XVI, Louis Philippe, and Directoire. Also wicker, painted furniture and garden furnishings, and more. Choice of wood and painted finishes. Very attractive styling. Delivery, if in stock, takes two to three weeks, or 12 weeks if ordered from France.

John Rosselli Antiques

European
Upper East Side

255 East 72nd Street
near 2nd Avenue / 737-2252
Weekdays 9:30am–6pm.

40	50	30	30
quality	style	service	value

The Edge: Antiques, reproductions, and modern decorative pieces. Three floors of decorative pieces: antiques from the 17th century on, reproductions, and modern furnishings. Prices to $20,000. No credit cards. *"Vast selection."*

Le Cadet de Gascogne
European
1015 Lexington Avenue
Upper East Side
near 73rd Street / 744-5925
Weekdays–Fri 10am–6pm; summer, Tues–Thurs 10am–6pm or by appointment.

The Edge: Quality French antique furniture from Louis XIV on. Many signed pieces. Also accessories, including paintings and objets d'art. No credit cards.

Le Decor Français
European
1006 Lexington Avenue
Upper East Side
near 72nd Street / 734-0032
Weekdays 9am–6pm, Sat 11am–6pm.

The Edge: A touch of Provence. Cozy shop featuring French fabrics in a living room setting.

Newel Art Galleries, Inc.
European
425 East 53rd Street
Midtown East
near 1st Avenue / 758-1970
Weekdays 9am–5pm.

| 43 | 48 | 50 | 35 |
| quality | style | service | value |

The Edge: Vast selection of antique furniture. Six full floors of antiques, ranging from Renaissance through art deco. Lots of English period furniture, including wicker and bamboo. Lovely garden furniture. Also a large selection of 18th- and 19th-century fireplace accessories. Wonderful decorative items. Newel favors the unique. One of the largest antique sources in the city. No credit cards.

Oak-Smith & Jones
European
1510 2nd Avenue
Upper East Side
near 79th Street / 327-3462
Mon–Sat 10am–8pm, Sun 11am–8pm.

| 36 | 37 | 41 | 35 |
| quality | style | service | value |

The Edge: Good prices for collectible (a.k.a. "used") furniture and accessories. Eclectic collection of furniture, including armoires converted to entertainment centers, upholstered furniture, tables, and chairs. Priced from $10 to $7,000+. *"Good selection of 'new antiques'." "Interesting furniture, value priced."*

Reymer-Jourdan Antiques
European
29 East 10th Street
Flatiron/East Village
near Broadway / 674-4470
Weekdays 10am–5:30pm, Sat noon–5pm (closed Sat June–Aug).

| 50 | 50 | 50 | 40 |
| quality | style | service | value |

The Edge: Excellent-quality continental and French 19th-century furniture. Favors Biedermeier, Directoire, and Empire. Among the items featured: a 1930s Hermès iron and leather bench at $5,500. Prices from $500 (for accessories) to $500,000. No credit cards. No delivery. Deluxe.

Calico Corners

Mon–Wed and Fri–Sat 9:30am–6pm,
Thurs 9:30am–8pm, Sun noon–5pm..

Fabric
Multiple locations

quality style service value

The Edge: Good fabric selection. Find fabrics for all your sewing and decorating needs. All major American and European lines, including the Ralph Lauren Fabric Collection. Will make up pillows. Sales are your best bet for good prices.

Locations: Connecticut: 1701 Post Road East, Westport (203-254-7904) / 683 Danbury Road, Wilton (203-762-5662) / **Long Island:** 333 Glen Cove Road, Lake Grove (516-742-6869) / **Westchester:** 1040 Mamaroneck Avenue, Mamaroneck (914-698-9141) / 681 East Main Street, Mt. Kisco (914-666-4486)

Harry Zarin Company

72 Allen Street
near Grand Street / 925-6112
Daily 9am–5:30pm.

Fabric
Lower East Side/Chinatown

quality style service value

The Edge: Vast selections of decorator fabrics. A huge inventory, 50,000 pieces of fabrics in stock, discounted 10% to 25% off retail. Don't forget to bargain to lower prices even further. Best for drapery and upholstery fabrics. Prices mostly from $3 to $35 per yard. *"Terrific selection of home-decorating fabrics." "The second-floor fabrics are the best buys."*

Hyman Hendler and Sons

67 West 38th Street
between 5th and 6th Avenues / 840-8393
Weekdays 9am–5:15pm, Sat 10am–2:30pm.

Fabric
Midtown West

quality style service value

The Edge: Fabulous quality and variety of color and patterns. Beautiful French and Swiss ribbons and tassels. No credit cards. Discounter. *"Any ribbon is possible."*

Intercoastal Textiles

480 Broadway
near Broome Street / 925-9235
Weekdays 9am–5pm; closed July 1–14.

Fabric
SoHo/TriBeCa

quality style service value

The Edge: Close-outs on quality, top decorator upholstery fabrics. Will recommend a source to make slipcovers. Large inventory. Unbelievable selections. Discounter.

Silk Surplus

243 East 59th Street, Suite 1B
near 3rd Avenue / 753-6511
Weekdays 10am–6pm, Sat 10am–5:30pm.

Fabric
Midtown East

quality style service value

The Edge: Outlet for Scalamandre close-outs. Source for Scalamandre fine fabrics, trimmings, and wallpaper. Periodic sales in the fall, starting in late summer. Priced from $5 to $100+ per yard.

50% off during sales, otherwise 10% off to designers. *"Excellent prices on best fabrics, limited quantities." "Good service. 50% off." "Not the selection it used to have."*

Tinsel Trading Company

Fabric
Midtown West

47 West 38th Street
between 5th and 6th Avenues / 730-1030
Weekdays 10am–5pm, Sat 11am–3pm (closed Sat July–Aug).

The Edge: Wonderful trims from the 1920s. Features (in every conceivable space) elaborate antique and contemporary as well—tassels and trims used for tiebacks, elaborate silk tiebacks, braids, cords, fringes, and more. Tassels made of gold and silver metallic threads.

Modern Supply Company

Fans
Lower Manhattan

19 Murray Street
between Broadway and Church Street / 267-0100
Weekdays 10am–5pm, Sat noon–5pm.

quality	style	service	value
50	10	30	50

The Edge: The definitive fan source. All kinds of fans, with and without lights.

Danny Alessandro Ltd. / Edwin Jackson, Inc.

Fireplace
Midtown East

146 East 57th Street
near Lexington Avenue / 421-1928
Weekday 10am–6pm; Apr–Aug,
weekdays 10am–5pm, Sat noon– 4pm.

quality	style	service	value
48	50	45	43

The Edge: Incredible selection of 17th-century and 18th-century fireplace mantels. Since 1979, six floors of fireplace mantels and equipment, with mantels in a wide range of styles, including art deco, contemporary, Early American, and 18th-century Louis XV. Also antique andirons, screens, and tools. A large selection of reproduction mantels and equipment. Custom orders are available. Prices range from $3,800 to $100,000. Deluxe.

William H. Jackson

Fireplace
Midtown East

210 East 58th Street
between 2nd and 3rd Avenues / 753-9400
Weekdays 9:30am–5pm.

quality	style	service	value
50	45	50	35

The Edge: Intricate and interesting fireplace equipment. Equipment includes fireplace mantels, andirons, screens, and fire sets. Specializes in antiques, but also sells reproduction equipment. No delivery.

Antique Cache

Garden & wicker
Midtown East

1050 2nd Avenue
near 55th Street / 752-0838
Weekdays 10:30am–5:30pm.

30	30	50	40
quality	style	service	value

The Edge: Antique bamboo furniture. Gallery 64 at the Manhattan Art and Antiques Center. Known for its antique English furniture and accessories. Accessories include desk sets, letter openers, pens and inkwells, and boxes.

April Cornell

Garden & wicker
Upper West Side

487 Columbus Avenue
between 83rd and 84th Streets / 799-4342
Mon–Sat 10am–8pm, Sun 11am–7pm.

47	40	40	40
quality	style	service	value

The Edge: Indian wicker furniture and fabrics. Store features Indian furniture and a large selection of Indian fabrics made into bedspreads and duvets. Also fabrics sold as piece goods. Prices for fine fabric bedding range from $100 to $400. *"Special things."*

Deutsch Wicker Furniture

Garden & wicker
Gramercy Park/Murray Hill

31 East 32nd Street
between Madison and Park Avenues / 683-8746
Weekdays 9am–5:30pm, Sat 10:30am–3:30pm.

35	35	25	40
quality	style	service	value

The Edge: Unbelievable selection of wicker furniture. For 30 years has featured wicker furniture. A huge inventory, over 6,000 pieces, with styles from Victorian to contemporary, imported from Hong Kong, Indonesia, Italy, and the Philippines.

Elizabeth Street Company

Garden & wicker
Multiple locations

Mon–Thurs 10am–6pm, Fri 10am–5pm.

50	50	50	40
quality	style	service	value

The Edge: Truly unique pieces. Best in class for garden ornamentation. Within the fenced garden (a lot rented from the city) expect to see garden furniture, ornaments, and statues. Some incredible items with prices into the mega thousands. Who would expect to find a garden in such an urban setting? Also an uptown shop with equally high-quality items.

Locations: SoHo/TriBeCa: 210 Elizabeth Street, at Prince Street (941-4800) / **Upper East Side:** 1176 2nd Avenue, at 62nd street (644-6969)

Farm & Garden Nursery

Garden & wicker
SoHo/TriBeCa

2 Avenue of the Americas
near White Street / 431-3577
Spring–summer, daily 9am–6pm; fall–winter, Tues–Sat 10am–5pm.

The Edge: Suburban nursery in the city. Fully stocked with shrubs, plants, soil, gardening gloves, equipment, etc. Features both indoor and outdoor plants.

Folly

Garden & wicker
SoHo/TriBeCa

13 White Street
near Church Street / 925-5012
Weekdays 11am–5pm.

The Edge: Amusing. Decorative garden antiques, most from the mid–18th century from around the world— England, France, Asia, and the U.S. Decorative items include planters, ornaments, seating, bird houses—wonderful things both for the interior and exterior of your home or office. No credit cards.

Gazebo

114 East 57th Street
between Park and Lexington Avenues / 832-7077
Mon–Sat 10am–7pm, Sun noon–6pm.

Garden & wicker
Midtown East

quality style service value

The Edge: Pricey but gorgeous quilts and wicker furniture. Features fine antique and reproduction white and natural wicker furniture and accessories. A large collection of handmade patchwork quilts complement the furniture; most are new, but made from traditional quilting patterns. The small selection of antique quilts is first-rate. Gift items include floral painted china, girls' smocked dresses, pastel rag rugs, and more. Dazzling handmade Christmas ornaments during the season. *"Very attractive store and things." "Expensive." "Enticing."*

Horticultural Society of New York

128 West 58th Street
between 6th and 7th Avenues / 757-0915
Weekdays 10am–6pm.

Garden & wicker
Midtown West

quality style service value

The Edge: A small greenhouse in the city. The greenhouse is filled with plants, bulbs, and books that are for sale. Frequent classes and lectures. Undertakes community projects for the city. Sponsors the New York Flower Show. Its huge library is open to the public. *"Great place to buy plants at good prices."*

Irreplaceable Artifacts

14 2nd Avenue
at Houston Street / 777-2900
Weekdays 10am–6pm, Sat–Sun 11am–5pm.

Garden & wicker
Flatiron/East Village

quality style service value

The Edge: Huge selection of one-of-a-kind accessories salvaged from old buildings. You'll likely find antique cast-iron garden benches, chairs, doors, fountains, and gates; antique bathroom fixtures; hardware in brass, copper, and crystal; stained-glass windows; mantels; and urns. Also sells new aluminum chairs made from the original Victorian molds. No credit cards.

Lexington Gardens

1011 Lexington Avenue
near 72nd Street / 861-4390
Weekdays 10am–6pm, Sat 11am–5pm (closed Sat June–Aug).

Garden & wicker
Upper East Side

quality style service value

The Edge: Fabulous dried arrangements. Antique and new garden furniture and accessories, plus English-style dried flower arrangements and garden books. At Christmas, outstanding hand-decorated angels and miniature Christmas trees. In addition, find mundane gardening equipment, including hoes, rakes, gloves, clippers, and watering cans.

Morgik Company

20 West 22nd Street

Garden & wicker
Gramercy Park/Murray Hill

between 5th and 6th Avenues / 463-0304
Weekdays 8am–4:30pm.

quality style service value

The Edge: Iron galore. Everyone needs the perfect source for wrought iron—chairs, gates, bookcases, and anything else of this substance. Beautiful things. Artisans in the shop repair and design new wrought-iron furnishings and gates for practically everyone—you see it everyplace. Custom work is turned around in less than a month, mostly.

New York Botanic Garden's Shop

Garden & wicker
Bronx

200 Southern Boulevard
near 200th Street, Bronx / 718-817-8723
Spring and summer, Tues–Fri 10am–5pm,
Sat–Sun 11am–6pm; fall and winter, Tues–Sun 10am–4pm.

quality style service value

The Edge: Call the Bronx for great gardening advice. You can call the New York Botanical Garden for its wonderful plant information service, which offers advice on any problem, including how to save annuals. *"Gracious, helpful, detailed plant and planting advice."*

Pimlico Way

Garden & wicker
Upper East Side

1028 Lexington Avenue
near 73rd Street / 439-7855
Mon–Sat 10am–5pm (closed Sat in summer).

quality style service value

The Edge: A large selection of faux bamboo furniture. Small-scale Victorian antique furniture and accessories, including fire tools. A large selection of faux bamboo furniture. Accessories include trays, brass candlesticks, vases, and picture frames (silver and shells).

Treillage Ltd.

Garden & wicker
Upper East Side

418 East 75th Street
between 1st and York Avenues / 535-2288
Weekdays 10am–6pm, Sat 10am–5pm (closed Sat July–Aug).

quality style service value

The Edge: Lovely English-feeling pieces. Features antique and reproduction Victorian garden furniture. Also the basics: very attractive terra-cotta pots as well as birdhouses, gardening aprons, gloves, plant markers, pottery, tools, and watering cans. Unusual pieces. Expensive. *"Beautiful, tasteful items for the garden and gardener."*

Wicker Garden

Garden & wicker
Upper East Side

1318 Madison Avenue
between 93rd and 94th Streets / 410-7000
Mon–Sat 10am–6pm by appointment,

quality style service value

The Edge: Broad selection of very beautiful wicker furniture. Incredibly expensive, antique white and natural wicker furniture in perfect condition. Wicker chairs from $300 to $5,000. A large selection of linens upstairs, some antique and others that look antique. Deluxe. *"High prices, beautiful goods." "Wonderful, attractive selection."*

A.F. Supply Corporation

22 West 21st Street
between 5th and 6th Avenues / 243-5400
Weekdays 8am–5pm and by appointment.

Hardware & fixtures
Gramercy Park/Murray Hill

48 | 38 | 23 | 23
quality style service value

The Edge: Luxury bathroom fixtures. Full line of luxury bathroom fixtures and hardware, ranging from toilets to saunas and spas. Over 100 American and Japanese lines. Decorator discount possible to 30%.

All Baths & Spas

159 Saw Mill River Road
Yonkers / 800-875-2600
Weekdays 9am–5:30pm.

Hardware & fixtures
Westchester

The Edge: Love the fixtures at the Carlyle and the Four Seasons? This is the source. Bathroom fixtures from all the major luxury lines—including Kohler, American Standard, Harrington Brass, and Caldera—are sold here. This is the source for the cast-iron whirlpool tubs at the Carlyle, and the saunas, steam baths, and tile spas at the Four Seasons Hotel.

American Steel Window Service

108 West 17th Street
between 6th and 7th Avenues / 242-8131
Weekdays 7:30am–4:30pm.

Hardware & fixtures
Chelsea

The Edge: Vintage window hardware to order. Bring in a piece of hardware and they'll either match it from their large stock of vintage pieces, supply a reproduction, or make a new piece. No credit cards.

Country Floors

15 East 16th Street
near 5th Avenue and Union Square / 627-8300
Mon–Wed and Fri 9am–6pm, Thurs 9am–8pm,
Sat 9am–5pm (closed Sat July– Aug).

Hardware & fixtures
Flatiron/East Village

45 | 47 | 40 | 33
quality style service value

The Edge: Designer ceramic tiles. Features a full range of designer patterns from plain to richly patterned and from every tile-producing country. Wonderful selection. *"Great selection, beautiful tiles, but you pay for it." "Such beautiful things, worth the expense."*

Eigen Plumbing Supply

236 West 17th Street
between 7th and 8th Avenues / 255-1200
Weekdays 6:30am–4:30pm.

Hardware & fixtures
Chelsea

The Edge: Where your super probably shops! A full range of plumbing supplies. Although professionals buy at Eigen, the staff can help you with your bathroom and kitchen problems. Eigen has the full American Standard showroom on-site. Telephone orders for customers who purchase with credit cards.

Garrett Wade

Hardware & fixtures
SoHo/TriBeCa

161 Avenue of the Americas
near Spring Street / 807-1155
Weekdays 9am–5:30pm, Sat 10am–3pm.

The Edge: Tools and hardware that can't be found anywhere else. Tools and hardware from around the world. Helpful staff. The catalog—over 200 pages long!—describes in detail the pieces' functions and advantages. Tools priced from $20 to $2,500 (for table saws).

George Taylor Specialties Company

Hardware & fixtures
SoHo/TriBeCa

100 Hudson Street
near Franklin Street / 226-5369
Mon–Wed 7:30am–5pm, Thurs 7:30am–6:30pm, Fri 7:30am–4pm.

The Edge: Stocks over 50,000 pieces of obsolete plumbing replacement parts or will make one to order. Specialties are antique hardware and bathroom fixtures and accessories in traditional styles. If none in stock is suitable, will manufacture a comparable part in its machine shop. If you can't get it here, it's unlikely you'll find it elsewhere. Decorator discounts to 25%.

Hammacher Schlemmer

Hardware & fixtures
Midtown East

147 East 57th Street
between Lexington and 3rd Avenues / 421-9000
Mon–Sat 10am–6pm.

quality style service value

The Edge: Strange gadgets galore. Since 1848. Offers a hard-to-categorize range. Includes all-in-one beach chair and carry cart, exercise equipment, luggage, miniature TV golf game, saunas, and much, much more. *"Unique inventory." "Like most Americans, I love gadgets!" "Fun to explore."*

Hastings

Hardware & fixtures
Flatiron/East Village

230 Park Avenue South
near 19th Street / 674-9700
Weekdays 9:30am–5:30pm, Sat 10am–5pm.

quality style service value

The Edge: High-style sleek kitchen and bathroom appliances and fixtures. Italian modern lines favored. Shop features ceramic tiles, mosaics, stones, shower/tub enclosures, and accessories. Designers are available to redo bathrooms and kitchens. Discounter. *"Fabulous hand-painted Mexican furniture and accessories. Much one-of-a-kind."*

Hold Everything

Hardware & fixtures
Upper East Side

1311 2nd Avenue
at 69th Street / 535-9446
Weekdays 10am–8pm, Sat 10am–7pm, Sun noon–6pm.

quality style service value

The Edge: Specializes in space savers. Another division of Pottery Barn and Williams-Sonoma. Space savers include containers, shelving, and other gadgets for the home. *"Wonderful theme. I stock up twice a year for my closets and storage room." "For the compulsively organized!"*

Howard Kaplan Antiques

Hardware & fixtures
Flatiron/East Village

827 Broadway
near 12th Street / 674-1000

Weekdays 9am–6pm.

quality style service value

The Edge: Antiques and reproductions of 18th- to 20th-century French and English bathroom furnishings. From necessities like bathtubs and sinks to accessories such as soap dishes and hardware. Sinks to $30,000! *"Unique inventory."*

Ideal Tile of Manhattan

405 East 51st Street
near 1st Avenue / 759-2339
Weekdays 9am–5pm, Sat 10am–5pm.

Hardware & fixtures
Midtown East

quality style service value

The Edge: Specializes in kitchen and bathroom tiles and counter tops. Features ceramic, porcelain, marble, granite, and terra-cotta tiles from Italy, Spain, and Portugal. Two designers on staff. Hand-painted pottery, platters, and vases. Not related to the West Side store. *"Excellent materials."*

Ideal Tile of Manhattan West

2048 Broadway
near 70th Street / 799-3600
Mon–Wed and Fri 10am–5:30pm, Thurs 10am–7pm, Sat 10am–4pm.

Hardware & fixtures
Upper West Side

The Edge: Tiles for your kitchen and bathroom. Find a wide variety of tiles, marble, and granite from Italy, Portugal, Spain, and other places. *"Excellent materials, but the staff could be more helpful."*

Janovic Plaza

Weekdays 7:30am–6:30pm, Sat 9am–6pm, Sun 11am–5pm.

Hardware & fixtures
Multiple locations

quality style service value

The Edge: Everything in moderately priced paper and paint. Find an enormous range of paints, wallpaper, and window treatments. Knowledgeable and helpful staff. Custom paint colors, of course.

Locations: Chelsea: 215 7th Avenue, near 23rd Street (645-5454) / **Gramercy Park/Murray Hill:** 292 3rd Avenue, between 22nd and 23rd Streets (982-6600) / **Midtown West:** 771 9th Avenue, near 52nd Street (245-3241) / **SoHo/TriBeCa:** 161 Avenue of the Americas, near Mulberry Street (627-1100) / **Upper East Side:** 1150 3rd Avenue, near 67th Street (772-1400) / 1555 3rd Avenue, between 86th and 87th Streets (289-6300) / **Upper West Side:** 159 West 72nd Street, near Broadway (595-2500) / 2475 Broadway, between 22nd and 23rd Streets (769-1440)

Kraft Hardware

306 East 61st Street
between 1st and 2nd Avenues / 838-2214
Weekdays 9am–5pm.

Hardware & fixtures
Upper East Side

quality style service value

The Edge: Mostly decorative hardware and plumbing. At 12,000 square feet, the city's largest hardware store. You'll find decorative brass items along with the basics: nails and screws, hand and power tools, plumbing and electrical supplies, paints and brushes, small appliances, and cleaning supplies. Also some upscale shower enclosures, sinks, toilets, and tubs. The majority of its customers are contractors and building maintenance staff and the sale staff seem to prefer professionals rather than the less experienced customer. *"I keep returning whenever I need decorative hardware. The help is good if you can snag a salesman."*

Nemo Tiles Company

48 East 21st Street
near Park Avenue South / 505-0009
Weekdays 9:30am–5:30pm, Sat 11am–4:30pm.

Hardware & fixtures
Gramercy Park/Murray Hill

quality style service value
50   40   40   40

The Edge: Vast tile selection. Showroom carries domestic and imported ceramic and marble tiles. Features top designers of hand-painted tiles from all over the world. Fixtures, hardware, and bathroom accessories in fine materials and styles complement the tiles.

P. E. Guerin, Inc.

23 Jane Street
between Greenwich Street and 8th Avenue / 243-5270
By appointment (closed the first two weeks in July).

Hardware & fixtures
Greenwich Village

quality style service value
50   50   38   45

The Edge: Handmade decorative hardware. Stocks handmade decorative hardware/fixtures in brass and bronze. Will copy or reproduce hardware. Priced from $9 per piece to tens of thousands of dollars. Reproduction jobs can be small. No credit cards. *"Expensive but worth it."*

Putnam Rolling Ladder Company

32 Howard Street
near Broadway / 226-5147
Weekdays 8:30am–4:15pm.

Hardware & fixtures
SoHo/TriBeCa

The Edge: Ladders in all shapes and sizes. Since 1905 it has been known for its custom-made ladders, including rolling library ladders (favored in grand old homes), in any hardwood finish. It also manufactures extension ladders, library carts, step stools, and steel ladders for industry, window cleaning, and home use. No credit cards.

Quarry Tile Marble and Granite, Inc.

128 East 32nd Street
between Park and Lexington Avenues / 679-2559
Weekdays 9am–5pm, Sat 11am–4pm (closed Sat July–Aug).

Hardware & fixtures
Gramercy Park/Murray Hill

The Edge: High-end kitchen and bathroom tiles and marbles from around the world. Find wallpaper, accessories, and fixtures to go with the marble and tile line. Also granite, limestone, and slate. Priced from $4 to $45 per square foot.

Sepco Industries

491 Wortman Avenue
near Linden Boulevard, Brooklyn / 718-257-2800
Weekdays 9am–5pm.

Hardware & fixtures
Brooklyn

The Edge: Wholesale fine hardware and bath accessories. Supplier of bath and kitchen faucets, fine hardware, and bath accessories. Modern but somewhat ornate styling. Lots of gilded options. Up to 50% off retail. Call toll free 800-842-7277 for catalog and customer service.

Sherle Wagner International
60 East 57th Street
near Madison Avenue / 758-3300
Weekdays 9:15am–5pm.

Hardware & fixtures
Midtown East

quality style service value

The Edge: Bathroom fixtures made in semiprecious materials with suitable hardware. Top-of-the-line bathroom fixtures offered in semiprecious stones with hand-painted porcelain bowls and crystal, marble, and gold-plated hardware. Fixtures in every possible material. Even the toilet bowls are decorated. Simple pedestal sinks without fixtures start at $4,000. No credit cards. Deluxe. *"Expensive."*

Simon's Hardware
421 3rd Avenue
near 29th Street / 532-9220
Mon–Wed and Fri 8am–5:30pm, Thurs 8am–7pm,
Sat 10am–6pm (Sat in summer to 5pm).

Hardware & fixtures
Gramercy Park/Murray Hill

quality style service value

The Edge: Everyday hardware as well as custom-made decorative fixtures. Styles range from antique brass reproductions to modern chrome and stainless steel. Offers a 20% discount to decorators. *"Best assortment of brass fixtures in New York." "Never has stock on hand, doesn't call back." "The clearance section is worth checking out."*

Solar Antique Tiles
971 1st Avenue
near 54th Street / 755-2403
By appointment.

Hardware & fixtures
Midtown East

The Edge: Unique antique tiles from the 14th-century. Tiles from the 14th-century to the 1920s. Original antique tiles and a reproduction line. Wide range of patterns from Dutch to Turkish. From $16 to $100 per tile. No credit cards.

Terra Verde Trading Company
120 Wooster Street
near Prince Street / 925-4533
Mon–Sat 11am–7pm, Sun noon–6pm.

Hardware & fixtures
SoHo/TriBeCa

quality style service value

The Edge: An ecological department store. Restricted to environmentally sound home and office products. Items sold include cleaning supplies and energy-saving appliances.

Tiles – A Refined Selection
42 West 15th Street
between 5th and 6th Avenues / 255-4450
Mon–Wed and Fri 9:30am–6pm, Thurs 9:30am–8pm, Sat 10am–5pm (closed Sat June–Aug).

Hardware & fixtures
Chelsea

The Edge: Large range of tiles. Quality glass tiles, granite, handmade tiles, limestone, marble, molded tiles, mosaics, and slate. High-end tiles favored by decorators but available to all. Prices $3 per square foot and up. Catalog for $20. No credit cards.

Waterworks

237 East 58th Street
between 2nd and 3rd Avenues / 371-9266
Weekdays 10am–5pm.

Hardware & fixtures
Midtown East

quality style service value

The Edge: English designer bathroom and kitchen fixtures and tiles. Specializes in traditional bathroom and kitchen fixtures, designer ceramic tiles, granite, and marble. The showroom has the full line on display. Architects and designers are the major customers, but open to the public. Also branches in Connecticut—Danbury, Greenwich, Westport.

Cobblestones

314 East 9th Street
between 1st and 2nd Avenues / 673-5372
Tues–Sat noon–7pm, Sun noon–5pm.

Kitchen
Flatiron/East Village

The Edge: Unique vintage collectibles. Vintage handbags, glassware, and kitchenware, plus linens (napkins, tablecloths, and 1930s and 1940s printed fruit and flower kitchen towels). No delivery.

Kitschen

380 Bleecker Street
near Christopher Street / 727-0430
Daily 1–8pm.

Kitchen
Greenwich Village

The Edge: Wonderful old-fashioned kitchen wares. From linens to cupboards, plus the basics. No delivery.

Lee Sam Kitchen & Bath

124 7th Avenue
near 18th Street / 243-6482
Mon–Wed and Fri 9:30am–6pm, Thurs 9:30am–8pm, Sat noon–5pm.

Kitchen
Chelsea

The Edge: One-stop shopping for kitchen and bathroom fixtures. All major brands of bathroom and kitchen hardware and fixtures. Lots of in-stock cabinets. Very large selection.

Pantry & Hearth

121 East 35th Street
near Lexington Avenue / 889-0026
By appointment.

Kitchen
Gramercy Park/Murray Hill

The Edge: Unique Early American hearth and home accessories and furniture. Features Early American furniture and related hearth and home accessories, including folk art. Mostly 18th and 19th century, with some rare Pilgrim period pieces. No credit cards.

Grand Brass Lamp Parts, Inc.

221 Grand Street
near Chatham Square / 226-2567
Tues–Wed and Fri–Sat 8am–5pm, Thurs 8am–8pm.

Light fixtures
SoHo/TriBeCa

The Edge: Parts to be found nowhere else. A good source for lamp replacement parts from chandelier crystals to glass globes. Stocks hundreds of parts and fixtures. Where the contractors go. *"No wonder it's so crowded—unique inventory, good prices."*

Jerrystyle
51 East 10th Street
between Broadway and University Place / 353-9480
Tues–Fri 11am–6pm, Sat 11am–5pm.

Light fixtures
Flatiron/East Village

The Edge: All forms of lighting. Unique designs favoring period styles from the 1930s to contemporary lighting fixtures. All the lighting is made by hand and requires six weeks for delivery. From $300 to $3,000.

Just Bulbs
936 Broadway
near 22nd Street / 228-7820
Mon–Wed and Fri 9am–6pm, Thurs 9am–7pm, Sat 10am–6pm.

Light fixtures
Gramercy Park/Murray Hill

The Edge: Any and every kind of lightbulb under the sun. The source for electric lights (American and European voltage) in dozens of hues. Priced from $5 to $30. *"It has all bulbs."* *"Terrific selection of unusual bulbs and a helpful staff to boot!"*

Lee's Studio
Weekdays 10am–6:30pm, Sat 10am–6pm.

Light fixtures
Multiple locations

The Edge: Wonderful contemporary designer lighting. Track and recessed lighting, halogen lamps, outdoor landscape fixtures, plus floor, table, and desk lamps and sconces. Reproductions of art deco and retro classics. Installation and repair services. Priced from $100 to thousands of dollars. Catalog $7. *"Great store for great lighting and accessories. It has everything—overwhelming."*

Locations: Midtown West: 1755 Broadway, near 56th Street (247-0110) / **Upper East Side:** 1069 3rd Avenue, near 63rd Street (371-1122)

Let There Be Neon City, Inc.
38 White Street
near Church Street / 226-4883
Weekdays 8:30am–5:30pm.

Light fixtures
SoHo/TriBeCa

The Edge: Custom neon lighting and signs. Allow two weeks to design and produce neon lighting.

Lightforms
Weekdays 11am–7pm, Sat 10am–6pm,
Sun noon–5pm (Sun from 1pm in summer).

Light fixtures
Multiple locations

quality style service value

The Edge: American and European lighting designs. Many styles, including overhead track lighting, traditional table lamps, floor lamps, and sconces. Prices on lamps range mostly from $59 to $300, but can go to the thousands of dollars. *"Good selection."*

Locations: Chelsea: 168 8th Avenue, near 18th Street (255-4664) / **Upper West Side:** 509 Amsterdam Avenue, near 85th Street (875-0407)

Lighting By Gregory
158 and 160 Bowery
near Delancey Street / 226-1276
Daily 9am–5:30pm.

Light fixtures
SoHo/TriBeCa

quality style service value

The Edge: Large selection of traditional and contemporary lighting. Two stores. Number 158 specializes in traditional lighting styles and number 160 mixes traditional with contemporary. Carries a large selection of well-known brands and will order any brand for you (even if it doesn't carry it) at close to wholesale prices. Priced from $10 to $3,000. *"The standard commercial inventory. Good prices."*

Lighting Plus
676 Broadway
near Great Jones Street / 979-2000
Mon–Sat 10am–7pm, Sun 11am–7pm.

Light fixtures
SoHo/TriBeCa

The Edge: Best for repairs. Sells anything connected with electricity. Will repair lighting fixtures if the materials are on hand. No delivery.

Marvin Alexander
315 East 62nd Street
near 2nd Avenue / 838-2320
Weekdays 9am–5pm.

Light fixtures
Upper East Side

quality style service value

The Edge: Breathtaking unique antique lighting treatments. Features distinctive 18th- to early 20th-century one-of-a-kind lighting fixtures. Chandeliers and sconces priced from $600 to $60,000. No credit cards. Deluxe.

Nesle
151 East 57th Street
near 3rd Avenue / 755-0515
Weekdays 9am–5pm.

Light fixtures
Midtown East

quality style service value

The Edge: Simply fabulous 18th- and 19th-century French crystal chandeliers and candelabra. Mostly high-end elaborate French crystal chandeliers and candelabra. Lots of very large, statement, exceptional, breathtaking museum-quality pieces. Deluxe. *"So beautiful."*

Price Glover, Inc.
59 East 79th Street, 3rd Floor
near Madison Avenue / 772-1740

Light fixtures
Upper East Side

Weekdays 10am–5pm.

quality style service value

The Edge: Antique and reproduction 18th- and 19th-century lighting devices. Lighting includes sconces (from $500), chandeliers ($4,300 to $18,000) and lanterns ($1,000 to $4,000). Also hurricane shades. No credit cards.

Rosetta Lighting & Supplies

Light fixtures
Midtown West

21 West 46th Street
between 5th and 6th Avenues / 719-4381
Mon–Wed and Fri 9am–6pm, Thurs 9am–7:30pm, Sat 9am–5pm.

quality style service value

The Edge: Good discounts on top-name lighting fixtures. Brands include Kovacs, Lightolier, and Stiffel. Special orders are taken; delivery service is available. To facilitate installations, a small inventory of electrical supplies. Priced from $2 to $5,000. 10% off. *"Convenient." "Great prices." "Wonderful inventory, especially for hard-to-find parts."*

Tudor Electrical Supply

Light fixtures
Midtown East

222 East 46 Street
between 2nd and 3rd Avenues / 867-7550
Mon–Thurs 8:30am–5pm, Fri 8:30am–4:30pm.

quality style service value

The Edge: Broad range of discounted electrical supplies. Features a wide variety of lightbulbs, lighting fixtures, and electrical supplies.

Uplift, Inc.

Light fixtures
Greenwich Village

506 Hudson Street
between Christopher and West 10th Streets / 929-3632
Daily noon–8pm.

The Edge: Unique art deco period lighting fixtures. Features a large collection of lighting fixtures from the 1930s, art deco, and Victorian eras— originals and reproductions, all in working order. Will restore lighting fixtures and/or sell lamp parts. Priced from $39 to $2,400.

Ad Hoc Softwares

Linens
SoHo/TriBeCa

410 West Broadway
near Spring Street / 925-2652
Mon–Sat 11am–7pm, Sun 11:30am–6pm.

quality style service value

The Edge: Household items with a high-tech style softened by traditional linens. Shop carries at-home wear, bath accessories, housewares, metal furniture, and table-top items (china and linens). Wonderful taste. Higher-end items. *"Lovely, but overpriced."*

Down Factory Outlet-America's Original Down Store

Linens
Midtown West

32 West 40th Street
between 5th and 6th Avenues / USA-DOWN
Tues 3–6pm, Wed–Thurs 10am–6pm, Fri 10am–noon.

The Edge: Discounted down! Sample and stock sale of down comforters, pillows, and duvet covers. Most people order by phone—to visit, call for an appointment for access to the wholesale showroom. Supplies fine stores and mail-order catalog companies.

E. Braun & Company

Linens
Upper East Side

717 Madison Avenue
near 63rd Street / 838-0650
Mon–Sat 10am–6pm (closed Sat July–Aug).

46	45	44	42
quality	style	service	value

The Edge: Exquisite Irish bed and table linens. Most are embroidered and lace trimmed in pastels or whites. Wonderful baby things, from layettes to hand-embroidered and smocked clothing and hand-knit sweaters. Unique custom linens priced from $500 to $1,000. *"Fine linens, old styles, excellent quality." "Helpful staff with good suggestions."*

Frette

Linens
Upper East Side

799 Madison Avenue
between 67th and 68th Streets / 988-5221
Weekdays 10am–6pm, Sat 10am–5:30pm.

50	50	40	30
quality	style	service	value

The Edge: Fine Italian bed, table, and bath linens. Expensive (but not as expensive as the French linens at Porthault) linens priced from $675 to $2,000 for sets. Deluxe. *"Expensive—but for this type of linen—good value."*

Harris Levy

Linens
Lower East Side/Chinatown

278 Grand Street
near Eldridge Street / 226-3102
Sun–Thurs 9am–5pm, Fri 9am–3:30pm.

40	31	27	34
quality	style	service	value

The Edge: Quality bed, bath, and table linens and accessories, discounted. Features basic to more expensive items. Can charge and send anywhere. Will monogram. 20% off. *"They carry current lines only—no discontinued items." "Still good value." "Prices like department store sales, but everyday."*

J. Schachter

Linens
Brooklyn

5 Cook Street
near Graham Avenue, Brooklyn / 718-384-2732
Mon–Thurs 9am–5pm, Fri 9am–1:30pm.

40	40	40	40
quality	style	service	value

The Edge: Will custom-make or adjust ready-made linens. Now in Williamsburg, Brooklyn, after generations on the Lower East Side. Adjustments include adding appliqués, embroidery lace, and monogramming. Will restuff, mend, and sew cushions to look like new. Works in cotton, lamb's wool, and polyester. Can make quilts in all sizes and in 20 different patterns. Discounter. *"I have my pillows filled religiously."*

Laytner's Linen and Home Center

Linens
Multiple locations

Weekdays 10am–7:30pm, Sat 10am–6:30pm, Sun noon–6pm.

41	39	34	33
quality	style	service	value

The Edge: A large selection of home furnishings in stock or available from catalogs. A wide selection of designer bed, bath, and table linens. A smaller Bed, Bath and Beyond. Top brands at retail, not discounted prices. *"Attentive sales staff."* *"Good basic household items. Not the latest styles."*

Locations: Upper East Side: 237 East 86th Street, between 2nd and 3rd Avenues (996-4439) / **Upper West Side:** 2270 Broadway, between 81st and 82nd Streets (724-0180)

Leron

750 Madison Avenue
near 65th Street / 753-6700
Weekdays 10am–6pm, Sat 10:30am–5pm (closed Sat July–Aug).

Linens
Upper East Side

quality style service value
48 44 44 43

The Edge: Hand-sewn, custom-made linens and lace lingerie. Linens and lingerie, often embroidered. Can order custom-designed linens and towels to match a fabric pattern in your home. Table linens can be made in any size and shape with hand lacework or other trims. Children's terry robes appliquéd with story-book characters. *"Beautiful linens from yesteryear."*

Porthault

18 East 69th Street
near Madison Avenue / 688-1660
Weekdays 10am–5:30pm, Sat 10am–5pm.

Linens
Upper East Side

quality style service value
47 47 44 43

The Edge: High high-end luxurious French linens. Features table and bed linens in over 600 ready-made and custom designs in scores of colors and weaves. Signature prints in printed terry towels, decorative accessories (including trays), table linens, wastebaskets, tissue-box covers, drawer liners, and room sprays. A set of standard queen-size sheets and two pillow cases are priced from $1,860 (printed patterns) to $3,000 (for embroidered sets), so go in January for the half-price sale! Also smocked dresses, rompers, shirts, and hooded terrycloth robes for children. Deluxe. *"Such quality, it's almost worth the cost!"* *"So beautiful, I wish I could afford it."*

Pratesi

829 Madison Avenue
near 69th Street / 288-2315
Mon–Sat 10am–6pm.

Linens
Upper East Side

quality style service value
50 47 42 39

The Edge: Beautiful top-of-the-line Italian linens. Crafted from the finest fabrics in classic styles. Twice-yearly sales. A standard set of queen-size sheets and two pillow cases priced from $1,080 to several thousand dollars. Deluxe. *"So expensive, but I still love to shop here!"* *"Quality well worth the high cost."* *"Only on sale!"*

Schweitzer Linens

Mon–Sat 10am–6pm.

Linens
Multiple locations

quality style service value
43 40 39 39

The Edge: Neighborhood shop offering nice linens. Quality standard name brands in bed, bath, and table linens, including Palace Royale and Wamsutta at a modest discount. Also items from Italy, France, Ireland, and Portugal made exclusively for the store. Towels can be made up in just about any color combination. Monogramming available. No delivery. *"Very expensive. Can often find the same stuff discounted in catalogs."*

Locations: Upper East Side: 1132 Madison Avenue, near 84th Street (249-8361) / 1053 Lexington Avenue, between 74th and 75th Streets (570-0236) / **Upper West Side:** 457 Columbus Avenue, between 81st and 82nd Streets (799-9629)

Town Bedding

205 8th Avenue
near 21st Street / 243-0426
Mon, Wed, and Fri 9am–8pm; Tues and Sat 9am–6pm; Thurs 9am–9pm; Sun 11am– 6pm.

Linens
Chelsea

The Edge: Charges and delivers major-brand bedding anywhere in the metropolitan area. Claims good prices on major brands—but wouldn't quote prices over the phone.

Trouvaille Française

737-6015
By appointment.

Linens
Upper East Side

45	45	45	35
quality	style	service	value

The Edge: Superb European bed linens. This tiny shop is on the top floor of the owner's brownstone. She gives out the address when you get an appointment. Features unique wedding gifts, mostly elegant antique bed linens and new bed linens imported from France and England. Also Victorian white adult and children's clothing. No credit cards. No delivery.

Blumka Gallery

209 East 72nd Street
between 2nd and 3rd Avenues / 734-3222
By appointment.

Medieval & Renaissance
Upper East Side

50	50	50	45
quality	style	service	value

The Edge: Medieval focus. Medieval art and sculpture alongside 15th- to early 17th-century furniture. Mostly walnut wood tables, medieval and Renaissance tapestries, Venetian glass goblets, and more. No credit cards. *"Rare stuff."*

L'Antiquaire & the Connoisseur, Inc.

36 East 73rd Street
between Madison and Park Avenues / 517-9176
Weekdays 9am–5:30pm.

Medieval & Renaissance
Upper East Side

50	50	50	40
quality	style	service	value

The Edge: Museum-quality medieval and Renaissance furnishings. French, Italian, and Spanish furniture, paintings, and decorative accessories, including tapestries from medieval to the 18th century. Wonderful Victorian painted pieces and old-master paintings. Same-day delivery depends on the customer. No credit cards. Deluxe. *"Such a beautiful shop."*

Office Furniture Heaven

22 West 19th Street
near 5th Avenue / 989-8600

Office
Chelsea

Weekdays 9am–6pm, Sat 9am–2pm.

The Edge: Used office furniture and close-outs of office furniture from top companies. Features more contemporary pieces.

Asian House
120 West 56th Street
between 6th and 7th Avenues / 581-2294
Mon–Sat 10am–6pm, Sun noon–5pm.

Oriental
Midtown West

The Edge: Asian decorative items. Since 1961, new and old porcelains, planters, vases, lamps, furniture, and screens from China, Japan, and Korea. Deluxe.

Chinese Arts & Antiques Ltd.
848 Broadway
between 13th & 14th Streets / 475-1141
Daily 10am–7pm.

Oriental
Flatiron/East Village

The Edge: Classic Chinese porcelains. Find a large selection of antique and new items, with excellent prices. Wonderful large planters in traditional patterns for $50. The shop specializes in Chinese antiques—porcelains, jade sculptures, ivory carvings, a small collection of Chinese furniture, and more.

Chinese Porcelain Company
475 Park Avenue
at 58th Street / 838-7744
Weekdays 10am–6pm, Sat 11am–5pm (closed Sat June–Aug).

Oriental
Midtown East

quality style service value

The Edge: Museum-quality Chinese antiques. Offers a wide range of early to 18th-century Chinese treasures, including carpets, ceramics, furniture, jade and ivory carving, lacquer, table screens, and more. Deluxe. *"Fabulous items, a must-see!"*

Dragon Gate Import and Export Company
1115 Broadway
near 25th Street / 691-8600
Daily 10am–6pm.

Oriental
Gramercy Park/Murray Hill

The Edge: Higher-end furniture imported from China. Some furnishings and antiques.

E&J Frankel Ltd.
1040 Madison Avenue
near 79th Street / 879-5733
Mon–Sat 10am–5:30pm.

Oriental
Upper East Side

quality style service value

The Edge: Quality Chinese and Japanese antiques. Asian, mostly Chinese and Japanese, antiques. Edith, of E. Frankel, chaired the Department of Far Eastern Studies at the New School. The collection includes antique accessories, furniture, jewelry, and paintings. Special exhibition (with a catalog) annually. Jewelry from $300 to several thousand dollars and furniture easily into the thousands of dollars. Deluxe.

Flying Cranes Antiques Ltd.

Oriental
Midtown East

1050 2nd Avenue
near 55th Street / 223-4600
Mon–Sat 10:30am–6pm (closed Sat–Sun July–Aug).

The Edge: Wonderful 18th- and 19th-century Japanese artifacts. Galleries 55 and 56 at the Manhattan Art & Antiques Center. An extensive collection of quality antiques from the 18th and 19th centuries. Mostly Japanese porcelains, ivories, cloisonné, and swords. Some ornate and beautiful Japanese silver. Truly unusual beautiful pieces."

J. J. Lally & Company Oriental Art

Oriental
Midtown East

41 East 57th Street, 14th Floor
between Madison and Park Avenues / 371-3380
Weekdays 9am–5pm, Sat 10am–4pm (closed Sat July–Aug).

The Edge: A small museum-quality collection of Chinese artifacts. Lally, formerly head of Sotheby's Chinese Art Department, specializes in early Chinese sculpture from the 5th millennium B.C. through the Song period. Some later works. Costly at $1,000 to $1 million, but items are museum quality. No credit cards. Deluxe.

Koreana Art and Antiques

Oriental
Upper East Side

963 Madison Avenue
near 75th Street / 249-0400
Mon–Sat 10am–6pm.

50 50 50 35
quality style service value

The Edge: Korean antiques from the 18th and 19th centuries. Since 1978, has offered antique Korean furniture and ceramics at prices from $1,000 to $20,000. No reproductions. Some pieces as early as the 13th and 14th centuries, but most from the 18th and 19th centuries.

Krishna Gallery of Asian Arts, Inc.

Oriental
Midtown East

153 East 57th Street
near Lexington Avenue / 249-1677
Mon–Sat 11am–6pm.

The Edge: Antiques and furniture from Tibet, Nepal, and India. Furniture, plus bronze and terra-cotta sculptures, Tanka (Tibetan paintings), Indian miniatures, and jewelry. Pieces from the 2nd century B.C. to 18th-century works. Prices run $100 to $15,000.

Naga Antiques Ltd.

Oriental
Upper East Side

145 East 61st Street
near Lexington Avenue / 593-2788
Weekdays 10am–5pm (Fri to 3pm July–Aug).

48 50 50 43
quality style service value

The Edge: Top-of-the-line 17th- to 19th-century Japanese antiques. A large selection of art, antique furniture, fine lacquerware, rare hand-painted screens, early ceramics, dolls, and unusual baskets. No credit cards. "*A shop to enjoy.*" "*The most beautiful Oriental furnishings and furniture.*"

Orientations Gallery Ltd.

Oriental
Upper East Side

802 Madison Avenue
between 67th and 68th Streets / 772-7705
Mon–Sat 11am–6pm.

The Edge: 18th- and 19th-century Japanese decorative arts. High-quality collectibles.

Ralph M. Chait Galleries

Oriental
Midtown East

12 East 56th Street
between Madison and 5th Avenues / 758-0937
Mon–Sat 10am–5:30pm (closed Sat June–Aug).

50	50	47	45
quality	style	service	value

The Edge: Museum-quality Chinese works of art. One of the top sources for early Chinese antiques, including bronze sculpture, crystal, export silver, jade, porcelains, pottery, and paintings. Priced from $1,000 to millions! Decorator discounts given if the galleries "have a relationship with the decorator." Deluxe. *"It's like being in a museum." "Wonderful."*

Weisbrod Chinese Art

Oriental
Midtown East

36 East 57th Street, 3rd Floor
near Madison Avenue / 319-1335
Weekdays 9:30am–5pm.

The Edge: Museum-quality classic Chinese antiques. Moved from the Carlyle Hotel to East 57th Street. Features museum-quality Oriental antiques, including jade, ancient Chinese bronzes, blue and white Chinese pottery, and Han dynasty porcelains. Some of our favorite pieces include Tang dynasty unglazed pottery, 6th-century limestone reliefs, and more. No credit cards. Deluxe.

America Hurrah

Quilts & quilting
Upper East Side

766 Madison Avenue, 3rd Floor
near 66 Street / 535-1930
Tues–Sat 11am–6pm (closed Sat June–Aug).

35	35	35	35
quality	style	service	value

The Edge: Museum-quality American antique quilts and Native American art. While most quilts are priced from $750 to $2,500, with some quilts at $2,500 to $25,000, it's best known for museum-quality collectible quilts at $100,000+. Lots of collectibles from the 1920s to 1940s. Also baskets, decoys, folk paintings, hooked rugs, painted furniture, and weather vanes. Cleans and restores antique rugs. Deluxe. No credit cards. *"Lovely staff."*

Laura Fisher / Antique Quilts & Americana

Quilts & quilting
Midtown East

1050 2nd Avenue
near 55th Street / 838-2596
Mon–Sat 11am–6pm or by appointment.

50	50	30	40
quality	style	service	value

The Edge: Gorgeous Early American quilts. Find antique quilts, hand-knit bedspreads, hooked rugs, European bedspreads, woolen coverlets, and more. Coverings and rugs are available in a wide range of colors, patterns, and sizes. Most items from the early 1800s to the 1940s. Prices into the thousands of dollars. *"Museum quality collection."*

Susan Parrish Antiques

Quilts & quilting
Greenwich Village

390 Bleecker Street
near Perry Street / 645-5020
Tues–Sat noon–6pm or by appointment.

The Edge: Large selection of beautiful antique American quilts. This shop with its country ambiance features antique Americana at affordable prices. Also American folk paintings from before 1850, and antique folk art and toys. Quilts from $200 to $35,000, with the majority priced from $500 to $3,000. No delivery.

Woodard & Greenstein

Quilts & quilting
Upper East Side

506 East 74th Street
near York Avenue / 794-9404
Weekdays 10:30am–6pm, Sat noon–4pm
(closed Sat July–Aug), or by appointment.

quality style service value

The Edge: Renowned collection of early 19th-century American quilts. Hundreds of antique and museum-quality quilts. Also painted and unpainted Shaker-style furniture and antique garden furnishings from England, France, and the U.S. Deluxe. *"The Woodards are such lovely people to buy from!"*

AFR (the Furniture Rental People)

Rentals
Midtown East

711 3rd Avenue
between 44th and 45th Streets / 867-2800
Mon–Sat 9am–6pm.

The Edge: Home and office furniture rentals. Provides accessories, electronics, and furnishings for home or office. Classic to modern styles with a three-month minimum rental. Delivery within 48 hours.

Churchill Corporate Services

Rentals
Gramercy Park/Murray Hill

6 East 32nd Street
between 5th and Madison Avenues / 686-0444
Mon–Thurs 9am–6pm, Fri 9am–4pm, Sun 11am–5pm.

The Edge: Rentals of traditional to contemporary furniture. Rents all household items, including furniture, housewares, and appliances. Free professional decorating advice available.

International Furniture Rentals

Rentals
Midtown East

345 Park Avenue
near 51st Street / 421-0340
Mon–Thurs 9am–5:45pm, Fri 9am–5:30pm, Sat by appointment.

The Edge: One of the largest furniture-rental companies. Rents furniture for both home and office. Maintains a free design service. Pulls everything together with accessories. Delivery within 48 hours.

Asia Minor Carpets, Inc.

Rugs & carpets
Midtown West

236 5th Avenue, 2nd Floor
near 28th Street / 447-9066
Weekdays 9:30am–5:30pm.

The Edge: Turkish flatweaves from carpets to covered furniture. A large selection of Turkish flatweaves, as well as semi-antique and new carpets. A large supply of pillows made from new kilims, as well as pillows made from old ones. Also furniture (benches, chairs, and ottomans) covered with kilims.

Beauvais Carpets

Rugs & carpets
Midtown East

201 East 57th Street, 2nd Floor
near 3rd Avenue / 688-2229
Weekdays 9am–5pm.

The Edge: Quality antique carpeting. For four generations, specializing in fine-quality antique European, Persian, Turkish, and Chinese carpets. No credit cards. Deluxe.

Beshar's

Rugs & carpets
Upper East Side

1513 1st Avenue
near 79th Street / 288-1998
Mon–Wed and Fri 10am–6pm, Thurs 10am–8pm, Sat 10am–4pm.

47 40 47 35
quality style service value

The Edge: Quality antique and new Oriental rugs. Offering antique and new Oriental and European rugs since 1898 at prices from $800 to $80,000. Specializes in Aubussons, Chinese, Persian, and French needlepoint. Now some antique accessories also. Also rug cleaning and restoring (call 718-292-3301).

Central Carpet

Rugs & carpets
Upper West Side

426 Columbus Avenue
near 81st Street / 362-5485
Mon–Wed and Fri–Sat 10am–7pm, Thurs 10am–8pm,
Sun 11am–6pm.

38 37 44 37
quality style service value

The Edge: A large selection of carpets. Carpets include Persians, Chinese, and Turkish kilims, plus contemporary floor coverings. *"Great resource, knowledgeable help."*

Doris Leslie Blau Gallery

Rugs & carpets
Midtown West

724 5th Avenue, 6th Floor
between 56th and 57th Streets / 586-5511
By appointment.

50 50 50 33
quality style service value

The Edge: Collector-quality Oriental carpets. Exquisite antique tapestries and top-of-the-line quality late 19th- to early 20th-century carpets. Best known for her Persian carpets, but also carries Aubussons, Savonneries, and needlepoints. When Chris Whittle was amassing, this was one favorite source. No credit cards. Deluxe. *"Expensive, but worth a visit." "Wonderful just to look."*

Lovelia Enterprises

Rugs & carpets
Midtown East

356 East 41st Street
in Tudor City / 490-0930
By appointment.

The Edge: 15th- to 19th-century reproduction tapestries and rugs. Imports tapestries and miniature rugs, including Aubusson and European Gobelins. Most are reproductions of 15th- to 19th-century designs. Also some tapestries with contemporary patterns. No credit cards. *"Good value, pretty rugs."*

Marvin Kagan, Inc.

Rugs & carpets
Midtown East

625 Madison Avenue, 2nd Floor
near 58th Street / 535-9000
Weekdays 9:30am–5:30pm, Sat 10am–5pm.

The Edge: Antique Oriental carpets. Carpets in all sizes, priced from $10,000 to $200,000. Fine antique carpets, including Kerman, Serapi, and Tabriz carpets, as well as semi-antique Aubussons, Persian, and Turkish rugs and tapestries.

Momeni International, Inc.

Rugs & carpets
Gramercy Park/Murray Hill

36 East 31st Street, 2nd Floor
near Park Avenue / 532-9577
Weekdays 9am–5pm.

The Edge: Oriental rugs sold wholesale or retail. Decorator discounts available. No credit cards.

Pasargad Carpets

Rugs & carpets
Gramercy Park/Murray Hill

105 Madison Avenue
near 30th Street / 684-4477
Weekdays 9am–6pm, Sat 10am–6pm, Sun 11am–5pm.

The Edge: One-of-a-kind Persian and Oriental carpets, from $100 to $100,000. Large selection. Repairs and cleans rugs also. Will buy or trade quality rugs.

Redi-Cut Carpets

Rugs & carpets
Lower Manhattan

208 East 23rd Street
near 2nd and 3rd Avenues / 685-3626
Weekdays 10am–8pm, Sat 10am–6pm, Sun noon–5pm.

quality style service value

The Edge: Top-quality remnants. A large selection of home and office carpeting at substantial savings. Installation within two days. Priced from $15 per yard. Discounter. *"Remainder items are an excellent buy."*

Rug Warehouse

Rugs & carpets
Upper West Side

220 West 80th Street, 2nd Floor
near Broadway / 787-6665
Mon–Wed and Fri–Sat 10am–6pm,
Thurs 10am–8pm Sun 11am–5pm

quality style service value

The Edge: New and antique rugs. Some handmade, but mostly machine-made, rugs from China, India, Pakistan, and Turkey at prices from $150 to $30,000, with some selected pieces to $100,000. There's an annual three-week sale where rugs are discounted 10% to 15%. Has seven-day return and consignment policies. Discounter.

Safavieh Carpets

153 Madison Avenue
near 32nd Street / 683-8399
Weekdays 9am–6pm, Sat 10am–6pm, Sun 11am–5pm.

Rugs & carpets
Gramercy Park/Murray Hill

quality style service value

The Edge: Good selection of quality rugs. Features Iranian, Indian, Pakistani, Turkish, Egyptian, and Chinese rugs. Prices range from $200 to $100,000. A 30% discount is offered to decorators. *"Really beautiful rugs." "You should bargain here."*

Sarajo

98 Prince Street
between Mercer and Greene Streets / 966-6156
Mon–Sat 11am–7pm, Sun noon–7pm.

Rugs & carpets
SoHo/TriBeCa

The Edge: Far Eastern antiques and decorative arts items. expensive rugs. Features Far Eastern antiques and decorative arts items. Prices to $12,000, but mostly less expensive rugs.

Vojtech Blau, Inc.

41 East 57th Street, 14th Floor
at Madison Avenue / 249-4525
Weekdays 9am–3pm.

Rugs & carpets
Midtown East

quality style service value

The Edge: Very fine 16th- to 18th-century tapestries and 18th-century Persian rugs. Favors antique Persian rugs, but also has fine linens, Aubussons, Savonneries, and Turkish and European carpets. Quality antique tapestries in a wide range of sizes and styles. A 20% discount is offered to decorators. No credit cards.

ABC Carpet and Home

888 Broadway
near 19th Street / 473-3000
Weekdays 10am–8pm, Sat 10am–7pm, Sun 11am–6:30pm.

Superstores
Flatiron/East Village

quality style service value

The Edge: Everything for the home. Great styling and products. One-stop shopping for the home, from bed and bath accessories to carpeting, linens, antique and reproduction furniture, and accessories from Europe, Scandinavia, Asia, and the Americas. Country pieces to formal. Excellent taste. Unbelievable selection. Decorators get a 10% discount. *"Good selection of everything." "Fabulous displays." "Expensive but unique." "The warehouse is great for carpet remnants." "Seems too pricey." "I was amazed that I could negotiate the price on an expensive carpet—try it yourself."*

Bed, Bath and Beyond

620 Avenue of the Americas
between 18th and 19th Streets / 255-3550

Superstores
Chelsea

Mon–Sat 9:30am–9pm, Sun 10am–8pm.

quality style service value

The Edge: A housewares supermarket. One-stop shopping in a store that takes up an entire block, 82,000 square feet. It carries all kitchen needs (cookware, dishes, gadgets, pots, pans), blankets, closetware, drapes, hampers, linens, pillows, picture frames, drapes, rugs, and more. Everything imaginable for the bedroom, bathroom, and kitchen. Okay (not discount) prices. *"A must for your child just off to college." "Lots of staples, nothing unusual." "Good for mass-market items for the bath." "Good selection, good price, fair service."*

Crate & Barrel

650 Madison Avenue
at 59th Street / 308-0011
Weekdays 10am–8pm, Sat 10am–7pm, Sun noon–6pm.

Superstores
Midtown East

quality style service value

The Edge: Attractive fresh-looking furnishings. Large store featuring very attractive furniture and gift items. Good selection and range of basic items. Gift items include Italian ceramics, table linens, glassware, picture frames, and more. Reasonable prices, with great furniture for first city apartments. In malls across the country and finally now in New York. *"Great variety that changes with the latest trends." "Good mass-produced articles."*

Gracious Home

1220 3rd Avenue
near 70th Street / 517-6300
Weekdays 8am–7pm, Sat 9am–7pm, Sun 10am–6pm.

Superstores
Upper East Side

quality style service value

The Edge: Beloved and shopped by virtually everyone. No store or service seems better known and better appreciated. The shop is large, well organized, and fully stocked. You name it, they have it: from nails and screws to appliances, cleaning supplies, curtains, linens, tool rental, and a repair department. The service is legendary, but you pay for it. *"Best selection on the Upper East Side for house- and hardware. Good sales help. Expensive." "Has just about everything. Terrific resource." "Overpriced, but excellent selection of housewares." "Can't beat it for quality, variety, and service." "Best decorative hardware selection in town."*

Fanelli Antique Timepieces

790 Madison Avenue, Suite 202
near 67th Street / 517-2300
Weekdays 11am–6pm, Sat 11am–5pm
(closed Sat June–Aug or by appointment).

Timepieces
Upper East Side

quality style service value

The Edge: Clocks from the 1880s to the 1920s. Sells and repairs antique clocks. Carries wonderful rare clocks, including gilded and jeweled clocks. Also quality vintage wristwatches. Favors European and American antique clocks. Also quality repairs.

Fossner Timepieces

1057 2nd Avenue
near 56th Street / 249-2600
Weekdays 10am–6pm, Sat 11am–4pm.

Timepieces
Midtown East

quality style service value

The Edge: Good selection of quality vintage watches. Buys and sells secondhand and vintage watches and clocks. Features Rolex, Patek Philippe, and Cartier, among other top designers. Fine watch repairs.

Time Will Tell
962 Madison Avenue
near 76th Street / 861-2663
Mon–Sat 10am–6pm.

Timepieces
Upper East Side

quality   style   service   value

The Edge: Vintage wristwatches from the 1910s to the 1970s. A large selection of vintage watches. All watches have the original works and are in working order. Features Cartier, Patek Philippe, Rolex, Vacheron & Constantin, and other top names. Does repairs. *"Interesting vintage watches."*

Alpha Puck Designs
139 Fulton Street, Room 210
near Nassau Street / 267-2561
By appointment.

Window treatments
Lower Manhattan

The Edge: Quality, reasonably priced window treatments and upholstery. Custom slipcovers, upholstery, and window treatments (Roman shades to drapes). The shop is oriented to designers. Requires a 50% cash deposit. Ask for Madeline Boutte. No credit cards.

Country Curtains
Main Street
Stockbridge / 800-876-6123
Daily 24 hours.

Window treatments
Mail/phone

quality   style   service   value

The Edge: Huge selection of inexpensive, ready-made mail-order curtains. Offers three types of catalogs, *Country Curtains* for casual, *Window Ways* for blinds and shades, and *City Curtains* containing 100 different styles, the latest looks, and nice hardware geared for apartment living. Great for apartment rentals when you don't want to invest in furniture and window treatments. Very responsive, providing good advice on how to hang curtains. A second phone line is 800-785-9215 (toll free), and a fax line is 413-243-0211. *"Good prices and good telephone help."*

Drapery Exchange, Inc.
1899 Post Road
Interstate 95 at Exit 11, Darien / 203-655-3844
Mon–Sat 10am–5pm.

Window treatments
Connecticut

quality   style   service   value

The Edge: Second to none for top-of-the-line draperies (including balloon shades) seeking a second life. The store sells—and therefore buys—used draperies in mint condition. All the top fabric houses appear here. The store prices the draperies, with half the proceeds going to the consignee. Mainly expensive drapes. The shop will arrange alterations so the treatments will fit your windows. Expensive for used, but top-quality new drapes cost even more. Drapes, even used, can run into the thousands of dollars. No credit cards. No delivery.

Just Shades

21 Spring Street
at Elizabeth Street / 966-2757
Thurs–Tues 9:30am–4pm.

Window treatments
SoHo/TriBeCa

quality	style	service	value
41	41	37	35

The Edge: Hundreds of appealing lamp shades in all shapes and fabrics. They specialize in lamp shades in every conceivable fabric, from burlap and parchment to linen and silk. Old shades can be recovered with your own fabric. "*Everything you need in shades—all styles and sizes.*"

Mardi Philips Design

31 Jane Street
near 8th Avenue / 242-2376
By appointment.

Window treatments
Greenwich Village

quality	style	service	value
50	50	10	50

The Edge: Elaborate custom window treatments. Specializes in Roman shades and elaborate custom curtain treatments, as well as cushions, pillows, and slipcovers. Roman shades for a 54- by 72-inch window start at $300, excluding fabric. Installation available for an extra charge. No credit cards.

Shades From the Midnight Sun

914-779-7237
By appointment

Window treatments
Mail/phone

The Edge: Custom-made shades. Caters to decorators and individuals. Can match shades to furniture and wallpaper. Shades from $60 to $900. A *New York Times* and *Martha Stewart Living* source.

Sheila's Interiors

323 Grand Street
between Allen and Orchard Streets / 966-1663
Sun–Thurs 9:30am–5pm, Fri 9am–2pm.

Window treatments
Lower East Side/Chinatown

quality	style	service	value
35	35	35	35

The Edge: Discounts decorator items. Stocks, or is able to order, a wide selection of wallpaper, fabrics, vertical and horizontal blinds, and shades. Can make up items into drapes, bedspreads, tablecloths, etc. Discounter. "*Good value.*"

Sundial-Schwartz

1582 1st Avenue
near 82nd Street / 289-4969
Weekdays 10am–5pm, Sat 10am–3pm (closed Sat June–Aug).

Window treatments
Upper East Side

The Edge: Features mirroring and window treatments. Sundial will install mirrors and remodel and resilver antique mirrors. Sells custom-design window treatments, blinds, shades, storm windows, and draperies. Discounter. "*Always reliable and helpful advice.*"

White Workroom

525 Broadway
near Spring Street / 941-5910
Weekdays 9am–6pm by appointment.

Window treatments
SoHo/TriBeCa

The Edge: A decorators' source for custom draperies. Will also do retail. A pair of side panels, with interlining and center-edge trim, for a nine-foot window starts at $350, fabric not included. No credit cards. Discounter.

The ratings: excellent very good good fair so-so

Home & home office

Art Station

144 West 27th Street
between 6th and 7th Avenues / 807-8000
Weekdays 8am–6:30pm, Sat 10am–3pm (closed Sat June–Aug).

Art supplies
Midtown West

The Edge: Everything for the artist. Complete range of supplies for the artist, including drawing tables, chairs, chalkboards, lamps, and framing. Weekly special sale items.

Arthur Brown & Bro., Inc.

2 West 46th Street
West of 5th Avenue / 575-5555
Weekdays 9am–6:30pm, Sat 10am–6pm.

Art supplies
Midtown West

43	43	38	35
quality	style	service	value

The Edge: Perhaps the city's largest art supply store. Extensive range of materials, including stationery, art supplies, FiloFaxes, leather goods, and framing materials. Great selection of pens by every major manufacturer, including Mont Blanc, Aurora, Namika, Bugatti, Dupont, Omas, Lamy, Waterman, Stipula, Tombo, Shaeffer, Cross, Creeks N' Creeks, Kenzo, Parker, and more. Extensive selection of antique writing instruments, all in working condition. Also a selection of technical pens—designed for artists, calligraphers, and musicians. Also offers custom framing.

Charrette

215 Lexington Avenue
near 33rd Street / 683-8822
Weekdays 8:30am–7pm, Sat 10am–5pm,
Sun noon–5pm (closed Sun July–Aug).

Art supplies
Gramercy Park/Murray Hill

45	43	40	43
quality	style	service	value

The Edge: Quality supplies for serious artists, draftsmen, etc. Offers quality supplies for architects, engineers, draftsmen, graphic designers, and artists. Catalog available, with substantial discounts on all major brands. Discounter. *"Great art supplies, reasonable prices."*

David Davis Fine Art Materials

65 Paris Street
near Pearl Street, Brooklyn / 718-237-1669
Weekdays 9:30am–6pm.

Art supplies
Brooklyn

The Edge: Quality supplies for professional artists. Wide selection of paints, quality brushes, handmade papers, pastels, drawing books, and papers. Davis will make stretchers and easels to any size.

New York Central Art Supply

62 3rd Avenue
near 11th Street / 473-7705
Mon–Sat 8:30am–6:30pm.

Art supplies
Flatiron/East Village

quality style service value

The Edge: Incredible selection of papers. In business since 1905. A large selection of imported and domestic papers, as well as brushes, canvas, drawing and drafting tools, drawing tables and lamps, easels, paints and stretchers, pens and inks, and printmaking supplies. The toll-free number is 800-950-6111.

Pearl Paint Company

308 Canal Street
near Church Street / 431-7932
Mon–Wed and Fri–Sat 9am–6pm,
Thurs 9am–7pm, Sun 9am–5:30pm.

Art supplies
SoHo/TriBeCa

quality style service value

The Edge: Six floors of discounted fine-arts products. Great selection. It claims to be the world's largest art-supply store. Stocks all major brands of art, graphic, craft, and stationery supplies, all discounted 20% to 70%. Prices to $6,000 for printing presses. Binds books as well. *"The perfect art store." "The best art supplies at the best prices." "Very helpful staff."*

Sam Flax

Weekdays 8:30-6:30 Sat 10-6 Sun noon-5.

Art supplies
Multiple locations

quality style service value

The Edge: Enormous inventory of quality art supplies. Sells an enormous stock of fine-art and drafting supplies, photographic equipment, drafting and drawing tables, storage units, carry cases, pens, picture frames, and fine papers. First-rate supplies and unique gifts at full retail price. *"Good selection of computer chairs." "Good service." "Good for mat and frame artwork."*

Locations: Chelsea: 12 West 20th Street, between 5th and 6th Avenues (620-3000) / **Midtown East:** 425 Park Avenue, between 54th and 55th Streets (620-3060) / **Midtown West:** 254 West 31st Street, between 8th and Broadway (630-0710) / **SoHo/TriBeCa:** 233 Spring Street, between 6th Avenue and Varick Street (675-3486) /

Utrecht Art and Drafting Supplies

111 4th Avenue
between 11th and 12th Streets / 777-5353
Mon–Sat 9am–6pm, Sun noon–5pm.

Art supplies
Flatiron/East Village

The Edge: Huge stock of art and drafting supplies at good prices. One of the largest art-supply houses in the country. Manufactures its own line of paint, canvas, and related products. Store boasts over 20,000 items carried at discount. Frequent sales reduce prices further. Popular with artists from the student to the professional.

Rafik Film and Video Tape Company

Film services
Flatiron/East Village

814 Broadway, 2nd Floor
between 11th and 12th Streets / 475-7884
Weekdays 9:30am–6:30pm.

The Edge: Videotape and film supplies. As well as supplies, they duplicate and edit videos, convert film to video, and convert foreign to U.S. format. No delivery. Discounter.

AAA American Flag

Flags
Midtown West

40 West 37th Street
near 6th Avenue / 279-3524
Mon–Thurs 8:30am–4pm, Fri 8:30am–3:30pm.

The Edge: Custom-made flags. Features custom-made corporate logos or family crests plus traditional flags, including assorted sizes of the American flag, state and city flags, and flags of more than 150 countries.

Ace Banner and Flag Company

Flags
Midtown West

107 West 27th Street
near 6th Avenue / 620-9111
Weekdays 7:30am–4pm.

The Edge: Custom display banners. Manufactures all types and sizes of custom display banners. Stocks U.S. and foreign flags. Clients include Carnegie Hall, Cartier, Columbia University, J. P. Morgan, and others. Priced from $12 to $2,000.

Florence Horowitz & Company

Marketing services
Brooklyn

525 East 72nd Street, Suite 28H
between York Avenue and the East River / 535-3055
By appointment.

quality style service value

The Edge: Find the best corporate gift. Florence Horowitz knows what's right for your corporate gift. She has a great sense of style and is cost-conscious and concerned about your bottom line. *"Flexible and easy to work with!"*

Solutions

Marketing services
Brooklyn

109 State Street
between Henry and Clinton Streets, Brooklyn / 718-855-5275
By appointment.

quality style service value

The Edge: Top talent that provides "pizzazz." A small team of writers and art directors who have created major advertising and marketing campaigns for clients such as Heineken, Jaguar, Yves St. Laurent, *Architectural Digest,* and others. Will develop marketing strategies and creative executions for your product or service on a cost-plus basis (actual production costs plus creative time billed by the hour, as law firms do). Very reasonable prices. *"Engaging, creative and clever!"*

Kinko's Copies
Daily 24 hours.

Printers
Multiple locations

quality style service value

The Edge: What did we do before Kinko's? They do it all—from straight copying jobs to creating poster boards and stationery. They do great work and are there all the time—so no excuses. Also faxing and computer services. *"How did we live without it?" "Good service."*

Locations: Flatiron/East Village: 24 East 12th Street, between University Place and 5th Avenue (924-0802) / **Gramercy Park/Murray Hill:** 191 Madison Avenue, near 35th Street (685-3449) / **Lower Manhattan:** 105 Duane Street, near West Broadway (406-1220) / **Midtown East:** 16 East 52nd Street, between 5th and Madison Avenues (308-2679) / **Midtown West:** 245 7th Avenue, near 61st Street (928-2675) / 232 West 54th Street, between Broadway and 8th Avenue (977-2679) / **Upper East Side:** 1122 Lexington Avenue, near 78th Street (682-5500) / **Upper West Side:** 2872 Broadway, between 111th and 112th Streets (316-3390)

Seeford Organization
75 Varick Street
between Canal and Watts Streets / 431-4000
Weekdays 7:30am–5:30pm.

Printers
SoHo/TriBeCa

The Edge: Quality printing services. Any size, any color, any typeface. No credit cards.

World-Wide Business Centres
575 Madison Avenue
between 56th and 57th Streets / 605-0200
Weekdays 9am–5:30pm, Sat–Sun by appointment.

Rentals
Midtown East

The Edge: Rents office space with full services. Services include conference rooms, desk space, private offices, receptionist, telephone answering, typists, and word processing. Operates a full-service travel agency.

Alpine Business Group
159 West 25th Street
between 6th and 7th Avenues / 213-8280
Weekdays 9am–5pm.

Stationery
Midtown West

The Edge: One-of-a-kind invitations. With a creative staff of illustrators—one-of-a-kind invitations are the house specialty.

Butch Krutchik Designs
112 East 83rd Street
between Park and Lexington Avenues / 734-0092
By appointment.

Stationery
Mail/phone

The Edge: Creative, handmade, pop-up invitations. Handmade invitations tending to the witty that arrive in a box. Very pricey at $25 per invitation. Takes four weeks to create and engrave. No credit cards. Deluxe.

Dempsey & Carroll

110 East 57th Street
between Lexington and Park Avenues / 486-7526
Weekdays 10am–6:30pm, Sat 10am–5:30pm.

Stationery
Midtown East

quality style service value

The Edge: Where tradition starts. Elegant engraved stationery in 30 lettering styles, plus party and wedding invitations, Christmas cards, birth announcements, engraved calling cards, business cards, letterhead, and note cards, as well as desk accessories. Meets all your needs. Deluxe.

Hudson Jam

Weekdays 8:30am–7pm, Sat–Sun 10am–6pm.

Stationery
Multiple locations

quality style service value

The Edge: Wide range of papers. From business to personal papers, including copies of top brands. If you wonder where those lifelike celebrity cardboard figures come from, come here. It features over 100 lifelike cardboard individuals, fun and realistic at $30, including Hillasy and Bill Clinton, Marilyn Monroe, John Wayne, and multiple Disney characters.

Locations: Chelsea: 611 Avenue of the Americas, between 17th and 18th Streets (255-4593) / **Midtown East:** 1100 2nd Avenue, near 58th Street (980-1999)

Hudson Street Papers

357 Bleecker Street
between 10th and Charles Streets / 229-1064
Mon–Thurs 11am–8pm, Fri noon–9pm,
Sat 11am–9pm, Sun noon–6pm.

Stationery
Greenwich Village

quality style service value

The Edge: European styling in paper and paper-related gifts. A large selection of European-style stationery and paper gift items, plus children's toys. No delivery.

Il Papiro

1021 Lexington Avenue
near 73rd Street / 288-9330
Weekdays 10am–6pm, Sat 10am–5:30pm.

Stationery
Upper East Side

quality style service value

The Edge: A touch of Florence with its wonderful marbleized paper products. Elegant stationery and accessories, including picture frames, tissue holders, desk accessories, address books, agendas, and photo albums.

Jamie Ostrow

876 Madison Avenue
between 71st and 72nd Streets / 734-8890
Mon–Sat 10am–6pm.

Stationery
Upper East Side

quality style service value

The Edge: Contemporary personalized stationery and invitations. Elegant stationery, Christmas cards, and invitations. Deluxe.

Joon

Stationery
Upper East Side

782 Lexington Avenue
at 61st Street / 935-1007
Weekdays 9:30am–6:30pm, Sat 10am–6pm.

The Edge: Large selection of the best pens discounted. Features one of the city's largest selections of pens from around the world—pens to use and pens to collect. Over 28 brands, including Caran D'Ache, Cartier, Dupont, Lamy, Le Boeuf, Marlen, Montblanc, Tombo, Yard O Led, Waterman, and others. Also pen accessories and an extensive FiloFax collection. Pens discounted 20% to 25%.

Kate's Paperie

Stationery
SoHo/TriBeCa

561 Broadway
near Prince Street / 941-9816
Weekdays 10:30am–7pm, Sat 10am–7pm, Sun 11am–6pm.

48	48	44	38
quality	style	service	value

The Edge: Wonderful papers and accessories. A well-stocked stationery store carrying agendas, boxes, cards, diaries, frames, holiday ornaments, leather address books, photo albums, stationery, wrapping papers, and more. *"Fabulous notes, cards, and gifts." "Enormous selection—beautiful items"*

Madison Signatures

Stationery
Upper East Side

743 Madison Avenue
at 64th Street / 717-1386
Weekdays 9:30am–6pm.

The Edge: Prints your stationery. Known for printing and engraving stationery, as well as writing instruments and desk accessories. A large FiloFax collection.

Montblanc Boutique

Stationery
Midtown East

595 Madison Avenue
near 57th Street / 223-8888
Mon–Sat 10am–6pm, Sun noon–5pm.

The Edge: Upscale stationery. $275+ for 100 engraved notes and plain envelopes.

Mrs. John L. Strong Company

Stationery
Upper East Side

699 Madison Avenue
between 62nd and 63rd Streets / 838-3775
By appointment.

50	48	45	30
quality	style	service	value

The Edge: Well known for beautiful traditional invitations. 100% cotton paper, with tissue paper to match or accent. Hand-lined envelopes, with inks and hand-engraved script selected by you. Beautiful wedding invitations and letter sheets. Engraving takes four to six weeks. Wedding invitations (classic size and styling) are priced at $860 for 100 invitations. Also sold at Barney's and Gumps in San Francisco. Deluxe. *"Pricey."*

Rebecca Moss
Stationery
Midtown East

510 Madison Avenue
near 53rd Street / 832-7671
Mon–Sat 10am–6pm.

The Edge: Unique writing instruments. The shop features a good selection of writing papers, invitations, and new and vintage pens. It has a calligraphy computer which can personalize invitations to look like handwritten calligraphy. Christmas 1995 *W* featured as "wonderful" its Radiowaves pen by Omas (for $650).

Costco Warehouse
Superstores
Multiple locations

Mon–Thurs 11am–8:30pm, Fri 11am–9pm,
Sat 9:30am–9pm, Sun 10am–6pm.
Opens at 10am weekdays for business members.

quality style service value

The Edge: Everything from office paper to baked goods—huge quantities at significant discounts. The only problem for New Yorkers is the huge quantity you must buy and the car you need to carry your purchases home. Terrific discounts, but significant storage required for their huge packages. Office supplies, food, cleaning supplies, computers, TVs, batteries, canned goods, health and beauty aids, tires, clothing, and more—all at discount. *Consumer Reports'* readers consistently rate them high for glasses and contact lenses. There's a $25 annual membership fee and it only accepts Discover and its own credit card, but the savings can be worth both the inconvenience and the trip. Call toll free 800-774-2678 to find a location near you. *"Every trip is an adventure!" "Of course it's great for office machines, telephones, and office supplies, but I love the prepared salmon filets—only $5.99 a pound."*

Locations: Brooklyn: 976 3rd Avenue, at 39th Street, Brooklyn (718-832-9300) / **New Jersey:** 80 South River Street, across from the warehouse., Hackensack (201-487-8674) / **Queens:** 3250 Vernon Boulevard, at Broadway, Long Island City (718-204-7443) / **Westchester:** 1 Joyce Road, New Rochelle (914-636-0029)

Staples the Office Superstore
Superstores
Multiple locations

Weekdays 7am–7pm, Sat 9am–6pm, Sun 11am–5pm.

quality style service value

The Edge: Large selection that meets most home office needs. From paper to computers, telephones to file folders—and of course, staples—the store has it all for the home office. Many locations and a helpful staff. 15% off. *"Large selection—good prices." "I've found its copying service very price competitive." "If you shop by phone and catalog, they'll match competitor's prices."*

Locations: Gramercy Park/Murray Hill: 16 East 34th Street, between 5th and Madison Avenues (683-8003) / 699 Avenue of the Americas, between 22nd and 23rd Streets (675-5379) / 345 Park Avenue South, at 26th Street (683-2959) / **Lower Manhattan:** 217 Broadway, at Vesey Street (346-9660) / **Midtown East:** 730 3rd Avenue, at 45th Street (867-9486) / 609 5th Avenue, entrance on 49th Street (593-0620) / 575 Lexington Avenue, between 51st and 52nd Streets (644-2118) / 205 East 42nd Street, at 3rd Avenue (697-4049) / **Midtown West:** 57 West 57th Street, at 6th Avenue (308-0561) / 250 West 34th Street, between 7th and 8th Avenues (629-3990) / 1075 Avenue of the

Americas, between 40th and 41st Streets (944-6744) / One Penn Plaza, between 7th and 8th Avenues on 34th Street (629-3990) / **SoHo/TriBeCa:** 350 Broadway, at Leonard Street (966-6694) / 490 Broadway, at Broome Street (219-1299)

Kroll Office Products

145 East 54th Street
off Lexington Avenue / 750-5300
Weekdays 8:30am–6pm, Sat 10am–6pm (closed Sat July–Aug).

Supplies
Midtown East

40	38	38	34
quality	style	service	value

The Edge: A standard office-supply store with an unbelievable range of supplies. Full range of office stationery, including multiple styles and price points in calendars, highlighters, pens, paper, office supplies, and furniture. Prices are okay. Ask for the corporate discount (10% to 15%), which is given to large customers. *"Great service." "They have all the basics." "Expensive."*

RTR Packaging Corporation

27 West 20th Street
between 5th and 6th Avenues / 620-0011
Tues and Thurs 10am–6pm.

Supplies
Chelsea

40	40	40	50
quality	style	service	value

The Edge: The best of the best wraps and ribbons—wholesale. A wholesale operation which is retail only Tuesday and Thursday. Find all your gift-packaging needs—paper, tissues, bags, boxes, ribbons, and more. Simply beautiful gift wrapping. Accepts credit cards for orders of $75 and up. Discounter.

State Office Supply Company

150 5th Avenue
near 20th Street / 243-8025
Weekdays 9am–5:30pm, Sat noon–5pm.

Supplies
Chelsea

40	30	30	40
quality	style	service	value

The Edge: State-of-the-art stationery and professional supplies.

The ratings: **50** excellent **40** very good **30** good **20** fair **10** so-so

Home renovation

We all know how difficult it is to find trustworthy, competent companies and individuals to do home repairs and renovations. This is doubly true for New York City! So we tapped the private files of friends and business associates for this chapter. The companies and individuals listed below were recommended by a single source. We believe them to be reliable, but we have not had personal experience with their work. **Before hiring anyone to do work on your home, ask for and check multiple references, examine the quality of work they have done and monitor closely the progress of the work they do for you. Inclusion in this category is not an endorsement or recommendation by the authors or publisher.**

Power Cooling, Inc.
4343 Vernon Boulevard
Long Island City / 718-784-1300
By appointment (24-hour answering service).

Air conditioning
Queens

The Edge: Good source to fill your heating and air-conditioning needs. Specialties are installation and repairs. *"Reliable and inexpensive."*

Paul Gleicher
7 West 22nd Street
between 6th and 7th Avenues / 462-2789
By appointment.

Architects
Gramercy Park/Murray Hill

The Edge: Architect. Specializes in brownstone restoration and renovation. *"Excellent."*

Spitzer and Associates
160 5th Avenue, Suite 611
near 21st Street / 924-7454
By appointment.

Architects
Gramercy Park/Murray Hill

The Edge: An architect who's easy to work with. *"Easy to work with. Understands clients' needs. Prices are moderate to high, but quality is excellent."*

Gothic Cabinet Craft
Mon–Wed 10am–8pm, Thurs–Fri 10am–9pm,
Sat 10am–7pm, Sun 11am–6pm.

Cabinetry/carpenters
Multiple locations

43	40	41	42
quality	style	service	value

The Edge: Furniture custom made to your specifications. Wall units, bookcases, murphy beds, kitchen cabinets, entertainment units—all can be made to your specifications. Also find a wide variety of unfinished furniture for every room in the house. *"Easy to work with."*

Locations: Chelsea: 360 6th Avenue, near Waverly Place (982-8539) / **Flatiron/East Village:** 104 3rd Avenue, at 13th Street (420-9556) / **Gramercy Park/Murray Hill:** 909 Broadway, near 21st Street (673-2270) / **Upper East Side:** 1601 2nd Avenue, at 83rd Street (472-7359) / 1655 2nd Avenue, at 86th Street (472-7359) / **Upper West Side:** 2543 Broadway, at 96th street (749-2020)

Island Sink

27 East Merrick Street
Valley Stream / 516-825-0486
Weekdays 8am–5pm, Sat 9am–1pm.

Cabinetry/carpenters
Long Island

The Edge: Detail-oriented cabinetry. Very good work, pays a great deal of attention to detail—fair prices. See Paul

Manhattan Cabinetry

Mon–Thurs 10am–7pm, Fri 10am–6pm,
Sat 10am–5:30pm, Sun noon–5:30pm.

Cabinetry/carpenters
Multiple locations

quality style service value

The Edge: You think of it and they'll build it. On-staff designers will help you design anything you can think of. Have kitchen cabinets, bedroom units, wall units, work centers, entertainment centers, or murphy beds built to your specs. All wood finishes, as well as mica and mirror.

Locations: Gramercy Park/Murray Hill: 455 Park Avenue South, near 31st Street (889-8808) / **Midtown East:** 227 East 59th Street, between 2nd and 3rd Avenues (750-9800) / **Upper East Side:** 1630 2nd Avenue, near 85th Street (772-8870)

Renovator - Peter E. Kilroy

145 Wyckoff Street
Brooklyn / 718-802-9105
By appointment.

Cabinetry/carpenters
Brooklyn

The Edge: Skilled carpenter. Prefers to work on architectural details, bookcases, and kitchens. Does small jobs, including replacing doors. *"Excellent quality at fair prices."*

Techline Studio

35 East 19th Street
between Broadway and Park Avenue South / 674-1813
Mon–Sat 10am-6pm, Sun noon–5pm.

Cabinetry/carpenters
Flatiron/East Village

quality style service value

The Edge: Custom, semi-custom and noncustom cabinetry. Affordable, versatile system of laminated furniture with wood veneer options. Clean, modern, functional components. The system begins with a basic bookshelf in 18" and 36" widths. Add doors and drawers to create storage. Assemble youself or they will install. Will replace any damaged or defective component for three years. *"Nice work—easy to work with—call Suzanne."*

Toledo Interiors

Cabinetry/carpenters
Brooklyn

1922 McDonald Avenue
Brooklyn / 718-349-3610
By appointment.

The Edge: Quality custom cabinetry. Eight-year-old custom-cabinetry company specializing in cedar closets and one-of-a-kind cabinetry from architectural designs.

Wood-O-Rama, Inc.

Cabinetry/carpenters
Upper West Side

238 West 108th Street
749-6438
Mon–Sat 9am–5:30pm.

The Edge: Molding heaven. Stocks over 700 moldings in oak, pine, poplar, mahogany, and plastic. It does kitchen cabinetry too.

Audio Design Associates

Electronics, etc.
Westchester

602-610 Mamaroneck Avenue
White Plains / 914-946-9595
Weekdays 9am–5pm by appointment.

quality style service value

The Edge: High-tech custom electronic systems. Makes and installs audiovisual equipment and home theaters. Integrates electronic systems, connecting pushbutton-controlled drapes, phones, and lights with room-to-room audiovisual systems. Touch screen for commands. $800 key pad that resembles a light switch and a volume control can change the station and dim the lights. Charges $125 per hour or $425 per day for labor. No credit cards.

Holland & Heim

Electronics, etc.
Midtown East

208 East 58th Street
between 2nd and 3rd Avenues / 980-6223
Weekdays 10am–6pm.

The Edge: Satisfy the Bill Gates in all of us—control your home with the touch of a button. Customized controls for your home so that with one switch you can control your home temperature, music, and lights; lower a screen; dim noise; etc. Expensive—most homes cost $10,000 plus.

Karp & Cantrell Audio & Video

Electronics, etc.
New Jersey

423 Center Avenue
Westwood / 201-666-0777
By appointment.

The Edge: Audio and video experts. Designs audio-video home theaters. No credit cards. *"Superior quality. Prices are fair. I recommend them highly."*

Agouti Consulting

Expediter
SoHo/TriBeCa

588 Broadway, Suite 705
near Houston Street / 941-8514

Weekdays 9am–5pm or by appointment.

The Edge: Expediter. Talk to Jack or Jackie. Able to facilitate getting building permits for construction projects. A specialist in dealing with the city for a Certificate of Occupancy. *"Superior service. Reasonable prices."*

Ed McCormack

Flooring
Connecticut

Connecticut / 203-735-1621
By appointment.

45 45 45 45
quality style service value

The Edge: Quality craftsmanship. Wonderful work laying ceramic tiles, including hand-crafted tiles which really take care to ensure that spacing is just right. Flexible to work with. *"Reasonable prices–among the best we found. But we chose him for the quality of the work we saw—and we're happy we did."*

J.P. Molyneux Studio Ltd.

Flooring
Upper East Side

29 East 69th Street
between Park and Madison Avenues / 628-0097
Weekdays 9am–6pm.

The Edge: Faux but fabulous. Floors painted to appear inlaid. Noted for doing Kips Bay show house, among other celebrated floors.

Janos P. Spitzer Flooring Company

Flooring
Chelsea

133 West 24th Street
between 6th and 7th Avenues / 627-1818
Weekdays 8am–4:30pm.

45 45 45 45
quality style service value

The Edge: Vintage designer floors Beautiful flooring with custom wood floors cut and designed by artisans. Prior to commencing work, Spitzer sketches out and shows to the customer a floor pattern that takes into consideration the size and use of the room. The showroom is stocked with samples of pattern styles and wood types, which include exotic flooring from around the globe. Custom floors cost $10 to $100 a square foot. Repairs and resanding available. *"The 'Van Gogh' of flooring. Expensive."*

New Wood Company

Flooring
Upper Upper East Side

22 East 105th Street
between Madison and 5th Avenues / 222-9332
Weekdays 8am–6pm.

45 45 45 45
quality style service value

The Edge: Custom flooring with an antique touch. Favors old wood sourced from the original floorboards in older homes. Designer patterns available to order, meeting clients' specifications. Can age new pieces to match older pieces. New oak floors start at $8 a square foot.

Peiser Hywood Berk, Inc.

Flooring
Midtown West

475 10th Avenue
between 36th and 37th Streets / 279-6900

Weekdays 9am–5pm.

The Edge: Enormous selection of flooring. The place to choose your floor from. The 4,000-square-foot gallery shows off a selection of 50 hardwood floors in simple to exotic woods in their natural shades, stained woods, and borders to go with all. Prices from $8 to $150 a square foot for antiqued "Parquet de Versailles."

Stanleyco., Inc.

63 Third Place, # 8
Brooklyn / 718-643-3938
By appointment.

**Flooring
Brooklyn**

45	45	45	45
quality	style	service	value

The Edge: Flooring contractor and refinisher. Talk to Stephen Clementi. He makes house calls to see what needs to be done. No credit cards. *"I recommend him highly. Reasonable prices."*

Terra Cotta Tile Service

914-359-7413
By appointment.

**Flooring
Westchester**

45	45	45	45
quality	style	service	value

The Edge: Terrific tile work. Everyone 'in-the-know' from Country Floors to tile manufacturers recommend Tony Viglietta for restoration and maintenance of wood and tile floors. East to work with and provides solid advice about what is right for your problem, even if he does not provide that service. Reasonable prices. No credit cards. *"Highly recommended—restored my terra cotta floor which I thought would have to be replaced."*

William J. Erbe Company

560 Barry Street
near Leggett Avenue / 249-6400
Weekdays 9am–3pm.

**Flooring
Bronx**

The Edge: For an antique look in flooring. Since 1908, well known for quality custom wood floors. Favors antique flooring imported from Europe. Pre-1830 floors go for $400 a square foot and are perishable to boot. Favors traditional French patterns.

Jane Gill

290 Riverside Drive, Apt 15B
near 101st Street / 316-6789
By appointment.

**Garden
Upper West Side**

The Edge: Horticulturist. Provides landscaping for terrace plantings. Favors using perennials and flowers for accent, but does work with trees and shrubs. Ask to see her portfolio. $100 consultation fee credited against future work. *"Superior quality. Pricey but worth it."*

ACM Engineering, P.C.

37 West 17th Street
between 5th and 6th Avenues / 924-3205
By appointment.

**General contractors
Chelsea**

The Edge: Construction engineers to manage your renovation. Consulting engineers and construction managers. Examples of their work include the new Sonia Rykiel boutique—completed on time and on budget.

Goldreich, Page & Throff
45 East 20th Street
near Park Avenue / 982-1410
By appointment.

General contractors
Flatiron/East Village

The Edge: Consulting engineer and general contractor on building projects. No credit cards. *"They offer excellent-quality workmanship at reasonable prices."*

Howard Haimes, Inc.
117 West 17th Street
between 6th and 7th Avenues / 807-7611
By appointment.

General contractors
Chelsea

The Edge: General contractor. Small high-quality construction firm. Works with the same subcontractors so the quality is consistent. Clients include Mayor Guiliani and the Swiss ambassador (his personal residence and the New York Mission to the U.N.), among others. Small to very large jobs undertaken. *"Superior quality. Reasonable prices. Very professional."*

Jack Henry & Company
321 East 54th Street
between 1st and 2nd Avenues / 888-6442
By appointment.

General contractors
Midtown East

The Edge: General contractor. Works all over the City but especially on in Upper East Side apartments and townhouses. High quality cabinetry and detailing. *"Superior quality. He's pricey, but worth it."*

Mid-City Construction
271 Columbia Street
Brooklyn / 718-875-3100
By appointment.

General contractors
Brooklyn

The Edge: General contractor. Talk to Pat Valcone. No credit cards. *"Excellent quality."*

Quadrant Construction
420 Lexington Avenue, Suite 1927
near 44th Street / 697-4007
Weekdays 8am–5pm.

General contractors
Midtown East

The Edge: General contractor. Mostly alterations of commercial and office buildings. No credit cards *"Excellent quality, but prices are high. Best for office work."*

Wm. Crawford Construction
560 Barry Street
between Leggett and Bruckner Boulevard, Bronx / 718-617-5390
Weekdays 7:30am–4:30pm.

General contractors
Bronx

The Edge: General contractor. Very high-end contractor. No credit cards. *"Superior quality, but very pricey."*

Amsterdam Corporation

Hardware & fixtures
Midtown East

150 East 58th Street
near 3rd Avenue / 644-1350
Weekdays 9am–5pm.

The Edge: Tile supplier and consultant. Talk to Barbara Berwick. She knows tiles and offers a wide selection. Prices are moderate. *"Easy to work with. Excellent quality."*

Jack Corcoran Marble Company

Marble & granite
Long Island

88 West Hills Road
off 7th Avenue, Huntington Station / 516-549-8207
Weekdays 8:30am–5pm.

The Edge: Marble and granite work. Features custom work for kitchens and bathrooms. *"Excellent quality at reasonable prices. Very professional to deal with."*

Classic Plastering and Tiling

Paint, plaster & tiles
Bronx

2353 Quimby Avenue
between Zegrea and Havemayer, Bronx / 718-824-4672
Weekdays 9am–5pm.

The Edge: Plastering and tiling contractor. *"Excellent quality at reasonable prices."*

Jane Kozlak

Paint, plaster & tiles
Connecticut

58 Laurel Lane
Simsbury / 203-658-7218
By appointment.

The Edge: Artist who paints sinks and tiles. This tile designer works on tiles that you provide. Then she'll paint them to your needs and fire them. Kozlak charges a $100 design fee and then by the hour for execution. See lots of her work at Country Floors and Waterworks, which stocks mostly 4½- to 6-inch-square works by Kozlak. For unique tiles, Kozlak will copy patterns to match wallpaper, fabrics, pictures, or whatever. Prices are better if you go to her direct; she will advise which tiles are appropriate. Prices for her predesigned tiles range from $12.50 to $95 per tile. There are lots of existing samples of things she does. Kozlak also designed the tiles in the Connecticut Governor's Mansion. *"Superior workmanship, but pricey."*

Pro-Tech Plumbing and Heating Corp.

Plumbing & heating
Queens

150-44 11th Avenue
between 150th Street and Clintonville, Whitestone / 718-767-9067
By appointment.

The Edge: Plumbing and heating work. Accepts credit cards. *"Superior quality at reasonable prices. The best!"*

John Venekamp
875-0441
By appointment.

Project manager
Mail/phone

quality style service value

The Edge: Construction and renovation manager. Represents the owner in managing the architect, contractor, co-op board, and buildings department. *"He makes those impossible projects easy and timely. First-rate." "Provides top-quality service. His prices are reasonable, considering the service."*

Albert Husted Studio
57 Front Street
Brooklyn / 718-625-6464
Weekdays 9am–5pm, Sat 11am–5pm by appointment.

Stained glass
Brooklyn

The Edge: Stained-glass expert. Repairs and washes stained glass. Charges by the job at about $100 per square foot. Sells museum-quality pieces and supplies for making and/or repairing stained glass. Works in churches, museums, and homes. Maintains a studio where on Saturday he teaches stained-glass workmanship (aimed at beginners) for $125 for five classes. Usually six to eight people in a class. *"Superior quality, reasonable prices. Superb stained-glass restoration." "Easy to work with. Makes beautiful pieces."*

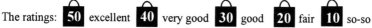 The ratings: **50** excellent **40** very good **30** good **20** fair **10** so-so

Leisure hours & parties

Ballooms-Balooms

147 Sullivan Street
between Prince and Houston Streets / 673-4007
Weekdays 10am–6pm, Sat noon–6pm.

Balloons
SoHo/TriBeCa

50	50	50	40
quality	style	service	value

The Edge: Customized imprinted balloons. Provides party balloons and party decorations. Will imprint balloons with names and logos. Priced at $64.13 for 50 balloons.

A Different Light Bookstore and Cafe

151 West 19th Street
near 7th Avenue / 989-4850
Daily 10am–midnight (cafe closes at 11:30pm).

Books & magazines
Chelsea

50	48	48	43
quality	style	service	value

The Edge: Gay and lesbian literature. Large selection (15,000 titles) of books and magazines of gay and lesbian interest from poetry to health, psychology, coming out, and parenting. Also find U.S. and foreign videos and a cafe and coffee bar. Offers movies on Sunday and readings three to four times weekly—see the event calendar at the store. *"Always open."*

A Photographer's Place

133 Mercer Street
between Prince and Spring Streets / 431-9358
Mon–Sat 11am–8pm, Sun noon–6pm.

Books & magazines
SoHo/TriBeCa

The Edge: For rare books, prints, and cameras, this is the place. Thousands of books, many rare, plus prints and a collection of vintage cameras and equipment.

A&S Magazines

308 West 40th Street
between 8th and 9th Avenues / 947-6313
Mon–Sat noon–7pm.

Books & magazines
Midtown West

The Edge: Collectible magazines. Stocks over 925,000 magazines, some of which go back to the 1920s. A great birthday idea— magazines from the week you were born. No credit cards.

Academy Book Store

10 West 18th Street
near 5th Avenue / 242-4848
Mon–Sat 10am–8pm, Sun 11am–7pm.

Books & magazines
Chelsea

quality style service value

The Edge: Used-book store. Specializes in out-of-print books. The annex (12 West 18th Street) features CDs, records, and tapes. *"Terrific source for used art books." "Great place."*

Action Comics

1551 2nd Avenue, 1st Floor
near 81st Street / 639-1976
Mon–Sat 11am–8pm, Sun 11am–6pm.

Books & magazines
Upper East Side

The Edge: Comics from the 1940s to date.

Alabaster Books

122 Fourth Avenue
between 12th & 13th Streets / 982-3550
Daily 10am–8pm.

Books & magazines
Flatiron/East Village

The Edge: Great for literature and the arts. Using Interloc, a subscription service, the shop can search databases of more than 1,000 used-book stores to seek out books. Well stocked in all areas, with a good selection of first editions and rare books. Best is its coverage of literature and the arts.

Appelfeld Gallery

1372 York Avenue
near 73rd Street / 988-7835
Weekdays 10am–5:30pm, Sat by appointment.

Books & magazines
Upper East Side

quality style service value

The Edge: Old-fashioned bookstore filled with rare books. Wonderful source for rare and out-of-print books, first editions, and some privately printed books. *"Great finds in leather books and classics."*

Applause Theater & Cinema Books

211 West 71st Street
between Broadway and West End Avenue / 496-7511
Mon–Sat 10am–8pm, Sun noon–6pm.

Books & magazines
Upper West Side

50	35	47	37

quality style service value

The Edge: Specializes in rare and out-of-print books on theater and cinema. A very large selection of these specialty books, plus videos. Trade and college bookstores purchase here at a 20% discount. *"A good browse with helpful staff." "The source for theater books."*

Archivia: The Decorative Arts Book Shop

944 Madison Avenue
between 74th and 75th Streets / 439-9194
Weekdays 10am–6pm, Sat 11am–5pm,

Books & magazines
Upper East Side

Sun noon–5pm (closed Sun July–Aug).

quality style service value

The Edge: Can you find a single source with more on the decorative arts? A wondrous collection of new and out-of-print books on the decorative arts, architecture, and garden design, plus some wonderful fashion editions. A full range of U.S. and foreign titles. If you need something, call Joan Gers or Cynthia Conigliaro.

Argosy Book Store

116 East 59th Street
between Lexington and Park Avenues / 753-4455
Weekdays 10am–6pm, Sat 10am–5pm (closed Sat May–Sept).

Books & magazines
Midtown East

quality style service value

The Edge: A broad selection of old and rare books. A large, comprehensive bookstore featuring autographs, botanicals, equestrian engravings, first editions, hard-to-find books, maps and prints (including Currier & Ives), and posters. For assistance, contact Judith Lowry. *"Good for browsing." "Great finds, huge print department." "Great place for unusual gifts."*

B. Dalton Bookseller

396 Avenue of the Americas
at 8th Street / 674-8780
Mon–Sat 9:30am–11pm, Sun noon–8pm.

Books & magazines
Chelsea

quality style service value

The Edge: Wide selection favoring best-sellers. Lots of choices. Favors contemporary books, best-sellers, and the like. A good source for remaindered books—the ones you meant to buy several years back are likely to be on sale on tables here. A division of Barnes & Noble.

Barnes & Noble

Mon–Sat 10am–8pm, Sun 10am–6pm.

Books & magazines
Multiple locations

quality style service value

The Edge: Great selection and a comfortable setting encourage browsing. From good reference sections to best-sellers, Barnes & Noble is known for great selections. Also a wide range of magazines. Better still are the comfortable lounge chairs and tables to settle in while you make your selection. The cafe in most stores adds civility to book browsing. Discounter. *"Citicorp location is very inviting and has a large collection." "Don't you miss the little bookshop?" "Community library!" "Superstores are the greatest thing to hit town!"*

Locations: Flatiron/East Village: 4 Astor Place, near Broadway (420-1322) / 33 East 17th Street, between 5th Avenue and Broadway (253-0810) / 105 5th Avenue, between 17th and 18th Streets (807-0099) / **Gramercy Park/Murray Hill:** 675 Avenue of the Americas, near 22nd Street (727-1227) / 385 5th Avenue, near 36th Street (779-7677) / **Midtown East:** 109 East 42nd Street, between Lexington and Park Avenues (695-1677) / 750 3rd Avenue, at 47th Street (697-2251) / 160 East 54th Street, near Lexington Avenue (750-8033) / **Midtown West:** 901 Avenue of the Americas, at 33rd Street (268-2505) / 600 5th Avenue, near 48th Street (765-0590) / One Penn Plaza, near 33rd Street (695-1677) / **Upper East Side:** 1280 Lexington Avenue, near 86th Street (423-9900) / 120 East 86th Street, between Park and Lexington Avenues (427-0686) / **Upper West Side:** 2289 Broadway, near 82nd Street (362-8835) / 1972 Broadway, near 67th Street (595-6859)

Barnes & Noble Sales Annex

Books & magazines
Chelsea

128 5th Avenue
near 18th Street / 691-3770
Weekdays 9:30am–8pm, Sat 9:30am–6:30pm, Sun 11am–6pm.

The Edge: Great bargains in used and remaindered books. Find two floors of books in 119 categories with prices starting at 69¢ up to hundreds of dollars. Price and selection make this store worth a trip if you're interested in more than just the current best-sellers.

Barnes & Noble for Kids

Books & magazines
Upper East Side

120 East 86th Street
between Park and Lexington Avenues / 427-0686
Mon–Sat 9am–9pm, Sun noon–9pm.

47 46 45 48
quality style service value

The Edge: Enormous selection of books for kids. A comfortable setting and a huge range of books for children. The only Barnes & Noble totally devoted to children's books. 20% off. *"Buy party gifts of books here." "They've set up a nice corner for children to read in."*

Bauman Rare Books

Books & magazines
Midtown East

301 Park Avenue
Waldorf Astoria Hotel at 50th Street / 759-8300
Mon–Sat 10am–7pm or by appointment.

45 45 45 40
quality style service value

The Edge: A broad selection of rare books. A good selection of early classic literature, history, philosophy, and science books. Also autographs and signed materials. Look for rare first editions, often inscribed.

Biography Bookshop

Books & magazines
Greenwich Village

400 Bleecker Street
near 11th Street / 807-8655
Mon–Thurs noon–8pm, Fri noon–10pm,
Sat 11am–11pm, Sun 11am–7pm.

The Edge: Mostly bios. A large, broad selection of biographies, autobiographies, and related materials. Some fiction and nonfiction now.

Bookberries

Books & magazines
Upper East Side

983 Lexington Avenue
near 71st Avenue / 794-9400
Daily 10:30am–6:30pm.

38 43 43 33
quality style service value

The Edge: Give thanks for neighborhood bookstores like this one. The side room is chock full of children's books. Clerks are friendly and special orders are accommodated quickly.

Books of Wonder

Books & magazines
Chelsea

16 West 18th Street
between 5th and 6th Avenues / 989-3270
Mon–Sat 11am–7pm, Sun 11:30am–6pm.

50 42 48 36
quality style service value

The Edge: A very special children's book shop. For children ages 4 to 8. Has an extensive *Wizard of Oz* section and, along with new titles, stocks rare, out-of-print, and vintage children's books. Readings every Sunday morning at 11:45am, with various artist signings. A newsletter announces all events. *"Great selection for children and kid-friendly!" "Terrific advice!"*

Borders Books

Books & magazines

Weekdays 7am–8:30pm, Sat 10am–8:30pm, Sun 11am–8:30pm.

Multiple locations

quality style service value

The Edge: Large selection and helpful staff. From best-sellers to arcane reference books to magazines, for children and adults, a wonderful depth of selection. *"Better than Barnes & Noble" "I prefer Barnes and Noble—I have found magazines here with their pages ripped out and books with coffee stains on them." "Interesting ever-changing sale sections."*

Locations: Lower Manhattan: 5 World Trade Center, at Church Street (839-8037) / **Midtown East:** 57th Street, at Park Avenue

Brunner/Mazel Bookshop

Books & magazines

19 Union Square West

Flatiron/East Village

near 15th Street / 924-3344
Weekdays 9am–6pm, Sat 10:30am–3:30pm.

The Edge: Features books on the behavioral sciences.

Calvary Bookstore

Books & magazines

139 West 57th Street

Midtown West

between 6th and 7th Avenues / 315-0230
Mon 10am–9pm, Tues and Thurs–Fri 10am–6pm, Wed 10am–7pm, Sun noon–2pm.

The Edge: Religious works of all descriptions. Wide range of books on all religions, printed in English and in a large range of foreign languages.

Chartwell Booksellers

Books & magazines

55 East 52nd Street

Midtown East

between Madison and Park Avenues / 308-0643
Weekdays 9:30am–6:30pm.

quality style service value

The Edge: An oasis. A very small bookstore featuring best-sellers and very select rare books. Good selection of best-sellers and art and design books. The rare-book collection is eclectic. Helpful staff.

Christian Publications Books & Supply Center

315 West 43rd Street

Books & magazines

between 8th and 9th Avenues / 582-4311

Midtown West

Mon–Wed and Sat 9:30am–6:45pm, Thurs–Fri 9:30am–7:45pm.

The Edge: Largest New York area publisher of Christian books. Also find videos and tapes.

City Books

Books & magazines
Lower Manhattan

1 Centre Street
669-8245
Weekdays 9am–5pm.

The Edge: Books about New York. Find *The Green Book,* which lists all city and state government and agency personnel and telephone numbers by function. Has all the code regulations plus books on the city and New York memorabilia. No credit cards.

Civilized Traveller

Books & magazines
Multiple locations

Mon–Sat 10am–9pm, Sun noon–7pm.

quality style service value

The Edge: Everything for travel. From books to packable rainwear to travel agents, pocket tailors, and portable showers.

Locations: Lower Manhattan: Two World Financial Center, at 225 Liberty Street (786-3301) / **Upper East Side:** 1072 3rd Avenue, near 63rd Street (758-8305) / **Upper West Side:** 2003 Broadway, near 68th Street (875-0306)

Coliseum Books, Inc.

Books & magazines
Midtown West

1771 Broadway
near 57th Street / 757-8381
Mon 8am–10pm, Tues–Thurs 8am–11pm, Fri 8am–11:30pm.

quality style service value

The Edge: A very wide selection. Good selection of best-sellers and general-interest books. Crammed full with books. *"Besides a great selection of books, has a terrific selection of puzzles, coloring books, and cutouts for kids, but you must dig for them." "They deserve our thanks, patronage, and business." "Great books, but everything leaves something to be desired. It just seems disorganized to me."*

Complete Traveller Bookstore

Books & magazines
Gramercy Park/Murray Hill

199 Madison Avenue
at 35th Street / 685-9007
Weekdays 9am–7pm, Sat 10am–6pm, Sun 11am–5pm.

quality style service value

The Edge: Travel guides about everywhere. A wide selection of new and out-of-print travel guides. Conventional to special-interest guides. Maps plus travel accessories, including money belts, converters, and alarm clocks. *"Knowledge and a good browse." "I always go here for my travel books—great selection."*

Doubleday Book Shop

Books & magazines
Midtown West

724 5th Avenue
at 57th Street / 397-0550
Mon–Sat 9am–11pm, Sun 11am–7pm.

quality style service value

The Edge: Selection A Barnes & Noble division, featuring general-interest books and best-sellers, of course.

Drama Bookshop

723 7th Avenue
near 48th Street / 944-0595
Mon–Tues and Thurs–Fri 9:30am–7pm, Wed 9:30am–8pm,
Sat 10:30am–5:30pm, Sun noon–5pm.

Books & magazines
Midtown West

quality style service value

The Edge: Specialty books on the theater and film. Scripts, scores, and books on people, practical matters, and culture.

Ex Libris

160A East 70th Street
near Lexington Avenue / 249-2618
By appointment.

Books & magazines
Upper East Side

The Edge: Rare and out-of-print avant-garde art books. Well-stocked shop specializing in rare and out-of-print books on 20th-century avant-garde art. Also graphics, illustrations, and posters. No credit cards.

Forbidden Planet

840 Broadway
near 13th Street / 473-1576
Daily 10am–8:30pm.

Books & magazines
Flatiron/East Village

quality style service value

The Edge: Terrific selection of books and magazines for science fiction enthusiasts. Department store for science fiction enthusiasts. Find a vast selection of books, comic books (American and Japanese), T-shirts, toys, etc. Also masks of all sorts and for all tastes, including scary masks great for Halloween and parties.

Glenn Horowitz Booksellers

19 East 76th Street
between 5th and Madison Avenues / 327-3538
Weekdays 9am–5pm.

Books & magazines
Upper East Side

quality style service value

The Edge: Rare books and manuscripts from the 18th to the 20th century. Features first editions. 20th-century American literature is a specialty. *"Beautiful, relaxing place to browse."*

Gotham Book Mart and Gallery

41 West 47th Street
between 5th and 6th Avenues / 719-4448
Weekdays 9:30am–6:30pm, Sat 9:30am–6pm.

Books & magazines
Midtown West

quality style service value

The Edge: Seen as an old friend by the reading set. Huge selection, including new books, but also rare out-of-print volumes. Lots of works on 20th- century literature and poetry. Also a large selection of contemporary first editions and magazines. The James Joyce Society meets here. It's also the place for Edward Gorey and modern Irish literature. *"Books everywhere—plus they have cats!" "Fun, rare finds." "Unusual finds."*

Gryphon Bookshop

2246 Broadway

Books & magazines
Upper West Side

between 80th and 81st Streets / 362-0706
Daily 10am–midnight.

quality style service value

The Edge: Large stock of more used, than rare, books. Stocks used and hard-to-find books. First editions of contemporary authors and poetry are a specialty. Will search for out-of-print books. *"Great fun—just don't mind the dust."*

H. P. Kraus

Books & magazines
Midtown East

16 East 46th Street
between 5th and Madison Avenues / 687-4808
Weekdays 9:30am–5pm.

quality style service value

The Edge: World-famous source for extremely rare early illustrated works. Features five floors of early printed volumes and illustrated works. Sells almost exclusively to libraries and academic institutions. Also extremely rare and early maps. *"Old-world atmosphere." "Large collection of fine maps—great!"*

Hacker Art Books

Books & magazines
Midtown West

45 West 57th Street, 5th Floor
between 5th and 6th Avenues / 688-7600
Mon–Sat 9am–6pm.

quality style service value

The Edge: Perhaps the city's largest inventory of scholarly works on art and architecture. Since 1937. A large selection of books, from old rare to new books on art and architecture. Also reprints. Bonus books and magazines offered with orders over $200.

Hagstrom Map and Travel Center

Books & magazines
Midtown West

57 West 43rd Street
between 5th and 6th Avenues / 398-1222
Weekdays 8:30am–5:45pm, Sat 10am–3pm.

quality style service value

The Edge: Nautical charts from Nova Scotia to Trinidad. A wide range of travel and travel-related items, including globes, books, atlases, nautical/aeronautical charts, and maps of all 50 states and overseas locations. Maps for all needs—hiking to travel.

Harmer Johnson Books Ltd.

Books & magazines
Upper East Side

21 East 65th Street, 4th Floor
between 5th and Madison Avenues / 535-9364
Weekdays 10:15am–5pm, Sat by appointment.

The Edge: Scholarly works on ancient art and archaeology of Africa, the Pacific, and the Americas. Rare, out-of-print, and current titles are featured, plus museum catalogs. Offers a search service. No credit cards.

Imperial Fine Books, Inc.

Books & magazines
Upper East Side

790 Madison Avenue
between 66th and 67th Streets / 861-6620
Mon–Sat 10:30am–6pm (closed Sat in June).

The Edge: Rare books, including illustrated children's books. Features signed first editions, illustrated volumes, and leather-bound sets. Also vintage children's books. Offers book binding, cleaning, restoration, and search services. Books start at $100.

International Center of Photography

Books & magazines
Upper East Side

1130 5th Avenue
near 94th Street / 860-1777
Tues 11am–8pm, Wed–Sun 11am–6pm.

quality style service value

The Edge: A must for photographers. Thousands of books and photo-related accessories (albums, frames, prints, and posters). *"Great resource."*

Irish Book Shop

Books & magazines
SoHo/TriBeCa

580 Broadway
near Prince Street / 274-1923
Weekdays 11am–5pm, Sat 1–4pm.

The Edge: Major supplier of Irish-language material in the United States. You'll find current titles to out-of-print, hard-to-find titles. Wide range of subjects. Also find engravings.

J. N. Bartfield Fine and Rare Books

Books & magazines
Midtown West

30 West 57th Street, 3rd Floor
between 5th and 6th Avenues / 245-8890
Weekdays 10am–5pm, Sat 10am–2:30pm (closed Sat July–Aug).

The Edge: Leather-bound books (single volumes and sets). Since 1937. Find illustrated editions of rare and old titles and first editions. A wide range of treasures.

Jewish Museum

Books & magazines
Upper East Side

1109 5th Avenue
near 92nd Street / 423-3200
Mon and Wed–Thurs 11am–5:45pm,
Tues 11am–8pm, Fri 11am–3pm, Sun 10am– 5:45pm.

quality style service value

The Edge: Judaica. Books and holiday celebratory items. Catalogs from its ever-changing exhibits.

Kinokuniya Bookstore

Books & magazines
Midtown West

10 West 49th Street
between 5th and 6th Avenues / 765-1461
Daily 10am–7:30pm.

quality style service value

The Edge: City's largest and most complete selection of Japanese books. This New York branch of a Japanese bookstore offers books in Japanese (and some in English). All subjects for those interested in Japan.

Kitchen Arts and Letters

Books & magazines
Upper East Side

1435 Lexington Avenue
between 93rd and 94th Streets / 876-5550
Mon 1–6pm, Tues–Fri 10am–6:30pm,
Sat 11am–6pm (closed Sat July–Aug).

quality style service value

The Edge: A bookstore dedicated to cooking and dining. More than 9,000 volumes on cooking, food, and wine. In addition to cookbooks, a large selection of restaurant guides and wine books, as well as food and cooking memorabilia such as restaurant postcards and vintage ads. Also an extensive collection of European books. *"The owner is a fabulous resource for the best cookbooks."*

Librairie de France / Libreria Hispanica

610 5th Avenue
between 49th and 50th Streets / 581-8810
Mon–Sat 10am–6:15pm.

Books & magazines
Midtown West

47 | 37 | 41 | 37
quality style service value

The Edge: French and Spanish books and dictionaries. Full range of French and Spanish books (children's, classic, best-sellers), books on tape, language tapes, Michelin travel guides, movies, and newspapers. One of the largest foreign-language bookstores in the city. *"Lots of books in the basement." "Rare service."*

Logos Bookstore

1575 York Avenue
at 84th Street / 517-7292
Weekdays 8am–8pm, Sat 10am–6pm, Sun noon–6pm.

Books & magazines
Upper East Side

45 | 45 | 46 | 43
quality style service value

The Edge: A much-needed Yorkville resource. Floor to ceiling books, ranging from children's, poetry, philosophy, history, business, and career to religious, spiritual, and New York City books— as well as best-sellers. *"Gracious neighborhood book shop."*

Madison Avenue Bookshop

833 Madison Avenue
between 69th and 70th Streets / 535-6130
Mon–Sat 10am–6pm.

Books & magazines
Upper East Side

41 | 39 | 37 | 35
quality style service value

The Edge: Old-world service. All the latest books, including a large selection of coffee-table books. Call, charge it to your house account, and have it delivered virtually immediately. Ask and get great recommendations from the staff. No credit cards.

Morton, the Interior Design Bookshop

989 3rd Avenue
near 59th Street / 421-9025
Mon–Sat 11am–7pm.

Books & magazines
Midtown East

44 | 43 | 37 | 42
quality style service value

The Edge: The source for design books. Near the D&D (Decorations & Design) building. Sells exclusively books on design, decoration, architecture, and gardening. All current titles, including coffee-table books. *"Crowded, but a terrific source for this type of material." "See Morton Dossik for advice."*

Movie Star News

134 West 18th Street
between 6th and 7th Avenues / 620-8160
Weekdays 10am–6pm, Sat 11am–6pm.

Books & magazines
Chelsea

The Edge: Posters, books, photos, and other cinema-related items.

Murder Ink

Mon–Sat 10am–7:30pm, Sun 11am–6pm.

Books & magazines
Multiple locations

quality style service value

The Edge: Just mysteries and wonderful staff recommendations. Houses one of New York's largest selections of mysteries, including rare and used books from the U.S. and England. The catalog lists staff picks, including children's and young adult mysteries. First editions. Publishers' overstocks at great prices. *"A must for those who love mysteries." "Jay Pearsall knows his stuff— see him for recommendations!"*

Locations: Upper East Side: 1467 2nd Avenue, near 76th Street (517-3222) / **Upper West Side:** 2486 Broadway, near 92nd Street (362-8905)

Mysterious Book Shop

129 West 56th Street
between 6th and 7th Avenues / 765-0900
Mon–Sat 11am–7pm.

Books & magazines
Midtown West

quality style service value

The Edge: A vast selection of mystery titles. Two floors of books. Find paperback books and best-sellers on the first floor and rare, out-of-print, and hard-to-find volumes, as well as signed first editions of contemporary authors, on the second floor. *"Relaxed, pleasant place to browse—they have it all for mystery lovers." "Otto Penzler gives great advice on what to read."*

NYU Health Sciences Bookstore

333 East 29th Street
between 1st and 2nd Avenues / 532-0756
Mon–Thurs 10am–7pm, Fri 10am–6pm, Sat 11am–5pm.

Books & magazines
Gramercy Park/Murray Hill

quality style service value

The Edge: The source for medical and veterinary books. The bookstore for NYU Medical School, so heavy on texts and reference books, as well as books on contemporary medical social issues. *"Great place to meet MDs!"*

New York Astrology Center

350 Lexington Avenue, Suite 402
corner of 40th Street / 949-7211
Weekdays 11am–6:30pm, Sat 11am–5pm.

Books & magazines
Gramercy Park/Murray Hill

The Edge: Books and software on astrology and New Age subjects.

New York Nautical Instrument & Service Corp.

140 West Broadway
between Duane and Thomas Streets / 962-4522
Weekdays 9am–5pm, Sat 9am–noon (closed Sat June–Aug).

Books & magazines
SoHo/TriBeCa

The Edge: Vast selection of nautical charts. Claim to have every nautical chart in the world in stock. Also nautical books and other gift items.

Océanie/Afrique Noire

Books & magazines
Midtown West

15 West 39th Street, 2nd Floor
near 5th Avenue / 840-8844
Weekdays 10am–5pm, Sat–Sun by appointment.

The Edge: Geographically focused art books. Features rare and out-of-print and current books on Africa, Oceania, Southeast Asia, and the Americas. Good source for old and new books on anthropology, contemporary art, history, and textiles, as well as auction and museum exhibition catalogs. Will purchase entire libraries as well as single books.

Old Print Shop

Books & magazines
Gramercy Park/Murray Hill

150 Lexington Avenue
between 29th and 30th Streets / 683-3950
Sept–June, Tues–Fri 9am–5pm, Sat 9am–4pm.
July–Aug, Mon–Thurs 9am– 5pm, Fri 9am–4pm.

48 quality 47 style 45 service 44 value

The Edge: 18th- to early 20th-century American prints. A good source for original Anton Schutz, Charles Frederick, and Currier & Ives prints, among others. Wonderful scenes of New York City at the turn of the century. Also a large collection of antique maps from all over the world. Some 19th-century French and English engravings. Frames prints well and also stocks reproduction and contemporary framing materials. *"Lots of good things, but you've got to look." "Vast selection— pricey, but fair." "Wonderful old world atmosphere."*

Oscar Wilde Memorial Bookshop

Books & magazines
Greenwich Village

15 Christopher Street
near 6th Avenue / 255-8097
Sun–Fri noon–8pm, Sat noon–9pm.

50 quality 35 style 35 service 35 value

The Edge: First gay bookstore in the city. Cramped but long-lived, with a good selection for its size." *"Good choices, wide selection."*

Pageant Book & Print Shop

Books & magazines
SoHo/TriBeCa

114 West Houston Street
near Thompson Street / 674-5296
Mon–Sat noon–8pm, Sun noon–7pm.

The Edge: Well stocked with literary collectibles. A special emphasis on American and early New York maps and 18th- and 19th-century engravings.

Paraclete Book Center

Books & magazines
Upper East Side

146 East 74th Street
near Lexington Avenue / 535-4050
Tues–Fri 10am–6pm, Sat 10am–5pm.

The Edge: Books for serious Christian scholars.

Perimeter

Books & magazines
SoHo/TriBeCa

146 Sullivan Street
near Houston Street / 529-2275

Mon–Sat noon–7pm.

The Edge: Hard-to-find titles on architecture, furniture, and design. Design books, plus unusual architectural posters, paper models, and postcards. Unique collection of books. The catalog features the 50 top sellers. International focus.

Printed Matter, Inc.

Books & magazines
SoHo/TriBeCa

77 Wooster Street
between Spring and Broome Streets / 925-0325
Tues–Fri 10am–6pm, Sat 11am–7pm.

The Edge: Exclusively artist's books. Features 3,500 titles covering primarily contemporary artists. Some signed books and some limited editions.

Rand McNally Map and Travel Store

Books & magazines
Midtown East

150 East 52nd Street
between 3rd and Lexington Avenues / 758-7488
Mon–Wed and Fri 9am–6pm, Thurs 9am–7pm,
Sat 11am–5pm, Sun noon–5pm.

45 | 38 | 38 | 38
quality style service value

The Edge: Vacation-planning guides to just about everywhere. Features vacation-planning guides, campground directories, games to amuse while traveling, and supplies like auto compasses, highway emergency kits, and rechargeable flashlights. Accessories include maps with an antique finish, globes, luggage, and gift items. From $45 to $7,000. *"Fun to poke around and plan trips."*

Richard B. Arkway, Inc.

Books & magazines
Midtown East

59 East 54th Street, Suite 62
between Park and Madison Avenues / 751-8135
Weekdays 9:30am–5pm.

The Edge: Specialty travel books. Features atlases, books, and maps dating from the 16th century.

Richard Stoddard – Performing Arts Books

Books & magazines
Flatiron/East Village

18 East 16th Street, Room 305
near 5th Avenue and Union Square / 645-9576
Mon–Tues and Thurs–Sat 11am–6pm (closed Sat June–Aug).

The Edge: 15,000 Broadway playbills plus rare theatrical materials. Out-of-print materials, plays, and technical titles. Outstanding collection of books covering the theater and original scenic and costume designs. Also books on film, dance, and the circus, plus autographs and general theater memorabilia. No delivery.

Rizzoli

Books & magazines
Multiple locations

Mon–Sat 10:30am–9pm, Sun noon–7pm.

48 | 46 | 41 | 36
quality style service value

The Edge: First-rate bookstore—big selection, great for browsing. Features best-sellers, coffee-table art/design books, and an international array of magazines. Also CDs. *"Very nice store and very nice books." "Beautiful books." "Fun place to shop, top quality, large selection."*

"Expensive, but they have it all!" "Great gift books." "Old-world atmosphere." "It's always a pleasure to spend time at Rizzoli—an oasis of civilization." "A New York institution."

Locations: Lower Manhattan: 3 World Financial Center, at Liberty Street (385-1400) / **Midtown West:** 31 West 57th Street, between 5th and 6th Avenues (759-2424) / **SoHo/TriBeCa:** 454 West Broadway, near Prince Street (674-1616)

Science Fiction Shop

Books & magazines
SoHo/TriBeCa

214 Sullivan Street
between West 3rd and Bleecker Streets / 473-3010
Weekdays 11am–8pm, Sat–Sun 11am–7pm.

The Edge: Science fiction and horror books. Large selection of books, tapes, and periodicals.

Shakespeare & Company Booksellers

Books & magazines
Flatiron/East Village

716 Broadway
at Washington Place / 529-1330
Sun–Thurs 10am–11pm, Fri–Sat 10am–midnight.

quality style service value

The Edge: Quality selection—80,000 volumes. Features both a range of general-interest topics and a wide range of special-interest books. Very strong literature section. Also find greeting cards, literary magazines, maps, and foreign magazines. *"Gracious and helpful sales staff."*

Spring Street Books

Books & magazines
SoHo/TriBeCa

169 Spring Street
between West Broadway and Thompson Streets / 219-3033
Mon–Thurs 10am–11pm, Fri 10am–midnight,
Sat–Sun 10am–10pm.

quality style service value

The Edge: Small, quality selection. An arty literary oasis in SoHo. Strong on literature and general-interest subjects. Also magazines, foreign periodicals, and greeting cards.

St. Marks Comics

Books & magazines
Flatiron/East Village

11 St. Marks Place
between 2nd and 3rd Avenues / 598-9439
Sun–Mon 11am–11pm, Tues–Sat 10am–1am.

quality style service value

The Edge: New and vintage comics.

Strand Book Store

Books & magazines
Multiple locations

Mon–Sat 9:30am–9:30pm, Sun 11am–9:30pm.

quality style service value

The Edge: Stocks more than eight million volumes. Very well known. A wide selection of books, including review copies of best-sellers at half price and current fiction and nonfiction. Features a large collection of art books. The rare book department is extensive. Kiosks are located at Fifth Avenue at 61st Street and the Tramway Plaza at 2nd Avenue. *"Always good for two hours. Great children's books." "Cramped, but good stuff." "Great new store on Fulton."*

Locations: Flatiron/East Village: 828 Broadway, near 12th Street (473-1452) / **Lower Manhattan:** 95 Fulton Street, between Willliams and Wall Streets (732-6070)

Stubbs Books & Prints, Inc.

330 East 59th Street
between 1st and 2nd Avenues / 772-3120
No set schedule—call ahead.

Books & magazines
Midtown East

quality style service value

The Edge: Rare and out-of-print books, mostly on architecture and the decorative arts, including landscaping. Many practical design books, including decorative suggestions, gardening tips, and books on fashion and cooking. *"Unique wonderful things. Good point of view." "See Jane Stubbs."*

Traveller's Bookstore

75 Rockefeller Plaza
near 52nd Street / 664-0995
Weekdays 9am–6pm, Sat 11am–5pm.

Books & magazines
Midtown West

quality style service value

The Edge: They have it all when you're on the move.

Union Theological Seminary Bookstore

3041 Broadway
near 121st Street / 280-1554
Mon and Wed–Fri 9:30am–5pm, Tues 9:30am–7pm.

Books & magazines
Upper Upper West Side

quality style service value

The Edge: Best for books on all aspects of religion. Located just inside the seminary. Caters to theology students. Also find books on comparative religions, politics, social sciences, and more.

Ursus Books & Prints

Weekdays 10am–6pm, Sat 11am–5pm (closed Sat July–Aug).

Books & magazines
Multiple locations

quality style service value

The Edge: Focus on rare art reference books for the sophisticated collector. Two locations— SoHo and the Upper East Side—feature 40,000 volumes with a focus on 19th- and 20th-century art and exhibition catalogs. Materials favored by libraries, universities, and serious students. The print department has more than 1,000 17th- to 19th- century prints, plus many decorative prints, engravings, and watercolors. Also a few out-of-print books on philosophy. *"Peter Kruas gives useful help."*

Locations: SoHo/TriBeCa: 375 West Broadway, near Broome Street (226-7858) / **Upper East Side:** 981 Madison Avenue, near 76th Street (772-8787)

Victor Kamkin, Inc.

925 Broadway
near 21st Street / 673-0776
Weekdays 9:30am–5:30pm, Sat 10am–5pm.

Books & magazines
Gramercy Park/Murray Hill

quality style service value

The Edge: Russian bookstore. The shop is filled with Russian titles printed in Cyrillic, with only 20% of the books in English. Includes current titles, children's books, dictionaries, historical works, and reference. Also classic painted wooden dolls, records, newspapers, and periodicals. No delivery. *"Not just for Russians!"*

Village Comics

Books & magazines
Multiple locations

Mon 11am–8pm, Tues and Thurs 11am–8:30pm,
Wed 10am–9pm, Fri 9am–9pm, Sat 10am–9pm, Sun 11am–7pm.

The Edge: Knickknacks for the younger set. Comics, T-shirts, trading cards, videos, limited-edition model kits, and more.

Locations: Midtown East: 118 East 59th Street, 2nd Floor, between Lexington and 3rd Avenues (759-6255) / **SoHo/TriBeCa:** 118 West 3rd Street, near MacDougal Street (475-9677)

Gryphon Record Shop

CDs, tapes & records
Upper West Side

251 West 72nd Street, 2nd Floor
between Broadway and West End Avenue / 874-1588
Mon–Sat 11am–7pm, Sun noon–6pm.

20	10	20	40
quality	style	service	value

The Edge: Large stock of rare records. Affiliated with Gryphon Bookshop. Features out-of-print and rare LPs. Classical and jazz labels are the specialty.

J&R Music World

CDs, tapes & records
Lower Manhattan

23 Park Row
near Broadway / 238-9000
Mon–Sat 9am–6:30pm, Sun 10:30am–6:30pm.

41	32	33	39
quality	style	service	value

The Edge: One stop shopping. A great source for audio, video, music, videos, and the like. Stocks a huge inventory of cameras, CD players, radios, stereos, tapes, televisions, and watches. Authorized dealer for Apple, AST, Canon, Hewlett-Packard, NEC, Toshiba, and more. Order by fax or phone—24 hours a day, seven days a week—call toll free 800-232-8180. 20% off. *"Good selection at low end of AV equipment." "I like catalog ordering."*

Jazz Record Center

CDs, tapes & records
Midtown West

236 West 26th Street, 8th Floor
between 7th and 8th Avenues / 675-4480
Labor Day–Memorial Day, Tues–Sat 10am–6pm; Memorial Day–Labor Day, Mon–Fri 10am–6pm.

The Edge: Everything you could want related to jazz. A source for rare to modern jazz cassettes, CDs, and records. Also printed materials, books, magazines, and posters. Huge inventory.

Music Inn

CDs, tapes & records
Greenwich Village

169 West 4th Street
near 6th Avenue / 243-5715
Tues–Sat 1–7pm.

The Edge: Ethnic records, along with sale and repair of musical instruments. Features African, English, Irish, and other folk music. Extensive offerings of jazz and blues recordings, even those out of print.

Nostalgia . . . and All That Jazz

CDs, tapes & records
SoHo/TriBeCa

217 Thompson Street
near Bleecker Street / 420-1940
Daily 1:30–9pm.

The Edge: Memorable old recordings. Jazz recordings, soundtracks of old movies, and recordings of early radio programs, plus a small collection of movie and jazz photographs and posters. No credit cards.

Rebel Rebel

CDs, tapes & records
Greenwich Village

319 Bleecker Street
near 7th Avenue / 989-0770
Weekdays 12:30–8pm, Sat–Sun 12:30–9pm.

The Edge: "Now" music—rock, alternative, and acid jazz. Find CDs, tapes, and records. No delivery.

Record Explosion

CDs, tapes & records
Multiple locations

Weekdays 9am–8:30pm, Sat 9am–9pm, Sun 10am–8pm.

The Edge: Broad selection of music. Standard pricing on all types of music from around the world. No delivery.

Locations: Lower Manhattan: 2 Broadway, near Battery Park (509-6444) / 176 Broadway, near John Street (693-1510) / **Midtown East:** 507 5th Avenue, near 42nd Street (661-6642) / **Midtown West:** 142 West 34th Street, near 7th Avenue (714-0450) / 384 5th Avenue, between 35th and 36th Streets (736-5624) / 469 7th Avenue, near 36th Street (643-1030)

Records Revisited

CDs, tapes & records
Midtown West

34 West 33rd Street, 2nd Floor
near Broadway / 695-7155
Weekdays 9am–5pm, Sat by appointment.

The Edge: One of the few sources still stocking 78-rpm records. A dying breed: an old-fashioned music store stocking records. You have to know what you want—it's not a place to browse. No credit cards.

Revolver Records

CDs, tapes & records
Chelsea

45 West 8th Street, 2nd Floor
near 6th Avenue / 982-6760
Daily 11am–10pm.

The Edge: Discounts soul, jazz, and rock CDs. Only CDs, but prices are good. No credit cards.

Sounds

CDs, tapes & records
Multiple locations

Mon–Thurs noon–10pm, Fri–Sat noon–11pm.

The Edge: Everything—rock, jazz, and classical. Good prices on new and used CDs. No credit cards. No delivery.

Locations: Flatiron/East Village: 16 St. Marks Place, between 2nd and 3rd Avenues (677-2727) / 20 St. Marks Place, between 2nd and 3rd Avenues (677-3444)

Tower Records & Video

CDs, tapes & records
Multiple locations

Daily 11am–11pm.

quality style service value
45   34   34   41

The Edge: Beloved for its selection of music and videos by those who can stand the environment. Low, low prices on music and videos. Great selection. No delivery. 20% off. *"Wonderful selection of records and tapes." "They always have what I want."*

Locations: Flatiron/East Village: 383 Lafayette Street, at 4th Street (505-1166) / **Midtown East:** 725 5th Avenue, near 56th Street (838-8110) / **Upper East Side:** 1535 3rd Avenue, at 86th Street (369-2500) / **Upper West Side:** 2107 Broadway, near 66th Street near Lincoln Center (799-2500)

Beauty & the Feast

Caterers
Midtown West

117-119 West 26th Street
between 6th and 7th Avenues / 691-6135
Weekdays 8am–6pm, Sat 9am–5pm.

The Edge: Reasonably priced Italian specialties. Seasonal Italian specialties are favored, including antipastos and pastas. Prices are reasonable at $20 per person.

Campagna Catering

Caterers
Upper East Side

24 East 21st Street
between Broadway and Park Avenue South / 460-0900
By appointment.

The Edge: A versatile caterer. An offshoot of the restaurant—Mark Strausman, the chef of Campagna, will do small dinners to mega events.

Catering Company

Caterers
Midtown West

215 West 29th Street
between 7th and 8th Avenues / 564-5370
Weekdays 9am–5:30pm.

The Edge: Full-service catering. Full-service catering and special event planning. Has orchestrated theme cocktail parties, awards banquets, and fund-raising events for various educational institutions.

Charlotte's Catering

Caterers
Lower Manhattan

146 Chambers Street
near West Broadway / 732-7939
Weekdays 10am–6pm or by appointment.

quality style service value
45   45   40   40

The Edge: Elegant excellent food. Expert full-service catering serves excellent food and provides flowers and waiters. Able to handle all events, including small dinners, dinner dances, business meetings, and wedding receptions. Corporate clients include Miramax Films and Lehman Bros. Will deliver takeout for small dinners. *"Pricey, but worth the convenience—call, order, and it's delivered to your door." "No muss, no fuss."*

Classic Fair Catering
Caterers
Lower Manhattan

125 Broadway
between Front and Water Streets / 574-7697
Weekdays by appointment.

The Edge: Party location caterer. Caterers to Ellis Island Immigration Museum, the Custom House, the Metropolitan Club, and other party locations.

Creative Edge Parties
Caterers
Greenwich Village

110 Barrow Street
near Washington Street / 741-3000
By appointment.

43 | 45 | 40 | 45
quality style service value

The Edge: Excellent creative food. Co-owner Robert Spiegel was Glorious Foods' sous-chef. Beautiful food served by well-trained, attractive help. Very beautiful and creative events. *"Still the best!" "They're so impressed with themselves, they become ludicrous."*

Feast and Fêtes
Caterers
Upper East Side

19 East 76th Street
between 5th and Madison Avenues / 737-2224
By appointment.

45 | 47 | 45 | 45
quality style service value

The Edge: Catering from Restaurant Daniel owner and partner. Jean-Christophe Le Picart joined Daniel Boulard, chef and co-owner of Restaurant Daniel and former chef of Le Cirque, to open Feast and Fêtes catering. How bad can it be?

Flavors Catering and Carry-out
Caterers
Chelsea

8 West 18th Street
near 5th Avenue / 647-1234
Weekdays 8am–6:30pm.

40 | 40 | 30 | 30
quality style service value

The Edge: From Texas- to Tuscany-style food. Specialties include polenta pie, roast vegetables, and excellent desserts. Will provide recipes on request. Takeout list includes 25 cold entrees, sandwiches, and hot items. Also offers a catering service, which is flexible and designed around your plans. A tasting room upstairs. *"Pricey, but worth it—great food." "Can be snooty."*

Fletcher Morgan's Provisions
Caterers
Gramercy Park/Murray Hill

432 West 19th Street
between 9th and 10th Avenues / 989-0724
By appointment.

The Edge: Versatile catering. From small dinner and cocktail parties for six or more to large corporate affairs. No minimum charges.

Gay Jordan
Caterers
Upper East Side

326 East 81st Street

between 1st and 2nd Avenues / 794-2248
By appointment.

quality style service value

The Edge: Up there with Glorious Food. Excellent classic French-style food. Parties for a minimum of 8 to 1,500. *"Catching up to Glorious Food."*

Glorious Food

504 East 74th Street
near York Avenue / 628-2320
Daily 9am–5pm.

Caterers
Upper East Side

quality style service value

The Edge: Sets the standard in catering. Impeccable food that's delicious, creative, and beautifully presented. Will cater for two to thousands of people at your choice of location. Celebrity clientele. Provides good-looking and well-trained staff who are mostly actors and actresses between engagements. Can accommodate 60 for dinner in its garden terrace setting or on its rooftop. Very expensive. *"Tops!" "They do great parties."*

Great Performances

287 Spring Street
near Hudson Street / 727-2424
By appointment.

Caterers
SoHo/TriBeCa

quality style service value

The Edge: Quality catering from crowds of 12 to hundreds. Professional-quality dining. *"Good job always." "Great New York City caterer."*

Harvest Gourmet

627-2712
By appointment.

Caterers
Mail/phone

The Edge: Caterer specializing in Californian and French cuisine. Chef Robert Stigman has been doing high-end dinners for the last three years. Dinner parties start at $45+ per person. Harvest Gourmet handles it all, including flowers. Also has a full-range food emporium, best for its good takeout, which favors soups, pasta salads, baked items, and simple meats.

Neuman & Bogdonoff

173 Christie Street
between Rivington and Delancey Streets / 228-2444
Weekdays 8am–5pm.

Caterers
Greenwich Village

quality style service value

The Edge: Very good, but not great, catering. Owned by the son of the owner of Rosedale Fish Market, which is one of the top fish stores in the city. Closed its takeout shop to focus on catering only. It's flexible but not surprising—the specialties include fish items (great poached salmon), as well as pasta dishes, salads, and basic meats and potatoes. Baked goods feature American classics. *"Expensive."*

New Creole Kitchen

241 West 97th Street
between Broadway and West End Avenue / 864-5381
Mon–Sat 10am–6pm.

Caterers
Upper West Side

quality style service value

The Edge: Créole catering. Specialties include catfish mousse, shrimp jambalaya pockets, tomato-basil corn tartlets, and shrimp gumbo. Menus are priced at $50 to $80 per person. Parties under 200 people are preferred.

Robbins and Wolfe Catering
521 West Street
near Horatio Street / 924-6500
Weekdays by appointment 9am–5pm.

Caterers
Greenwich Village

quality style service value

The Edge: Excellent food served well. Celebrity clientele. Attractive, innovative food.

Robert Swingle
360 West 22nd Street
at 9th Avenue / 353-8848
By appointment

Caterers
Chelsea

The Edge: Caterer with the personal touch. Does in-house catering for Christie's. Excellent personal service.

Taste Caterers
113 Horatio Street
near West Street / 255-8571
By appointment.

Caterers
Greenwich Village

quality style service value

The Edge: Good food. Favors simple California-style cuisine.

Tentation Catering
47 East 19th Street
between Park Avenue South and Broadway / 353-0070
Weekdays by appointment 9am–6pm.

Caterers
Flatiron/East Village

quality style service value

The Edge: Consistently very good French food. Dinners for 8 to 2,000. The food tastes as exceptional as it looks.

Washington Street
433 Washington Street
near Vesey Street / 925-5119
Weekdays 8am–6pm.

Caterers
SoHo/TriBeCa

The Edge: Caters at Chelsea Piers. One of the caterers recommended by Chelsea Piers.

Yura
1645 3rd Avenue
between 92nd and 93rd Streets / 860-8060
Weekdays 7am–8pm, Sat–Sun 8am–7pm.

Caterers
Upper East Side

quality style service value

The Edge: When's she's good, she's great. Catering and takeout featuring "comfort food." Offers chicken salad, tuna salad, fried chicken, meatloaf, and macaroni and cheese. Desserts appear to be a first love and include angelfood cake with bittersweet-chocolate icing, apple crisp, and baked muffins. When available, try the poached-plum fruit dessert—it's in a class by itself. *"Tops for food, but not always consistent."*

Abrons Arts Center

466 Grand Street
near Pitt Street / 598-0400
Schedule varies by activity.

Classes & activities
Lower East Side

50 | 50 | 50 | 50
quality style service value

The Edge: The Lower East Side's answer to the 92nd Street Y. While it has a smaller number of programs than the 92nd Street Y, the Henry Street Settlement's Abrons Art Center offers an array of classes and workshops in drama, music, and the visual arts. Classes are reasonable. A sampling includes: drawing and painting at 10 sessions for $150 or book arts/printmaking (all levels) at 10 sessions for $90. Offers private music lessons in just about everything (bassoon, flute, saxophone, clarinet, bass/electric bass, guitar, trumpet, trombone, cello, oboe, vibes, kettle drums, piano, violin, French horn, recorder), including voice. The charge is $16.50 per hour for nonneighborhood students and $15 per hour for neighborhood students. Offers small-group lessons for six students or fewer. Also a summer arts camp program for children ages 6 to 12. The recently redone theater is a jewel and presents a variety of drama, jazz, and opera programs. *"The best."*

After School Workshop

45 East 81st Street at PS 6
between Park and Madison Avenues / 734-7620
Daily 3–6pm.

Classes & activities
Upper East Side

The Edge: Wonderful educational activities for children. Get help with homework at reading and math workshops, plus classes on computers, arts and crafts, baking, theater training, sports, and games. After-school workshops are $140, or $15 per half hour of private tutoring.

Alliance of Resident Theatres

131 Varick Street, Room 904
near Spring Street / 989-5257
Weekdays 10am–6pm.

Classes & activities
SoHo/TriBeCa

The Edge: Hot seats and news on discounts to Off Broadway. Also called A.R.T., this is an advocacy group for about 250 of New York City's not-for-profit theater groups. Publishes bimonthly *Hot Seats,* which features the Passport to Off Broadway program providing discount coupons (subject to ticket availability) to Off Broadway plays. Discounts range from 10% to 50% and are redeemable at scores of plays currently. No credit cards.

Art Students League

215 West 57th Street
near Broadway / 247-4510
Weekdays 8:30am–8pm, Sat 8:30am–3pm, Sun 1–3:30pm.

Classes & activities
Midtown West

30 | 20 | 20 | 40
quality style service value

The Edge: Art courses taught by master artists. Courses in various aspects of drawing, including anatomy, are offered on Saturday and Sunday. Half and full day programs. No credit cards.

Ballet Academy East
Classes & activities
Upper East Side

1651 3rd Avenue
near 92nd Street / 410-9140
Children, daily 9am–6pm; adults, daily 9am–2pm and 6–9pm.

The Edge: Top-notch mother-and-child classes. Classes for children ages 2 and up. Pre-ballet classes for ages 2 to 5 years and ballet classes for all ages to adult. Each class has two teachers and a pianist. Vans run from many private schools. Now offering classes for boys.

Central Park Activities Manhattan Urban Rangers
Classes & activities
Upper East Side

1234 5th Avenue
starting at 59th Street / 427-4040
Daily during daylight hours.

quality style service value

The Edge: Manhattan's indispensable playground. Find 90-minute walks and talks led by urban park rangers, on subjects ranging from geology to birdwatching, every Sunday at 2pm, rain or shine. Also find tours Tuesday through Sunday at various times between 10am and 4:30pm. The carousel is open Monday through Friday from 10:30am to 4:30pm and on Saturday and Sunday from 10:30am to 5:30pm. The Central Park Zoo features wildlife exhibitions and a wonderful children's zoo, open Monday through Friday from 10am to 5pm and Saturday, Sunday, and holidays from 10:30am to 5:30pm. The Hechscher Puppet House at the Hechscher Playground presents puppet shows Monday through Friday at 10:30am and noon; reservations are required. No credit cards. *"Best outdoor place in the city!"*

Children's Acting Academy
Classes & activities
Upper East Side

1050 5th Avenue
near 87th Street / 860-7101
Weekdays after 3:30pm.

The Edge: Acting classes for children. For 25 years, acting classes for 5- to 17-year-olds, after school and during the summer. Monica May, the director, trained at Lee Strasberg's Theater Institute. Her summer theater program includes 2-, 4-, and 6- week classes covering different topics each week. Students go to Broadway and Off Broadway shows and study plays and authors from Shakespeare to Simon.

Children's Museum of Manhattan
Classes & activities
Upper West Side

212 West 83rd Street
between Amsterdam Avenue and Broadway / 721-1223
Wed–Sun 10am–5pm; also Tues in July.

40 43 43 45
quality style service value

The Edge: Just for children, but adults will appreciate the museum too. Wonderful museum for children. The shop has books and science items for children and .the merchandise changes to complement the exhibits. *"A great activity center. Well supervised and educational." "My granddaughter loves it."*

Children's Museum of the Arts
Classes & activities
SoHo/TriBeCa

72 Spring Street
near Broadway / 941-9198
Tues–Wed and Fri–Sun 11am–5pm, Thurs 11am–7pm.

quality style service value

The Edge: A museum just for children. For children up to 10 years old. Ever-changing exhibitions. Workshops every hour on the hour in painting, drawing, and mask making, among other topics. Weekend workshops for children over age 6 are included in the admission fee of $5 per child ($4 on weekdays) plus $1 materials fee. No credit cards.

China Institute
125 East 65th Street
near Lexington Avenue / 744-8181
Per class schedule.

Classes & activities
Upper East Side

38 35 32 38
quality style service value

The Edge: A wide range of Chinese courses. A wonderful place to explore your interest in China. Excellent language, poetry, and cooking classes. Our favorite courses include a one-month, intensive, day-long, five-days-per-week Mandarin course that's given in the summer. Also explore the Mandarin classes for children. The six-session group cooking class, given in the institute's well-equipped kitchen, is hands-on and costs $300. *"Wonderful courses and teachers—especially Ben Wang."*

Cooper Union
30 Cooper Square
at 3rd Avenue and 7th Street / 353-4195
Weekend classes.

Classes & activities
Flatiron/East Village

The Edge: Art classes for all. Beginners' drawing class meets on Saturday mornings. A range of classes for more advanced students also.

Craft Studio
1657 3rd Avenue
between 92nd and 93rd Streets / 831-6626
By appontment.

Classes & activities
Upper East Side

45 45 45 45
quality style service value

The Edge: Salvation from those birthday party woes. Barbara Mindel is a miracle worker—making sure you no longer fret over birthday parties for your children. Parties fro 12 range from $315 to $575. They include activities, where the guests make something to take home. The parties end with cake and juice or other foods as requested. *"A happening my daughter wouldn't miss."* *"Thank goodness for the Craft Studio!"*

Diller-Quale
24 East 95th Street
between 5th and Madison Avenues / 369-1484
Schedule varies.

Classes & activities
Upper East Side

50 50 50 50
quality style service value

The Edge: Music and art lessons for all ages. Devoted to music, voice, and the arts. Provides after-school/after-work programs for all ages. Offers individual and group lessons for instruments (including cello, violin, clarinet, and piano), voice, and art classes one to three times per week. No credit cards.

Greenwich House Pottery
16 Jones Street
between Bleecker and West 4th Streets / 242-4106

Classes & activities
Greenwich Village

Day and evening classes.

quality style service value

The Edge: Pottery classes. Pottery classes are available six days a week, with day and evening sessions. For all ages from 3 years old and up! *"A pottery studio in New York. Great and fun to visit. Nice quaint building and nice craft shows."*

Ice Studio, Inc.

Classes & activities
Upper East Side

1034 Lexington Avenue
near 73rd Street / 535-0304
Call for the current schedule of skating sessions.

The Edge: Tiny year-round ice rink located on the second floor of a brownstone. Offers lessons and skate rentals. Lessons are $35 per half hour. No credit cards.

International Wine Center

Classes & activities
Midtown West

231 West 29th Street, Suite 210
between 7th and 8th Avenues / 268-7517
Weekday evenings per schedule. Office, weekdays 9:30am–5:30pm.

The Edge: For the serious wine lover, blind wine tastings over lunch. Tastings and lunches featured for serious amateurs. Priced at $235 for tastings with lunch.

James Beard Foundation

Classes & activities
Chelsea

167 West 12th Street
near 7th Avenue / 675-4984
Call for current schedule.

quality style service value

The Edge: Special dining events for members and their guests throughout the U.S. Restaurant news and recommendations, but best of all, features dinners planned around special wines, seasonal specialties, and occasions. *"Great events and information."*

Joan Victor Studio

Classes & activities
Upper East Side

863 Park Avenue
between 77th and 78th Streets / 988-2773
Day and evening classes.

The Edge: Drawing lessons salon style. Drawing classes in a studio setting with a small group of six to eight students. Lessons given once a week for 10 weeks. Beginning and intermediate classes are offered.

Julliard Placement Bureau

Classes & activities
Upper West Side

60 Lincoln Center Plaza
near 65th Street / 799-5000
Weekdays 9:30am–8pm, Sat 10am–7pm, Sun noon–5pm.

The Edge: Professional training by day, amateur education by night. The evening division features lectures on music, applied music, and ear and voice training. Over 300 courses are offered each semester, including a survey course on music. Will provide recommendations for piano teachers. Also has a store selling music, books, CDs, and tapes.

Karen Lee

Classes & activities
Upper West Side

142 West End Avenue, Apartment 30V
at 66th Street / 787-2227
By appointment for catering. Morning classes 11am–2pm; evening classes 6–9pm.

The Edge: The source for Chinese cooking. Known for her excellent Chinese catering as well, but her reach goes beyond that to Italian and an eclectic mix of other international fare she calls "fusion." For 24 years has offered small (limited to nine students) cooking classes called Fusion Cooking, Mostly Italian, the Occasional Vegetarian, and Traditional Chinese. Students participate fully in making the meal and eat the results! Classes run $450 for four three-hour sessions or $125 for an individual class. Requires a $300 deposit.

Lenox Hill Neighborhood House

Classes & activities
Upper East Side

331 East 70th Street
near 1st Avenue / 744-5022
Weekdays 6:30am–9:30pm, Sat–Sun 9am–5pm.

quality style service value

The Edge: Toddler and parenting group activities. Activities, including playtime, gym tots, and aqua tots for ages 1½ to 3½ years. Also age-appropriate arts and crafts, games, gymnastics, and swimming activities; Head Start comprehensive early-childhood programs; and teen program for 12- to 18-year olds. Offers weekend computer groups for ages 5 to 18 and gymnastics groups for children ages 3½ to 8. Of course, adult programs too. Wonderful pool. *"Good resource. No-frills value."*

Little Orchestra Society

Classes & activities
Midtown West

220 West 42nd Street, 18th Floor
near 7th Avenue / 704-2100
Scheduled performances.

quality style service value

The Edge: Peabody Award–winning concerts for children. Happy Concerts for children ages 5 to 12 are at Avery Fisher Hall in Lincoln Center on Saturday. The Lolli-Pops Concerts for children ages 3 to 5, at Florence Gould Hall at the French Institute/Alliance Française, involve youngsters who conduct the orchestra and play along on toy trumpets and tambourines. *"A music lover's must."*

Mannes College of Music

Classes & activities
Upper West Side

150 West 85th Street
near Amsterdam Avenue / 580-0210
Mon–Sat 9am–4pm, Sun 9am–6pm.

quality style service value

The Edge: Great instruction for the professional or the amateur. Individually designed programs for adults. Instruction for virtually all classical instruments and voice. Special programs for children ages 4 to 18. Small classes, private and semiprivate lessons, orchestral and jazz studies, and piano teacher referrals. Classes on weekday afternoons and all day Saturday. *"Produces fine musicians and performers."*

Marymount Manhattan College

Classes & activities
Upper East Side

221 East 71st Street
near 2nd Avenue / 517-0564
Evenings and weekends.

quality style service value

The Edge: Neighborhood school featuring practical courses. Offers over 200 courses covering a wide range of topics, including the ancient world, art history, play writing, and public relations in the entertainment industry. Focus is on expanding horizons and teaching and reinforcing the fundamentals, such as hands-on computer training, communication skills, and writing. Offers certificate programs. For the body: exercise programs featuring low-impact aerobics and swimming in a heated 20- by 60-foot pool. Special tots to teens and over-65 programs. *"Offers a lot to the neighborhood."*

Metropolitan Museum of Art

1000 5th Avenue
near 82nd Street / 879-5500
Tues–Thurs and Sun 9:30am–5:30pm, Fri–Sat 9:30am–8:45pm.

Classes & activities
Upper East Side

49 quality 46 style 42 service 45 value

The Edge: For the soul—world-class art and instruction. A wonderful permanent art collection and special exhibits. Art and music appreciation courses and concerts, gallery lectures, and special children's programs. Member's discount. *"A great New York resource." "Terrific courses— especially Rosamond Bernier's. Don't miss her."*

National Academy of Design

5 East 89th Street
east of 5th Avenue / 996-1908
Mon–Thurs 8:30am–8pm, Fri–Sat 8:30am–1pm.

Classes & activities
Upper East Side

48 quality 48 style 43 service 42 value

The Edge: Top instruction using live models. Three-hour courses in figure drawing, both clothed and unclothed figures, are conducted on Saturday and Sunday. Half-day (3½ hours) to full-day (7 hours) programs. No credit cards. *"Excellent art school." "Very fine exhibits."*

New School

66 West 12th Street
near 5th Avenue / 229-5630
Per current course schedule.

Classes & activities
Chelsea

35 quality 35 style 33 service 40 value

The Edge: 1,500 courses. If they don't have it, does it exist? Offers courses in business, communications, computers, culinary arts, foreign languages, humanities, music history and appreciation, science, social sciences, theater arts, and writing. In addition, special events include a workshop at the Met, career planning, and cooking, plus its distinguished lecturer series and concert programs. Courses for certificate or degree programs. *"Extensive classes." "A New York institution." "Comprehensive catalog, but needs better organization."*

New York Academy of Art

111 Franklin Street
near Church Street / 966-0300
Per schedule.

Classes & activities
SoHo/TriBeCa

50 quality 50 style 50 service 50 value

The Edge: Classic painting well taught. A basic course, Old Master Drawing: Methods and Materials, is offered on 12 Saturdays in three-hour afternoon sessions. Also two uninstructed sketch courses are available for students of all levels who come in and draw the model of the day (models pose for 5- and 20-minute intervals) throughout a three-hour period or for a long pose session in which the model changes the pose only once over the three hours. *"Has a very fine museum."*

New York Choral Society

881 7th Avenue, Studio 1201
at 57th Street / 247-3878
Per schedule.

Classes & activities
Midtown West

quality style service value

The Edge: Classical choral concerts at Carnegie or Avery Fisher Hall. Tickets priced from $12 to $42. Major upcoming events at Avery Fisher Hall include Mahler's 8th Symphony on February 1, 1998, and Berlioz's *Damnation of Faust* on April 19, 1998. Call for details on these and their other concerts. *"Great music."*

New York University School of Continuing Education

50 West 4th Street
Shimkin Hall, near 5th Avenue / 998-7171
Primarily evenings and weekends.

Classes & activities
Flatiron/East Village

quality style service value

The Edge: 2,000 courses leading to degrees. Career focus! Courses days, nights, and Saturday and Sunday on a wide range of topics, including career (business, real estate) and life enhancement (arts and humanities). Offers more than 2,000 courses for credit and more than 100 certificates, specialized diplomas, undergraduate degrees, and master's degrees. Free career nights, open houses, and other special events. *"Good programs to keep one busy."*

92nd Street Y

1395 Lexington Avenue
near 92nd Street / 996-1100
Varies by activity, but there's always something going on.

Classes & activities
Upper East Side

quality style service value

The Edge: A neighborhood treasure offering everything. You name it, they have it—from culture to sports to children's programs. Lectures from the Who's Who in their field—for example, hear Studs Terkel, Charlton Heston, Wendy Wasserstein, Philip Johnson, and Caroline Kennedy. Adult programs, including Jewish education, great world of ideas, personal growth, career and finance, language and writing, art, music, dance, 60+ programs, tours and travel, dance, health, fitness, and sports. The health and fitness center has aerobics classes and a full gym and pool. Yearly fitness membership is $884, or $95 monthly. Theater, concerts, and a full children's program are also available. *"Wonderful facilities and teachers." "Great concerts." "Hurry—their Lyrics and Lyricists Program tickets go fast."*

Parents League

115 East 82nd Street
near Lexington Avenue / 737-7385
Mon and Wed–Thurs 9am–4pm, Tues 9am–6pm,
Fri 9am–midnight.

Classes & activities
Upper East Side

quality style service value

The Edge: Knowledgeable parent-advisors will consult candidly on topics of interest. One of the best city resources for parents. A nonprofit organization which shares information between parents on topics of interest like choosing a school, locating a summer camp, finding a babysitter, selecting after-school activities, and teen travel. Publishes the *Parents League Calendar and Guide to NY*, the *Parents League Review, The Toddler Book* and the *Parents League News. "Provides a real service."*

Peter Kump's School of Culinary Arts

Classes & activities
Upper East Side

307 East 92nd Street
near 2nd Avenue / 410-5152
Evening and weekend classes.

The Edge: International chefs share their secrets. Names you know teaching bread baking, buffet dishes, cake decoration, spa cuisine, French bistro cooking, Italian, Japanese, Mexican, Vietnamese, wine tasting, and more. Evening, Saturday, and weekend workshops.

Playspace

Classes & activities
Upper West Side

2473 Broadway
near 92nd Street / 769-2300
Mon–Sat 9:30am–6pm, Sun 10am–6pm.

The Edge: Indoor playground for children plus a cafe area for parents. 15 play areas, including a bridge with a 20-foot crawling tunnel in the shape of a train and a screened tree house. Party packages are $129 Monday through Friday or $169 on Saturday and Sunday for 10 children, plus $11.95 for each additional child. Package includes a staff person. For children to 6 years old.

Pratt Institute of Art

Classes & activities
SoHo/TriBeCa

295 Lafayette Street, 2nd Floor
near Houston Street / 925-8481
Per course schedule.

The Edge: Training by the instructors to the professionals. Basic drawing is offered on Saturday mornings in a 10-week course.

Spanish Institute

Classes & activities
Upper East Side

684 Park Avenue
between 68th and 69th Streets / 628-0420
Per class schedule.

quality style service value

The Edge: Spanish classes every day but Sunday. All levels, day and evening classes, every day but Sunday. Group, semiprivate, and private lessons. Conversational, business, medical, and social service terminology. Cultural courses. Nine-week programs. Translation services available. 30% discount for seniors in the day program.

Userfriendly

Classes & activities
Upper West Side

139 West 72nd Street
between Columbus and Amsterdam Avenues / 580-4433
Mon–Thurs 9am–10pm, Fri 9am–6pm, Sat 11am–7pm, Sun noon–8pm.

The Edge: The place to learn how. Private training and practice opportunities in WordPerfect, Lotus 1-2-3, Microsoft Word, and many other programs. Training includes private sessions followed by the opportunity to practice, with the best rates at off-peak hours. Three hours of one-on-one instruction and three hours of practice cost $189.

Wines & Spirits

Classes & activities
Gramercy Park/Murray Hill

203 East 29th Street
between 2nd and 3rd Avenues / 718-263-3134
Per course schedule.

The Edge: Fine wine classes. This year, Harriet Lembeck's wine and spirit courses (10 weeks on wine and 4 on spirits) will be moving to her own historic 1789 townhouse in Manhattan. Classes met for 2½ hours per week. Charges are $525 for the 10-week course and $700 for all 14 weeks.

YWCA

610 Lexington Avenue
at 53rd Street / 735-9731
Weekdays 6:30am–9pm; Sat–Sun 10am–4pm for classes,
6–9pm for gym (closed Sun July–Aug).

Classes & activities
Midtown East

quality   style   service   value

The Edge: In midtown, both a great sports facility and the Crafts Students League. Call for its catalog. The swimming pool is gorgeous and not always crowded. Exercise programs are tailored to busy career people. The Crafts Students League offers programs in crafts and fine arts, teaching basic and master craft techniques in well-equipped studios. Other programs focus on careers. "*Lots of activities for kids.*"

Stacks Rare Coins

123 West 57th Street
near 6th Avenue / 582-2580
Weekdays 10am–5pm.

Coins & stamps
Midtown West

quality   style   service   value

The Edge: Ten coin auctions per year. One of the largest rare-coin dealers in the country. Also find rare seals and paper money. For serious collectors. No credit cards. No delivery.

Diana Gould Ltd.

826 Scarsdale Avenue
Scarsdale / 914-725-3844
Mon–Sat 9am–5pm.

Coordinators
Westchester

quality   style   service   value

The Edge: Stylish arrangements that fit the mood of your occasion. Her staff of 50 can handle it all—provide set design, artwork, floral designs, lighting, and entertainment, as well as the menu that makes it all come together. For over 20 years—flowers that make the party. "*Expensive.*"

Dorothy Wako

686-5569
Weekdays by appointment.

Coordinators
Mail/phone

quality   style   service   value

The Edge: Stylistically tops. Flower designs for all events from dinner parties to major society events. Clients have included Dominick Dunne and Julia Roberts. For a Greenwich, Conn., garden wedding, they planted a traditional English garden with the feel of a country cottage. Prices start at $85 and up for a simple dinner party arrangement. Accepts American Express only. Deluxe.

Gourmet Advisory Service, Inc.

315 East 68th Street
near 2nd Avenue / 535-0005

Coordinators
Upper East Side

By appointment.

The Edge: Party designer with strong food skills. Harriet Rose Katz and her team can put it all together—food, music (jazz bands, classical quartets, cabaret singers), caterers, florists, invitations, and accessories. They're a pleasure to deal with. You may have known them as Liaison, Unlimited. Very expensive. Deluxe.

Mood Food Ltd.

263 West 12th Street
between 8th Street and Greenwich Avenue / 243-4245
Mon–Sat 10am–7pm.

Coordinators
Greenwich Village

The Edge: Does it all well. From charity to corporate events, from formal to theme, they make it happen. Can arrange everything from food to security.

Perl & Berliner

260 Columbia Avenue
Ft. Lee / 201-224-0034
Weekdays 9am–5pm for appointments.

Coordinators
New Jersey

The Edge: Creative party skills. Owned by Gail Perl and Carol Berliner. Handled the wedding of Leonard Stern's son Emanuel at the Central Park Zoo and Al Roker's wedding. 25 years' experience. Events for 50 to 1,700. No credit cards.

Philip Baloun Designs

340 West 55th Street
near 9th Avenue / 307-1675
By appointment.

Coordinators
Midtown West

The Edge: Ability to transform entire spaces into theatrical other worlds. Celebrity clients include the Metropolitan Opera. Views itself as floral decoration specialists. No credit cards.

Renny - Design for Entertaining

505 Park Avenue
near 59th Street / 288-7000
Mon–Sat 9am–6pm (to 5pm in summer).

Coordinators
Midtown East

The Edge: Orchids are a specialty. Romantic arrangements. Also plants and trees. Known for planning dramatic party events. Handles rental of props and the regulars—linens, crystal, and dishes. Gorgeous things. Celebrity clients include Brooke Astor, the Newhouses, the Agnellis, and the Safras, among others. Renny runs a plant-maintenance and landscaping service. Many of the flowers are grown for him in Bucks County, Penn. Arrangements start at $50. *"Unusual, beautiful arrangements—expensive, but worth it."*

Robert Isabell

410 West 13th Street
near Washington Street / 645-7767
Weekdays 9am–6pm for appointments.

Coordinators
Greenwich Village

The Edge: The Glorious Food of florists—periodic sales of items left over from major events. Coordinates flowers, lighting, and sound effects. Top of the line with matching attitude. Did the Steinberg-Tisch wedding and Random House's party in the Winter Garden celebrating the launch of Avedon's autobiography, but best known for doing the celebrated Miller (of the Duty Free Shops) daughters' multi-million-dollar weddings. Event planners, no walk-in business. No credit cards. Deluxe.

Table of Contents

Coordinators
Flatiron/East Village

73 5th Avenue
at 15th Street / 620-0622
Weekdays 9:30am–5:30pm.

The Edge: Full event planning. Event planner Ilene Landers does it all from her Fifth Avenue loft space. Menus tend to be traditional, befitting the occasion.

Dance Manhattan

Dance
Chelsea

39 West 19th Street, Fifth floor
between 5th and 6th Avenues / 807-0802
Evening classes.

The Edge: Learn ballroom dancing. Classes in multiple dance styles, from basic to advanced techniques, including the waltz, Milonguero-style tango, and Argentine waltz, among others. A four-week course (one hour per week) costs $60; two courses, $95.

Chuckles and Friends

Entertainment
Upper West Side

496-6228
By appointment.

The Edge: Entertainment for children ages 5 to 10. Chuckles will come to you with entertainment that includes balloons, magic, puppets, music, and face paints. Features games, including relay races, for older children. Parents can choose a character (Chuckles, Minnie and Mickey Mouse, Cinderella and Peter Pan) and have the party planned around that character. $165 per hour. No credit cards.

Party Poopers

Entertainment
SoHo/TriBeCa

104 Reade Street
near West Broadway / 587-9030
Weekdays 10am–6pm for bookings.

The Edge: Parties to go, and even better—a private party at their place. Theme parties for younger children, ages 1 to 4, include fairytale land, superhero adventure, medieval party, beauty parlor/fashion show, and Mother Goose nursery rhymes. Themes for older children include game show, spookhouse, dance party, secret agent, and whodunit. Various facilities are available, including a 1,100-square-foot room, a 2,200- square-foot room, or both combined. Will provide cake, snacks, drinks, and loot bags. An at-home party option is available. No credit cards.

Silly Billy

10 West 15th Street, Suite 222
between 5th and 6th Avenues / 645-1299
By appointment.

Entertainment
Mail/phone

quality style service value

The Edge: Great party entertainment for toddlers to age 11. Provides entertainers for parties, including clowns, balloon sculpture, and magic. No credit cards. *"Great for kids' parties."*

Antony Todd

307 7th Avenue, Suite 1506
between 27th and 28th Streets / 367-7363
By appointment

Florists
Mail/phone

The Edge: For that "just-picked" look. Did the glorious arrangements for the New York Public Library centennial fund-raiser. Pulls together unusual combinations that work. Will also deliver flowers to you daily.

Belle Fleur

53 West 72nd Street, 2nd Floor
between Central Park West and Columbus Avenue / 688-6371
Weekdays by appointment 9am–6:30pm.

Florists
Upper West Side

The Edge: Flowers with old English look. The gift card is hand-calligraphed and sealed with a hand-pressed flower.

Decor Floral

227 West 29th Street
between 7th and 8th Avenues / 463-8091
By appointment.

Florists
Midtown West

The Edge: The place to buy if you loved the Kips Bay Show House flowers. Favors statement flowers—opulent and romantic. Designer Thom prefers statement arrangements—large and grand. Prices $50 for a small bouquet to over $100 for something significant.

Elan Flowers

148 Duane Street
at West Broadway / 343-2426
By appointment.

Florists
SoHo/TriBeCa

The Edge: Slightly less expensive for classic European-style bouquets. Features stylish flowers in attractive arrangements in vibrant colors priced from $45, plus delivery. The flowers often have a Victorian style. Sources flowers from Holland and France.

Irene Hayes Wadley & Smythe LeMoult

One Rockefeller Plaza
between 48th and 49th Streets / 247-0051
Weekdays 8am–6pm, Sat 8am–noon.

Florists
Midtown West

quality style service value

The Edge: Flowers for every event and setting. Something for every occasion, from flowers for your home or office to major events— weddings and conventions and the like. Expect to find fresh and dried flowers and fruit and gourmet baskets, which can be sent around the corner or around the world. *"Beautiful arrangements, but very expensive."*

Les Fleurs de Maxim's

680 Madison Avenue
near 61st Street / 752-9889
Mon–Sat 10am–6pm.

Florists
Upper East Side

42	40	44	40
quality	style	service	value

The Edge: Very attractive flowers. Pierre Cardin is the founder and owner. Does single arrangements to settings for weddings or smaller dinners.

Melonie de France

160 East 56th Street
between 3rd Avenue and Lexington Avenues / 935-4343
Mon–Sat 10am–6pm.

Florists
Midtown East

40	40	40	35
quality	style	service	value

The Edge: Wonderful dried flowers. Beautiful dried-flower arrangements. Imported from France where they have shops in Nice and Cannes. Wonderful arrangements, including big bouquets and topiaries.

Michael George

315 East 57th Street
between 1st and 2nd Avenues / 751-0689
Weekdays 8am–6:30pm.

Florists
Midtown East

The Edge: Sleek Japanese-style flowers. Calvin Klein's source for flowers.

Paul Bott Beautiful Flowers

1305 Madison Avenue
near 92nd Street / 369-4000
Weekdays 9am–5pm and by appointment.

Florists
Upper East Side

45	45	45	40
quality	style	service	value

The Edge: Great flowers. Features very creative, wonderful flowers nestled in tissues and cellophane. Fresh and dried flowers and plants available. Celebrity clients include William Simon (for his daughter's wedding).

Preston Bailey

88 Lexington Avenue, Studio 16C
between 26th and 27th Streets / 683-0035
Mon–Sat 8am–5pm.

Florists
Gramercy Park/Murray Hill

The Edge: Romantic-style florist. Loves to use roses and peonies giving an *Age of Innocence* feeling.

Ronaldo Maia

27 East 67th Street
near Madison Avenue / 288-1049

Florists
Upper East Side

Mon–Sat 9am–6pm.

quality style service value

The Edge: **Gorgeous Oriental floral styles.** Delicate floral styles in wonderful containers.

Simpson & Company and Florist West

852 10th Avenue
near 56th Street / 772-6670
Weekdays 9am–6pm, Sat 9am–1pm.

Florists
Midtown West

The Edge: **Unusual flowers and dried arrangements.** Features flowers, plants, freeze-dried flowers, fruits, and vegetables in arrangements. Recommended to us but still unknown to our survey panel. Let us know what you think.

Spring Street Garden

186½ Spring Street
near Thompson Street / 966-2015
Mon–Sat 11:30am–7pm.

Florists
SoHo/TriBeCa

The Edge: **Pretty flowers, which appear to be priced about 20% less than at other top florists.** Less fussy, simple arrangements.

Surroundings

224 West 79th Street
near Broadway / 580-8982
Weekdays 10am–7pm, Sat 10am–6pm.

Florists
Upper West Side

quality style service value

The Edge: **Attractive romantic arrangements.** Gift baskets also, which can be customized. Imported flowers only. $50 minimum.

VSF

204 West 10th Street
near Bleecker Street / 206-7236
Mon and Sat 10am–5pm, Tues–Fri 10am–7pm.

Florists
Greenwich Village

quality style service value

The Edge: **English garden look.** Favors Dutch flowers. Pricey but gorgeous. *"Beautiful flowers, but staff had attitude."*

Venamy Orchids

Route 22 North
Brewster / 800-362-3612
Mon–Sat 9am–6pm, Sun 10am–4pm.

Florists
Westchester

quality style service value

The Edge: **Hundreds and hundreds of orchids on display.** Sells decorative pots and baskets to complement arrangements. Wedding and event orchid displays are a specialty. Delivers to New York City, Fairfield, and Westchester and will ship throughout the U.S. Provides expert advice and care. A designer/decorator is on the staff. $30 minimum for arrangements. A good-size plant of blooming orchids is priced from $26 to $50+. Wonderful quality. Discounter. *"Good prices."*

Zeze

398 East 52nd Street
near 1st Avenue / 753-7767
Weekdays 8am–6pm.

Florists
Midtown East

quality style service value

The Edge: Dramatic arrangements with a touch of whimsy. Wide variety of orchids and flowers. A large selection of vases is the core ingredient of the dramatic arrangements. $50 minimum, plus delivery ($7 to $15 in Manhattan), $75 minimum outside Manhattan.

Asphalt Green, the Murphy Center

555 East 90th Street
at York Avenue / 369-8890
Weekdays 5:30am–10pm, Sat–Sun 8am–8pm.

Gyms
Upper East Side

quality style service value

The Edge: A splendid sports facility with a huge array of fitness classes, aquatic activities, and sports. Used by schools, groups, and individuals of all ages (infant to senior). Fees $35 to $150, depending on the class of membership and age of the member. A wonderful neighborhood attraction. *"Excellent facility in an inaccessible neighborhood." "Nice atmosphere."*

Atrium Club

115 East 57th Street
near Park Avenue / 688-9840
Weekdays 6am–10pm, Sat–Sun 6am–11pm.

Gyms
Midtown East

quality style service value

The Edge: Exercise in a convenient location. Three floors offering aerobics (over 70 classes), cardiovascular equipment, a 30- by 40-foot lap pool (often crowded), a sun deck, and a restaurant. Initiation fee is $300, then $113 monthly. Convenient location. Older crowd. No credit cards. *"Easiest place to get to!" "1980s washout!"*

Cardio Fitness Center

Weekdays 6:30am–9:30pm.

Gyms
Multiple locations

quality style service value

The Edge: In and out in one hour. Leave your sneakers—they provide the workout clothing. An unassuming, service-oriented, get-it-done (in one hour) club. It's never too crowded. Provides functional blue workout shorts and gray shirts. Best are the individually designed programs updated quarterly. CNN is available to keep you amused at all times. If you don't come in, they call to remind you. Good range of equipment, including treadmills, Lifecycles, Stairmasters, Nordic Track, and weight equipment. Personal trainers are on call to provide advice. $1,600 per year. Very expensive. Deluxe. *"Needs classes. Very expensive." "Good no-frills workout place." "Great for us middle-aged women!"*

Locations: Lower Manhattan: 79 Maiden Lane, near Williams Street (943-1510) / **Midtown East:** 345 Park Avenue, near 52nd Street (838-4570) / 885 3rd Avenue, near 54th Street (888-2120) / 200 Park Avenue, 3rd Floor, near 44th Street (682-4440) / **Midtown West:** 9 West 57th Street, near 5th Avenue (753-3980) / 1221 Avenue of the Americas, near 49th Street (840-8240)

Central Park Challenges

Gyms
Upper East Side

5th Avenue
near 96th Street mid Central Park / 348-4867
Various times during the day. Call for information regarding specific programs.

The Edge: Rock climbing in Central Park. Rock-climbing classes in Central Park for anyone at least 12 years old. Sessions include the Challenge Program (rock climbing for ages 14 and up) and Team Building (less physical, trust activities). Sunday classes (10am to 1pm) are $200 for four classes. Classes are limited to groups of 15. The climbing course, geared for beginners to advanced climbers, covers various climbing techniques, balance, and safety and uses the park's designed outdoor and indoor walls. No credit cards.

Chelsea Piers Sports Complex

Gyms
Chelsea

23rd Street and the Hudson River
between 17th & 23rd Streets / 336-6000
Weekdays 6am–11pm, Sat–Sun 8am–9pm.

quality	style	service	value
40	38	38	38

The Edge: You name it, they offer it. Four piers converted into an enormous all-encompassing sports complex including a Golf Center, Sports Center, in-line skating rink, Gymnastic Center, Maritime Center, roller rink, film and sound stage, and several restaurants. The Golf Center has 52 all-weather driving stalls on four levels, a 200-yard fairway with target greens, and a small putting area. The Sports Center features the city's largest indoor running track (a quarter mile) and largest rock climbing wall (10,000 square feet), three basketball courts, a boxing ring, and an indoor infield. There are also 4,000 square feet of aerobics studios, spa services, over 100 fitness classes a week, wellness seminars and workshops, and sport-specific and personal training. A fabulous array of sports opportunities! *"Lousy location—hard to get there without a cab." "Love the golf facility." "I've been to several seven-year-old parties here—big but okay." "Too bad it's not midtown and too bad there's not a direct bus from midtown."*

Club La Raquette

Gyms
Midtown West

119 West 56th Street
in the Parker Meridien Hotel near 7th Avenue / 245-1144
Weekdays 6am–11pm, Sat–Sun 7am–8pm.

quality	style	service	value
23	24	24	25

The Edge: Full gym facility at the Parker Meridien Hotel. Offers full gym facilities, aerobics, and a pool.

Crunch

Gyms
Multiple locations

Weekdays 6:30am–10pm, Sat–Sun 8am–8pm.

quality	style	service	value
43	45	33	40

The Edge: Gym combining exercise and entertainment. Focus is the cross-training circuit. A full gym with cardiovascular machines, free weights, classes, massage, personal training, rock-climbing walls, boxing, video theater, and a wide range of classes. $20 per day without membership, $949 per year if you decide to join. *"Too crowded and sweaty." "Gives corporate discounts."*

Locations: Flatiron/East Village: 54 East 13th Street, between University Place and Broadway (475-2018) / 404 Lafayette Street, near 4th Street (614-0120) / 88 University Place, near Broadway (620-7867) / **Greenwich Village:** 666 Greenwich Street, near Christopher Street (366-3725) /

Midtown East: 1109 2nd Avenue, between 58th and 59th Streets (758-3434) / **Upper West Side:** 162 West 83rd Street, near Amsterdam Avenue (875-1902)

David Barton Gym

552 Avenue of the Americas
between 15th and 16th Streets / 727-0004
Weekdays 6am–midnight, Sat 9am–9pm, Sun 10am–11pm.

Gyms
Chelsea

quality style service value

The Edge: 10,000-square-foot space with custom-built gym equipment. The focus is on weights and abdominal classes. Fee is $659 per year, with personal training extra. Celebrity clientele. *"Luxury workout place."*

Downtown Athletic Club

19 West Street
near Battery Place / 425-7000
Weekdays 6am–8:30pm, Sat–Sun 9am–5pm.

Gyms
Lower Manhattan

quality style service value

The Edge: Downtown club. Offers a full-service gym and a great pool. Serves the Wall Street crowd. Also a restaurant and rooms. $1,800 per year.

Drago's Gymnasium

50 West 57th Street
between 5th and 6th Avenues / 757-0724
Weekdays 7am–8pm, Sat 8am–2pm.

Gyms
Midtown West

quality style service value

The Edge: Pilates methodology. A no-frills gym, featuring small gymnastics classes limited to six people using the Pilates method. Favored by dancers and people with injuries. $18 for group classes, $40 for a private class, and $35 for first-time use. Reduce the price by buying multiple sessions. No credit cards.

Equinox Fitness Club

Mon–Thurs 6am–11pm, Fri 6am–10pm, Sat–Sun 8am–9pm.

Gyms
Multiple locations

36	33	30	28

quality style service value

The Edge: An attractive 18,000-square-foot spot to sweat. Machines for every interest, including Cybex weight training, Stairmasters, recumbent bikes, and more. Cost $825 per year ($82 monthly), plus $295 initiation. *"Pre-Reebok."*

Locations: Flatiron/East Village: 897 Broadway, near 19th Street (780-9300) / **Upper West Side:** 344 Amsterdam Avenue, near 76th Street (721-4200)

Excelsior Athletic Club

301 East 57th Street
between 1st and 2nd Avenues / 688-5280
Weekdays 6am–10pm, Sat–Sun 7am–7:30pm.

Gyms
Midtown East

33	33	27	30

quality style service value

The Edge: Luxurious upscale health club. Luxurious health club with 60 aerobics classes a week, outdoor summer sun deck, 30 new pieces of Cybex equipment, and best of all, the domed swimming pool. Not too congested because membership is limited. Full membership is $950 per year. Check out the less expensive day membership at $750 a year or $72 a month for weekday 9am to 5pm usage.

Executive Fitness Center

3 World Trade Center, 22nd Floor
near Vesey Street / 466-9266
Weekdays 6am–9:30pm, Sat–Sun 8am–7pm.

Gyms
Lower Manhattan

35	30	25	30
quality	style	service	value

The Edge: Full-service health club. Over 50 pieces of equipment in the gym, plus a wonderful pool. Personal trainers. Aerobics.

Lotte Berk Method

23 East 67th Street
near Madison Avenue / 288-6613
Weekdays 7:15am–8pm, Sat 8:30am–2pm, Sun 9:30am–2pm.

Gyms
Upper East Side

40	40	40	40
quality	style	service	value

The Edge: Great workouts! 60-minute sessions for $18 per session in small classes of not more than 10 to 12 women. Wonderful for tightening all those places that need it. No credit cards. *"Not Radu, but good."*

Manhattan Plaza Health Club

482 West 43rd Street
near 10th Avenue / 563-7001
Weekdays 6:30am–10pm, Sat–Sun 8:30am–7pm.

Gyms
Midtown West

50	50	40	30
quality	style	service	value

The Edge: A gym that has it all but location. Located in the heart of Times Square. Offers aerobics, a climbing wall 20 feet high with 30 available routes, Cybex bikes, Stairmasters, and treadmills, plus a glass-enclosed swimming pool and sun deck. Fees are $875 per year or $195 initiation plus $67 a month. *"Very clean and excellently maintained."*

New York Athletic Club

180 Central Park South
near 59th Street / 247-5100
Hours depend on department, but front desk open 24 hours daily.

Gyms
Midtown West

50	48	45	38
quality	style	service	value

The Edge: Great facilities, finally open to women. It finally admitted women! The sponsorship of three members is required, as well as a three- to four-month wait to get in after the interview. Personal trainers, weight equipment, and Olympic-size pool are the big attractions. No credit cards.

New York Health and Racquet Club

Weekdays 6am–10pm, Sat 9am–6pm.

Gyms
Multiple locations

40	40	35	35
quality	style	service	value

The Edge: Convenience and good equipment. Eight locations offering a range of activities, including basketball, racquetball, squash, strength, and free weights and equipment, including swimming pools, cardiovascular equipment, and spa facilities. Corporate memberships reduce charges. Can be crowded at prime times.

Locations: Flatiron/East Village: 24 East 13th Street, at 5th Avenue (924-4600) / **Lower Manhattan:** 39 Whitehall Street, near the South Street Seaport (269-9800) / 3 New York Plaza, (424-4653) / **Midtown East:** 132 East 45th Street, near 3rd Avenue (986-3100) / 20 East 50th Street, near 5th Avenue (593-1500) / **Midtown West:** 110 West 56th Street, near 6th Avenue (541-7200) / **Upper East Side:** 1433 York Avenue, near 76th Street (737-6666)

New York Sports Club

Mon–Thurs 6:30am–9pm, Fri 6:30am–8pm, Sat–Sun 8am–10pm.

Gyms
Multiple locations

quality   style   service   value

The Edge: Work out on the latest equipment at this widely available health club. Many locations, offering classes for all levels of aerobics, plus the latest cardiovascular equipment, many types of programs, and classes as well as pools. *"Crowded at times." "Incredibly convenient with so many locations."*

Locations: Midtown West: 404 5th Avenue, at 37th Street (594-3120) / 1601 Broadway, at 49th Street (977-8880) / 50 West 34th Street, at 6th Avenue (868-0820) / 1601 Broadway, at 49th Street (265-0995) / **Midtown East:** 380 Madison Avenue, (983-0303) / 541 Lexington Avenue, at 49th Street (838-2102) / **SoHo/TriBeCa:** 151 Reade Street, (571-1000) / **Upper East Side:** 349 East 76th Street, at 2nd Avenue (288-5700) / **Upper West Side:** 258 West 80th Street, at Broadway (873-1500)

Peninsula New York Spa

700 5th Avenue
at 55th Street / 247-2200
Weekdays 6am–9:30pm, Sat–Sun 8:30am–7pm.

Gyms
Midtown West

quality   style   service   value

The Edge: The ultimate. A gorgeous three-level gym and treatment facility. The gym includes all the latest equipment in a three-level club with spectacular views of the city and one of the most pleasant interiors. Saunas, steam rooms, and a swimming pool help you unwind. To get even more gorgeous: a full range of services, from body and scalp treatments and massages to hair-styling provided by the spa's Melange salon. Lunch and snacks are available for even more pampering. Cushy robes, and juice and fruit abound. *"Treat a bride-to-be—like Canyon Ranch in New York."*

Pumping Iron Gym

403 East 91st Street
between 1st and York Avenues / 996-5444
Weekdays 6am–11:30pm, Sat–Sun 8am–8pm.

Gyms
Upper East Side

quality   style   service   value

The Edge: Weightlifting for beginners to pros. Weightlifting for beginners, with a separate aerobics program on two floors, one for weights and the other for cardiovascular equipment. Personal trainers available. Membership fees are $72.80 a month or $624 per year. No credit cards. *"No-nonsense gym—inexpensive."*

Reebok's Sport Club New York

160 Columbus Avenue
near 67th Street / 362-6800
Mon–Thurs 5am–11pm, Fri 5am–10pm, Sat Sun 8am–8pm.

Gyms
Upper West Side

quality style service value

The Edge: One of New York's finest new facilities. A 140,000-square-foot gym on the Upper West Side, including a large pool with underwater music, a 45-foot climbing wall, and two regulation-size basketball courts. Also includes a full salon and spa. $950 initiation fee, then $135 per month. *"Chic till next year." "Great club, beautiful but expensive."*

Sports Training Institute

575 Lexington Avenue
at 51st Street / 752-7111
Weekdays 5:30am–9pm, Sat 8:30am–2pm.

Gyms
Midtown East

The Edge: Only one-on-one personal trainers. No frills, just work. Facilities include a stretch room, cardiovascular room, and weight room. Initial evaluation $250, then $42.50 to $50 per session with a personal trainer.

Vertical Club

Weekdays 6am–10pm, Sat–Sun 9am–6pm.

Gyms
Multiple locations

quality style service value

The Edge: Where the young chic go to meet and sweat. Offers a good range of equipment and facilities, including a full spa, pool, and track at multiple locations. The East 61st Street location is best. Sometimes its promotions offer two years for the price of one year at $1,400. 60 to 80 classes per week. *"Noisy."*

Locations: Midtown East: 335 Madison Avenue, near 43rd Street (983-5320) / **Midtown West:** 139 West 32nd Street, between 6th and 7th Avenues (465-1750) / 350 West 50th Street, between 8th and 9th Avenues (265-9400) / **Upper East Side:** 330 East 61st Street, between 1st and 2nd Avenues (355-5100)

World Gym

Weekdays 24 hours (closes Fri at midnight), Sat–Sun 7am–9pm.

Gyms
Multiple locations

quality style service value

The Edge: Offers 140 gym classes per week. Five different levels of aerobics, body boxing and yoga, a full range of cardiovascular equipment, and personal trainers. $796 per year.

Locations: SoHo/TriBeCa: 232 Mercer Street, between Bleecker and West 3rd Streets (780-7407) / **Upper West Side:** 1926 Broadway, between 64th and 65th Streets (874-0942)

YMCA (West Side)

5 West 63rd Street
between Central Park West and Broadway / 787-4400
Weekdays 6:30am–10pm, Sat 8am–8pm, Sun 9am–7pm.

Gyms
Upper West Side

quality style service value

The Edge: Complete gym facilities, plus swimming. Upper West Side health club offering two full-size pools (one for lane swimmers and one for instruction only), 120 classes per week, Universal machines/free weights, plus personal trainers at $90 for three one-hour sessions. Membership is $684 per year or $57 per month. Also a pottery studio and family and children's activities. *"Great pool, good gym."*

Downtown Rifle & Pistol Club
24 Murray Street
near Church Street / 233-5420
Daily 9am–9pm.

Hunting
Lower Manhattan

The Edge: New York's private pistol club. Membership club. You'll need a license (they'll help) for a pistol. Sells pistols and guns and provides instruction and target practice. Fees are $500 the first year, $350 thereafter. No daily passes.

Diamond Ice
473-6784
Mon–Sat 6:30am–6:30pm.

Ice
Mail/phone

quality style service value

The Edge: Buckets of ice. Reliable delivery service for buckets of ice ($14 a bucket) and non-alcoholic soft drinks and seltzer (a case of liter bottles is about $20). *"They've never let me down! 20 years of service."*

Abigail Kirsch
By appointment.

Locations
Multiple locations

quality style service value

The Edge: Attractive setting and pretty decor. Catering and party services at the Pratt Mansion (its New York townhouse), at Tappan Hill (a gray stone mansion that was formerly Mark Twain's home) in Westchester, or at its newest location, at the New York Botanical Gardens, which will have a formal ballroom (being built now) as well as the more rustic Snuff Mill in the gardens. All settings are divine. Started booking the Botanical Gardens in April 1997. The Pratt Mansion holds 150, and Tappan Hill, 300. No credit cards. *"The Tower Club dinner at the Bronx Botanical Gardens was excellent—particularly given the numbers they served."*

Locations: Bronx: New York Botanical Gardens, Southern Boulevard near Mosholu Parkway, Bronx (718-220-0300) / **Upper East Side:** 1026 5th Avenue, near 84th Street (744-4486) / **Westchester:** 81 Highland Avenue, Tarrytown (914-631-3030)

American Museum of Natural History
Central Park West
at West 79th Street / 769-5350
By appointment.

Locations
Upper West Side

quality style service value

The Edge: Theme parties. The museum's party range is wide, from elegant corporate and private functions to theme parties centered around a craft activity. Party bags can be drawn from the gift shops. Sells a wide selection of activity kits, dinosaur books, plush toys, posters, scale models, and T-shirts. Multiple areas with space to accommodate thousands. *"Great gift shop, but upstairs has declined in terms of variety and selection." "Dinosaurs, history, and jewelry!" "Dinosaur exhibit is a child's dream."*

Americas Society

680 Park Avenue
near 68th Street / 744-6650
By appointment.

Locations
Upper East Side

quality style service value

The Edge: Wonderful setting. The main salon, the Simon Bolivar Room, is decorated with crystal chandeliers and gilt-framed mirrors. Events for 40 to 300. Members only. Expensive. No credit cards.

Boathouse in Central Park

5th Avenue & 72nd Street
in Central Park / 988-0575
By appointment.

Locations
Upper East Side

quality style service value

The Edge: Gorgeous classic New York park view—too bad you have to eat there. A very institutional interior and often dreadful food. The adjacent cafe can compete with your privacy (although you can include it in your party). But what makes this place are the Central Park lake and New York skyline views and English garden pavilion setting. Not air-conditioned, so can be uncomfortable in rain or hot weather. In summer, arrange for the gondola for your quests to take out on the lake. The Pavilion seats 250, and up to 500 if you rent the cafe also. *"Nice atmosphere, but the food is not great." "Good location, great sunsets, average food."*

Burden Mansion

1 East 91st Street
near 5th Avenue / 722-4745
By appointment.

Locations
Upper East Side

quality style service value

The Edge: Majestic and special setting. Part of the Convent of the Sacred Heart. Excellent food, service, and style. Can accommodate up to 150. Expensive. No credit cards. *"Delightful spot for informal parties."*

Ellis Island Immigration Museum

344-0996
Daily 9:30am–5:15pm.

Locations
Lower Manhattan

quality style service value

The Edge: Where most of us stepped off from. For those huge parties—up to 2,000 guests. Great for nostalgia, space, and views. *"Pricey party, but great views and good displays." "Very interesting—great renovation."*

Empire State Building Observatories

350 5th Avenue
at 34th Street / 736-3100

Locations
Midtown West

By appointment.

quality style service value

The Edge: Wonderful views. In the 80th-floor Sky Lobby or the 86th-floor West Lounge—good locations for an intimate dinner for 40 or cocktails for 225. No credit cards. *"The best Manhattan view."* *"Can't beat the view, but can beat everything else!"*

Equitable Tower

787 7th Avenue
near 51st Street / 554-2833
By appointment.

Locations
Midtown West

quality style service value

The Edge: Spectacular skyline views in an elegant, but businesslike, setting. Corporate club by day, events by night. Can accommodate 400 people and four parties at the same time. Expensive. Deluxe. No credit cards. *"Particularly suited to corporate gatherings."* *"Expensive."*

Essex House Hotel Nikko New York

160 Central Park South
near 6th Avenue / 484-5144
Weekdays 9am–6pm.

Locations
Midtown West

quality style service value

The Edge: Elegant ballroom, quality cuisine and service. Less expensive than the St. Regis. Can accommodate 300 quests. Only one function at a time. Deluxe. *"Bring back the DP Champagne Brunch."* *"Expensive."*

Georgian Suite

1-A East 77th Street
between 5th and Madison Avenues / 734-1468
By appointment.

Locations
Upper East Side

quality style service value

The Edge: Intimate setting. Elegant room in a 5th Avenue apartment building. No credit cards. Deluxe.

Hotel Plaza Athenee

37 East 64th Street
near 5th Avenue / 793-9100
By appointment.

Locations
Upper East Side

quality style service value

The Edge: Elegant rooms. Three elegant private rooms plus the Louis XV–style restaurant, Le Régence, are available for dinner and cocktails. The Trianon, with six windows overlooking 64th Street, connects to a parlor that can be used for a cocktail reception. It holds for 100 for a seated dinner and 75 for cocktails. A private dining room adjacent to the Le Régence can seat an additional 30 or hold an additional 40 for cocktails. French cuisine is the specialty. *"Great breakfast showings."*

Hudson River Club

4 World Financial Center
250 Vesey Street / 786-1500

Locations
Lower Manhattan

Mon–Sat 11:30am–2:30pm and 5–10pm.

quality style service value

The Edge: Incredible views. The food is good, but the views and the interior space are outstanding. *"Incredible river views." "Expensive." "An office building makes a sterile entrance for a personal party."*

Linda Kaye's Birthdaybakers, Party Makers

195 East 76th Street
near 3rd Avenue / 288-7112
By appointment.

Locations
Upper East Side

quality style service value

The Edge: Creative children's parties. Party planning for all styles, ages, and occasions in its own party room or in your house. Rents tables and chairs for children's parties, and designs and makes costumes. Can arrange unique off- premises theme parties all over the city.

Lowell

28 East 63rd Street
between Park and Madison Avenues / 838-1400
By appointment.

Locations
Upper East Side

quality style service value

The Edge: A perfect location for small weddings. European styling, intimate feel—the Pembroke Room, which resembles an English sitting room, can accommodate 75 for cocktails or 40 for dinner. Menu prepared by the Post House Restaurant or prepare your own.

Manhattan Penthouse

45 Downing Street
near Bleecker Street / 627-8838
By appointment.

Locations
Greenwich Village

quality style service value

The Edge: Good views, moderate prices. Open 7,000-square-foot space, entire top floor with good views on all sides. Features acceptable, but not great, French, American, and international cuisine. One party at a time.

Mark

25 East 77th Street
at Madison Avenue / 744-4300
By appointment.

Locations
Upper East Side

quality style service value

The Edge: Feels like you're dining in a townhouse. The banquet rooms have the feel of dining in a townhouse. A glass-roofed greenhouse with 3,500 square feet of banquet space accommodates 150 for a seated dinner or 230 for cocktails.

New York Palace Hotel

455 Madison Avenue
between 50th and 51 Streets / 888-7000
By appointment.

Locations
Midtown East

quality style service value

The Edge: Elegant old-world decor. The Versailles Ballroom is an oval room under a 16-foot ceiling featuring murals. The ballroom accommodates up to 250 for a reception and dinner. The

Trianon Room can accommodate 200 for a reception or 140 for a seated dinner. The difficulty in the space is that the two rooms are not adjacent, which means trekking through the hotel to go between the rooms. *"Very nice since the renovation."*

Paint the Town Red

853 Broadway
at 14th Street / 677-3173
Weekdays 9am–5:30pm.

Locations
Flatiron/East Village

The Edge: Information about locations and caterers. Sources party locations—it's paid by the hotel/location when you book your party. Will also suggest caterers.

Palm House at the Brooklyn Botanic Garden

1000 Washington Avenue
near Eastern Parkway, Brooklyn / 718-398-2400
By appointment.

Locations
Brooklyn

quality style service value

The Edge: Beautiful setting in the gardens of the Brooklyn Botanical Garden. The settings capitalize on the celebrated gardens, Victorian greenhouse, and beautiful inside garden pavilions. Food is good. No credit cards. *"Interesting and beautiful place." "Can be hot." "Expensive." "Competent staff and of course, a beautiful spot."*

Peninsula New York

700 5th Avenue
at 55th Street / 247-2200
Daily 24 hours.

Locations
Midtown West

quality style service value

The Edge: Old-world charm and elegance for your parties. At this internationally known hotel you'll find old-world charm and elegance. The interior features Beaux Arts styling. The catering is first-rate. The Pen-Top Bar and Terrace provide panoramic views of the city. Facilities accommodate 200 for cocktails or 120 for dinner.

Plaza Hotel

768 5th Avenue
at 59th Street / 546-5380
Weekdays by appointment 9am–6pm, Sat 9am–3pm.

Locations
Midtown West

quality style service value

The Edge: The legendary Plaza. Can accommodate 500 (in the large Baroque Ballroom) to small numbers. 18 functions are possible at a time. A plan is underway to upgrade the hotel amenities, including its food, and restore some of the legendary rooms, including the Palm Court. *"Old New York atmosphere. Expensive." "Beautiful location and magnificent architecture." "Breakfast for the 'movers and shakers'."*

Puck Building

295 Lafayette Street
at Houston Street / 274-8900
Weekdays 9:30am–5:30pm, Sat by appointment.

Locations
SoHo/TriBeCa

quality style service value

The Edge: Attractive space. Very good food and service. The grand ballroom and the building itself are divine, albeit more architecturally striking than intimate. Events for 50 to 1,000. No credit cards. *"Beautiful outside and inside."*

Ritz Carlton
112 Central Park South
between 6th and 7th Avenues / 757-1900
By appointment.

Locations
Midtown West

The Edge: Lovely space overlooking Central Park. A spot for 10 to 150 people overlooking Central Park, with a wonderful wrap-around balcony.

St. Regis
2 East 55th Street
near 5th Avenue / 753-4500
Weekdays 9am–5pm.

Locations
Midtown East

The Edge: A top spot for weddings, priced accordingly. Completely redone. Absolutely gorgeous space, with quality food and attentive service. Accommodates up to 150 for dinner and 600 for cocktails. Very expensive. No credit cards.

Stanhope Hotel
995 5th Avenue
near 81st Street / 288-5800
By appointment.

Locations
Upper East Side

The Edge: A favorite for small, intimate, quality weddings. Perfection for small weddings— good food, service, and atmosphere. Two functions are possible at a time, with the largest accommodating 120. Moderately expensive. *"Beautiful location." "Expensive."*

24 Fifth Avenue Ballroom
24 5th Avenue
near 9th Street / 254-1300
By appointment.

Locations
Flatiron/East Village

The Edge: An elegant art deco glass-enclosed cafe ballroom, overlooking Fifth Avenue. The ballroom has a sunken dance floor which accommodates 500, plus space for an outdoor party. Holds only one party at a time, at a cost of $90+ per person. No credit cards.

21 Club
21 West 52nd Street
near 5th Avenue / 582-7200
Mon–Sat noon–10:15pm.

Locations
Midtown West

The Edge: A New York institution—very masculine and clublike. The food is very good, never great, as long as you keep it simple—grilled meats and wonderful shrimp cocktails in an elegant townhouse setting. The service is legendary. Accommodates 240 quests maximum. Seven functions are possible and are often going at the same time. Very expensive. *"Great rooms, good buzz, okay food." "Very helpful staff."*

200 Fifth Club

200 5th Avenue
near 23rd Street / 675-2080
By appointment.

Locations
Gramercy Park/Murray Hill

quality style service value

The Edge: One function at a time and reasonable prices. At the Toy Building, find a baroque-style ballroom, high ceilings, and a cocktail-hour space that can accommodate 500 people. Provides full-service party planning, customizes menus, and will hold only one party at a time. Moderate prices. *"Convenient location." "Fair prices."*

Waldorf-Astoria Hotel

301 Park Avenue
between 49th and 50th Streets / 872-4700
By appointment.

Locations
Midtown East

quality style service value

The Edge: Good food, and prices are negotiable. Still a good place to host a big event. The food is good and the hotel is attractive.

Asia Society Bookstore

725 Park Avenue
near 70th Street / 288-6400
Mon–Wed and Fri 10am–6:30pm, Thurs 10am–8:30pm,
Sat 11am–6pm, Sun noon– 5pm.

Museum shops
Upper East Side

quality style service value

The Edge: The selection! A great collection of books and moderately priced Asian crafts. Find books that cover all aspects of Asia, including art, culture, dictionaries, history, language tutorials, religion, and travel. Books and gifts for children and adults. Gift items include contemporary baskets, hand-blocked Indian scarves, Javanese shadow puppets, jewelry, note paper, stoneware, and vases. *"Good selection."*

Cathedral of St. John the Divine

1047 Amsterdam Avenue
near 112th Street / 222-7200
Daily 9am–5pm.

Museum shops
Upper West Side

quality style service value

The Edge: All gifts related somehow to the Bible, the cathedral, or St. John. Hand-painted/hand-carved reproductions galore of church ornamentation, religious folk art, and, at Christmas, tree ornaments. Wonderful Noah's Ark guests—stuffed and cuddly. *"Our treasure."*

Metropolitan Museum of Art Gift Shop

Tues–Thurs and Sun 9:30am–5:15pm, Fri–Sat 9:30am–8:45pm.

Museum shops
Multiple locations

quality style service value

The Edge: Lovely inexpensive gifts, particularly jewelry and scarves. A huge gift store, featuring books (serious art books, guide books, cooking and travel guides) and decorative objects (jewelry, accessories, tableware, and art pieces) that are reproductions of works of art in the Met.

Wonderful jewelry, both costume and real. Also children's games and books. Members' discount. *"A great solution for stylish gifts." "Good for gifts and note cards." "Great books and pretty cards." "Great gift resource."*

Locations: SoHo/TriBeCa: 113 Prince Street, between Greene and Wooster Streets (614-3000) / **Upper East Side:** 1000 5th Avenue, near 82nd Street (650-2911) / **Midtown West:** 15 West 49th Street, near Rockefeller Center (332-1360) / **Upper Upper West Side:** Fort Tryon Park near the Cloisters, at 190th Street (650-2277) / **Midtown West:** 151 West 34th Street, Macy's Herald Square (268-7266)

Museum of American Folk Art

62 West 50th Street
near 6th Avenue / 247-5611
Mon–Sat 10:30am–5:30pm.

Museum shops
Midtown West

quality style service value

The Edge: The best in handicrafts. Features one-of-a-kind handmade items from the decorative to the practical, designed by artisans and craftspeople. *"Delightful gifts and ideas in the gift shop. Good books."*

Museum of Modern Art, the MOMA Design Store

44 West 53rd Street
West of 5th Avenue / 708-9800
Mon–Wed and Sat 10am–6pm,
Thurs–Fri 10am–8pm, Sun 11am–6pm.

Museum shops
Midtown West

quality style service value

The Edge: The best for contemporary works. Located across from the museum, the shop features the best of modern designs, including furniture, jewelry, lighting, and small gift items. Sells authorized versions of furniture by many of the greats, including Breuer, Eames, Frank Lloyd Wright, Le Corbusier, Mies van der Rohe, and Noguchi. Bold area rugs complement the furniture. At the bookstore, find art books, posters, publications, and slides of the collection. *"Interesting inventory." "Nice things for the house." "Nice furniture, if you can afford it." "Wonderful shows. Garden cafeteria is often unpleasantly crowded." "Great stuff, but pricey."*

Museum of the City of New York Gift Shop

5th Avenue
near 103rd Street / 534-1672
Wed–Sat 10am–5pm, Sun 1–5pm.

Museum shops
Upper Upper East Side

quality style service value

The Edge: Books, guides, maps, and novels about the city. For children, tiny inexpensive toys, and for adults, prints, photographs, and guides.

National Museum of the American Indian

Old U.S. Custom House - Bowling Green
near Whitehall Street / 825-6700
Thurs 10am–8pm, Fri–Wed 10am–4:45pm.

Museum shops
Lower Manhattan

quality style service value

The Edge: One-of-a-kind Native North and South American crafts. Features traditional Native American crafts, including rugs, baskets, pottery, and jewelry (silver and turquoise), as well as books for adults and children.

New York Public Library Shop

Museum shops
Midtown West

5th Avenue
between 40th and 42nd Street / 930-0678
Tues–Wed 11am–6pm, Thurs-Sat 11am–6pm.

quality style service value

The Edge: Patience and Fortitude, the lions that guard the library entrance. Gifts evoking yesteryear are wonderful as house gifts. Find stationery items from note cards to calendars to address books. The styling is classic. For children, find Winnie the Pooh diaries, alphabet books, illustrated children's classic books, games, and more. *"For cool gifts."*

Pierpont Morgan Library

Museum shops
Gramercy Park/Murray Hill

29 East 36th Street
near Park Avenue / 685-0008
Tues–Fri 10:30am–4:45pm, Sat 10:30am–5:45pm,
Sun noon–5:45pm.

quality style service value

The Edge: Books and cards that relate to the library's collection. Includes facsimile editions of manuscripts and scores from the collection. Wonderful gift items, including books, reproductions of drawings and botanical prints, and more that relate to the collection. *"Nice ambiance."*

South Street Seaport Museum Shop

Museum shops
Lower Manhattan

207 Front Street
near South Street / 480-4951
Daily 10am–6pm.

quality style service value

The Edge: Caters to tourists, offering books and toys. Find navigational maps of the New York area waters, maritime books (including the Patrick O'Brian series), tourist T-shirts, and children's toys.

Studio Museum in Harlem

Museum shops
Upper Upper West Side

144 West 125th Street
near Adam Clayton Powell Boulevard / 864-0014
Wed–Fri 10am–4:45pm, Sat–Sun 1–5:45pm.

The Edge: The source for African items. Features handicrafts and art from Africa and black America. An ever-changing assortment of books, carvings, fabrics, pottery, traditional to contemporary jewelry, toys, and weavings.

Ukrainian Museum

Museum shops
Flatiron/East Village

203 2nd Avenue
near 12th Street / 228-0110
Wed–Sun 1–5pm.

The Edge: Ukrainian Easter eggs plus supplies to make Easter eggs. Features contemporary and traditional Ukrainian crafts, including Easter eggs, elaborate embroidered blouses, table linens, and more. No credit cards.

United Nations Gift Shop

Museum shops
Midtown East

United Nations Headquarters

1st Avenue and 46th Street / 963-7700
Daily 9am–5pm.

The Edge: Handicrafts from around the world on the lower level of the U.N. headquarters.
Hundreds of inexpensive items, including hand-carved animals, pin cushions, coin pursues, puzzles,
and a large selection of jewelry in all price ranges.

Whitney Museum's Store Next Door

943 Madison Avenue
near 75th Street / 606-0200
Tues–Wed and Fri–Sun 11am–6pm, Thurs 11am–8pm.

Museum shops
Upper East Side

The Edge: American designs related to the current exhibits. Furniture and accessories for the
home and the individual created by top American talent. No delivery. *"Unique gift items." "Love it!
Not cheap, but wonderful things."*

Carmine Street Guitar Shop

42 Carmine Street
near Bedford Street / 691-8400
Mon–Sat 11am–7pm.

Musical instruments
Greenwich Village

The Edge: Custom-made guitars. For amateurs and professionals, the source for both new and
used electric and acoustic guitars. Priced from $250 to $1,250. Stocks Gibson, Rickenbacker, Jerry
Jones, and Washburn, as well as custom guitars.

Detrich Pianos

211 West 58th Street
between Broadway and 7th Avenue / 245-1234
Weekdays 10am–6pm, Sat 10am–4pm.

Musical instruments
Midtown West

The Edge: One of the few city places that can refinish and rebuild pianos. Rents, tunes, and
repairs antique and new pianos. Carries a stock of contemporary music boxes in the shape of pianos
made in porcelain, metal, and plastic that play classical or pop tunes. *"I used them for antique piano
restoration."*

Manny's (Musical Instruments)

156 West 48th Street
between 6th and 7th Avenues / 819-0576
Mon–Wed and Fri–Sat 10am–6pm, Thurs 10am–7pm.

Musical instruments
Midtown West

The Edge: Wide range of musical instruments. Can refer you to teachers and classes.

Piano Store

158 Ludlow Street
near Stanton Street / 674-5555
Weekdays 10am–6pm, Sat 10am–4pm.

Musical instruments
Lower East Side/Chinatown

The Edge: Large stock of antique and used pianos. Just pianos, from the plain to the "grand."

Pro Piano
Musical instruments
Greenwich Village

85 Jane Street
near West 12th Street / 206-8794
Weekdays 9am–5:30pm, Sat 10am–4pm.

The Edge: Large selection of pianos to rent. All major brands of pianos. Priced from $2,000 to $90,000. Will refer you to teachers and classes.

Harry Hanson
Personal trainers
SoHo/TriBeCa

63 Greene Street
near Spring Street / 431-7682
Weekdays 6am–9pm, Sat–Sun 8am–2pm.

45	45	45	45
quality	style	service	value

The Edge: Top trainers. One-on-one focus. 3,000 square feet of work space. Celebrity clients have included top models like Naomi Cambell and Linda Evangelista and, reportedly, John F. Kennedy Jr. There are 11 trainers on staff who always work one-on-one with you. The focus is on low-impact aerobics. Cost is $45 per hour, or $2,700 for 60 sessions. Body-fat test. Nutritional information. Deluxe. *"Where the models sweat!"*

Joseph D. Tonti
Personal trainers
Upper West Side

280 Riverside Drive
near 100th Street / 662-4679
By appointment.

The Edge: Personal trainer. Bodybuilding and training charges on a sliding scale. No credit cards. *"Gets you off your duff!"*

Larry Tan
Personal trainers
Midtown East

225 East 57th Street
near 3rd Avenue / 753-7280
By appointment.

The Edge: A kung fu master. Tan has evolved a system of stress reduction through individually designed art forms. Private or group lessons. No credit cards. *"A great learning experience."*

Plus One Fitness Clinic
Personal trainers
Multiple locations

Weekdays 6am–9pm.

The Edge: Provides suitable personal trainers. One-on-one training for $65 an hour.

Locations: Lower Manhattan: 200 Liberty Street, near South Street (945-2525) / **Midtown East:** 301 Park Avenue, the Waldorf-Astoria, near 49th Street (355-3000) / **SoHo/TriBeCa:** 106 Crosby Street, near Prince Street (334-1116)

Radu's Physical Culture Studio
Personal trainers
Midtown West

24 West 57th Street, 2nd Floor
between 5th and 6th Avenues / 581-1995
Mon, Wed, and Fri 7am–7pm; Tues and Thurs 8am–7pm;

Sat–Sun noon–10pm.

quality style service value

The Edge: Strenuous physical training. Physical trainer to Calvin Klein and Cindy Crawford. Very strenuous. $65 per hour with staff member and $100 with Radu. Deluxe. *"The best in town."*

Beth Green Studio

60 Riverside Drive
580-1928
By appointment.

Photographs & video
Mail/phone

quality style service value

The Edge: Recommended photographer. Beth Green, a former editor of *Newsweek,* focuses on photographing people in their many roles. She specializes in photographing women and backlights a woman's hair for a more glamorous look. Also specializes in photographing corporate executives. Stylist on staff. No credit cards. *"Wonderful for those special occasion photos!"*

Don Pollard Photography

400 Central Park West, #12V
749-3228
By appointment.

Photographs & video
Mail/phone

The Edge: Recommended photographer. Don Pollard focuses on portraits, both personal and large family groups and corporate special events. He has done work for the Museum of Modern Art, the Metropolitan Museum of Art, NYU, and the State of New York. He even took a family portrait for Mario Cuomo when he was Governor. *"Will come to your home or office for your portrait—very convenient!"*

Lyn Hughes Photography

114 West 27th Street, Apt. 6N
between 6th and 7th Avenues / 645-8417
By appointment.

Photographs & video
Mail/phone

The Edge: Good photographer. For weddings and special occasions. No credit cards.

Mary Hilliard

120 East 85th Street
between Park and Lexington Avenues / 879-7839
By appointment.

Photographs & video
Mail/phone

The Edge: Excellent photographer. Specializes in shooting weddings, charity galas, and opening-night events.

Rob Fraser Photography

211 Thompson Street
near Bleecker Street / 941-0433
By appointment.

Photographs & video
SoHo/TriBeCa

quality style service value

The Edge: He must be great—he was used by the editor of *Brides* magazine for her wedding. Excellent photographer who does weddings, society events, and executive portraits. Shot the University of Pennsylvania board of directors and other major corporate executives. No credit cards.

"Black and white and color—he does it all well. Great candid photography." "The pictures couldn't have looked better, and he was easy to work with."

Party Rentals

22 East 72nd Street
between 5th and Madison Avenues / 594-8510
By appointment.

Rentals
Upper East Side

quality style service value

The Edge: Used by Glorious Foods. First-rate rentals and excellent service. Exceptional china, linens, and crystal available. $300 minimum. No delivery.

Posh Party / Broadway Party Rental

888 10th Avenue
269-2666
Weekdays 7am–5pm.

Rentals
Mail/phone

The Edge: Quality party necessities. A large assortment, including tableware, chairs, and linens.

Props for Today

330 West 34th Street
between 8th and 9th Avenues / 244-9600
Appointments are recommended for the best service.

Rentals
Midtown West

The Edge: A large inventory of party rental items. Furniture, accessories, and table settings for great theme parties. $100 minimum.

Ruth Fischl

156 West 28th Street
between 6th and 7th Avenues / 929-3586
Weekdays 8am–5pm.

Rentals
Midtown West

The Edge: If you've been at top social events, you've seen her stuff. The place to rent silver ice buckets, silver charger plates, candelabras, vases, linens, and the like—everything you need for parties. It's not the stuff you'd see at ordinary rental places: for example, the linens include damask or metallic tapestry linens. Fischl helps set the stage at such events as the post–Grammy Award ball, MOMA events, and the like.

Something Different

107-111 Penn Avenue
Patterson / 201-742-1779
Weekdays 9am–5pm.

Rentals
New Jersey

50 50 50 50

quality style service value

The Edge: Wonderful party rentals. Quality tablecloths in a good selection of colors and patterns. Ballroom chairs in assorted colors. Attractive service plates (emerald-green glass, cobalt-blue glass, crystal), 30-inch candelabra, and whatever else you need. No minimum order required.

Claremont Riding Academy

175 West 89th Street
near Amsterdam Avenue / 724-5100
Weekdays 6:30am–10pm, Sat–Sun 6:30am–5pm.

Riding
Upper West Side

43	43	43	43

quality style service value

The Edge: Riding in Central Park. In business since 1892. Provides riding in Central Park for experienced riders or group and private classes in the stable. Teaches all skill levels and offers equestrian programs. *"A 'bit of the barn' in New York City." "The half-day summer program was terrific for my preteen horse-mad daughter."*

Manhattan Sailing School

393 South End Avenue
786-0400
In season, weekday evenings until sunset, Sat–Sun during daylight.

Sailing
Lower Manhattan

The Edge: Sailing lessons in New York Harbor. Owns and maintains a fleet of J-24s docked at the North Cove Yacht Harbor in Battery Park City. Offers classes in basic sailing, coastal cruising, racing, and bare-boat chartering. Permission to charter sailboats from the school is granted after students reach the Skipper's Club level. After students learn the fundamentals, there are opportunities to participate in harbor events like competing on teams in the International Yacht Club Challenge. The sailing school gives lessons at $395 for groups of three or four. Courses are given on weekend days and weekday nights on a J-24.

Barnard Bartending

854-4650
By appointment.

Service help
Mail/phone

40	40	45	50

quality style service value

The Edge: Always reliable, and the nicest students show up. This women's college can provide bartenders, waitresses, and just general help. Well trained, as they're required to take a bartending course. Inexpensive, at $13 per hour the fee is $2 per hour less than Columbia Bartending! No credit cards.

Columbia Bartending Agency

854-4537
By appointment.

Service help
Mail/phone

40	40	45	45

quality style service value

The Edge: Always reliable, and the nicest students show up. Can provide bartenders, waiters, waitresses, and just general help. Well trained, as they're required to take a bartending course. Inexpensive at $15 per hour. No credit cards.

Rockefeller Center Ice Skating Rink

601 5th Avenue
between 49th and 50th Streets / 757-5730
Weekdays 9am–10pm, Sat 8:30am–midnight,
Sun 8:30am–10pm. Closed spring–fall.

Skating
Midtown West

quality style service value

The Edge: Skating among the skyscrapers. Everyone's favorite rink, though small. Admission is $6 to $8.50, depending on the time of week and the skater's age; skate rental is $4 and lessons are $23 per half hour. Can arrange birthday parties. "*A lot of fun. Beautiful but very crowded.*" "*Try it for your casual evening function. Nothing else like it.*"

Sky Rink

Chelsea Pier
Pier 61 / 336-6100
Session schedule varies depending on season.

Skating
Chelsea

quality style service value

The Edge: One of the largest indoor ice rinks. Admission per session: $9 for adults and $7 for children under 12. Lessons are $25 per half hour. $4 for skate rentals. No credit cards. "*Good family fun.*"

Wollman Skating Rink

Central Park
East 59th Street and 5th Avenue / 396-1010
Mon–Thurs 10am–6pm, Fri 10am–10pm, Sat–Sun 11am–6pm.

Skating
Upper East Side

quality style service value

The Edge: New York's largest rink. Offers outdoor ice skating in the winter, from October through March, and roller skating during the spring and summer. Telephone reservations for lessons only. Individual lessons are $56 per hour or $28 for a half hour; group lessons are $150 for 13 weeks. Admission is $6 for adults and $3 for children under 12 years. Rentals are $3 for ice skates and $6 for in-line roller skates. A credit card or $100 cash or a valid passport serves as a refundable deposit for roller skate rentals. The skate shop sells apparel, skates, and T-shirts. A small cafe offers hot chocolate, pizza, and the like.

East River Tennis Club

44-02 Vernon Blvd.
Long Island City / 718-784-0600
Daily 7:30am–9pm.

Tennis
Queens

quality style service value

The Edge: Tennis courts. 20 Hard-Tru tennis courts, match-up games, and a bus service from the city ($6 each way, departing every hour on the half hour).

Midtown Tennis Club

341 8th Avenue
near 27th Street / 989-8572
Weekdays 7am–10pm, Sat–Sun 8am–8pm.

Tennis
Midtown West

The Edge: Great courts, midtown location. Eight Har-Tru courts where group and private lessons are available. You must reserve to play, with fees from $35 to $50 an hour or $700 to $1,300 per 20-week session, depending on the hour. Offers an advanced league on Wednesday from 8 to 10:30pm (at $45 per hour), Friday-night parties, the "stroke of the week," and adult camp.

New York Racquet & Tennis Club

370 Park Avenue
near 52nd Street / 753-9700
Weekdays 7am–11pm, Sat–Sun 10:30am–6pm.

Tennis
Midtown East

The Edge: Where the elite meet to smash. A private club for which a new member must be proposed and seconded by two members. Primarily a social club with racquetball and court tennis. Also fitness facilities. No credit cards. Deluxe.

River Club

447 East 52nd Street
near 1st Avenue / 751-0100
Daily 24 hours.

Tennis
Midtown East

47	40	43	37
quality	style	service	value

The Edge: The club where old New York money "hangs." Beautiful private club with excellent facilities. Must be sponsored for membership and it can be difficult to join. A social club (1,000 members) with health facilities, including swimming and tennis. No credit cards. Deluxe.

Sylvia and Danny Kaye Playhouse

695 Park Avenue
69th Street near Hunter College / 772-5207
Evening and weekend performances.
Box office open Tues–Sat noon–6pm, Sun noon– 3pm,
and one hour before each performance.

Theater
Upper East Side

45	33	37	40
quality	style	service	value

The Edge: Moderately priced entertainment in a jewel of a theater. $20 tickets (range from $10 to $45), members' prices about $15, and student tickets at $10. The membership arrangement is simple—just buy tickets to three performances of your choice and you're a member. The playhouse features music, dance, and theater, plus excellent children's productions and performers, including the Paper Bag Players. *"Wonderful dance performances here."*

TKTS

Matinee tickets daily 10am–2pm;
matinee and evening tickets, daily 5–8pm.

Theater
Multiple locations

37	30	34	43
quality	style	service	value

The Edge: Discount tickets to much of what's currently on Broadway. What a deal—tickets at 35% to 50% off box office prices! Tickets are available on the day of the performance (matinee and evening, uptown) or the evening before (matinees, downtown). *"Great on Fridays in the summer"*

Locations: Lower Manhattan: 2 World Trade Center, mezzanine level, near Vesey Street /
Midtown West: Broadway, at 47th Street

Theatre Development Fund

Theater
Midtown West

1501 Broadway, Suite 2110
near 44th Street / 221-0013
Weekdays 10am–6pm.

quality style service value

The Edge: Reduced-price tickets by mail for students, teachers, and retirees. Offers multiple services for theater lovers. Runs TKTS, two discount ticket centers where tickets are sold at 25% to 50% off box office prices (see above). Students, teachers, and retired people can receive an application to join TDF by sending in a self-addressed stamped envelope. TDF offers reduced-price tickets to a host of new Broadway and Off Broadway plays. No credit cards. *"Terrific discount theater tickets for teachers and students."*

Davidoff of Geneva

Tobacco
Midtown East

535 Madison Avenue
near 54th Street / 751-9060
Mon–Wed and Fri 9:30am–6:30pm,
Thurs 10am–7:30pm, Sat 10am–6pm.

quality style service value

The Edge: Stocks fine tobacco products, pipes, and smoking accessories. Hand-rolled cigars from Honduras, humidors in silver and/or mahogany, porcelain tobacco jars, tobacco pouches of lamb nappa, and attaché cases with removable cigar humidors. *"If you want cigars, this is the place."*

J.R. Tobacco

Tobacco
Lower Manhattan

219 Broadway
near Vesey Street / 233-6620
Weekdays 7:45am–5pm.

quality style service value

The Edge: Perfume and cigars at 20% to 50% off retail. Huge selection, thousands of cigar brands and all the top fragrances discounted. No price quotes given over the phone, but claim to offer a discount of 20% and more. Call toll free 800-572-4427 for mail order and catalog.

Nat Sherman

Tobacco
Midtown West

500 5th Avenue
at 42nd Street / 764-5000
Weekdays 9am–7pm, Sat 10am–5:30pm, Sun 11am–5pm.

quality style service value

The Edge: An old-line/old-time smoke shop. Specializes in custom-blended cigarettes and pipe tobaccos, pipes and pipe accessories, and of course, the current craze—cigars. Also expect to find humidors. *"Great cigars!" "Expensive." "Not what it used to be."*

A Bear's Place

Toys, games & hobbies
Upper East Side

789 Lexington Avenue
near 61st Street / 826-6465
Weekdays 9am–7pm, Sat 10am–6pm, Sun 10am–5pm.

quality style service value

The Edge: Upscale children's furniture and toys. Unique wood and upholstered furniture. Toys include bicycles, trucks, and specialty dolls.

Allcraft Tool and Supply Company

Toys, games & hobbies
Midtown West

45 West 46th Street, 3rd Floor
near 6th Avenue / 840-1860
Mon–Wed and Fri 9:30am–5pm, Thurs 10am–6pm.

The Edge: Everything you need to make fine jewelry. Features a complete line of tools and supplies for jewelry making, including silver and metal smithing, wax casting, and more. The best source in the city for enameling supplies. Catalog available by calling 718-789-2800.

America's Hobby Center

Toys, games & hobbies
Chelsea

146 West 22nd Street
near 7th Avenue / 675-8922
Weekdays 9am–5:30pm, Sat 9am–3:30pm.

The Edge: The source for model builders. You name the transport, they have the kit and supplies.

B. Shackman

Toys, games & hobbies
Flatiron/East Village

85 5th Avenue
at 16th Street / 989-5162
Weekdays 9am–5pm, Sat 10am–4pm, Sun noon–6pm.

quality style service value

The Edge: Everything for the dollhouse. For dollhouse furnishings and reproductions of vintage windup toys. *"My 10-year-old's favorite place."*

Back Pages Antiques

Toys, games & hobbies
SoHo/TriBeCa

125 Greene Street
between Prince and Houston Streets / 460-5998
Mon–Sat 9am–6pm, Sun noon–6pm.

The Edge: Arcade items, gambling devices, and jukeboxes. No credit cards.

Bear Hugs & Baby Dolls

Toys, games & hobbies
Upper East Side

311 East 81st Street
between 1st and 2nd Avenues / 717-1514
Tues–Wed and Fri–Sat 10am–6pm, Thurs 11am–7pm, Sun noon–5pm (closed Sun July–Aug).

The Edge: Bears for all occasions. A great source for Muffy Vander Bear, its accessories, and wonderful cuddly animals.

Big City Kite Company

Toys, games & hobbies
Upper East Side

1210 Lexington Avenue
near 81st Street / 472-2623
Mon–Wed and Fri 11am–6:30pm, Thurs 11am–7:30pm, Sat 10am–6pm, Sun noon– 5pm.

The Edge: Performance stunt kites. Features kites made in a range of fabrics (from paper to silk), from here and around the world, as well as other flying toys. Also a huge dart selection. Kite repair service available.

Ceramic Supply of New York & New Jersey

Toys, games & hobbies
New Jersey

7 Route 46 West
Lodi / 800-723-7264
Mon–Wed and Fri 9am–5pm, Thurs 9am–9pm.

The Edge: The source for potters. For potters—supplies, equipment, and lessons, all in one place.

Compleat Strategist

Mon–Wed and Fri–Sat 10:30am–6pm, Thurs 10:30am–9pm.

Toys, games & hobbies
Multiple locations

quality style service value

The Edge: Large selection of strategy games. Specializes in military games covering just about every battle and every period in military history. Also chess and backgammon sets, Risk, and Monopoly. No delivery. *"Very pricey." "Great for browsing."*

Locations: Gramercy Park/Murray Hill: 11 East 33rd Street, between 5th and Madison Avenues (685-3880) / **Midtown West:** 630 5th Avenue, between 50th and 51st Streets (265-7449) / 320 West 57th Street, between 8th and 9th Avenues (582-1272)

Dollhouse Antics

Toys, games & hobbies
Upper East Side

1343 Madison Avenue
near 94th Street / 876-2288
Weekdays 11am–5:30pm, Sat 11am–5pm;
also Sun in Dec before Christmas (call for hours).

quality style service value

The Edge: Dollhouse registry. For children and collectors, the biggest miniatures store in the city, featuring furniture and dollhouses, with carpenters on the premises to restore pieces. Large range of miniatures, from top of the line to lower end, with styles from Colonial to Victorian to contemporary. Some pieces are complete with electricity. Gift registry service.

Enchanted Forest

Toys, games & hobbies
SoHo/TriBeCa

85 Mercer Street
between Spring and Broome Streets / 925-6677
Mon–Sat 11am–7pm, Sun noon–6pm.

The Edge: Like coming into a forest. A magical spot for children focusing on animal themes. Features unique lifelike animals, kaleidoscopes, wooden musical instruments, and books. What makes it more fun for children is passing through trees, bridges, and waterfalls to shop. The toll-free number is 800-456-4449.

Erica Wilson

Toys, games & hobbies
Upper East Side

717 Madison Avenue
near 63rd Street / 832-7290
Mon–Wed and Fri–Sat 10am–6pm, Thurs 10am–7pm.

quality style service value

The Edge: The best selection of needlepoint patterns. Known by all for her top-quality (and top-priced) needlework patterns and wools. Also patterns for hand-knit sweaters. Blocking and mounting services. *"Expensive."*

FAO Schwarz

Toys, games & hobbies
Midtown East

5th Avenue
between 58th and 59th Streets / 644-9400
Mon–Wed 10am–6pm, Thurs–Sat 10am–7pm, Sun 11am–6pm.

44	46	35	31
quality	style	service	value

The Edge: A five-star city attraction. An unbelievable range of toys, including the Barbie Boutique, electric trains, life-size stuffed animals, and battery-operated toys, plus all the latest rages. No wonder FAO is the place all out-of-towners and grandparents must visit. *"Best toy store in the world. It's like a museum." "Can't get the kids to leave!" "Love to visit, but I still buy from Toys 'R' Us, which has better prices."*

Flosso-Hornmann Magic Company

Toys, games & hobbies
Midtown West

45 West 34th Street, Room 607
between 5th and 6th Avenues / 279-6079
Weekdays 10am–5pm, Sat 10am–4pm.

The Edge: You name the trick, this shop has it. The city's oldest magic shop, founded in 1869. You'll find magic acts, books, manuals, historical treatises, and equipment.

Game Show

Toys, games & hobbies
Multiple locations

Mon–Wed and Fri–Sat noon–7pm,
Thurs noon–8pm, Sun noon–5pm.

The Edge: Adult toys. An extensive selection of games and puzzles arranged by category from real estate to politics.

Locations: Chelsea: 474 Avenue of the Americas, near 12th Street (633-6328) / **Upper East Side:** 1240 Lexington Avenue, between 83rd and 84th Streets (472-8011)

Gampel Supply

Toys, games & hobbies
Midtown West

11 West 37th Street
near 5th Avenue / 398-9222
Weekdays 9am–5pm.

The Edge: Craft jewelry and tools. Everything (tools included) to make fine and costume jewelry and related crafts. Beads and pearls sold below retail price. Wide range of sizes, colors, and shapes.

Jan's Hobby Shop

Toys, games & hobbies
Upper East Side

1557 York Avenue
between 82nd and 83rd Streets / 861-5075
Mon–Sat 10am–7pm, Sun noon–5pm.

The Edge: Big selection of model kits. Hobby shop features kits for remote-controlled airplanes, cars, ships, and tanks. Also makes models and showcases for models.

Jimson's

Toys, games & hobbies
Flatiron/East Village

28 East 18th Street

near Broadway / 477-3386
Weekdays 9:30am–5:30pm, Sat 10am–3pm.

The Edge: Wholesale novelty shop selling gags and tricks.

Leekan Designs, Inc.
93 Mercer Street
near Spring Street / 226-7226
Sun–Fri noon—6pm, Sat 11am–7pm.

Toys, games & hobbies
SoHo/TriBeCa

The Edge: Hundreds of types of antique and new beads. Unique bead collection, including bone, brass, copper, crystal, glass, horn, quartz, semiprecious stones, and silver.

Little Rickie
49½ 1st Avenue
near 3rd Street / 505-6467
Mon–Sat 11am–8pm, Sun noon–7pm.

Toys, games & hobbies
Flatiron/East Village

quality style service value

The Edge: Unique pop culture nostalgia. Find 1950s memorabilia, including Elvis items and classic toys.

Marion & Company
147 West 26th Street
near 6th Avenue / 727-8900
Weekdays 8am–5:30pm, Sat 10am–4pm.

Toys, games & hobbies
Midtown West

The Edge: Gambling equipment and games. Find casino equipment such as tables, chairs, and slot machines, as well as games such as chess, backgammon, dominoes, and cards.

Mary Arnold Toys
962 Lexington Avenue
near 70th Street / 744-8510
Weekdays 9am–6pm, Sat 10am–5pm.

Toys, games & hobbies
Upper East Side

quality style service value

The Edge: An old-fashioned, personable neighborhood toy store with all the latest toys. A neighborhood treasure for more than 60 years. Sells the full range of hot new and classic toys, with a good selection of dolls and trucks. You can call and have gifts sent. The staff gives great advice on what's right for all ages. Great wrapping papers. *"Good neighborhood store and value. Courteous."*

Myron Toback
25 West 47th Street
between 5th and 6th Avenues / 398-8300
Weekdays 8am–4pm. Closed July 1–14 and Dec 25–Jan 1.

Toys, games & hobbies
Midtown West

quality style service value

The Edge: Large selections of jewelry tools and materials. Sells bangles and gold, gold-filled, and silver chains by the yard, as well as bindings, plate wire, tools, and supplies. Make it yourself.

Penny Whistle Toys
Mon–Sat 10am–7pm, Sun 11am–5pm.

Toys, games & hobbies
Multiple locations

The Edge: Upscale store with unique children's toys, especially craft kits. Large selection of good children's gifts, including craft kits, jigsaw puzzles, toy cars, trucks, and dolls.

Locations: Upper East Side: 1283 Madison Avenue, near 91st Street (369-3868) / **Upper West Side:** 448 Columbus Avenue, near 81st Street (873-9090)

Red Caboose

23 West 45th Street
between 5th and 6th Avenues / 575-0155
Weekdays 10:45am–7pm, Sat 10:45am–5pm.

Toys, games & hobbies
Midtown West

The Edge: New and old model railroads. New and antique trains, including vintage Lionel and American Flyer models, and remote-controlled cars and boats. Also construction models. Great selection and range.

Star Magic Space Age Gifts

Mon–Sat 10am–10pm, Sun 11am–9pm.

Toys, games & hobbies
Multiple locations

32 quality | 36 style | 33 service | 34 value

The Edge: The stars steal the show here. Features maps of the stars and constellations, and telescopes in all sizes. Also books, games, and toys—all related to the stars. *"Cluttered fun place with inexpensive doodads, weird small toys, masks (impossible to describe) for adults and kids. Great party items and stocking stuffers."*

Locations: Flatiron/East Village: 745 Broadway, near 8th Street (228-7770) / **Upper East Side:** 1256 Lexington Avenue, near 85th Street (988-0300) / **Upper West Side:** 275 Amsterdam Avenue, near 73rd Street (769-2020)

Toys "R" Us

Mon, Thurs and Fri 9am–9pm, Tues–Wed and Sat 9am–8pm.

Toys, games & hobbies
Multiple locations

42 quality | 25 style | 22 service | 38 value

The Edge: Likely to be the lowest prices in town for toys. The country's largest toy chain finally made it to New York. All the latest toys, bikes, wagons, cars, and crafts. Don't expect help and, at Christmas, it's every parent on their own. No delivery. Discounter. *"Best buy." "I'm a regular and have been successful here. The prices are good!"*

Locations: Flatiron/East Village: 2430 Union Square East, between 15th and 16th Streets (674-8697) / **Midtown West:** 1293 Broadway, near 34th Street (594-8697)

Village Chess Shop

230 Thompson Street
near West 3rd Street / 475-8130
Daily noon–midnight.

Toys, games & hobbies
SoHo/TriBeCa

The Edge: Competitive chess games and everything for the chess aficionado. Come to play for about $2 per hour or to buy basic to special chess sets. Find unusual chess sets (in brass, ebony, onyx, pewter, and more), as well as backgammon and cribbage sets.

West Side Kids

Toys, games & hobbies
Upper West Side

498 Amsterdam Avenue
near 84th Street / 496-7282
Mon–Sat 10am–7pm, Sun noon–6pm.

The Edge: Quality books and educational toys for young children. Books and educational toys, along with videos, puppet theaters, arts and crafts supplies, and the standard toys and party favors. Find inexpensive stocking-stuffer toys at the front of the store.

Woolgathering

Toys, games & hobbies
Upper East Side

318 East 84th Street
between 1st and 2nd Avenues / 734-4747
Tues–Fri 10:30am–6pm, Sat 10:30am–5pm.

quality style service value

The Edge: Everything for the knitter. A small shop with a good variety of different types of yarns. Instructions given. Has samples of handmade things to show different designs and styles. Offers workshops and instruction. Custom sweaters available for sale or design to order. *"Good neighborhood knittery."*

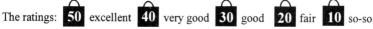

The ratings: **50** excellent **40** very good **30** good **20** fair **10** so-so

Personal & repair services

Air Care

Air conditioning
Queens

5830 Maspeth
Maspeth / 718-894-8313
Weekdays 9am–5pm.

The Edge: Keeps you cool with clean air conditioners. Air conditioners need to be cleaned at times to ensure proper circulation of air. Bring your air conditioner in for a lower price, or have it picked up, serviced, and returned—in less than a week. Will also store air conditioners for the winter. No credit cards.

Autobahn Service Center

Car
Upper East Side

421 East 91st Street
near 1st Avenue / 289-5800
Weekdays 6:30am–6pm.

40	40	40	40
quality	style	service	value

The Edge: Honest car repairs. Great for foreign cars. No delivery. *"Good car repairs—reliable."*

Asian Art Gallery

China, crystal & silver
Midtown East

136 East 57th Street, 7th Floor
near Lexington Avenue / 688-7243
Weekdays 9:30am–5pm or by appointment.

The Edge: Best for restorations of lacquer and ceramic. Also offers a full range of high-end antique furniture. Discounts offered to dealers and decorators. No credit cards.

Center Art Studio

China, crystal & silver
Midtown West

250 West 54th Street, Room 901
between Broadway and 8th Avenue / 247-3550
By appointment.

The Edge: Quality repairs of china and glass. If an object is not too small and is in fewer than 50 pieces, it can be reassembled. About half the company's repairs are on ceramics and porcelains. Color and patterns can be matched. Also works with precious stones. Will pack and crate items for shipment.

Glass Restorations

1597 York Avenue
between 84th and 85th Streets / 517-3287
Weekdays 9:30am–5pm.

China, crystal & silver
Upper East Side

quality style service value

The Edge: Excellent repairs on all types of glass. Mr. Jochec, the owner, trained in Czechoslovakia, has fine craft skills. Minimum of two weeks to restore a glass piece. No credit cards.

Hess Restorations

200 Park Avenue South
near 17th Street / 260-2255
Weekdays 10am–4pm (by appointment after 4pm).

China, crystal & silver
Flatiron/East Village

quality style service value

The Edge: The restorer recommended by Tiffany and the Metropolitan Museum of Art
Restores china, crystal, ivory, lacquer, porcelain, silver, tortoise shell, sculptures, and objets d'art. Replaces blue glass liners for antique silver salt dishes and ice buckets. Accepts shipments of items to be repaired. Will send an estimate. No credit cards.

Sano Studio

767 Lexington Avenue
near 60th Street / 759-6131
Weekdays 10am–5pm, Sat–Sun by appointment.

China, crystal & silver
Upper East Side

quality style service value

The Edge: Repairs antique porcelain. 18 years in the business of restoring ceramic and porcelain pieces. Minimum repair $50.

Vic Rothman for Stained Glass

161 Varick Street
at Van Dam / 255-2551
By appointment.

China, crystal & silver
Mail/phone

The Edge: Noted expert for stained-glass repair. He has 20+ years of experience. He worked on St. Paul's Chapel at Columbia University and the Lalique windows at Henri Bendel. Does residential projects also. No credit cards.

Best Domestic

310 Madison Avenue, Suite 1517
near 42nd Street / 685-0351
Weekdays 9am–5pm.

Cleaning
Midtown East

The Edge: Cleaning agency with very reasonable fees. Cleaning services—maids and butlers provided on short notice, and also good help who can prepare and/or serve and clean up after meals. Rates are $10 an hour (four-hour minimum), plus a $25 fee paid by the customer to the agency. Prices higher during holidays.

Crosstown Shade and Glass

Cleaning
Upper West Side

200 West 86th Street
between Amsterdam and Broadway / 787-8040
Tues and Thurs 9am–7pm, Wed and Fri 9am–5pm, Sat 9am–4pm.

The Edge: Washes and repairs venetian blinds.

NY Little Elves

Cleaning
Mail/phone

271E 10th Avenue, Suite 21A
673-5507
Mon–Sat 8am–6pm.

The Edge: Teams of maids. Weekly and biweekly maid service provided. Maid service is $19.50 per hour (plus tax), with a four-hour minimum. To get it done fast, teams of people can be sent. Also does post-renovation cleaning.

Tiecrafters

Cleaning
Midtown West

252 West 29th Street
between 6th and 7th Avenues / 629-5800
Weekdays 9am–5pm.

47	43	43	43
quality	style	service	value

The Edge: Restores soiled and spotted ties. Restores and repairs neckwear. Will dye, widen, straighten, and/or clean ties.

New York Closet Company

Closet design
Upper East Side

1458 3rd Avenue
near 83rd Street / 439-9500
Mon–Sat 11am–6pm.

45	45	45	45
quality	style	service	value

The Edge: Organize your closet with melamine and wire systems. Functional melamine and wire closet systems tailored to maximize your closet space. Partitions cost $8 to $10 per foot, with a $250 minimum.

Aero Studios

Decorators
SoHo/TriBeCa

132 Spring Street
near Greene Street / 966-1500
Weekdays 11am–6pm.

47	50	47	20
quality	style	service	value

The Edge: Fashionable design firm. Design firm in SoHo. 60% of its work is residential and 40% commercial. Clients have included Ralph and Ricky Lauren, the James Danziger Gallery, and the Donna Karan Company. Also has a design store in SoHo with an impressive array of eclectic antiques and reproductions, and many stocking stuffers. Vintage photographs.

Dial-A-Decorator

Decorators
Mail/phone

54 Riverside Drive
496-7076
By appointment.

The Edge: Call in your decorating questions. Barbara Landsman takes your decorating questions over the phone. Will provide a scaled floor plan to your measurements. Send a video or a letter and photographs and a check. Call for a telephone appointment and she does the rest! Charges $125 for two rooms (or three rooms if it's a living room, dining room, and one other room). No time limit to your call. *"So convenient!"*

Drake Design

140 East 56th Street
between 3rd and Lexington Avenues / 754-3099
By appointment.

Decorators
Midtown East

quality style service value

The Edge: A genius with color and style. Listed in *Vanity Fare* as Generation X's equivalent of Mario Buatta, Mark Hampton, etc. Wonderful style, color sense, cooperative and flexible, so don't be alarmed if he shows up in his Rolls. Charges wholesale plus a design fee. No credit cards. *"Despite our modest (for him) budget, he was patient and clever, making our home a dream. Easy to call for freshening up ideas."*

John Barman, Inc.

225 East 57th Street
between 2nd and 3rd Avenues / 838-9443
By appointment.

Decorators
Mail/phone

quality style service value

The Edge: For that New York look. Strong designer who listens and gets it done well. Favors classic styling with contemporary elements. Particularly strong at delivering a sophisticated New York look. Wholesale plus a design fee. No credit cards. *"Modern and chic style."*

Martin Albert Interiors

9 East 19th Street
between 5th and Broadway / 673-8000
Weekdays 10am–6pm, Sat 10am–5pm
(closed Sat in summer), Sun noon–5pm.

Decorators
Flatiron/East Village

quality style service value

The Edge: Wonderful up-to-the-minute fabrics. Wonderful fabrics, including this year's look— mesh and metallics.

Richard's Interior Design

1390 Lexington Avenue
near 92nd Street / 831-9000
Mon–Wed and Fri 10am–6pm, Thurs 10am–7pm, Sat 10am–5pm.

Decorators
Upper East Side

quality style service value

The Edge: Wonderful selection for your reupholstery needs. Find over 10,000 decorator fabrics, including tapestries, damasks, stripes, plaids, silks, velvets, and floral chintzes. All first-quality. Prices are competitive. Will do upholstered furniture, reupholstery, slipcovers, and draperies. Top home consultation and installation available. *"I go to its twice-yearly sale for upholstery, etc."*

Use What You Have

145 East 74th Street
near 3rd Avenue / 288-8888
Weekdays by appointment.

Decorators
Upper East Side

quality style service value

The Edge: Decorating advice on making the most of what you have. Pay per room or on an hourly basis. Advice is given on how to complete and finish a room or revise and move around what you already have to make it look new and better. Reasonably priced. No credit cards. *"Wonderful service. Things are moved around, a few new items suggested, and you have a 'decorated' look. Good value!"*

E.C. Electronics

Electronics, etc.
Midtown West

253 West 51st Street
near 8th Avenue / 586-6156
Weekdays 9:30am–6pm, Sat 10am–4pm.

The Edge: Authorized service center for 15 brands of electronic equipment. Brands include Aiwa, Fuji, Hitachi, and Sony. Accepts credit cards.

F & C Electronics

Electronics, etc.
Upper West Side

233 West 77th Street
between Broadway and West End Avenue / 874-7722
Weekdays 10am–7pm, Sat 10am–5pm.

The Edge: Reliable stereo repairs. Stereo repairs, generally completed within two weeks. Free estimates, but you must bring in your stereo.

Pyramid Electronics Ltd.

Electronics, etc.
Upper East Side

353 East 76th Street
between 1st and 2nd Avenues / 628-6500
Weekdays 8am–5:30pm, Sat 9am–5pm.

40	40	40	20
quality	style	service	value

The Edge: Repairs VCRs and TVs. Accepts credit cards and delivers.

Rent-A-Phone

Electronics, etc.
Lower Manhattan

One World Trade Center
near Vesey Street / 524-9700
Weekdays 9am–5pm.

The Edge: Rents cellular phones. Rentals are $5 per day. Usage charges are $1.25 per minute within the five boroughs, $1.75 in the U.S. outside New York, and $2 per minute in Canada. Accepts credit cards. No delivery.

Acme Exterminating

Exterminator
Midtown West

460 9th Avenue
between 35th and 36th Streets / 594-9230
Weekdays 8am–5pm.

The Edge: Handles all bug problems. Services homes, offices, stores, museums, and hospitals. No credit cards.

Fountain Pen Hospital

Fountain pens
Lower Manhattan

10 Warren Street
opposite City Hall / 964-0580
Weekdays 8am–5:45pm.

The Edge: Will fix your favorite pen. Sells and repairs pens and other writing instruments. Sells fine writing instruments worldwide, including the limited-edition Sole Pen by Aurora.

Antique Furniture Workroom

Furniture
Midtown West

210 11th Avenue, 9th Floor
683-0551
Weekdays 8am–4pm.

The Edge: Reliable furniture restoration. Along with furniture restoration, gold-leafing and caning. Estimates are given in your home based on the hours required for the work. No credit cards.

Authentic Porcelain Refinishing

Furniture
Queens

51-30 40th Avenue
Woodside / 718-726-1481
Weekdays 9am–6pm.

The Edge: Porcelain repairs like new. Specializes in bathtub refinishing. Sprays wood cabinets and metal furniture. Has color charts or can match colors. Will make house calls with a $225 minimum order. No credit cards.

Custom Spraying and Reglazing Company

Furniture
Staten Island

386 Nome Avenue
Staten Island / 718-494-3751
Mon–Sat 9am–5pm.

The Edge: Gives metal furniture new life! Recently started using the electrostatic refinishing process, which attracts paints to metal molecularly. $150 job minimum. Custom colors are possible. Family-run business.

E.C.R. Antique Conservation and Restoration

Furniture
Midtown West

515 West 29th Street, 5th Floor
between 10th and 11th Avenues / 643-0388
Weekdays 9am–4:30pm.

The Edge: A Martha Stewart source. Quality repairs, including cleaning and polishing, refilling antique pieces, and duplicating turnings from existing pieces. Repairs chairs (tightening and gluing) and more. Repairs start at $175, including cleaning and polishing.

Juan Angel Pogonza Restoration

Furniture
Midtown West

526 West 26th Street, Studio 915
between 10th and 11th Avenues / 691-6251
Weekdays 9am–5pm.

40	50	40	30
quality	style	service	value

The Edge: Expert restoration of European furniture and furnishings. Specializes in restoring European, French, and continental furniture and furnishings. Charges by the hour. Will arrange pickup and delivery of your piece for an additional charge. Provides in-home estimates for a fee; in-shop estimates are free of charge. No credit cards.

Metro Sofa Service

Furniture
Westchester

242 Albany Avenue
Thornwood / 914-769-2178
By appointment

The Edge: They'll make it right if your sofa can't fit in the elevator. You paid for it, it's too big, but never mind, they'll get it in. Known for disassembling and reassembling furniture better than new. Reasonably priced. No credit cards.

Stone Services, Inc.

Furniture
Mail/phone

Offices in the five boroughs and Westchester
1455 Cromwell Avenue, Bronx / 718-293-2055
Weekdays 8am–6pm.

The Edge: Spray-paints furniture. Specializes in spray-painting furniture. Offers a variety of finishes, from simple enamels used on household woodwork to costly high-tech paints like Imron, which is very strong, durable, and flexible. If an object is rusted or dented, Stone Service will reshape and sand it. Also spray-paints furniture, sculptures, wicker, wood, etc. No credit cards.

Traditional Line

Furniture
Chelsea

143 West 21st Street
between 6th and 7th Avenues / 627-3555
Weekdays 8:30am–5pm.

The Edge: Quality restoration. The company has been around long enough to establish its reputation for doing quality restorations from simple jobs to marquetry repairs. Charges $60 an hour. No credit cards.

York End Caning

Furniture
Upper East Side

454 East 84th Street
between 1st and York Avenues / 288-6843
Weekdays 9am–6pm, Sat 9am–2pm (closed Sat in summer).

40	33	43	40
quality	style	service	value

The Edge: Hand- and machine-caning. Can create a new cane seat to match an old back. Can match the weave and will stain the weave to match the old. No credit cards.

Manhattan Band

Jewelry & watches
Midtown West

10 West 47th Street
between 5th and 6th Avenues / 869-3828
Weekdays 9am–5pm.

47	45	48	50
quality	style	service	value

The Edge: Great repairs. You can trust them with anything—from small pieces to priceless family heirlooms. Also a wonderful selection of watches to purchase at excellent prices.

Rissin's Jewelry Clinic

4 West 47th Street
near 5th Avenue / 575-1098
Mon–Tues and Thurs 9:30am–5pm for retail customers.

Jewelry & watches
Midtown West

quality style service value
45 25 47 48

The Edge: Quality repairs from a most reliable source. Joe Rissin, the quintessential New Yorker, talks very fast and is very proud of his work— repairing jewelry from costume to Fabergé. Has worked for the British Museum (King Tut exhibit), the Brooklyn Museum, the Guggenheim, and the Jewish Museum, among others. Joe is a gemologist and a platinum-trained jeweler. His wife, Toby, specializes in pearl stringing. He's known for repairs of antiques, but also repairs eyeglasses, and gives them priority since "they're a necessity." Appraisals for $60 to $65 per hour. Gives estimates. Accepts checks from customers he knows. Be prepared to wait at times. Joe pays attention to your detailed requests, no matter how small. No credit cards. *"He was able to fix my husband's Tiffany gold pen—something Tiffany's could not do." "I gave him my mother's 55-year-old diamond wedding band to restore. He made it look as if it just came new from the original jewelry store. And the price was very reasonable."*

Sanko Cultured Pearls

45 West 47th Street
between 6th and 7th Avenues / 819-0585
Weekdays 9am–5pm.

Jewelry & watches
Midtown West

The Edge: Great for pearl restringing. Features a large selection of cultured pearls in various sizes, colors, and levels of perfection for sale. And of course, pearl restringing. No credit cards. No delivery.

City Knickerbocker

781 8th Avenue
near 47th Street / 586-3939
Weekdays 8am–5pm.

Light fixtures
Midtown West

quality style service value
40 40 40 40

The Edge: Lamp repair and rewiring. For four generations since 1906, quality lamp repairs, rewiring, replating, and remodeling. Accepts credit cards.

Crown Limousine

544 West 48th Street
between 10th and 11th Avenues / 246-2626
By appointment.

Limo rentals
Midtown West

quality style service value
30 30 30 20

The Edge: Great value. For the service, inexpensive—$30 an hour (two-hour minimum). Features late-model Lincoln town cars driven by uniformed chauffeurs and equipped with cellular phones. Call to make a reservation.

Express Car

1729 1st Avenue
831-8900

Limo rentals
Mail/phone

By appointment 24 hours daily.

quality style service value

The Edge: Good car service and reasonable prices. . *"The best!"*

London Towncars

40-14 23rd Street
Long Island City / 800-221-4009
By appointment 24 hours daily.

Limo rentals
Mail/phone

quality style service value

The Edge: High-quality reliable service, but you pay for it. Over 100 dark-blue Buick Park Avenues with burgundy leather interiors, plus a cadre of stretch limos. All cars feature phones and uniformed drivers. Used by Citicorp executives and CBS celebrities. 24-hour advance notice is suggested, but last-minute calls have frequently been met. Deluxe. *"Best car service in Manhattan." "Expensive but incredibly reliable."*

Robert's Big Apple Limousine Service

253-4546
Daily 24 hours.

Limo rentals
Mail/phone

The Edge: Chauffeur-driven luxury. Best of all, the chauffeur-driven antique cars (Bentley or Rolls-Royce Silver Shadow or Silver Cloud) at $90 an hour plus. Stretch limousines are also available starting at $50 an hour.

TWR Express

472-4868
Daily 24 hours.

Limo rentals
Mail/phone

quality style service value

The Edge: Reliable transportation. Over 400 Lincoln Continentals to take you anywhere. Prices are a reasonable $30 to $35 an hour, and limousines at $58 hour. Cars are stationed at local airports. 24-hour advance notice required for stretch limos. Deluxe.

Vital Transportation

468-4825
Daily 24 hours.

Limo rentals
Mail/phone

The Edge: A large fleet of recent model Lincoln town cars and Cadillacs. Drivers wear dark suits. All cars have car phones. Deluxe.

AAA Locksmiths

44 West 46th Street
near 6th Avenue / 840-3939
Mon–Thurs 8am–5:30pm, Fri 8am–5pm.

Locksmiths
Midtown West

The Edge: Reliable. 50+ years' experience. Clients include Citibank. No credit cards. *"Reliable."*

Artbag Creations, Inc.

Luggage & handbags
Upper East Side

735 Madison Avenue
near 64th Street / 744-2720
Mon–Sat 9:15am–5:45pm.

The Edge: Noted for quality repairs. Can repair and rework fine leather goods. Repairs zippers, restitches, and repairs or duplicates handles. Can modify leather items to add compartments or hidden pockets. Will custom-make bags and briefcases. Sells new handbags, belts, and buckles as well.

Carnegie Luggage

Luggage & handbags
Midtown West

1392 Avenue of the Americas
between 56th and 57th Streets / 586-8210
Weekdays 9am–5:45pm, Sat 9am–5pm.

The Edge: Luggage repairs. Work done immediately or in one to three hours, if it's an emergency.

John R. Gerardo

Luggage & handbags
Midtown West

30 West 31st Street
between Broadway and 5th Avenue / 695-6955
Weekdays 9am–5pm, Sat 10am–2pm (closed Sat Apr–Aug).

The Edge: Custom repair work on handbags and luggage. Beloved by *Vogue*. Repairs (does emergency work) include handles, locks, patches, and zippers. Best known for work on Louis Vuitton, but also lots of high-end luggage. Also sells a full range of luggage. Same-day delivery available for some items.

Kay Leather Goods Repair Service

Luggage & handbags
Gramercy Park/Murray Hill

333 5th Avenue
near 33rd Street / 481-5579
Weekdays 9am–5pm.

The Edge: Repairs and makes quality leather goods. Find attaché cases, belts, and handbags.

Modern Leather Goods

Luggage & handbags
Midtown West

2 West 32nd Street, 4th Floor
between 5th Avenues and Broadway / 947-7770
Weekdays 8:30am–5pm, Sat 9am–2pm.

The Edge: Expert leather repairs. Repairs handbags, luggage, and the like. Will duplicate your worn-out belts, handbags, or attaché cases. Recommended by the *New York Times, Vogue,* and top leather companies for its moderately priced, excellent work. Prices start at $12 to fix a zipper.

Superior Repair Center

Luggage & handbags
Multiple locations

Mon–Wed 10am–7pm, Thurs 10am–8pm,
Fri 10am–6pm, Sat 10am–3pm.

The Edge: Superior leather repair. Widely known. Fixes handbags, luggage, and the like. Excellent work at good prices. *"Top repair shops send their work here." "I was disappointed in a recent repair."*

Locations: Gramercy Park/Murray Hill: 133 Lexington Avenue, near 29th Street (889-7211) / **Upper West Side:** 138 West 72nd Street, near Broadway (769-2099)

International Retinning & Copper Repair
Metals
Midtown West

525 West 26th Street
between 10th and 11th Avenues / 244-4896
Weekdays 9am–5pm.

The Edge: One of the only places in Manhattan to get metal objects refurbished. Fixes, restores, or makes new handles, lids, etc. for virtually all metals (no aluminum or stainless steel). Known for making sheet-metal planter liners for window boxes. Pickup for work costing more than $300. No credit cards.

Thome Silversmiths
Metals
Midtown West

49 West 37th Street, Room 605
between 5th and 6th Avenues / 764-5426
Weekdays 8:30am–1pm and 2:30–5:30pm.

50	40	50	40
quality	style	service	value

The Edge: Metal restoration. Cleans, repairs, and replates silver, silver plate, copper, brass, pewter, and gold. Can repair velvet backs of picture frames. No credit cards.

Authorized Repair Service
Miscellaneous
Midtown West

30 West 57th Street, 2nd Floor
between 5th and 6th Avenues / 586-0947
Mon–Tues and Thurs–Fri 9am–5pm, Wed 9am–6pm, Sat 10am–3:30pm.

The Edge: A virtual hospital for lighters, pens, and shavers. Buys, sells, and services antique (from the 1800s) lighters and pens.

Down East Service Center
Miscellaneous
SoHo/TriBeCa

50 Spring Street
near Lafayette Street / 925-2632
Weekdays 11am–6pm.

The Edge: The source for repairs of camping equipment. Repairs backpacks, hiking boots, hiking equipment, mosquito netting, overnight bags, sleeping equipment, and tents.

French-American Reweaving Company
Miscellaneous
Midtown West

119 West 57th Street, Room 1406
between 6th and 7th Avenues / 765-4670
Weekdays 10:30am–5:30pm, Sat 11am–2pm.

The Edge: A lifesaver for fabrics. In business for 60 years. Will repair and mend knits and scarves, plus a range of fabrics, including silks and leathers. Quality work. Prices depend on the state of the fabric. No credit cards.

Henry Westpfal and Company
Miscellaneous
Midtown West
105 West 30th Street
between 6th and 7th Avenues / 563-5990
Weekdays 9am–6pm.

The Edge: The sharpest edge! Sells scissors (from cuticle cutters to leather-working tools). Also stocks left-handed tools. Sharpens everything.

MicroEcologies
Miscellaneous
Upper East Side
141 East 61st Street, 2nd floor
at Lexington Avenue / 755-3265
Weekdays 9am–6pm, Sat 10am–6pm, or by appointment at your home/office.

The Edge: Makes sure your environment is safe. Makes house/office calls to search out environmental hazards—mold, lead poisoning, asbestos, and other potential hazards. Consultation fee starts at $250.

Big John Moving
Movers
Upper East Side
1602 1st Avenue
near 83rd Street / 734-3300
Weekdays 9am–5pm.

quality	style	service	value
40	35	40	43

The Edge: Careful movers. Also sells moving supplies, boxes, wraps, paper, etc. No credit cards. *"Reasonable and careful."*

Brownstone Brothers Moving & Storage
Movers
Upper East Side
426 East 91st Street
between 1st and York Avenues / 289-1511
Weekdays 9am–5:30pm, Sat 9am–1pm.

quality	style	service	value
48	40	48	48

The Edge: Widely used and no complaints. Expensive, but careful movers. Very service-oriented. *"Careful and helpful. Tops!"*

Vogel Brothers Trucking
Movers
Mail/phone
347-5417
Weekdays--Fri 9am–5pm. Moves by appointment.

quality	style	service	value
45	-	48	48

The Edge: They do the Spence-Chapin Thrift Shop pickups. Reliable and careful movers. *"Prompt and responsive."*

Micro-Ovens of New York

970 Woodmansten Place
near Bogart Avenue, Bronx / 718-823-7101
Weekdays 8:30am–5:30pm, Sat 9am–noon.

Ovens
Bronx

The Edge: Fixes microwaves. Since 1976 an authorized service center for 10 oven makers, including Amana, Panasonic, and Sharp. Makes house calls all over the metropolitan area. No credit cards.

Galowitz Photographics

50 East 13th Street
between Broadway and University Place / 505-7190
Weekdays 8:15am–5:30pm, Sat 10am–4pm
(closed Sat Memorial Day–Labor Day).

Personal services
Flatiron/East Village

quality style service value

The Edge: Everything for your photographs. Top-quality full-service photo lab—makes old photos updated. Does large blowups, good for parties or business events.

It's Easy

10 Rockefeller Plaza
between 5th and 6th Avenues / 586-8880
Weekdays 8:30am–6pm.

Personal services
Midtown West

quality style service value

The Edge: Will do those "wait-in-line" chores for you. Cuts through the red tape if you need renewal with passports, visas, etc. Will wait in line for you for all sorts of needs. Deluxe.

Passport Plus

20 East 49th Street, 3rd Floor
between 5th and Madison Avenues / 759-5540
Weekdays 9:30am–5pm.

Personal services
Midtown East

The Edge: The wife we all need. Handles arranging visas; birth, death, and marriage certificates; and such.

Saved by the Bell Corporation

11 Riverside Drive
near 73rd Street / 874-5457
Weekdays 9am–7pm.

Personal services
Upper West Side

The Edge: Finally, the part-time wife we dream of having. Specialties include corporate relocations, delivery arrangements, party planning, personal shopping, and help with organizational problems. Provides personal and professional services on an ad hoc, very flexible basis. No credit cards.

Chanit Roston

Portraits
Mail/phone

Midtown studio
or in your home / 628-1310
By appointment

The Edge: Recommended portrait painter. Formerly the resident portrait painter at Guerney's in Montauk and at the Guild Hall Museum in East Hampton, Chanit has taught portraiture. She works in oil or water color, will work from photographs, and will travel. Very reasonable prices.

Michael Fischer

Portraits
Midtown West

601 West 26th Street, 18th Floor
between 11th and 12th Avenues / 645-9848
By appointment

The Edge: Portrait painter. Academically trained painter and sculptor who paints portraits. For a single subject, head and shoulders, expect to pay over $2,000; for two-person portraits, about $4,000. The artist works from Polaroids he takes at his studio or your home. Travel expenses are additional.

Cohen Carpet Cleaning

Rugs & carpets
Mail/phone

663-6902
By appointment.

The Edge: Reliable and honest carpet cleaning. One-man operation. Very reliable. Can leave him alone in your house with anything. Very expensive. No credit cards.

Costikyan Ltd.

Rugs & carpets
Queens

2813 14th Street
at 28th Avenue, Long Island City / 800-247-7847
Weekdays 9am–5pm.

50	50	50	50
quality	style	service	value

The Edge: Hand-cleaning for priceless Oriental rugs. Quality carpet cleaning. Reasonable prices. No credit cards. *"I trust them with my expensive Orientals. Dependable."*

Elite Carpet and Upholstery Cleaning

Rugs & carpets
Queens

23 Adams Street
East Rockaway / 516-887-5437
Weekdays 9am–6pm.

The Edge: Carpet and upholstery cleaning for 15 years. Charges $20 per square foot for dry cleaning. Carpet cleaning charges are per room. Pickup and delivery are available at no extra charge. Also fire and flood restoration.

Long Island Carpet Cleaners

Rugs & carpets
Brooklyn

301 Norman Avenue
at Morgan, Brooklyn / 718-383-7000

Weekdays 8am–6pm, Sat 9am–1pm.

quality style service value

The Edge: Upholstery and carpet cleaning done at your home or office. In business for 76 years. On-site carpet and upholstery cleaning.

Crown Machine Service

2792 Broadway
near 108th Street / 663-8968
Weekdays 9am–6pm, Sat 9am–4pm.

Sewing machines
Upper West Side

The Edge: One of New York's largest sewing machine repair shops. Authorized dealer for Elna, Pfaff, Singer, Viking, and White machines. Services and rents machines, and even makes house calls. Cleaning and oiling starts at $30. Weekly rentals start at $25. Add $10 to the bill for house calls.

Park East Sewing Center

3206 43rd Street
Garden City / 718-721-7510
Daily 10am–6pm.

Sewing machines
Long Island

The Edge: Repairs and sells sewing machines. Cleaning and oiling start at $35. Free estimates given. An authorized dealer for Bernina, White, and New Home. A long-time Manhattan staple, recently moved to Queens.

B. Nelson Shoe Corporation

1221 Avenue of the Americas
C-2 level, McGraw-Hill Building / 869-3552
Weekdays 7:30am–5:15pm.

Shoe repair
Midtown West

The Edge: Excellent shoe-repair shop. Quality repairs. Excellent recommendations. If it isn't worth it, they tell you.

Evelyn and San

400 East 83rd Street
near 1st Avenue / 628-7618
Weekdays 8am–6pm, Sat 8am–5pm.

Shoe repair
Upper East Side

The Edge: Shoe restoration and dyeing. A good neighborhood source for quality shoe repairs. No credit cards. No delivery.

Jim's Shoe Repair

50 East 59th Street
between Madison and Park Avenues / 355-8259
Weekdays 8am–5:45pm, Sat 9am–3:45pm.

Shoe repair
Midtown East

quality style service value

The Edge: Excellent shoe repair. Everyone knows and recommends Jim's. Almost always crowded. No deliveries. *"Can fix and repair any shoe. If it's crowded, you can wait forever. But advice and work are wonderful."*

Top Service

845 7th Avenue
near 54th Street / 765-3190
Weekdays 8am–6pm, Sat 9am–1pm.

Shoe repair
Midtown West

The Edge: Updates old shoes to look stylish. Effective at updating old shoes to look stylish. Possibilities include adding platforms to flat-soled shoes and sneakers; changing buckles, trims, straps; and recovering heels. Also dyes shoes to match clothing and cleans fabric shoes. Works for designers and was featured in the April 1995 *Martha Stewart Living*.

Alfonso Sciortino Custom Alterations

57 West 57th Street, Suite 609A
near 6th Avenue / 888-2846
Daily 10am–6pm.

Tailors
Midtown West

The Edge: Top alterations. One-man operation that offers good tailoring. No credit cards. No delivery.

Eddie Egras

125 West 72nd Street
near Amsterdam Avenue / 595-1596
Weekdays by appointment 9:30am–7pm.

Tailors
Upper West Side

The Edge: Men's tailor. No credit cards. No delivery. *"Dependable and reasonably priced."*

John's European Boutique

118 East 59th Street, 2nd Floor
near Park Avenue / 752-2239
Weekdays 9am–6pm, Sat 10am–1pm.

Tailors
Midtown East

quality style service value

The Edge: Quality tailoring. Does a lot of work for department stores and boutiques. No credit cards. No delivery. *"Fairly priced and terrific tailoring."*

Peppino

780 Lexington Avenue
near 60th Street / 832-3844
Weekdays 8:30am–6:30pm, Sat 10am–4pm.

Tailors
Upper East Side

The Edge: Excellent alterations at a fair price. No credit cards.

Forsyth Decorations

Upholsterers
Lower East Side/Chinatown

100 Forsyth Street
between Grand and Broome Streets / 226-3624
Sun–Thurs 9:30am–5pm, Fri 9am–noon.

The Edge: Custom fabric work. You provide the fabrics and they'll do custom work, from cushions to window treatments to slipcovers. Everything is made to order—there's no store inventory. No credit cards. No delivery. Discounter.

International Decorators

Upholsterers
Brooklyn

141 Spencer Street
Brooklyn / 718-522-7434
Call for appointment.

The Edge: Reasonably priced upholsterer. Excellent work at unbelievably low prices. Delivery and pickup are included in the price.

Laser Interiors

Upholsterers
Brooklyn

250 44th Street, 3rd Floor
455-5500
Weekdays 9am–5pm.

The Edge: Well-priced upholsterering. Talk to Jeff at Laser Interiors. Good work at excellent prices.

Pembrooke & Ives

Upholsterers
SoHo/TriBeCa

149 Wooster Street
near Houston Street / 995-0555
Weekdays by appointment 9am–5pm.

quality   style   service   value

The Edge: Good tailoring and details, often whimsical. A choice upholsterer, featuring skirts with box or pencil pleats, shirred skirts, and/or buttons. Prices for custom slipcovers start at $500, not including fabric. No credit cards.

Upholstery Unlimited, Inc.

Upholsterers
Midtown West

138 West 25th Street, 11th Floor
between 6th and 7th Avenues / 924-1230
By appointment.

The Edge: Superior-quality upholstery with reasonable prices. Upholstery and drapery specialists. No credit cards.

The ratings: 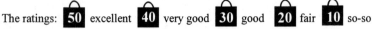 excellent very good good fair so-so

Pet services & supplies

ASPCA

Adoption
Upper East Side

424 East 92nd Street
near 1st Avenue / 876-7700
Weekdays 11am–7pm, Sun noon–5pm for adoptions.
Weekdays 8:30am–7pm, Sat 8:30am–3pm for animal hospital.

quality style service value

The Edge: Great source for pets. Wonderful selection of animals needing a home. Adoption of animals is a two-way process. The ASPCA interviews you and all members of your family to ensure that the pet you choose suits your lifestyle, meaning that the pet's needs are well met. Some people are turned down. Fee includes medical exam, initial shots, and neutering. A Behavior Health Line is available to help you settle the animal into your home. If the animal has health needs, veterinary care is provided. Prices are $55 for a dog and $45 for a cat. Also training classes are offered, group lessons at $230 for eight weekly classes ($175 if ASPCA dog). No delivery.

Bide-A-Wee Home Association

Adoption
Gramercy Park/Murray Hill

410 East 38th Street
near 1st Avenue / 532-4455
Mon–Sat 10am–6pm, Sun 10am–5pm.

quality style service value

The Edge: Great source for pets. Wonderful selection of animals needing a home. Fee of $55 for dogs and cats under six months ($30 for older animals) includes medical exam, initial shots, and neutering. Two forms of ID, as well as proof of employment and your current address, are required to adopt. Dog training, offered Thursday evenings 7–8pm, costs $200 for seven sessions. No delivery. No credit cards.

Canine College

Boarding
Connecticut

40 Marchant Road
West Redding / 203-938-2124
Daily 24-hour dog boarding. By appointment.

quality style service value

The Edge: A Relais et Châteaux experience for your pets. These folks have a way with pets. In existence for over 50 years, the place is top-drawer, gorgeous. Boarding, training, and grooming services are available. Large private indoor and outdoor runs. Heating and air conditioning make runs comfortable in all weather. Special-handling options include individual play time with staff. Training is a one-week (plus) formalized program. Manhattan pickup and delivery. No credit cards. *"My pet thinks this is camp!"*

Bow-Wow Bakery

336 East 54th Street
between 1st and 2nd Avenues / 230-1988
Weekdays 11am–7pm, Sat 11am–6pm, Sun noon–5pm.
Call ahead since hours change seasonally.

Grooming & supplies
Midtown East

quality style service value

The Edge: Glorious foods for the pet set. Favorites to celebrate your pet's special occasions—birthday cakes, quiches, and pizzas. Baked items made from real chicken liver, chicken stock, bananas, and apples. Beyond food, carries clothing, beds, and basics for your pet. Recently added tuna muffins for your favorite cat. Cookies $6.50 per baker's dozen or 70¢ each. Jumbo bones $8.50 per bakers dozen or $1 each. *"Perfect house gift for your favorite dog owner"*. *"Expensive."*

Groomer Direct

1989 Transit Way
at Route 31, Brockport / 800-551-5048
Weekdays 8am–8pm, Sat 8am–11pm, Sun 10am–7pm.

Grooming & supplies
Mail/phone

quality style service value

The Edge: All the basics at close-to-wholesale prices. Discounts all the necessities for your pets. The catalog features crates, leads and collars, toys, treats, and grooming supplies. Orders under $50 are subject to a $5 service charge. Discounter.

Karens for People + Pets

1195 Lexington Avenue
near 81st Street / 472-9440
Weekdays 8am–6pm, Sat 9am–6pm.

Grooming & supplies
Upper East Side

The Edge: Elegance for the family's favorites. Known for the quality of its grooming care (uses hypoallergenic products), the salon sells its products and grooming supplies plus accessories for people and pets.

Petography, Inc.

25 Central Park West, Suite 3A
between 62nd and 63rd Streets / 245-0914
By appointment

Photographs & video
Upper West Side

The Edge: Perfect portraits of your pets. Devoted to creating beautiful photographs of pets and people with their pets. Portraits are taken in your home, their setting, or any setting you choose. Creative. A portion of the proceeds from each Petography photo session is donated to an animal cause. Jim Dratfield is the master photographer. Prices start at $550.

Pet Cab

631 West 130th Street
near Broadway / 491-5313
By appointment.

Transportation
Upper Upper West Side

quality style service value

The Edge: If only yellow taxis were as good. Can and will take your pet anywhere. Chauffeurs pets, crated or not, in good health or emergency transportation for injured pets. Can handle dogs, cats, birds, you name it. Has served the ASPCA and the Animal Medical Center, among others. Has stretchers for emergency cases. Can handle aggressive dogs (muzzles are an extra charge). Prices are $38 an hour. Minimum charge $22. No credit cards.

Pet Taxi
227 East 56th Street
between 2nd and 3rd Avenues / 755-1757
On call 24 hours daily.

Transportation
Midtown East

quality style service value

The Edge: Transportation for you and your pet. Gets you both where you need to go. Stretchers are available for ill pets. Can rent pet carriers for air rides here. Fully bonded and insured. $20 for a standard one-way trip.

Animal Medical Center
510 East 62nd Street
between FDR Drive and York Avenue / 838-8100
Daily 24 hours.

Veterinarians
Upper East Side

42 | 33 | 34 | 35
quality style service value

The Edge: They've seen it all, done it all. The best! The city's most extensive animal hospital. Staffed and operating 24 hours a day. Specialists are available in everything, 22 subspecialties. They offer routine veterinary care and emergency treatment. A true city treasure. *"For ordinary regular visits, I prefer a private vet. Normally a long wait to be seen and a bit of a factory. They have all the newest equipment though, and terrific trauma treatment." "They saved my cat's life in the early-morning hours."*

Manhattan Veterinary Clinic
240 East 80th Street
near 2nd Avenue / 988-1000
Daily 8am–6pm (emergency services 6pm–1am).

Veterinarians
Upper East Side

40 | 35 | 35 | 35
quality style service value

The Edge: High-tech, caring hospital. Dr. Marder, director. Full-time working hospital with staff veterinarians with diagnostic skills (internal medicine) and surgery. Staff surgeon is Dr. Greene. *"Nice staff, great service."*

New York Veterinary Hospital
150 East 74th Street
between Lexington and 3rd Avenues / 717-7222
Weekdays 8:30am–7pm, Sat–Sun 8:30am–1pm.

Veterinarians
Upper East Side

The Edge: High-tech hospital. Dr. Kessler, senior veterinarian, plus two other resident vets. Maintains quality hospital facilities. Technicians are on site until midnight. Makes house calls. Will board animals to 70 pounds. No run, but walks three times daily. They deliver on Monday, Wednesday, and Friday.

Park East Animal Hospital
52 East 64th Street

Veterinarians
Upper East Side

near Park Avenue / 832-8417
Appointments: Mon–Thurs 9am–8pm,
Fri–Sat 9am–5:30pm, Sun 10:30am–3pm.

quality style service value

The Edge: 24-hour emergency care and vets who make house calls. Dr. Berman, senior director at the hospital, plus two other vets. Hospital is open 24 hours a day. Technician or vet is on site at all times. The veterinarians make house calls when necessary, and offer at-home nursing care. Facilities are state of the art, with good postoperative recovery equipment. Limited boarding. Delivery in Manhattan.

University Animal Hospital

Veterinarians
Upper East Side

354 East 66th Street
near 1st Avenue / 288-8884
Weekdays 8am–8pm, Sat 9am–4pm by appointment.

The Edge: Vets on call 24 hours per day. Dr. Lawrence Zola is the senior vet here. Two vets are on staff. 24-hour emergency care with doctors on premises or on call 24 hours per day.

Yorkville Animal Hospital

Veterinarians
Upper East Side

227 East 84th Street
near 2nd Avenue / 249-8802
Weekdays 9–11:30am and 3:30–5:30pm, Sat 9am–2pm.

The Edge: Full animal hospital. Performs surgery, dentistry, and grooming, all on site. Three vets are on staff. Boards small to medium-size dogs with play time available in an outdoor run. Prices are $22 per day for dogs and $18 per day for cats.

Jim Buck School for Dogs

Walking
Mail/phone

410-2825
By appointment.

The Edge: An old-standby dog-walking service. These could be the guys you see mornings with the packs of dogs in tow. Pick up your dog every morning for two hours of training and exercise. Interviews required for pets to ensure they fit into the group. In business for more than 35 years. No credit cards.

Urban Animal

Walking
Mail/phone

969-8506
Daily by appointment.

quality style service value

The Edge: TLC for your beloved pets. Since 1991 these folks have been providing tender, loving care for your pets. Individualized walks (one or two dogs at a time). Serves over 200 clients. Weekday prices are $12 for half-hour walk increasing to $20 for an hour walk. Discounts for more than 10 walks per week. Provides boarding in staff members' homes for dogs and cats—prices are $30 per night for toys and elderly dogs, $38 per night for standard dogs, increasing to $45 for unneutered male dogs and puppies, and include four walks per day. They'll also arrange housesitting at $25 per night, if your pet doesn't like to leave home! Staff is hired based on three references and a trial co-walk test with the owners of Urban Animal. If you need a pet, give them a call as these folks periodically adopt strays and seek good homes for their adoptees. No credit cards.

Sample sales

Accento Marzoto

650 5th Avenue, 17th Floor
between 51st and 52nd Streets / 541-8856
Weekdays 9am–5:30pm.

Clothing
Midtown West

The Edge: Missoni Donna and Studio 0001. Sample and stock sale of Missoni Donna and Studio 0001 by Ferre plus other Italian designers of the same quality. Prices $50 to $300. No credit cards. No delivery.

Adrianna Papell

498 7th Avenue, 6th Floor
at 36th Street / 695-5244
Weekdays 9am–5:30pm. Call Rufus for an appointment.

Clothing
Midtown West

35	40	40	35
quality	style	service	value

The Edge: Moderate lines. Mostly sample sizes (size 8). Daytime dresses to evening wear. No credit cards. *"The usual."*

Agem - European Designers

134 West 37th Street, 2nd Floor
between Broadway and 7th Avenues / 947-8748
Call for sales dates and times.

Clothing
Gramercy Park/Murray Hill

The Edge: European styling. European designer clothing—Gianni Versace, Istante, Fendi, and other European designers. Sample sales run by SSS Sales. No delivery.

Alberene Scottish Cashmeres

435 5th Avenue, 3rd Floor
between 38th and 39th Streets / 689-0151
Weekdays 10am–6pm, Sat 10am–4pm.

Clothing
Gramercy Park/Murray Hill

The Edge: More affordable cashmere. Scottish cashmeres at a third to half the prices at Madison Avenue designer shops. Expect to find sweaters, coats, capes in all styles and colors. Also scarves, throws, gloves, socks, and more. Cashmere to four plys. Custom orders available.

Ann Taylor

1372 Broadway, 5th Floor
between 37th and 38th Streets / 536-4500
Call for sales dates and times.

Clothing
Midtown West

The Edge: Merchandise that's sold at Ann Taylor and The Limited. Mostly sizes 2 to 10, some size 12 possibly. No credit cards. No delivery.

Arnold Scassi

681 5th Avenue
near 54th Street / 755-5105
Weekdays by appointment.

Clothing
Midtown East

quality style service value

The Edge: From Barbara Bush to Hillary Clinton, the first ladies' source for gowns. Lean, sensual evening gowns. American couturier known for his custom evening wear. Priced from $10,000 to $20,000. Customers only by recommendation, but it can't hurt to call, since this is the '90s and customers are at a premium. No credit cards. No delivery. Deluxe.

Augustus Suiting

134 West 37th Street, 2nd Floor
between Broadway and 7th Avenues / 947-8748
Call for sales dates and times.

Clothing
Gramercy Park/Murray Hill

quality style service value

The Edge: Conservative for the office. Suits in wool crepe and gabardine. Blazers to be coordinated with skirts and slacks. Solids, tweeds, and herringbone fabrics. Sizes 2 to 14. Sample sales run by SSS Sales. No delivery.

Balinger*Gold

Call for sale dates and times.

Clothing
Multiple locations

The Edge: The source for handlooms. Known for its custom-handloomed jackets, pants, skirts, dresses, two-piece dresses, and handknit sweaters. Sizes 4 to 16. Prices $50 to $450. Accepts credit cards. Delivers.

Locations: Midtown West: 134 West 37th Street, 2nd Floor, between Broadway and 7th Avenues (947-8748) / 1441 Broadway, 28th Floor, between 40th and 41st Streets (730-7880)

Barbara Koto

501 7th Avenue, Suite 206
between 37th and 38th Streets / 997-7747
By appointment.

Clothing
Midtown West

The Edge: Custom handloomed clothing. Known for its custom-handloomed jackets, pants, skirts, dresses, two-piece dresses, and handknit sweaters. Sizes 2 to 16. Prices $50 to $450 are at least half of retail.

Betsey Johnson

134 West 37th Street, 2nd Floor
between Broadway and 7th Avenue / 947-8748
Call for sales dates and times.

Clothing
Gramercy Park/Murray Hill

The Edge: You know her collection. Fun prints in Lycra/Spandex and year-round knitwear. Sample sales run by SSS Sales. No delivery. *"Fun for the teens."*

Bicci by Florine Wachter

530 7th Avenue, 12th Floor
near 38th Street / 764-1466
Weekdays 8:30am–6pm.

Clothing
Midtown West

quality style service value

The Edge: Reasonable work uniforms. Three-piece rayon pantsuits retail $430 to $500 (from $200 wholesale). Fabrics are wool crepes, suedes, some rayon-crepe combinations. No credit cards.

Burberrys Collection

Clothing
Midtown West

512 7th Avenue, 7th Floor
between 37th and 38th Streets / 221-0988
Call for sale dates and times.

47	40	43	47
quality	style	service	value

The Edge: Better prices than at outlets or any of sales. Tailored clothing—kilts, blazers, cotton shirts, dresses, and more. No delivery.

CXI/Chapter 11

Clothing
Midtown West

533 7th Avenue
between 38th and 39th Streets / 944-7070
Weekdays 9am–5pm.

The Edge: You have to work to find what you want—but great prices. Sports clothing in moderate price ranges—blazers, sweaters, skirts, blouses, T-shirts, and similar items. Fabrics are cottons, linens, and rayons. Prices $10 to $150. Expect high-fashion sportswear. Limited try-ons possible.

Calida

Clothing
Gramercy Park/Murray Hill

180 Madison Avenue, Suite 1402
between 33rd and 34th Streets / 889-5003
Call to be put on the mailing list.

The Edge: Value for the basics. Panties, T-shirts, bras, and sleepwear. Prices start at one-third of retail. No credit cards. No delivery.

Carolina Herrera

Clothing
Midtown West

48 West 38th Street, 3rd Floor
between 5th and 6th Avenues / 575-0557
By appointment

35	35	35	30
quality	style	service	value

The Edge: Elegance. Sample room open for retail customers. Contact Patty Rose. Expect to find Herrera's elegant timeless evening wear. Simply gorgeous classic things. No delivery. No credit cards. *"Contact Patty Rose." "Still expensive."*

Celine

Clothing
Gramercy Park/Murray Hill

134 West 37th Street, 2nd Floor
between Broadway and 7th Avenues / 947-8748
Call for sale dates and times.

50	40	30	40
quality	style	service	value

The Edge: French elegance—very high quality. The collection for ladies who lunch—shoes, handbags, dresses, and suits. Suits and dresses that are normally $900 plus start at $200. Sizes 2 to 12. Sample sales run by SSS Sales. No delivery. *"I paid $225 for a suit that retailed at $850 plus."*

Central Park West

Clothing
Gramercy Park/Murray Hill

134 West 37th Street, 2nd Floor

between Broadway and 7th Avenues / 947-8748
Call for sale dates and times.

The Edge: Glamour for those with great bodies. Great source for separates with an emphasis on the new body-hugging styling. Knits of Lycra, Spandex/cotton in leggings, riding pants, tops, vests, and similar casuals. Sample sales run by SSS Sales. No delivery.

Cinzia Rocca / Couture Helene

Clothing
Midtown West

530 7th Avenue, 28th Floor
between 38th and 39th Streets / 944-6027
Call for sale dates and times.

The Edge: Features Italian coats and suits and Belgium faux furs at below-wholesale prices. Best prices on wearables from the just-past season. Faux furs include leopard, mink, beaver, Persian lamb—some reversible. Tailored classic suits. Petite and regular sizes. Checks accepted with two forms of ID. No delivery. No credit cards.

Cynthia Rowley

Clothing
Gramercy Park/Murray Hill

134 West 37th Street, 2nd floor
between Broadway and Seventh Avenue / 947-8748
Call for sale dates and times.

quality style service value

The Edge: An update, elegant Jackie O look. Deep discounts on her line. Dresses and coordinates to party or play in. No try-ons. Now complementing her line is a limited selection of home accessories, including picture frames. Sample sales run by SSS Sales. No delivery. *"Cute dresses."*

Cynthia Steffe / Francess & Rita

Clothing
Gramercy Park/Murray Hill

134 West 37th Street, 2nd Floor
between Broadway and 7th Avenues / 947-8748
Call for sale dates and times.

quality style service value

The Edge: For the executive woman. Crepe suits in pastel and basic colors plus blazers, pants, skirts (long and short lengths), and blouses. Sample sales run by SSS Sales. Sizes 2 to 14. *"The suits are beautiful and stylish."*

David Glazer

Clothing
Flatiron/East Village

85 5th Avenue, 11th Floor
at 16th Street / 691-5100
Weekdays 9am–5pm. Sample sales twice per year in May–June and Nov–Dec. Call for an appointment—ask for Josephine.

The Edge: Top Italian lines. Represents over 20 designers, including Dolce Gabana, Gianni Versace, Jeans by Dolce & Gabanna, Istante by Gianni, and the like. Over 4,000 samples but in limited sizes. No delivery.

Donna Karan/DKNY

Clothing
Midtown West

40 West 40th Street
between 5th and 6th Avenues / 789-1500
Sample sales in June and Dec.

quality style service value

The Edge: All of Donna. Donna's various lines—sample and stock sale—with great finds. The crowds are unreal. Go early for the best options. No strollers allowed. No delivery. *"Great suits and fun clothes." "Fabulous prices on sample sizes only. Otherwise prices are close to department store sale prices." From a size 6 respondent: "Sample sweaters were excellent value. DKNY line good value, but Donna Karan couture stil seemed very expensive."*

E.V.A. Diffusion, Inc.

225 West 39th Street, 3rd Floor
between 7th and 8th Avenues / 719-1731
Weekdays 9am–5pm.

Clothing
Midtown West

The Edge: Louis Feraud off-price. Exceptional designer clothing from casual to evening wear. Expect to find fine slacks ($100), suits ($350), to cocktail dresses ($295). E.V.A. is Louis Feraud's exclusive off-price outlet. What it has in the Feraud collection is at wholesale prices or less. Other French designers also. Sizes 4 to 16. No delivery.

Elizabeth Knits

526 7th Avenue, 3rd Floor
between 38th and 39th Streets / 221-6006
Call for sale dates and times.

Clothing
Midtown West

The Edge: Knits for ladies. Knitwear sold at Neiman Marcus and other quality specialty stores. Knits are 76% wool and 24% rayon. Suits are made to order and take three weeks. Prices are $260 for suits and $236 for dresses. Great for the business woman on airplanes and the like. No credit cards. No delivery.

Emanuel Ungaro

11 Madison Avenue
between 24th and 25th Streets / 683-1000
Call for sale dates and times.

Clothing
Gramercy Park/Murray Hill

The Edge: Mostly Emanuel items. A great collection of timeless clothing. Sizes 2 to 16. No delivery.

Erik Stewart

1441 Broadway, 34th Floor
between 40th and 41st Streets / 944-9096
Call for sale dates and times.

Clothing
Midtown West

The Edge: Great sweaters. Huge assortment of sweaters—twin sets, tweeds, boucles, chenilles, and more. Prices are great—from $20 to $60. Sizes 4 to 14. No try-ons. No credit cards. No delivery. *"Great cotton sweaters."*

Ermenegildo Zegna

134 West 37th Street, 2nd Floor
between Broadway and 7th Avenues / 947-8748
Call for sale dates and times.

Clothing
Gramercy Park/Murray Hill

The Edge: Divine for men. Mostly accessories. Lots of ties. Sample sales run by SSS Sales. No delivery.

Escada

Clothing
Midtown West

40 West 40th Street, Ground Floor
between 5th and 6th Avenues / 767-9296
Call for sale dates and times.

The Edge: The whole lines. Expect to find the full range of their lines including Escada, Laurel, Escada Sport, Badgley Mischka, and Nic Janik. Sizes 4 to 14. No delivery. *"Very well organized. Long waiting lines. 25% off."*

European Classic

Clothing
Midtown West

48 West 37th Street, 11th Floor
between 5th and 6th Avenues / 629-3991
December, daily 9am–7:30pm.

30	30	20	30
quality	style	service	value

The Edge: Warehouse sale of fine Italian clothing. Clothes by Emilio Visconti. Mostly men's items, though some things for women—5,000 suits plus jackets, tuxedos, overcoats, blazers, shirts, sweaters, shearlings, ties, and belts. Sizes 36 to 50. Prices are $250 to $350.

Flossie Designs

Clothing
Midtown West

575 8th Avenue, Suite 504
at 38th Street / 967-3062
Weekdays 10am–6pm.

The Edge: Eclectic collection. Designer blouses in a variety of fabrics, including cotton and satins, and a range of accessories—scarves and shawls. Also table accessories, including napkins, in assorted prints and trims. Sizes 4 to 12. No credit cards. No delivery.

French Collection / Nicole Farhi

Clothing
Midtown West

512 7th Avenue, 42nd Floor
between 37th and 38th Streets / 221-3157
Call for sale dates and times.

The Edge: You know the look. Contemporary sportswear designed and made in London. Full collection. No try-ons. No delivery.

Front Femme N.Y.

Clothing
Midtown East

19 East 48th Street, 6th Floor
between 5th and Madison Avenues / 832-4633
Call for sale dates and times.

The Edge: Very high-styled luxury. Tops for women and men in viscose. The Rex Tech line for men is in cotton and sold at Bendel and Takashimaya. No delivery.

Genny USA, Inc.

Clothing
Midtown West

650 5th Avenue, 18th Floor
at 52nd Street / 245-4860
Call to be put on the mailing list.

50	50	40	50
quality	style	service	value

The Edge: Great sexy designs. Daytime to evening, designer clothing by Genny, Byblos, Complice, and Gennyway. Great designers. Everything from day to evening wear, including slacks, jackets, sweaters, skirts, and coats. No credit cards. No delivery. *"With Byblos. My favorite clothing sample sale. Great style; good prices. 70% off retail."*

Giesswein
Clothing
Midtown West

499 7th Avenue, 14th Floor
between 36th and 37th Streets / 629-3260
Call for sale dates and times.

The Edge: Classic Austrian outerwear. Expect to find outerwear, wool sweaters, wool challis skirts, and more from this well-known Austrian manufacturer. Known for its Loden coat, available in navy, Loden green, and camel for ladies and in navy and green for men. The coats are available in sizes 6 to 16. No delivery.

Gispa/Marina Spadafora
Clothing
Midtown West

530 7th Avenue, 15th Floor
between 38th and 39th Streets / 869-2888
Call for sale dates and times.

quality style service value

The Edge: Fashion-forward sportswear. Find sweaters, leggings, knit jackets, and more. Prices are $20 to $120. No credit cards. No delivery.

Givenchy Couture
Clothing
Upper East Side

21 East 75th Street, 3rd Floor
between 5th and Madison Avenues / 772-1322
Call to be put on the mailing list.

The Edge: Elegance Sizes 2 to 14—items from the just-past season. No delivery. No credit cards.

Gottex
Clothing
Midtown West

240 West 40th Street, 2nd floor
between 7th and 8th Avenues / 921-8585
Call to be put on the mailing list.

quality style service value

The Edge: Beautiful bathing suits. Enormous selection of bathing suits and covers. Sizes 6 to 18 for women and sizes 4 to 16 for girls. Some men's swimwear. No delivery. *"Quality-made bathing suits." "Nice sales."*

Gruppo Americano
Clothing
Midtown West

512 7th Avenue, 36th Floor
between 37th and 38th Streets / 819-9161
Call to be put on the mailing list.

quality style service value

The Edge: Great value and style to boot. Gruppo manufactures some of the best labels, including Emanuelle, so you'll never know what you'll find there. Prior season merchandise is way below retail (75% off). Jackets from $50, skirts and blouses from $29. Velvets, leathers, and wonderful accessories (scarves, shawls). Suits from $160. This year's statement stretch velvets. No delivery. *"Hit or miss, but prices are good." "When great, really unbelievable."*

Isabel Ardee
247 West 37th Street, 7th Floor
between 7th and 8th Avenues / 302-1002
Sale at end of year. Call to be put on the mailing list.

Clothing
Midtown West

The Edge: Young clothing. Synthetic fabrics—triacetate, rayon, wool blends, flannels, wool crepe, and chiffon fabrics favored. Sportswear favored with prices from $30 to $160. No delivery.

Isabel Toledo
277 5th Avenue, 5th Floor
between 28th and 29th Streets / 685-0948
Weekdays 9am–5pm.

Clothing
Gramercy Park/Murray Hill

The Edge: Young finely tailored clothing as sold at Barneys. Features suits and jersey dresses at least half of retail.

Isabella Company, Inc.
1412 Broadway, Suite 1200
between 39th and 40th Streets / 302-2055
Call to be put on the mailing list.

Clothing
Midtown West

The Edge: Great high-end designer fashion. Features Basler, Bianca, and La Squadra, plus others, featuring top-of-the-line fabrics in tailored styles. Sizes 4 to 18. Prices are $80 to $300. No delivery.

Jamak
200 West 70th Street, Suite 12C
at Amsterdam Avenue / 787-0278
Mar and Dec.

Clothing
Upper West Side

The Edge: American designer clothing. Some separates made from excellent Italian fabrics. You never know what you'll find: silk scarves and cut velvets; silk sweaters in multiple colors and 525 Made in America bed throws; long and short dresses, cropped tops, slim pants, skirts, jackets, and blouses. Limited selection of Donna Karan accessories. Something for everyone, with prices mostly from $50 to $179. Sizes 2 to 14. No delivery.

Jill Stuart
275 West 39th Street, 10th Floor
between 7th and 8th Avenues / 921-2600
Weekdays 9:30am–6pm.

Clothing
Midtown West

The Edge: Hot young looks Something for everyone—from children to adults. The look is "today." Features mostly women's clothing sizes 2 to 12. Priced from $100 to $1,000 for suits, dresses, skirts, jackets, etc. Last sale featured great satin slip dresses ($68 to $129). Faux fur backpacks are $58. Call to get on the mailing list announcing the next sale.

Joanna Mastroianni
530 7th Avenue, 26th Floor
between 38th and 39th Streets / 764-0840
Call for sale dates and times.

Clothing
Midtown West

The Edge: Sexy statement clothing for day into night. Best known for its couture evening collection, but also dresses and suits. Very luxurious fabrics. Silk brocade suits and coat dresses, wool suits, and evening wear favoring silk chiffon and chantilly laces. Very expensive—even wholesale gowns from $1,800. Closeout rack $50 to 200. Deluxe. No delivery. No credit cards. *"Sensational clothing which will ensure that you'll be noticed."*

Jolene

Clothing
Midtown West

112 West 34th Street, 9th Floor
between Broadway and 7th Avenue / 695-5151
Call for sale dates and times or watch for ads.

The Edge: For dresses. Dresses and a limited selection of sportswear. No credit cards. No delivery.

Jones New York Wool Coats

Clothing
Midtown West

1411 Broadway
between 39th and 40th Streets / 840-8350
December, Mon 10am–4pm.

quality style service value

The Edge: Jones for all! Wool coats and jackets from Jones New York. Sizes 2 to 16. Prices are great, with coats starting at $200 and short coats at $150. No credit cards. No deliveries.

KL by Karl Lagerfeld/Steilmann

Clothing
Gramercy Park/Murray Hill

y34 West 37th Street, 2nd Floor
between Broadway and 7th Avenues / 719-5548
Call to be put on the mailing list.

quality style service value

The Edge: Lagerfeld Sportswear to coats. Stock sizes 4 to 14 and sample sizes 6 to 10—great selection of this designer's duds. No delivery. *"25% off." "Sample sale excellent value." "Overstocks are what's there." "KL line better design and quality than Steilmann."*

Kenneth Barnard Rainwear

Clothing
Midtown West

350 5th Avenue, Suite 3013
at 34th Street / 268-1520
Weekdays 9am–5pm.

The Edge: Necessities for the elements. Men's outerwear. Sizes 34 to 36. Wholesale prices $50 to $160. No credit cards.

Kim & Kelly

Clothing
Midtown West

525 7th Avenue, 17th Floor
between 38th and 39th Streets / 997-3258
Watch for newspaper ads.

The Edge: Sexy knits for all occasions Knits in sweaters to dresses. Prices from $40 to $160. Sizes S–M–L. No credit cards. No delivery.

Klurk

Clothing
Gramercy Park/Murray Hill

1123 Broadway
at 25th Street / 229-9227

Call for sale dates and times.

The Edge: The Rocker Chic look in knitwear. Sweaters from $60, coats from $100. No delivery.

Lauren Hansen
1410 Broadway, 30th Floor
between 38th and 39th Streets / 398-1270
Call to be put on the mailing list.

Clothing
Midtown West

The Edge: Inexpensive sweaters. Most about $25. Sizes S–M–L. No credit cards. No delivery.

Linda Richards
512 7th Avenue
between 38th and 39th Streets / 382-2257
December sales.

Clothing
Midtown West

The Edge: New York casualwear. Semi-annual warehouse sale. Features European-inspired women's designer sportswear and coats. For winter favors gabardine, cashmere, mohair, and lambswool. Prices $20 to $289. No delivery.

Lorenza
240 West 35th Street, Suite 702
between 7th and 8th Avenues / 244-3920
Call for sale dates and times.

Clothing
Midtown West

The Edge: Bridge line classics. Designer novelty jackets and blazers. Also pants and skirts. Velvets, silks, chenilles, boucles, and more. Conservative styling. Luxurious Italian and French fabrics. Jackets retail for $200 to $400, wholesale at $29 to $119. Pants, regularly $159 retail at $59 to $79. Sizes 2 to 16 regular and petites. No delivery. No credit cards.

Lulu Bravo
512 7th Avenue, 39th Floor
between 37th and 38th Streets / 302-0610
Call for sale dates and times.

Clothing
Midtown West

The Edge: Daytime separates in today's fabrics. Some knitwear in the same daytime look. Also an evening collection of dresses and suits. Sizes 4 to 16. No credit cards.

M.A. Rabinowitz
40 East 34th Street, Suite 1216
between 5th and Madison Avenues / 679-8344
Call to be put on the mailing list.

Clothing
Gramercy Park/Murray Hill

The Edge: High-end lingerie. Lingerie from some of the best of the French—Lejaby, Le Mystère, Huit, Pastunette, Chantal Thomas, and others. Legwear from Gerbe, Janira, and Le Bourget. Hair accessories from Evita Peroni. Swimwear from Huit and Cacharel. Prices $2 to $25. No delivery. No credit cards.

Magali Collection
498 7th Avenue, 12th Floor
between 36th and 37th Streets / 239-9055

Clothing
Midtown West

Call for sales dates and times.

The Edge: Inexpensive lines. Two-piece suits, dresses, and separates. Sizes 4 to 18. Very low prices—$35 to $95. No credit cards. No delivery.

Magaschoni

Clothing
Gramercy Park/Murray Hill

134 West 37th Street, 2nd Floor
between Broadway and 7th Avenues / 947-8748
Call for sale dates and times.

The Edge: Suits, knits, and outerwear. Suits in crepe and wool gabardine. Sample sales run by SSS Sales. Sizes 2 to 14. No delivery.

Malo Cashmere

Clothing
Multiple locations

Call for sale dates and times.

quality style service value
47   47   33   43

The Edge: Must have collection. Top-quality, best designer's cashmeres from Malo, Gentry, Portofino, and Saverio Palatella. Also leather handbags. No delivery. *"Great buys at 50% off."*

Locations: Midtown West: 745 5th Avenue, #1225, at 58th Street (753-7015) / 745 5th Avenue, Suite 3100, between 57th and 58th Streets (753-7015)

Maria Ficalora Knitwear Ltd.

Clothing
Gramercy Park/Murray Hill

34 West 22nd Street, 4th Floor
between 5th and 6th Avenues / 645-6905
Call for sale dates and times.

The Edge: Knits galore. No delivery.

Mark Eisen

Clothing
Gramercy Park/Murray Hill

134 West 37th Street, 2nd Floor
between Broadway and 7th Avenues / 947-8748
Call for sale dates and times.

The Edge: Young new designer. Find women's suits, knitwear, evening wear, and more. Sample sales run by SSS Sales. Sizes 2 to 14. No delivery.

Mary McCadden Couture / Collection MMcF

240 West 35th Street, 17th Floor
between 7th and 8th Avenues / 736-4078
Call for sale dates and times.

Clothing
Midtown West

The Edge: Her distinctive line. The time to find bargains from her couture and more moderate collection. Prices are $100 to $1,500. Sizes 2 to 14. No credit cards. No delivery.

Mevisto

134 West 37th Street, 2nd Floor
between Broadway and 7th Avenue / 947-8748
Call for sale dates and times.

Clothing
Gramercy Park/Murray Hill

quality style service value

The Edge: Nice for the office. Rayon and wool crepes, matte jersey, and velvet suits and separates. Suits and dresses. Sample sales run by SSS Sales. Sizes 2 to 14. No delivery. *"I have a few of their suits—they last forever."*

Michael Kors

55o 7th Avenue, 7th Floor
between 39th and 40th Streets / 221-1950
Call for sale dates and times.

Clothing
Midtown West

quality style service value

The Edge: Kors galore. Elegant designer clothing. No delivery. *"Wonderful finds at 50% off."*

Michael Simon

134 West 37th Street, 2nd Floor
between Broadway and 7th Avenue / 947-8748
Call for sale dates and times.

Clothing
Gramercy Park/Murray Hill

quality style service value

The Edge: Stylish showy sweaters—day and evening. Some beaded, some embroidered, some with each. No try-ons. Sample sales run by SSS Sales. No delivery. *"Cheap sweaters; stylish young-looking."*

Nanette Lepore/Robespierre

225 West 35th Street
between 7th and 8th Avenues / 594-0012
Call to be put on the mailing list.

Clothing
Midtown West

The Edge: Festive cocktail dresses—from rhumba dresses to gilded lace dresses. Also tailored suits and A-line dresses for work. No credit cards. No delivery.

New Frontier

244 West 39th Street, 5th Floor
between 7th and 8th Avenues / 947-8748
Call for sale dates and times.

Clothing
Midtown West

The Edge: The source for blazers, stretch pants, and suits in pastel colors and neutrals. Find Polar fleece, stretch velour, stretch twills, denim, and more. Sizes 4 to 14, XS to L. Prices $10 to $200. Sample sales run by SSS Sales. No delivery.

Norma Kamali

134 West 37th Street, 2nd Floor
between Broadway and 7th Avenues / 947-8748
Call for sale dates and times.

Clothing
Gramercy Park/Murray Hill

quality style service value

The Edge: Kamali exclusively. Her collection, with past-season clothing priced from $79 to $199. Sample sales run by SSS Sales. No delivery.

Onward Kashiyama

499 7th Avenue, 14th Floor
between 36th and 37th Streets / 629-6100
Call to be put on the mailing list.

Clothing
Midtown West

The Edge: Cutting-edge samples. The source for Jean Paul Gaultier, Helmet Lange, and others wholesale. No delivery.

P.H.D.

80 West 40th Street, 2nd Floor
between 5th and 6th Avenues / 719-0221
Call for sale dates and times.

Clothing
Midtown West

The Edge: Young and fun. Young designer lines, including Laundry Industry, Ventilo, Grass Roots, Moreno Martini da Firenze, Spirit of the Lake, Big Star, Blue System, Majestic, Roberto Collina, Peter Hadley, Totem Swimwear, and Tracy Reese. No delivery. No credit cards.

Paco and Celeste

3 East 54th Street, 12th Floor
between 5th and Madison Avenues / 308-9023
Call to be put on the mailing list.

Clothing
Midtown East

The Edge: Luggage, carry-ons, handbags, backpacks. Find leather, suede, nylon, etc. No delivery. No credit cards.

Per Lui Per Lei

525 7th Avenue, 19th Floor
at 38th Street / 302-8484
Call to be put on the mailing list.

Clothing
Midtown West

The Edge: Semi-annual sample and stock sale. Features current labels from the collection. Expect to find washable silk in blazers, pants, skirts, shirts, T-shirts, and silk sweaters. All sizes. Prices $10 to $150. No credit cards. No delivery.

Philippe Adec Equipment and Nima Knits

209 West 38th Street, 2nd Floor
between 7th and 8th Avenues / 391-8070
Call to be put on the mailing list.

Clothing
Midtown West

The Edge: Fashionable shirts and dresses in silk, satin, velvet, and cotton. Sample and stock sale. Collection features trousers, skirts, blazers, dresses, and outerwear in wool blends and silks. Novelty knits plus pullovers. Use freight elevator only. No credit cards. No delivery.

Regina Porter

500 7th Avenue
at 38th Street / 354-5250
Call for sale dates and times.

Clothing
Midtown West

The Edge: Moderately priced sportswear. Find blouses, skirts, pants, and jackets priced at $40 to $75—about half of wholesale. Sizes 4 to 16. Call Chris for an appointment. No delivery.

Rena Lange
Clothing
Midtown West

730 5th Avenue, 10th Floor
between 56th and 57th Streets / 262-8065
Call to be put on the mailing list.

The Edge: Glamour wholesale. Gorgeous day to evening clothing by this noted designer. No delivery. *"Go early—the best selection flies out."*

Renfrew Collection Ltd.
Clothing
Gramercy Park/Murray Hill

214 West 39th Street, Suite 905
between 7th and 8th Avenues / 944-4030
Call to be put on the mailing list.

The Edge: Shirts in brilliant colors made in fine wools and silks—in a soft feel. Semi-annual sample and stock sale. Items from the just-past season. Expect to find trousers, jackets, and shirts for women. For children and men, some sweaters. Sizes 2 to 16, S to XL. Prices are $25 to $150. No delivery.

Robert Danes
Clothing
SoHo/TriBeCa

476 Broome Street, 2nd Floor
between Wooster and Greene Streets / 941-5680
Call to be put on the mailing list.

The Edge: High end. Designer clothing made in fabulous fabrics—silk crepe, wools, silk georgettes, and jacquards in colors and classic browns and blacks. This designer will take you from day (skirts, suits, and dresses) to evening (gowns). Featured in *Elle, W,* and *WWD,* among others. Sizes 2 to 10. No credit cards. No delivery.

Roy Ogden
Clothing
Midtown West

570 7th Avenue
near 41st Street / 575-8806
Weekdays 10am–7pm, Sat 11am–4pm (ring bell).

The Edge: Tailored classic clothing. Featured in *New York* magazine for its tailored clothing cut in classic styles out of fine fabrics in good colors. The collection includes blazers, skirts, slacks (cashmere and wool blends), dresses, and coats offered at 50% off retail prices. Discounter. No delivery.

SSS Sales
Clothing
Gramercy Park/Murray Hill

134 West 37th Street, 2nd Floor
between Broadway and 7th Avenues / 947-8748
Mon noon–6pm, Tues–Fri 10am–6pm.

The Edge: You never know! Tends to feature more moderate lines. From children's items to those for grandma—something for everyone—from sportswear to evening clothing. Every week new merchandise. Runs sample sales for many manufacturers, including Augustus Suiting, Balinger*Gold, Betsey Johnson, Celine, Urban Outfitters, Cynthia Steffe/Francess & Rita, Mag/Magaschoni, Mark Eisen, Mevisto, Norma Kamali, Premise, 525 Made in America, Michael Simon, Nicole Miller Accessories, Steilmann, Tricots St. Raphael, Kenar, Cynthia Rowley, Item, Wilke Rodriguez, and more. Known for deep discounts. No delivery.

Sanyo by Carol Cohen

512 7th Avenue, 7th Floor
between 37th and 38th Streets / 869-2990
Call to be put on the mailing list.

Clothing
Midtown West

quality style service value

The Edge: Outerwear. Microfiber balmacans, trenches, and swing raincoats. Coats made from gabardines and more. Great velvet quilted jackets. Sizes 2 to 16 and petite 0 to 12 for women and a full range of sizes for men. Men's rainwear, with or without button-in warmers.

Sergio Pellari

46 West 55th Street, 4th Floor
between 5th and 6th Avenues / 582-0200
By appointment.

Clothing
Midtown West

The Edge: For the young. Clothing by Marina Martin, Villa Nova, and Speak Easy. Call Nina for an appointment. No credit cards. No delivery.

Showroom Seven

498 7th Avenue, 24th Floor
between 36th and 37th Streets / 643-4810
Call to be put on the mailing list.

Clothing
Midtown West

quality style service value

The Edge: Young—cutting edge. Sample and stock items in small sizes only. Mostly for women (sizes 4 to 10), occasionally for men. Favors contemporary European and domestic designer sportswear and accessories. Designers include Ghost, Erickson Beamon (jewelry designer for Anna Sui and Richard Tyler), Lianne Barnes, Severin, Genius, Dilettante, Russell Bennett, Cesar Galindo, Stephen Jones Hats, Ann Turk (exotic leather handbags), Beverly Mehl, Eva Branca, Amaya, Violeta Villacorta, Whistles clothing, and Nancy Severin Venetian lace dresses. No delivery.

Soiffer/Haskin, Inc.

767-9296
Weekdays 9am–5pm only on sales dates.

Clothing
Mail/phone

quality style service value

The Edge: Runs the sales for some of the greats. Represents Escada, DKNY, Emanuel, and Emanuel Ungaro, among others, at periodic sample sales, some of which are held at the Parsons School of Design. Call for their announcements. Discounter. No delivery. *"30% off."*

Staff USA, Inc.

495 Broadway, 5th Floor
corner of Broome Street / 925-9700
Call for sale dates and times.

Clothing
SoHo/TriBeCa

The Edge: Today's hot designers. Features hot designers, including Vivienne Westwood Red, Vivienne Westwood Man, Costume National, Costume Homme, Alberto Viana for New York Industries, Gym, Oliver by Valentino, NN Studio, and more. Prices from $20 to $350. Sizes 2 to 12. Expect to find suits, shirts, slacks, dresses, skirts, and jackets. No delivery.

Steve Fabrikant

550 7th Avenue, 24th Floor

Clothing
Midtown West

between 39th and 40th Streets / 869-6777
Call to be put on the mailing list.

quality style service value

The Edge: Looks and travels well. Sample and stock items from Steve's current collection of easy-to-wear elegant knits—dresses, suits, and sports separates. Great for the office. Check out his styles at Bergdorf, which maintains a designer shop devoted to his collection. Fans of Fabrikant include Jane Pauley, Deborah Norville, and others on the go who always look good. Once a month one-day-only sample sale. No credit cards. No delivery. *"Always finds."*

Subito
390 5th Avenue, Suite 611
at 36th Street / 290-2646
Call to be put on the mailing list.

Clothing
Midtown West

The Edge: Haute Italian wholesale. You know the labels—the big ones with the sample sale providing prices at least 50% of wholesale. Retail prices on suits $1,100 to $2,200 and blouses up to $400. Substantial savings on top items. Expect to find at times Dolce & Gabbana, Genny, and more—below wholesale. These are the people who were the first to discover and discount high-end European designer clothing—remember Damages on Madison Avenue?. No credit cards. No delivery.

Susan Lazar
214 West 39th Street, Suite 505
between 7th and 8th Avenues / 302-5888
Weekdays 9am–5:30pm.

Clothing
Midtown West

The Edge: Young and nice. Coats, sweaters, jackets, pants, skirts, and more. Prices $60 to $400. No delivery. *"Up-and-coming designer—great suits."*

Sylvia Heisel
230 West 39th Street, 3rd Floor
between 7th and 8th Avenues / 719-3916
Call to be put on the mailing list.

Clothing
Midtown West

The Edge: The Barneys look. Heisel sells to Barneys, so expect its clean lines with clothing made of jersey and silk fabrics. No delivery.

TSE Cashmere
525 7th Avenue, 19th Floor
at 38th Street / 921-3600
Call for sale dates and times.

Clothing
Midtown West

quality style service value

The Edge: So comfy. Lovely sweaters, slacks, and sweat suits in cashmere, cashmere blends, and wool. Colors are seasonal. No delivery. *"SoHo sale." "Not much there—but 50% off."*

Tocca
134 West 37th Street, 2nd Floor
between Broadway and 7th Avenue / 947-8748
Call for sale dates and times.

Clothing
Gramercy Park/Murray Hill

The Edge: Designer dresses and sportswear. Find twin sweater sets, bags, and more. Sample sales run by SSS Sales. No delivery.

Ungaro

650 5th Avenue, 35th Floor
at 52nd Street / 826-9800
Call to be put on the mailing list.

Clothing
Midtown West

quality style service value

The Edge: Ungaro's collection. The couture line at incredible prices: suits for $500 to $800, blouses for $200—still expensive! No delivery.

Vera Porter

488 7th Avenue, Suite 10K
between 36th and 37th Streets / 971-0209
By appointment

Clothing
Midtown West

quality style service value

The Edge: Sonia Rykiel and St. John styling. Custom-fit handloomed knitwear for day to evening wear. Elegant contemporary jackets, pants, skirts, tunics, sweaters, vests, coats, and dresses in natural blends. Hundreds of color options. No delivery. *"Classic clothing that could go anywhere. Some new-looking, others with an older matronly style." "Great for work, particularly those travel days."*

Vestimenta

41 East 57th Street, Suite 903
between 5th and Madison Avenues / 207-8100
Call for sale dates and times.

Clothing
Midtown East

quality style service value

The Edge: Sold in Barneys and selected boutiques. The best Italian looks for men and women. Expect classic tailored clothing to wear to the office and casual dinners at the boss's. Great fabrics and tailoring. No delivery. *"Limited selection, but lovely—50% off."*

Via Madison

244 Madison Avenue
between 37th and 38th Streets / 599-3533
Weekdays 10am–7pm, Sat 11am–6pm.

Clothing
Gramercy Park/Murray Hill

quality style service value

The Edge: Fine Italian clothing for women as well as contemporary domestic fashions. Italian fabrics and styling—wool and cashmere coats ($295), wool suits with pants or skirts ($195), and for around $100, slack and skirt separates and sweaters and scarves in many styles, colors, and fabrics. Prices are about a third to a half of retail.

Votre Nom

214 West 39th Street, Suite 804
between 7th and 8th Avenues / 764-3200
Call to be put on the mailing list.

Clothing
Midtown West

The Edge: Great for the dating crowd. Great casualwear, including linen/viscose separates, leggings, blouses, wool and cashmere blazers, and more. Sizes 4 to 14. Prices $86 to $200. No credit cards. No delivery.

Weekend Exercise Company

Clothing
Midtown West

58 West 40th Street, 16th Floor
between 5th and 6th Avenues / 354-0143
Call for sale dates and times.

The Edge: Dress to sweat. Leotards, bike shorts, leggings, unitards, active shorts, crop tops, kids' bodywear—everything to sweat right. Labels include Marika, Marika Sport, Performance Barishnikov, Barishnikov Studio, Barishnikov Dance, and Toughwear. No credit cards. No delivery.

Wippette Rainthings

Clothing
Midtown West

500 7th Avenue, 14th Floor
between 37th and 38th Streets / 852-4900
Annual sale. Call to be put on the mailing list.

The Edge: Stylish outerwear. Features vinyl rainwear for men, women, and children. Prices from $15 to $25. No delivery.

Yves Saint Laurent & Christian La Croix

Clothing
Midtown East

543 Madison Avenue, 3rd Floor
between 54th and 55th Streets / 478-0700
Call for sale dates and times.

50	50	40	50
quality	style	service	value

The Edge: Yves is always appropriate. Sportswear and evening wear of these greats offered from their just-past season. Sizes 2 to 16. Also find costume jewelry, handbags, scarves, belts, and ties. Great selection. Prices are 50% below wholesale. *"Very high-end clothes". "There's lots of St. Laurent's second line vs. couture or ready-to-wear. Much cheaper—suits go for $300 to $400. You'll find LaCroix at good discounts." "Much for evening as well as day." "Go early."*

Zanella

Clothing
Midtown East

681 5th Avenue, 7th Floor
between 53rd and 54th Streets / 371-2121
Call for sale dates and times.

The Edge: Timeless Italian clothing for both women and men. Expect to find separates for women and suits, sportscoats, trousers, shirts, and knits for men. Impeccable design, detail, and fabrics. No delivery.

Accessory Street / Designs on Travel / Dolcetta

Clothing-accessories
Midtown West

350 Fifth Avenue, Suite 2101
Empire State Building, at 34th Street / 868-9700
Month of December; call for times.

The Edge: Full range of accessories. Find silk scarves, handbags, small leather items, and travel/cosmetic bags. Sample and stock sale. No credit cards. No delivery.

Allyn & Co.

Clothing-accessories
Gramercy Park/Murray Hill

8 East 36th Street, 4th Floor
between 5th and Madison Avenues / 532-5400
Annually in December. Call for dates.

The Edge: Christmas stocking stuffers. Sample and stock sale. Annual sale in December, in time for Christmas gift giving. Expect to find handbags, scarves, belts, and jewelry. Prices start at $5. No credit cards. No delivery.

Carey Adina, Inc.

Clothing-accessories
Midtown East

5 East 57th Street, 14th Floor
between 5th and Madison Avenues / 755-5234
Call for sale dates and times.

quality style service value

The Edge: The source for special-occasion bags. From day to executive to evening bags, find glamour in satin, velvet, or leathers in interesting shapes (including the heart bag, now in various sizes) and matching designs. Priced from $50 to $350 for leather or fabric. Will do custom work, but will not copy others' designs. Will repair her own bags. Offers sample sales at Christmas for a select group only. No delivery.

Carolina Amato, Inc.

Clothing-accessories
Gramercy Park/Murray Hill

389 5th Avenue, Suite 707
at 36th Street / 532-8413
Call for sale dates and times.

The Edge: Gloves galore. Gloves, gloves, gloves. From cashmere knit gloves and mittens to bridal glove samples for brides, bridesmaids, and flower girls. Prices start at $5, with the cashmere gloves at $10 to $15 (retail at $25 to $35). No delivery.

Chelsey Imports Ltd.

Clothing-accessories
Midtown West

392 5th Avenue, Suite 900
at 36th Street / 244-5858
Annual sale; call to get on the mailing list.

The Edge: Scarves, capes, shawls, and wraps for day or evening. Fabrics include chenilles, printed velvets, cut velvets, cashmeres, wool, jacquards, silk/wool challis, silk chiffons, and silk. No delivery.

Colette Malouf

Clothing-accessories
SoHo/TriBeCa

594 Broadway, Suite 1216
near Houston Street / 941-9588
Call for sale dates and times.

The Edge: Wonderful hair accessories. Featured at Bendel, Saks, and Harrods for $18 to $125, just $5 to $40 at the sample sale. Some bridal pieces. No credit cards. No delivery.

Couture Cafe

Clothing-accessories
Gramercy Park/Murray Hill

431 5th Avenue
near 39th Street / 213-4353
Call to be placed on mailing list.

quality style service value

The Edge: Accessories sourced from young new designers. Expect to find hats, gloves, and jewelry at about 25% of retail. Excellent styles as you'd expect to find at Bendel and Zitomer. Also pants suits for more casual wear. Prices $20 to $150. No credit cards. No delivery.

Dayne DuVall, Inc.
54 West 39th Street, 10th Floor
between 5th and 6th Avenues / 768-2444
Call for sale dates and times.

Clothing-accessories
Midtown West

The Edge: Stylish accessories. Delicate jewelry, scarves, and handbags as featured in *Style, People, Mademoiselle, Elle,* and *Vogue* and sold at Saks, Neiman Marcus, and the like. Prices $5 to $100. Home accessories include pillows, picture frames, vases, and more. No delivery.

Echo Design Group
10 East 40th Street, 16th Floor
between 5th and Madison Avenues / 686-8771
Call for sale dates and times.

Clothing-accessories
Gramercy Park/Murray Hill

The Edge: Lots of different scarves and ties. Echo is the scarf licensee for many designers, including Ralph Lauren, so you never know whose scarves you may find. Sale features silk and wool scarves for ladies and ties for men. No delivery. *"Great sales."*

Eric Javits Hats
406 West 31st Street, 3rd Floor West
between 9th and 10th Avenues / 374-4287
Advertises sales.

Clothing-accessories
Midtown West

quality style service value

The Edge: Classic hats. You know them—gorgeous hats as featured at the best department stores such as Saks. No delivery. *"Exclusive, crowded, but what a bargain." "40% off." "Sales are on Sunday, so the Orthodox crowd floods the store."*

Estee Einstein
184 2nd Avenue, Suite 1B
at 12th Street / 677-2360
Call for sale dates and times.

Clothing-accessories
Flatiron/East Village

quality style service value

The Edge: High-end hats. Hats as seen in *WWD, Elle,* and elsewhere. Day to evening statement hats. No credit cards. No delivery. *"Beautiful unique things."*

Etcetera Accessories
433 5th Avenue, 4th Floor
between 38th and 39th Streets / 684-4144
Call for sale dates and times.

Clothing-accessories
Gramercy Park/Murray Hill

quality style service value

The Edge: Great to make your look. Accessories—belts, scarves, hats, handbags—favoring a contemporary look. Prices $5 to $25. No credit cards. No delivery. *"I love this store—I practically live there."*

525 Made in America
134 West 37th Street, 2nd Floor
between Broadway and Seventh Avenue / 947-8748
Call for sale dates and times.

Clothing-accessories
Gramercy Park/Murray Hill

quality style service value

The Edge: Lovely comfys. Sweaters, blankets, and scarves for everyone in your family. No try-ons. Sample sales run by SSS Sales. No delivery. *"Trendy, bright popular colors and patterns. 15% off."*

Frou and Princess Foufou

Clothing-accessories
Midtown West

236 West 26th Street, Suite 303
between 7th and 8th Avenues / 633-2066
Call to be put on the mailing list.

The Edge: Hip young looks Two young designers who feature hats, bags, scarves, and hair accessories sold at Barneys, Intermix, and Big Drop. Prices a fraction of retail. No credit cards. No delivery.

ICV/Sarti Imports

Clothing-accessories
Midtown West

12 West 57th Street, Penthouse
at 5th Avenue / 757-0500
Call to be put on the mailing list.

The Edge: High-end accessories. Sale favors fine Italian accessories—Ferre, Desmo, Fornasetti— including handbags, evening bags, briefcases, agendas, belts, wallets, key chains, and more in calfskin, printed crocodile, and lizard and other fine fabrics, plus scarves and shawls. Prices from $65 to $395. No delivery.

Jeffrey Aronoff, Inc.

Clothing-accessories
Gramercy Park/Murray Hill

16 West 23rd Street, 2nd Floor
between 5th and 6th Avenues / 645-3155
Call for sales dates and times.

quality style service value

The Edge: Divine accessories for you and the house. Coty award winner sells his wonderful scarves and throws at Saks, Neiman Marcus, and Bergdorf, among other places. Merchandise featured in *Architectural Digest, Elle, Decor,* and *House Beautiful.* Retail prices range from $210 to $385; prices here are more than half of retail. Chenille throws regularly $510 to $990, wholesale here at $340 to $660—great taste. No delivery.

Judith Leiber

Clothing-accessories
Midtown West

20 West 33rd Street, 2nd Floor
between 5th and 6th Avenues / 736-4244
Call for sales dates and times.

quality style service value

The Edge: Celebrity collectibles. Sold at all the finest shops. Known for her fabulous evening handbags, including her signature miniatures—animal purses encrusted with Austrian crystals. Her collection includes leather handbags for day, small leather items, belts, jewelry boxes, and now jewelry. Very, very expensive, even at wholesale. No credit cards. No delivery. *"If you ever wanted one, this is the sale, 50% off." "Everyone stands on 'long lines'—but worth the wait."*

Lisette Handbags

Clothing-accessories
Gramercy Park/Murray Hill

1 East 33rd Street, 11th Floor
between 5th and Madison Avenues / 684-6272
Call for time and watch for ads.

The Edge: Moderate handbags. Good prices on handbags—$25 to $45 for fabric and synthetic bags to $55 to $95 for leathers. Also some leather items priced $8 to $48. Savings are less than half of retail. No credit cards. No delivery.

M + J Savitt, Inc.

Clothing-accessories
Midtown West

10 West 46th Street, Suite 1301
between 5th and 6th Avenues / 869-5228
Call for times or watch for ads.

The Edge: At all the department stores. From sterling-silver designer jewelry to 18-karat gold and cubic zirconia and pearls—a wide range of styles and prices. No delivery.

The Edge: Nice chapeaus. High-fashion hand-blocked straw hats and linen caps to winter wools. Featured on the cover of *Vanity Fair*. Something for everyone. No credit cards.

Matkins Hats Ltd.

Clothing-accessories
Midtown West

212 West 35th Street, 12th Floor
between 7th and 8th Avenues / 594-6666
Call for sale dates and times.

The Edge: Designer hats featured in *Harpers Bazaar,* the *New York Times Magazine* fashion issue, and on the cover of *Vanity Fair*. For women: animal prints, feathered hats, and furs, including fox, lamb, beaver, etc. For men: both veloured fur felt and flat fur felt. All hand-blocked. No credit cards. No delivery.

Nancy Marshall Second Edition Ltd.

Clothing-accessories
Midtown West

15 West 36th Street, 8th Floor
near 5th Avenue / 465-2104
Call for sales dates and times.

The Edge: Accessories for you and your home. Styling is antique Victorian costume jewelry. Lovely French enameled accessories. Also home accessories from bookmarks to desk accessories. No delivery. No credit cards.

Nicole Miller Accessories

Clothing-accessories
Gramercy Park/Murray Hill

134 West 37th Street, 2nd Floor
between Broadway and 7th Avenue / 947-8748
Call for sale dates and times.

quality style service value

The Edge: Nicole glamour. Discounts on her accessories—wallets, makeup bags, memo books, umbrellas (in all sizes, including children's sizes), ties, and more. Also some Erik Stewart sweaters. Sample sales run by SSS Sales. No delivery. *"Her ties, scarves, etc. are all original."*

Nina Footwear/Delman

Clothing-accessories
Midtown West

730 5th Avenue, 8th Floor
between 56th and 57th Streets / 399-2323
Call to be put on the mailing list.

The Edge: The Bergdorf look. Classic Delman loafers, flats, sandals, and pumps at $75 to $85, less than half of retail prices. Sizes mostly 6 to 10M, 7 to 9N. Summer sandals, platforms, and espadrilles at $20 to $50. No delivery. *"Always the best designers, fabulous service."*

Pancaldi

Clothing-accessories
Midtown East

41 East 57th Street
between Madison and Park Avenues / 755-2212
Sales twice annually: Mar–Apr and Sept–Oct.

quality style service value

The Edge: Run don't walk—high-end chic now affordable Wonderful showroom sales twice a year. Shoes mostly by Isaac Mizrahi, Pancaldi, and Escada on sale in the showroom in sizes 5 to 10M, with some AA and some samples in size 6B. Shoe prices are unbelievable—under $100 for shoes that sell retail for several hundred dollars. Expect to find long lines—but the wait is often worth it. Cash only. No delivery. *"I can't resist—call me Imelda."*

Patricia Underwood

Clothing-accessories
Midtown West

242 West 36th Street, 11th Floor
between 7th and 8th Avenues / 268-3774
Call for sale dates and times.

quality style service value

The Edge: Simple stunning hats. Hats sold at the best department stores only. Prices around $100 wholesale. No credit cards. No delivery.

Portolano

Clothing-accessories
Midtown West

32 West 39th Street, 5th Floor
between 5th and 6th Avenues / 719-4403
Call to be put on the mailing list.

The Edge: Fine accessories. Find gloves, small leather goods, handbags, silk ties, hosiery, and some sweaters. Gloves—cashmere, silk, and lambswool linings from all the finest companies, including Fendi and Moschino. Prices start at $5. No delivery.

R.J. Graziano's, Inc.

Clothing-accessories
Gramercy Park/Murray Hill

389 5th Avenue, 3rd Floor
at 36th Street / 685-3737
Call for sale dates and times.

quality style service value

The Edge: Costume jewelry and accessories with an antique look. Many with semiprecious stones. Prices are $5 to $50. No credit cards. No delivery.

Rafael Sanchez

Clothing-accessories
Midtown West

35 West 35th Street, 7th Floor
between 5th and 6th Avenues / 967-8214
Call for sale dates and times.

The Edge: You know the line. See the bags at Bergdorf and Bendel. Handbags retail for $350 and up, wholesale at $75 to $400. No credit cards. No delivery.

Shalimar Accessories

Clothing-accessories
Gramercy Park/Murray Hill

10 East 39th Street
between 5th and Madison Avenues / 685-8087
Sales twice annually,
May–Jul and Oct–Dec: Tues and Thurs noon–6pm.

quality style service value

The Edge: European made silk and cashmere lined gloves. Wonderful showroom sales twice a year for Fall and Spring fashions. These are the gloves sold at over 350 retail outlets, including Nordstroms, Brooks and Bloomingdales, but here at wholesale prices. Designers include Issac Mizrahi, Ellen Tracy, Norma Kamali, Adrienne Vittadini, and Vera Wang. Find classic leather gloves, lined in silk or cashmere and cashmere as well as wool gloves, scarves, and hats. *"Such beautiful gloves—as good as buying in Florence."*

Sharif / Jay Herbert / American Handbags

Clothing-accessories
Gramercy Park/Murray Hill

33 East 33rd Street, 4th Floor
between Madison and Park Avenues / 679-7373
Call to be put on the mailing list.

The Edge: Basic handbags and small leather goods. No credit cards. No delivery.

Sola

Clothing-accessories
Gramercy Park/Murray Hill

162 5th Avenue, Suite 1009
at 21st Street / 620-0988
Call to be put on the mailing list.

quality style service value

The Edge: Bags, jewelry, and scarves. Expect to find Maria V. Pinto RTW accessories, Carrie Forbes handbags, Pazuki scarves, Camilla Ridley scarves, and Dorian Webb semiprecious and Venetian glass jewelry and Hat Attack hats. Prices $30 to $300. No delivery.

Sondra Roberts Ltd.

Clothing-accessories
Gramercy Park/Murray Hill

383 5th Avenue, 6th Floor
at 36th Street / 696-9726
Call for sale dates and times.

The Edge: High-fashion handbags. Also find belts, small leather goods, briefcases, and carry-alls. No credit cards. No delivery.

To Boot Warehouse

Clothing-accessories
Greenwich Village

603 Washington Street
between Morton and Leroy Streets / 463-0438
Call for sale dates and times.

quality style service value

The Edge: Lots of their standards. Mostly men's shoes, some women's. Prices are less than half of what their stores sell shoes for. Shoes and boots from the current and earlier seasons. No credit cards. No delivery.

Tracy Watts

Clothing-accessories
Chelsea

305 West 20th Street, Lower Level
between 8th and 9th Avenues / 727-7349
Weekdays 10am–6pm.

The Edge: Today's look. Hats as featured in *Vogue, W,* and the *New York Times Magazine* fashion issue, among other publications, and at fine stores, including Barneys. No credit cards.

Two Girls NYC

411 FIfth Avenue, Suite 803
between 36th and 37th Streets / 481-3559
Call for sale dates and times.

Clothing-accessories
Gramercy Park/Murray Hill

The Edge: Seasonal themed chapeaus. Hats, scarves, boas, and flower pins made from suedes, velvets, tweeds, fake furs, and taffetas. Lots of fun designs, including hats with holiday themes—Halloween and Christmas. Prices from $3 to $75. No credit cards. No delivery.

Walter Katten, Inc.

10 East 33rd Street
between 5th and Madison Avenues / 679-7898
Call for sale dates and times.

Clothing-accessories
Gramercy Park/Murray Hill

The Edge: Italian handbags. In leathers (calfskin and soft nappa) and also alligator, ostrich, and lizard in classic styles. Prices from $85 (versus retail prices from $250). No credit cards. No delivery.

Flapdoodles

112 West 34th Street, Suite 819
between Broadway and 7th Avenue / 643-0801
Call for sale dates and times.

Clothing-children
Midtown West

quality   style   service   value

The Edge: Great kidswear—an adorable line. Sample sale only. Infants to 12 months; girls and boys to 6 years. No credit cards. No delivery.

Richard B. Kutner

131 West 33rd Street, Suite 301
between 6th and 7th Avenues / 594-3740
Call for sale dates and times.

Clothing-children
Midtown West

quality   style   service   value

The Edge: Nice lines. Features European children's wear sold in all the best boutiques. No credit cards. No delivery. *"David Charles dresses. French baby dresses."*

Showroom

131 West 33rd Street
between 6th and 7th Avenues / 947-3443
Call for sale dates and times.

Clothing-children
Midtown West

The Edge: Better children's lines. By appointment only. No credit cards. No delivery.

Toning Plus

1407 Broadway, Lower Level
between 38th and 39th Streets / 947-8748
Call for sale dates and times.

Clothing-children
Midtown West

The Edge: Great children's lines. Flapdoodles, Fungraphics, Les Touts Petits, Harley Davidson, Converse, Sam & Libby, and more. A full range of clothing to take your children everywhere. Sizes infant to preteen. Sample sales run by SSS Sales. No delivery.

Fernando Sanchez
5 West 19th Street, 7th Floor
between 5th and 6th Avenues / 929-5060
Call for sale dates and times.

Clothing-lingerie
Chelsea

The Edge: Lovely things. Wonderful sensuous lingerie. No delivery.

Gruppa Intermoda
180 Madison Avenue, Suite 1602
between 33rd and 34th Streets / 213-4599
Weekdays 8:30am–5pm.

Clothing-lingerie
Gramercy Park/Murray Hill

The Edge: Top lingerie lines. Call Lucy for an appointment to buy wonderful hose and lingerie. Available are hose, lingerie, and underwear. In legwear, Moschino leggings and hose, Christian Lacroix hosiery, and Nina Ricci hose. Lingerie is sourced from Italy, France, and Belgium. Labels include Ravage, Etincelle, Stafunia, Nina Ricci, Lisanza, and Ritralti. Prices $20 to $65. No delivery.

Hanky Panky
303 Park Avenue South
between 26th and 27th Streets / 725-4996
Call to be put on the mailing list.

Clothing-lingerie
Gramercy Park/Murray Hill

quality	style	service	value
40	45	28	40

The Edge: Underwear so light you forget you're wearing any. Children's clothing and underwear for women. The underwear is slinky and light—you won't know it's there. No credit cards. No delivery. *"Sells me full boxes anytime."*

Hanro
40 East 34th Street, 2nd Floor
between 5th and Madison Avenues / 532-3320
Call to be put on the mailing list.

Clothing-lingerie
Gramercy Park/Murray Hill

quality	style	service	value
50	40	25	47

The Edge: Hanro luxury at unbelievable prices. Mostly samples. Expect to find Hanro underwear, bras, and camisoles. Items go fast, so get there early or expect to find everything gone. It's a madhouse, but worth it if you have fortitude. No try-ons. No delivery. No credit cards.

Joe Boxer
1466 Broadway, Suite 207
at 42nd Street / 354-2727
Call to be put on the mailing list.

Clothing-lingerie
Midtown West

quality	style	service	value
45	45	35	30

The Edge: Boxers for all. Boxers for all. Mostly a men's place with boxers, pajamas, and T-shirts in flannel, cotton jersey, and silk. For women and kids, some pajamas too. Prices are $10 to $40. Sizes S to XL. No credit cards. No delivery. *"Good loungewear/sleepwear!"*

Natori Company

600 Secaucus Road
Secaucus / 201-319-0777
Call for sale dates and times.

Clothing-lingerie
New Jersey

quality style service value

The Edge: Lovely lingerie. Warehouse sale, featuring nightgowns to robes at low prices (from $50 for robes). No delivery. *"Elegant—overpriced—available at Century 21." "The prettiest and best for lingerie."*

A la Menthe

236 West 26th Street, Suite 1002
between 7th and 8th Avenues / 675-4651
Call to be put on the mailing list.

Furniture & furnishings
Midtown West

The Edge: Accessories imported from Casablanca. Expect to find mosaic tabletops, wooden tissue boxes, pillows, lanterns, and wrought-iron chairs and screens. Check out her wares at such stores as ABC Carpet & Home, Felissimo, and Portico, among others. Checks accepted. No credit cards. No delivery.

Annie J

180 Varik Street, 8th Floor
at Charleston Street / 741-0112
Call to be put on the mailing list.

Furniture & furnishings
Greenwich Village

The Edge: Festive linen and fabric accessories for the holidays and all occasions. Expect to find lovely Christmas holiday offerings from Christmas tree skirts and stockings to tablecloths and metallic holiday linens. In the regular collection: festive linens, textured boucle throws, cotton chenille throws, and cotton and velvet pillows. Prices from $3 to $100. No delivery.

Area, Inc.

180 Varik Street, 9th Floor
at King Street / 924-7084
Call to be put on the mailing list.

Furniture & furnishings
Greenwich Village

The Edge: Linen linens. Find pure linen linens and linen/cotton duvet covers, sheets, pillowcases, shams, tablecloths, napkins, hand towels, and more. An array in solids, stripes, textures, and modern embroideries. Contemporary Swedish vases and candleholders in crystal. Prices are $10 to $300. No delivery. No credit cards.

Bay Linens

152 Madison Avenue, 16th Floor
between 32nd and 33rd Streets / 725-2002
Call to be put on the mailing list.

Furniture & furnishings
Gramercy Park/Murray Hill

quality style service value

The Edge: Upper-end linens and bedware. Find throws, napkins, place mats, and home accessories. Duvet covers in floral chintz, stripes, and plaids. Luxurious quality—with sample sale prices heavily discounted. Line carried at Bloomingdale's, Bed, Bath & Beyond, and Linen 'n

Things. Call to be put on the mailing list for the sample sales, which are held once or twice a year. No credit cards. No delivery.

Casafina

301 Fields Lane
Brewster / 914-277-5700
Quarterly special sales.

Furniture & furnishings
Westchester

quality style service value

The Edge: Nice presents. Warehouse sale quarterly, featuring hand-painted ceramic china and giftware items. Below-wholesale prices. No delivery. *"Some nice things, most ordinary."*

Dan Levy Ceramics

155 West 29th Street, Suite 3N
between 6th and 7th Avenues / 268-0878
Call to be put on the mailing list.

Furniture & furnishings
Midtown West

The Edge: Fine porcelains. Porcelains, as found in Bergdorf, including dinnerware and gift items such as bowls, and platters, as well as bathroom accessories. No credit cards. No delivery.

Donghia

485 Broadway, 4th Floor
between Grand and Broome Streets / 925-2777
Advertises sales in paper.

Furniture & furnishings
SoHo/TriBeCa

quality style service value

The Edge: Top items for the home. This designer's collection includes wall coverings, textiles, and furniture. Definitely check this out—he's a fabulous designer. No credit cards.

Ellen Evans Collection / Terrafirma Ceramics

152 West 25th Street, 11th Floor
between 6th and 7th Avenues / 645-7600
Call for sale dates and times.

Furniture & furnishings
Midtown West

The Edge: Handcrafted dinner- and tableware. Find dinnerware, trays, platters, bowls, vases, planters, and wine accessories sold worldwide at fine stores and as featured in *Gourmet, New York* magazine's "Best Bets" column, *Food & Wine, Modern Bride, Victoria, Better Homes & Garden,* and *Bon Appetit* magazine. Offers samples, seconds, and overstocked items. No delivery.

George Dell, Inc.

151 West 25th Street, Ground Floor
between 6th and 7th Avenues / 206-8460
Call to be put on the mailing list.

Furniture & furnishings
Midtown West

The Edge: Chairs, table bases, étagères, and accessories. No delivery.

George Milos Co., Inc.

158 West 29th Street, 4th Floor
at 7th Avenue / 594-5096
Call for sale dates and times.

Furniture & furnishings
Midtown West

The Edge: Custom leather and wood humidors. Also find Italian leather desk accessories, picture frames, jewelry boxes, and more. No credit cards. No delivery.

Jabara Group, Inc.
295 5th Avenue, Suite 1213
at 31st Street / 545-7642
Sales held at hotels in New York City. Call to be put on the mailing list.

Furniture & furnishings
Gramercy Park/Murray Hill

The Edge: Fine linens plus holiday linens. Find Christmas stockings, tree skirts, and the like. Home accessories include handmade needlepoint pillows; linens include tablecloths, place mats, runners, and napkins in prints, imported embroidery, and other fabric patterns.

James Cole Company
41 West 25th Street, Ground Floor
between Broadway and 6th Avenue / 741-1500
Annual sale. Call to be put on the mailing list.

Furniture & furnishings
Gramercy Park/Murray Hill

The Edge: Christmas ornaments. No credit cards. No delivery.

Kimberly House Ltd.
168 Madison Avenue, 7th Floor
at 33rd Street / 779-3434
Call to be put on the mailing list.

Furniture & furnishings
Gramercy Park/Murray Hill

The Edge: Fine linens. Accessories for the home, including fine linens for all, tableware, serving pieces, frames, carving sets, and more. Prices are $4 to $500. Materials are fine Egyptian cottons, hand-embroidered designs, bright fruits, florals, and hand-painted items. No delivery.

MU/H
121 East 24th Street, #4R
between Park and Lexington Avenues / 366-4740
Weekdays 9am–5pm, Sat–Sun by appointment.

Furniture & furnishings
Gramercy Park/Murray Hill

The Edge: Home accessories from many designers. A 4,500-square-foot loft space filled with home accessories, antiques, and antique clothing collected for sale by a group of designers. Home accessories include silk napkins and place mats priced from $10 and less. Antique furnishings from the 1880s and a large selection of vintage clothing that date from the 1920s. No credit cards.

Marble Arch Designs
380 Lafayette Street, 2nd Floor
at Great Jones Street / 777-3011
Call to be put on the mailing list.

Furniture & furnishings
Flatiron/East Village

The Edge: Wonderful accessories as sold at Barneys and Adrien Linford. Expect to find napkins, pillows, throws, and tablecloths. Prices from 50¢ to $130—at least half of retail. No credit cards. No delivery.

Mark Rossi
668 Greenwich Street, Suite 339
between Christopher and Barrow Streets / 924-0522

Furniture & furnishings
Greenwich Village

Call to be put on the mailing list.

The Edge: Items featured in *Metropolitan Home* **and** *Bon Appetit.* Expect to find hand-finished and handcrafted home furnishings and giftware such as stone carved and stone-inlaid coasters, dish towels, barware, bath accessories, linen hand towels, napkins and napkin rings, and more. Prices $1 to $150. No credit cards. No delivery.

Paula Sweet

Furniture & furnishings
SoHo/TriBeCa

95 Morton Street, 7th Floor
between Greenwich and Washington Streets / 989-0822
By appointment.

48	48	35	48
quality	style	service	value

The Edge: Lovely things you now can't live without. Elegant home furnishings, including table linens, decorative pillows, throws, and bed coverings. Accessories emphasize the finest fabrics, from plaid flannels to delicate floral designs to creamy white cotton with gold trim. You've seen the line at all the best places—Bergdorf, Neiman Marcus, and the like, and featured in *InStyle, Bon Appetit,* and *Gourmet* magazines. No delivery. *"Not to be missed—an opportunity!"*

Angela Cummings

Jewelry & watches
Midtown West

730 5th Avenue, Suite 1602
between 55th and 56th Streets / 757-7841
Call for sale dates and times.

50	50	40	35
quality	style	service	value

The Edge: Angela at 50% off. Her wonderful collection of sterling-silver, 18-karat-gold inlay jewelry, scarves, and other accessories from her just-past season. Wonderful looks—sold at Bergorf, among other top stores. No credit cards. No delivery. *"Still expensive."*

Antique Source

Jewelry & watches
Gramercy Park/Murray Hill

271 Madison Avenue, Suite 1008
between 39th and 40th Streets / 681-9142
By appointment.

The Edge: Treasures, if you search. Antique and vintage women's jewelry, men's jewelry, fountain pens, and items. Prices from $15 to $400. No delivery.

Ben Amun Co., Inc.

Jewelry & watches
Midtown West

246 West 38th Street., Suite 12A
between 7th and 8th Avenues / 944-6480
Call for sale dates and times.

The Edge: Wide range of looks. From contemporary, hot-fashion-statement jewelry and belts to the classics—pearls. Sample and stock sale. No credit cards. No delivery.

Catherine Stein

Jewelry & watches
Midtown West

8 West 38th Street, 3rd Floor
between 5th and 6th Avenues / 840-1188
Call for sale dates and times.

The Edge: Jewelry combining turquoise, vintage glass, and pearls. A collection of Stein/Blye sterling-silver rings, earrings, and necklaces also. No delivery. No credit cards.

Ciner Fashion Jewelry

20 West 37th Street, 10th Floor
between 5th and 6th Avenues / 947-3770
Once-a-year special sale—two days only

Jewelry & watches
Midtown West

quality style service value

The Edge: Faux showpiece. Once-a-year, pre-Christmas showroom sale. Wonderful costume jewelry pieces—50%+ off retail. You'll find earrings, bracelets, necklaces, and gold-plated jewelry at reasonable prices (earrings, $30; pins, $35; and necklaces, $95 to $200). Favorites are the wonderful Austrian crystal combinations and the large crystal peony pin (looks like vintage Tiffany). Discounter. No delivery. No credit cards. *"Looks like the real stuff." "See it at Saks."*

David Dubin Ltd.

37 West 39th Street, 11th Floor
between 5th and 6th Avenues / 382-0109
Annual sale; call for dates and times.

Jewelry & watches
Midtown West

The Edge: Today's look. Contemporary jewelry in sterling silver in combination with semiprecious stones. Also costume jewelry in gold-tone and silver-tone finishes. Annual sample and stock sale. Prices $5 to $50. No credit cards. No delivery.

Gerard Yosca

39 West 38th Street, 12th Floor
between 5th and 6th Avenues / 302-4349
Call to be put on the mailing list.

Jewelry & watches
Midtown West

The Edge: If you liked Alicia Silverstone's jewelry in *Clueless* **or Sharon Stone's barrettes— this is the source.** Great costume jewels priced retail around $100—with periodic sales bringing prices down to 70% of retail. No credit cards. No delivery.

Lucy Isaacs Designer Jewelry Sample Sale

24 West 40th Street, 9th Floor
between 5th and 6th Avenues / 302-3454
Call for sale dates and times.

Jewelry & watches
Midtown West

The Edge: Annual sample sale of designer jewelry. Collection includes jewels mixed with sterling silver, semiprecious stones, and antique glass. Prices $1 to $180. No credit cards. No delivery.

Magnificent Costume Jewelry, Inc.

654 Madison Avenue, Suite 1703
between 60th and 61st Streets / 750-5379
Call for sale dates and times.

Jewelry & watches
Upper East Side

The Edge: Fine costume jewelry, including faux pearls and rhinestone jewelry. Sold at fine department and specialty stores. Prices $20 to $200. No delivery.

Miguel Ases Designer Jewelry

Jewelry & watches
Midtown West

25 West 31st Street, Suite 705
between 5th Avenue and Broadway / 629-7815
Call for sale dates and times.

The Edge: Classic designs. Expect to find semiprecious stones, freshwater pearls, Austrian crystal on sterling-silver and gold-filled jewelry. The collection is sold at Saks, Bendel, Nordstrom, and the like. Prices $10 to $150. No credit cards. No delivery.

Miriam Haskell

Jewelry & watches
Midtown West

49 West 37th Street, 7th Floor
between 5th and 6th Avenues / 764-3332
Call to be put on the mailing list.

50 50 45 50
quality style service value

The Edge: Classic '30s styling. Sample, one-of-a-kind pieces, discontinued items, and production overruns of her classic jewelry. Wonderful pearls alone and in combinations with rhinestones. Prices are at least half of retail. Checks accepted with two forms of ID. No delivery. No credit cards. *"My favorite jewelry sample sale. Great designs." "Earrings are 50% to 70% off retail. Wide selection."*

Nancy & Rise Ltd.

Jewelry & watches
Midtown West

48 West 48th Street, Suite 1002
between 5th and 6th Avenues / 391-1484
Call for sales dates and times.

45 40 20 45
quality style service value

The Edge: Very elegant selections. Exquisite fine jewels sold at the best department stores. Expect to find a wide selection of jewelry in sterling silver, vermeil, amber, and sterling two-tone styles. For men: cufflinks, key rings, and money clips. Prices $12 to $200. No delivery. *"Excellent-looking jewels which are special gifts for all."*

Paloma Picasso

Jewelry & watches
Midtown West

37 West 57th Street, 5th Floor
between 5th and 6th Avenues / 421-2260
Call to be put on the mailing list.

43 43 33 35
quality style service value

The Edge: Paloma's finest. Her signature collection of jewelry, belts, handbags, and scarves. Prices from $25 to $300. No delivery.

Patti Horn

Jewelry & watches
Multiple locations

Call to be put on the mailing list.

The Edge: Elegant jewelry. Much with semiprecious stones. Prices $10 to $40. No credit cards. No delivery.

Locations: SoHo/TriBeCa: 63 Greene Street, Suite 605, between Spring and Broome Streets (431-6622) / 80 Thompson Street, between Spring and Broome Streets (334-9244)

Roxanne Assoulin

Jewelry & watches
Midtown West

39 West 37th Street, 15th Floor
between 5th and 6th Avenues / 869-5090

Call to be put on the mailing list.

The Edge: One-of-a-kind runway pieces. Find leather chokers, evening jewels, pearls, hair accessories, and day jewels with a classic look. Prices from $5 to $100. No credit cards. No delivery.

Stephen Dweck Jewelry

Jewelry & watches
Midtown West

21 West 38th Street, 17th Floor
between 5th and 6th Avenues / 764-3039
Call for sale dates and times.

quality   style   service   value

The Edge: Elegant jewelry. Featured in *Vogue, Harper's Bazaar,* and *Mirabella.* Jewelry in sterling silver and bronze mixed with semiprecious stones and natural minerals. Jewelry and belts in classic styles. No delivery. *"Love his stuff."*

Swank, Inc.

Jewelry & watches
Gramercy Park/Murray Hill

90 Park Avenue, 19th Floor
between 39th and 40th Streets / 867-2600
Call to be put on the mailing list.

The Edge: Accessories sold everywhere. The Swank line, which includes Anne Klein, Pierre Cardin, and Colours by Alexander Julian. For women: designer jewelry. For men: also jewelry, wallets, belts, and braces. No delivery.

Blue Duck Shearling Company

Leathers
Midtown West

463 7th Avenue, Suite 702
corner 35th Street / 268-3122
Call for sale dates and times.

The Edge: Medium-quality shearling coats. Okay prices—with great prices on sale dates. Open to the public for the season, starting in the fall. Custom orders accommodated. No credit cards. No delivery.

Denimax by DM Emporio

Leathers
Midtown West

333 7th Avenue, 2nd Floor
between 28th and 29th Streets / 290-2600
Call for sale dates and times.

The Edge: Spanish shearlings to check out. Very fine Spanish shearlings manufactured in its own plant. A very large selection sold at all the best department stores and boutiques. Sizes XS to XXL. Prices from $600 to $2,500. No delivery.

Grownbeans, Inc.

Leathers
Flatiron/East Village

41 Union Square West, Suite 218
at 17th Street / 989-3486
Weekdays 9am–5pm.

The Edge: Leather and suede custom clothing. Priced from $150 to $1,950. No credit cards.

Gus Goodman, Inc.
Leathers
Midtown West

333 7th Avenue, 10th Floor
near 29th Street / 244-7422
Call to be put on the mailing list.

The Edge: Fur-lined coats and jackets and reversible coats in a large number of combinations. Find various furs and silks and leathers. Furs range from nutria to mink. Also shearlings.

Sara Vicci
Leathers
Brooklyn

464 Avenue U
near East 5th Street, Brooklyn / 718-645-2877
Mon–Wed 10am–6pm, Thurs 10am–6:30pm, Fri 10am–3pm, Sun noon–5pm.

The Edge: Accessories for him and her. For him: belts and humidors—humidors imported from Agreseti (Italy), with prices starting at $150 for pocket humidors made of burlwood up to larger models which hold up to 300 cigars. For her: imported handbags by all the greats, including Goldpfeil and Paloma Picasso, and from not-as-well-known Italian designers. Scarves in silk and challis from Dolce and Gabanna, Adrienne Landau, Nina Ricci, and Karl Lagerfeld. Scarf prices start at $22. Discounter.

Shearling Selection New York
Leathers
Midtown West

224 West 35th Street, Suite 200
btween 7th and 8th Avenues / 268-3844
Weekdays 9am–5pm, Sat 10am–3pm.

The Edge: A wholesale outlet. Features wholesale Spanish Merino shearling outerwear, including jackets and coats. Coats that retail for $2,195 to $2,695 sell here for less than $1,000 to $1,500. No delivery.

Trussardi
Leathers
Midtown West

745 5th Avenue, Suite 601
between 57th and 58th Streets / 541-6780
Call to be put on the mailing list.

The Edge: Haute Italian. Italian designer leather items, including clothing (skirts, coats, and more) and accessories priced at wholesale prices—at least half of retail to much, much more. Checks accepted with ID. No credit cards. No delivery.

Tuscany & Company
Leathers
Midtown West

12 West 57th Street
west of 5th Avenue / 307-1258
Weekdays 9am–5pm.

48	48	40	48
quality	style	service	value

The Edge: A treasured source for top Italian leathers and shearlings. A distributor to top department stores and the finest Madison Avenue stores and boutiques of fine Italian leather and shearling jackets and coats. Mostly women's, some men's. Half of retail prices. Great selection. No credit cards. No delivery. *"Ask for Antonio Di Capua." "Great, great things."*

ZBO International Corp.
Leathers
Midtown West

512 7th Avenue, 2nd Floor
between 37th and 38th Streets / 944-0655

Call to be put on the mailing list.

The Edge: End-of-season sale on Spanish shearlings. Some 30 colors to choose from. Prices $800 to $1,600. Sizes 6 to 13. No delivery.

The ratings: excellent very good good fair so-so

Sporting goods

Bicycle & Fitness Equipment Store
242-244 East 79th Street
near 3rd Avenue / 249-9344
Weekdays 9:30am–8pm, Sat–Sun 9am–7pm.

Bicycles
Upper East Side

The Edge: Sells and rents all types of bikes and skates (roller and in-line). Competitive prices, with last year's models offering the best values. Also standard exercise equipment, including treadmills and aerobic bikes. Good bike repairs. Bike and skate rentals are $6 an hour or $21 a day. No delivery.

Bicycle Habitat
244 Lafayette Street
near Prince Street / 431-3315
Mon–Thurs 10am–7pm, Fri 10am–6:30pm, Sat–Sun 10am–6pm.

Bicycles
SoHo/TriBeCa

The Edge: Best bikes and repair classes. This bike store stocks Diamond Back, Mongoose, Trek, and UniVega. Bikes priced from $200 to $3,000. You can find cycling accessories and clothing. Good repairs. The store also offers a $150 seven-week repair class which usually meets on Wednesday evenings from 7:30 to 9:30. Bike rentals from $25 per day.

Bicycle Renaissance
430 Columbus Avenue
between 80th and 81st Streets / 724-2350
Weekdays 10am–7:30pm, Sat 10am–6pm, Sun 10am–5pm.

Bicycles
Upper West Side

The Edge: Full-service bike shop. Find top brands of city, racing, and touring bikes, as well as custom bikes. Also clothing and accessories. Excellent service and repairs. Stocks over 100 parts.

Conrad's Bike Shop
25 Tudor City Place
near 41st Street / 697-6966
Mon–Sat 11am–7pm.

Bicycles
Midtown East

45	45	48	35
quality	style	service	value

The Edge: For the serious biker—service, top bikes. Carries only the best frames, bicycles, and parts. Mostly European bikes, with prices to $1,600. The shop is known for its top service and excellent staff. Also find the clothing and accessories that befit a $1,600 bike! *"The Tiffany of bike shops!"*

Larry & Jeff's Bicycles Plus
Daily 10am–7pm.

Bicycles
Multiple locations

The Edge: Full-service bike shop. Features every type of bicycle from touring to sports and racing bikes. Brands include Cannondale, Diamond Back, Jamis, GT, and Mongoose. Bikes priced from $100. Rentals $7 per hour and $25 per day. All kinds of accessories, clothing, and shoes to complement.

Locations: Upper East Side: 1400 3rd Avenue, near 79th Street (794-2929) / 1690 2nd Avenue, between 87th and 88th Streets (722-2201)

TogaBikes
110 West End Avenue
near 64th Street / 799-9625
Mon–Wed and Fri 11am–7pm, Thurs 11am–8pm, Sat 10am–6pm, Sun 11am–6pm.

Bicycles
Upper West Side

The Edge: Among New York's largest and oldest bike shops. Features repairs and equipment. Find touring, sport, city, and triathlon bikes, including American Flyer, Colnago Lite Speed, Merlin, Kestrel, Specialized Cannondale, Gary Fisher, and Marin. Bikes priced from $259 to $8,000 (custom bikes). Rentals from $35 per day. Discounts 10% to 20% on prior season's bikes. Free emergency repair and maintenance class open to all on the first and third Tuesdays of the month at 7:15pm. Sells clothing and shoes also. Its Web site is www.togabikes.com. E-mail is info@togabikes.com.

Blatt Billiards
809 Broadway
near 11th Street / 674-8855
Weekdays 9am–6pm, Sat 10am–4pm (closed Sat July–Aug).

Billiards
Flatiron/East Village

The Edge: Billiard heaven. Since 1923 nothing appears to have changed. Largest collection of antique, custom, and contemporary pool tables and cues. Regulation dart boards and darts.

V. Loria & Sons
178 Bowery
near Delancey Street / 925-0300
Weekdays 10:30am–6pm, Sat 10:30am–4pm.

Billiards
SoHo/TriBeCa

The Edge: The place for billiard equipment. Since 1912 the source for indoor games, including billiards, poker, Ping-Pong and gaming tables, pinball machines, and bowling equipment. Find new, used, and custom tables. Gear for all these sports and games, including bags, balls, shoes, and accessories.

Tents & Trails
21 Park Place
between Church Street and Broadway / 227-1760
Mon–Wed and Sat 9:30am–6pm,
Thurs–Fri 9:30am–7pm, Sun noon–6pm.

Camping
Lower Manhattan

quality style service value

The Edge: Top-of-the-line source for camping supplies to buy or rent. Three floors packed with camping equipment and survival gear for sale or rent. Also clothing in all sizes, from children to adults. Find hiking boots, down jackets, jeans, backpacks, camping stoves, sleeping bags, tents, and ropes. No delivery.

Capezio

Mon–Wed and Fri 9:30am–6:30pm, Thurs 9:30am–7pm, Sat 9:30am–6pm, Sun 11:30am–5pm.

Dance
Multiple locations

quality style service value

The Edge: Selection—everything for the dancer. Full line of dance wear (shoes and clothing), athletic wear, and fashion shoes. Traditional and timeless.

Locations: Midtown West: 1650 Broadway, 2nd Floor, near West 51st Street (245-2130) / **Upper East Side:** 136 East 61st Street, between Lexington and Park Avenues (758-8833) / 1651 3rd Avenue, near 92nd Street (348-7210)

Freed of London

922 7th Avenue
near 58th Street / 489-1055
Mon–Sat 10am–6pm.

Dance
Midtown West

quality style service value

The Edge: The dance establishment's source. Established London supplier of equipment and costumes for the dance community (ballet, gymnastics, tap, jazz, and ballroom dancing), plus period shoes. Full range of dance wear, including shoes, leg warmers, leotards, skirts, and tutus. Keeps a complete line of regulation wear for the Royal Ballet. *"The only place for dance wear."*

Repetto

215 Little Falls Road
Fairfield / 201-785-9292
Weekdays 9:30am–6pm.

Dance
New Jersey

The Edge: French manufacturer of classic dance wear and accessories. Everything for the dance professional, as well as exercise clothing for aerobics, gymnastics, and jazz. Ballet wear for boys and girls to adults. Catalog costs $3.

DMI Dartmart, Inc.

160 West 26th Street
near 6th Avenue / 366-6981
Weekdays 10am–8pm, Sat 11am–5pm.

Darts
Midtown West

The Edge: A good source for darts and all indoor games. Features a wide selection of darts, boards, cabinets, and team shirts. Darts up to $165 per set. Find indoor games, quality pool tables (at $1,200) and cues, Ping-Pong tables, and air-hockey equipment.

Dart Shop Limited

30 East 20th Street
between Park Avenue South and Broadway / 533-8684
Weekdays noon–6pm, Sat 11am–5pm.

Darts
Flatiron/East Village

quality style service value

The Edge: The only store in Manhattan devoted solely to darts and darting equipment. Equipment includes tournament-quality cabinets, boards, and scoreboards for pros and amateurs. Priced from $6.50 to $160.

Nautica

216 Columbus Avenue
near 70th Street / 496-0933
Mon–Sat 10am–8pm, Sun noon–7pm.

Diving
Upper West Side

The Edge: Sells only Nautica goods—equipment, clothing, and themed items. Find men's clothing, cologne, diving watches, plus equipment.

Pan Aqua Diving

460 West 43rd Street
near 10th Avenues / 736-3483
Weekdays noon–7pm, Sat 10am–7pm, Sun noon–5pm.

Diving
Midtown West

The Edge: Divers' dreams start here. Top-quality diving gear—air compressors, depth gauges, dive planners, gloves, fins, tanks, and wet suits. Find Henderson, Oceanic, O'Neill, ScubaPro, Sea Quest, and Tusa equipment. Large price range available.

Scuba Network

124 East 57th Street
between Park and Lexington Avenues / 750-9160
Mon–Tues and Thurs 10:30am–7pm, Wed and Fri 10:30am–8pm,
Sat 10:30am–6pm, Sun noon–4pm.

Diving
Midtown East

The Edge: Tops in equipment. Features top-quality scuba-diving equipment, plus books and travel guides. No delivery.

Barbara Gee Danskin Center

Mon–Sat 10:30am–7:30pm, Sun 1–6pm.

Exercise
Multiple locations

The Edge: 10% off on a full line of exercise wear. Features exercise and dance wear, underwear, lingerie, and hosiery. 10% to 20% off for Danskin tights and leotards. Lingerie and underwear is mostly Hanes.

Locations: Upper West Side: 2487 Broadway, near 82nd Street (769-1564) / 2282½ Broadway, at 82nd Street (769-2923)

Gym Source

40 East 52nd Street
between Park and Madison Avenues / 688-4222
Weekdays 9am–6pm, Sat 10am–5pm (closed Sat July–Aug).

Exercise
Midtown East

The Edge: One of the city's best exercise-equipment sources. A 7,000-square-foot showroom with a huge selection of all major brands of exercise equipment, including treadmills, Lifecycles, stair climbers, weight machines, rowers, and more. Will rent equipment with a one-month minimum. The staff will help you design an exercise room for a home or office gym with the equipment that best meets your own goals.

Nordic Track

650 Madison Avenue
between 59th and 60th Streets / 688-3883
Mon–Wed and Fri–Sat 10am–6pm, Thurs 10am–8pm,
Sun noon–5pm.

Exercise
Midtown East

The Edge: The original cross-country ski machine. Exercise equipment meeting all needs, plus exercise apparel and footwear. Spa and message products are also available. *"Best buy for quality."*

Women's Workout Gear

78 7th Avenue
near 17th Street / 627-1117
Weekdays 11am–6:30pm, Sat 11am–6pm, Sun 1:30–5:30pm.

Exercise
Chelsea

The Edge: Workout gear for all occasions. Features sports clothing; aerobics and running gear; walking, running, and aerobic shoes; bathing suits and goggles; sports bras; weights and exercise mats. Brands include City Lights, Fast Forward, Gilda Marx, Speedo, and its own label. No delivery.

Blade Fencing

212 West 15th Street
near 7th Avenue / 620-0114
Weekdays 10am–7pm, Sat 11am–3pm.

Fencing
Chelsea

The Edge: Meets all fencing needs. Instruction, plus all the equipment, clothing, and books required to fence in style.

Capitol Fishing Tackle Company

218 West 23rd Street
near 7th Avenue / 929-6132
Mon–Wed and Fri 9am–6pm, Thurs 9am–7pm, Sat 9am–5pm.

Fishing
Chelsea

The Edge: For the serious saltwater angler. The oldest (since 1897) fishing-tackle store in the city. Top-quality equipment includes rods, reels, lures, lines, and accessories, with special emphasis on deep-sea saltwater equipment. A good source for inexpensive beginner equipment. A wide range of equipment priced from $2.95 to $800. *"Really fine for saltwater."*

Orvis

355 Madison Avenue
near 45th Street / 697-3133
Weekdays 9am–6pm, Sat 10am–5pm.

Fishing
Midtown East

The Edge: Known for its hunting and fishing lines, plus great lessons. Features a complete line of fly-fishing reels, rods, lures, and accessories, including bags, fishing vests and jackets, hip boots, and waders. Hunting equipment includes guns and equipment for bird hunting. Casual country and safari clothing. Gift items feature fishing- and hunting-motif items. Best of all are Orvis's trips and fishing lessons. *"Great for fishing flies, but clothes are outdated."*

Urban Angler Ltd.

118 East 25th Street, 3rd Floor
between Park and Lexington Avenues / 979-7600
Mon–Tues and Thurs–Fri 10am–6pm, Wed 10am–7pm, Sat 10am–5pm.

Fishing
Gramercy Park/Murray Hill

The Edge: Everything for the fly fisherman. Find rods of all weights, lines, leaders, flies, vises, tying tools, hooks, wading equipment, nets, and accessories including luggage, eyewear, vests, knives, and more. Books about fly fishing and travel—planned trips to destinations around the globe.

Foot-Joy Shoes

7 East 52nd Street
between 5th and Madison Avenues / 753-8522
Weekdays 10am–5:30pm, Sat 10am–5pm.

Golf
Midtown East

quality style service value

The Edge: Enormous variety of golf shoes. More than 150 styles, from saddle to wing tip. Some shoes with cleats, some without. Also golf gloves and socks.

New York Golf Center, Inc

131 West 35th Street
near Broadway / 564-2255
Daily 10am–7pm in winter, 10am–8pm in summer.

Golf
Midtown West

quality style service value

The Edge: Large selection favored by golf pros and amateurs. Selection includes Callaway, Honma, Ping, Top-Flite, Titleist, and Wilson. Shop features clubs, bags, balls, shoes, and accessories. They say they offer a 30% discount.

Richard Metz Golf Studio

425 Madison Avenue, 3rd Floor
near 49th Street / 759-6940
Mon–Thurs 10am–8pm, Fri 10am–7pm, Sat 10am–5pm.

Golf
Midtown East

quality style service value

The Edge: Pro shop with practice cages and putting greens. Golfer heaven. Find the latest, top-quality balls, clubs, golf bags, shoes, and clothing, plus golfing books and videotapes. Lessons and practice area plus equipment all in one location. Offers instruction at $350 for 10 lessons. *"Better for men—not enough choice for women."*

World of Golf

147 East 47th Street, 2nd Floor
between Lexington and 3rd Avenues / 755-9398
Mon–Sat 9am–7pm.

Golf
Midtown East

quality style service value

The Edge: A New York pro shop. Carries a full range of golf equipment, including clubs, bags, shoes, and clothing for the younger set, women, and men. A very large selection of all the best names. Also practice aids, books, and videos. Discounter.

John Jovino Gun Shop

Guns
SoHo/TriBeCa

5 Centre Market Place
near Grand Street / 925-4881
Weekdays 10am–6pm, Sat 10am–3pm.

The Edge: New York's gun shop. Since 1911 has featured handguns, rifles, shotguns, and accessories, including ammunition and bulletproof vests. Authorized warranty repair station for virtually all gun manufacturers. Carries most major brands of guns, priced from $100 to $1,000.

Hunting World / Angler's World

Hunting
Midtown East

16 East 53rd Street
between 5th and Madison Avenues / 755-3400
Mon–Sat 10am–6pm.

quality style service value

The Edge: Everything you'll need for a safari or fishing trip. Offers clothing and sporting gear, including a full line of fishing equipment. Clothing includes safari jackets, slacks, hats, shooting bags, shoes, and clay shooter vests. Luggage with its logo and jewelry. *"More for show than sport."*

Goldberg's Marine

Marine
Midtown West

12 West 37th Street
between 5th and 6th Avenues / 594-6065
Mon–Sat 9am–6pm, Sun 10am–5pm.

quality style service value

The Edge: New York's source for boaters. Features one of the largest selections in the city of fishing devices and nautical gear. Find the simplest personal equipment (books, clocks, clothing) to sports needs (diving, fishing, waterskiing) to everything for your boat (china to electronics). *"Best prices, and they have it all."*

Miller's Harness Company

Riding
Gramercy Park/Murray Hill

117 East 24th Street
near Park Avenue / 673-1400
Mon–Wed and Fri–Sat 10am–6pm, Thurs 10am–7pm.

quality style service value

The Edge: Full-line, world-class equestrian store. Features proper riding gear and saddles. Offers all major brands, including Crosby and Hermès. Books, videos, and gift items—practical to horsy motif. *"Good selection for English-style riders."*

Super Runners Shop

1337 Lexington Avenue
near 89th Street / 369-6010
Mon–Wed and Fri 10am–7pm, Thurs 10am–9pm,
Sat 10am–6pm, Sun noon–5pm.

Running
Upper East Side

quality style service value

The Edge: One of the best running stores in the city. Features shoes, running gear, and accessories (goggles, sunglasses, and watches). Most major brands. No delivery. *"Very knowledgeable salespeople. It has the sneaker that's right for you."*

Blades West

120 West 72nd Street
near Columbus Avenue / 787-3911
Mon–Sat 10am–8pm, Sun 10am–6pm.

Skating
Upper West Side

The Edge: Meets all blade and board needs. Features a full range of bodyboards, skates, skateboards, snowboards, and surfboards for sale or rent—plus outfits to match. Maintains a full repair shop on premises.

Peck and Goodie Skates

917 8th Avenue
near 54th Street / 246-6123
Mon–Sat 10am–8pm, Sun 10am–6pm.

Skating
Midtown West

The Edge: Could be the city's finest skate shop. Carries the best equipment for novice to expert in figure, hockey, and in-line skates, equipment, and apparel. Hockey skate brands include Bauer, CCM Mega, Riedell, and Spteri. Figure-skating brands include Don Jackson, Riedell, and Teri. In-line skating brands include K2, Miller, Oxygen, Rollerblade, and Viking. Rents in-line skates for $15 per day. Offers skate sharpening and repairs.

Bogner

821 Madison Avenue
near 68th Street / 472-0266
Mon–Sat 10am–6pm.

Skiing
Upper East Side

quality style service value

The Edge: High-fashion ski wear. Also some après-ski wear. The "in" colors change each year. Look for golf and tennis wear outside the ski season. Bogner designs only. Very expensive. *"Great-looking clothes and colors."*

Scandinavian Ski Shop

40 West 57th Street
between 5th and 6th Avenues / 757-8524
Mon–Wed and Fri–Sat 10am–6pm,
Thurs 10am–6:30pm, Sun 11am–5:30pm.

Skiing
Midtown West

40 32 36 34

quality style service value

The Edge: More practical than glamorous ski equipment and clothing. Best known for its ski equipment and ski wear, but also offers tennis, hiking, skating, and swimwear, depending on the season. Three full floors. All top ski lines are featured, including Obermeyer, Emmegi, VdeV, Bogner, LaFont, Postcard, and MCM. Children's and adult sizes. *"Good selection."*

Soccer Sport Supply Company

Soccer
Upper East Side

1745 1st Avenue
between 90th and 91st Streets / 427-6050
Weekdays 10am–6pm, Sat 10am–3pm.

The Edge: The name says it all. New York's specialist in soccer and rugby equipment. Find shoes, team equipment, and uniforms for basketball, lacrosse, rugby, soccer, and softball.

Collector's Stadium

Sports-general
Lower Manhattan

17 Warren Street
opposite City Hall / 353-1531
Daily 11am–7pm.

The Edge: Anything and everything for collectors. Devoted to sports and comic book memorabilia. Anything the collector would want from autographed baseballs ranging in price from $300 per baseball to over $1,000 for a Michael Jordan autographed ball. Good gift items include Game 1 pieces (clothing actually worn by players at games) and less expensive items such as baseball caps in more than 200 team styles. Items go back to 1890. Old and new comics for kids and adult comic book lovers.

Eastern Mountain Sports

Sports-general
Multiple locations

Weekdays 10am–9pm, Sat 10am–6pm, Sun noon–6pm.

48	40	43	40
quality	style	service	value

The Edge: No-frills, well-priced sturdy clothing and equipment. Basic and functional. Climbing, backpacking, and camping clothing and equipment. Complete stock of mountaineering and downhill and cross-country skiing equipment.

Locations: SoHo/TriBeCa: 611 Broadway, near Houston Street (505-9860) / **Upper West Side:** 20 West 61st Street, near Broadway (397-4860)

Eisner Brothers

Sports-general
Lower East Side/Chinatown

75 Essex Street
between Delancey and Broome Streets / 475-6868
Mon–Thurs 8:30am–6:30pm, Fri 8:30am–3pm, Sun 8:30am–4:30pm.

The Edge: Source for NBA, NHL, and collegiate team items. Sells wholesale licensed team merchandise. Find caps, sweatshirts, team jackets, and more. Sizes toddlers through adult extra-large. Inexpensive. No credit cards.

G&S Sporting Goods

Sports-general
Lower East Side/Chinatown

43 Essex Street

near Grand Street / 777-7590
Sun–Fri 9am–6pm.

The Edge: Good prices on the basics—athletic clothing, footwear, and equipment. Find sneakers by Converse, Keds, LA Gear, New Balance, Nike, and Reebok. Regulation balls for all sports. Also pool cues and accessories, Ping-Pong, badminton, racquetball, and sleeping bags. No golf or ski equipment. No delivery. Discounter.

Gerry Cosby and Company

Sports-general
Midtown West

3 Pennsylvania Plaza
at Madison Square Garden / 563-6464
Weekdays 9:30am–6:30pm, Sat 9:30am–6pm, Sun noon–5pm.
Open daily starting three hours before sports events.

The Edge: Pro sports apparel. Features a large selection of pro sports jerseys, and NFL- and NBA-licensed apparel and souvenirs. Makes protective and sports gear designed for professional use for most sports, including baseball, basketball, football, hockey, and lacrosse. Discounter.

Modell's Sporting Goods

Sports-general
Multiple locations

Weekdays 8:30am–6:30pm, Sat 9am–4pm, Sun 11am–4pm.

quality style service value
40 34 30 38

The Edge: Large range of moderately priced sporting equipment and clothing. A chain of 70 stores. One of the city's largest sources for gear for almost all sports. Features all major brands, with a seasonal focus. Discounter.

Locations: Lower Manhattan: 200 Broadway, near John Street (962-6200) / 280 Broadway, near John Street (962-6200) / **Midtown East:** 51 East 42nd Street, between 5th and Madison Avenues (661-4242) / **Midtown West:** 601 Avenue of the Americas, near 32nd Street (594-1830)

Paragon Sporting Goods

Sports-general
Flatiron/East Village

867 Broadway
at 18th Street / 255-8036
Mon–Sat 10am–8pm, Sun 11am–6:30pm.

quality style service value
42 38 33 36

The Edge: Could be the best—certainly the most comprehensive—sports shop in the city. Over 80,000 square feet on three full floors dedicated to equipment and clothing for the serious sportsman. You name the sport and it has the top-brand equipment and clothing, no matter the season. Also binoculars, down vests, and sunglasses. Selection is often unique. Prices are full list. *"New York's finest sports shop." "Helpful staff in most areas but shoes." "Multi-department approach makes checkout and returns a nightmare."*

Spiegel Sporting Goods

Sports-general
Lower Manhattan

105 Nassau Street
near Fulton Street / 227-8400
Weekdays 10am–6pm, Sat 11am–5pm.

quality style service value
30 30 30 30

The Edge: Equipment for just about any sport. Since 1916. Known for its special sale prices, which can make items among the lowest priced in the city. When it commits to selling inexpensively, it does just that. No delivery. *"Great prices, but limited selection."*

Cameo Water Wear

Swimming
Upper East Side

1349 3rd Avenue
near 77th Street / 570-6606
Weekdays 10am–8pm, Sat 10am–6pm, Sun noon–6pm.

The Edge: Swimwear always available. Swimwear and coverups available in all seasons and in misses' sizes 6 to 16 to make the most of what you've got. All the leading names and hundreds of suits. No delivery.

Fila of Madison Avenue

Tennis
Upper East Side

831 Madison Avenue
near 69th Street / 737-3452
Mon–Wed and Fri–Sat 10am–6pm, Thurs 10am–7pm.

40	30	30	30
quality	style	service	value

The Edge: Fashionable sports garb. From summer to winter, great-looking sportswear. Find tennis workout clothes and swimwear in summer, ski wear in winter.

Mason's Tennis Mart

Tennis
Midtown West

911 7th Avenue
near 57th Street / 757-5374
Weekdays 10am–7pm, Sat 10am–6pm.

30	30	30	30
quality	style	service	value

The Edge: Racquets and clothes for pros. Great selection in top equipment and clothing. Traditional styling favored. Sells bags, balls, ball machines, and racquets. Same-day racquet stringing.

The ratings: **50** excellent **40** very good **30** good **20** fair **10** so-so
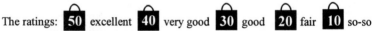

Travel & vacation

Air Facility
712-1769
Weekdays 9am–4:30pm.

Discount
Mail/phone

The Edge: For those who can travel light—courier flights. Courier-flight options to Central and South America. Open an account by calling—no charge to register.

Capital Reservations
1730 Rhode Island Avenue NW, Suite 1114
at 17th Street, Washington / 800-847-4832
Weekdays 9am–6pm, Sat 9am–1pm.

Discount
Mail/phone

The Edge: Discounts Washington, D.C.–area hotels. Offers discounts from 30% to 50% on 70 Washington, D.C.–area one-star to five-star hotels on its list. Hotels include the Willard and the Ritz. Confirmation numbers are given. Cancellation policy varies by hotel (most require 24 hours' notice for full refund).

Central Reservation Services
11420 North Kendall Drive, Suite 108
Miami / 800-950-0232
Daily 24 hours.

Discount
Mail/phone

The Edge: Discounts on more moderate U.S. hotels and car rentals. Offers good rates at two-star hotels. Discounts from 10% to 40%. Gives confirmation numbers.

Cheap Tickets, Inc.
800-377-1000
Weekdays 8:30am–10pm, Sat–Sun 10am–7pm.

Discount
Mail/phone

The Edge: The name says it all. Check it out for both domestic and international discount tickets for air travel, cruises, and car rentals. Overnight ticket delivery. Major airlines only.

Discount Travel International
169 West 84th Street
between Columbus and Amsterdam Avenues / 362-3636
Weekdays 10am–8pm, Sat 10am–4pm.

Discount
Upper West Side

The Edge: For those who can travel light—courier flights. Courier-service options to the Far East, South and Central America, and Western and Eastern Europe—everyplace you'd want to go. Lots of options. Sometimes two of you can fly on the same flight by working for different shipping services. No fees to join. A recorded announcement lists available fares—plus it has a travel agency for hotels and other services.

East-West Express

718-656-6246
Weekdays 11am–2:30pm.

Discount
Mail/phone

The Edge: For those who can travel light—courier flights. Courier-flight options to Australia via Los Angeles and New York. You'll need to book early— two months in advance is recommended.

Halbart Express

147-05 176th Street
Jamaica / 718-656-8189
Weekdays 8am–5pm.

Discount
Mail/phone

The Edge: Best deals for last-minute travelers. A wide range of locations to travel to—Europe and Asia, occasionally South America.

Moment's Notice

7301 New Utrecht Avenue
near 73rd Street, Brooklyn / 718-234-6295
Daily 9am–5:30pm.

Discount
Mail/phone

The Edge: A clearinghouse for unsold tour and cruise-line tickets. In business for 30 years. A $25 membership fee is required for their discounts. Provides updates on opportunities. Hotline at 212-873-0908.

Quikbook

381 Park Avenue South
near 28th Street / 789-9887
Weekdays 9am–5pm. Fax service 24 hours daily at 212-532-1556.

Discount
Mail/phone

The Edge: Discounts hotel rooms in 21 cities. Offers discounted rates of 40% to 70% off regular walk-in rates for hotels in 21 cities in a wide variety of price ranges. Confirmation number by mail or phone. In New York, offers discounts at the Empire (moderate) to the Helmsley and Drake (first class).

Room Exchange

450 7th Avenue
near 35th Street / 846-7000
Weekdays 9am–5:30pm.

Discount
Mail/phone

The Edge: Discounts on hotel rooms. Offers discounts on 23,000 hotels in the U.S., Bermuda, Canada, Europe, Mexico, and the Caribbean. Confirmation numbers provided and the traveler is billed direct. Cancellation possible 48 hours in advance in the U.S. and seven days in advance elsewhere.

San Francisco Reservations / Topaz Hotel Service

22 Second Street, 4th Floor
San Francisco / 800-677-1550
Daily 7am–11pm Pacific Time.

Discount
Mail/phone

quality   style   service   value

The Edge: Discounts San Francisco hotels. Offers discounts of 5% to 50% at 225 hotels in the San Francisco Bay Area, budget to deluxe. Confirmation numbers provided. The individual hotels set the cancellation policy. Service is difficult at times—expect to be put on hold.

Travel Bargains
2250 Butler Pike
Plymouth / 800-872-8385
Weekdays 8am–midnight Eastern Time.

Discount
Mail/phone

The Edge: Discounts domestic and international flights. Long waits for service.

Virgin Express / Vex Wholesale Express
JFK International Airport
Jamaica / 718-244-7244
Weekdays 8am–6pm.

Discount
Mail/phone

The Edge: Courier flights to London. Plan early. With its several flights a day, you can vacation essentially together—although starting on different flights. Departures from JFK or Newark to Heathrow. You can take your full luggage allotment.

White Travel
127 Park Road West
Hartford / 800-547-4790
Weekdays 9am–5pm.

Discount
Mail/phone

The Edge: Deals on cruises. Wide range of cruises offered at 5% to 65% off the cost of sailing.

The ratings: **50** excellent **40** very good **30** good **20** fair **10** so-so

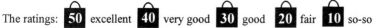

Index

—A—

—E—

—H—

James Robinson, 195
Jamie Ostrow, 252
Jan's Hobby Shop, 324
Jana Starr Antiques, 80
Jane Gill, 260
Jane Kozlak, 262
Jane Wilson-Marquis, 4
Janos P. Spitzer Flooring Company, 259
Janovic Plaza, 227
Jay's Perfume Bar, 107
Jazz Record Center, 279
Jean's Silversmiths, 195
Jean Hoffman, 81
Jean Laporte L'Artisan Parfumeur, 107
Jefferson Market, 129, 142
Jeffrey Aronoff, Inc., 369
Jekyll and Hyde Ltd., 29
Jensen-Lewis, 203
Jerrystyle, 231
jewelry & watches, 59–70, 334–335, 378–381
jewelry & watches–costume, 68–70
jewelry & watches–supply, 70
Jewelry Display of New York, 70
Jewish Museum, 272
Jill Stuart, 356
Jim's Shoe Repair, 342
Jim Buck School for Dogs, 348
Jimson's, 324
Joan & David, 77, 88, 89
Joan Victor Studio, 288
Joanna Mastroianni, 356
Jobson's Luggage, 74
Jodamo International Ltd., 29
Joe's Dairy, 135
Joe's Ninth Avenue Meat Market, 142
Joe Boxer, 374
John's European Boutique, 343
John Anthony, 46
John Barman, Inc., 331
John Fluevog Shoes, 90
John Jovino Gun Shop, 390
John R. Gerardo, 337
John Rosselli Antiques, 171
John Rosselli International, 171
John Venekamp, 263
Joia Interiors, Inc., 188
Jolene, 357
Jones New York Wool Coats, 357
Joon, 253
Joovay, 99
Joseph, 37
Joseph D. Tonti, 315
Josie Atplace, 64

Juan Angel Pogonza Restoration, 333
Judith Leiber, 369
Judith Leiber on Madison, 74
Judith Ripka Jewellery, 64
Julie Artisan's Gallery, 1
Julius Caruso Salon, 110
Julliard Placement Bureau, 288
Just Bulbs, 231
Just Once Ltd., 4
Just Shades, 246

—K—

K&D Wines & Liquors, 165
Kadouri & Son, Inc., 132
Kalustyan Orient Export Trading, 149
Kam Man Food Products, 151
Kanae + Onyx, 37
Karen Lee, 289
Karens for People + Pets, 346
Karl Kemp & Associates Ltd., 215
Karp & Cantrell Audio & Video, 258
Katagiri and Company, 152
Kate's Paperie, 253
Kate Spade, 74
Kavanagh's Designer Resale Shop, 81
Kay Leather Goods Repair Service, 337
Kenar, 37
Kenneth's Salon, 111
Kenneth Barnard Rainwear, 357
Kenneth Cole, 90
Kentshire Galleries, 216
Kenzo, 11, 49
Kidding Around, 24
Kids "R" Us, 25
Kids Are Magic, 25
Kiehl's, 107
Kim & Kelly, 357
Kimberly House Ltd., 377
Kinko's Copies, 251
Kinokuniya Bookstore, 272
kitchen, 230
Kitchen Arts and Letters, 272
Kitschen, 230
KL by Karl Lagerfeld/Steilmann, 357
Klein's of Monticello, 38
Kleinfeld and Son, 4
Klurk, 357
Kmart, 50
Knoll, 203
Kordol Fabrics, 53
Koreana Art and Antiques, 238
Kossar's Bialystoker Kuchen Bakery, 130
Kraft Hardware, 227

—M—

New York Astrology Center, 274
New York Athletic Club, 302
New York Botanic Garden's Shop, 224
New York Central Art Supply, 249
New York Choral Society, 291
New York Closet Company, 330
New York Exchange for Women's Work, 1
New York Firefighter's Friend, 2
New York Golf Center, Inc., 389
New York Health and Racquet Club, 302
New York Nautical Instrument & Service
    Corp., 274
New York Palace Hotel, 308
New York Public Library Shop, 313
New York Racquet & Tennis Club, 320
New York Sports Club, 303
New York University School of Continuing
    Education, 291
New York Veterinary Hospital, 347
Newel Art Galleries, Inc., 219
Niall Smith, 215
Nicole Miller, 40, 370
Nicole Miller Accessories, 370
Nicolina of New York, 82
Niels Bamberger, 198
Nina Footwear/Delman, 370
Nine West, 92
9th Avenue Cheese Market, 136
Ninth Avenue International Foods, 156
99X, 92
92nd Street Y, 291
Noelle Day Spa, 115
Nordic Track, 388
Norma Kamali, 360
North Carolina Furniture Showrooms, 204
Nostalgia . . . and All That Jazz, 280
Novello, 156
Nuovo Melodrom, 204
NY Little Elves, 330
NYU Health Sciences Bookstore, 274

—O—

Oak-Smith & Jones, 219
Ocean Sea Food, 143
Océanie/Afrique Noire, 275
office, 236–237
Office Furniture Heaven, 236
Old Navy Clothing Company, 17
Old Print Shop, 275
Olden Camera, 212
Oldies, Goldies & Moldies, 188
Omo Norma Kamali, 21
Once Upon a Tart, 161

One of a Kind Bride, 5
One-of-a-Kind, 47
Only Hearts, 2
Onward Kashiyama, 361
Open Pantry, 138
Oppenheimer Meats, Inc., 144
Ora Feder Lingerie, 100
Oren's Daily Roast, 138
Oribe, 112
Oriental, 151–153, 237–239
Orientations Gallery Ltd., 239
Orrefors, 198
Orvis, 388
Orwasher's Bakery, 130
Oscar Wilde Memorial Bookshop, 275
Ottomanelli & Sons Prime Meat Market,
    144
Ottomanelli Brothers, 144
Out of the Closet Thrift Shop, 82
outlet center, 77
ovens, 340

—P—

P. E. Guerin, Inc., 228
P.H.D., 361
Pace Collection, 205
Pace Wildenstein Gallery, 186
Paco and Celeste, 361
Pageant Book & Print Shop, 275
Paint the Town Red, 309
paint, plaster & tiles, 262
Palm House at the Brooklyn Botanic
    Garden, 309
Paloma Picasso, 380
Pan Am Sportswear and Menswear, 18
Pan Aqua Diving, 387
Pancaldi, 371
Pantry & Hearth, 230
Paraclete Book Center, 275
Paradise Market, 153
Paragon Sporting Goods, 393
Parents League, 291
Park Avenue Liquors, 165
Park East Animal Hospital, 347
Park East Kosher Butcher, 144
Park East Sewing Center, 342
Paron Fabrics, 54
Party Poopers, 295
Party Rentals, 317
Pasargad Carpets, 242
Passport Plus, 340
Patisserie Claude, 125
Patisserie Lanciani, 126

S. Wyler, Inc., 199
Sable's, 119
Sacco Shoes, 93
Safavieh Carpets, 243
Sahadi Importing Company, Inc., 156
sailing, 318
Saint Laurent Rive Gauche, 41
Saint Laurie Ltd., 13
Saint Remy, 174
Saity Jewelry, 66
Saks Fifth Avenue, 51
Sally Hawkins Gallery, 66
Salumeria Biellese, 145
Salvatore Macri, 112
Sam Flax, 249
Samantha Jones Lingerie, 101
sample sales, 349–383
San Francisco Reservations / Topaz Hotel
    Service, 396
Sander Witlin, 6
Sanko Cultured Pearls, 335
Sano Studio, 329
Sant Ambroeus Ltd., 127
Sanyo by Carol Cohen, 363
Sara Vicci, 382
Sarajo, 243
Saved by the Bell Corporation, 340
Scandinavian Ski Shop, 391
Schachner Fashions, 101
Schaller & Weber, 146
Schatzie's Prime Meats, 146
Schweitzer Linens, 235
Science Fiction Shop, 277
Scoop, 21
Scott Jordan Furniture, 205
Screaming Mimi's, 83
Scuba Network, 387
Scully & Scully, 199
Sea Breeze Fishmarket, 146
Seaman Schepps, 67
Searle, 41
Secaucus Outlets, 77
Secondhand Rose, 180
SEE Ltd., 205
Seeford Organization, 251
Sensuous Bean, 138
Sepco Industries, 228
Serendipity, 175
Sergio Pellari, 363
service help, 318
sewing machines, 342
Shabby Chic, 205
Shades From the Midnight Sun, 246

Shakespeare & Company Booksellers, 277
Shalimar Accessories, 371
Sharif / Jay Herbert / American Handbags,
    372
Sharper Image, 212
Shearling Selection New York, 382
Sheila's Interiors, 246
Sherle Wagner International, 229
Sherry-Lehmann Wine & Spirits Merchants,
    166
Shirt Store, 84
shirts & blouses, 84–85
Shoe City, 93
shoe repair, 342–343
shoes, socks & stockings, 85–96
Shoofly, 93
Showroom, 373
Showroom Seven, 363
Shulie's, 41
Sigerson Morrison, 94
Silk Surplus, 220
Silly Billy, 296
Simon's Hardware, 229
Simon Pearce, 200
Simpson & Company and Florist West, 298
67 Wine & Spirits Merchants, 166
skating, 319, 391
skiing, 391–392
Sky Rink, 319
Slatkin & Company, 175
soccer, 392
Soccer Sport Supply Company, 392
Software Etc., 213
So-Good, 7
Soiffer/Haskin, Inc., 363
Sola, 372
Solanee, Inc., 200
Solar Antique Tiles, 229
Sole of Italy, 94
Solutions, 250
Something Different, 317
Sondra Roberts Ltd., 372
Sotheby's, 189
Sound City, 213
Sounds, 280
South Street Seaport Museum Shop, 313
Space Kiddets, 26
Spanish Institute, 292
special sizes, 96–97
Spectra Research Group, 213
Spence-Chapin Thrift Shop, 83
Spiegel Sporting Goods, 393
Spitzer and Associates, 256